Global Political Economy

Second edition

Edited by John Ravenhill

OXFORD
UNIVERSITY PRESS

OXFORD
UNIVERSITY PRESS

Great Clarendon Street, Oxford OX2 6DP

Oxford University Press is a department of the University of Oxford.
It furthers the University's objective of excellence in research, scholarship,
and education by publishing worldwide in

Oxford New York

Auckland Cape Town Dar es Salaam Hong Kong Karachi
Kuala Lumpur Madrid Melbourne Mexico City Nairobi
New Delhi Shanghai Taipei Toronto

With offices in

Argentina Austria Brazil Chile Czech Republic France Greece
Guatemala Hungary Italy Japan Poland Portugal Singapore
South Korea Switzerland Thailand Turkey Ukraine Vietnam

Oxford is a registered trade mark of Oxford University Press
in the UK and in certain other countries

Published in the United States
by Oxford University Press Inc., New York

First published 2005

Second edition 2008

British Library Cataloguing in Publication Data

Data available

Library of Congress Cataloging in Publication Data

Global Political Economy / edited by John Ravenhill.—2nd ed.
       p. cm.
   Includes bibliographical references and index.
   ISBN-13: 978-0-19-929203-5
   1. Globalization—Economic aspects.   2. International economic relations.
   3. International finance.   I. Ravenhill, John.
   HF1359.G577 2008
   337—dc22

                                                                2007032943

Typeset by Laserwords Private Limited, Chennai, India
Printed in Italy on acid-free paper by Legoprint S.p.A

ISBN 978-0-19-929203-5

10 9 8 7 6 5 4 3 2

Preface

It is always gratifying to authors when the first edition of a book does sufficiently well that publishers request the preparation of a second edition. In commissioning this second edition, Oxford University Press sought reviews of its predecessor from a dozen readers. In response to their suggestions, and to feedback from others who have assigned the book to their classes, several significant changes were made for the second edition. A new chapter was added that examines the historical origins and subsequent intellectual lineages of major theoretical approaches to the study of global political economy. And a new chapter on international production networks provides a detailed examination of their role in driving globalization.

As I noted in the Preface to the first edition of the book, students in IPE courses often are concerned about their lack of background in economics. While we provide concise explanations in this book for all of the key concepts that we use (and the book contains a comprehensive glossary), students often want to go beyond this basic information to improve their knowledge of economics. The following books are useful introductions, written with the non-specialist in mind:

James Gerber, *International Economics,* 4th edn (Addison-Wesley, 2007).

Graham Bannock *et al., The Penguin Dictionary of Economics,* 7th edn (Penguin, 2004).

Donald Rutherford, *Routledge Dictionary of Economics* (Routledge, 2002).

Donald Rutherford, *Economics: The Key Concepts* (Routledge, 2007).

For those who are comfortable with basic economic concepts, the following are the best introductory overviews of major theoretical approaches to international economics:

Paul Krugman and Maurice Obstfeld, *International Economics: Theory and Practice,* 7th edn (Addison-Wesley, 2005).

Peter B. Kenen, *The International Economy*, 4th edn (Cambridge University Press, 2000).

John Ravenhill
Canberra, September 2007.

Acknowledgements

Preparation of a volume of this size is a major task, which would not have been possible without generous support from the Department of International Relations, Research School of Pacific and Asian Studies, Australian National University. I am grateful to the Head of Department, Chris Reus-Smit, for making research assistance and funding available. Mary-Louise Hickey did her customary excellent job in preparing the manuscript to OUP's requirements, maintaining her good humour throughout. Miwa Hirono was meticulous in chasing up copyright owners for permissions to reproduce tables and figures.

I am grateful to the authors for the work they have put into their chapters, and for complying with the tight schedule required in publishing a book of this type. Besides valuing the positive feedback from readers commissioned by the Press, I am particularly grateful to Iain Hardie of the University of Edinburgh for his detailed comments on many of the chapters.

My principal debt, as always, is to my wife, Stefa Wirga, who has provided encouragement and support throughout the project from its original conceptualization.

We are grateful to those listed below for permission to reproduce copyrighted material:

Figure 5.1 from Department of Trade and Industry (UK), 'Average Industrial Tariffs in Developed Countries since 1947', *The Government's Expenditure Plans* (Her Majesty's Stationery Office, 2000), chapter 8. Reprinted with the permission of Her Majesty's Stationery Office.

Figure 6.2 from World Trade Organization, Committee on Regional Trade Agreements, 'Mapping of Regional Trade Agreements: Note by the Secretariat', WT/REG/W/41 (Geneva: World Trade Organization, 2000), chart 2. Reprinted with the permission of the World Trade Organization.

Table 6.3 from J. Crawford and R. V. Fiorentino, 'The Changing Landscape of Regional Trade Agreements', Discussion Paper No. 8 (Geneva: World Trade Organization Publication, 2005), Table 1. Reprinted with the permission of the World Trade Organization.

Figures 8.1, 8.2 and *8.6* from data in B. Eichengreen and M. Bordo, 'Crises Now and Then: What Lessons from the Last Era of Financial Globalization', NBER Working Paper No. 8716 (Cambridge, Mass.: National Bureau of Economic Research, January 2002), tables 5, 6, and 7. Reprinted with the permission of the authors.

Table 9.3 from P. H. Lindert and J. G. Williamson, 'Does Globalization Make the World More Unequal?', in M. D. Bordo, A. M. Taylor, and J. G. Williamson (eds), *Globalization in Historical Perspective* (Chicago, Ill.: University of Chicago Press, 2003), table 5.1. Reprinted with the permission of the University of Chicago Press and the authors.

Figure 12.1 and *Table 12.3* from B. Milanovic, *World Apart: Measuring International and Global Inequality* (Princeton: Princeton University Press, 2005), figure 10.1 and table 7.3. Reprinted with the permission of Princeton University Press and the author.

Figure 12.2 from United Nations, *World Economic and Social Survey 2006: Diverging Growth and Development* (New York: United Nations, 2005), figure O.1. Reprinted with the permission of the United Nations.

Figure 12.3 from P. Edward, 'The Ethical Poverty Line: A Moral Quantification of Absolute Poverty', *Third World Quarterly*, 27/2 (2006): 377–93, figure 1. Reprinted with the permission of Taylor & Francis Ltd. (http://www.informaworld.com).

Figure 12.4 from S. Dorrick and M. Akmal, 'Contradictory Trends in Global Income Inequality: A Tale of Two Biases', *Review of Income and Wealth*, 51/2 (2005): 201–29, figure 7A. Reprinted with the permission of Wiley-Blackwell.

Table 12.4 from S. Lall, 'Reinventing Industrial Strategy: The Role of Government Policy in Building Industrial Competitiveness', G-24 Discussion Paper Series No. 28 (New York: United Nations, April 2004), figure 1.

Figures 13.1, 13.2, and *13.5* to *13.8* from UNCTAD (Secretariat of the United Nations Conference on Trade and Development), *Trade and Development Report 2006*, UNCTAD.TDR/2006 (New York and Geneva: United Nations), figures 1.A2, 3.7, 3.10, 3.8, and 3.2.

Figure 13.4 from UNCTAD (Secretariat of the United Nations Conference on Trade and Development), '2005: A Pivotal Year for Commodity Prices?'
[http://www.unctad.org/Templates/Page.asp?intItemID=3732&lang=1] Monthly Price Indices by Commodity Groups. Reprinted with the permissions of Infocomm, Market Information in the Commodities Area, and Commodity Price Statistics (CPS).

Table 13.1 from M. Gautam, *Debt Relief for the Poorest: An OED Review of the HIPC Initiative* (Washington, DC: Operations Evaluation Department, World Bank, 2003). Reprinted with the permission of the World Bank.

Appendix 13.1 from I. Bencheikh, A.-L. Henry-Greard, S. Rinaldi, and L. von Trapp, 'A Parliamentarian's guide to the World Bank'
[http://siteresources.worldbank.org/EXTPARLIAMENTARIANS/Resources/Parliamentarians_Book_Revised.pdf], figure 3.1. Reprinted with the permission of the World Bank.

Guided Tour of Textbook Features

This text is enriched with a range of learning tools to help you navigate the text material and reinforce your knowledge of global political economy. This guided tour shows you how to get the most out of your textbook package.

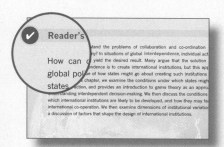

Reader's Guides

Reader's Guides at the beginning of every chapter set the scene for upcoming themes and issues to be discussed, and indicate the scope of coverage within each chapter topic.

Boxes

A number of topics benefit from further explanation or exploration in a way that does not disrupt the flow of the main text. Throughout the book boxes provide you with extra information on particular topics to complement your understanding of the main chapter text.

Key Points

Each main chapter section ends with a set of Key Points that summarize the most important arguments developed within each chapter topic.

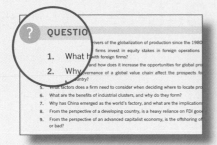

Questions

A set of carefully devised questions has been provided to help you assess your comprehension of core themes and may also be used as the basis of seminar discussion and coursework.

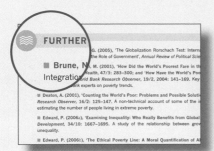

Further Reading

To take your learning further, reading lists have been provided as a guide to find out more about the issues raised within each chapter topic and to help you locate the key academic literature in the field.

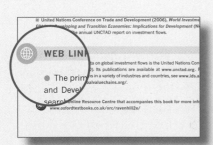

Web Links

At the end of most chapters you will find an annotated summary of useful websites that will be instrumental in further research.

Glossary Terms

Key terms are blue in the text and are defined in a glossary at the end of the text to aid you in exam revision.

Guided Tour of the Online Resource Centre

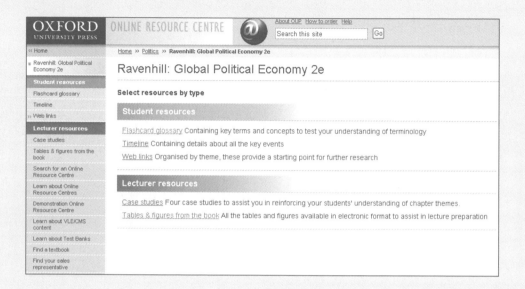

@ **www.oxfordtextbooks.co.uk/orc/ravenhill2e/**

The Online Resource Centre that accompanies this book provides students and lecturers with ready-to-use teaching and learning materials.

Timeline

A timeline has been provided so that you can find out about key events.

Web Links

Additional annotated web links organized by theme.

Flashcard Glossary

A series of interactive flashcards containing key terms and concepts have been provided to test your understanding of terminology.

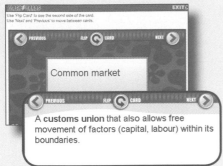

Case Studies (lecturers only)

Four case studies are included on the following topics: the integration of the former Soviet bloc into the global financial system; the Heavily Indebted Poor Countries initiative; the Doha Development Round of the WTO; and the role of the emerging economies of Brazil, Russia, India, and China.

Brief Contents

Detailed Contents

List of Figures

List of Boxes

List of Tables

Abbreviations

ACP	Africa, the Caribbean and the Pacific
ACU	Asian Currency Unit
AFL–CIO	American Federation of Labor–Congress of Industrial Organizations
AFTA	ASEAN Free Trade Area
ANZCERTA	Australia–New Zealand Closer Economic Relations Trade Agreement
APEC	Asia-Pacific Economic Cooperation
ASEAN	Association of Southeast Asian Nations
BIS	Bank for International Settlements
BRICS	The 'new globilizers': Brazil, Russia, India, China
CAP	Common Agricultural Policy
CARICOM	Caribbean Community and Common Market
CEO	Chief executive officer
CERDS	Charter of Economic Rights and Duties of States
CFA	Communauté Financière Africaine (African Financial Community)
CFCs	chlorofluorocarbons
COCOM	Coordinating Committee for Multilateral Export Controls
COMECON	Council of Mutual Economic Assistance
COMESA	Common Market for Eastern and Southern Africa
CPR	Common pool resources
CSAs	country specific advantages
CUSFTA/CUSTA	Canada–US Free Trade Agreement
DAC	Development Assistance Committee
DDA	Doha Development Agenda
DSF	Debt Sustainability Framework
DSU	Dispute Settlement Understanding
ECLA	Economic Commission for Latin America
ECOSOC	[United Nations] Economic and Social Council
ECSC	European Coal and Steel Community
EC	European Community
ECU	European Currency Unit
EEC	European Economic Community
EFTA	European Free Trade Association
EMS	electronic manufacturing service
EPA	Environmental Protection Agency
EPZs	Export Processing Zones
EU	European Union
FDI	foreign direct investment
FSA	firm-specific advantages
FSC	Forest Stewardship Council

ABBREVIATIONS

FSF	Financial Stability Forum
G77	Group of Seventy-Seven
GATS	General Agreement on Trade in Services
GATT	General Agreement on Tariffs and Trade
GCC	Gulf Cooperation Council
GDP	gross domestic product
GEF	Global Environment Facility
GEIs	global economic institutions
GEMs	global economic multilaterals
GM	General Motors
GNP	gross national product
GPE	global political economy
HIPC	Heavily Indebted Poor Countries Initiative
IAIS	International Association of Insurance Supervisors
IBM	International Business Machines
IBRD	International Bank for Reconstruction and Development
ICP	International Comparison Project
ICSID	International Centre for Settlement of Investment Disputes
IDA	International Development Association
IFC	[World Bank] International Finance Corporation
IFI	international financial institution
ILO	International Labour Organization
IMF	International Monetary Fund
IOSCO	International Organization of Securities Commissions
IPCC	Intergovernmental Panel on Climate Change
IPE	international political economy
ISI	import substitution industrialization
ISO	International Organization for Standardization
ITA	Information Technology Agreement (WTO)
ITO	International Trade Organization
ITTO	International Tropical Timber Organization
JFC	[World Bank–Civil Society] Joint Facilitation Committee
JV	joint venture
LDCs	less developed countries
LIC	Low-income country
LLDC	Landlocked developing countries
LMU	Latin Monetary Union
M&As	Mergers and acquisitions
MAI	[OECD] Multilateral Agreement on Investment
MDGs	Millennium Development Goals
MDRI	Multilateral Debt Relief Initiative
MEOs	multilateral economic organizations
MERCOSUR	Common Market of the South
MFA	Multifibre Arrangement

MFN	most-favoured nation
MIC	middle-income country
MIGA	[World Bank] Multilateral Investment Guarantee Agency
MNC	multinational corporation
MNE	multinational enterprise
NAFTA	North American Free Trade Agreement
NAM	non-aligned movement
NAMA	non-agriculture market access
NEC	Nippon Electric Company
NGOs	non-governmental organizations
NIEs	newly industrializing economies
NIEO	New International Economic Order
NTBs	non-tariff barriers
NTMs	non-tariff measures
OECD	Organization for Economic Co-operation and Development
OEMs	original equipment manufacturers
OPEC	Organization of Petroleum Exporting Countries
PC	personal computer
PGA	Peoples' Global Action
PIER	politics of international economic relations
POPs	persistent organic pollutants
PPP	purchasing power parity
PRSPs	Poverty Reduction Strategy Papers
PSIA	Poverty and Social Impact Analysis
PTA	preferential trade agreement
PWC	Post-Washington Consensus
PWT	Penn World Tables
R&D	research and development
RNGMA	Regional Nature of Global Multinational Activity Survey
RTAA	Reciprocal Trade Agreements Act
RTA	regional trading agreement
SADCC	Southern African Development Coordination Conference
SDR	Special Drawing Rights
SIDS	Small Island Developing States
SMEs	small and medium-sized enterprise
SMU	Scandinavian Monetary Union
SSA	Sub-Saharan Africa
TNC	transnational corporation
TPRM	Trade Policy Review Mechanism
TRIMs	trade-related investment measures
TRIPs	trade-related aspects of intellectual property rights
UN	United Nations Organization
UNCED	United Nations Conference on the Environment and Development
UNCTAD	United Nations Conference on Trade and Development

UNEP	United Nations Environment Programme
UNIDO	United Nations Industrial Development Organization
USAID	United States Agency for International Development
VW	Volkswagen
WC	Washington Consensus
WEU	Western European Union
WIDER	[UN] World Institute for Development Economics Research
WTO	World Trade Organization

About the Contributors

Vinod K Aggarwal is Professor of Political Science, Affiliated Professor of Business and Public Policy at the Haas School of Business, and Director of the Berkeley APEC Study Center at the University of California, Berkeley. His publications include *Liberal Protectionism* (University of California Press), *Debt Games* (Cambridge University Press), and *Bilateral Trade Agreements in the Asia-Pacific* (Routledge).

Peter Dauvergne is Professor of Political Science and Canada Research Chair in Global Environmental Politics at the University of British Columbia, Vancouver, Canada. His publications include *Shadows in the Forest* (MIT Press) and *Loggers and Degradation in the Asia-Pacific* (Cambridge University Press).

Cédric Dupont is Professor of Political Science at the Graduate Institute of International Studies, Geneva. He is also Director of the Centre on Alpine Environment and Society at the Kurt Bösch University Institute in Sion, Switzerland. He has published in journals including the *European Journal of International Relations* and the *International Political Science Review*.

Colin Hay is Professor of Political Analysis at the University of Sheffield, UK. His recent publications include *Why We Hate Politics* (Polity Press), *Political Analysis* (Palgrave), *The State* (Palgrave), *European Politics* (Oxford University Press) and *Demystifying Globalization* (Palgrave).

Eric Helleiner is CIGI Chair in International Governance at the University of Waterloo, Ontario Canada. His publications include *States and the Reemergence of Global Finance* and *The Making of National Money* (both from Cornell University Press), as well as *Towards North American Monetary Union?* (McGill-Queen's University Press).

Michael J Hiscox is Professor of Government, Harvard University. His publications include *International Trade and Political Conflict* (Princeton University Press).

Anthony McGrew is Professor of International Relations and Head of the School of Social Sciences at the University of Southampton, UK. His recent publications include *Globalization/Anti-Globalization: Beyond the Great Divide* (2007), *Globalization Theory* (2007), and *Globalization: Human Security and Development* (2006) (all published by Polity Press).

Louis W Pauly is Director of the Centre for International Studies, University of Toronto, where he also holds the Canada Research Chair in Globalization and Governance. His publications include *Opening Financial Markets* and *Who Elected the Bankers?* (both Cornell University Press).

John Ravenhill is Professor in the Department of International Relations, Research School of Pacific and Asian Studies, Australian National University. His publications include *APEC and the Construction of Pacific Rim Regionalism*, and *The Asian Financial Crisis and the Architecture of Global Finance* (both Cambridge University Press).

Caroline Thomas is Deputy Vice Chancellor and Professor of Global Politics at the University of Southampton, UK. Her publications include *Global Governance, Development and Human Security* (Pluto) and *Globalization and the South* (St. Martin's Press).

Eric Thun is Peter Moores Lecturer in Chinese Business Studies at Oxford University's Saïd Business School. His publications include *Changing Lanes in China: Foreign Direct Investment, Local Governments and Auto Sector Development* (Cambridge University Press).

Robert Hunter Wade is Professor of Political Economy, Development Studies Institute, London School of Economics. His publications include *Governing the Market* (Princeton University Press), *Village Republics* (Cambridge University Press), and *Irrigation and Agricultural Politics in South Korea* (Westview Press).

Matthew Watson is Associate Professor (Reader) in Political Economy, Department of Politics and International Studies, University of Warwick, UK. His publications include *The Political Economy of International Capital Mobility* (Palgrave Macmillan), while the argument in the current contribution is more closely related to his previous book, *Foundations of International Political Economy* (Palgrave Macmillan).

Gilbert R Winham is Emeritus Professor of Political Science and Adjunct Professor, Faculty of Law, Dalhousie University, Halifax, Nova Scotia, Canada. His publications include *International Trade and the Tokyo Round Negotiation* (Princeton University Press) and *The Evolution of International Trade Agreements* (University of Toronto Press).

PART 1

Theoretical Approaches to Global Political Economy

1

The Study of Global Political Economy

JOHN RAVENHILL

 Chapter Contents

 Reader's Guide

The contemporary international economic system is more closely integrated than in any previous era. The East Asian financial crisis provides a clear illustration of the relationship between trade, finance, international institutions, and the problems that governments face in coping with the problems generated by complex interdependence.

Before 1945, the spectacular increase in economic integration that had occurred over the previous century was not accompanied by institutionalized governmental collaboration on economic matters. International trade patterns also changed very little over several centuries before 1945. The end of the Second World War marked a significant disjunction: global economic institutions were created, and the transnational corporation emerged as a major actor in international economic relations.

Since the emergence of international political economy (IPE) as a major subfield of the study of international relations in the early 1970s, IPE scholars have generated an enormous literature that has been the product of the employment of a wide variety of theories and methods. Most introductions to the study of IPE have divided the theoretical approaches to the subject into three categories: liberalism, nationalism, and Marxism. This threefold typology is of limited utility today, given the overlap between many of the approaches classified in different categories, and the wealth of theories and methodologies applied in the contemporary study of global political economy.

Prologue: Thailand and the East Asian Financial Crisis

When the government of Thailand was forced in July 1997 to break the long-standing fixed exchange rate between the local currency, (the baht) and the US dollar, its action precipitated what soon became known as the Asian financial crisis. The Thai economy had enjoyed one of the highest rates of growth in the world over the previous decade: observers frequently referred to Thailand as one of the new Asian tigers, or 'second-tier' newly industrializing economies (NIEs). The record of the central bank—the Bank of Thailand—had been praised widely as a model of responsible economic management. Yet plaudits for the country's economic record afforded no protection when the sentiment of the financial markets turned against it. Local and foreign investors alike rushed to move their money out of the country, fearing that if they did not move quickly, the Bank of Thailand's foreign exchange reserves would be exhausted and they would be left empty-handed. The government had no alternative but to allow the market to determine the value of the currency, and to turn to the International Monetary Fund (IMF) and to other governments for loans of foreign exchange. By the end of the year, the value of the baht had collapsed to close to half its level at the end of June.

Other countries quickly became embroiled in the crisis. Korea, one of the original 'Gang of Four' newly industrializing economies, a country whose phenomenal economic success had seen its annual per capita income rise from around $50 in the 1950s to close to $10,000 in the mid-1990s, endured its worst recession since the country's civil war at the start of the 1950s: the value of its currency collapsed; living standards fell precipitously; and a significant number of the country's largest companies became bankrupt when financial institutions were unable to continue to provide them with loans. The effects of the crisis went far beyond the East Asian region itself. Instability in financial markets spread as far as Brazil and Russia, even though the developments in Asia did not have a significant direct impact on these economies, and their underlying economic fundamentals were quite different from those in the crisis-hit countries of East Asia. Given East Asia's increasing prominence as the 'workshop of the world', the crisis was a significant factor in a slowing in the growth of international trade in 1998 (this increased by only 3.5 per cent, compared with 10 per cent in the previous year) (WTO 1999a). Reduced levels of economic activity in East Asia also caused a drop in the prices of raw materials for African and South American exporters (World Bank 1999b).

At a fundamental level, the origins of the crisis illustrate the close interrelationship between the trade and financial spheres. Thailand's economic success in the previous decade owed much to the relocation of manufacturing industry from North-East Asia to relatively low-cost South-East Asian countries. This move had been precipitated by the appreciation of the currencies of Japan, Korea, and Taiwan, following an agreement (the Plaza Accord, named after the New York hotel in which the 1985 meeting took place) on exchange-rate realignment among the Group of Seven industrialized countries (see Box 1.1). Many of the exports of the three North-East Asian economies were already facing cost pressures as a consequence of the rising prices of both labour and land; these were intensified when the exchange-rate realignments raised the cost of their goods in their export markets. These pressures prompted massive flows of foreign direct investment from North-East Asia into South-East Asia as Japanese, Korean, and Taiwanese manufacturers sought to take advantage of the relatively low costs in their Southern neighbours (Bernard and Ravenhill 1995). The structure of the Thai

BOX 1.1

The Group of Seven/Group of Eight

The Group of Seven (G7) industrialized countries was established in 1975, the first of a series of annual meetings where politicians and officials from the world's leading economies discussed issues relating to macroeconomic policy co-ordination, trade and financial policies, and relations with developing countries.

Six countries were present at the initial meeting in Rambouillet: Britain, France, (West) Germany, Italy, Japan, and the United States. Canada joined the group in 1976, at its second meeting. In 1977, the group allowed participation by a representative of the European Community. From 1994 onwards, the G7 met with representatives of Russia at each of its meetings; at the Birmingham meeting in 1998, Russia was accorded full membership, transforming the G7 into the G8.

For more details on the G7/G8, see www.g7.utoronto.ca/

economy was transformed in the process: whereas, in 1980, manufactures contributed only a-quarter of the total value of Thailand's exports, by 1990 this figure had reached 63 per cent.

In the first half of the 1990s, Thailand not only received substantial inflows of **foreign direct investment** (FDI—the acquisition abroad by companies of physical assets such as plant and equipment) but also very large volumes of bank lending and **portfolio investment** (funds invested in debt securities such as bonds, and investment in company equities of insufficient size to give control over the company). Unlike FDI, these flows could easily be reversed through the non-renewal of loans (most of which were short-term). The growth in bank lending and portfolio flows reflected changes on both the supply and demand sides of international finance, and in technology. On the supply side, the principal development was the growth in Western industrialized countries of pension funds with enormous sums to invest; moreover, to meet the needs of their clients and to capitalize on an increasingly globalized market, both existing and new financial institutions developed ever more complicated financial instruments. Secure satellite communications made it possible for financial institutions to move funds around the world instantaneously.

On the demand side, access to these new sources of lending appeared to offer economies such as

Thailand a relatively low-cost source of funds to supplement domestic savings. Countries undergoing industrialization—whether the United States and Russia in the nineteenth century, or Brazil today—have always used foreign borrowing to bridge the gap between actual domestic savings and desired levels of investment. And, in the first half of the 1990s, foreign borrowing was particularly attractive because loans from international sources frequently carried lower interest rates than money available domestically. Like many other developing countries seeking to attract foreign capital, Thailand in the late 1980s took steps to liberalize and deregulate its financial sector. It soon became apparent, however, that a large portion of the loans flooding into Thailand were not being used for productive purposes: rather, they were fuelling speculation in real estate and the stock market. Banks, largely freed from government oversight, were lending recklessly and incurring substantial volumes of non-performing loans. The domestic inflation that resulted from the speculative investments in turn reduced the competitiveness of Thailand's exports.

Had Thailand, like most industrialized countries from the early 1970s onwards, maintained a flexible exchange rate, then depreciation of its currency could have compensated in international markets for the rise in the domestic prices of its products. But Thailand, like a large number of less developed economies, had chosen to maintain a fixed exchange rate between its currency and that of its largest export market, the United States. The loss of competitiveness of Thailand's exports because of domestic inflation was compounded by a depreciation of the exchange rates of some of its competitors. The value of the Japanese yen fell against the US dollar (and consequently also the Thai baht, because of the fixed exchange rate between the dollar and the Thai currency) in the mid-1990s. The products of Thai subsidiaries of Japanese companies became more expensive in the Japanese market. Consequently, a number of Japanese firms shifted their production back to Japan. And China, emerging in the 1990s as a significant competitor to Thailand and other South-East Asian economies in the production of labour-intensive products, devalued its currency, the renminbi (or yuan), in 1994, placing further pressure on Thailand's export earnings.

The combination of domestic inflation, a fixed exchange rate, the depreciation of the currencies of competitors, and massive inflows of short-term capital proved catastrophic for the Thai economy. By 1996, because of the loss of competitiveness of its exports, the country was running a large trade deficit. Investors began to fear that the government would be forced to devalue the baht—which would have led to foreign exchange losses for them. And here the sheer quantity of short-term lending exacerbated the panic among investors: the volume of short-term loans exceeded the central bank's total holdings of foreign currencies, so it was rational for individual investors to scramble to move their money out of Thailand before the Bank's foreign exchange holdings were exhausted. The withdrawal of funds forced the Thai government to float the baht and to seek loans from the IMF and foreign governments to stabilize the economy. Thailand negotiated a package that gave it access to $3.9 billion of IMF money, and a further $12.7 billion, mainly from other governments, of which the Japanese government provided $4 billion (for further discussion of the Thai experience, see Warr (1998) and Haggard and MacIntyre (2000)).

The involvement of the International Monetary Fund in crisis-hit Asian economies proved particularly controversial. Many observers believed that the conditions that the IMF attached to its loans were unnecessarily intrusive, that the policies it prescribed were inappropriate for the particular problems the East Asian economies faced, and that the Fund was conspiring with the US Treasury and Wall Street to open up the East Asian economies to foreign influence (see, from a variety of perspectives, Wade and Veneroso 1998; Eichengreen 2000; Stiglitz 2002). Criticism of the policies of the international financial institutions' response to the East Asian crises caused both the IMF and the World Bank to review their policies, and in turn led to a significant increase in the transparency of their operations (for further discussion of the international financial institutions and debt crises, see Pauly, Chapter 8 in this volume). But the unhappiness of East Asian governments at what they perceived to be an unsympathetic response to their difficulties, not just by the international financial institutions but also by most Western governments, also prompted new efforts to provide regional mechanisms to support economies in crisis. While an initial proposal from the Japanese government for an Asian Monetary Fund failed, in part because of opposition from the United States, this was followed up by agreement on a series of bilateral arrangements between the central banks of East Asian governments to loan foreign currencies to one another should they experience a foreign exchange crisis. The momentum established by these proposals carried over to foster the negotiation of new regional trade treaties among the East Asian economies.

The East Asian economic crises provide an excellent illustration of many of the themes of this book:

- the growing interdependence of countries in a globalizing economy;
- the speed with which developments in one part of the world economy are transmitted to others;

- the increased significance of private actors in the contemporary global economy, especially in the financial sector;

- the way in which crises prompt governments to seek collaboration at both regional and global level to regulate international markets—but concurrently the difficulties that states have in co-ordinating their behaviours to take effective action;

- the vulnerability of the contemporary global financial system to periodic crises;

- the significant role of the international financial institutions (the World Bank and the International Monetary Fund) in responding to crises in less developed economies;

- the manner in which the increased severity of financial crises, and other developments in the trade and financial relationships between industrialized and less developed economies, have had an impact on poverty and inequality (from 1996 to 1998, for example, the incidence of poverty increased by 80 per cent in Indonesia, and doubled in South Korea);

- the relationship between economy and environment (the crisis in Indonesia, for example, that followed quickly on the heels of that in Thailand, and which led to the Indonesian currency, the rupiah, to lose 80 per cent of its value, in the words of a report by the US Department of Energy (Energy Information Administration 2001) 'accelerated natural resource depletion as environmental regulations were set aside and people opted for less expensive and environmentally damaging production and harvesting methods'); and

- the growing significance of civic groups in articulating alternative approaches on many economic issues from those favoured by states and corporate actors.

Although, as will become evident in later chapters, contributors to this book hold a variety of perspectives on the question of whether there is such a thing as a 'global' economy, all would accept that we live in a *globalizing* economy that differs in some fundamental ways from anything that the world has previously experienced. The following section briefly sketches how the world economy evolved to reach its present state.

The World Economy Pre-1914

The 'modern world economy', most historians agree, came into existence in the late-fifteenth and sixteenth centuries. This was a period in which despotic monarchs in Western Europe, seeking to consolidate their power against both internal and external foes, pushed to extend the boundaries of markets. In this era of mercantilism, political power was equated with wealth, and wealth with power (Viner 1948). Wealth, in the form of bullion generated by trade surpluses or seized from enemies, enabled monarchs to build the administrative apparatus of their states, and to

finance the construction of military forces. The new concentration of military power could be projected, both internally and externally, to extract further resources. The consolidation of the state went hand in hand with the extension of markets. Gradually, most parts of the world were enmeshed in a Euro-centric economy, as suppliers of raw materials and 'luxury' goods. Britain adopted domestic reforms largely pioneered by the Netherlands (which had the world's highest per capita income in the seventeenth and eighteenth centuries) to supplant the Dutch in many world markets: armed conflict and the use of the Navigation Acts (1651–1849), which restricted the use of foreign vessels in British trade, enabled it to monopolize trade with its ever-expanding empire.

The era of mercantilism did not, however, bring a notable increase in overall global wealth. Before 1820, per capita incomes in most parts of the world were not significantly different from those of the previous eight *centuries* (they increased by less than an average of one-tenth of 1 per cent each year between 1700 and 1820). And despite the striking extension of the global market during the seventeenth and eighteenth centuries, the vast majority of commerce continued to be conducted within individual localities until the advent of the Industrial Revolution. The introduction of steam power revolutionized transportation, both internally and internationally. And in the second half of the nineteenth century, further technological advances—the introduction of refrigerated ships, the laying of submarine telegraph cables—contributed to a 'shrinking' of the world and to a deepening of the international division of labour. The value of world exports grew tenfold (from a relatively small base) between 1820 and 1870: from 1870 to 1913, world exports grew at an annual average rate of 3.4 per cent, substantially above the 2.1 annual increase in world GDP (Maddison 2001: 262, table B-19; and 362, table F-4).

Trade was becoming increasingly important to world welfare, yet the pattern of international commerce in 1913—indeed, even in 1945—was not dramatically different from that of the eighteenth century. The industrialized countries of the world—essentially a Western European core to which had been added the United States and Japan by the turn of the twentieth century—exported principally manufactured goods while the rest of the world supplied agricultural products and raw materials to feed the industrialized countries' workforces and to fuel their manufacturing plants (as a relative latecomer to industrialization, and an economy with significant comparative advantage in agricultural production, the United States was an exception to this generalization: cotton remained the

single most important export for the United States in 1913, contributing nearly twice the value of exports of machinery and iron and steel combined; it was not until 1930 that machinery exports exceeded those of cotton, although by 1910 the USA had become a net exporter of manufactured goods (data from Mitchell 1993: 504, table E3; and Irwin 2003)).

With the exception of the United States, trade among the industrialized countries in manufactured goods remained relatively unimportant. In 1913, for example, agricultural products and other primary products constituted two-thirds of the total imports of the United Kingdom. To be sure, some changes had occurred in the composition of imports. Although the 'luxury' imports of the previous centuries—sugar, tea, coffee, and tobacco—had become staples in the diet of the new urban working and middle classes, their aggregate importance in European imports had shrunk relative to other commodities, notably wheat and flour, butter and vegetable oils, and meat (Offer 1989: 82, table 6.1).

For the early European industrializers, trade with their colonies, dominions, or with the other lands of recent European settlement, such as Argentina, was more important than trade with other industrialized countries. For the United Kingdom, a larger share of imports was contributed by Argentina, Australia, Canada, and India together than by the United States, despite the latter's importance in British imports of cotton for its burgeoning textiles industry. These four countries also took five times the American share of British exports in 1913 (Mitchell 1992: 644, table E2). Similarly, Algeria was a larger market for French exports in 1913 than was the United States.

Tariffs continued to constitute a significant barrier to international trade, even in what is often termed the 'golden age' of liberalism before 1914. Most industrialized countries (the significant exceptions being the United Kingdom and the Netherlands) had actually raised the level of their tariffs in the last three decades of the nineteenth century to protect their domestic producers against the increasing import competition that had been facilitated

BOX 1.2

Most-Favoured Nation Status

Under the **most-favoured nation** (MFN) principle, a government is obliged to grant to any trading partner with which it has signed an agreement treatment equivalent to the best ('most preferred') it offers to any of its partners. For example, if France had a trade treaty with Germany in which it had reduced its tariffs on imports of German steel to 8 per cent, it would be obliged, under the most-favoured nation principle, if it signed a trade treaty with the United States, to reduce its tariffs on imports of US steel also to 8 per cent. The MFN principle is the foundation for non-discrimination in international trade, and is often asserted to be the 'cornerstone' of the post-1945 trade regime (see Winham, Chapter 5 in this volume). The MFN principle makes a significant contribution to depoliticizing trade relations because (a) countries are obliged to give equivalent treatment to all trading partners, regardless of their economic power; and (b) countries cannot discriminate in their treatment of the trade of certain partners simply because they do not like the political complexion or policies of the governments of these countries.

by lower transport costs. In 1913, the average tariff level in Germany and Japan was 12 per cent, in France 16 per cent, and in the United States 32.5 per cent (Maddison 1989: 47, table 4.4). The post-1870 increase in tariffs offset some of the gains from lower transportation costs. Lindert and Williamson (2001) estimate that nearly three-quarters of the closer integration of markets that occurred in the century before the outbreak of the First World War is attributable to these lower transport costs (see Table 9.3 in McGrew, Chapter 9 in this volume).

Governments continued to erect barriers to the movement of goods in the second part of the nineteenth century, but capital and people moved relatively freely across the globe, their mobility facilitated by developments in transportation and communication. From 1820 to 1913, 26 million people migrated from Europe to the United States, Canada, Australia, New Zealand, Argentina, and Brazil. Five million Indians followed the British flag in migrating to Burma, Malaya, Sri Lanka, and Africa while an even larger number of Chinese are estimated to have migrated to other countries on the Western Pacific rim (Maddison 2001: 98). The opening up of the lands of 'new settlement' required massive capital investments—in railways in particular. By 1913, the United Kingdom, France, and Germany had investments abroad totalling over $33 billion: after the 1870s, Britain invested more

than half its savings abroad, and the income from its foreign investments in 1913 was equivalent to almost 10 per cent of all the goods and services produced domestically (Maddison 2001: 100).

The spectacular growth in international economic integration was not accompanied by any significant institutionalization of intergovernmental collaboration. Even though the Anglo-French Cobden–Chevalier Treaty of 1860 had introduced the principle of most-favoured nation status into international trade agreements (see Box 1.2), governments conducted trade negotiations on a bilateral basis rather than under the auspices of an international institution.

The international financial system was similarly characterized by a lack of institutionalization. The rapid growth of economic integration was facilitated by the international adoption of the gold standard (see Box 1.3). The origins of the nineteenth-century gold standard lay in action by the Bank of England in 1821 to make all its notes convertible into gold (although Britain had operated a de facto gold standard from as early as 1717). The United States, though formally on a bimetallic (gold and silver) standard, switched to a de facto gold standard in 1834 and turned this into a de jure arrangement in 1900. Germany and other industrializing economies followed suit in the 1870s. Because every country fixed the value of its national currency in

BOX 1.3

The Gold Standard

A gold standard exists when a country fixes the price of its domestic currency in terms of a specific amount of gold. National money (which may or may not consist of gold coins, because other metallic coins and banknotes were also used in some countries) and bank deposits would be freely convertible into gold at the specified price.

Under the gold standard, because the level of each country's economic activity is determined by its money supply, which in turn rested on its gold holdings, a disequilibrium in its **balance of trade** in principle would be self-correcting. Let us assume, for example, that Britain is running a trade deficit with the United States because inflation in Britain has made its exports relatively unattractive to US consumers. Because British exports do not cover the full costs of imports from the United States, British authorities would have to transfer gold to the US Treasury. This transfer would reduce the money supply, and hence the level of economic activity in Britain, having a deflationary effect on the domestic economy, and depress its demand for imports. In the United States, the opposite would occur: an inflow of gold would boost the money supply, thereby generating additional economic activity in the United States and increasing inflationary pressures there. Higher levels of economic activity would increase the country's demand for imports. Changes in the money supplies in the two countries brought about by the transfer of gold therefore would bring their demand for goods back into balance and lead to a restoration of the ratio of the two countries' prices to that reflected in the exchange rate between their currencies.

In principle, the gold standard should act to restore equilibrium automatically in international payments. Central banks, however, were also expected to facilitate adjustment by raising their interest rates when countries were suffering a payments deficit (thereby further dampening domestic economic activities and making domestic investments more attractive to foreigners) and, conversely, to lower interest rates when their economies' were experiencing a payments surplus. For most of the period from 1870 to 1914, the Bank of England played by the rules of the game fairly consistently. Other central banks—including those of France and Belgium—did not. They frequently intervened to attempt to shield the domestic economy from the effects of gold flows (to 'sterilize' their effects) by buying or selling securities (thereby reducing or increasing the volume of gold circulating in the domestic economy).

The gold standard was vulnerable to shocks, which were often transmitted quickly from one country to another. The discovery of gold in California in 1848, for example, led to an increase in the US money supply, domestic inflation, and an outflow of gold to its trade partners, which in turn raised their domestic price levels. Countries on the periphery were particularly vulnerable to shocks: interest-rate increases in the industrialized countries, for example, often drew capital from the periphery, leaving the peripheral countries with the major burden of adjustment.

For further discussion, see Eichengreen (1985) and Officer (2001).

terms of gold, each currency had a fixed exchange rate against every other in the system (assume, for example, that the United States sets the value of its currency as $100 per ounce of gold, while the United Kingdom sets its value at £50 per ounce of gold: the exchange rate between the two currencies would be £1 = $2).

The great contribution of the gold standard to facilitating international commerce was that economic agents generally did not have to worry about foreign exchange risks: the possibility that

the value of the currency of a foreign country would change *vis-à-vis* their domestic currency and thus, for example, reduce the value of their foreign investments. British investors in American railways could be confident that the dollars they had bought with their sterling investments would buy the same amount of sterling at the date their investment matured, and that the US Treasury would convert the dollars back into gold at this time. Meanwhile, they received interest on the sums invested. Confidence in the gold standard rested not on any international institution but rather on the commitment of individual governments to maintain the opportunity for individuals to convert their domestic currencies into gold at a fixed exchange rate. Ultimately, the implementation of the gold standard rested on the assumption that governments had both the capacity and the will to impose economic pain on their domestic populations when deflation was needed in order to bring their economy back into equilibrium. These domestic costs became less acceptable with the rise of working-class political representation, and with the growth of expectations that a fundamental responsibility of governments was to ensure domestic full employment.

KEY POINTS

- The modern world economy came into existence in the fifteenth and sixteenth centuries.

- Despite the significant changes that occurred in the three centuries before the outbreak of the First World War, the fundamental composition and direction of international trade remained unchanged.

- Neither in the field of trade nor of finance was any significant international institution constructed in the years before 1914.

- Advances in technology were the main driving force behind the integration of markets, and they facilitated the enormous growth in investment and migration in the nineteenth century.

- The great merit of the gold standard was that it provided certainty for international transactions because, to a great extent, it removed the risk of foreign exchange losses.

The World Economy in the Inter-War Period

The outbreak of the First World War was a devastating blow to cosmopolitan liberalism: it destroyed the credibility of the liberal argument that economic interdependence in itself would be sufficient to foster an era of peaceful coexistence among states. The war brought to an end an era of unprecedented economic interdependence among the leading industrial countries. As discussed in the chapters by McGrew and Hay in this book, for many industrialized economies, indicators of economic openness and interdependence did not regain their pre-First World War levels until the 1970s.

The war devastated the economies of Europe: subsequent political instability compounded economic disruptions. Economic reconstruction was further complicated by demands that Germany make reparations for its aggression, and that Britain and other European countries repay their wartime borrowings from the United States. The economic chaos of the inter-war years was a sorry reflection of the inability of governments to agree on measures to restore economic stability, and their resort to beggar-thy-neighbour policies in their efforts to alleviate domestic economic distress. Although the collapse of international trade in the 1930s is the feature of the inter-war economy that figures most prominently in stories of this era, the most fundamental problem of the period was the inability of states to construct a viable international financial system.

The international gold standard broke down with the outbreak of war in August 1914, when a speculative attack on sterling caused the Bank of England to impose exchange controls—a refusal to convert sterling into gold and a de facto ban on gold exports. Other countries followed suit. Leading countries agreed to reinstate a modified version of the international gold standard in 1925. They failed to act consistently, however, in re-establishing the link between national currencies and gold. The United Kingdom restored the convertibility of sterling at the pre-war gold price despite the domestic inflation that had occurred in the intervening decade: the consequence was that sterling was generally reckoned to be overvalued by at least 10 per cent, making British exports uncompetitive; it proved very difficult for the British government to establish an equilibrium in its balance of payments without imposing severe deflation domestically. Other countries—notably France, Belgium, and Italy—restored convertibility of their currencies at a much lower price of gold than had prevailed before 1914.

The resulting misalignment of currencies was compounded by higher trade barriers than had existed before 1914, the absence of a country/central bank with the resources and the will to provide leadership to the system, and by a failure of central banks to play by the 'rules of the game' of the gold standard. Their inclination to intervene to 'sterilize' the domestic impact of international gold flows was symptomatic of a more fundamental underlying problem: in an era when the working class had been fully enfranchised, when trade unions had become important players in political systems, especially in Western Europe, and when governments were expected to take responsibility for maintaining full employment and promoting domestic economic welfare, the subordination of the domestic economy to the dictates of global markets in the form of the international gold standard was no longer politically acceptable. Polanyi (1944) is the classic statement of this argument; on the misguided attempts by Britain to restore the convertibility of sterling at pre-1914 levels, see Keynes (1925).

The abandonment of the international gold standard followed another speculative attack on sterling in the middle of 1931. The Bank of England lost much of its reserves in July and August of that year, and Britain abandoned the gold standard in September, a move that precipitated a sharp depreciation of the pound (testimony to its overvaluation in the brief period in which the gold standard was restored). Other countries again quickly followed in breaking the link between their currencies and gold. By then, the world economy was in depression, following the shocks to the world economy transmitted from the United States after the Wall Street collapse of October 1929. The gold standard almost certainly exacerbated the effects of the depression, because government efforts to maintain the link between their currencies and gold constrained the use of expansionary (inflationary) policies to combat unemployment and low levels of domestic demand (Eichengreen 1992).

The world economy was already in depression before the US Congress, in response to concerns about the intensification of import competition for domestic farmers, passed the Smoot–Hawley Tariff of 1930. This raised US tariffs to historically high levels (an average *ad valorem* tariff of 41 per cent, although tariff rates were already very high as a result of the Tariff Act of 1922, the Fordney–McCumber Tariff). Retaliation from US trading partners quickly followed, with the European countries giving preferential tariff treatment to their colonies. The value of world trade declined by two-thirds between 1929 and 1934, and became increasingly concentrated in closed imperial blocks.

As in the pre-1914 period, international institutions played no significant role in the governance of international economic matters. The League of Nations had established an Economic and Financial Organization with subcommittees on the various areas of international economic relations. It enjoyed success in the early 1920s in co-ordinating a financial reconstruction package of $ 26 million for Austria. It also held various conferences aimed at facilitating trade by promoting common standards on customs procedures, compilation of economic statistics, and so on. But the economic and political disarray of the inter-war period simply overwhelmed the League's limited resources and legitimacy: the move to restore international economic collaboration awaited effective action by the world's leading economy, the United States. This began with the passage by Congress in 1934 of the Reciprocal Trade Agreements Act (RTAA), which gave the president the authority to negotiate foreign trade agreements (without Congressional approval). The RTAA and the subsequent signature before 1939 of trade agreements with twenty of America's trading partners laid the foundations for the multilateral system that emerged after the Second World War (the reasons why US trade policy changed so dramatically between 1930 and 1934 have been a focus of significant recent work in international political economy; see Hiscox 1999; Irwin and Kroszner 1997).

KEY POINTS

- Misalignment of exchange rates contributed to the problems of economic adjustment in the 1920s.

- The world economy was already in recession before tariffs were raised in the early 1930s—but higher tariffs exacerbated the decline in international trade.

- States did not negotiate any significant institutionalization of international economic relations in the inter-war period.

The World Economy Post-1945

The world economy that emerged after the Second World War was qualitatively different from anything experienced before. John Ruggie, a leading contemporary theorist of political economy, has identified two fundamental principles that distinguish the post-war economy from its predecessors: the adoption of what Ruggie (1982), following Polanyi (1944), terms embedded liberalism, and a commitment to multilateralism (Ruggie 1992).

Embedded liberalism refers to the compromise that governments made after 1945 between safeguarding their domestic economic objectives, especially a commitment to maintaining full employment, and an opening up of the domestic economy to allow for the restoration of international trade and investment. The 'embedding' of the commitment to economic openness—the liberal element—within domestic economic and political objectives was attained through the inclusion of provisions in the rules of international trade and finance that would allow governments to opt out, on a temporary basis, from their international commitments should these threaten fundamental domestic economic objectives. Moreover, an acknowledgement of the legitimacy of governments giving priority to the pursuit of domestic economic objectives was also written into the rules of the game. The adoption of the principle of embedded liberalism was an acknowledgement by governments that international economic collaboration rested on their capacity to maintain domestic political consensus—and that international economic collaboration was, fundamentally, a political bargain. This recognition explains, for example, why the agricultural sector was for many years excluded from trade liberalization: the domestic political costs for governments of negotiating freer trade in agricultural products were judged to be so high as to jeopardize otherwise politically feasible trade liberalization in other sectors.

The institutionalization of international economic co-operation is another fundamental change in international economic relations in the post-war period. In neither the period of relative stability of the pre-First World War gold standard era nor in the chaos of the 1930s did leading economies create significant international economic institutions. A commitment to multilateralism is one of the defining characteristics of the post-1945 order. For Ruggie (1992: 571), multilateralism is not merely a matter of numbers—it involves collaboration among three or more states, not necessarily all members of the system—but it also has a *qualitative* element in that the co-ordination of relations is on 'the basis of "generalized" principles of conduct—that is, principles which specify appropriate conduct for a class of actions, without regard to the particularistic interests of the parties or the strategic exigencies that may exist in any specific occurrence'. A classic example is the most-favoured nation principle, with its requirement that products from all trading partners must be treated in the same manner regardless of the characteristics of the countries involved. This principle for the conduct of trade contrasts, for example, with the largely bilateral trade agreements of the inter-war years, where governments, rather than applying a generalized principle to their trade relations, discriminated in their treatment of individual trading partners.

The commitment to multilateralism that developed in the late 1930s and during the Second World War bore immediate fruit in the founding of the Bretton Woods multilateral financial institutions: the International Monetary Fund, and the World Bank (see Box 1.4). Note, however, that these global or universal institutions, membership of which is open to all states in the international system, are just one form of multilateralism. For the whole of the period since 1945, but especially since the mid-1990s, regional institutions have also played an important role in international economic (as well as security) affairs (Ravenhill, Chapter 6 in this volume). States have enmeshed themselves increasingly in a dense web of multilateral institutions.

The unprecedented rates of economic growth achieved in the years after 1945 attest to the success of the pursuit of multilateral economic collaboration in this period. Global gross domestic product (GDP) grew at close to 5 per cent in the period 1950–73. Although the recessions that followed the oil price rises of 1973–4 and 1979–80, and the debt crises that afflicted Latin America and Africa, contributed to a slowing of growth in the quarter-century after 1973, world GDP nonetheless grew

---

BOX 1.4

Bretton Woods

In 1944, the Western allies brought together their principal economic advisers for a conference at the Mount Washington Hotel in the village of Bretton Woods, New Hampshire, to chart the future of the international economy in the post-war period. The forty-four governments represented at what was officially known as the United Nations Monetary and Financial Conference agreed on the principles that would govern international finance in the post-war years, and to create two major international institutions to assist in the management of these arrangements: the International Monetary Fund; and the World Bank (formally known as the International Bank for Reconstruction and Development). For details of the discussions at the conference see Dormael (1978) (excerpted at www.imfsite.org/origins/confer.html; see also www.yale.edu/lawweb/avalon/decade/decad047.htm).

These institutions and the rules for managing international finance that were agreed became known collectively as the Bretton Woods regimes. In 1947, a United Nations Conference on Trade and Employment in Havana, Cuba, drew up a charter (www.globefield.com/havana.htm) for an International Trade Organization (ITO), to complement the Bretton Woods financial institutions. The ITO never came to fruition, however—see Winham, Chapter 5 in this volume.

at an average of 3 per cent per annum, a faster rate than during any period before 1945 (Maddison 2001: 262, table 8–19). Moreover, world trade grew more rapidly than world production: world exports expanded by close to 8 per cent per annum in the years 1950–73, and by 5 per cent annually in the subsequent twenty-five-year period (Maddison 2001: 362, table F-4). The internationalized sector consequently grew in importance in most economies, with important implications for the balance of domestic political interests on trade policy issues (see Hiscox, Chapter 4 in this volume).

Aggregate rates of growth, however, disguised substantial variations across different regions of the world economy. The gap between rich and poor widened substantially (see Figure 1.1). In 1500, little difference had existed in per capita incomes across various regions of the world. Incomes per head in the United States did not exceed those of China until the second quarter of the eighteenth century.

By the third quarter of the nineteenth century, however, a marked gap had developed between incomes per capita in the United States and Western Europe on the one hand, and those of the rest of the world. Per capita incomes in Africa and in most parts of Asia stagnated (and in China actually regressed for a century). Despite the economic turmoil and slower rates of growth of the inter-war years, the absolute gap between the industrialized economies and the rest of the world continued to widen: the divergence increased rapidly in the post-1945 era. Only a handful of previously less developed countries, mostly in East Asia, made significant progress in closing the gap. Africa, meanwhile, became increasingly detached from the globalizing economy: its exports, measured in constant prices, barely expanded in the years between 1973 and 1990. The poor export performance contributed to falls in per capita income that occurred in the majority of years between 1973 and 1998. By the latter date,

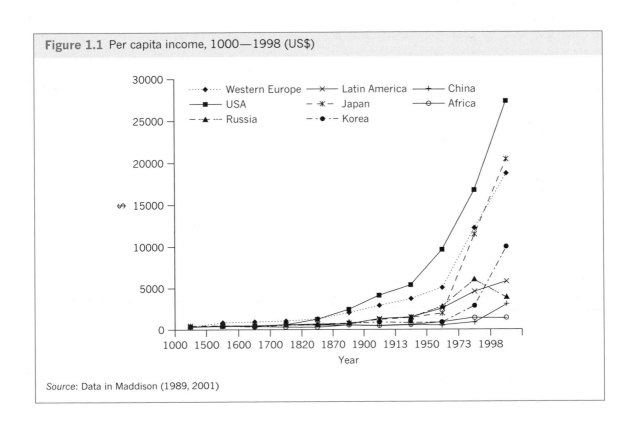

Figure 1.1 Per capita income, 1000—1998 (US$)

Source: Data in Maddison (1989, 2001)

the average per capita income in Africa was no more than Western Europe had experienced in 1820 (all data drawn from Maddison 2001). Growing international inequality has been a fundamental part of the modern globalizing economy (see the chapters by Wade and Thomas in this volume).

Another defining characteristic of the post-1945 international economy was the growth in the number of transnational corporations (TNCs—also referred to in some chapters of this volume as multinational enterprises). A growth of significant private economic enterprises with international operations had accompanied the emergence of the modern world economy in the fifteenth century. These, however, were primarily trading companies, such as the East India Company, specializing in moving goods between national markets. And when foreign investment took off in earnest, in the half-century before the First World War, the vast majority of it was portfolio investment—that is, investment in bonds and other financial instruments that did not give investors management control over the borrowing company. Companies that engaged in foreign direct investment—that is, the ownership and management of assets in more than one country for the purposes of production of goods or services (the definition of a TNC)—were relative rarities before 1945 (with some notable exceptions, such as the major oil companies and IBM). In the post-Second World War years, FDI took off, and has grown more rapidly than either production or international trade (see Thun, Chapter 11 in this volume).

The TNC has become the key actor in the globalizing economy. By 2005, it was estimated that there were 77,000 TNCs in operation, controlling more than 770,000 subsidiaries worldwide. The global stock of FDI amounted to more than $10 trillion, and the value added by TNC subsidiaries was equal to about 10 per cent of the world's GDP. Moreover, sales by the subsidiaries of TNCs were nearly double the total value of world trade: an estimated $22 trillion compared to a figure of $12.6 trillion for all world exports (all data from UNCTAD 2006b: xvii, 9). Whereas in the period before 1960, the vast majority of FDI and TNCs came from the United

States, in subsequent years the American presence has been supplemented by corporations with their headquarters in Europe, Japan, Korea, and, increasingly, in less developed countries such as Brazil and India (for further discussion, see Dicken 2003).

The activities of TNCs, in turn, have transformed the nature of international trade fundamentally. In particular, the composition of trade has changed dramatically since 1945. Whereas in the inter-war years the composition of trade differed little from that of the previous centuries—that is, it was based on the exchange of raw materials and agricultural products for manufactured goods, since the post-war reconstruction of Europe and Japan, the principal component of trade has been the international exchange of manufactured goods. At first, this trade was primarily among the industrialized countries. In many instances it involved intra-industry trade, that is, the international exchange of products from the same industry. For example, intra-industry trade occurs when Sweden exports Volvos cars to Germany and imports BMW vehicles from Germany. As this example suggests, product differentiation by brand name often provides the basis for intra-industry trade, and bears little resemblance to the comparative advantage-based explanation for trade that underlies conventional economic theory. This change in the composition of world trade has been associated with the growing role of TNCs. They now account for two-thirds of global trade: trade among the various subsidiaries of TNCs—that is, trade within the same firm—constitutes fully a third of all world trade.

Since the 1980s, in particular, less developed countries have also been integrated into the international production networks led by TNCs (see Thun, Chapter 11 in this volume). An increasing number of developing countries have changed the structure of their tariffs to give preference to the processing and assembling of components that are exported subsequently. The World Trade Organization estimates that such processing activities account for more than 80 per cent of the exports of the Dominican Republic, close to 60 per cent of the exports of China, and nearly 50 per cent of the exports of Mexico (WTO 2000*a*). This participation in global production networks is the most significant factor in a dramatic change in the commodity composition of the exports of less developing countries. Contrary to some popular impressions, by the end of the 1990s, manufactured exports constituted 70 per cent of the total exports from the developing world. The share of manufactures in their exports had increased threefold since the end of the 1970s (UNCTAD 2001: xviii).

Reference to these less developed economies provides a timely reminder of another dramatic change in international economic relations since 1945—a huge augmentation in the number of independent states in the system. As noted in Box 1.4, only forty-four countries were represented at the Bretton Woods conference, which was dominated by the industrialized countries of Europe and North America, but also included a few of the long-independent countries of Central and South America. Within two decades, almost all of the colonies of the European countries had gained their independence. This development had profound implications for the international system. One was simply the consequence of an increase in both the number of states and in the diversity of the international community: the number of states in the system more than doubled. Collaboration in international economic relations and the management of various dimensions of this collaboration became increasingly complex, illustrated very clearly in the

trade sphere by the difficulties in negotiating the Uruguay and Doha Rounds of WTO talks (see Winham, Chapter 5 in this volume, for details of these discussions; and Aggarwal and Dupont, Chapter 3, for a discussion of the problems that larger numbers pose for collaboration). The growth in the number of less developed countries also brought institutional change, most notably in the foundation of the United Nations Conference on Trade and Development (UNCTAD) in 1964. And the new arithmetic in the international system generally, and particularly within the United Nations system, contributed to a change in international norms with the adoption, first, of decolonization (Jackson 1993), and then of development as core norms of the modern system.

Another defining characteristic of the contemporary system contributed to the enshrining of the development norm—the vast expansion in the number of non-governmental organizations (NGOs), many of which were focused on the alleviation of poverty (for further discussion of this topic, see the chapters in this volume by Wade and Thomas). NGOs have also been prominent in global environmental affairs (see Dauvergne, Chapter 14 in this volume). Relations between industrialized and less developed countries, and issues relating to global poverty and inequality, emerged as an important dimension of the study of international political economy, the evolution of which is discussed in the next section of this chapter.

KEY POINTS

The post-war international economy was qualitatively different from anything that preceded it, on several dimensions:

- states made a commitment to multilateralism, reflected in the construction of institutions at the global and regional levels;

- the world economy grew at unprecedented rates after 1945—the internationalized component of economies became more significant as trade and foreign investment grew more rapidly than production;

- TNCs and foreign direct investment (FDI) emerged as key agents in the process of internationalization;

- the composition and direction of international trade changed dramatically, with intra-industry trade among industrialized economies constituting the vast majority of aggregate world trade; and

- the number of countries in the international system rose substantially.

The Study of Global Political Economy

The emergence of international political economy as a distinct subfield

International political economy (IPE) developed as a significant subfield in the study of international relations in the 1970s. As has so often been the case in political science, the emergence of a new subject area was a response both to real world changes and to trends in theorizing within and outside the discipline (see Box 1.5).

In the early 1970s, the global economy entered a period of turbulence following an unprecedented period of stable economic growth. The 'long boom' from the early post-war years through to 1970 benefited developed and less developed economies alike. Because of the comparative stability of this period, it was commonplace to regard international economic relations as a relatively uncontentious

issue area that could be left to technocrats to manage. All this changed in the late 1960s, however, when the US economy encountered increasing problems because its commitment to a fixed exchange rate constrained its policy options at a time when domestic inflation was being fuelled by high levels of government expenditure—domestically, on social programmes, and internationally on the pursuit of the Vietnam War. In August 1971, a new era of instability in the global economy was ushered in when the Nixon administration unilaterally devalued the dollar (for further discussion, see Helleiner, Chapter 7 in this volume). In doing so, it set in train events that were to end the system of fixed exchange rates, one of the pillars of the Bretton Woods financial regime.

The new instability in international finance reinforced perceptions that the global economy was about to enter an era of significant upheaval.

BOX 1.5

What's in a Name? International Versus Global Political Economy

When IPE emerged as a major focus for students of international relations, it inherited the rather misleading adjective 'international' as the leading word in its title. Commentators have often pointed out that 'international' relations is a misnomer for its subject matter in that it confuses 'nation' with 'state', and fails to acknowledge the significance of private actors in global politics. But labels, like institutions, are often 'sticky'—once adopted, it is difficult to displace them even if a better alternative is available. The abbreviation IPE has become synonymous with the field of study. Even though we prefer 'global political economy' for the title of the book because it reflects more accurately the contemporary subject matter of this field, many of the contributors follow conventional usage in employing the abbreviation IPE and in referring to 'international' political economy.

While the study of international political economy achieved a new prominence in the 1970s, a variety of work in what would now be recognized as the field of IPE was published much earlier than this. A prominent example is Albert Hirschman's (1945) study of Germany's economic relations with its East European neighbours. Much of the work in the field of development economics that blossomed in the post-war period included significant political and international components. And the Marxist tradition of political economy remained vibrant, particularly in Europe.

To confuse matters, the study of economics was known in the eighteenth and nineteenth centuries as political economy (see, for example, John Stuart Mill's *The Principles of Political Economy*). The titles of some leading journals in the field of economics—for example, the *Journal of Political Economy*, first published in 1892—reflect this older usage.

Commodity prices had risen substantially in the early 1970s; Western concerns about the future availability and pricing of raw materials were compounded by the success of the Organization of the Petroleum Exporting Countries (OPEC) during the Arab–Israeli war of 1973 in substantially increasing the price of crude oil. Less developed countries believed that they could use their new-found 'commodity power' to engineer a dramatic restructuring of international economic regimes, a demand they made through calls at the United Nations for a New International Economic Order (NIEO–see Thomas, Chapter 13 in this volume). Industrialized economies were already having difficulty in coping with a surge in imports of manufactured goods from Japan and the East Asian NIEs, causing them to revert to various measures to protect their domestic industries, in disregard of their obligations under the international trade regime. In trade and finance regimes alike, new pressures were causing governments to seek to rewrite the rules governing international economic interactions.

At this time of the greatest instability in international economic relations since the depression of the 1930s, inter-state relations in the security realm, which had been the principal focus of the study of post-war international relations, appeared to be on the verge of entering a new era of collaboration. The United States was winding down its involvement in Indo-China; Henry Kissinger was negotiating détente with the Soviet Union; and President Nixon's visit to China in 1972 appeared to presage a new epoch in which China would be integrated peacefully into the international system. For many scholars of international relations, the traditional agenda of the discipline was incomplete, and the preoccupation of the dominant, realist approach with security issues and military power seemed increasingly irrelevant to the new international environment (Keohane and Nye 1972; Morse 1976).

The new turbulence in international economic relations prompted political scientists to take an interest in a subject matter that had previously been left largely to economists. It was not, as

some commentators have suggested, that international economic relations had suddenly become politicized. Politics and asymmetries in power had always underlain the structure of global economic relations, seen, for example, in the content of the various financial regimes negotiated at Bretton Woods. Rather, what was novel was that the turbulence of the early 1970s suggested that the fundamental rules of the game were suddenly open for renegotiation.

Political scientists' new interest in international economic relations also coincided with the abandonment by the economics profession of what had previously been taught and researched as institutional economics: as the discipline of economics aspired to more 'scientific' approaches through the application of statistical and mathematical models, so increasingly it abandoned the study of international economic institutions. Political scientists discovered a vacuum that they quickly filled: the field of international political economy was born.

What is IPE?

International political economy is a field of enquiry, a subject matter whose central focus is the interrelationship between public and private power in the allocation of scarce resources. It is not a specific approach or set of approaches to studying this subject matter (as we shall see, the full range of theoretical and methodological approaches from international and comparative politics has been applied to the study of international political economy).

Like other branches of the discipline, IPE seeks to answer the classic questions posed in Harold D. Lasswell's (1936) definition of politics: *who gets what, when, and how?* This definition identifies explicitly questions of *distribution* as being central to the study of politics. It also points implicitly to the importance of power—the concept that is at the heart of the study of political science—in determining outcomes. Power, of course, takes various forms: it is classically defined in terms of relationships—the capacity of one actor to change the behaviour of another (Dahl 1963). But power is also exercised in the capacity of actors to set agendas (Bachrach and Baratz 1970; Lukes 1974), and to structure the rules in various areas of international economic relations so as to privilege some actors and to disadvantage others (Strange 1988).

Consider, for example, the international financial regime. As the world's largest economy (and single most important market for many other countries in the global system), the United States has been able, over the years, to exercise relational power: to force changes in the behaviour of other countries—notably, to accept changes in their exchange rates (as, for example, in the Nixon administration's breaking of the fixed exchange rate between the dollar and gold, and, as discussed at the beginning of this chapter, the forced appreciation of the North-East Asian currencies against the dollar following the Plaza Accord). The rules of the international financial regime have also been structured so that they privilege the more economically developed states in the system: not only do the wealthy industrialized economies enjoy more votes within the IMF and the World Bank under the weighted voting system employed in the two major international financial institutions (IFIs) (Box 1.6), but the industrialized economies also (in part because of arrangements they have negotiated among themselves) largely escape the discipline imposed by the IMF on countries that run persistent balance of payments deficits. No industrialized country has sought assistance from the IMF since Britain and Italy did so in 1976. Despite running huge deficits in its balance of payments, the United States has not been subject to IMF discipline, because it can take advantage of the international acceptability of the dollar and print more money to finance its trade deficits.

Besides a focus on questions of distribution and of power, two of the fundamental concerns of political science, students of international political economy have also been preoccupied with one of the central issues in the study of international relations: which conditions are more favourable for the evolution of co-operation among states in an environment where no central enforcement agency is present?

For many observers, this problem of 'co-operation under anarchy' is even more pertinent in the economic than in the security realm. This is because greater potential exists in the economic sphere, particularly under conditions of interdependence, for co-operation on a win–win basis, but states have a considerable temptation to 'cheat' by attempting to exploit concessions made by others while not fully responding in kind (see Aggarwal and Dupont, Chapter 3 in this volume).

Much of the early IPE work in the 1970s and early 1980s, particularly in North America, married two of these central concerns—the distribution of power within the global economy, and the potential for states to engage in collaboration. Conducted at a time when many perceived US economic power to be waning, this work focused on the link between hegemony and an open global economy (see Box 1.7).

Approaches to the study of global political economy

Following the publication of Robert Gilpin's (1987) magisterial overview of the then-emerging field of international political economy, most introductions to the subject have identified three principal categories of theoretical approaches to IPE. In Gilpin's original terminology (he changed some of his labels in the updated version of his book (Gilpin 2001)), these were liberalism, nationalism, and Marxism. Of these three labels, only liberalism has been used universally in other categorizations. Other writers have substituted 'statism', 'mercantilism', 'realism' or 'economic nationalism' for nationalism. The approaches that Gilpin subsumed under the label Marxism have variously been identified as 'radical', 'critical', 'structuralist', 'dependency', 'underdevelopment', and 'world systems'.

In itself, the use of a variety of labels points to one of the problems with the 'trichotomous' categorization of approaches to the study of IPE: the (sometimes misleading) lumping together of substantially different perspectives within a single category. Moreover, the trichotomous categorization

BOX 1.6

Voting in the International Financial Institutions

When the allied powers decided at Bretton Woods to create two international financial institutions, they agreed on a formula for voting rights that represented a compromise between the principle of sovereign equality and the realities of markedly unequal economic power. Members' voting power has two components: 'basic votes', assigned equally to all members; and (a much larger number) of weighted votes that are linked directly to the money members subscribed to the two institutions. Quotas have been adjusted since the post-Second World War period (1940s) as the membership of the institutions has expanded, but the G7 industrialized countries still control 45 per cent of the votes in the IMF, while more than forty African countries together have less than 5 per cent of the total votes.

Eight countries—China, France, Germany, Japan, Russia, Saudi Arabia, the United Kingdom, and the United States—have their own representative on the twenty-four-member IMF Executive Board, which is responsible for the day-to-day running of the institution. Others are arranged in various groups with a single executive director casting their collective votes. Five executive directors represent individual countries on the seventeen-member World Bank Executive Board: the United States, Japan, Germany, France, and the United Kingdom; the remaining twelve directors represent the Bank's other 180 member states.

In the IMF, 'Ordinary' Decisions require a simple majority whereas 'Special' Decisions require an 85 per cent 'supermajority'. The United States, with slightly less than 17 per cent of the total votes at the IMF, can unilaterally block 'Special Decisions', such as changes in the IMF's Charter or use of its holdings of gold. Voting, however, is relatively rare, with most decisions being carried by consensus.

Criticisms of the failure of IMF quotas and voting rights to reflect the growing significance of developing economies were voiced increasingly after the East Asian financial crises. This criticism led to proposals to reform quotas and to increase the number of basic votes assigned to each country. The first stage was an 'ad hoc' increase in the quotas of China, Korea, Mexico and Turkey (ranging from about a 20 per cent increase for Turkey to about 80 per cent for Korea), to take effect in 2007. Further re-negotiations of quotas have been scheduled for 2007–8.

By convention, since the foundation of the two IFIs, the United States has nominated the president of the World Bank, and (West) European countries the managing director of the IMF. In an unusual move in 2000, however, the Clinton administration in the US vetoed the German government's first-choice nominee for the post of managing director of the IMF. Although the appointment of the nominees is subject to a formal vote within the Fund and the Bank, other members have only the option of either voting for or against the nominated candidate rather than proposing alternative names.

The Washington, DC, location of the two IFIs facilitates US influence over their operations. For more detailed discussion of the representativeness and accountability of the IFIs, see Woods (2003).

A list of the members of the IMF and their voting rights can be found at www.imf.org/external/np/sec/memdir/members.htm. (Unlike the IFIs, the World Trade Organization operates on the principle of one member, one vote, but its members have never voted: decision-making is by consensus, see Winham, Chapter 5 in this volume.)

does not capture the wealth of methodological and theoretical approaches used in the contemporary study of IPE, or provide an accurate signpost to the breadth of fascinating questions that currently preoccupies researchers in the field. For these reasons, we do not use such conventional categorization in this book. So common is the trichotomy in introductions to IPE, however, that

it is worth investing a little time in understanding the underlying foundations of the categorization. Matthew Watson's chapter in this volume examines the historical origins and subsequent intellectual lineage of the principal theoretical perspectives on IPE.

Much of the best work in international political economy in recent years has been concerned

BOX 1.7

Power and Collaboration

The theory of **hegemonic stability** suggests that international economic collaboration in pursuit of an open (or liberal) economic order is most likely to occur when the global economy is dominated by a single power (because this country, the hegemon, will have both the desire and the capacity to support an open economic system—the dominant economy is likely to benefit most from free trade; moreover, its relatively large size will give it leverage over other states in the system). Theorists pointed to the experience of the mid-nineteenth century, when Britain was the hegemonic power, and to the period of US dominance from 1945 to 1971, as demonstrating the relationship between hegemony and an open world economy. In contrast, the inter-war period, when no single country enjoyed equivalent pre-eminence, was characterized by a breakdown in international economic collaboration. The decline in the relative position of the US economy in the 1960s, following the rebuilding of the Western European and Japanese economies, appeared to coincide with renewed closure (a rise in protectionism in response to imports from Japan and the East Asian NIEs) and the general turbulence in global economic regimes noted above.

Subsequently, however, the hegemonic stability argument was undermined both by trends in the real world and by new theoretical work. In the 1990s, countries extended their collaboration on international economic matters, especially in trade, despite a relatively more even dispersion of economic power in the global system.

For statements of the hegemonic stability argument, see Kindleberger (1973) and Krasner (1976); for alternative theoretical perspectives see Keohane (1984, 1997) and Snidal (1985b). For further discussion, see Aggarwal and Dupont, Chapter 3 in this volume.

less with prescription than with explanation—for example, how differences in political institutions shape policy decisions, and why some sectors of the economy are more successful than others in seeking protection (see Hiscox, Chapter 4 in this volume); why it is easier for states to collaborate on some issues rather than others (see Aggarwal and Dupont, Chapter 3 in this volume); why states have increasingly pursued trade agreements at the regional instead of the global level (Ravenhill, Chapter 6 in this volume); why states have been unable to agree on an effective regime for dealing with international debt (Pauly, Chapter 8 in this volume); and why some global environments regimes are effective while others are not (Dauvergne, Chapter 14 in this volume). Of course, policy prescriptions often follow from such theoretically informed analysis, and they are far more specific than those of the 'get the state out of the market' variety.

Since the early 1980s, the study of international political economy has been enriched by the application of a diverse array of theoretical and methodological approaches, but neither their subject-matter nor the methodologies employed allow easy categorization. Take, for example, the role of ideas in shaping policy agendas, in helping states to reach agreement in various international negotiations, and in legitimizing current economic, political, and social structures. Ideas have been the central focus of work firmly within the Marxist tradition, which builds on the arguments of the former Italian communist party leader, Antonio Gramsci, on how ideas help ruling classes to legitimate their domination (Cox 1987; Gill 1990). But ideas have also been pivotal to quite different approaches, drawing on the work of the German sociologist, Max Weber; work from this perspective examines the role that ideas play in defining the range of policy options that governments consider, and in providing a focal point for agreement in international negotiations (Hall 1989; Goldstein and Keohane 1993; Garrett and Lange 1996). Also derived from Weberian analysis are constructivist approaches, which emphasize the significance of ideas in constituting actors' perceptions of their interests and identities, rather than taking these for granted—examples of the application of constructivist analysis to IPE include Colin Hay, Chapter 10 in this volume, Haas (1992), Hay and Rosamond (2002). Burch and Denemark (1997). And cross-fertilization has occurred across different approaches—for example, the Gramscian idea of hegemony has been used by writers from a non-Marxist perspective, such as Ikenberry and Kupchan (1990), and finds resonance in Joseph Nye's (1990) concept of 'soft' power.

Likewise, turning to methodology, we find similar methods employed by scholars from dramatically different theoretical traditions. Consider rational choice approaches, for example. Since the mid-1990s, rational choice has dominated many areas of the study of political science, particularly in universities in the United States. Its origins lie in economic theory; the focus is primarily on individuals, the factors that lead them to choose preferred courses of action, and how strategic interaction generates uncertainty. In IPE, rational choice analysis has been prominent in the recent study of why international institutions, including the European Union, take particular forms, what the effects of institutions are, and why some institutions survive longer than others (Frey 1984; Martin 1992 Garrett and Weingast 1993). Vaubel (1986, 1991) has applied rational choice analysis in an examination of the behaviour of the officials of the IMF. Such work is very much in the mainstream of contemporary political science. But rational choice methods have also been applied by theorists working within the Marxist tradition—for example, Roemer (1988), and Carver and Thomas (1995).

Although rational choice methods have become dominant in some circles within North American political science, a large number of scholars of IPE would find it difficult to accept the argument of one proponent of rational choice methods that IPE 'is today characterized by growing consensus on theories, methods, analytical frameworks, and important questions' (Martin 2002: 244). Diversity in ontology, epistemology, and methodology continues to characterize the international study of global political economy (see Box 1.8). Many scholars find this rich mix of theories and methodologies a cause for celebration rather than concern. This is certainly the view of the contributors to this volume, which reflects much of the current lively debate in the study of IPE.

The first part of this volume looks at some of the approaches that have addressed the key concerns of theorists of IPE: what conditions are most conducive to the emergence of collaborative behaviour among states on economic issues, and what are the determinants of the foreign economic policies of states? It then examines the evolution of trade relations, first at the global and then at the regional level. Chapter 7 reviews the development of the global financial regime since 1944; the following chapter addresses the causes of financial crises and the reasons why international collaboration to date has been ineffective in devising strategies to combat them.

BOX 1.8

Epistemology, Ontology, and Methodology

Epistemology addresses the issues of what knowledge is and how it is acquired. **Ontology** is the study of being, addressing the question of what is there, what are the essential features of an object. **Methodology** refers to a procedure or set of procedures used to study a subject matter.

The chapters in the second half of the book that examine various aspects of the debate about globalization: whether in fact the contemporary economy is global and whether it differs, qualitatively or quantitatively, from previous eras of economic interdependence; the role of international production networks in driving globalization; the consequences of enhanced globalization for the policy options available to states; the impact of globalization on world poverty and inequality; how globalization has changed the relations between industrialized and less developed economies; and the impact of globalization on the environment.

KEY POINTS

- The field of international political economy emerged in the early 1970s in response to developments in the world economy, in international security, and in the study of economics and international relations.

- IPE is best defined by its subject matter rather than as a particular theory or methodology.

- Approaches to the study of IPE have conventionally been divided into the three categories of liberalism, nationalism, and Marxism.

- This trichotomous division is of questionable contemporary utility because of the variation in approaches included within each of the three categories.

- The contemporary study of IPE is characterized by the application of a wealth of theories and methodologies.

- Most of the contemporary work in IPE focuses on positive theory; that is, attempting to explain why things happen, rather than on policy prescription.

QUESTIONS

1. What were the principal reasons why the Thai economy experienced a financial crisis in 1997?

2. What are the implications of the East Asian financial crisis for the contemporary world economy?

3. What were the principal features of the classical period of mercantilism?

4. What were the reasons for rapid economic growth in the nineteenth century?

5. How did the gold standard operate automatically to bring the payments position of countries into equilibrium?

6. What were the principal reasons for the breakdown of international economic relations in the inter-war period?

7. What are the defining characteristics of the post-1945 world economy?

8. What factors led to the emergence of IPE as a significant field of study?

9. What is IPE?

10. What are the main weaknesses with the traditional threefold categorization of approaches to IPE?

■ **Cohen, B. J. (1977),** *Organizing the World's Money: The Political Economy of International Monetary Relations* **(New York. Basic Books).** The first major study from an IPE perspective of global financial relations.

■ **Cooper, R. N. (1968),** *The Economics of Interdependence* **(New York. Columbia University Press).** A pioneering work that laid the foundations for the emergence of IPE as a significant field of enquiry in the 1970s.

■ **Crane, G. T., and Amawi, A. (eds) (1997),** *The Theoretical Evolution of International Political Economy: A Reader,* **2nd edn (New York. Oxford University Press).** An excellent compilation of selections from classical and contemporary writing on international political economy.

■ **Gilpin, R. (1987),** *The Political Economy of International Relations* **(Princeton; NJ. Princeton University Press).** The most theoretically sophisticated of the early introductory books on IPE.

■ **Hirschman, A. O. (1945),** *National Power and the Structure of Foreign Trade* **(Berkeley and Los Angeles: University of California Press).** A pioneering study of the relationship between power and the foreign economic relations of Nazi Germany.

■ **Keohane, R. O. (1984),** *After Hegemony: Cooperation and Discord in the World Political Economy* **(Princeton, NJ. Princeton University Press).** The most thorough assessment of the relationship between the distribution of power and collaboration among states on international economic matters.

■ **Maddison, A. (2001),** *The World Economy: A Millennial Perspective* **(Paris: Development Centre of the Organization for Economic Co-operation and Development).** Excellent source of historical statistics on the development of the world economy.

■ **Palan, R. (ed.) (2000),** *Global Political Economy: Contemporary Theories* **(London: Routledge).** The most comprehensive survey of contemporary theoretical approaches to global political economy.

■ **Schwartz, H. M. (2000),** *States Versus Markets: The Emergence of a Global Economy,* **2nd edn. (London: Macmillan).** Provides an unusual historical perspective on the contemporary global economy by tracing its development since the 1500s, with emphasis placed on the links between the emergence of the modern state and the modern global economy.

■ **Strange, S. (1971),** *Sterling and British Policy: A Political Study of an International Currency in Decline* **(London: Oxford University Press).** A pioneering work on the relationship between politics and international financial policies.

■ **Strange, S. (1988).** *States and Markets* **(London: Pinter).** An idiosyncratic introduction to global political economy that is organized around the theme of structural power.

■ **Wallerstein, I. (1974).** *The Modern World-System* **(New York: Academic Press).** The first volume of a multi-part work examining the emergence of the modern world economy.

 WEB LINKS

● **www.g7.utoronto.ca**   University of Toronto G8 Information Centre.

● **www.imf.org**   International Monetary Fund.

- **www.worldbank.org** World Bank.

- **www.unctad.org** United Nations Conference on Trade and Development (UNCTAD).

- **www.opec.org** Organization of the Petroleum Exporting Countries.

- **www.eh.net/encyclopedia/article/officer.gold.standard** Gold Standard—EH.Net Encyclopedia.

- **www.amosweb.com/gls** Glossary of economic terms.

 Visit the Online Resource Centre that accompanies this book for more information:
www.oxfordtextbooks.co.uk/orc/ravenhill2e/

2 Theoretical Traditions in Global Political Economy

MATTHEW WATSON

Chapter Contents

- Introduction
- The Trichotomous Structure of Teaching IPE
- The Contested Label of 'Realist' IPE
- The Contested Label of 'Marxist' IPE
- The Mis-Specified Roots of Liberal IPE
- Beyond the Trichotomous Structure of Teaching IPE
- Basic Heuristic Distinctions for Appraising IPE Research
- Analytical Distinctions to Sub-Divide the Field
- Disciplinary Distinctions to Sub-Divide the Field
- Conclusion

Reader's Guide

The chapter focuses on the historical origins and the subsequent intellectual lineage of different theoretical positions within contemporary global political economy (GPE). The search for such origins is important, because it reminds us that contemporary perspectives are part of a longer tradition of thought. By heeding this reminder, GPE is shown to be a highly variegated subject field, encapsulating many different positions born of different theoretical traditions and rooted in different analytical claims. A number of ways of thinking about the divisions in the field are then reviewed as a means of demonstrating why it is important to comprehend how one method of undertaking research in GPE relates to another. To understand the subject field as a whole is to grasp how the separate positions within it fit together. The most commonly used distinction to be found in introductory courses in GPE is that between liberalism, realism, and Marxism. However, this trichotomy is shown to be inappropriate because, by attempting to categorize all contributions to debates in one of these three camps, it obscures many of GPE's most noteworthy theoretical subtleties. Appropriate ways of thinking about the major divisions in the field must avoid rigid lines of demarcation and must capture the sense of being able to move fluidly between different positions which share similar historical origins. The chapter ends by showing how this might be done. By combining analytical and disciplinary distinctions it is possible to understand the subject field as a whole without resorting to artificially constructed divisions within it.

Introduction

More academics than ever before practice GPE and describe themselves as global political economists. The courses they run feed into degree programmes which consequently have a more substantial GPE component than at any time in the past. This means that many more students are now taught GPE and encouraged to identify major issues of world politics as problems in global political economy.

My task in this chapter is to provide a broad overview of the subject field of GPE as a whole: (*i*) to uncover the shared analytical commitments that make one researcher's work readily recognizable to another researcher specifically as a component of global political economy; as well as (*ii*) to make clear the primary theoretical and analytical divisions that fragment the field into one of competing approaches. I shall attempt to do so by exploring the historical antecedents of various perspectives in international political economy (IPE), out of which the more recent designation of GPE has arisen.

At their core, GPE and IPE are very much the same; some researchers prefer one name rather than the other. The difference in terminology corresponds mainly to a matter of timing. The use of the name GPE is a recent phenomenon, reflecting the assumption that an important global dimension has been introduced into world economic affairs since the 1980s. For those who accept that the world economy has effectively been globalized in the intervening period, the designation of GPE makes a good deal of sense. In this chapter, though, as I will be focusing largely on the theoretical origins of the subject field and the historical antecedents of those origins, the GPE designation has less resonance. The origins of the subject field date to the early 1970s, a time before anyone talked about globalization. As a consequence, at that time, all the people working in the field called the subject international political economy. For this reason, in what follows I shall use the designation IPE rather than GPE, albeit noting

that, as GPE is merely a recent manifestation of modern IPE, the historical antecedents of the two are exactly the same.

The task of exploring the historical antecedents of various perspectives in IPE is far from straightforward. First, any attempt to create self-contained categories that serve to synthesize many individuals' work into a single approach with a single label necessarily involves a process of both abstraction and generalization. At most, it is possible to provide heuristic categories in order to underscore the idea that there are particular, as well as discrete, ways of doing IPE. But these heuristic categories seem to trip something of a psychological trigger among researchers within the field. While most are content to apply such categories to the work of others, they are less likely to think that any heuristic category captures the essence of their own work adequately, and they are likely to attack such categorization as a crude attempt at pigeonholing.

Second, and perhaps more importantly, the way in which IPE is taught is often different from the way it is researched, even though its teachers and researchers are the same people. When making this claim, I have in mind once again the heuristic categories that are appealed to in order to make sense of the internal divisions within the subject field. In general, when IPE is taught, one set of distinctions is used as a way of allowing students to grasp what divides one group of scholars from another. However, international political economists use another set of distinctions entirely when debating among themselves the different practices that define the separate approaches to IPE as a scholarly pursuit. In other words, one set of heuristic categories underpins the teaching of IPE and an altogether different set categories underpins academic appraisals of what it means to be doing IPE.

From the above, then, it seems as though IPE possesses a potentially dual identity and, moreover, there might be two distinct dimensions to it. The task I have accepted in this chapter—to try to impose some sort of typological order on the diverse field of IPE—therefore represents a large undertaking. I am in no position to do anything about the psychological trigger that allows international political economists to use heuristic categories to understand other people's work, but deny that such categories offer helpful representations of their own. The most I can do is to note this problem and then move on. The chapter will therefore focus on the curious predilection of international political economists to appeal to different heuristic categories when teaching the subject field than when appraising how it is researched. I begin with the way in which IPE is traditionally taught.

The Trichotomous Structure of Teaching IPE

If one were to take a representative sample of all the introductory courses taught in IPE, one would doubtless be struck by how they build on almost identical foundations. The same is true of the vast majority of textbooks recommended as companions to the lecture series through which students first develop a sense of what it means to be doing IPE. Through these two central pillars of learning about IPE, students are encouraged to believe that all possible positions on the nature of the world economy must have an affinity with one of the trichotomous poles of liberalism, realism, and Marxism (see, for example, Woods 2001a; Goddard *et al.* 2003; O'Brien and Williams 2004). Viewed in such a way, every intellectual contribution by international political economists must therefore reflect a pure variant of one of these approaches, or it must gravitate towards it to a greater or lesser degree.

The contentious nature of the trichotomy

The general similarity in syllabases does not mean, however, that the trichotomous structure of introductory IPE teaching is unchallenged by those who reflect on such matters. Indeed, my motivation for discussing the trichotomy is to pick up on the developing trend for it to be referred to critically (see, for example, Ravenhill 2005: 18–25). In general, we find that for every person who uses the distinction between liberalism, realism, and Marxism to organize their introductions to IPE, there is another person who wonders openly about whether this is the best way to proceed. It is one of the ironies of the field that sometimes these two 'people' are in fact the same person playing two distinct roles. Many of the most fervent advocates of transcending the trichotomous structure of teaching IPE in fact replicate that structure in their own lecture courses, presumably in recognition that this is the way things are usually done in IPE. The distinction between liberalism, realism, and Marxism thus continues to exert a highly significant influence on students' first exposure to the subject field.

So, what might be wrong with the trichotomous structure of teaching IPE? At the very least, we can be forgiven for presuming that there might be something wrong with it, such is the acerbic language with which critics describe both it and its effects. Perhaps most pointedly, Craig Murphy and Roger Tooze (1991: 6) describe the tendency to train students to think in terms of liberalism versus realism versus Marxism as a 'tripartite pedagogical framework', where the similarity in sound between the words 'tripartite' and 'apartheid' is surely more than coincidence. Under an apartheid political system people are packaged up into neat little boxes based on ascriptive characteristics linked to skin colour, and their life chances are shaped according to a perceived need to keep them apart physically. By extension, under IPE's tripartite pedagogical framework, theoretical perspectives undergo a similar packaging process, whereby they are treated as being mutually exclusive and students feel pressure to take sides on the question of which one to align with.

However, theories in IPE are not like sports teams. They are not something to support in an act of uncritical allegiance; they are something both to appeal to and to confront in the search for plausible insights into the nature of the world. The presentation of theories when teaching introductory IPE can hence be used for two distinct purposes. On the one hand, this can merely be about facilitating students' desire to learn more for themselves about the theoretical bases of IPE's competing approaches, and on the other, it can be about grooming students to become devotees of a particular position before they are equipped with the knowledge to make such a choice. The trichotomous structure of teaching IPE might inadvertently encourage the latter effect, at least in so far as each of the three core perspectives is presented in opposition to (that is, *versus*) the other two. Given the frequency with which this happens, Murphy and Tooze (1991: 6) conclude that the tripartite pedagogical framework is so often 'inappropriately used by scholars as something more than a tool for the beginning student'.

Treating IPE theories as ideologies

The accusation, then, is that overly rigid demarcations in introductory texts between liberal, realist, and Marxist IPE create a learning context more conducive to tutoring advocacy of one particular perspective than to helping students develop a broad-based and reflexive understanding of the subject field as a whole. This is perhaps best illustrated by Robert Gilpin's *The Political Economy of International Relations* (1987), which is still widely used as a teaching companion within the field, despite now being twenty years old (see Denemark

and O'Brien 1997). Gilpin describes liberalism, realism, and Marxism as 'the three ideologies' of IPE (1987: 25).

The choice of descriptor is important. He could have called liberalism, realism, and Marxism three separate starting points for IPE. But this would have implied that at some stage students would be required to branch out from those starting points in order to comprehend what is at stake by beginning there, as well as to understand what needs to be done to soften initial assumptions so as to meet the challenge of other perspectives. Equally, he could have called liberalism, realism, and Marxism three separate theoretical bases for understanding the world on which international political economists are asked to comment. But the art of working within a theoretical perspective is always to question the limits that perspective imposes on original thought. So, to have called them theoretical bases would have implied a commitment to tackling issues which serve continually to destabilize the certainty with which the theory can speak about the world.

Instead of these alternative appellations, then, Gilpin uses the word 'ideology' to describe liberal, realist, and Marxist IPE. As he readily admits (1987: 25–26), he does so in an attempt to capture a sense of self-contained, coherent world views, capable of imposing meaning on any experience of the world, and equally capable of encapsulating whole systems of thought and belief. It is interesting to note that, in his updated version of the book (Gilpin 2001), Gilpin drops the trichotomous approach from his discussion of what it means to be doing IPE. This is in recognition of his increasing dissatisfaction that the choice of using one of the three ideologies of IPE rested not on an assumption by its adherents that it was based on sounder principles, as much as it being consistent with the adherents' normative preferences.

In Gilpin's treatment, IPE scholars are ideologues first and foremost, rather than theorists who attempt to abide by the standards of observational science. While theories are, of course, never value-neutral, and while they can also generate their own devotees, they do not do so in the same way or with the same effect as ideologies. An ideology cleanses an experience of alternative explanations and, in this manner, narrows potential understandings rather than enlarges their scope. Hence, it makes a difference whether students are presented with liberalism, realism, and Marxism as three possible points of theoretical departure for IPE, or as the three ideologies of IPE.

The tendency to emphasise the latter—as identified and latterly as lamented by Gilpin—puts me in mind of Thomas Kuhn's classic study, *The Structure of Scientific Revolutions* (Kuhn 1970), where he attempts to explain progress in scientific knowledge via the move from one 'paradigm' to another. (Indeed, at one point, Gilpin hints directly that what he means by an 'ideology' is exactly the same as what Kuhn means by a scientific paradigm.) For Kuhn, science is undoubtedly a social process (see, for example, Hoyningen-Huene 1993). This means that progression in science does not equate to an ever closer approximation to an external, existential truth, as much as to an ever-fuller explication of the framework of understanding into which existing members of the scientific community have been socialized (see, for example, Margolis 1993). The key act of agency that allows scientific norms to be passed down from one generation of scholars to the next therefore lies in the formative training that young scientists receive. In turn, Kuhn suggests that training is a matter of familiarizing scientists with particular habits of thought which conform to the existing structure of explanation. This is about developing learned intuitions, as it were. And the route to developing such intuitions focuses on exposing young scientists to a series of 'exemplars'. By being asked to solve the exemplars' associated puzzles in a particular way, the tenets of the prevailing scientific world view become embedded in young scientists' minds (Kuhn 1970: 186–192).

The main difference between Kuhn's scientific exemplars and teaching the foundations of IPE is that, for Kuhn, the cognitive power of exemplars is concentrated in their ability to unify the scientific mindset around homogeneous and internally consistent principles of explanation. No such effects

are visible when teaching the foundations of IPE as ideologies. They are presented purposefully as competing foundations leading to competing ideologies and, in this respect, the contrast with scientific unity comes to the fore. Each of Gilpin's ideologies of IPE is taught through, and rests on, different exemplars. For liberalism, the exemplars relate to real-life instances in which market-based economic organization has led to more efficient outcomes; for realism, the exemplars relate to real-life instances in which one can detect the influence of power politics on inter-state economic affairs; for Marxism, the exemplars relate to real-life instances in which economic relationships of production, distribution, and exchange conform to deep societal structures of class-based exploitation.

Beyond these differences in content, however, the role of the exemplars has exactly the same effect in Gilpin's ideologies of IPE as it does in Kuhn's notion of scientific progress. They are designed specifically to inculcate habits of mind, which then act as cognitive shortcuts for understanding the events one is asked to explain. For exmple, if one has been trained by liberalism's exemplars to treat all questions of market structure as attempts to allocate resources in the most productive manner possible, then one's learned intuition when confronted with evidence of changes to the world market structure will be to respond by offering a post hoc explanation of how those changes can be expected to lead to enhanced economic efficiency. Equally, if one has been trained by realism's exemplars to treat all questions of market structure as epiphenomena of the prevailing balance of inter-state power in world politics, then one's learned intuition when confronted with evidence of changes to the world market structure will be to respond by offering a post hoc explanation of how those changes can be expected to produce economic gains for powerful states *vis-à-vis* weaker states. Finally, if one has been trained by Marxism's exemplars to treat all questions of market structure as attempts to institutionalize class-based economic asymmetries, then one's learned intuition when confronted with evidence of changes to the world market structure will be to respond by offering a post hoc explanation of how those changes can be expected to further subjugate a proletarian class struggling to escape the logic of capitalism. In all of these instances, students' exposure to and interaction with the exemplars normalizes the way in which they view the world and restricts the scope of their explanations of it.

There is nothing necessarily wrong with teaching introductory IPE as a menu of alternative approaches, as long as the aim is not to produce devotees of a certain approach before students understand how the separate approaches to the subject field fit together, and how their historical antecedents relate to one another. The alternative is to ensure that students are trained adequately in the historical antecedents before building up an understanding of how this informs contemporary approaches to the subject. The benefit of the latter is that it requires students to engage with the diverse

foundations of different ways of doing IPE rather than simply attaching themselves prematurely to one way and then learning its major arguments by rote.

> **KEY POINTS**
>
> - Introductory IPE teaching usually revolves around a presumed trichotomy which defines the field: liberalism versus realism versus Marxism.
>
> - The separate positions in the trichotomy are often presented as ideologies (requiring true believers) rather than as theories (requiring constant reflection and reformulation).
>
> - Each 'ideology' is taught through its own constitutive exemplars, thus encouraging students to accept its way of viewing the world without extensive theoretical reflection of the strengths and weaknesses of the approach.

The Contested Label of 'Realist' IPE

A further criticism of the trichotomous structure of teaching IPE is that there are noticeable disagreements about the preferred nomenclature for at least two of IPE's three ostensible poles. These disagreements arise from the fact that different approaches are often lumped together under the same label in the absence of overt recognition that they do in fact have different origins. The label 'liberalism' is the only one of the three that is generally immune to challenge. The other two are discussed using a variety of terms. While I have used 'realism' so far in this chapter to describe the approach that emphasizes the importance of inter-state rivalry to the conduct of world economic affairs, other descriptors have also been deployed. The realist approach has also often been termed the 'statist' approach, the 'mercantilist' approach, or the 'nationalist' approach.

In much the same way, what I have called 'Marxism' in order to capture the intellectual origins of an approach that does not take the social basis of capitalism for granted also goes by other names. Within the IPE literature one also sees this style of scholarship being described as 'structuralist', 'radical', or 'critical'.

What, then, is in a name? At first glance, these differences may appear to be of only superficial concern, and this will certainly be the case if all of them describe the same basic way of doing things. However, when we scratch the surface of the name tags we quickly realize that this is not necessarily the case, particularly when we seek to learn more about their intellectual origins and associated intellectual histories. Further investigation is therefore required.

The IR foundations of realist and statist IPE

Looking first at the 'realist' approach, the descriptor 'realist' is used to signal the similarities with international relations (IR) realism. Indeed, here IPE is simply a subset of IR. The theories and methods of IR realism are simply transposed on to subject matters that link states economically. IR realists talk about the essential struggle between states for power, prestige and influence in the 'high' political arenas of diplomacy and warfare (see, for example, Viotti and Kauppi 1993; ch. 2). IPE realists also work with a conception of the world in which states struggle instinctively for power, prestige, and influence, but their focus is on the 'low' political arenas associated with commercial and financial pre-eminence (see, for example, Lee 2008). Even the language of IR realism is incorporated readily into IPE. Thus, for example, IPE realists intuitively turn issues of contemporary concern in world economic affairs into problems of international economic diplomacy and trade wars.

The intellectual lineage of IPE realism can thus be traced to the founding texts of modern IR realism. It represents an attempt to synthesize two separate strands of thought, described by R. B. J. Walker (1993: 108–122) as structural realism and historical realism. Modern structural realists tend to follow Hans Morgenthau's pioneering lead (1948/1960) in anthropomorphizing the state and therefore treating state behaviour as epiphenomenal of essential human behaviour. By making the further assumption that it is human nature to be self-serving and to chase gains solely for oneself, combatively self-interested actions are consequently inscribed into the very logic of state behaviour. By contrast, modern historical realists work within a tradition that originates with E. H. Carr (1939/1946). Here, the emphasis is on developing historically contextualized explanations for how the instinct for combatively self-interested actions might be balanced in any given instance by the perceived need for a state to demonstrate to rival states that it is acting within the bounds of international political norms. The structural logic of state behaviour might therefore always be offset by historically conditioned concerns for turning away from exercising full-on aggression towards other states.

The two IR realist traditions, one starting with Morgenthau and the other with Carr, translate readily into IPE realism. On the one hand, it is assumed that states are concerned solely with their own interests when calculating their preferred stance in international economic negotiations (that is, the realist tradition that begins with Morgenthau). On the other hand, it is also assumed that states will want to avoid triggering retaliatory actions from other states, as this is likely to harm domestic producers and consumers, and thus work against the national economic interest (that is, the realist tradition that begins with Carr). The easiest way to prevent the precipitation of openly aggressive behaviour from other states is to show that one is acting in accordance with the prevailing international economic norms. These are the norms that are both inscribed into and defended by the actions of international institutions, thereby setting the context for global economic governance. In contemporary times, they include respect for the right of others to engage in free trade (as enshrined in the operating credo of the World Trade Organization) and a commitment to liberalizing financial flows and open capital accounts (as enshrined in the operating credo of the International Monetary Fund).

The alternative label 'statist' IPE applies to exactly the same style of scholarship as that captured by the label 'realist' IPE. Once again, the intellectual lineage of the approach can be traced back to its foundations in IR realism. The difference in nomenclature is to be explained merely by an attempt to place even more emphasis on the ontological basis of the theories that define the approach (that is, on the common assumptions its adherents share about the fundamental nature of the world). As Stephen Krasner, one of the leading proponents of this style of IPE, suggests (1994: 17), it is assumed that 'states are the ontological givens in the system'. The world that statist IPE describes is, at heart, a world of states, and every other aspect of that world is merely subsidiary to the existence, activities, and decisions of states. Other influential actors, such as large corporate bodies or regulatory institutions, are either constituted directly by states or have their capabilities delegated to them by the decisions of states. From this perspective, to focus on world economic affairs is necessarily to prioritize the study of the actions of states. The statist approach provides no new methods of understanding of its own, theorizing actual state behaviour in exactly the same way as realism. In IPE, then, 'realism' and 'statism' serve as acceptable synonyms for one another.

There is also a tendency for introductory texts to treat 'mercantilism' and 'nationalism' as further synonyms for 'realism' and 'statism'. However, this is not a move that should be endorsed unquestioningly. While it is certainly the case that all four lead to very similar explanations of contemporary issues in world economic affairs, this does not mean that they are in essence identical approaches. At least, they have different intellectual lineages. The foundations of realism and statism in IPE take us back to the origins of modern IR realism. While many have attempted to read proto-realist arguments back into classical political texts going as far back as the Ancient Greeks, this has generally been to impose post hoc coherence on disparate arguments that were not designed in their original form as fully specified theories of realism. The latter endeavour occurred much later, with the exposition of a modern form of realism which attempted to describe the specific exigencies of the modern world. As such, realism and statism emerge from distinctively twentieth-century traditions of thought, and thus they are infused with twentieth-century political priorities. The same is not true, however, for mercantilism or nationalism. Neither originates from within IR scholarship, and neither is the historical product of twentieth-century politics.

The political economy foundations of mercantilist and nationalist IPE

The 'mercantilist' approach is a political economy perspective on the question of the state's role in economic life. It differs from realism's IR perspective on the same question in terms of its focus. For realists, the most important issue is how states manage their economic affairs in international politics. This can be thought of as an outward-looking perspective on the role of the state, whereby its search for economic power, prestige and influence is condensed into those moments in which it projects itself on to the world stage in order to interact with other states. By contrast, mercantilism can be thought of as a more inward-looking perspective on the role of the state, concentrating on how it organizes domestic economic arrangements in order to develop the economic resources that give it a more credible bargaining position in international negotiations. For mercantilists, then, the most important issue is how states create the domestic economic basis for ensuring that they can punch their weight subsequently in international politics.

Mercantilism was the dominant approach in political economy prior to the publication of Adam Smith's *Wealth of Nations* in 1776, and Smith devoted a significant proportion of its 950 pages to an attempt to refute its core propositions (Smith 1776/1981). For 250 years from 1500, mercantilism informed almost all of the theory of the economy and the practice of economic policy (Backhouse 2002: ch. 3). It is therefore linked inextricably to the conditions in which large-scale commercial societies developed in Europe and the earliest experiences of industrialization occurred. Unlike modern realist and statist traditions, then, which incorporate the 'high' political priorities of twentieth-century world affairs, mercantilism reflects the 'low' political priorities of nations seeking to industrialize (Blaug 1996).

Arguably the two most important contributions to mercantilist thought, certainly in its anglophone variant, are to be found in Thomas Mun's *England's Treasure by Forraign Trade* (1664/1928) and Bernard Mandeville's *Fable of the Bees* (1714/1755). At the very least, these were the two publications that drew so much of Smith's attention in his efforts to construct a credible counter-argument. Mun's treatise was a celebration of England's eminent position in seventeenth-century international trade relations. Mun attributed English success to a strong state capable of structuring the country's commercial activities so as to produce continual trade surpluses. Imports were discouraged by the use of tariffs, quotas and subsidies, but the relative strength of the state was sufficient to ensure (through military means if necessary) that similarly restrictive practices were not imposed against English goods and, as a consequence, exports were not discouraged to the same extent as imports. The result was a net inflow of precious metals as other countries serviced their trade deficits with England. For the mercantilists, the hoarding of precious metals made possible by trade surpluses was the measure of the nation's wealth, not the overall productive capacity of the economy as a whole.

Mandeville extended Mun's analysis to argue that, while hoarding of precious metals was the primary objective of the state's economic policy, the state should also ensure that its citizens did not follow its lead by attempting to hoard their wealth. He suggested that individual saving might well be seen as a private virtue, but that it was in fact a public vice. The impetus for export activity could only be maintained under the full utilization of domestic productive potential, and this in turn required the state to be on its guard against domestic under-consumption. Such situations were most likely to ensue when individuals chose to save rather than spend any new income they earned, so every effort had to be made to encourage spending, with the state acting coercively if necessary.

The 'nationalist' approach in IPE accepts the same precepts as those that underpin the 'mercantilist' approach. The main difference between the two is the time at which they originated (Landreth and Colander 1994). The mercantilist approach pre-dates Smith's *Wealth of Nations*, while the nationalist approach is grounded in the historical conditions that were evident in the middle of the nineteenth century. By that time, English eminence in world economic affairs had turned into British pre-eminence. Britain was not only the primary exporter of tradable goods within world markets; it had also successfully exported its *laissez-faire* ideology of free trade. It was these same principles that formed the basis of the classical economics that Smith had counterposed successfully as an alternative to mercantilist principles, and had then been taken on by later generations of classical economists such as Thomas Malthus, William Thornton, David Ricardo, J. S. Mill, and Nassau William Senior.

Against this came a restatement of fundamental mercantilist belief, contextualized by the accusation that 'British' classical economics served primarily as an ideological support for British interests in maintaining a liberal international trading order. The seminal text in this respect is Friedrich List's *National System of Political Economy* (1841/1977) (although Eric Helleiner has recently shown (2005) that List might only be one of a number of starting points for the tradition of economic nationalism, albeit the most important one). List argued that institutionalized free trade worked well for Britain in the middle of the nineteenth century, because Britain's more advanced level of economic development meant that it had productivity advantages that helped it to dominate world markets in tradable goods. By contrast, *laissez-faire* was less appropriate for countries at a lower level of development, because they did not have the acquired productive capacity to be able to compete with Britain on an equal footing. According to List, the solution was to operate a nationalist policy that would stifle imports, favour domestic industry, and help eventually to close the productivity gap with Britain.

The four separate strands of realist IPE therefore divide neatly into two pairs. Realism and statism both have their origins in modern IR theory, taking their most basic understandings of the world from that theory; while mercantilism and nationalism both have their origins in older, pre-classical traditions of political economy, being similarly influenced by their intellectual lineage. However, it would be a mistake to suggest that all four were anything other than recognizably part of the same tradition of scholarship. All understand the state to be the privileged actor in world economic affairs, and all understand the primary issues of international economic management to be about devising institutional forms in which states can struggle with one another in the hope of securing relative gains. This degree of congruity is nowhere evident, however, in the other approach in the trichotomous structure of teaching IPE, where we see contestation over the most appropriate descriptive label: that of Marxism.

> **KEY POINTS**
>
> - The label 'realist' is deceptive in so far as it implies a homogenized area of study, when in fact it covers a number of different positions, often with contrasting historical and disciplinary origins.
>
> - 'Realism' should actually be disaggregated into four distinct positions: 'realist', 'statist', 'mercantilist', and 'nationalist'.
>
> - All four of these positions focus on optimal state strategies designed to enhance capitalist accumulation in the interests of increasing the state's power and prestige on the international stage.

The Contested Label of 'Marxist' IPE

The label 'Marxism' itself contains no surprises. Clearly, it refers to interventions into IPE debates that draw direct inspiration from the work of Karl Marx. Some contributions are rooted in the normative Marx, who makes the avowedly political case for a new type of society. The lineage here is usually to *The Communist Manifesto* (Marx and Engels 1848/1948). Others, however, are rooted in the analytical Marx, who makes the intellectual case for breaking with the liberal traditions of classical economics. The lineage here is usually to the *Grundrisse* (Marx 1973) or to *Kapital* (Marx 1930). Despite this difference, all are united in their refusal to take the social basis of capitalism for granted, and on their determination to ask searching questions about the likely effects of the capitalist system on those who have to construct their lives within it. The broad church of realist perspectives all ask how the state might be able to structure the capitalist system so that it can gain relative to other states. By contrast, those who find their inspiration in Marx ask why society should be expected to consent to the reproduction of the capitalist system in the first place.

The foundations of Marx's political economy

The whole of Marx's political economy is grounded in the opening premise that the capitalist system can only be a dynamic entity when the needs of that system are prioritized forcibly over the rights of individuals to live as autonomous human beings. The reproduction of the capitalist system overrides that autonomy by turning individuals into a functional part of the system. We may believe that we work to satisfy basic existential needs, that we work to be able to finance leisure time, or that we work to provide ourselves with the material possessions we associate with a life of comfort. According to Marx, however, within a capitalist system we in fact work in order to preserve the smooth running of the system itself. In effect, we are little more than tiny cogs in a huge machine, and it is the well-being of the machine that takes precedence over the defence of truly human existence. In Marx's view, the incorporation of the individual as a commodified input into the capitalist system necessarily comes at the cost of dehumanizing effects.

Marx works within the basic Hegelian position, which states that individuals' activities in the world change both the world on which they act and who they themselves are. The novelty in his argument lies in his insistence that it is the practical activities associated with the production process that matter most in this respect. Individuals are socialized into the necessity of production, before being coerced into a social structure that facilitates specifically capitalist production. Once there, the requirement is to live a regimented life, consisting primarily of the endless repetition of basic work tasks, so that standardized commodity production can take place. Obedience is paramount, and creativity in productive practices is discouraged, for fear that it will corrupt the standardization of commodities.

Given this, it is easy to see why Marx thought that the act of labour was so important to life in a capitalist society. The subjugation of the needs of the individual to the reproduction of the capitalist system in effect reduces the essence of human life to mere labouring activities. But even then, Marx was eager to show that labourers do not receive full recompense for the value of their labouring activities. He drew a politically charged distinction between labour and labour power, arguing that the average capitalist will always seek to reduce wages as far as possible, until they become the equivalent of labour power, even though it is labour that is physically expended in the production process. Labour power represents the costs of sustaining the workers who have been incorporated into the capitalist system. Yet it is labour that adds value to the commodities being produced, and thereby creates the potential for the capitalist to take profit out of the system. The more that capitalists are able to enforce a structural difference between labour and labour power, the more assured are those capitalists of being able to reward themselves with handsome profits. Marx described this as the logic of surplus value extraction, and he believed it to be a fundamental logic inscribed into the very essence of the capitalist system. The basic idea here is that, in order to ensure the dynamism that guarantees its survival as a system, employers under capitalism must require employees to add more economic value in production than they are recompensed for in terms of wages.

This, of course, is also a logic of exploitation. The contractual basis of the wage labour nexus defends a situation in which workers remain unpaid for part of the work they are obliged to do. A procedural injustice is clearly perpetrated in this instance and, given that this experience is fundamental to the reproduction of capitalism as a functioning system, for Marx, capitalism could never be just. Indeed, the whole essence of capitalism, according to Marx, is that it forcibly submits the vast majority of any given society to implicit consent to the injustices that are committed against them. This is the point of departure for the political Marx to advocate the move to a brand new society capable of transcending the logic of exploitation on which capitalism depends. The organizational basis for prosecuting such a move arises from the fact that exploitation and injustice are not solitary experiences under capitalism. Rather, they are experiences that are shared to a greater or lesser degree by everyone within society who has to work to finance their own subsistence. Marx thus depicts society as riven into two classes relating to their respective positions in the production process. On the one hand there are the capitalists—the bourgeoisie—who benefit from the surplus value extraction that permeates right to the heart of the capitalist system. On the other hand there are the workers—the proletariat—who bear the indignity of having surplus value forcibly extracted from them.

Modern 'structuralist' interpretations of Marx's political economy

Proponents of Marxist IPE have stayed remarkably loyal to Marx's original analytical formulations in the 150 years since they were initially devised. They seek to uncover exploitative dynamics in modern processes of international production, and they present such dynamics as infringements of global justice. Thus, they might investigate the way in which large companies with multinational operating facilities today make profits for themselves and their shareholders, focusing in particular on the potential for labour power to command different prices in different countries, and on how this creates opportunities for multinational corporations to enforce ever-greater discrepancies between the labour they command and the labour power they are obliged to recompense. The policy-making apparatus of the state might always be called upon to defend workers' rights and to meliorate the tendency towards proletarian exploitation. Yet Marxist IPE scholars have pointed increasingly to the development of a transnational capitalist class as a byproduct of the contemporary trend towards globalization (see, for example, van der Pijl 1998; Sklair 2001). Members of a transnational capitalist class have allegiance to no state and are therefore able increasingly to escape the bounds of regulatory policies introduced by state managers in the interests of workers' rights. If this is true, then the fundamental antagonism between bourgeoisie and proletariat identified by Marx is likely to be experienced in its purest form today within specifically international production processes.

The 'structuralist' approach to IPE is a close cousin of the 'Marxist' approach, at least in so far as it accepts Marx's basic position on the exploitative nature of capitalism. The difference between the two is primarily one of emphasis. Structuralists tend to pay less attention to reconstructing Marx's explanatory framework in its own terms, because their real point of departure is to be found in Lenin's efforts to internationalize fundamental Marxian themes (Lenin 1917/1996). In a pamphlet of the same name, Lenin argued that imperialism had become the 'highest stage of capitalism' by the start of the twentieth century, and that, as such, the new dynamism within the capitalist system centred on the relationship between states. Marx's original class-based analysis was retained, but Lenin asked how class-based relationships had been transformed now that capitalism had become a world system.

He argued that domestic bourgeoisies in advanced European countries had increasingly become international bourgeoisies through their willingness to strike class compromises at home. Their acquiescence to the granting of workers' rights domestically was met by a need to increase the level of surplus value extraction overseas in the interests of maintaining underlying levels of profitability for the national economy as a whole. Colonial links provided the ideal political context in which this could be achieved. As a consequence, imperialism was seen to have important economic effects both at home and abroad. Given the willingness of many scholars to treat contemporary conditions of globalization as just the latest phase of economic imperialism (see, for example, Hoogvelt 1997; Hardt and Negri 2000; Petras and Veltmeyer 2001), the structuralist approach to IPE has retained many adherents. They are usually to be found today practising either World Systems Theory or Dependency Theory. In its most up-to-date guise, World Systems Theory is based on the assumption that the world divides into economic regions of core, periphery, and semi-periphery (see, for example, Wallerstein 1979), while Dependency Theory is based on the assumption that the continued distorted development of certain countries results from the need to defend the conditions that have led to the development trajectory of more economically advanced countries (see, for example, dos Santos 1970).

'Radical' and 'critical' extensions of Marxist IPE

It is at this point, however, that the generic similarities between these four approaches end. While a close familial resemblance underpins Marxism and structuralism, the labels 'radical' and 'critical' IPE are intended to imply something else. It is clear that Marxism and structuralism are both radical (in that they represent overt political challenges to the capitalist system) and critical (in that their adherents refuse to accept the continued reproduction of that system as a given). But the purpose of the labels 'radical' and 'critical' is to suggest that these features are not owned exclusively by approaches that appeal to Marx for their intellectual inspiration. This is shown by the increasing prominence of feminist, green and poststructuralist scholars, all of whom argue that radical and critical features are just as prominent in their work (see Box 2.1). Indeed, for many of these scholars, the Marxian lineage is something to critique rather than to celebrate, as it is accused of over-emphasising class-based economic relationships—centred around the needs of a distinctively male industrial working class at that—and thus of obscuring the political

significance of other elements of the social relations of production. The argument is that class now matters less to the process of identity construction than at previous times, so class-based explanations now have less intellectual purchase than they once had.

Many of these radical approaches to IPE have their origins in the turn towards Critical Theory in IR since the 1980s. As a philosophical movement, Critical Theory dates from the 1930s and the Frankfurt School interventions focusing on the essentially political nature of all social scientific explanations. However, in IR, the origins of Critical Theory are more usually traced to Robert Cox's selective

---

BOX 2.1

Feminist International Political Economy

Feminists have every much as entitlement to the labels 'radical IPE' and 'critical IPE' as have Marxists. Feminist approaches to the subject field are certainly radical in their assertions that the capitalist system is founded on the reproduction of patriarchal social relations and, as such, the system itself should be a focus for concerted political challenge. They are also certainly critical in their related concerns to show that the dual structures of a capitalist economy and a patriarchal society are anything but natural. Rather, the continued existence of these structures requires decisive political interventions on the part of those who have privileged access to public decision-making bodies. As such, they must both be seen as conscious political choices.

Many feminists accept the basic Marxist proposition that the capitalist economy is rooted inextricably in the exploitation of those whose labours are functional to its reproduction. Indeed, for those feminists who seek to emphasize the economic basis of everyday life in their explanations of the subordinate social position of women, there is much to commend in an integrated Marxist–feminist perspective. Almost all feminists, however, wish to push beyond the Marxist conception of society, which overlooks the issue of gender in order to focus solely on the interaction of economic classes. In Marx's original analysis of the dynamics of capitalist reproduction, it is the male industrial working class that is the main agent of historical change, and this focus has been retained by

the majority of modern-day Marxists. The aim is to show how systems of ostensibly free exchange have been established on the back of the forced extraction of surplus value from the working class. The focus of feminist IPE is different. Here, the aim is to show how systems of ostensibly free exchange have been established on the back of social norms that involve deeply gendered assumptions about family role specialization.

The ability of women to participate fully in the economy—whether as consumer or producer—is constrained by the tasks they are required to undertake in support of basic family structures. Whereas the Marxist conception of labour refers only to paid work in the formal economy, feminists' extended conception of labour also includes unpaid work undertaken in the home, without which the maintenance of the workforce in the formal economy could not be guaranteed. Economy and society are therefore not distinct entities but rather interdependent spheres of human existence. As a consequence, any attempt to reproduce economic relations in their distinctively capitalist form is also likely to involve reproducing social relations in their distinctively patriarchal form. According to feminists, to truly engage with either radical or critical IPE requires explicit and simultaneous theorization of both dimensions of reproduction (that is, economic and social) within the context of everyday life.

appropriation of Frankfurt School theory than to the foundations of that theory itself. In the early 1980s, Cox attempted to create renewed space for radical approaches to IR by juxtaposing the transformative intentions of radical approaches with what he termed the 'problem solving' goals of non-radical approaches (Cox 1981). Cox had detected an ever-sharper concentration of research activities in IR on increasingly technical questions of system management: how best to organize the relationship between states in order to minimize the potential for violence between them, and how best to integrate states into an international system whose emergent properties emphasized liberal concerns for co-operation in the interests of meeting common goals. In this way, IR had been focused on finding solutions to systemic problems which served to defend the most basic structure of world affairs. That is, it took the world increasingly as it found it, and stopped asking more profound questions concerning the political and moral legitimacy of that world. Cox's appeal to a critical theoretical tradition should therefore be seen as an effort to refocus IR on these existential issues.

This appeal translated readily into IPE. Cox's own work asked how the basic structure of world affairs was predicated upon the forced institutionalization of social relations of production consistent with capitalist accumulation (see, for example, Cox with Sinclair 1996). As such, it was an attempt to get IR scholars to ask questions more usually associated with IPE. His aim was to show that the dominant problem-solving tradition in IR was inattentive to issues of economic organization, either nationally or internationally. It was consequently closed to political or moral critiques of capitalism and it had no basis to engage with radical perspectives on the social relations of capitalist production. In Cox's terms, it simply had to take the continued reproduction of capitalist accumulation for granted. It could ask how to manage the relationship between states so that possible tensions embedded within the very nature of accumulation might be alleviated. But it had no basis from which to understand the social implications of those tensions as a need to argue for the move to an alternative type of society. Critical Theory's attraction was precisely that it was able to offer a grounding for such an argument.

What Marxism shares with realism, then, is that it is not a single homogeneous approach to IPE as much as a collection of a number of like-minded approaches, each of which confirms the same basic view of the world but individually have different intellectual starting points. The only element of IPE's trichotomous structure not to embody such heterogeneity is liberalism. In the way that it is taught through introductory texts, liberal IPE appears to be a homogeneous body of thought derived from a single intellectual starting point. Even here, though, things are more complicated than they seem at first glance. As the next section shows, the ostensible homogeneity of liberal IPE arises primarily from a superficial understanding of its origins, which consequently misrepresents the intellectual lineage of the approach.

KEY POINTS

- The label 'Marxist' is deceptive in so far as it implies a homogenized area of study, when in fact it covers a number of different positions, often with contrasting historical and disciplinary origins, and sometimes constituted as a direct challenge to Marxism's focus on the male industrial working class.

- 'Marxism' should be disaggregated into four distinct positions: 'Marxist', 'structuralist', 'radical' and 'critical'.

- All four of these positions focus on the social relations of production, and ask how state strategies designed to enhance capitalist accumulation require the forced subordination of certain sectors of society (either domestic or international).

The Mis-Specified Roots of Liberal IPE

Most IPE textbooks trace the origins of the liberal approach to the birth of the British tradition of classical political economy, identifying a generally unbroken heritage that leads right back to the second half of the eighteenth century. More specifically, credit is given first to Adam Smith, and then to David Ricardo, as the founders of this approach. The textbook reading of liberalism reduces the significance of Smith to his identification of an 'invisible hand' that enables market economies to become self-regulating entities. From Ricardo, it takes the notion of **comparative advantage** in order to explain how invisible hand dynamics can expand global economic welfare by encouraging countries to specialize in producing what they are best at, and then trading goods freely in open markets. Add to this the insight of mid-nineteenth-century advocates of *laissez-faire*, such as Richard Cobden and John Bright, that countries trading with one another enjoy a more peaceful existence, and this constitutes the three bases of liberalism as taught through most IPE texts.

However, to reduce the work of Smith and Ricardo to one argument each is to overlook the nuances in their arguments and to misinvoke them as the forefathers of a purely economic liberalism. The label 'liberalism' is not contested in the teaching of IPE, then, in the same way as are the labels of 'realism' and 'Marxism'. Yet the implied homogeneity of liberalism in fact constitutes another difficulty, because what is taught as liberalism is not what emerges if we trace back the intellectual origins of the approach in the manner recommended by the textbooks.

Unpacking Smithian liberalism

Taking Smith first, there is no reason to deny that he was responsible for writing two of the most important treatises outlining the foundations of Enlightenment liberalism: *The Theory of Moral Sentiments* (1759/1982) and *The Wealth of Nations* (1776/1981). Yet the approach which Smith provides involves a complex synthesis of an ontological liberalism (outlining how the world works along liberal principles of economic organization) and a deontological liberalism (outlining how the world *should* be made to work in accordance with liberal philosophical principles—deontology being that branch of knowledge concerned with the rights and duties of individuals). By reducing the whole of his contribution to the single notion of the invisible hand, however, all that remains is a particular reading of Smith's ontological liberalism. In almost all textbooks on the subject, the invisible hand is assumed to be an economic metaphor explaining how a liberal capitalist system provides the basis of its own internal co-ordination (see, for example, Dunne 2001; Steans and Pettiford 2001; O'Brien and Williams 2004; Scholte 2005). But in the chapters of *The Wealth of Nations* in which such dynamics are discussed—Book One, chs. 5–7—Smith makes it clear that a self-regulating liberal economy is an ideal-type only; that is, it is not intended to be a description of conditions that one should expect to find in the real world. Rather, it is the hypothetical state of affairs that would arise were one able to remove all the messiness of the real world from one's contemplations about it.

For the ideal-type to be realized, according to Smith, the 'market price' of every commodity in circulation in the economy would have to equal its 'natural price'. He defines the natural price as that which exactly covers the value of labour input into the commodity's production plus the value of the entrepreneurial costs shouldered by the capitalist. In such a situation, he says, 'The commodity is then sold precisely for what it is worth, or for what it really costs the person who brings it to market' (1776/1981: 72). But he also says that in almost every real-world circumstance, we should not expect the natural price to prevail and that the market price will be somewhat higher than it.

The reason for this is that the business classes have shown themselves to be almost pathologically incapable of acting according to the demands of a genuinely liberal economy, thereby allowing the market to set prices at their natural rate. He accuses the business classes of fundamentally illiberal activities of conspicuous profit-taking from the economy, thus ensuring that market prices exceed natural prices. A similar dynamic is evident in Marx's analysis of surplus value extraction discussed previously, but in Smith's analysis it is the consumer who acts as the capitalist's source of surplus value by being required to pay above natural prices, rather than the worker, who is only recompensed for labour power and not full labour. As such, Smith's ontological liberalism applies at most to the hypothetical circumstances he describes within his theoretical model. It does not apply to circumstances which he believed might be experienced in practice. The invisible hand interpretation of Smith that appears in IPE textbooks is therefore of strictly limited application.

Moreover, the invisible hand interpretation also crowds out the extensive attention that Smith pays to deontological liberalism. This focus is most evident when he discusses the constitution of the individual as a moral agent, and how this translates into either a functioning or a dysfunctional society. (This is the principal theme of *The Theory of Moral Sentiments*.) Smith is keen to emphasize that only certain moral dispositions are consistent with life lived tolerably within a liberal society, and, in general, these reduce to those that are fashioned out of the sentiment of propriety (Smith 1759/1982; Part 1). In order to encourage behaviour consistent with the sentiment of propriety, Smith thought that it was necessary to design social institutions which rewarded a certain moderation of action. Such instincts are more difficult to instil when social relations are played out at a distance, because the relative anonymity of those relations is an impediment to anything other than partial behaviour by the individual. However, for Smith, excessive partiality to oneself which cannot be regulated by the sentiment of propriety undermines tolerable existence in a liberal society.

Smith therefore praises deliberate acts of impartiality and insists that all individuals should experience dutiful sensations to act with conscience. Conspicuously self-motivated actions cannot be approved of unless they also serve to promote the wider ends of society (West 1976). According to Smith, all individuals must internalize the image of the good society, to ensure that they live within the bounds of acceptable social behaviour (Raphael and Macfie 1982). Partiality of the self is thereby juxtaposed with the possibility of learning the instinct towards impartiality through incorporating the image of the good society into one's most basic world view. Human fallibility can potentially be balanced by tutoring oneself to exercise restraint of the selfish passions. Such restraint, when it comes from within, is called by Smith 'self-command'.

When Smith's clear preference for a society populated by individuals who are capable of exercising self-command is taken into consideration, it becomes evident that only by taking his notion of the invisible hand out of context can his work be read as an unequivocal endorsement of a market-based liberalism. It is certainly the case that he accepted the potential gains in dynamism that could be made if an economy was organized along market lines, especially if the illiberal activities of the business classes could be eradicated. But he also thought that socialization into market norms could be a distraction to individuals who were seeking to exercise self-command. After all, the dynamism of the market economy comes from individuals deliberately ignoring the promptings of self-command and immersing themselves in the acquisitive culture that market life makes possible. The material privileges enjoyed by a successful individual in market society makes conspicuously self-motivated actions all the more likely. The more that they act in this way, the greater the consumption possibilities they open up for themselves, and the greater the temptation to renege on society-building commitments associated with self-command.

Moreover, so much activity in a market economy takes place at arm's length from genuine face-to-face human relationships, being conducted through the impersonal guise of the price mechanism. This is becoming ever truer in contemporary times, as the scope of globalization stretches economic relations further across space. Yet this creates situations which Smith associated with reduced likelihood for the instinct for propriety to be incorporated into the individual's moral dispositions. As such, it also corresponds to situations in which a tolerable life led within a liberal society becomes less likely.

Adam Smith's ontological liberalism is therefore often directly at odds with his deontological liberalism: the acculturating features of the market economy appear to be consistent with his ontological liberalism, but directly antithetical to his deontological liberalism. How, then, might we summarize his overall position? The very least we should do is to recognize the stress he placed on the need for all individuals to develop virtuous dispositions associated with moral propriety. From this perspective, all of his work apart from the first of the five books of *The Wealth of Nations* seems to be an expression of concern about the probably corrupting effects of the market economy on the individual as moral agent. The typical IPE textbook reading of Smith's liberalism ignores this aspect of his work by concentrating instead on the 'invisible hand', which is taken to be a metaphor for uncritical support of the existence of market institutions. As such, it rests on shaky foundations.

Indeed, if we were to focus solely on Smith's deontological liberalism and his desire for all individuals to teach themselves the virtues of morally praiseworthy behaviour, then he looks less like the arch-advocate of the classical liberal position and more like the type of critical theorist reviewed in a previous section of this chapter. He certainly meets the two standards that today influence whether one's work will be judged to be part of the critical IPE literature. On the one hand, he refuses to take the social relations of capitalism as a given,

and he worries incessantly about what effect the continual exposure to the cultural norms of the market economy will have on the moral make-up of the individual. On the other hand, he argues that remedial action is necessary, in the form of personal self-command, whenever market life threatens to corrupt the individual's sentiment of propriety. He thus focuses at least as much attention on the desirability of political mobilization against the personal attributes of market life as he does on the desirability of political mobilization for them. In this way, he has as much in common with the critics of the liberal position as it appears in IPE as he does with its advocates. Smith's liberalism is therefore not the route to a self-contained and hermetically-sealed liberal position in IPE, as much as a bridge between such a position and some of the supposedly contrary positions already discussed. The image of a trichotomous structure of liberalism versus realism versus Marxism is consequently much more difficult to maintain once we scratch the surface of the more superficial readings of Smith's liberalism.

Unpacking Ricardian liberalism

The same is also true of David Ricardo's liberalism. Ricardo made a seminal contribution to the evolution of classical political economy in his *Principles of Political Economy and Taxation* (1817/2002), where he sought to put many of Smith's insights from Book One of *The Wealth of Nations* into a more rigorous logical framework. This, remember, was the only part of Smith's entire work in which he adopted the perspective of ontological liberalism without trying to balance this with his deontological liberalism. Book One of *The Wealth of Nations* thus represents the only glimpse of Smith as a pure economic theorist, and it was in this tradition that Ricardo operated, attempting to sharpen the clarity of Smith's theoretical model of a functioning market economy. Among this commitment to generating a fully specified hypothetical model of a purely self-regulating economy, one can find the passages for which Ricardo is cited most frequently in IPE texts as one of the founders of liberalism (see, for example, Grieco and Ikenberry 2003; Brawley 2005; Oatley 2006). These are to be found in Chapter VII, entitled 'On Foreign Trade', as it is here that Ricardo develops the notion of comparative advantage as a means of arguing the case for free trade.

Almost 200 years later, this notion still provides the theoretical backbone for economists' discussions of the dynamics of international trade. Part of its continuing appeal is that it is founded on a small number of simple assumptions, all of which correspond to what we are most likely to accept as empirical givens about the world. Ricardo assumed that different economies are differently endowed: some countries have climates specifically suited to certain types of agricultural production; others have developed expertise in financial services and now have a solid banking structure; and others still concentrate the capital accumulation process in the production of manufactured goods. He further assumed that countries should specialize economically in what they already do best, thus increasing their existing lead over other countries in these areas.

This is the logic of comparative advantage, and Ricardo argued that modern economic production should be organized in each country on the basis of comparative advantage. To back this point, he showed—as a matter of logic, supported by elementary arithmetic—that welfare gains were available, both for the world as a whole and for every country in it, as long as a system of comparative advantage was supported by an institutionalized structure of free trade among nations. This was true even if one country had an **absolute advantage** over others in producing all categories of goods. The implication was that countries should specialize economically in what they do best, and reap the gains from this by trading the produce of their specialization in an unrestricted manner with other countries.

This is as far as the vast majority of IPE texts get with Ricardo, which means that they fail to contextualize adequately his notion of comparative advantage. Beneath his theory of international trade, and acting as direct political inspiration to

it, is a deep-seated contempt for the commercial policy enacted in the Britain of his day. Ricardo objected most forcefully to the influence that an unaccountable cadre of landowners had been able to exert over commercial policy. At one point in his treatise he even calls the landowning classes 'parasites' in his attempt to signal as clearly as possible that they were responsible for the immiseration of others through their illiberal and wholly self-serving activities (Landreth and Colander 1994).

Ricardo's anger centred on the continuation of the Corn Laws (see Box 4.1, Chapter 4 on page 99). These had been laws introduced during the Napoleonic Wars, ensuring British agricultural producers guaranteed prices for basic foodstuffs, so that they could continue to meet demand for them amid fears of French blockades of imported grain. The end of the Napoleonic Wars, though, did not lead to the repeal of the Corn Laws. The landowning classes benefited handsomely from guaranteed prices to agricultural producers, and they wanted this situation to be maintained in the face of potentially cheaper foodstuffs being imported from abroad. They used their position as parliamentarians to defend the gains they made from the Corn Laws, slapping high tariffs on imported grain in order to protect the price floor underpinning the grain produced on their land. Ricardo's notion of comparative advantage was devised specifically to demonstrate that maintaining the Corn Laws represented an affront to economic logic, as Britain would be noticeably better off specializing in the production of manufacturing goods and using the money that resulted from their export to import cheaper foreign foodstuffs.

Ricardo drew a powerful political distinction between those who (legitimately) took earned rewards out of the economy and those who (illegitimately) enjoyed unearned rewards. Both the labouring and manufacturing classes had his sympathy, because both worked for their rewards, and he judged this to be earned income. The earned income for labourers is their wages, and the earned income for manufacturers is a normal rate of profit to reflect their entrepreneurial risks. (This is a similar reward to what Smith had in mind as the acceptable return to cover the costs of entrepreneurship in his structure of natural prices.) By contrast, the landowning classes attracted Ricardo's condemnation. They took excessive amounts of rent from the economy, where rent is the return to owners of land. The amount of money that landowners could extract from the economy in rent was facilitated by the price floor on basic foodstuffs introduced by the Corn Laws, but they had to do no work to receive these rents. They were eligible for them simply because of the good fortune of having been born into a landowning family. Ricardo consequently judged this to be unearned income.

It is clear, then, that Ricardo's liberal economic model is underpinned by a class-based understanding of society. This is usually not recognized in IPE treatments of Ricardo, which depict him as being about free trade and nothing else. By undertaking a more thorough reading of his work, though, it becomes increasingly difficult to sustain the image of 'liberalism' as taught in IPE. At the very least, it is necessary to acknowledge the links between Ricardo's liberalism and other positions in IPE's trichotomous structure (as, of course, was also the case with Smith's liberalism). Ricardo's overt politicization of economic theory through his use of a class-based interpretation of society is particularly noteworthy. If we were to focus primarily on this, then we would probably be forced to reposition Ricardo in the critical camp, such was his desire to use economic theory to overturn the established political order of society. Indeed, the class analysis in his work signals

clear intellectual similarities with a critical tradition that links directly with Marx. The great Cambridge economist, Piero Sraffa, certainly recognized this link, describing Ricardo as a 'proto-Marxian' (Sraffa 1951/1981). So too did the Nobel Laureate in Economics, Paul Samuelson, albeit from the opposite direction, describing Marx as a 'minor Ricardian' (Samuelson 1987). Marx takes from Ricardo the assumptions that society is divided along class lines, that different classes receive different types of reward from the economy, and that the political power of price determination allows some classes to set the market price of economic rewards to their own advantage and to the detriment of other classes.

KEY POINTS

- What is presented as the liberal position in introductory IPE texts is in truth little more than the amalgamation of a single idea from Adam Smith (the invisible hand) and a single idea from David Ricardo (comparative advantage).

- Reading Smith's work more widely shows that he stopped well short of unequivocally endorsing economic liberalism, because he was concerned about the morally degrading impact on the character of individuals resulting from their incorporation into a market economy.

- Reading Ricardo's work more widely shows that he also stopped well short of unequivocally endorsing economic liberalism, because he was concerned about the impact of capitalism's power-brokers on the ability to operate society in line with meritocratic principles.

Beyond the Trichotomous Structure of Teaching IPE

So, where does this leave us? The trichotomy of liberalism versus realism versus Marxism remains the standard fare of introductory IPE teaching. It is through the series of oppositions between the three approaches that students are taught the basic concepts of the subject field, and these continue to be the primary points of reference as students are gradually exposed to more complex concepts. The trichotomous structure is thus an extremely powerful tool for training students who are new to the subject field to think in particular ways, and to develop particular theoretical intuitions.

But is it defensible in its own terms? My argument thus far in this chapter is that it almost certainly is not. It matters, for a number of reasons, that we are accurate when it comes to specifying the historical roots of the contemporary theories on which we base our work. If this specification is questionable, then the intellectual lineage that acts as a defence of the contemporary position is equally questionable. Contemporary theories are not free-floating entities, but are necessarily part of historically grounded traditions of thought. If the claim to belong to a certain tradition cannot be sustained under close textual scrutiny, then the contemporary theory immediately loses both its historical anchoring and part of its validation to talk authoritatively about the world as it is encountered today. And by this measure we must doubt whether realism, Marxism or liberalism hold the clear-cut and tightly contained positions that they appear to hold in introductory IPE texts (see Table 2.1).

Table 2.1 Disaggregating the Trichotomy of Liberalism Versus Realism Versus Marxism

Conventional labelling	Disaggregated labelling	Key focus	Historical origins in recognized political economy traditions
Liberalism	Ontological liberalism	The aim is to understand the real economic features of an ideal-type liberal system in which individuals enjoy autonomy in the decisions as to how to expend their economic resources.	First generation: Adam Smith, *Wealth of Nations*, Book 1, 1776; David Ricardo, *Principles of Political Economy*, Chapters I–VII, 1817. Second generation: William Stanley Jevons, *Theory of Political Economy*, 1871.
	Deontological liberalism	The social regulation of economic affairs is highlighted, so as to prevent socialization into market norms from leading to the moral, communal, cultural, or spiritual decay of society.	Originally: Adam Smith, *Theory of Moral Sentiments*, 1759; *Wealth of Nations*, Books 2–5, 1776; David Ricardo, *Principles of Political Economy*, Chapters VIII–End, 1817. Modern Reincarnation: Amartya Sen, *Development as Freedom*, 1999.
Realism	Realism	The international economy is understood to be an anarchical environment in which states struggle against one another for economic power, prestige and influence.	This is not really a political economy perspective on world economic affairs, so there is no obvious historical lineage back to classic political economy texts. Modern text: Robert Gilpin, *The Political Economy of International Relations*, 1987.
	Statism	The role of the state is emphasized in the conduct of international economic negotiations, with each state seeking to make gains relative to other states.	As above, this is not really a political economy perspective on world economic affairs, so there is no obvious historical lineage back to classic political economy texts. Modern text: Stephen Krasner, *Defending the National Interest*, 1978.

Table 2.1 (*continued*)

Conventional labelling	Disaggregated labelling	Key focus	Historical origins in recognized political economy traditions
	Mercantilism	Policy-makers are advised to use state power in an attempt to suppress import penetration, but also to prevent reciprocal restrictive practices from other states.	Thomas Mun, *England's Treasure by Forraign Trade*, 1664; Bernard Mandeville, *Fable of the Bees*, 1714.
	Nationalism	Resuscitating the mercantilist focus, nationalist political economy arose from concerns that *laissez-faire* was an ideology that only the most powerful could afford to support.	Friedrich List, *National System of Political Economy*, 1841.
Marxism	Marxism	The ownership of the means of capitalist production divides society into two fundamentally antagonistic classes: those who own the means of production (the bourgeoisie), and those who are forced to sell their labour to the owners (the proletariat).	Karl Marx, *Grundrisse*, not published in English until 1973, but clearly written a long time before that, given that Marx died in 1883. Karl Marx, *Capital*, the authoritative fourth edition was published posthumously by his literary executor, Friedrich Engels, in 1890.
	Structuralism	The aim is to internationalize Marx's core concepts in order to discover how the relationship between bourgeoisie and proletariat plays out across space once capitalism becomes a genuine world system.	Vladimir Ilyich Lenin, *What Is to Be Done?*, 1902; Vladimir Ilyich Lenin, *Imperialism, the Highest Stage of Capitalism*, 1917.
	Radical	The analysis revolves around attempts to show that the dispossessed (however defined) suffer their fate specifically because of the logic of capitalism, with a view to arguing the case for a move beyond current economic conditions.	This is a combination of myriad modern perspectives on the world, each of which is linked indelibly to contemporary experiences. As such, it is not a single position with a corresponding singular lineage back to a historical tradition of political economy.
	Critical	The social relations of capitalist production are argued to be contingent features of the modern world and not a natural phenomenon inscribed into the very essence of economic life.	As above, there are many critical positions to be adopted in IPE, so the issue of a singular lineage back to a historical tradition of political economy does not really arise. Most cited modern link: Robert Cox, *Production, Power and World Order*, 1987.

- *Realism*   It has been shown that realism is not a single approach, but rather an amalgam of at least four ('realist', 'statist', 'mercantilist' and 'nationalist'). These four share many of the same basic theoretical features, but crucially each has distinct historical roots, which is what makes them different approaches in the first place. To mix and match between them, as if to imply that they are all synonymous with one another, is therefore to muddle the historical roots and to leave the resulting theoretical claims less securely anchored. Greater clarity would be introduced into theoretical debates were these four approaches to be treated as separate entities, and were their different intellectual lineages to be recognized as such. But this would also be responsible for removing the clarity of one of the three poles of IPE's trichotomous structure of teaching.

- *Marxism*   Exactly the same can be said about the Marxist approach. Perhaps even more clearly, this in truth is four approaches ('Marxist', 'structuralist', 'radical' and 'critical'), not one, where some of those believing that they are doing radical and critical IPE do so specifically so that they can set themselves in opposition to elements of the Marxist world view. Again, the most convincing case is to argue for keeping these four approaches separate, and for acknowledging explicitly their different historical roots. But this would also be at the expense of the clarity of one of the three poles of IPE's trichotomous structure of teaching.

- *Liberalism*   The same problem is not as evident here of conflating distinct intellectual lineages

inaccurately and presenting them as a single, unified approach. However, another problem of at least equal significance does arise: definite historical roots are claimed for liberal IPE but, on closer inspection, these roots are shown to be constructed on the basis of a superficial reading of the texts to which they claim allegiance. This means that the clarity of the third pole of IPE's trichotomous structure of teaching also rests on intellectually dubious bases. Either the clarity can be preserved, or a more secure intellectual anchorage can be targeted.

Overall, then, two of the three poles of IPE's trichotomous structure of teaching are poorly specified as single approaches, and the third is poorly specified in its own terms. There are many more theoretical and analytical connections between the separate ways of doing IPE than the trichotomous structure of teaching the subject field allows. Indeed, that structure attempts to negate the very possibility of identifying connections by attempting to force the subject field into a series of mutually exclusive positions. This suggests that it is not the most useful way of trying to devise heuristic distinctions for making sense of how the separate interventions into IPE debates fit in with one another and are positioned in relation to one another.

So, if this is not the most appropriate manner to proceed, then what might be? One way of answering this is to look, not at the distinctions through which IPE is taught, but at the way in which IPE scholars' research is appraised. It is to this issue that I turn in the remainder of the chapter.

Basic Heuristic Distinctions for Appraising IPE Research

The first thing to note is that there is no single, generally accepted method of appraising the subject field in terms of basic themes of research. The IPE literature is by no means over-populated with attempts to summarize what it means to be doing IPE by reviewing the field as a whole. But most of the people who have attempted this have devised their own classificatory schema for identifying the major analytical, theoretical and disciplinary divisions in IPE research. I shall begin with the twofold separation of the field advocated by Robert Denemark and Robert O'Brien (1997). The reason for starting here is that their argument is constructed on the back of a significant volume of survey data which they collected from researchers in the field. Their point of departure was to ask IPE scholars what it meant *to them* to be doing IPE. So the categories they devise in order to explain the primary divisions within the field come, as it were, straight from the horse's mouth.

'Traditional' versus 'inclusive' IPE

From their respondents' descriptions of what they consider IPE to be, Denemark and O'Brien suggest that IPE is divided broadly down the middle. On one side of this partition we find those who practice what they call 'traditional IPE'. Here, the goal is to treat IPE as a subset of IR more generally and, as such, the historical roots of the two subject fields are treated as being one and the same. Yet this leaves us in something of a bind. Modern IR is overwhelmingly a twentieth-century phenomenon, but political economy has a much longer heritage than this. In its modern guise alone, it stretches back at least to the second half of the eighteenth century. To treat the historical roots of the two subject fields as being coterminous, then, is to lose sight immediately of pre-twentieth-century political economy. However, contemporary IPE theories quite clearly claim allegiance to political economy traditions whose historical roots precede those of modern IR (liberalism, Marxism, mercantilism, and nationalism, to name but a few). Denemark and O'Brien's traditional IPE therefore falls foul of many of the objections that can be raised against the liberal pole of IPE's trichotomous structure of teaching. It lacks adequate historical anchorage with respect to its own political economy traditions.

Susan Strange has also identified a similar trend for IPE to be practised in this way: that is, for it to

be treated simply as a subset of IR scholarship and to be inattentive to its own political economy history. Here, the aim is merely to explain the political dynamics of the inter-state system on matters of an economic nature. Given such a goal, the theories and methods of modern IR are quite adequate, and there is no need to look into the divergent historical roots of IR and IPE. Strange (1998a) argues that this reduces IPE to the economic branch of foreign policy studies and, for this reason, she refuses even to describe it as IPE per se. Instead, she prefers to call it the 'PIER' approach, where PIER stands for the politics of international economic relations.

On the other side of Denemark and O'Brien's partition they place what they call 'inclusive IPE'. This is to be distinguished from traditional IPE primarily by the extent to which it treats IR and IPE as two entirely separate undertakings. In this way, the historical roots of IPE can be thought about more clearly because there is no need to tie them to the less extensive historical roots of IR. Practitioners of this approach cite as a particular influence Cox's entreaties to disentangle IPE from explanatory frameworks that give sole precedence to the role of the state and, as a consequence, they take seriously the impact of social forces in shaping both the context and the conduct of world economic affairs (Cox 1981).

This opens up contemporary IPE to active engagement with the classical political economy tradition originating in the work of Adam Smith, as well as the radical economics tradition originating in the work of Karl Marx, because both traditions accept that the role of social forces is crucial in the production of economic outcomes. For Smith, the social forces that mattered most were those that impacted on the constitution of the individual as a moral agent; for Marx, they were those that impacted on the division of society into economic classes. Strange is also more satisfied with this style of scholarship and, in particular, its potential for re-establishing the link between IPE and its historical roots in the tradition of political economy. At the very least, she deigns to call this IPE proper.

The straw man characteristics of traditional IPE

Perhaps the most obvious drawback of the descriptive labels used both by Denemark and O'Brien, and by Strange, is that it is very difficult to imagine circumstances in which IPE scholars would willingly assign their work to the category the labellers have in mind, as the less appropriate way of undertaking research in IPE. We have to be clear that the labels themselves infer that there is a preferred way and a non-preferred way (that is, an effectual and an ineffectual way) of doing IPE. For Denemark and O'Brien, the preferred way is to be practising 'inclusive IPE', while for Strange it is to be practising IPE proper rather than some foreign economic policy studies imitation of IPE. All practitioners within the field are likely to want to align their own work with the preferred label, no matter the extent to which others would want to impose the alternative designation.

For example, to be described as a 'traditional' scholar would not be treated as a compliment by most academics. They would much prefer their work to be seen as cutting-edge, as politically and intellectually challenging, and as being on the cusp of conceptual and theoretical innovations within the field. In other words, most academics would seek to define their own contribution in exactly the opposite way from what is implied by the label 'traditional' scholarship. There is no reason to think that IPE scholars are any different in this respect and, for that reason, Denemark and O'Brien's category of traditional IPE is one with which exceptionally few IPE scholars would wish consciously to associate their work. Given the choice that comes with the self-designation of labels, almost all would prefer to be seen in the more favourable light of being 'inclusive' scholars.

The same point can be made even more forcefully in relation to Strange's labels. To align oneself with her PIER approach is to deny that one's work even deserves to be categorized as IPE proper. Yet, why should any IPE scholar invite this rather damning characterization on to their own work? Hence, the search must continue for appropriate heuristic distinctions that help us to understand the generic differences between one way of practising IPE and another.

KEY POINTS

- Denemark and O'Brien's distinction between 'traditional IPE' and 'inclusive IPE' finds a direct corollary in Strange's distinction between PIER approaches and IPE proper.

- Many of the distinctions from IPE's trichotomous structure of teaching also reappear in the divisions identified by Denemark and O'Brien and by Strange, especially the suggestion that there are those who focus all their analytical energies at the level of the state, and those who look elsewhere for the basis of their analysis.

- Neither Denemark and O'Brien's nor Strange's labels are neutral, because each imply that there is a right approach and a wrong approach to IPE.

Analytical Distinctions to Sub-Divide the Field

Another place to begin in the search for suitable heuristic distinctions is Craig Murphy and Douglas Nelson's desire to distinguish between an 'IO School' and a 'British School' of IPE (Murphy and Nelson 2001). The meanings of these labels are not self-evident and, at one level, they might even invite confusion. They certainly require more explanation, which is what they will receive in due course. But, for now, the important thing to note is that they have one great advantage as a means of appraising the subject field over the rival classificatory schema favoured both by Denmark and O'Brien and by Strange. The latter two rely on labels that are clearly not neutral in their application, but are designed deliberately to deliver followers. By contrast, Murphy and Nelson's distinction between an IO School and a British School is an attempt to divide the field analytically, and it thus offers a more neutral description of two different analytical starting points for conducting research in IPE. It is a means of recognizing these divergent starting points rather than saying that one is necessarily right and the other wrong.

The 'IO' and 'British' schools of IPE

As 'IO' refers to *International Organization*, the leading US-based journal in the field, and as the IO School is purposefully juxtaposed with the British School, notice is served of a possible 'Atlantic divide' in IPE. But this does not mean that all US scholars share an unreflexive, almost pre-conscious, allegiance to the IO School; nor does it mean that all scholars working in US universities, irrespective of their country of origin, share a similar affiliation. It is merely to point to the fact that the vast majority of scholarly IPE journals published in the US have followed the lead of *International Organization* in prioritizing a particular conception of research within the field.

Similarly, the label 'British School' should not be understood too literally, at least not to infer homogeneity of approach in all IPE that originates geographically in the UK. Once again, it is the editorial policy of leading journals that gives meaning to the label, and that editorial policy attracts work submitted from all over the world. It is intended to capture the sense that the major journals published in the UK have been set up in (often conscious) opposition to the style of IPE scholarship that features so prominently in the major journals published in the US. It therefore provides a potential home for work that might not otherwise be published.

In the first instance, the division to which Murphy and Nelson want to draw attention is largely methodological. Authors whose work is consistent with the IO School approach tend to link economic outcomes to interests, and this is achieved most often through the application of a largely mechanistic rational choice framework. Economic agents are assumed to satisfy their interests in a manner that imposes the logic of utility maximization on their actions. What is true of individuals' economic behaviour is also considered to be true of economic policy. States are assumed to have readily identifiable interests, and to be constituted in such a way as to have the cognitive capacities of a utility-maximizing agent. As a consequence, policy decisions are treated as a rational response to a national interest that is relatively straightforward both to define and to act upon, and whose identification with the will of the people is thought to be largely uncontroversial.

IPE within the IO School tradition is able to focus on the standard political question of 'who gets what and how', but it reduces its answers to that question to those that are consistent with a rationalist framework that can say almost nothing about social influences on the construction of economic identities. As an individual's behaviour is conceptually indistinguishable from that of states in so far as both are orientated towards a pre-given structure of interests, every agent within the economy will be seeking to ensure that they emerge from economic activity—either as an individual or as a country—with a sense of having gained at someone else's expense. Policy outcomes can therefore be reduced to the prevailing balance of interests within society (either domestically or internationally).

By contrast, British School scholars tend to focus less on matters of policy than do their IO School counterparts, and they reject the idea that all issues of concern to the student of IPE can be reduced to models of rational agential choice. They concentrate instead on how choice of agent is itself shaped by the social structures of the economic environment in which it is attempted. Individuals' economic behaviour is thus not understood as a purely rational response to external circumstances which in themselves do nothing to condition how economic agents think about the choices available to them. Rather, behaviour is assumed to reflect social aspirations, aspirations arise as a consequence of socially constituted identities, and the process of identity formation responds to complex dynamics of acculturation to embedded economic norms.

From this standpoint, neither individuals' interests nor the national interest can be discerned from observing the outcomes of economic behaviour that must be assumed, by definition, to be utility maximizing. Interests precede behaviour, and are linked not to a process of rational calculation but to the place of the individual within the social life of the community. Of particular importance to the British School is the question of how both identities and interests reflect the structure of distribution within society. In this respect, British School scholars are equally happy to work with a conception of either national or international society. They ask either how the structure of distribution nationally affects economic identities and interests nationally, or how the structure of distribution internationally affects economic identities and interests internationally. The tendency to write about issues of distributive justice domestically in the former becomes transformed into the tendency to write about issues of distributive justice globally in the latter.

This is also to focus on the question of 'who gets what and how', but this might be the only underlying property shared by the IO and British Schools of IPE. The British School asks how initial economic endowments arise from culturally specific relationships between economy and society, while the IO School asks how those endowments are expended in an attempt to maximize utility. The IO School treats IPE generically as the study of constrained utility maximization problems under conditions of rational choice, while the British School treats IPE as the study of the philosophy of social organization across various spatial scales of economic life. The IO

School prioritizes exchange relations as the essence of the economy, and it models policy decisions as direct analogues of economic exchange. By contrast, the British School prioritizes distributive relations, and theorizes policy decisions as reflections of the underlying balance of social forces.

Drawbacks of the Murphy and Nelson approach

If there are problems with the Murphy and Nelson designation, then these are twofold. From the perspective of the current review, the most obvious one is that of over-homogenization (in much the same way that the liberalism/realism/Marxism trichotomy is guilty of over-homogenization). The concern when using the either/or distinction between the IO School and the British School is that many interventions into IPE debates will lose their individuality if they can only be thought of as reflecting one half or the other of a binary opposition. In practice, on both sides of the IO School/British School divide, what is presented as a single position is in fact an amalgam of a large number of different positions, many of which will involve ignoring the other school altogether and instead challenging other positions from within the same school. What can be made to look like an internally homogeneous school for the sake of analytical abstraction subsequently fragments into a series of often mutually antagonistic theoretical claims when viewed more closely.

In addition to this, the Murphy and Nelson designation prioritizes the contemporary practices of IPE and it understands these solely on their own terms. From my perspective, what is most obviously missing here is a ready way to link contemporary pursuits within IPE to their historical roots via a direct intellectual lineage. The two-schools approach refers only to ways in which IPE might be undertaken in the present. Its labels offer few clues about how the two schools correspond to established, yet competing, historical traditions in political economy. The designation emphasizes contemporary theories, contemporary methods and contemporary approaches, presenting the choice between the two schools as one that mirrors the most obvious methodological dispute in contemporary social science: will one accept the convenience of rational choice theory as a modelling technique, or demand a more philosophically reflexive account of human agency?

At one level, this focus on the contemporary is entirely understandable. After all, almost every appraisal of the subject field begins by commenting on IPE's youth relative to other fields (see, for example, Gill and Law 1988; Onuf 1997; Pearson and Rochester 1998; Dash *et al.* 2003). The field was forged amid attempts to explain events that were a particular feature of distinctively modern times. Specifically, the recent manifestation of IPE results from concerns to reflect on the future of world economic affairs following the collapse of the **Bretton Woods** system of international economic management in the early 1970s (see, for example, Krasner 1976; Gilpin 1987; Frieden and Lake 1995; Grieco and Ikenberry 2003). Given this intimate connection between the birth of IPE and the onset of the most recent phase of the modern world, it could conceivably be said that contemporary theories, methods and approaches are all that is required to understand that world.

Yet this would be to overlook an important point already raised on a number of occasions in the current chapter. This is that contemporary approaches are not free-floating entities; they are not without their own history and they cannot be understood other than in relation to the historical traditions of thought of which they are a part. To treat contemporary approaches in their own self-referential terms is to deny them their intellectual heritage, and to strip them of the historical anchoring that comes from recognizing their lineage. As such, the labels IO School and British School, while useful, are also not without their limits. Consequently, the search should probably continue for the most appropriate heuristic distinctions for understanding the subject field of IPE in its entirety.

> **KEY POINTS**
>
> - The distinction between the IO School and the British School of IPE is an attempt to divide the field in relation to its major underlying analytical themes.
>
> - The difference between the two comes down primarily to their position on whether to accept rational choice theory as the dominant methodology for the field: IO School practitioners do, but British School practitioners do not.
>
> - This distinction tells us a lot about what distinguishes one contemporary group of practitioners from another, but it does not tell us about the historical origins of those different practices.

Disciplinary Distinctions to Sub-Divide the Field

My preference is to distinguish between two broad approaches to IPE, one of which is the 'international relations' approach, and the other the 'political economy' approach (Watson 2005: ch. 1). The advantage of using this classificatory schema is that it divides the subject field on the basis of its disciplinary starting point.

As such, there is no necessary tendency to privilege modern forms of study, and thus to divorce those forms from their historical roots. In fact, the reason for using a heuristic distinction emphasizing disciplinary starting points is precisely to signal the importance of different intellectual lineages.

The disciplinary basis of the Atlantic divide

There are, of course, different ways of practising both IR and political economy. No simple mapping procedure exists, then, through which we can say that Morphy and Nelson's Atlantic divide translates into a dispute between those who treat IPE as a subset of IR and those who treat it as a subset of political economy. We can detect both IR and political economy perspectives in the IO School tradition. Equally, we can also detect both IR and political economy perspectives in the British School tradition. The disciplinary distinction between IR and political economy perspectives can therefore be used alongside the analytical distinction between the IO School and the British School. The result is a two-by-two table (see Table 2.2).

Thus there is no need to treat the disciplinary distinction between the IR and political economy perspectives and the analytical distinction between the IO School and the British School as being mutually exclusive. Indeed, by using the two distinctions in conjunction with one another it is possible to devise a more nuanced picture of the subject field of IPE. The four sets of distinctions drawn by Denemark and O'Brien; Strange; Murphy and Nelson; and Watson in their different depictions of the field all share one important property: they are all 'either/or' characterizations, in which to be practising IPE is either to be doing one thing or another. A logic of opposition is thus implied, whereby alternative approaches must necessarily be at loggerheads with one another. Yet, as soon as we try to integrate the latter two depictions into a single characterization, the sense of an oppositional logic dividing the field in two immediately begins to recede.

Most obviously, integrating the Murphy and Nelson and the Watson distinctions into a single classificatory schema doubles the number of generic positions one can expect to find within IPE. Table 2.2, as is clear to see, is a four-cell table rather than a two-cell, suggesting that there are at least four generic types of IPE for the student to discover and

to work with. Moreover, the movement between two adjacent cells in Table 2.2 is likely to be much more fluid than across a binary opposition. This is because adjacent cells share one important constitutive feature. Reading across the page, adjacent cells are either both part of the IO School or both part of the British School, and, as such, they have underlying analytical assumptions in common. Reading down the page, adjacent cells are either both part of the IR perspective or both part of the political economy perspective, and, as such, they have an underlying disciplinary pedigree in common. This implies that there might well be significant IPE content to be found in the borderlands between adjacent cells, which is a possibility that immediately becomes less easy to contemplate if we revert to thinking about the subject field through the lens of an oppositional logic.

Further reflections on the liberalism/realism/Marxism trichotomy

The four-cell approach to appraising IPE research also allows us to turn our attention back to the liberalism versus realism versus Marxism trichotomy used so extensively in teaching the fundamentals of the field. The trichotomy is usually presented as three mutually exclusive traditions of thought, which can only be understood in opposition to one another. In other words, we learn most about the arguments that proponents of one position are likely to make by knowing what proponents of the other two positions would *not* argue. The mental map of the field that arises from this characterization is triangular in shape, with liberalism, realism, and Marxism occupying the three corners, and the rest of the field being pretty much barren land. A very different mental map emerges, however, if we try instead to locate the disaggregated view of the trichotomy outlined in earlier sections of the chapter on to the four-cell approach outlined in Table 2.2. The result is shown in Table 2.3. The single lines

Table 2.2 A Four-Cell Approach for Appraising IPE

<table>
<tr><td rowspan="2"></td><td rowspan="2"></td><td colspan="2">Disciplinary distinctions (Watson 2005)</td></tr>
<tr><td>International relations</td><td>Political economy</td></tr>
<tr><td rowspan="2">Analytical heuristic distinctions (Murphy and Nelson 2001)</td><td>IO School</td><td>The aim is to model relationships between states as a zero-sum game played by rational actors. The substantive context in which the game takes place is international economic negotiations (at the World Trade Organization, for example; or at the G8). These contexts are not understood as dialogic forums in which negotiators come together in democratic discussions to decide what is best for the world as a whole. Any pronouncements of this nature are seen as a smokescreen to disguise the enactment of a narrowly defined national interest. International economic negotiations are therefore treated as competitive environments in which states struggle for supremacy. At times they might make concessions to one another, but only if this is seen as the most likely strategy to elicit the greatest gains.</td><td>The aim is to model relationships between economic agents as a zero-sum game played out by rational actors. The substantive context in which these relationships are explored is highly varied. They include the interactions between the firm and its shareholders, labour and management, consumers and consumption culture, development ideals and the World Bank and International Monetary Fund, etc. At all times, these interactions are understood as competitive struggles in which each side is trying to impose its interest on the other. Cessation of struggle only occurs in the event of interests being aligned. The goal of all actors is to maximize the utility arising from their economic activities, and they will act upon such a goal largely without reference to their long-term interests.</td></tr>
<tr><td>British School</td><td>The aim is to uncover the sources of both the state's hard and soft power, with a view to demonstrating how these translate into important economic resources. As above, the substantive context of study is most likely to be international economic negotiations, but here it is believed that the outcomes of the negotiations are influenced by more than the representatives around the table enacting the national interest. Outcomes are also influenced by the prevailing ideological climate, so it is also necessary to show how the dominant world view arose, and how it is reproduced in the interactions between state and non-state actors. There are circumstances in which non-state actors might be the primary recipients of gains, and this could even be at the expense of states.</td><td>The aim is to explore the link between established modes of economic thinking and the practices of everyday economic life. In particular, it is to specify the mechanisms (political, cultural, cognitive) through which individuals are socialized into creating patterns of life that replicate directly the implied behavioural traits embedded in economic theory. Economic theory is thus presented as an ideological intervention into the world rather than a politically neutral description of relationships within that world. A range of actors carry the premises of economic theory in their intentions, and disseminate them more widely within society through their day-to-day practices. But these practices are also challenged by counter-cultural movements seeking to contest their influence on everyday life. The economy is thus necessarily an arena of social struggle.</td></tr>
</table>

Table 2.3 Mapping IPE's Trichotomy on to the Four-Cell Approach to the Field

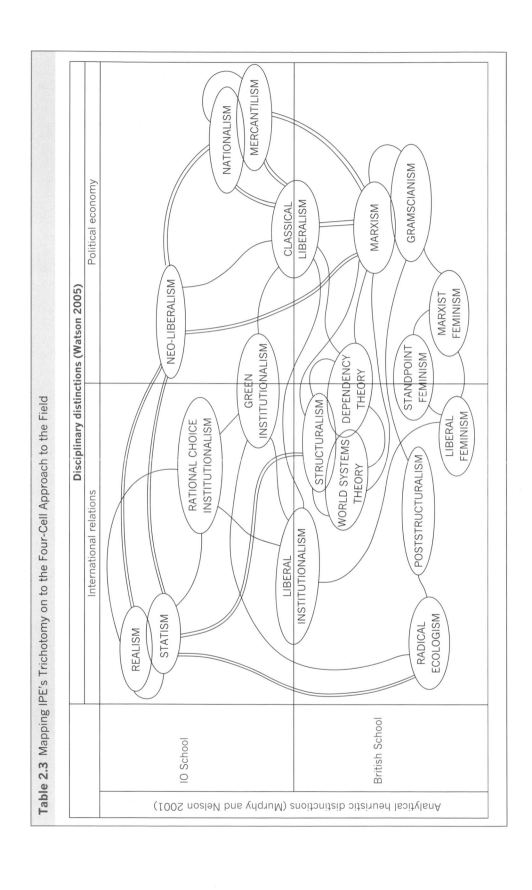

Disciplinary distinctions (Watson 2005)

International relations | Political economy

IO School

British School

Analytical heuristic distinctions (Murphy and Nelson 2001)

REALISM
STATISM
RATIONAL CHOICE INSTITUTIONALISM
NEO-LIBERALISM
CLASSICAL LIBERALISM
NATIONALISM
MERCANTILISM
GREEN INSTITUTIONALISM
MARXISM
GRAMSCIANISM
LIBERAL INSTITUTIONALISM
STRUCTURALISM
WORLD SYSTEMS THEORY
DEPENDENCY THEORY
STANDPOINT FEMINISM
MARXIST FEMINISM
POSTSTRUCTURALISM
LIBERAL FEMINISM
RADICAL ECOLOGISM

connecting different positions (both within cells and across the boundaries of adjacent cells) show positions which have much in common with one another, whereas the double lines connecting different positions show instances in which one position was created as a direct refutation of another.

As before, what emerges in this instance is a much more fluid conception of the field than is implied by the trichotomous structure of introductory IPE teaching. Many of the individual approaches to the subject field themselves traverse a boundary between adjacent cells, while many more are closely linked to approaches located in other cells. By re-presenting the liberalism versus realism versus Marxism trichotomy as a series of false demarcations between what are in any case amalgams of heterogeneous positions, it is much more possible to focus on the nature of those links than it is using the standard presentation of the trichotomy, in which no such links are presumed to exist. Even in those instances in which the fluidity of the subject field breaks down because one position is established in direct opposition to another, this is as likely to occur within the context of a single cell as across a boundary dividing two cells.

The result is a pictorial warning that cautions against the reification of simple clear-cut divisions in the complex and diverse theoretical underpinnings of the field as a whole. The picture of IPE thus created is much messier than the one at the start of the chapter. Yet this in itself is no bad thing, because it provides a more representative characterization of the field than one that is guilty of pigeonholing contributions to the literature into neat, but incommensurable, little boxes. Academic instinct is always to push the limits of theoretical arguments as far as they will go: to extend the previous analogy, to attempt to think outside the box. This is no less true of IPE than it is of any other subject field. The rigid reification of theoretical demarcations therefore deprives the analyst of IPE of a sense of the ebb and flow of theoretical arguments over time. None of the positions represented in Table 2.3 will be fixed beyond the short term. Their centres will remain pretty much where they are in their current cells, but their outermost boundaries will shift under the influence of future theoretical innovations. Some of the approaches will appear to move closer together in the future, as their respective boundaries converge on increasingly common theoretical underpinnings. But it is just as likely that others will appear to move further apart.

Beyond heuristic distinctions altogether?

Having muddied the waters of clear-cut distinctions in the representation of the field outlined above, it is next necessary to ask whether we should be thinking in terms of heuristic distinctions at all. By reflecting further on the Watson distinction between the IR and political economy perspectives, it is more than possible to conclude that we should not. That distinction appears to suggest that only half of IPE scholars work with political economy assumptions, yet by scratching the surface of this claim we might be able to show that this is not in fact the case. The question that needs to be asked of scholars working within the IR perspective is whether they fail to work with political economy assumptions when practising their IPE, or whether they merely fail to acknowledge the basis of their political economy assumptions in a consciously reflexive way?

When we read Table 2.2 across the page, we see that IO School IPE can be practised from both an IR and a political economy perspective. But this does not mean that the IO School's IR perspective is devoid of any political economy essence. In common with the IO School's political economy perspective, it treats IPE as the study of constrained utility maximization problems under conditions of rational choice. And this most basic way of conceptualizing issues of concern within the subject field implies that it is rooted in a particular form of economic thinking, because it very much mirrors the patterns of scholarship we encounter in neoclassical economics. The only difference between the two IO School cousins is that this intellectual lineage is more readily acknowledged in the political economy perspective than it is in the IR perspective. It would be much more usual, for example, for those adopting theoretical positions in the upper-right cell of Table 2.3 to comment openly on their historical roots in neoclassical economics than it would be for those adopting theoretical positions in the upper-left cell to do the same.

A similar story can be told in relation to British School IPE. It too can be practised from both an IR perspective and a political economy perspective, and here too there is more than initially meets the eye with the IR perspective. Both camps within the British School treat IPE as the study of the philosophy of social organization with respect to everyday economic life. This most basic way of conceptualizing the issues of concern within the subject field also leads us back to a particular form of economic thinking. It very much mirrors the patterns of scholarship we encounter in classical political economy, the tradition that was dominant before the onset of the era of neoclassical economics in the 1870s (Heilbroner 2000). As before, the big difference here is probably only one of emphasis, with those working in the political economy perspective of the British School more readily acknowledging the intellectual lineage of contemporary positions than those working in the IR perspective. We would not expect, for example, modern-day Marxists to do anything other than acknowledge the intellectual debt that their specific brand of IPE owes to Marx's political economy. In contrast, it would be much less usual to see anyone adopting a theoretical position from the bottom-left cell of Table 2.3 reflecting openly on the classical political economy origins of their position.

It is a significant finding that Murphy and Nelson's two schools of IPE have origins in, and replicate, the analytical style of two very different traditions of economic thought, because these historical differences feed through directly today into different scholarly intentions embedded right at the heart of contemporary IPE's two schools. It is important, then, to say a few words about the differences between classical political economy and neoclassical economics.

Historians of economic thought usually treat the shift from classical political economy to neoclassical economics as one from an outdated to a thoroughly state-of-the-art way of studying economic relations (see, for example, Blaug 1996; Backhouse 2002). After all, classical political economy was the dominant tradition until the so-called 'Marginalist Revolution' of the 1870s (see Box 2.2), whereupon economists have typically followed the premises of neoclassical theory (see, for example, Robinson 1964; Barber 1991). Yet, what counts as a pathbreaking moment in appraisals of economics should not necessarily lead us to dismiss the insights that can be gleaned about IPE from continuing to follow the original path. The two subject fields are orientated around different intentions and different goals, so it is perfectly understandable that appraisals of them will emphasize different issues as being decisive to their respective historical developments. Given this, for current purposes, classical political economy and neoclassical economics will be presented as being equally valid and appropriate ways of thinking about economic relations. The aim of what follows is merely to demonstrate the different types of intellectual commitments involved in choosing one over the other, and, by extension, in choosing one contemporary school of IPE over the other.

Starting with classical political economy, it developed historically as an open field of scholarship, whereby practitioners argued strongly for their own position but were content to accept a plurality of theories and methods for the field as a whole. The labour theory of value—which in general states that the one true price of a good reflects the amount and quantity of labour expended in its production—provides a consistent point of departure for most classical political economists. However, it is specified in a variety of ways depending on the normative perspective adopted by the theorist. The labour theory of value has both intuitive and normative appeal, because it provides a means of passing judgement on the intrinsic value of a commodity, which can then be compared with its actual selling price. Analytical divergences arise within the

BOX 2.2

Significance of the Marginalist Revolution for Contemporary IPE

Neoclassical economics has divergent origins, but it also has a distinctive core. That core emerges from the assumption that all economic actions result from 'constrained maximization' decisions. Agents are necessarily constrained, because they will not have a limitless supply of money, and they will also have competing claims on whatever money they do have. But within this context it is assumed that they will attempt to allocate their available resources to the best possible outcome. According to neoclassical economics, this is the outcome that maximizes utility, where utility is a technical economic term for the degree of pleasure that can be derived from commodity production. It is not claimed that economic agents in fact undertake the complex calculations required to show that choices always follow the fully rational utility maximizing option. Instead, it is simply assumed that it is human instinct to necessarily adopt mechanistically rational behavioural traits and, as a consequence, all actions must automatically be utility maximizing, whether the agent is conscious of having targeted such motivations or not.

This might sound familiar even for someone who is approaching neoclassical economics for the very first time. This is because it is exactly the same structure of argument as for rational choice theory. While the latter's proponents do not always reflect explicitly on the intellectual origins of their position, the roots of rational choice theory in fact stem directly from neoclassical economics. The choices described by rational choice theory are not choices at all in the literal sense of the word, because they do not follow from a process of reflection about how best to orientate behaviour within the context of the social relationships in which it is contemplated. Instead, it is modelled as an instinctive selection of the utility maximizing option in the interests of self-preferment.

It is important that the link is made between rational choice theory and neoclassical economics when engaged in appraisals of the subject field of IPE, because so many contemporary international political economists adopt rational choice theory as their chosen methodology. This is particularly true of those researchers with North American training, which once again raises the possibility of an Atlantic divide in IPE. For its proponents, rational choice theory is a universal methodology that transcends the selection of key concepts and theoretical frameworks. By remaining steadfast in the assertion that all economic actions must necessarily entail the goal of utility maximization, it is possible to align almost any concept or framework with the core claims of rational choice theory. Thus the exemplars through which individual positions are taught in IPE (as discussed previously in this chapter) lose an element of their pedagogical power, because each can be re-described in rational choice theory terms.

For its critics, though, this can only be achieved by trying too hard to squeeze other arguments into a rational choice framework where they might not fit comfortably. The assumption of utility maximization leads to an entirely decontextualized theory of action, in so far as it removes the economic agent from the social relationships in which he or she is involved. Rational choice theoretical perspectives in IPE can only describe situations in which individuals can in some way be assumed to be beyond society. But there are no circumstances in which an individual can truly be said to exist in such a state. Rational choice theoretical perspectives can still be defended in pragmatic terms, because they provide a convenient means of constructing straightforward hypotheses against which to compare observations drawn from the real world. However, such hypotheses might always be susceptible to the charge of superficiality. As they can only ever be abstractions of the actual decisions with which people are faced in their everyday lives, they can never capture on their own the full complexity of the social totality in which international economic processes are embedded.

---

labour theory of value, though, depending on what, precisely, is meant by labour.

For some, especially those whose classical political economy begins with Marx, the labour theory of value is just that: the intrinsic value of a commodity is determined by the inputs workers provide for the production process via their labour, and by nothing else. For others, though, entrepreneurial labour should also be reflected in the price of a commodity (this is a feature of Smith's concept of natural prices) and so should the organizational labour provided by the firm (this is a feature of Ricardo's defence of profits). Today, in order to emphasize the significance of the so-called knowledge economy, some would say that intellectual labour should also be accounted for in the dynamics of price formation. There is thus no single labour theory of value, and hence no scientific unity in the approach. But this did not matter to the classical political economists. For them, the search for scientific unity was less important than was the possibility of dialogue between theorists with different world views. (Indeed, the labour theory of value could not have taken its many divergent forms were it not for this sense of later generations of theorists engaging with and talking directly to the conceptual legacies of earlier generations of theorists.)

This sense of priority is entirely reversed within neoclassical economics, where scientific unity is a much more important feature of the day-to-day practice of economists. Neoclassical economics is therefore more closed as a field of scholarship than is classical political economy. Its practitioners have tended to coalesce around set theories and methods, and what internal debate there is bears little upon the core precepts of the field. Neoclassical economics focuses almost all of its attention on instances in which behaviour can have a rational calculus of costs and benefits imposed upon it.

The aim is to use this calculus to offer a detached, objective description of economic events which matches the standards of scientific rigour by being cleansed of the disruptive influence of philosophical debate (Schumpeter 1954/1994). The analyst is thus able to comment on economic affairs from beyond the boundaries of his/her own particular world view. Such concerns relegate the significance of clear normative position-taking, thus providing economic enquiry with a technical veneer. The methodologist of economics (and father of John Maynard Keynes), John Neville Keynes, once distinguished between the 'science' and the 'art' of economics, in order to emphasize that economists' attempts to engage in methodologically rigorous enquiry (the science) must also be set within the

context of explicit acknowledgement that all economic enquiry is always undertaken with specific purposes in mind (the art) (Keynes 1891/1970). David Colander has picked up on this distinction to suggest that the current dominance of neoclassical theory equates with 'the lost art of economics' (Colander 2001). Economic theory always proceeds according to preconceived social ends but, in trying to emphasize the purely technical prerequisites of modern theory, this is something that neoclassical economics attempts to disguise.

The different degrees of openness between the two broad traditions of economic thought are also replicated in the two schools of IPE that they inform. Members of the IO School tend to construct their analyses of the world (whether loosely or more formally) on rational choice theory grounds. They might still disagree on their prescriptions for future political action, depending on which social and economic factors they choose to include in their understanding of the utility function. But there is broad agreement on questions of **ontology** (viewing the interaction between economic agents and their world as constrained utility maximization problems), questions of methodology (imposing implicit values on the costs and benefits of a particular decision in order to explain, after the event, how that decision conforms to a rational calculus), and questions of theory (reducing economic identity to an epiphenomenon of self-interest). This gives the appearance of a relatively closed body of thought, in which academic progress rests on the ever more precise specification of the dynamics involved, rather than reflexive analysis of the essence of political economy itself.

By contrast, the British School is much more avowedly a broad church. Perhaps the only unifying point for its practitioners is collective agreement on what it is not, which involves the conscious rejection of both the starting point and the style of analysis of the IO School. Beyond that, though, there is considerable diversity of content between the different positions associated with the British School. These range from ontological disputes about the nature of the world (for example, between various strands of structuralist thought and an increasingly prominent post-structuralist trend), to theoretical disputes about how to conceptualize the economy in its most fundamental form (for example, whether to start with the act of production or the social relations of production), and normative disputes about the most important aspect of the economy's social structure (for example, whether to emphasize gender, class, race, religion and so on).

Much therefore hinges on recognizing the significance of the Marginalist Revolution in the 1870s, as it is this that divides the political economy roots of IO School and British School IPE. Neoclassical economics is itself a complex amalgam of positions that possess a familial resemblance but otherwise have different theoretical emphases (see Watson 2005: ch. 2). There are even three distinct starting points for neoclassical theory, to be found in the contrasting work of William Stanley Jevons (1871/1970), Carl Menger (1871/1950), and Léon Walras (1874/1984). As these three worked out of Manchester, Vienna and Lausanne, respectively, there were rival English-speaking, German-speaking and French-speaking traditions of neoclassical economics right from the start. However, despite these differences, all three traditions have a similar core in a recognized way of thinking, and it is this that has subsequently filtered through to influence the analytical style of contemporary IO School IPE.

The core of neoclassical economics is given its clearest enunciation in Jevons' *Theory of Political Economy*. It comes in the form of an anti-productionist reworking of the classical political economists' theory of value. The classical political economists had assumed that all commodities had an intrinsic value. Moreover, to the extent that this intrinsic value was a reflection of both the quantity and the different types of labour embedded in the commodity via the production process, they were happy to endorse a labour theory of value. The classical political economists therefore highlighted the significance of production to the inscription of value upon a commodity. Jevons took exception to this way of thinking, insisting that the intrinsic

value of a commodity does not determine its price but, on the contrary, we can use the price at which it was exchanged to make plausible inferences about its value. This is because the price at which it was exchanged will reveal the degree of utility the consumer will expect to enjoy from its purchase (that is, the higher the purchase price, the more the expected utility; the lower the purchase price, the less the expected utility). And Jevons was adamant that value is entirely dependent upon utility (1871/1970: 77).

Hence Jevons creates an analytical framework in which little significance can be accorded to the process of production. It is for this reason that practitioners of contemporary British School IPE have to go back to pre-Jevonian political economy to discover ways of thinking that enable them to begin their analyses with the social relations of production. Instead, Jevons focuses the gaze of subsequent generations of neoclassical economists on the process of consumption, as he believes that it is here that value is imposed on commodities through the price consumers are willing to pay in expectation of the utility they will subsequently experience. Rather than accept the classical political economists' emphasis on relations of production, then, Jevons devised a new analytical framework that emphasized the moment at which a commodity is exchanged (and, therefore, he emphasized exchange relations more generally).

Thus established, Jevons' framework has two crucial effects, and both of these can be detected clearly in contemporary IO School IPE. First, it embeds utility maximization as both the language of economics and the intuitive basis of economic enquiry. As outlined previously, proponents of the IO School treat all issues in IPE as constrained utility maximization problems (that is, how one actor might be a successful utility maximizer in circumstances in which all other actors are trying to do the same). Second, Jevons' framework reduces all events of economic significance to the moment of exchange. Within contemporary IPE, IO School practitioners also attempt to model all events of economic significance in terms of their underlying exchange relations. International economic negotiations are certainly understood in this way, whereby the negotiating environment is one to which negotiators bring bargaining resources in an attempt to influence outcomes to their own advantage. International labour relations, international corporate governance issues, and international environmental treaties can also be thought of in this way: how can one side shape the exchange relation to enable that side to benefit the most?

The birth of neoclassical economics should therefore be seen as a decisive historical moment for contemporary IPE, even though it occurred exactly a century before the birth of international political economy. This is almost never recognized explicitly in appraisals of IPE, but it is nonetheless true, because the introduction of neoclassical theory into the subject field of economics created a decisive fissure in that field. Those who followed the key insights of neoclassical economics were performing a fundamentally different type of economic enquiry from their classical political economy forebears, and nothing has been achieved since the 1870s to reunite these two traditions. The same fissure also informs many of the key differences that create the

sense of a heterogeneous field of IPE today. These are differences in analytical instincts, in fundamental ways of setting up problems of international economic significance, in the most basic view of the world, and in underlying methodology. And at heart these differences are rooted historically in the split between neoclassical economics and classical political economy.

KEY POINTS

- A more fluid and dynamic conception of the field arises from integrating analytical and disciplinary distinctions in an attempt to tease out the links between one position and another.

- Most people working from an IR perspective in IPE fail to recognize explicitly the political economy traditions in which they are located, but more can be learnt about their approaches by recognizing these links formally.

- The decisive break in the history of economic thought engendered by the Marginalist Revolution in the 1870s also has important implications for the way in which IPE is researched today.

Conclusion

So, what can be distilled from this tour around the subject field of IPE? Perhaps the most obvious thing to note is the astonishing degree of growth of IPE since its inception in the early 1970s. It now incorporates the work of so many people and creates bridges to so many other cognate social scientific subject fields that it is impossible to do justice to every conceivable way of practising IPE within the confines of a single chapter. My only hope is that I might have whetted the appetites of students to find out more for themselves of what can be discovered within the IPE literature. Beyond that, two principal conclusions arise from the preceding pages.

First, it is clear that IPE is anything other than a united field of study. To my mind, this is a point in its favour rather than something to be lamented. There are some prominent scholars who might not agree, given their position that progress in the field will only be possible when there is consensus on key concepts, principles and methods of enquiry. But this plea for uniformity of approach comes with obvious costs. After all, united subject fields are ones in which the space for genuine intellectual debate is squeezed to a minimum. For me, though, IPE is not only about describing the world as it is at the present time; it is also about describing how the world might be in the future. This means that debate is the lifeblood of the field and that, to flourish, the field must necessarily stop short of being united. Moreover, subject fields that revolve around the reproduction of set themes, theories and methods leave little to the creativity of individual theorists. It is surely something to celebrate that few IPE theorists could claim to have been hampered seriously in this way; they are free to display their intellectual creativity in whatever manner they deem best.

Recognizing the laudable nature of IPE being an openly diverse field is one thing. However, trying to impose typological order on those differences is an altogether more difficult task. As the preceding analysis has shown, this can be attempted in many ways, but each classificatory schema appears to run into its own problems. Moreover, they also all appear to share an even more important common drawback. The second major conclusion of the chapter is that any attempt to impose typological order on the field runs the risk of introducing overly rigid, and often false, lines of demarcation which lead to the artificial segregation of the field. What emerges is often a stereotype of the positions that define the field, rather than an accurate account of the field itself. The stereotypes fall down in large part because they are insufficiently attentive to the historical roots of the positions under review and, once a discussion of those roots is re-instated, it can be shown that the movement between positions is often much more fluid than the rigid demarcations of the stereotypes allow.

This is not an argument against categorization per se—and, given the preceding analysis, how could it be? Rather, it is a plea for the open acknowledgement of the limitations of all typologies. They can only ever act as guides to further reflection and as means of opening up more sophisticated understandings of the field as a whole. In particular, they should be used to facilitate attempts to transcend overly homogenized depictions of the major divisions within the field, even though it is the typologies themselves that promote such images of homogeneity.

The main lesson to be learned in this respect—and, indeed, the main message of the chapter as a whole—is that awareness of the historical roots of contemporary IPE is a prerequisite of practising IPE successfully. Such awareness matters because, without it, it is impossible to trace the intellectual lineage of contemporary positions and, in the absence of the ability to do that, contemporary positions are stripped of their own origins. The result is positions with inadequate historical moorings, debates between which are always likely to be grounded inappropriately. History matters, then, and a historical turn to situate IPE more assuredly within the context of its political economy origins is very much to be advocated.

? **QUESTIONS**

1. Why might it be important to know how the major theoretical and analytical positions in IPE compare, sometimes linking directly to one another and sometimes being constructed in direct opposition?

2. What can be gained in our understanding of contemporary IPE by attempting to uncover the historical roots of the political economy traditions in which modern positions are located? In other words, why should we read classic texts?

3. To what extent does the trichotomous structure of liberalism versus realism versus Marxism obscure the significance of societal cleavages such as gender, race, and religion?

4. Do we have to conclude that IPE's trichotomy is constructed by reading off supposedly universal theories from the particular historical development of distinctively Western economies? That is, does it take the development profile of Western market capitalism and treat it as a generic feature of economic life, thus implying that all other countries will also have the same experience?

5. What are the main features of mercantilist political economy? Can we point to examples in the modern world of mercantilist insights continuing to inform the management of international economic affairs?

6. Is Marxism still relevant in contemporary IPE? What features of the world that Marx described are still recognizably with us today?

7. Would it be appropriate to describe the economics of globalization simply as the operation of a global 'invisible hand'? If not, what does this do to the usual characterization of globalization as a liberal project?

8. Should we agree with Susan Strange, and argue that the study of foreign economic policy is not IPE proper, because it has no historical lineage to a recognizable tradition in political economy?

9. How convincing is the characterization of an 'Atlantic Divide' within contemporary IPE?

10. To what extent do many IPE theorists incorporate the key insights of neoclassical economics without acknowledging explicitly that this is what they are doing?

 FURTHER READING

General

■ **Watson, M. (2005),** *Foundations of International Political Economy* **(Basingstoke: Palgrave Macmillan).** This is for students who find my account of the practice of IPE convincing, as the themes of the current chapter are surveyed in much greater depth here.

History of economic ideas

■ **Backhouse, R. (2002),** *The Penguin History of Economics* **(London: Penguin).** A further book that could be used as a substitute for either Heilbroner or Barber.

■ **Barber, W. (2001),** *A History of Economic Thought,* **reprinted edn (London: Penguin).** As with Heilbroner, this book is written with the beginning student in mind, and as such is a more accessible introduction to the history of economic ideas than those that address the student who already has some training in economics.

■ **Blaug, M. (1996),** *Economic Theory in Retrospect,* **5th edn (Cambridge: Cambridge University Press).** This is arguably *the* most comprehensive account of the different ways in which the economy has been studied in the history of economic thought. However, it is written from a perspective which assumes that the student has some prior background in economics debates, but this will not necessarily be the case for beginning IPE students.

■ **Heilbroner, R. (2000),** *The Worldly Philosophers: The Lives, Times, and Ideas of the Great Economic Thinkers,* **7th edn (London: Penguin).** This is an accessible text where the author's aim is not to dazzle his readers with the technicalities of the argument, but to bring the basic ideas he is discussing to life.

■ **Landreth, H., and Colander, D. (1994),** *History of Economic Thought*, **3rd edn (Boston, Mass.: Houghton Mifflin).** This book covers much of the same territory as Blaug, and would serve as a more than acceptable substitute for it. Again, though, it is written assuming that the reader has some background training in the theories, methods, and language of economics.

■ **Robinson, J. (1964),** *Economic Philosophy*, **revised edn (Harmondsworth: Penguin).** This is written less as an introduction to the history of economic ideas but more as an attempt by the author to carve out her own view of how economic analysis should proceed. Nonetheless, it is a very good read and students will learn much from it.

■ **Samuels, W., Biddle, J., and Davis, J. (eds) (2007),** *A Companion to the History of Economic Thought*, **2nd edn (Oxford: Blackwell).** This is a new book, offering extensive commentary and criticism on existing attempts to provide a plausible historiography of economic ideas. Thirty-nine chapters cover nearly 700 pages of scholars writing on their research specialisms, but, as before, this probably is not for students without prior knowledge of rudimentary economic debates.

Introductions to the classical political economists

■ **Heilbroner, R. (1986),** *The Essential Adam Smith* **(New York: W. W. Norton).** This is a very good introduction to the work of Adam Smith. Students do not need to read all of Smith's published work, because Heilbroner provides excerpts from it, each of which is preceded by a useful introduction.

■ **Hollander, S. (1987),** *Classical Economics* **(Oxford: Basil Blackwell).** This is a very good introduction to the field of classical political economy as a whole. However, there is a chance that beginning IPE students might find it a little bit daunting, as it is written by a respected economist for an audience that has some familiarity with the rudiments of economics.

■ **Wheen, F. (1999),** *Karl Marx* **(London: Fourth Estate).** This is perhaps the most readable of all biographies of Marx, and it tries to draw out the intellectual inspiration underpinning his work from a broader assessment of his life.

■ **Wolff, J. (2002),** *Why Read Marx Today?* **(New York: Oxford University Press).** This is an introductory book about Marx's ideas, and will not present the non-economist with similar problems to those they might experience when reading Hollander. The content of the book follows directly from the self-explanatory title.

Classic texts

Despite all the above advice on further reading, nothing beats the rewards that come from going back to a classic text and discovering what is in it for oneself. I would very much advocate, then, that students attempt to familiarize themselves with at least some of the classic texts mentioned by name in this chapter, details of which are given in Table 2.1.

 WEB LINKS

● **www.unc.edu/depts/econ/byrns_web/EC434/HET/biographies.htm** An electronic encyclopaedia allowing students easy access to thumbnail sketches of the most important figures in the history of economic ideas. Further searching of the site reveals an extensive glossary of economic terms and theories.

● **www.blupete.com/Literature/Biographies/Philosophy/BiosEcon.htm**   Students can work their way around the alphabetical listings on this site to find the bibliographies of most of the great economists in history, plus excerpts from their work.

● **econc10.bu.edu/economic_systems/Theory/theory_frame.htm**   This is a comprehensive site for anyone wishing to learn more about economics. It allows students to visit, among others, sections on both classical political economy and neoclassical economics.

● **www.marxists.org/subject/economy/index.htm**   This is a comprehensive site that allows students to explore both Marx's work and his reflections on the context in which his work was written. Importantly, it also contains links to a detailed glossary of terms to be found in the writings of Marxist political economists.

● **www.epistemelinks.com/Main/Philosophers.aspx?PhilCode=Smit**   This is another comprehensive site, providing the student with a large number of links to further sites containing Adam Smith archives. A similar archive is available through the www.marxists.org website listed above.

 Visit the Online Resource Centre that accompanies this book for more information: **www.oxfordtextbooks.co.uk/orc/ravenhill2e/**

3

Collaboration and Co-Ordination in the Global Political Economy

VINOD K AGGARWAL AND CÉDRIC DUPONT

Chapter Contents

- Introduction
- Globalization and the Need for International Co-operation
- International Co-operation: a Strategic Interdependence Approach
- International Co-operation: a Variety of Solutions
- The Formation and Evolution of Institutions
- Conclusion

Reader's Guide

How can one understand the problems of collaboration and co-ordination in the global political economy? In situations of global **interdependence**, individual action by states often does not yield the desired result. Many argue that the solution to the problem of interdependence is to create international institutions, but this approach itself raises the issue of how states might go about creating such institutions in the first place. In this chapter, we examine the conditions under which states might wish to take joint action, and provides an introduction to game theory as an approach to understanding interdependent decision-making. We then discuss the conditions under which international institutions are likely to be developed, and how they may facilitate international co-operation. We then examine dimensions of institutional variation, with a discussion of factors that shape the design of international institutions.

Introduction

It is now commonplace to hear about the phenomenon of globalization. Much of the current analytical debate on globalization has its roots in the international political economy literature on interdependence of the early 1970s (Cooper 1972; Keohane and Nye 1977). At that time, political scientists began to identify the characteristics of the changing global economy, including increased flows of goods and money across national boundaries as well as the rise of non-state actors as a challenge to traditional conceptions of international politics.

Although increasing interdependence among states was a relatively new phenomenon when considered against the baseline of the 1950s, high levels of interdependence had existed in earlier historical periods, including the period prior to the First World War (Bordo *et al.* 1999; McGrew, Chapter 9 in this volume). This interdependence, however, was not matched by high levels of institutionalization, standing in stark contrast to the post-Second-World-War Bretton Woods organizations of the International Monetary Fund (IMF), the World Bank, and the General Agreement on Tariffs and Trade (GATT, and its successor, the World Trade Organization). The problems that institutions such as the IMF faced with the breakdown of the Bretton Woods dollar-based standard in 1971, the movement towards trade protectionism that appeared to undermine the GATT, and instability in the oil market with the 1973–4 oil crisis also drove the debate on interdependence in the early 1970s.

A key issue in considering the implications of interdependence revolves around the question of how to achieve collaboration and co-ordination among states. In particular, scholars have focused on how states respond to perceived problems in the global economy that they cannot deal with on their own. An important starting point is to distinguish interdependence from interconnectedness based on the costs of interaction. 'Where interactions do not have significant costly effects, there is simply interconnectedness' (Keohane and Nye 1977: 9). With costly effects (or high benefits), however, we can consider countries as being mutually dependent on each other, or interdependent. In attempting to cope with interdependence, then, countries will be faced with making decisions that will have a direct effect on their well-being, and thus the sharing of costs and benefits can potentially be controversial.

In this chapter, we consider the problem of collaboration by first characterizing situations that might require states to work with each other to achieve a desired outcome. We then focus on basic game theory as an analytical tool to tackle the nature of collaboration and co-ordination efforts. Finally, we consider how institutions might play a role in enhancing the prospects for co-operative behaviour.

Globalization and the Need for International Co-operation

According to international economics textbooks, worldwide economic openness has clear benefits.

Integrated world markets help to ensure an optimal allocation of factors of production, and therefore help to maximize both aggregate world welfare and individual national welfare. By contrast, sealing off national borders fosters economic inefficiency, and has negative consequences for poverty alleviation and development prospects. Yet, in practice, the benefits of globalization cannot always be realized by states pursuing independent policies; co-operative action is required.

The process of global integration forces significant adjustments in production patterns across states. In particular, the changing distribution of costs and benefits from trade liberalization can result in strong political opposition both for and against further liberalization. Adjustment has been made the more difficult in that it leads to unpredictable outcomes and instability in the prices of traded goods. This has proved particularly problematical for many of the lowest-income countries, because they often rely on one or two commodities for the bulk of their exports. Not only have the prices of most non-fuel commodities been volatile, but they have also been declining over recent decades because of longer and deeper slumps than booms (Cashin *et al.* 1999). Ultra-specialization in some of those commodities has therefore, on the one hand, brought severe adjustment costs and, on the other, failed to provide stable and increasing revenues. Developing countries that rely on the export of manufactures have also faced significant adjustment challenges. For example, many Latin-American countries are increasingly facing a loss of market share in the United States and Europe with the rapid rise of the Chinese export juggernaut.

Liberal analysts often argue that countries will be able to manage the process of adjusting to a rapidly shifting division of labour. From their perspective, the prospect of growth in a large number of newly competitive sectors, combined with state capacity to provide social and fiscal transfers, should serve as means of addressing the challenges of world competition. Yet developing countries, in particular the poorest among them, often have a pre-industrial economic structure. As a consequence, economic openness has brought about a radical transformation of their socio-economic structures, particularly

in rural areas, leading to massive migration flows to urban areas. The state structures of developing states are often simply unable to cope with such a rapid and radical transformation. This has led to chaos and, in many instances, to famine and violence as well as to further political instability and insecurity. For their part, rich countries often face strong domestic lobbies in agriculture, textiles, steel, and other, older, sectors of the economy, creating pressure for trade distorting restrictions of various kinds, including subsidies, tariffs, quotas, voluntary export restraints, and the like (see Hiscox, Chapter 4 in this volume).

Given these political constraints, countries may either be unwilling, or unable by themselves to sustain processes of economic liberalization. In that it would be difficult to renege openly and fully on previous commitments, they may be tempted to gain time by shirking on the implementation of their commitments. While others would continue to implement fully their market opening commitments, theirs could be slowed or halted. But their counterparts might find this unacceptable, and react by reneging on their own commitments, leading to an action–reaction cycle that slows global integration and decreases economic welfare. International cooperative action may therefore be required to avoid the unfortunate effects of this temptation to free ride. What factors might affect the likelihood that countries will engage in free riding? One key indicator of the temptation to free ride is a country's socio-political organization and economic flexibility. On the socio-political dimension, the political insulation of governments from lobbying by those who are affected by adjustment costs can ease the process of economic liberalization, as was the case in the first wave of globalization in the second half of the nineteenth century, when few countries had democratic systems of government. But with the spread of democracy, such political insulation has diminished drastically. Another way to make liberalization politically palatable has been the development in some countries of corporatist deals among the government, unions and business to share the costs of adjustment. The temptation to free ride also depends on the economies of countries, and on its flexibility, particularly regarding labour markets, as well as labour skill levels. More generally, countries with deregulated markets, and few and lean state-owned companies, should be less tempted to free ride on the globalization process, because adjustment would be less costly.

International co-operation may also be required to remedy what we call the inhibiting fear that countries might feel when facing a decision either to engage in economic liberalization or to continue it. Although countries might be convinced that liberalization will yield benefits, they may be hesitant to risk the instability that might come from the ebb and flows of the international market. This fear is particularly problematical in the domain of financial liberalization. In contrast to trade integration, financial integration has produced sudden and violent shocks to national economies (see Pauly, Chapter 8 in this volume). The massive increase in capital flows since the early 1990s has been accompanied by extreme volatility, particularly for developing countries that have been experiencing sharp fluctuations in the flow of short-term capital (Calvo and Talvi 2005; Edwards 2005). As John Ravenhill discusses in Chapter 1, the series of crises that hit Southeast Asia in the period 1997–8 led to drastic economic contractions. South Korea's growth rate dropped seven percentage points below its pre-crisis, five-year-average growth rate; Indonesia's performance was similar; and Thailand's was even worse (Bordo and Eichengreen 2002). Recent work following the Asian financial crises and the Argentinean crisis in 2001, both at the aggregate and case-specific levels, has shown that governments are highly vulnerable to such profound economic contractions. On average, the chances of leaders losing office in the six months immediately following a currency crash seem to be twice as likely as at other times (Frankel 2005). Economic globalization has created profound and far-reaching policy challenges to states that, in turn, have had an impact on key pillars of their economic and political organization.

International co-operative action in the financial realm may reassure countries with promises of

assistance, either by individual states or international institutions, before or during difficult times. This may facilitate states' adjustment efforts in responding to shocks, and prevent them from taking the wrong action at the wrong time, which could lead to massive negative contagion effects. As with trade, the need for international support varies across countries, depending on the socio-political and economic characteristics we have discussed. The inadequate response of rich states and financial institutions to the problems faced by countries affected by the financial crises of the late 1990s has led many countries to build up rapidly their holdings of foreign reserves to counter speculative attacks on their currency. Reserves now amount to almost 30 per cent of developing countries' gross domestic product (GDP), enough to finance eight months' imports (Rodrik 2006). But this individual response has come at a significant price. Most central banks hold foreign exchange reserves in the form of low-yielding, short-term US Treasury (and other) securities; and the accumulation of reserves by developing countries created an important opportunity cost (the difference between what governments might have earned by investing these assets elsewhere versus keeping them in low-yielding securities). In most cases, for example, investing the same amount in the domestic economy would have yielded a significantly higher return. According to a recent study, the income loss caused by this difference in yields amounts to close to 1 per cent of GDP (Rodrik 2006). Leaving aside the question of whether this insurance against the vagaries of financial integration comes at an acceptable price, such a solution is only available to a small number of countries, and therefore is not a viable alternative to international action to provide liquidity to countries facing financial crises.

Finally, when countries address the issues of 'temptation to free ride' and 'inhibiting fear', they may encounter a third problem—how to negotiate the distribution of gains and losses from a possible agreement. This where to meet problem can be seen in cases of international co-operation such as a decision on how much to contribute to common support funds, how and to what extent to intervene in currency markets, and in the trade-off between quotas, tariffs, and subsidies in trade negotiations. For example, as part of the bargaining over the creation of a **common pool of resources** to support financial stability, there is likely to be considerable debate about the criteria to be used to determine individual countries' contributions. This burden-sharing decision has often been a problem historically. Intervention in currency markets is also controversial. Although some national intervention to maintain stable currencies may be warranted as it helps governments to obtain various national economic objectives, such as controlling the rate

of inflation, the USA has often accused Japan and China (and other East Asian states) of manipulating their exchange rate to gain a competitive advantage in trade.

Burden-sharing problems may also be part of the problem of trade liberalization. A good example has been the ongoing conflict for many years with respect to the reduction of agricultural support schemes that have been used by developed countries (and often by developing countries as well) to protect their farmers. Addressing the free riding temptation has been hampered by the difficulty of finding an agreement at a lower level of support.

BOX 3.1

Goods and the Problem of Collaboration

In examining the problem of international collaboration, we can use the concept of 'types of goods' to examine more rigorously the problem of incentives to free ride, fear that one's counterparts will fail to follow good policies, and the distributive conflicts that might ensue over where to meet. In a capitalist economy, private firms produce goods such as wheat, clothing, computers, and services such as financial products, insurance, and the like. Such goods are generally referred to as **private goods**, based on two characteristics: the goods are generally excludable and are not joint in consumption. The concept of *excludable* means that goods can be withheld from those who do not pay for them; *not joint in consumption* means that when a consumer utilizes the good, it is exhausted and cannot be used by others without there being additional production.

In addition to private goods, other goods may be desired, such as national defence or parks. These goods are characterized by the lack of ability to create exclusion and the jointness of their consumption, and they are known as **public goods**. Because anyone can have access to these goods once they are produced, consumers will misrepresent their demand for such goods as they can obtain them once they are produced and 'free ride'. In such cases, the private sector will not produce public goods, and governments will coerce citizens to pay for such goods through mechanisms such as taxation.

If a good is characterized by lack of exclusion and lack of jointness, then such a good is referred to as a common pool resource. Examples of such goods include fish in the oceans, or even, as a limiting case, a public park. Thus, if the ocean is overfished, fish will cease to reproduce and die out. Similarly, while parks are often seen as public goods, too many users of a park create crowding, which impairs the enjoyment of the good for others. Private actors will be particularly reluctant to produce such goods, and even governments will be concerned about the problem of too many users.

Finally, **inclusive club goods** refer to goods that may be excludable and yet be joint in consumption. These include goods such as software, music, and literature, which the private sector has a great incentive to produce. Once a unit of the good is produced, it can be distributed at either little or no cost. Indeed, firms may quickly develop a monopoly in the production of such goods if they are the first movers who make the good, and thus face regulation. For example, if a firm launches a satellite to beam television programmes to consumers, while the initial cost of securing a rocket to put the satellite in orbit will be great, once the satellite is in operation, the programmes can be disseminated to large numbers of consumers. Private firms will generally attempt to regulate consumption by encoding the transmission to prevent free riding. Alternatively, governments may simply regulate the

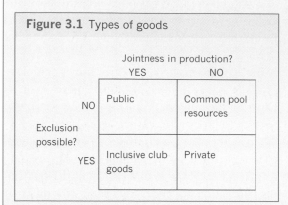

Figure 3.1 Types of goods

| | Jointness in production? | |
	YES	NO
Exclusion possible? **NO**	Public	Common pool resources
YES	Inclusive club goods	Private

industry and consumer behaviour to prevent consumption without paying (for example, penalties for copyright infringement). Figure 3.1 summarizes the four types of goods.

How do the problems of creating various types of goods play out in the international arena, and what obstacles do states face in achieving co-operation? Consider the case of co-operation with respect to avoiding damage to the ozone layer. Chlorofluorocarbons (CFCs) and other chlorine- and bromine-containing compounds have many uses, including as coolants, in aerosols, as cleaning agents, and as solvents. Yet by the early 1970s, scientists began to argue that such compounds could damage the ozone layer that protects the earth from the harmful ultraviolet radiation that has been implicated in skin cancer. By the early 1980s, there was increasing scientific consensus that these products were causing destruction of the ozone layer. Yet, because CFCs have many valuable uses, the debate over how to reduce or eliminate these products became an internationally contentious issue.

The public goods nature of the problem can be seen in the incentives to free ride by various countries who wish to benefit from the reduction in emissions of CFCs but do not want to bear the costs of reducing their production. There may also be distributive conflict ('where to meet') as actors debate the levels of production for rich and poor countries.

With respect to crowding, at the extreme, protecting the ozone layer has common pool resource properties, because jointness may be impaired if one country produces a huge amount of emissions that damages the ozone layer. Responding to demands for action by activists and governments to stop the destruction of the ozone layer, an initial treaty was signed by twenty countries in Vienna in 1985. And the Montreal Protocol was negotiated in 1987 and ratified in 1989.

With respect to inclusive club goods, the debate over standards also illustrates the problem of 'where to meet'. If a firm convinces its government to advocate the choice of its standard in international negotiations, the firm may be able to gain a significant advantage over its competitors. Even less firm-driven choices may influence costs and benefits, and lead to possible conflict. For example, the choice of English as the international language for use in international air traffic control imposes costs on those pilots who do not have an adequate command of English and who must therefore spend time and effort to learn the language (see Stein 1982).

KEY POINTS

- International co-operation can help to address three typical problems associated with the process of global integration: a temptation to free ride, an inhibiting fear, and a need to find meeting points in situations where collaboration will produce differing costs and benefits to governments.

- A country's need for international co-operation depends on its socio-political structure as well as on the structure and flexibility of its economy.

- Different types of problems associated with the process of global integration call for different solutions to address these three typical problems, ranging from the provision of binding rules to facilitating mechanisms.

International Co-operation: a Strategic Interdependence Approach

Our discussion so far has highlighted the potentially important role of international co-operation in enhancing the prospects for global economic integration. Yet, as the 'where to meet problem' shows, such co-operation may itself entail varying costs and benefits for participating states, and its successful negotiation is therefore not a foregone conclusion. To explore further the challenges of international co-operation, we can utilize a game theoretic approach to examine interdependent decision-making. A country's choice depends both on its cost/benefit evaluation of the various outcomes, and on its expectations regarding the choices of other actors. Game theory provides useful

---

BOX 3.2

Game Theory and its Critics

Game theory has become a standard tool for analysis of situations of interdependence in social sciences. Aside from its predictive aim, game theory has a strong appeal for anyone engaged in explanation, investigation, or prescription. It often makes ostensibly puzzling processes intelligible, without attributing causality to factors such as the incompetence, irresponsibility, or lack of concern of decision-makers.

Whatever its value, however, the use of game theory poses severe methodological problems that have prompted intense debates in the literature. Critics have traditionally emphasized (1) the over-stretching of the concept of rationality and (2) the gap between abstract theoretical concepts and real phenomena. Regarding the notion of rationality, most applications of game theory assume that players, interacting under conditions of imperfect information, possess a very high computational ability. To make their decisions, players must evaluate a host of possible worlds on the basis of the knowledge commonly shared with others, or privately known. This kind of situation often implies that players engage in comparative reasoning about a large set of possible worlds. Leeway in their interpretation often leads to a myriad of possible equilibria, which significantly decreases the predictive power of game theory. To avoid this indeterminacy, most game theorists have refined the concept of 'rationality' to allow the selection of one, or very few, equilibria among the vast initial array. For example, one might assume that people always choose to buy the cheapest product available (even though we know

that many people buy based on brand name, reputation, or other factors) because it makes the choices of actors easier to map. Most of these refinements to the concept of rationality thus lack empirical grounding.

A more recent controversy has focused on the empirical contribution of rational choice approaches to politics, including game-theoretic work. A variety of pathologies have prevented rational choice theory from improving our understanding of politics. In particular, rational choice theorists are, according to these critics, method-driven rather than problem-driven. In other words, instead of focusing on building models that reflect accurately decision-making in the real world, game theorists (according to critics) are more concerned with constructing elegant models rather than matching the models to real world situations. As a consequence, game theorists tend to neglect issues of empirical testing, which allegedly undermine the scientific value of rational choice theory.

Although there clearly remain weaknesses in most game theoretic analyses of international relations, the link between theory and empirics has clearly improved since the mid-1990s. Users of game theory have used different techniques to check the validity of their models, based on a comparison with reality. The dominant approach has been indirect testing through statistical analysis using either large-N data sets or a series of case studies. Another approach has been to use case studies to trace the behavioural attitude of actors and check them with the specific predictions derived from models.

tools to analyse actors' behaviour in such a context. Key features of actors' interactions are captured through 'games' describing the choices available to actors (players in the game), their evaluations of potential outcomes, and the information they have when they make their choices (see Box 3.2).

To keep this chapter's discussion of game theory as uncomplicated as possible, we focus on simple games with two people and two strategies per person. We further assume that actors have extensive knowledge of the other actor's preferences, but that they cannot observe his or her actual choices. Obviously, in real-life situations, actors may have less information about preferences and/or may be able to observe the other's behaviour. Our modelling choices may appear to over-simplify real-life examples but, as several authors have already shown, simple models can clearly reveal the decisions that governments face in attempting to deal with fundamental aspects of interdependence (Cooper 1975; Snidal 1985a; Martin 1992; Zürn 1992; Aggarwal and Dupont 1999).

Each of the three typical problems discussed in the previous discussion can be depicted with a specific game. We address them in turn, and then focus on situations that represent mixed situations.

'Free riding temptation': the Prisoner's Dilemma

As we have seen, global economic integration remains fragile as a result of countries' political difficulties in implementing potentially costly changes in economic policy. They may be tempted to free ride on others' policy changes, to take advantage of gains from their trading partners opening markets, which may in turn affect others' policy choices, and possibly bring an end to global economic liberalization. This situation is nicely captured with the game called the Prisoner's Dilemma.

The Prisoner's Dilemma models a situation in which two individuals are involved in a robbery and are then caught near the scene of the crime. The District Attorney (the DA or prosecutor) does

not have sufficient evidence to convict either of the suspects of robbery unless at least one of them reveals additional information to him, but he has some evidence to convict both of them of a lesser crime (for example, reckless driving, or carrying a firearm). The DA wants more information to convict both suspects for a long period. The two prisoners are placed in separate interrogation rooms. The DA tells each prisoner that if they confess and reveal the truth, they will get a much lighter sentence. If both prisoners confess, however (strategy S2 in the game depicted in Figure 3.2), they each get a heavier sentence than they would have received if they had both remained silent (strategy S1 in Figure 3.2), when they would have been charged with the lesser crime (when both confess, the DA has the evidence to convict both on the more serious offences). Confessing to the DA could bring the minimal sentence if the other one does not confess, but could also lead to a lengthier sentence if the other does confess. Remaining silent, on the other hand, may lead either to a moderate sanction if the other prisoner remains silent, or the maximum penalty if the other one speaks to the attorney. Facing this situation, and unable to communicate, the logical strategy for both prisoners is to choose to confess. They do so because confessing to the DA is individually always a safer strategy than remaining silent. The key point of the Prisoner's Dilemma game is that actors may face a structure of interaction that prevents them from reaching a

Figure 3.2 Prisoner's Dilemma game (ordinal form)

		Player Beta	
		S1	S2
Player Alpha	S1	3, 3	1, 4
	S2	4, 1	**2, 2**

Note: Nash Equilibrium in bold

co-operative solution even though such a solution would be optimal for both of them.

This story can be generalized using the game depicted in Figure 3.2. The numbers in the various cells indicate the preferences of players on an ordinal ranking scale, with 4 being the most preferred situation and 1 the least preferred. In the following figures, the first number in each box refers to Player Alpha's preference, while the second number refers to Player Beta's preference (thus '4, 1' is Alpha's most preferred outcome and Beta's least preferred outcome).

As Figure 3.2 shows, both players have a dominant strategy (confess, Strategy 2) that leads to what is called the Nash Equilibrium outcome, which is in the lower right cell of the matrix. A Nash Equilibrium is an outcome in which neither of the players can improve his or her situation by changing his/her individual strategy. But if both switch to Strategy 1 (remain silent) together, both players will secure a better outcome (upper-left cell). Yet, ironically, this collectively optimal situation is unstable, because each actor can improve his or her own welfare by individually switching strategy to the cells in the upper right or lower left corners of the matrix.

Within international political economy, the Prisoner's Dilemma has been widely used to illustrate the problem of reciprocal trade liberalization (Grossman and Helpman 1995; Hoekman and Kosteki 1995; Maggi 1999). The difficulties in monitoring partners' trade policies, and the potential political benefits to governments from open export markets and closed domestic markets often push states to back out of their commitments to reciprocate trade liberalization measures. As Conybeare (1984) shows, this argument applies in particular to countries with large domestic markets, as these countries are less dependent on the success of trade liberalization (this makes the utilities of the lower right cell in Figure 3.2 relatively acceptable), and such countries can also affect world prices positively through their tariff policy (imposing a tariff on imports lowers the price that other countries will receive for their exports). For smaller countries, though, the Prisoner's Dilemma is not an adequate depiction of their trade situations. Rather, smaller countries tend to have preferences that reflect the game of chicken, a situation we discuss below.

Another typical application of the Prisoner's Dilemma in international political economy has been in examining the collective management of resources. Whereas countries producing particular commodities traded on world markets would prefer a situation where they all manage production so as to keep prices sufficiently high (by forming a cartel such as OPEC—the Organization of Petroleum Exporting Countries), individual countries face the temptation to 'cheat' by increasing extraction or production of those commodities so as to maximize their individual income. As a result, acting collectively to keep commodity prices stable (for commodities such as coffee, tin, and even oil) has been a daunting task, particularly for developing countries.

'Inhibiting fear': assurance games

The second typical problem that countries seeking to enter international co-operation face comes from the uncertainty of benefits and costs linked to integration in the world economy. Global economic integration brings its full benefits when most countries are part of it and adopt appropriate policies. When some countries make mistakes, or if liberalization policies lose momentum, international markets may react abruptly. If states become paralysed by this likelihood, the whole world may revert to a much lower level of integration. This situation is best modelled through another category of game—assurance games.

One specific example of an assurance game is 'Stag Hunt', depicted in Figure 3.3. The name of the game comes from the story of two hunters chasing a stag. They go out before dawn and take positions on different sides of an area where they think a stag is hiding. They have a mutual understanding to shoot only at the stag (strategy S1 in the game depicted in Figure 3.3). Shooting at any other wild animal, say, a hare (strategy S2), would lead them

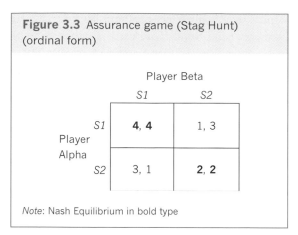

Figure 3.3 Assurance game (Stag Hunt) (ordinal form)

Player Beta

		S1	S2
Player Alpha	S1	**4, 4**	1, 3
	S2	3, 1	**2, 2**

Note: Nash Equilibrium in bold type

to miss shooting the stag because the stag would be frightened by the noise and stay put in its hiding place. As time goes by and dawn arrives, however, both hunters start thinking that going back home with a hare might be better than continuing to wait for the stag to come out of hiding. If each of them thinks that the other one will eventually yield to the temptation to shoot at a hare, they will both end up killing a hare—a better outcome than not catching anything, but clearly much less attractive than sharing a stag.

In Stag Hunt, players share a single most preferred outcome, but they do not have dominant strategies. As a result, there is a second, Pareto-deficient, equilibrium outcome. In such a game, reaching the Pareto-efficient equilibrium is not a foregone conclusion. Doubts about the willingness of one's counterpart to choose strategy S1 (shoot the stag) might push a player to choose strategy S2 (shoot a hare), which guarantees the highest minimal gain for that individual. Yet such an outcome is rather unlikely because of the attraction of the upper-left cell. In contrast to the Prisoner's Dilemma game, it is not the temptation to reap additional gains that may prevent actors from being in the upper-left cell of the game, but their anticipation of a possible mistake or unintentional move by the other one.

Financial globalization has features of a stag hunt game. With increasing capital flows among countries, global capital markets become deeper

and provide greater opportunities for individual countries. Yet, policy mistakes by some countries may quickly destabilize markets. Fear of the potential negative impact of such a destabilization may lead countries to implement measures to slow down or restrict capital movements. Such a move may lead to changes in other actors' expectations and quickly drive the world, or at least a region of the world, to a much lower level of integration. This new situation could have the advantage of being less risky for countries, but is unlikely to bring as many opportunities for investment, and therefore reduce growth prospects.

'Where to meet': co-ordination games

Whereas market liberalization is essential for global economic integration and increased prosperity, sustainable global integration requires some market supervision. This supervision in turn requires co-operative action by countries. The difficulty, however, is that there are often many ways to supervise markets, and countries may differ on their preferred co-ordination point because potential solutions vary in their costs and benefits. This strategic context corresponds to a co-ordination game. In the specific game depicted in Figure 3.4, actors have to choose from among Pareto-efficient outcomes (Pareto-efficient outcomes are defined as outcomes from which no actor could become better off without worsening the payoffs to another actor). Its name, 'Battle of the Sexes', comes from the story of a husband and wife who have to decide where to spend their evening after work. They either can go to the opera or watch a football match. Neither spouse derives much pleasure from being without the other one, but they differ on the best choice. The husband would prefer to watch football (strategy S1 in Figure 3.4), whereas the wife would prefer the opera (strategy S2 in Figure 3.4). In the story, both are leaving work and have to rush to either the stadium or the opera house. They cannot communicate with each other (say the batteries of their cell phones are

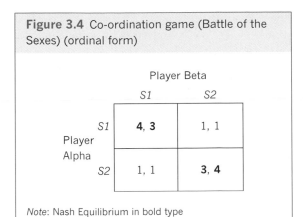

Figure 3.4 Co-ordination game (Battle of the Sexes) (ordinal form)

Player Beta

		S1	S2
Player Alpha	S1	**4, 3**	1, 1
	S2	1, 1	**3, 4**

Note: Nash Equilibrium in bold type

dead!), and have to meet at one of the locations. If each of them follows their preferred solution, they end up at different locations, which both regard as a bad outcome. Perversely, if both of them want to please the other one by choosing the location that they know that their partner prefers, they also end up being separated. Thus, they have in some way to co-ordinate implicitly, with one making a concession and the other receiving his/her first choice. Figure 3.4 provides a generalization of that story.

In the Battle of the Sexes, neither of the players has a dominant strategy. Player Alpha prefers to play Strategy 1 when Player Beta chooses Strategy 1, and prefers Strategy 2 when Player Alpha chooses strategy 2. With Player Beta having the same preferences as Alpha, the game has two equilibrium outcomes—the upper-left and lower-right cells in Figure 3.4. These two outcomes are clearly Pareto-superior to the two other possible outcomes, but actors will disagree on which one to choose. Player Alpha prefers the upper-left cell, whereas Player Beta prefers to end up in the lower-right cell. Both players want to avoid being separated, but each player prefers a different outcome.

In international political economy, efforts by developed countries to choose mutually compatible macroeconomic policies typically reflect games of co-ordination (Putnam and Bayle 1987). For example, when there is high volatility on financial and exchange rate markets, co-ordinated responses by leading countries would often be best, but each

country would like to choose the policy mix that best fits its own domestic constraints. Another prominent example is the choice of international monetary system (Cooper 1975). Discussions between the USA and Great Britain during the Second World War regarding the architecture of the future international economic order revealed that, while both countries agreed on the absolute need for co-ordination, they fought over the details of the new order, with each trying to impose its own plan. A more recent example was the debate within the European Union over the design of monetary union, which saw Britain, France and Germany proposing different solutions for some economic and monetary convergence between member states, as well as for rules of fiscal behaviour within the monetary union (Wolf and Zangl 1996).

Mixed situations: Chicken, Called Bluff, and Suasion

We now turn to games that capture situations in which more than one typical problem of co-operation may be present, or in which the actors may view the structure of the problem differently. We begin with the game of Chicken, which combines the features of the temptation to free ride as well as distributive tensions between the actors. This game, depicted in Figure 3.5, builds on the story of two cars, travelling in opposite directions, speeding down the middle of the road towards one another. Inside each car sits a driver who wants to impress his/her passenger that he/she is a tough person (that is, demonstrate resolve). The best way to do this is to continue driving straight down the middle of the road (strategy S2 in the game depicted in Figure 3.5)—even when the car coming in the opposite direction comes dangerously close. Yet, if at least one driver does not swerve, the outcome will be disastrous and both cars will crash, killing everyone. To avoid this unfortunate outcome, at least one driver will have to yield and swerve (strategy S1 in Figure 3.5), but both would like the other one to be the 'Chicken' who swerves.

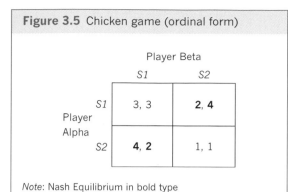

Figure 3.5 Chicken game (ordinal form)

Player Beta

		S1	S2
Player Alpha	S1	3, 3	**2, 4**
	S2	**4, 2**	1, 1

Note: Nash Equilibrium in bold type

Figure 3.6 Called Bluff (ordinal form)

Player Beta

		S1	S2
Player Alpha	S1	3, 3	1, 4
	S2	**4, 2**	2, 1

Note: Nash Equilibrium in bold type

The distributive tension between two equilibrium outcomes is a typical feature of the co-ordination games discussed above. But, in contrast to those games, the game of Chicken has a third outcome that is collectively optimal—the compromise solution in the upper-left cell. As in the Prisoner's Dilemma, however, this outcome is not stable, and actors have a strong temptation to revert to one of the two equilibria represented in boldface in Figure 3.5. As such, the Chicken game helps to capture more complex situations faced by countries attempting to engage in international co-operation (Stein 1982).

In the context of the global political economy, Chicken games are useful depictions of the complex structure of burden-sharing that occurs within a group of powerful players. For example, when there is monetary and financial stability in the global economy, the USA and the EU may tend to resist making public commitments to international co-operation unless there is a clear sign that the other party will act similarly. Getting out of a trade negotiation stalemate or dispute can also be a Chicken-like situation, in which each actor is unwilling to agree on any asymmetric solutions.

Up this point, we have only considered cases where actors have symmetrical preferences. We now examine two interesting *asymmetric* games, the first of which has one player whose preferences are those of the Prisoner's Dilemma game, and a second player with a structure of preferences of the Chicken game. The resulting asymmetric game, known as the game of 'Called Bluff', is depicted in Figure 3.6.

Player Alpha has Prisoners' Dilemma preferences, with a dominant strategy to play S2, whereas Player Beta has Chicken preferences, with a preferred choice of S2 if Alpha chooses S1, and a choice of S1, if Alpha chooses S2. Yet, in this game, becuase of the asymmetry in payoffs, Beta knows that Alpha has a dominant strategy of S2, Beta should therefore choose S1, leading to the equilibrium outcome in the lower-left cell in Figure 3.6. Here, Player Alpha gets his/her most preferred outcome, whereas Player Beta gets his/her second-worst outcome. This scenario can be used to analyse situations where stronger countries or actors can take advantage of another's weakness and shift the burden of cost of co-operative action on to the weaker party. This outcome is caused by the difference in actors' sensitivity (vulnerability) to the need for co-operation itself. The player with less dependence on the need for co-operation (Alpha in Figure 3.6) is able to free ride on the other player (Beta in Figure 3.6). Given the lack of capacity of the weaker actor to sustain co-operation alone, this often leads to a breakdown of international action.

A good illustration of this situation is the monetary policy of Germany and Japan in the 1960s, in the context of the Bretton Woods fixed exchange rate system. The stronger player, the United States, asked these countries to revalue their currencies to help boost the competitiveness of US exports and relieve the pressure on the dollar. These countries refused to undertake significant re-evaluations, which had increasingly costly implications for the US economy and, ultimately under the Nixon administration, the USA simply forced the burden of adjustment on to the weaker countries by breaking the link between the dollar and gold, and imposing a 10 per cent across-the-board tariff. This action led to the end of the Bretton Woods system (see Helleiner, Chapter 7 in this volume).

A second case of asymmetry is a game with one player having preferences orientated towards co-operation and the other having Chicken preferences. In the game of 'Suasion', Player Beta has preferences similar to a player in the Chicken game, but Player Alpha has preferences that are typical of another game, the game of Harmony. The basic feature of Harmony games (see Figure 3.7) is that both players not only dislike acting separately (as in the case of co-ordination games) but they also do not differ on the best outcome. They both therefore have a dominant strategy to do the same thing. Co-operation is, so to speak, naturally guaranteed (as, for example, in nineteenth-century liberal assumptions about international economic relations).

Combining a player with Chicken preferences and a player with Harmony preferences yields the game depicted in Figure 3.8, known as the game of 'Suasion' (Martin 1992). The predicted outcome of the Suasion game shares some similarity with that of the game of Called Bluff that was illustrated in Figure 3.6. Both games feature a situation in which one player achieves his/her most preferred outcome. However, the difference between these two games

Figure 3.8 Suasion (ordinal form)

Player Beta

		S1	S2
Player Alpha	S1	4, 3	**3, 4**
	S2	2, 2	1, 1

Note: Nash Equilibrium in bold type

is that, in Suasion, the 'stronger' player gets his/her second-best outcome, which results from the choice of a dominant strategy by the Alpha. Put into the context of international co-operation, this clearly reflects a situation in which an actor perceives the benefits of international action to be much more than its associated costs. Because this actor (Alpha) absolutely wants to carry through action at the international level, and is assumed to have the capability to do so, other actors (Beta) are in a situation whereby they will let Alpha undertake the bulk of the effort, and will enjoy the benefits at low cost or no cost to themselves.

One can view this as a situation as one of the tyranny of the weak, which is in sharp contrast to the game of Called Bluff. Note, however, that the stronger player is not forced into an asymmetric outcome by the behaviour of the weak one, but by his/her own preferences. From this perspective, the Suasion game features an opportunistic attitude by the weak player rather than a deliberately tyrannical outlook. Martin (1992) argues that this game illustrates the Western world's restriction of technology exports to the Soviet Union during the Cold War. Control of technology sales to the Soviet bloc was done through the Coordinating Committee for multilateral Export Controls (COCOM). Within it, however, the United States had a dominant strategy to control technology, whereas European states were more opportunistic. They could benefit from sales to the Soviet bloc without jeopardizing the overall balance of power between the two blocs.

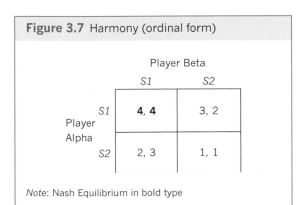

Figure 3.7 Harmony (ordinal form)

Player Beta

		S1	S2
Player Alpha	S1	**4, 4**	3, 2
	S2	2, 3	1, 1

Note: Nash Equilibrium in bold type

The USA was dissatisfied with this situation and had to persuade Europeans to participate fully in COCOM.

More generally, this type of game relates to situations where one actor (or group of actors) can undertake actions that are immune (to some degree) to the free riding behaviour of other countries.

For example, tax havens in small countries have been 'tolerated' by bigger countries as long as the latter could use capital movement restrictions to secure financial stability. When capital restrictions were dismantled, there were significant increases in the efforts to circumvent the free riding behaviour of tax havens.

KEY POINTS

- Each of the typical problems of international co-operation can be viewed through the lens of strategic decision-making.

- Game theory can help us to analyse interdependent decision making.

- Co-operation can be expected to fail, because of actors' incentives to cheat, actors' sensitivities to distribution issues, or to lack of confidence in the other actor's behaviour.

- Problems of distribution and free riding may be combined in real-world situations; some games are able to model these combinations.

- Differences in resources or in the perceived need for co-operation result in situations of asymmetric burden sharing.

International Co-operation: a Variety of Solutions

The discussion of co-operation problems in the global political economy highlights the varied nature of the challenges facing actors. We now turn to the question of how to address these challenges. In particular, we focus on the role that international institutions can play in addressing co-operation problems. Our analysis begins with situations where the problems can be addressed without institutions, and then turns to cases where institutions help the process of co-operation.

International action without international institutions

In most of the games we have examined, individual actions by both players lead, or may lead, to an outcome we can characterize as collectively optimal, because there is no welfare loss. Yet this notion

of optimality tends to be short-sighted because the asymmetric outcomes of the Called Bluff, Suasion, Chicken, and even co-ordination, games are optimal only in terms of a narrow view of *collective welfare*. Such a conception of welfare does not obviate the problems of the distribution of gains that may either make the road to agreement difficult, or plague the likelihood of collaboration. As we discuss below, institutions may play useful roles in addressing these problems, but collaboration may also occur through individual actions.

Individual, decentralized, action can also be optimal in the thorny case of the Prisoner's Dilemma. Yet, for this to happen, we must relax the base-line assumption that players play the game only once, and allow them to have repeated interactions over time (Axelrod and Keohane 1986; Taylor 1987; Sandler 1992; Cornes and Sandler 1996). When players expect to meet again in the future, they may be more willing to co-operate. Yet even under such conditions of iteration, however, co-operation is not a foregone conclusion. For example, if the expected net value of co-operation is too low (for example, actors may overly discount the importance of future iterations because of a dire economic or political situation for governments in the country), the temptation to free ride cannot be overcome. The Prisoner's Dilemma (PD) demonstrates that, if defection by one actor generates high costs for the other actor (resulting in a lengthy prison sentence in PD), or if actors cannot gather information easily, they may not achieve a Pareto optimal outcome.

Applied to the case of trade liberalization, repeated interaction is not sufficient to ensure co-operative behaviour for governments under heavy domestic pressure, as the temptation to reap immediate political gains through defection may simply be too great. Domestic pressure may be particularly high in democratic countries, where economic groups or citizens have easy access to the political sphere; in countries with a political system that tends to favour coalitional governments; or in countries without strongly embedded social consultation mechanisms. Conversely, the cost of defection may be too high when actors invest heavily in co-operative efforts and value the outcome produced by co-operation. In such cases, they are significantly more reluctant to jeopardize co-operation, even if others have indulged in free riding behaviour.

A world without international institutions is also not universally effective in securing the exchange of goods. As long as trading partners have access to other markets for their products, an institution-free world can work in the context of global trade, because countries can simply turn to another market if a breach occurs in the trading relationship. Yet, if there is only one partner interested in the goods produced, or if it would be more costly to trade with other partners, such an option does not exist. If a country cannot threaten to sell its goods elsewhere, another country may take advantage of it. Another important qualification for successful

institution-free contexts is if one (or both) of the parties has made relation-specific investments. In such a case, these investments will discourage defection and may encourage co-operative behaviour.

What other factors might impede co-operation when actors cannot rely on international institutions? Monitoring will be much more difficult if states only have limited information-gathering capability. If an actor has so little information that, for example, it is unsure whether the other actor 'defected' on the last round, then the prospect of repeated interactions does not increase the chances of co-operation. Similarly, an expanding number of states, with an expanding range of trade products using increasingly sophisticated policies to intervene in markets, makes monitoring trade policies increasingly difficult. It is therefore more difficult to detect non-compliance without the help of a third party.

The role of institutions

As our discussion above suggests, actors may need help to sustain collectively optimal outcomes. One way in which individuals might be able to co-ordinate their choices to achieve desired goals could be through the creation or use of international institutions or regimes. International regimes have been defined broadly as 'sets of principles, norms, rules and decision making procedures upon which actors' expectations converge' (Krasner 1983). To refine this definition, we can distinguish between the principles and norms—the 'meta-regime' (Aggarwal 1985)—and the regime itself, defined as the rules and procedures that allow us to distinguish between two very different types of constraints on the behaviour of states. In this case, we can use the term 'institution' to refer to the combination of meta-regime and regime—rather than Krasner's definition. Note that an institution is not the same thing as an international organization: one can find areas of international collaboration where there are well-defined principles, norms, rules and procedures for actors' behaviour in the absence of an organization such as the IMF. We structure our discussion below around three major functions of institutions.

First, institutions can act as channels for the third-party enforcement of agreements. To overcome successfully players' temptation to free ride, international institutions should be strong—meaning that member countries should have specific and binding obligations. In particular, agreements that credibly restrain actors' temptation to free ride in trade and monetary policy, for example, need to rely on some sort of enforcement mechanism delegated to an international institution. At its strongest expression, in the European Union or the WTO, such a mechanism relies on an organization (the EU has two such entities, the Commission, and the Court of Justice) with supranational power to monitor, evaluate, and sanction (if needed) the behaviour of its members.

The chances of a co-operative agreement can also be enhanced through a different kind of centralization—one that ensures a prompt and undistorted dissemination of information. This type of facility helps to identify the requirements of multilateral action, and protects against possible defections. Enforcement can also be achieved either through positive incentives, as when the IMF provides funds to countries that are following its policy recommendations, or through punitive action, as when the WTO rules against a particular state policy.

Second, international institutions can help to craft responses to situations characterized by distributive tensions among states. They can help states choose one among several collective outcomes, and eliminate some sharply asymmetric outcomes. Institutions may also be useful for gathering information about the preferences of actors, and, through appropriate use of agenda setting, may help find focal point solutions for both cost sharing and benefit splitting. Institutions with a firmly and widely established meta-regime tend to perform these tasks extremely well. In contrast, institutions lacking a strong meta-regime may have difficulty in generating possible solutions that are attractive

to all members. This has often been considered as the source of difficulties for the GATT and its successor, the WTO. Deep disagreements among GATT members led to the creation of another forum—the United Nations Conference on Trade and Development (UNCTAD)—in the 1960s, and to serious hurdles in the negotiations of the extension of the scope of GATT/WTO, as revealed recently during the Doha Round of negotiations. The members of UNCTAD had shared principles and norms that they felt were not importantly addressed in GATT/WTO.

Third, international institutions can do a lot to allay actors' fear or reluctance to engage in co-operative behaviour. Rather than enforcing a particular outcome, institutions should enable actors to reach it (by pooling resources, for example). To help the integration of developing countries into the global financial system, the IMF provides cheap credit opportunities through the contributions subscribed by all members. The World Bank finances the development of basic infrastructure in developing countries to help them reduce poverty. At the European regional level, the European Monetary System (EMS) has relied on a decentralized system of very short lending facilities among members to help them defend the parity grid that tightened them together.

To address enforcement and distribution problems, institutions can establish rights for members that either define mechanisms of exclusion or determine compensation schemes. In relation to our previous discussion of games and co-operation, careful institutional design can sometimes 'privatize' the benefits of co-operation, reducing the temptation to free ride. The reduction of trade barriers almost always applies to countries that belong to particular clubs, be they regional (see Ravenhill, Chapter 6 in this volume) or global. Assigning rights and obligations can also produce decentralized co-operation when institutions also provide information about the preferences of actors and reduce the costs of their discussions to their minimum. When actors are more certain about who owns and is responsible for what (a result of the assignment of rights and obligations), co-operation may result.

Under these conditions, as Coase (1960) suggests, actors do not need any centralized power to remedy the problem of negative externalities (situations where an individual's action has a negative effect on the well-being of another individual in ways that need not be paid for according to the existing definition of property rights) (Conybeare 1980; Keohane 1984) but should find a mutually satisfactory solution through financial compensation. The crucial aspect, in the Coasian framework, is establishing liabilities for externalities. The history of international monetary agreements provides several examples of the difficulties associated with determining satisfactory schemes assigning responsibilities to the involved parties. For instance, the collapse of the fixed exchange rate systems was largely a result of the inability of IMF members to redistribute the burden of adjustment from the USA to Germany and Japan. Difficulties in the so-called European Snake in the early 1970s induced member states to design the EMS in such a way as to put the responsibility on strong currency members (in particular, on Germany) to intervene as much as weak currency members in defending existing parities.

Our brief discussion of the roles of institutions reveals the value associated with information gathering and dissemination. Long-term enforcement requires the identification of prospects for defection, finding a focal point based on the constellation of positions, and informing actors of the overall global context. Therefore, a major activity of international institutions is to collect information about actors' behaviour, preferences, and the state of the international environment.

KEY POINTS

- Institutions are key instruments for resolving enforcement, distribution, and assurance problems.

- Institutions help assign rights and obligations to benefactors of co-operation as well as in defining those benefactors.

- Institutions help make the international scene an information-rich environment.

The Formation and Evolution of Institutions

We have seen that institutions can help co-operation in several ways. But how might institutions be formed in the first place? And what factors may have an impact on the design of institutions? We begin with a broad discussion from the literature on international relations and then turn to more specific issues. In examining institutions, five different approaches in international relations have been brought to bear on this problem: neo-realism; neo-realist institutionalism; neo-liberal institutionalism; cognitivism; and radical constructivism (Aggarwal 1998—the term radical constructivism was first used by Haas 1992).

Neo-realists assume that, in an anarchic international system, states must rely primarily on their own resources to ensure their security. For neo-realist scholars, therefore, regimes and international institutions have no significant role in international relations because power considerations are predominant in an anarchic world (Waltz 1979; Mearsheimer 1990). In this view, as we have discussed earlier, collaboration will only be sustainable if states value future interactions highly, have symmetric resources, and are highly interdependent.

Still within a power-based tradition, though, some scholars have examined changes in, and the effects of, international institutions. In this literature, labelled neo-realist institutionalism, the central concern is on how regimes affect the distribution of costs and benefits of state interaction. For analysts in this school (Krasner 1983, 1991; Aggarwal 1985; Knight 1992), institutions have distributional consequences (in other words, the benefits of co-operation may be unequal) and can be used as devices to seek and maintain asymmetric gains. They can, more broadly, help to control other actors' behaviour, both at home and abroad (Aggarwal 1985). For example, within the domestic context, state elites can argue that their hands are tied and thus attempt to circumvent pressure for particular actions from domestic actors. Examples of this include the Mexican government signing on to the North American Free Trade Agreement (NAFTA) (tying the hands of the Mexican government to a more open market posture in the face of domestic protectionist groups) or the American use of the Multifibre Arrangement (MFA) to prevent textile and apparel interests from pressing for excessive protection.

A central theme in this literature has been the role of hegemonic powers in fostering the development of institutions through both positive and negative incentives (Kindleberger 1973; Gilpin 1975; Krasner 1976). Benevolent hegemons, for example, may provide public goods (a special type of good—for example, national defence, that cannot practically be withheld from an individual without withholding it from all (the 'non-excludability criterion'), and for which the marginal cost of an additional person consuming them, once they have been produced, is zero (the 'non-rival consumption' criterion)), because their large size makes it worthwhile for them to take action on their own to overcome collective action problems. But while suggesting that regimes may form when powerful states desire them, this approach does not tell us much about the nature of regimes. Moreover, scholars in this school overemphasize tensions arising from differences in the distribution of benefits between actors, and downplay the possibility that actors may not necessarily and as acutely think in comparative terms, but focus

on the positive impact of institutions on their situations. Finally, this approach has little to say about actors' desire to pursue multilateral versus bilateral solutions to accomplish their ends.

Building on these criticisms of the neo-realist approach, neo-liberal institutionalists have examined the specific incentives for states to create institutions—as opposed to simply engaging in *ad hoc* bargaining. This body of work, taking off from seminal research by Oliver Williamson, examines the role of institutions in lowering the costs involved in choosing, organizing, negotiating, and entering into an agreement (what he calls transaction costs), and has garnered a considerable following in the field of international relations (Keohane 1984). As we have seen, institutions provide many useful functions in helping actors to co-ordinate their actions or achieve collaboration. This theoretical approach assumes that collaborative action is primarily demand driven—that is, actors will create institutions because they are useful—but does not really specify a mechanism for how they would go about creating them.

An important theme of this work has been how existing institutions may constrain future institutional developments (Keohane and Nye 1977; Keohane 1984). One aspect of this constraint is the possibility that existing institutions with a broad mandate will affect the negotiation of more specific institutions, leading to the 'nesting' of regimes within one another (Aggarwal 1985). Thus, while the notion of transaction costs and sunk costs (the investments that actors have made in specific institutions) are central elements in this thinking, the role of regimes in providing states with information and reducing organizational costs can be distinguished from the role of existing institutions in constraining future actions.

A fourth approach to examining institutional innovation and change puts an emphasis on the role of expert consensus and the interplay of experts and politicians (Haas 1980; Haas 1992). New knowledge and cognitive understandings may lead decision-makers to calculate their interests differently. For example, work by Ernst Haas focused on the efforts of politicians to use linkages across various issues (sometimes from quite distinct areas) to create new issue packages in international negotiations. The objective is to provide benefits to all, in an effort to facilitate the formation of international regimes (Haas 1980).

Lastly, 'radical constructivists', while focusing on the role of ideas, argue that reality is in fact constructed in the minds of decision-makers. These scholars, drawing on Ernst Haas's work, go much further than Haas in suggesting that 'power and interest do not have effects apart from the shared knowledge that constitutes them as such' (Wendt 1995: 74). Analysts in this school see norms and values as being dominant causal forces, and ascribe considerable power to institutions in not only constraining actors, but also in fundamentally altering how they conceive of their basic interests. In summarizing their view, Peter Haas notes that this school argues that 'there is no "objective" basis for identifying material reality and all claims for objectivity are therefore suspect' (Haas 1992: 21).

The subjective element in states' decision-making makes it more difficult to evaluate objectively the role that institutions might play, or how they might be constructed.

The characteristics of international institutions

The five general approaches discussed above are a useful starting point for the understanding of how institutions are created, and of the key drivers of their subsequent evolution, but they are clearly of limited help in understanding specific variations in the forms of institutions. Based on the existing literature and on our own work, we characterize institutions in terms of their membership, the stringency of their rules (the degree to which they constrain state behaviour), their scope, the extent of delegation of power from member states to institutional bodies, and the centralization of tasks within the institution.

BOX 3.3

IMF and WTO: Selected Organizational Characteristics

Created to promote international monetary co-operation, the International Monetary Fund exerts a surveillance function over member states' financial and economic policies and provides financial and technical assistance to member states. Day-to-day business is conducted by the Executive Board, a body with 24 Executive Directors representing directly or indirectly all members. The IMF's five largest shareholders—the USA, Japan, Germany, France and the United Kingdom—along with China, Russia, and Saudi Arabia have their own seats, whereas the other 16 Executive Directors are elected by groups of countries. The Executive Board is empowered by the Board of Governors, the highest authority of the IMF in which each member has a seat. To assist it in the conduct of IMF affairs, the Executive Board in turn selects a Managing Director who is the chief of the operating staff of the Fund, roughly 2800 employees with half of them being economists.

Within the Executive Board, the normal *de jure* decision making mode is simple majority, but important issues are decided by qualified majority, either 70 per cent (suspension of one member's rights in case of non-respect of obligations) or by 85 per cent (for instance modification of quotas, change in the seats of the Executive Board, or provisions for general exchange arrangements). Qualified majority voting increases the power of the biggest contributors, in particular the US, which has a veto power over issues requiring 85 per cent majority decisions. *De facto*, however, voting rarely occurs in the Executive Board. Instead, Executive Directors use consensus to adopt decisions.

The institutional structure of the WTO differs significantly from the IMF model. It reflects very clearly what the organization considers to be its primary role—a forum for the negotiation of trade liberalization agreements. The WTO's principal institutional structures are a ministerial Conference meeting every two years; the General Council; and three councils in the area of goods, services, and intellectual property. All members have a seat in these councils. The default decision-making mode is consensus, but decisions may also be made by unanimity (suspension of MFN treatment), with a 75 per cent majority (interpretation of an existing multilateral agreement, or a waiver of an obligation for a particular country) or a two-thirds majority (for instance, the admission of new members).

The WTO General Council also serves as the Trade Policy Review Body that reviews member states' trade policies. Reviews are conducted on the basis of a policy statement by the Member under review and a report prepared by economists in the WTO Secretariat. That Secretariat, headed by a director-general, has around 630 staff and its main function is one of administrative and technical support for WTO councils, committees and working groups.

Delegation of authority in the WTO is therefore restricted to the mechanism for solving trade disputes between members. Delegation is conferred first to small groups of experts (3 or 5) who are established when members fail to settle disputes in conciliatory way. Panel members are independent individuals under instruction from no government. Their role is to make an objective assessment of the dispute and issue a report with findings and recommendations (establishing the legality of member states' policies in the case under dispute). This report has then to be adopted by the General Council serving as the Dispute Settlement Body. The latter, however, can only reject the panel report by consensus.

The second body with delegated authority from the member state is the Appellate Body, which review appeals made by member states on panel reports. The seven members of the Appellate Body serve for four-year terms and are legal experts with international standing. The appeal can uphold, modify, or reverse the panel's legal findings and conclusions. As in the case of panel reports, the appeal report must be endorsed by the Dispute Settlement Body. Rejection is only possible by consensus.

For more information, http://www.wto.org; and http://www.imf.org

The Bretton Woods institutions, the WTO, and UNCTAD have quasi-universal *membership*. By contrast, the Group of Seven most industrialized countries has welcomed only one new member since the 1970s (Russia formally joined the Group in 1997, transforming it into the G8). Similarly, most regional integration arrangements have remained as select clubs, with limited membership (see Ravenhill, Chapter 6 in this volume). Membership also varies in terms of the types of actors who can participate. While most institutions remain state-centric, some have started to include private actors: for example, the Financial Stability Forum (FSF) was created in 1999 to promote international financial stability groups' representatives from national ministries, international financial institutions, and sector-specific groups (insurance, accounting standards, securities commissions). Controversy continues at the WTO over whether non-state actors should be permitted to participate in deliberations (for other efforts paying particular attention to membership issues see Sandler 1992; Koremenos *et al.* 2001; Aggarwal and Dupont 2002).

The second dimension, *stringency of rules*, covers both the precision and the obligation of rules in the literature on legalization of world politics (see Aggarwal 1985 on regime strength; and Abbot and Snidal 2000 on legalization). From this perspective, authors have often contrasted the so-called European and Asian models of regional economic integration. The first is built upon a wide set of specific and binding rules (called the *acquis communautaire* in the jargon of European integration) whereas the second is built upon declarations, intentions and voluntary commitments (Ravenhill 1995, 2001). The lack of any precise and concise definition of a balance of payments problem in the IMF had a severe effect on the constraining power of this institution in attempts to preventing its members from running imbalances.

Third, we consider the *scope* of agreements defined as issue coverage (Aggarwal 1985; Koremenos *et al.* 2001). The evolution of the GATT from its origins in 1947 to the creation of WTO in 1995 reveals an important increase in the scope of the agreements. Whereas GATT focused initially on the liberalization of trade in goods, the WTO covers services and agriculture, as well as trade-related aspects of intellectual property rights and investment (see Winham, Chapter 5 in this volume). Similarly, the G7/G8 agenda has expanded drastically, from a focus on macro-economic management to a broad range of international security and economic issues, including terrorism, energy, environment, and arms control. At the other end of the range, one finds sector-specific institutions such as the International Organization of Securities Commissions, the International Association of Insurance Supervisors, and the International Accounting Standards Board as well as product-specific organizations such as the International Coffee Organization, the International Cocoa Organization, the International Copper Study Group, and the International Sugar Organization.

The fourth dimension is the extent of *institutional delegation*, the authority ceded by members to an institution, a dimension central to several existing studies (Abbot and Snidal 2000; McCall Smith 2000; Dupont and Hefeker 2001). International agreements may or may not include the creation of institutional organs, and these organs may or may not be given some autonomy by members in making new rules, or monitoring and enforcing existing ones.

The extent of delegation may vary significantly across organs of the same institution. For example, while the dispute settlement process in the WTO features an independent appellate body, the governing body of the organization—the General Council—relies on consensus decision-making, and the members have kept the size and the prerogatives of the secretariat to a minimum. At the regional level, the extent of delegation distinguishes the European Union strongly from the small secretariats found in other regional institutions. Whereas the EU includes organs with supranational power, governments remain in full control of negotiation and implementation processes in most other regional agreements, including NAFTA, the Association of Southeast Asian Nations (ASEAN), and the Asia-Pacific Economic Cooperation (APEC) grouping.

A fifth dimension is *institutional centralization* (Koremenos *et al.* 2001). Is there a concentration of tasks performed by a single institutional entity? Centralization may refer to such tasks as the diffusion of information, monitoring of members' behaviour, or the imposition of sanctions, as well as the adoption of new rules or the modification of existing ones. Strong administrative bodies are natural candidates for the centralization of many tasks, as exemplified by the case of the European Commission in the European Union, or the administration of the IMF or the World Bank. Yet, in the latter two, key decisions and tasks go through the Executive Board with a limited membership of 24 countries or groups of countries represented by Executive Directors chosen by member states (see Helleiner, Chapter 7 in this volume).

It is often difficult to understand these five dimensions as being separate, but they are conceptually distinct. As an example, although it is hard to imagine an agreement with lax rules and high delegation, strict rules do not necessarily imply high delegation (good examples are the numerous bilateral treaties on investment, and to a lesser extent bilateral free trade treaties). Similarly, centralization and delegation may reinforce each other, but neither requires the other. Conferences or councils of heads of governments and states centralize most of the activities of several regional economic organizations (including monitoring, and dispute settlement). Yet decision-making remains either consensual (where no state dissents publicly from the agreement) or based on unanimity.

Explaining institutional design

How can one account for institutional variation on these five dimensions? Consistent with a functionalist approach to the study of international institutions, we should expect the five dimensions to be affected by the types of problems that institutions should address (Stein 1982; Snidal 1985*a*; Aggarwal and Dupont 1999; Koremenos *et al.* 2001). In Table 3.1 (on page 88), we link our three

Table 3.1 From Problems to Institutional Solutions

	'Free riding temptation'	'Inhibiting fear'	'Where to meet'
Strategic game	Prisoner's Dilemma	Stag Hunt (assurance games)	Battle of the Sexes
Illustrations	Trade liberalization Debt rescheduling	Financial integration Trade specialization	Managing adjustments Multilateral negotiations
Role(s) of institutions	Channel to enforce contracts • monitoring/surveillance • sanctioning mechanisms • policy transfer	Enhancers of co-operation • pools of resources • suppliers of knowledge and capacity	Providers of solutions to distributive conflicts • negotiation forums • agenda setting • linkages
Examples of institutional solutions	*Monitoring/surveillance*: Articles IV and VIII of IMF; Trade Policy Review mechanism WTO *'Sanction'*: IMF Conditionality IMF; WTO DSB's authorization of sanctions *Policy transfer*: Common Trade policy and Economic and Monetary Union in the European Union	*Pools of resources*: quota system in IMF *Suppliers of knowledge and capacity*: WTO (technical co-operation); World Bank; IMF; UNCTAD	*Negotiation forums*: WTO General Council; Executive Boards IMF and World Bank; UNCTAD *Agenda setting*: IMF and World Bank staff

typical problems with specific roles for international institutions. Keeping these in mind, the 'temptation to free ride' problem is the one that clearly calls for strong rules, with delegation and centralization to international bodies. Co-operation is difficult, and thus requires relatively strong institutions. In such cases, membership tends to be restricted to well-'socialized' governments. An inclusive membership makes monitoring more difficult and costly, and thus creates many opportunities for members to free ride.

As for scope, on the one hand, enforcement of the agreements is more likely to occur when institutions have a broad scope and are able to connect different issues ('issue linkage'). Linkages across issues help to deter defection on a single issue when actors have broad interests (Lohmann 1997; McGinnis 1986).

For example, members of the WTO cannot subscribe to the agreement on goods (GATT) without also accepting the agreement on services (GATS) as well as the agreements on intellectual property rights TRIPs and investment TRIMs, and the dispute-settlement mechanism. On the other hand, adding issues to an institution's agenda requires a strong capacity to monitor behaviour, which may often simply not be present.

The 'inhibiting fear' and 'where to meet' problems call for quite different institutional features. For these cases, there is a positive link with centralization for the pooling of resources, knowledge and information provision, or the reduction of the costs of negotiations. Addressing the 'inhibiting fear' may require some clear and binding rules on access to resources and knowledge. Yet, in these cases, restricting the size of membership may not be a strong prerequisite for success. Solving distribution problems may require a softening of rules to allow some room for different interpretations of the agreements. Delegation of power is not essential in either situation, apart from the potential benefit of agenda-setting power to find mutually acceptable solutions.

As for scope, there is no clear link between 'inhibiting fear' and issue coverage. But a diverse set of issues can provide greater ground for compromise when players have different preferences, and when they do not assign equal value to all the issues. For example, trade liberalization and monetary co-operation in the European Community has often been facilitated by the development of social or regional policies or packages to 'compensate' countries that might not immediately be major beneficiaries of the other policies. But, as the case of agriculture in the GATT/WTO shows, having different issues on the agenda is not helpful when countries categorically exclude certain issues from consideration in making trade-offs. Finally, with respect to membership, selected, restrictive groupings tend to reinforce the fear of being left out, and thus should be avoided to address the 'inhibiting fear' problem. As for problems of distribution, more members may on the one hand help in the quest for new solutions. Yet new members may also add as many new conflicts as complementarities among players.

As we have seen, then, different types of problems call for appropriate institutional design. Although focusing on general tendencies in institutional design in view of the problems they need to address provides a useful first step, we are still faced with some anomalies. For example, given that trade liberalization is widely portrayed as embodying a 'temptation to free ride', how can one explain that some institutions (for example, the European Free Trade Association) that focus on trade liberalization have remained informal, and thus lack organs with delegated power? Why is it that some institutions do not have clear rules and preconditions for membership (for example, GATT/WTO or the

EU until the early 1990s)? And, lastly, why do some countries prefer very loose rules in designing institutions (such as ASEAN and APEC)?

To increase our ability to understand such choices, we can consider three other key influences. First, an important issue is what we call *potential participants* in the institution. In particular, the number of these actors and their relative power—two factors considered by Koremenos *et al.* (2001) as well as their overall financial and 'social' capital (Ostrom 2000) influence the design of institutions. Relatively little concern about membership rules in GATT 1947 can be accounted for by the fact that the international system was much smaller and more homogeneous than the one that emerged in the 1960s as a result of decolonization. Similarly, the need to define strict criteria for entering the EU only became salient when the Iron Curtain fell and former communist countries with still very different political systems expressed an interest in joining the EU.

Turning to the financial and social capital among potential actors, the disparities in size of financial reserves held by East Asian agreement surely explains the very decentralized form of the regional financing arrangement known as the Chiang Mai Initiative (an East Asian institution intended to provide emergency finance to member economies facing a run on their currencies). In turn, the fact that there has been little formalization of relationships between central banks in the developed, democratic world, builds upon a joint understanding and on a high level of expertise in ways of addressing problems.

Second, the *information and knowledge available to actors* affects institutional design. Institutions comprised of actors with rich and reliable information usually require less centralization or less delegation (Coase 1960; Williamson 1975; Koremenos *et al.* 2001), as illustrated with the loose structure of the European Free Trade Association from its creation in 1960 to its upgrading in 1993. The founding members of that association—the United Kingdom, Denmark, Norway, Sweden, Austria, Switzerland, and Portugal—did not have the mutual distrust that characterized French–German relation in the EC, and information from partner countries was thus considered by all members to be rich and reliable. Existing knowledge about the issue area(s) covered by the agreement may affect the stringency of rules, the delegation of power, issue scope, and membership. Poor knowledge about the issues at stake tends to make actors wary of making hard commitments (rules and delegation)—a tendency particularly present in the discussions in the domain of the environment (see Dauvergne, Chapter 14 in this volume). Better knowledge may affect issue scope and the contours of membership. Whereas the politics of trade liberalization may call for careful selection of members for inclusion in the WTO, the widespread belief in the veracity of international trade theory (which argues that global membership yields the greatest efficiency in the allocation of resources) helps to account for the pressure increasingly to universalize membership in this institution.

Third, and finally, we can focus on the *outside institutional setting*. When actors create new institutions, they generally do not do so in a vacuum. Thus, when new institutions are developed, they must often be reconciled with existing ones. One approach to achieving such reconciliation is by nesting broader and narrower institutions in a hierarchical fashion. Another means of achieving harmony among institutions is through an institutional division of labour, or 'horizontal' linkages (Aggarwal 1998). The challenge of institutional reconciliation is not, however, unique to the creation of new ones. In lieu of creating new institutions, policy-makers might also modify existing institutions for new purposes. For example, faced by seemingly intractable balance of payments problems in Africa in the 1990s, the IMF developed new structural adjustment facilities that overlapped substantially with those of the World Bank. When modifying institutions, members must therefore also focus on issues of institutional compatibility. Moreover, bargaining over institutional modification is likely to be influenced strongly by existing institutions.

A few examples will illustrate these ideas. One can think about the problem of reconciling institutions from both an issue area and a regional perspective (Oye 1992; Gamble and Payne 1996; Lawrence 1996a). Nested institutions in an issue area are illustrated nicely by the relationship between the international regime for textile and apparel trade (the Long Term Arrangement on Cotton Textiles and its successor arrangement, the Multifibres Arrangement) with respect to the broader regime in which it is nested, the GATT. When the Executive Branch in the USA faced pressure from domestic protectionist interests at the same time as international pressures to keep its market open, the American administration promoted the formation of a sector-specific international regime under GATT auspices. This 'nesting' effort ensured a high degree of conformity with both the GATT's principles and norms as well as with its rules and procedures (Aggarwal 1985, 1994). Although the textile regime deviated from some of the GATT's norms in permitting discriminatory treatment of developing countries' exports, it did adopt and adapt the most-favoured nation norm, which called for developed countries to treat all developing countries in a similar way.

The Asia-Pacific Economic Cooperation grouping (APEC), created in 1989, illustrates the concept of regional nesting. APEC's founding members were extremely worried about undermining the GATT, and sought to reconcile these two institutions by focusing on the notion of 'open regionalism'—that is, the creation of APEC would not bar others from benefiting from any ensuing liberalization in the region. APEC members saw this non-discriminatory liberalization as a better alternative to using Article 24 of the GATT, which permits the formation of discriminatory free trade areas and customs unions, to justify this accord (see Ravenhill, Chapter 6 in this volume). Rather than forming an institution that could conflict with the promotion of GATT initiatives, therefore, APEC founding members attempted to construct an institution that would complement the GATT. Furthermore, APEC members wanted to avoid undermining existing sub-regional organizations, in particular ASEAN. This clearly restricted the level of obligation and delegation that could be transferred to the newly created pan-regional organization (Dupont 1998).

An alternative mode of reconciling institutions would be simply to create 'horizontal' institutions to deal with separate but related activities, as exemplified by the division of labour between the GATT and the Bretton Woods monetary system (IMF and World Bank). In creating institutions for the post-Second-World-War era, policy-makers were concerned about a return to the 1930s period of competitive devaluations, marked by an inward turn among states and the use of protectionist measures. These 'beggar-thy-neighbour' policies were found across economic issue areas, and individual action by each state worked to the detriment of all. As a consequence, the founders of the Bretton Woods monetary system also changed their focus to creating institutions that would help to encourage trade liberalization. By promoting fixed exchange rates through the IMF and liberalization of trade through the GATT, policy-makers hoped that this horizontal institutional division of labour between complementary institutions would lead to freer trade.

Finally, on a regional basis, one can see the development of the European Economic Coal and Steel Community and the Western European Union (WEU) as horizontal organizations. The first was orientated towards strengthening European co-operation in economic matters (which, of course, had important security implications), while the WEU sought to develop a co-ordinated European defence effort.

Conclusion

This chapter has sought to provide a systematic analysis of the problem of collaboration in global political economy through the lenses of types of problems, games, and institutions. We have seen that states may need to collaborate or to co-ordinate their actions to keep economic globalization on track because they may face problems of free riding, an inhibiting fear that their efforts will lead to instability for their economy, and the need to find co-ordination points that have varying costs and benefits to the participants.

The problem of free riding or the difficulty of finding a co-ordination equilibrium is a common one on a number of issues, including trade, monetary co-operation, the environment, human rights, and the like. Despite some limitations, game theory provides a useful insight into the diverse sets of problems states may face in collaborating or in co-ordinating their actions. One of the most commonly used games, the Prisoner's Dilemma, has been utilized to show that, in many issue areas, actors have a strong incentive to defect despite the potential joint gains that they might receive. Yet, as we have shown, many problems in international political economy are not PD games, but instead may be better characterized as Chicken, Assurance, Suasion, or even Harmony games. By examining carefully the types of problems actors face in a particular issue area—the structure of payoffs—game theory provides insight into the constraints on joint action.

It is worth keeping in mind that the preferences that go into creating games are often assumed by many analysts—particularly those in the neo-realist institutionalist and neo-liberal institutionalist camps. Where do preferences come from, and are such preferences amenable to change? It is on this dimension that constructivist arguments focusing on the role of experts, changing knowledge, and possible shifts in preferences through learning may provide a significant insight that can help us to create more logically compelling games.

Once we can establish the basic game structure that actors face, we can better examine the role institutions might play in ensuring more favourable outcomes. In some cases, contrary to the perspective often taken by neo-institutionalists, institutions may not really be necessary to ensure co-operative state action. Hence we examined the types of situations in which self-help might lead to a positive outcome versus those in which institutions might play a genuinely useful role in overcoming problems of collective action.

The role of institutions in fostering collaboration itself produces two puzzles: first, how might states collaborate in the first place to create institutions? This in itself raises an analytical problem that various theories have attempted to address. As we have seen, hegemons may have strong incentives to create institutions to constrain the behaviour of other actors, and possibly their own domestic lobbies. Other approaches, such as neo-liberal institutionalism, focus on the strong incentives that major states may have in creating institutions, and suggest that small numbers of actors may be able to overcome the usual collective action problems that might lead to free riding behaviour. To better understand the process of institutional design, we focused on five dimensions to characterize institutions: membership; the stringency of their rules; their scope; the extent of delegation of power from member states to institutional bodies; and the centralization of tasks within the institution. The types of problems actors face can partially account for specific institutional characteristics. Yet other factors also influence the design of institutions. These include the potential participants in the specific issue area, the knowledge and information available to actors, and the pre-existing institutional context. In particular, with respect to the latter factor, the Asian financial crisis of 1997–8 and the current proliferation of trade agreements raises an important issue about reconciling new and old institutions. The Asian financial crisis generated considerable conflict when some Asian countries sought to create an Asian Monetary Fund. In the end, this effort faltered in the face of IMF and US opposition, but East Asian countries have since sought aggressively to create regional institutions. In trade, the problems of the Doha Round have been followed by a renewed push to move away from broad, multilateral institutions to bilateral free trade agreements and regional accords. The extent to which such arrangements will further undermine the WTO remains a crucial question that will have important implications for prospects of continued economic liberalization in the global economy.

? QUESTIONS

1. Why does globalization increase the pressure for international collaboration?
2. What is the most frequent problem of collaboration in global political economy?
3. What is the thorniest situation of collaboration in global political economy?
4. How can game theory help us understand problems of collaboration?
5. Can enforcement really be carried out in international political economy?
6. How can institutions help overcome obstacles to collaboration?
7. What is the link between the types of problems that countries face in the global economy and their choice of an institution?

8. What are some key characteristics that can be used to describe international institutions?

9. What theories or variables help to account for the choice of specific international institutional characteristics?

 FURTHER READING

■ Aggarwal, V. K. (ed.) (1998), *Institutional Designs for a Complex World: Bargaining, Linkages and Nesting* (Ithaca, NY: Cornell University Press). A collective volume that focuses on the relationships between institutions and the stability of dense institutional settings.

■ Aggarwal, V. K. and Dupont, C. (1999), 'Goods, Games and Institutions', *International Political Science Review*, 20/4: 393–409. The original and technical presentation of our theory that links goods, games and institutions.

■ Cooper, R. N. (ed.) (1989), *Can Nations Agree*? (Washington, DC: Brookings Institution). An insightful collection of work on co-ordination attempts of economic policies among nations outside of institutional settings.

■ Hasenclever, A., Mayer, P., and Rittberger, V. (1997), *Theories of International Regimes* (Cambridge: Cambridge University Press). A collective volume on recent developments on theories of international regimes with application to all domains of international politics.

■ Kaul, I., Grunberg, I., and Stern, M. A. (eds) (1999), *Global Public Goods: International Cooperation in the 21st Century* (New York: Oxford University Press). A collective volume with a range of examples of global public goods in economics, politics, environment with interesting lessons for the future provision of such goods.

■ Keohane, R. O. (1984), *After Hegemony: Cooperation and Discord in the World Political Economy* (Princeton, NJ: Princeton University Press). The classic work on the links between regime change and change in power distribution.

■ Koremenos, B., Lipson, C., and Snidal, D. (2001), 'The Rational Design of International Institutions', *International Organization*, 55/4: 761–799. Introductory article to the latest collective work on institutional design, using insights from game theory and considering various facets of institutions.

■ Krasner, S. D. (ed.) (1983), *International Regimes* (Ithaca, NY: Cornell University Press). The seminal collective volume on international regimes that includes the classic definition of regimes as well as a range of examples in various domains of international politics.

■ Olson, M. (1965), *The Logic of Collective Action: Public Goods and the Theory of Groups* (Cambridge, MA: Harvard University Press). Classic work on collective action and the conditions under which groups of actors may produce public goods.

■ Sandler, T. (1992), *Collective Action: Theory and Applications* (Ann Arbor, Mich.: University of Michigan Press). A comprehensive treatment of the problem of collective action using both basic and advanced formal analytical tools.

■ Snidal, D. (1985), 'Coordination versus Prisoners' Dilemma: Implications for International Co-operation and Regimes', *American Political Science Review*, 79/4: 923–942. The seminal article on the contrast between PD and co-ordination games applied to international relations.

■ **Taylor, M. (1987),** *The Possibility of Cooperation* **(Cambridge: Cambridge University Press).** An advanced treatment of the problem of co-operation using repeated games.

■ **Yarbrough, B. V., and Yarbrough, R. M. (1992),** *Cooperation and Governance in International Trade: The Strategic Organizational Approach* **(Princeton, NJ: Princeton University Press).** An elegant analysis of the problem of governance in trade approached through the lens of transaction costs.

 ## WEB LINKS

● Game theory   **www.gametheory.net/**
                http://william-king.www.drexel.edu/top/eco/game/game.html
● Global public goods   **http://www.globalpublicgoods.org**

 Visit the Online Resource Centre that accompanies this book for more information:
www.oxfordtextbooks.co.uk/orc/ravenhill2e/

4

The Domestic Sources of Foreign Economic Policies

MICHAEL J HISCOX

Chapter Contents

- Introduction
- Policy Preferences
- Institutions
- Conclusions, Extensions, and Complications
- Appendix

Reader's Guide

How should a nation manage its economic ties with the rest of the world? How should the government regulate the flow of goods, people, and investment to and from foreign nations? Debates over foreign economic policies are a recurring, often volatile, feature of national politics in all countries. Indeed, how governments should now be dealing with the multiple facets of 'globalization' is perhaps the single most pressing political issue of our time. It is an issue that has been debated in international institutions, national legislatures, and lecture halls across the world; it has mobilized nationalist populist movements at one end of the political spectrum, and transnational environmental and human rights organizations at the other; and it has led to violent protests and demonstrations in the streets of Seattle, Melbourne, Washington, Genoa, and New York. What are the battle lines in these political debates? How are policies decided in different countries? How do differences in political institutions shape these policy decisions? And how do new ideas and information about policy options filter into politics? This chapter examines each of these questions, focusing on the domestic politics of trade, immigration, investment, and exchange rates.

Introduction

Each government must make choices about how best to manage the way its own economy is linked to the global economy. It must choose whether to open the national market to international trade, whether to liberalize trade with some nations more than with others, and whether to allow more trade in some sectors of the economy than in others. Each government must also decide whether to restrict international flows of investment in different sectors, and whether to regulate immigration and emigration by different types of workers. And it must either fix the exchange rate for the national currency or allow the rate to fluctuate to some degree, in response to supply and demand in international financial markets.

Of course, if every government always made the same choices in all these areas of policy, things would be very simple for us as scholars (and much more predictable for the citizens of the world). But governments in different countries, and at different moments in history, have often chosen radically different foreign economic policies. Some have closed off their national economies almost completely from the rest of the world, imposing strict limits on trade, immigration, and investment—an example is China in the 1960s, which kept itself isolated almost completely from the rest of the world's economies. In other situations, governments have adopted the opposite approach, allowing virtually unfettered economic exchange between their citizens and foreigners—ironically, Hong Kong in the 1960s may be the best example of this type of extreme openness. Most governments today adopt a mixture of policies that fall somewhere in the middle ground between these two extremes, imposing selective controls on activities that affect some sectors of their economy, and restricting exchanges with some foreign countries more than with others. Understanding why governments make the particular choices they do requires careful attention

to the political pressures they face from different domestic groups and the political institutions that regulate the way collective decisions are made and implemented.

Politics, we know, is all about who gets what, when, and how. Different individuals and groups in every society typically have very different views about what their government should do when it comes to setting the policies that regulate international trade, immigration, investment, and exchange rates. These competing demands must be reconciled in some way by the political institutions that govern policy-making. To really understand the domestic origins of foreign economic policies we thus need to perform two critical tasks:

1. Identify or map the policy preferences of different groups in the domestic economy.

2. Specify how political institutions determine the way these preferences are aggregated or converted into actual government decisions.

The first step will require some *economic* analysis. How people are affected by their nation's ties with the global economy, and thus what types of policies they prefer to manage those ties, depends primarily on how they make their living. Steelworkers, for example, typically have very different views from wheat farmers about most foreign economic policies, because these policies rarely affect the steel and wheat industries in a similar fashion. Of critical importance here are the types of assets that individuals own, and how the income earned from these assets is affected by different policy choices.

The second step calls for *political* analysis. How political representatives are elected, how groups organize to lobby or otherwise influence politicians, and how policies are proposed, debated, amended, and passed in legislatures, and then implemented by government agencies, all depend on the structure of political institutions. Democratically elected leaders face very different institutional constraints from military dictators, of course, and even among democracies there is quite a wide range of institutional variation that can have a large impact on the behaviour of policy-makers.

These two analytical steps put together like this, combining both economic and political analysis in tandem, are generally referred to as the *political economy* approach to the study of policy outcomes. In the next two sections we shall consider each of the two analytical steps in some detail, examining the domestic sources of policies in the areas of trade, immigration, investment, and exchange rates. We shall then shift gears a little, and consider the ways in which ideas and information might affect policy-making. We shall also discuss linkages between the different policy dimensions and non-economic issues, focusing on environmental and human rights concerns, and how they feature in debates over foreign economic policies. Finally, in the conclusion, to link all this to the discussion of international collaboration and co-ordination in the previous chapter, we shall consider briefly the impact of domestic politics on bargaining over economic issues between governments at the international level.

Policy Preferences

The guiding assumption here is that, when it comes to taking positions on how to regulate ties with the global economy, individuals and groups are fundamentally concerned with how different policy choices affect their incomes. Of course, people may also have important non-material concerns that affect their attitudes toward foreign economic policies. Many people are concerned about the ways in which globalization affects national security, for example, and they worry about its impact on traditional cultures, on the world's environment, and on human rights; and these concerns may have a direct impact on their views about the regulation of international trade, immigration, and investment. We shall discuss some of these important considerations in more detail later in the chapter. But we begin here with the simplest possible framework in which economic policies are evaluated only in terms of their economic effects. Given that organized producer groups have almost always been the most vocal participants in domestic debates about foreign economic policies, and the debates themselves have been couched mainly in economic terms, this seems an appropriate way to begin.

Trade

The dramatic growth in international trade over the last few decades has intensified political debate over the costs and benefits of trade openness. In the United States, the controversy surrounding the creation of the North American Free Trade Agreement (NAFTA) in 1993 was especially intense, and similar arguments have arisen in Europe over the issue of enlargement of the European Union, and over attempts to reform the Common Agricultural Policy (CAP). Rapid trade policy reforms have also generated a significant political backlash in many developing nations, and recent years have witnessed violent protests and demonstrations by groups from a variety of countries that hope to disrupt meetings of the World Trade Organization (WTO). Political leaders around the world frequently voice concerns about the negative effects of trade, and the need to protect their firms and workers from foreign competition.

What is behind all this political fuss and bother? At first glance it may seem puzzling that there is so much conflict over trade. After all, the most famous insight from international economics is the proof that trade provides mutual gains; that is, when countries exchange goods and services they are all generally better off. Trade allows each country to specialize in producing those goods and services in which it has a comparative advantage, and in doing so world welfare is improved (see Appendix 4.1 on page 132).

While there are gains from trade for all countries *in the aggregate*, what makes trade so controversial is that, among individuals within each country, trade creates winners and losers. How trade affects different individuals depends on how they earn their living. To flesh out this story, economists have traditionally relied on a very simple theory of trade devised by two Swedish economists, Eli Heckscher and Bertil Ohlin. In the Heckscher–Ohlin model of trade, each nation's comparative advantage is traced to its particular endowments of different factors of production: that is, basic inputs such as land, labour, and capital that are used in different proportions in the production of different goods and services. Since the costs of these inputs in each country will depend on their availability, differences in factor endowments across countries will create differences in comparative advantage. Each country will tend to export items whose production requires intensive use of the factors with which it is abundantly endowed relative to other nations; conversely, each country will import goods whose production requires intensive use of factors that are relatively scarce. Countries well endowed with land, such as Australia and Canada, are expected to export agricultural products (for example, wheat and wool), while importing products that require the intensive use of labour (for example, textiles and footwear) from more labour-abundant economies like China and India. The advanced economies of Europe, Japan, and the United States, well endowed with capital relative to the rest of the world, should export capital-intensive products (for example, automobiles and pharmaceuticals), while importing labour-intensive goods from less developed trading partners where supplies of capital are scarce compared to supplies of labour.

Building on this simple model of trade, Wolfgang Stolper and Paul Samuelson (1941) derived a famous theorem in 1941 that outlined the likely effects of trade on the real incomes of different sets of individuals within any economy. According to the Stolper–Samuelson theorem, trade benefits those who own the factors of production with which the economy is relatively well endowed, but hurts owners of scarce factors. The reasoning is straightforward: by encouraging specialization in each economy in export-orientated types of production, trade increases the demand for locally abundant factors (and bids up the earnings of those who own those factors), while reducing demand for locally scarce factors (and lowering the earnings of owners of such factors). In Australia and Canada, the theorem tells us, landowners should benefit most from trade, while workers can expect lower real wages as a consequence of increased imports of labour-intensive goods. In Europe, Japan, and the United States, the theorem predicts a fairly simple class division over trade: the trade issue should benefit owners of capital at the expense of workers. The converse should hold in relatively labour-abundant (and capital-scarce) developing economies such as China and India, where trade will raise the wages of workers relative to the profits earned by local owners of capital.

By revealing how trade benefits some people while making others worse off, the Stolper–Samuelson theorem thus accounts for why trade is such a divisive political issue. The theorem also provides a neat way to map the policy preferences of individuals in each economy. In each nation, owners of locally *abundant* factors should support greater trade openness, while owners of locally *scarce* factors should be protectionist.

There is a good deal of evidence in the histories of political conflict over trade in a variety of nations that fits with this simple prediction (see Rogowski 1989). In Australia, for example, the first national elections in 1901 were fought between a Free Trade party, representing predominantly rural voters, and a Protectionist party supported overwhelmingly by urban owners of capital and labour.

A very similar kind of political division characterized most debates over trade policy in Canada in the late nineteenth century, with support for trade openness emanating mainly from farmers in the western provinces. In Europe and Japan, in contrast, much of the opposition to trade over the last century or so has come from agricultural interests, anxious to block cheap imports of farm products from abroad. In the United States and Europe, at least since the 1960s, labour unions have voiced some of the loudest opposition to trade openness and called for import restrictions aimed at protecting jobs in labour-intensive industries threatened by foreign competition.

On the other hand, political divisions and coalitions in trade politics often appear to contradict this simple model of preferences. It is quite common to see workers and owners in the same industry banding together to lobby for protective import barriers, for example, in contemporary debates about policy in Europe and the United States, even though the Stolper–Samuelson theorem tells us that capital and labour are supposed to have directly opposing views about trade in these economies. So what is going on here? The critical problem is that the theorem is derived by assuming that factors of production are highly mobile between different industries in each economy. An alternative approach to mapping the effects of trade on incomes, often referred to as the **specific factors model** allows instead that it can be quite costly to move factors of production between different sectors in the economy. That is, different types of land, labour skills, and capital equipment often have a very limited or specific use

BOX 4.1

The Repeal of the Corn Laws

The story of the repeal of Britain's protectionist Corn Laws in 1846 is perhaps still the best-known example of a political clash over trade policy that fits nicely with the **Stolper–Samuelson theorem**. With the revival of foreign trade after the Napoleonic Wars, policy debates in Britain began to focus on the protectionist Corn Laws that restricted importation of various grains (wheat, rye, barley, and oats, as well as peas and beans), defended resolutely by the landowning elite. Pressure for reform came most strongly from manufacturers, especially textile producers in Leicester and Manchester, anxious to reduce labour costs (see McCord 1958). It was these manufacturers who formed the leadership of the Anti-Corn Law League in 1838, and a cotton manufacturer, Richard Cobden, became the League's most famous advocate. The push for reform soon drew a larger following among both the urban middle and working classes, and attracted support from the working-class Chartist reform movement, which organized the 'bigger loaf' campaign in the 1840s. The effects were soon felt in Parliament, transformed by the Great Reform Act of 1832 and the enfranchisement of voters in the large industrial centres of the West Riding. Cobden himself entered Parliament in 1841, campaigning with the cry 'You must untax the people's bread!' and the League stepped up its campaign with a storm of pamphlets, petition drives, public meetings, and addresses to labour unions. The widespread economic distress of the early 1840s had a great impact on the Tory prime minister, Robert Peel. He introduced a sliding scale for grain duties in 1841 and then reduced those rates in 1842 and 1844, in an attempt to ease the food crisis, but this aroused fierce opposition from landed interests and from within Conservative ranks. The failure of the potato crop in 1845, and the ensuing food crisis, gave Peel the pretext to go further. Amid reports of widespread starvation, the prime minister pushed through a bill to repeal the Corn Laws altogether, with support from both Liberals and Radicals. The conflict over repeal split the Conservatives irrevocably. Once 'purified' of their Peelite faction, the Tories (known for years as the Protectionists) were increasingly isolated on the trade issue in Parliament. Peel's supporters, including William Gladstone, gravitated to the Liberals, and their free-trade platform drew on an immense base of support among urban industrialists, the middle classes, and workers. Gladstone's first budget as prime minister in 1860 effectively eliminated all remaining protectionist duties in Britain.

(or range of uses) to which they can be put when it comes to making products. The plant and machinery used in modern manufacturing industries is very specialized: the presses used to stamp out automobile bodies are designed only for that purpose, for example, and cannot be adapted easily or quickly to perform other tasks. Steel factories cannot easily be converted into pharmaceutical factories or software design houses. Nor can steelworkers quickly adapt their skills and become chemical engineers or computer programmers.

In the specific factors model, the real incomes of different individuals are tied very closely to the fortunes of the particular industries in which they make their living. Individuals employed or invested in export industries benefit from trade according to this model, while those who are attached to import-competing industries are harmed (see Jones 1971; Mussa 1974). In the advanced economies of Europe and the United States, the implication is that owners and employees in export-orientated industries such as aerospace, pharmaceuticals, computer software, construction equipment, and financial services, should be much more supportive of trade than their counterparts in, say, the steel, textiles, and footwear industries, which face intense pressure from import competition. There is much evidence supporting these predictions in the real world of trade politics, especially in the debates over trade in the most advanced economies, where technologies (and the skills that complement them) have become increasingly specialized in many different manufacturing and service industries, and even in various areas of agriculture and mining production (see Magee 1980; Hiscox 2002). In the recent debates over regional and multilateral trade agreements in the United States, for example, some of the most vociferous opposition to removing barriers to trade has come from owners and workers aligned together in the steel and textile industries.

The leading research on the political economy of trade now assumes routinely that the specific factors approach is the most appropriate way to think about trade policy preferences, at least in the contemporary context in the advanced economies

(see Grossman and Helpman 1994; Rodrik 1995), so we shall rely on it for the most part in the discussions below. This model, it is worth noting, is still nested within the broader Heckscher–Ohlin theory that explains trade according to differences in factor endowments. Newer theories of trade, motivated by some clear evidence that not all trade seems to fit well with this simple endowments-based theory (for example, Europe, Japan, and the United States all importing automobiles from each other), have made some significant departures from the standard Heckscher–Ohlin framework. One innovation is to allow that technologies of production and tastes among consumers may vary substantially across countries. Such differences might affect the types of products an economy will be likely to export and import, but the predictions about trade policy preferences derived from the specific factors approach are not otherwise affected: individuals engaged in export industries favour trade, while those in import-competing industries oppose trade. A more complicated innovation in trade theory allows for the possibility of economies of scale. In some industries requiring large investments of capital, the largest firms may enjoy such a dramatic cost advantage over smaller firms that those markets tend to be dominated by only a few, very large, corporations. In such cases, in which firms compete with one another and with foreign rivals for different market niches, trade may have different effects for firms in the same industry. These types of complexities are difficult to incorporate into a broadly applicable model of trade, however, so we shall not pursue them here. Although it might be pointed out that large firms that enjoy economies of scale in production also tend to engage in foreign investment, locating parts of their enterprise in different nations. Below we shall discuss the political implications of this type of multinational investment in more detail.

Immigration

Of course globalization is not simply a matter of trade in goods and services; it also involves international flows of the factors of production themselves—the migration of workers between nations, and international investment and lending that transfers capital across borders. There is not a radical difference between how we analyse these phenomena and how we examine trade, but neither is the analysis identical in terms of the economic effects and the policy preferences we anticipate for different sets of individuals within each nation.

Political debates about immigration policy have been rising in volume and intensity in recent years in almost all Western economies. On the one hand, immigration is seen by many as an economic and cultural lifeline that can supply firms in key industries with skilled workers while also injecting new artistic and intellectual life into the nation. On the other hand, many people are concerned that immigrants take jobs away from local workers and create ethnic enclaves that can balkanize a nation and lead to more crime and other social ills. These latter concerns have encouraged the recent imposition of much tighter immigration controls in many countries, while also nurturing the growth of extremist anti-immigrant political movements in several European countries and increasing the incidence of hate crimes directed toward immigrants. The debate seems certain to continue in the years ahead, and to grow fiercer.

Historically, immigration has almost always been more politically controversial than has trade. The issue is still so sensitive that tight restrictions on immigration are nearly universal. Again, as with limits on trade, such restrictions make little sense if we look only at the *aggregate* welfare effects of international labour flows. It is easy to demonstrate that when labour is free to migrate to countries where it can be more productive (and earn correspondingly higher wages), there will be an increase in total world output of goods and services (see Krugman and Obstfeld 2000: ch. 7). And total output must also increase in any economy that allows more immigrants to enter. This expansion in production makes it possible, in principle, for everyone to enjoy higher standards of living. Migration flows can actually serve the same economic purpose as trade flows, responding to price signals to improve economic efficiency. Indeed, in the standard Heckscher–Ohlin model of trade described above, trade is simply a function of country differences in endowments of labour and other factors, and so international movements of goods and factors are in fact substitutes for one another. Countries abundantly endowed with labour, such as China and India, and in which wages are thus quite low compared to wages paid elsewhere, are not only natural suppliers of labour-intensive exports for the world market, they are also natural suppliers of labour itself (that is, emigrants).

As we already know, however, what matters most for politics is not that aggregate welfare gains are possible from exchanges (of goods or factors) between economies; what matters most is that some people gain and others lose. Which individuals are most likely to oppose immigration? Again, the standard economic analysis emphasizes the importance of the different types of productive factors—including land and capital, as above, with an additional distinction made between high-skilled labour (or 'human capital') and low-skilled or blue-collar labour. What is critical, as you will have already guessed, is the impact that immigration can have on relative supplies of factors of production in the local economy. If immigrants have low skill levels, as is typically assumed when discussing the effects of immigration in the advanced economies of Europe and North America, allowing more immigration will increase the local supply of low-skilled labour relative to other factors. The effect is to lower the real wages of all low-skilled workers, as the new arrivals price themselves into employment by accepting lower pay, while raising the real earnings for local owners of land, capital, and skills, as demand for these other factors increases. Of course, if a nation only allows *high-skilled* workers to immigrate, the effect will be lower real wages for high-skilled workers, but higher real earnings for low-skilled workers and owners of land and capital.

The basic results from this simple model of the impact of immigration—often referred to as 'factor-proportions' analysis (see Borjas *et al.* 1996;

Borjas 1999)—are widely applicable. Immigration always harms local workers with similar skill levels to those of the arriving workers, while benefiting local owners of other factors. Even if we allow for high levels of trade, which can partially offset the impact of immigration as economies adjust to the change in factor supplies by importing less of some goods that can now be produced locally at a lower cost, the effects are always in the same direction—although they may become very small in size, and even disappear altogether, if the local economy is small relative to other economies (Leamer and Levinsohn 1995). The effects are even generally the same if we allow that the skills of workers can be highly 'specific' to particular industries, though the impact of immigration on earnings will be larger for high-skilled (specific) workers in some industries than in others. Any inflow of unskilled labour will be especially valuable for high-skilled workers in sectors that use unskilled labour more intensively, for example, but it will still benefit all high-skilled workers since output (and demand for their skills) will rise in each industry. Conversely, an inflow of any type of high-skilled labour will generate the largest decline in earnings for high-skilled workers in the same industry (those who own the same specific skills as the immigrants). But it will also hurt high-skilled workers in other industries in the local economy whose earnings will suffer, albeit in a relatively minor way, as demand for their types of specific skills falls in response to the expansion taking place in the industry into which the skilled immigrants have moved.

So again, we have a very simple and generally applicable way of identifying the policy preferences of individuals. Individuals can be expected to oppose any policy that would permit immigration of foreign workers with similar skill levels, but they will support other types of immigration. Individuals who make their living from ownership of land and capital are likely to be the strongest supporters of more open immigration laws. If we look at the political debates over immigration laws in particular countries, the general alignment of interests seems to fit rather well with these expectations. Typically,

the most vocal opposition to changes in immigration laws that would permit more low-skilled immigration comes from labour unions representing blue-collar workers. In the United States, for example, the AFL–CIO has traditionally taken a very tough stance in favour of restrictive immigration laws and border control measures aimed at stemming illegal immigration into the country from Mexico (Tichenor 2002: 209). American business and farm associations have taken a very different position, often lobbying for more lenient treatment of illegal immigrants and for larger quotas in various non-immigrant working visa categories. In similar fashion, trade union federations in Britain, France, and Germany have raised protests about enlargement of the European Union and the possible influx of low-skilled workers into their economies from new member countries in Southern and Eastern Europe. High-skilled workers have not shied away from immigration politics either, often lobbying to restrict inflows of immigrants with skills that match their own and would thus pose a competitive threat in the local labour market—the American Medical Association, for example, the organization that represents doctors in the United States, has pushed hard in recent years to limit the number of foreign doctors granted visa status while also making it more difficult for them to obtain licences to practice (see Box 4.2).

This simple approach to the political economy of immigration restrictions is very useful, at least as a first step towards understanding the political forces that are likely to shape policy outcomes. It is extremely difficult, however, to analyse the politics of immigration without examining non-economic concerns among individuals related to questions of culture and identity. Immigration policy, after all, has a profound impact on who makes up the nation itself. In this way it is quite different from trade policy. A great deal of recent research suggests that divisions among individuals over immigration policy are most strongly related to fundamental differences in cultural values associated with ethnic and racial tolerance and cosmopolitanism (for example, Espenshade and

Calhoun 1993; Citrin *et al.* 1997; McLaren 2001). This question of whether preferences related to non-economic issues have a profound effect on attitudes towards foreign economic policies is one that we shall return to below.

Foreign investment

Capital can also move from one country to another. These movements usually do not take the form of a physical relocation of some existing buildings and machinery from a site in one nation to another site abroad (the equivalent to worker migration). Instead, they take the form of financial transactions between citizens of different nations that transfer ownership rights over assets: a firm in one country buys facilities abroad that it can operate as a subsidiary, for example, or individuals in one country buy shares in foreign companies, or a bank in one country lends money to foreign firms. All such transactions increase the stock of capital available for productive use in one country, and decrease the stock of capital in another country.

The dramatic increase in the volume of international capital flows since the 1960s, outstripping the increase in trade, has had a profound impact on the international economy. Short-term flows of capital in the form of portfolio investment (purchases of company shares and other forms of securities, including government bonds), which can change direction quite rapidly in response to news and speculation about changing macroeconomic conditions and possible adjustments in exchange rates, have had a major impact on the choices governments can make when it comes to monetary and exchange-rate policies (see Pauly, Chapter 8 in this volume). Longer-term capital flows in the form of 'direct foreign investment' (where the purchase of foreign assets by a firm based in one country gives it ownership control of a firm located on foreign soil), have perhaps been even more politically controversial since the activities of these multinational firms have had major and highly visible effects in the host nations in which they manage affiliates (see Thun, Chapter 11 in this volume). Many critics of multinational corporations fear that the economic leverage enjoyed by these firms, especially in small,

---

BOX 4.2

The 'New World' Closes its Doors to Immigrants

Beginning in the 1840s and 1850s, there was a huge surge in emigration from England, Ireland, and other parts of Europe and Asia to the 'New World' economies in North and South America and Australasia, where labour was relatively scarce and wage rates comparatively high. The rudimentary border controls and open policy towards immigrants in these frontier economies meant that labour flows responded quite quickly to economic events—and, in particular, to gold rushes and other 'booms' associated with the construction of railways and the birth of new industries. Over time, however, as labour unions became more organized and politically influential in the New World economies, greater restrictions were imposed on immigration. The political pressure for limits on immigration became especially strong during economic recessions, when local rates of unemployment

often rose swiftly, and labour groups blamed new immigrants for taking jobs away from 'native' workers (see Goldin 1994). Between the 1880s and the 1920s, all the New World economies gradually closed themselves off to immigration (see O'Rourke and Williamson 1999). In the United States, the first bans were imposed on Chinese immigrants in 1882, and then on all Asian immigrants in 1917, when a tough literacy test was also introduced as a way of limiting inflows of low-skilled workers. In 1921, the Emergency Quota Act placed severe restrictions on all new arrivals. The strongest political support for these measures came from north-eastern states with highly urbanized populations working in manufacturing industries, where labour unions were particularly well organized and vocal.

ping nations, can undermine national ...es aimed at improving environment stand-...and human rights. The political debate over direct foreign investment is thus highly charged.

Tight restrictions on both short- and long-term investment by foreigners have been quite common historically, although the controls have been much less strict than those typically imposed on immigration. Clearly, these controls cannot be motivated by a desire for economic efficiency. If such controls are removed and capital is allowed to move freely to those locations in which it is used most productively (and where it will be rewarded, as a result, with higher earnings), it is easy to show that the total output of goods and services will be increased in both the country to which the capital is flowing and in the world economy as a whole. Again, this expansion in aggregate production makes it possible, in principle, to raise the standard of living for people everywhere. International investment, just like the migration of workers examined above, can serve the same economic purpose that is otherwise served by trade. International flows of capital substitute for the exports of capital-intensive goods and services in the benchmark Heckscher–Ohlin model. In general, then, we can expect that the advanced industrial economies of Europe and the United States, which have abundant local supplies of capital for investment, and in which rates of return on capital are thus quite low compared with earnings elsewhere, are the natural suppliers of capital (as well as capital-intensive goods) to poorer nations, in which capital is in relatively scarce supply.

One point worth making here about the likely direction of capital flows concerns the distinction between lending and portfolio flows of capital and direct foreign investment (see Ravenhill, Chapter 1 in this volume). It is reasonable to imagine that the former types of international investment are driven purely by the quest to maximize (risk-adjusted) rates of return on capital, in line with the Heckscher–Ohlin model. With the caveat that capital-poor developing countries are often politically unstable, and high levels of risk can deter investors, we should nevertheless expect large flows

of capital from the industrial nations to the developing world. It is much less clear that economy-wide differences in rates of return are critical for explaining patterns in direct foreign investment. There is certainly a considerable amount of direct investment by European, American, and Japanese firms in developing nations, with many firms setting up a 'vertical' multinational structure of enterprises that locates land or labour-intensive parts of the production process in developing nations. But the vast bulk of direct foreign investment in the modern world economy in fact takes the form of capital flows between the industrial economies themselves, with firms creating 'horizontal' structures in which similar functions are performed in facilities in different locations (see Graham and Krugman 1995: 36). This type of investment does not fit well with the standard Heckscher–Ohlin predictions based on factor endowments, and is best explained instead by the special advantages that firms in some industries gain by jumping borders (and trade barriers), and by internalizing transactions within the firm itself. Firms that rely heavily on specialized technologies, and management and marketing expertise, may have a hard time selling these kinds of intangible assets to foreign companies it would like to work with as suppliers or distributors; instead, it may make far more sense to keep all these relationships within the firm (see Hymer 1976; Caves 1982). Many of these types of horizontal multinational firms also appear to have been established to secure access to foreign markets into which they might not otherwise be able to sell because they faced trade barriers. This 'tariff-jumping' motive was a big factor in motivating Japanese auto firms to set up manufacturing facilities in both Europe and North America beginning in the 1980s. The implication is that there is often a strong connection between the effects of trade policies and investment (and investment restrictions), a topic we shall return to in the final section of the chapter (see also Thun, Chapter 11 in this volume).

Now, putting aside the aggregate welfare gains that international movements of capital make possible, which individuals are likely to benefit from such capital flows, and which individuals will lose out? Here we can simply apply the logic of the same 'factor proportions' approach we used above to outline the effects of immigration. We might distinguish between different types of capital, in the same way that we distinguished between low- and high-skilled labour above, and set apart lending and short-term or portfolio investment flows from direct foreign investment. But to keep things simple here, we shall just consider them all as a single form of capital. What is critical here, of course, is the impact that inflows of any foreign capital have on relative supplies of factors of production in the local economy. Allowing more inflows of capital from abroad will increase the local supply of capital relative to other factors, and thus lower real returns for local owners of capital. At the same time, inflows of investment will raise the real earnings of local owners of land and labour by increasing demand for these other factors of production.

Again, even allowing for the fact that trade flows can partially offset the impact of international movements of factors of production—economies may adjust by importing lower quantities of some goods that are now less costly to produce at home—the direction of the effects on the incomes of different groups is always the same. Local owners of capital are disadvantaged by inflows of foreign capital; while local landowners and workers (in all categories) are better off. These effects may diminish in size in cases in which the local economy is small relative to others, as we noted above when discussing the income effects of immigration, but they are always working in the same direction. And again, in parallel with the analysis of immigration flows, these income effects are not affected drastically by allowing that capital can take forms that are highly 'specific' to particular industries—though the effects may be larger for owners of some types of capital than others. This is especially relevant when we think about direct foreign investment, which typically involves the relocation of a particular set of manufacturing or marketing activities that require very specific types of technologies in a particular industry. An inflow of any type of specific capital will, of course, result in a decline in earnings for local owners of capital in the same industry; it will also hurt all others who own specific types of capital used in different industries—in a more marginal way, of course—as demand for their assets will fall in response to the expansion taking place in the industry favoured by foreign investment.

We can thus expect that policies allowing greater inflows of foreign capital will be strongly opposed by individuals who own capital in the local economy, but such policies will be supported by local landowners and workers. There is some evidence that does fit well with these basic predictions. Perhaps the best example involves the way European and American auto companies have supported restrictions on the operations of local affiliates of their Japanese rivals since the 1980s. In Europe, auto firms pushed hard for an agreement with Japan that included cars produced in Japanese affiliates within the limits set on the total Japanese market share of the European auto market. In the United States, after some initial hesitation (perhaps reflecting the fact that they had themselves set up numerous foreign transplant firms around the world) the US auto firms supported a variety of proposals for 'domestic content' laws that would have placed local affiliates of Japanese auto makers at a considerable disadvantage by disrupting their relationships with parts suppliers at home (Crystal 2003). The 'big three' American firms (Ford, General Motors, and Chrysler) also seized the opportunity to demand high local content requirements in the **rules of origin** for autos in the negotiations over the 1993 North American Free Trade Agreement, ensuring that they would have a major advantage over Japanese transplants producing cars in Mexico for the North American market. Interestingly, the workers we would expect to be strongly supportive of incoming Japanese investment in the auto industry, represented by the United Auto Workers union, were in fact quite lukewarm—perhaps because they had long advocated that tough domestic content rules be applied to American firms, to prevent them from transplanting their parts manufacturing facilities to Canada and Mexico, and perhaps also in response to concerns that the foreign transplants setting up in southern American states such as Tennessee (Nissan) and Kentucky (Toyota) were not employing union members.

Foreign investment tends to be even more politically controversial in developing nations, where the behaviour of large foreign corporations can have profound effects on the local economy and on local politics. One particular concern among critics of multinational firms has been the role that several large corporations have apparently played in supporting authoritarian governments that have restricted political organization among labour groups, limited growth in wage rates, and permitted firms to mistreat workers and pollute the environment (see Evans 1979; Klein 2002). While the evidence is not very clear, in some cases, local owners of capital may well have muted their opposition to investments by foreign firms in order to support authoritarian policies adopted by military regimes: in Nigeria, for example, where Shell (the European oil company) has long been the major foreign investor, or more recently in Myanmar, where Unocal (an American oil and gas firm) is the key foreign player. But the basic competitive tension between local capitalists and foreign firms (whose entry into the economy bids down local profits) is typically very obvious even in these unstable and non-democratic environments, as local firms have often encouraged their governments to impose severe restrictions on foreign investments, including onerous regulations stipulating that foreign firms use local rather than imported inputs, exclusion from key sectors of the economy, and even nationalization (seizure) of firms' assets (Jenkins 1987: 172). Newer evidence suggests that, as we might expect given the preferences of labour in capital-poor developing nations, left-wing governments backed by organized labour have made the strongest efforts to lure foreign firms to make investments (Pinto 2003).

So far we have considered only the issue of whether governments relax restrictions on *inflows* of foreign capital. Of course, governments can and often do act to influence how much investment flows out of their economies. And the same holds for labour flows, as governments often try to affect *emigration* as well as immigration—many governments, in countries as diverse as Australia, Canada, and India, are worried about a 'brain drain' of skilled workers and professionals, for example, and have adopted a range of policies to discourage or tax such labour flows. But the issue of outward direct investment, often involving the 'outsourcing' of jobs by multinational firms to their affiliates in labour-abundant (low-wage) nations, has become an especially salient political issue recently in Europe and the United States. The political divisions over the issue are largely what we expect from the factor proportions theory: those who own capital are strongly opposed to any restrictions on their ability to invest it abroad in order to earn higher profits, but restrictions on outward investment are strongly supported by local workers, who understand that capital outflows will reduce their real earnings. In the United States, for example, the most ardent advocates of legislation that would raise the tax burden on profits earned abroad by American corporations has been the AFL–CIO and those workers among its membership that have been hit hardest by outsourcing (for example, labour unions in the textile and auto industries). Interestingly, these labour unions have often had support from environmental and human rights groups concerned that competition among developing countries to attract new investments from multinational firms may produce a race to the bottom in environmental and labour standards. Coalitions of labour unions and human rights groups have waged campaigns to try to force US corporations to adhere to strict codes of conduct abroad. We shall discuss these types of multi-issue political coalitions below.

Exchange rates

Of course, a critical difference between transactions that take place between individuals living in the same country and transactions between people in different countries is that the latter require that people can convert one national currency into another. If a firm in Australia wants to import DVDs from a film studio in the United States, for example, it will need to exchange its Australian dollars for US dollars to pay the American company. The rate at which this conversion takes place will obviously affect the transaction: the more Australian dollars it takes to buy the number of US dollars required (the price of the DVDs), the more costly are the imports for movie-loving Australian buyers. All the trade and investment transactions taking place every day in the world economy are affected by the rates at which currencies are exchanged.

Before the First World War, almost all governments fixed the value of their currency in terms of gold, thereby creating an international monetary system in which all rates of conversion between individual currencies were held constant (for further discussion of this international **gold standard**, see Ravenhill, Box 1.3, page 10 in this volume). Between the Second World War and 1973, most currencies were fixed in value to the US dollar, the most important currency in the post-war world economy. In this system, often referred to as the **Bretton Woods** system (see Ravehnhill, Box 1.4,

page 14 in this volume), the United States agreed to guarantee the value of the dollar by committing to exchange dollars for gold at a set price of $35 per ounce. Since 1973, when the Nixon administration officially abandoned the fixed rate between the dollar and gold, all the major currencies have essentially been allowed to fluctuate freely in value in world financial markets (see Helleiner, Chapter 7 in this volume). Among developing nations, however, many governments continue to fix the value of their currency in terms of dollars or another of the major currencies (see Frieden *et al.* 2001). And groups of nations in different regions of the world, including the members of the European Union, have made separate efforts to stabilize exchange rates at the regional level, even progressing to the adoption of a common regional currency.

The fundamental choice each government must make involves decided whether to allow the value of the national currency to fluctuate freely in response to market demand and supply, or instead fix the value of the currency in terms of some other currency or external standard—typically, the currency of a major trading partner or, as was common in the

BOX 4.3

Investment, Imperialism, and the 'Race for Africa'

Beginning in the 1870s, vast quantities of investment capital flowed from the centres of finance in Western Europe to the rest of the world, providing the capital necessary to develop railways and telegraph networks, ports, and new mining industries in eastern and central Europe, the Americas, and much of Asia. Beginning in the 1880s, the political context in which these foreign investments were made began to change drastically as an intense race developed among the major powers for political control of territories in Africa and Eastern Asia. Governments in Britain, France, Germany, and Belgium made imperial expansion in these regions their most urgent foreign policy priority. Seizing political control of territories in which there was often no clear or stable governing authority, or at least not one capable of defending the area from conquest by outside force, was a way to

safeguard the investments that were being made in these territories (mostly in the production of raw materials, such as cotton, silk, rubber, vegetable oils, and other products of tropical climates, as well as railways and ports, that were all very vulnerable to seizure). These imperial policies were supported most strongly by financial interests and conservative parties, typically backed by commercial and shipping industries as well, and by military leaders anxious about the security implications of falling behind rivals in the control of strategic territories and ports. British economist, J. A. Hobson (1902/1948), and following him, Lenin (1917/1996), famously interpreted the imperial expansion of this time as the natural consequence of owners of capital needing access to new investment opportunities overseas; imperialism was, in Hobson's terms, 'excessive capital in search of investment'.

past, gold (a precious metal valued highly in most societies throughout history). When a government chooses to fix the value of the national currency, it sets the official rate of exchange and commits itself to buy the currency at that fixed rate when requested to by private actors or foreign governments. Between a 'pure float' and a fixed exchange rate there are intermediate options: a government can choose a target value for the exchange rate and only allow the currency to fluctuate in value within some range around the target rate. The wider this range, of course, the more policy approximates floating the currency.

When it comes to trade, immigration, and investment, economists agree almost universally on the policy choice that is best for maximizing national (and world) output, and hence general standards of living: removing barriers to all types of international exchange is optimal, because it allows resources to be allocated in the most productive way. There is no similar consensus, however, on the best approach to currency policy. Fixing the exchange rate has both pros and cons, and it is not always clear which are larger. By eliminating fluctuations in the exchange rate, fixing makes international trade and investment less costly for firms and individuals, since they will not need to worry that the benefits from these international transactions will be affected adversely by some sudden, unexpected shift in exchange rates. By doing away with exchange-rate risk, fixing allows the economy to benefit more fully from international trade and investment. But what is the downside? What does the government give up by pledging to buy or sell its own currency on request at the official rate of exchange? The answer, in short, is control over **monetary policy**.

A nation's monetary policy regulates the supply of money (and the associated cost of credit) in order to manage aggregate levels of economic activity, and hence levels of inflation and unemployment. Governments typically use monetary policy to counter economic cycles: they expand the supply of money and lower the cost of credit during recessions to increase economic activity and promote job creation, and restrict the supply of money and raise the cost

of borrowing during 'booms' to slow economic activity and control inflation. When a government commits to fixing the exchange rate, it effectively gives up the ability to tailor monetary policy to manage domestic economic conditions. To see why, just imagine what happens to money supply if, at the given exchange rate, the nation's residents spend more on foreign goods, services and assets in any given period than foreigners buy from firms and individuals in that nation: the country's **balance of payments**, which registers the value of all transactions with the rest of the world, will be in deficit. This means that that there is less overall demand for the country's currency than for the currencies of other countries (needed for residents to buy foreign products and assets). To satisfy this excess demand for foreign currencies and to maintain the exchange rate at the fixed level, the government will be a net buyer of its own currency, selling off its reserves of foreign currencies (or gold). The automatic effect of maintaining the fixed exchange rate in these conditions, then, is to reduce the total supply of the nation's money in circulation and slow domestic economic activity. Just the opposite should occur when the nation runs a balance of payments surplus: excess demand for its currency compared to other currencies will require that the government increases the supply of its money in circulation, thus stimulating economic activity.

In effect, then, fixing the value of the currency makes monetary policy a hostage to exchange-rate policy. Even if a government sets the exchange rate at a level that it hopes will generate no balance of payments deficits or surpluses, since the balance of international transactions in any period will depend heavily on external economic conditions and events in foreign countries, it has very little control. A recession abroad, for example, will reduce purchases of a nation's products by foreigners and lead to a deficit in the balance of payments, and so, if currency values are fixed firmly, this recession will be 'transmitted' to the home nation by the subsequent reduction in its money supply.

The crux of the choice between fixed and floating exchange rates is the choice between stability and policy control: a stable exchange rate will increase the economic benefits attainable from international trade and investment, but this requires giving up the ability to adjust monetary policy to suit domestic economic conditions. Governments in the most advanced economies have generally decided that policy control is more important to them than exchange-rate stability, at least since the early 1970s. Governments in smaller, developing nations have mainly chosen exchange-rate stability over policy control. In part this is because these countries tend to rely more heavily on trade and foreign investment as sources of economic growth. This choice is also more attractive for governments in smaller countries trying to defeat chronic inflation. Government promises to deal with runaway inflation in these countries may not be regarded as credible by private actors if governments in the past have shown a tendency to act irresponsibly (for example, by printing and spending large amounts of money) when facing electoral challenges. Since the expectations that private actors have about government policy feed directly into the prices (and wages) set, inflationary expectations can have devastating effects. In such circumstances, fixing the nation's currency in terms of the currency of a major trading partner with a comparatively low rate of inflation can serve an important function, providing a way for the government to commit itself more credibly to a low-inflation monetary policy. In essence, by committing to keep the exchange rate fixed, the government is ceding control of monetary policy in a very clear and visible way, and anchoring inflation at home to the inflation rate in the partner country (see Giavazzi and Pagano 1988; Broz and Frieden 2001).

In terms of the effects on aggregate welfare, the wisdom of fixing exchange rates is thus not always crystal clear. The best or most preferred policy for different sets of individuals within each country can similarly be difficult to identify. Consider first the case in which we assume that factors of production are mobile between sectors in the domestic economy (they are not 'specific' to particular sectors), and so we can apply the logic of the Stolper–Samuelson theorem and factor-proportions analysis. Since exchange-rate volatility serves, in effect, as an added barrier or cost to international trade and investment flows, we have a place to begin when trying to map the policy preferences of individuals: in each economy, owners of locally abundant factors are more likely to support a fixed exchange rate, while owners of locally scarce factors are more likely to prefer a floating rate. In the capital-abundant, labour-scarce advanced economies of Europe and the United States, we might thus expect a simple class division over exchange-rate policy: fixed rates benefit owners of capital at the expense of workers. We could expect the reverse alignment of class interests in the labour-abundant, capital-scarce economies of, say, China and India. In such countries, greater exchange-rate certainty should encourage more trade and greater inflows of foreign investment, and both types of international flows will benefit workers at the expense of local owners of capital.

But here we cannot think about exchange-rate stability without also thinking about monetary policy control. In general, workers might be expected to oppose fixed exchange rates in most circumstances, since they are likely to bear greater costs than others when monetary policy can no longer be used to avert economic downturns resulting in higher levels of unemployment. Owners of capital, on the other hand, care less about unemployment rates than they do about keeping inflation in check, which is typically much easier for the government to achieve (as noted above) when monetary policy is committed to keeping the exchange rate fixed. Just as in the case for the nation as whole, then, owners of labour and owners of capital may have to make a difficult choice about where they stand in terms of the trade-off between the effects of greater currency stability and less monetary policy control. In contemporary, labour-scarce Europe, for example, workers would seem to be better off along both dimensions if exchange rates were more flexible, while owners of capital should prefer fixed rates. There is some evidence that fits with this interpretation. Labour unions in Western European countries generally provided the most vocal opposition to government policies aimed at fixing or stabilizing exchange rates in the 1970s and 1980s, particularly in France and Italy. But the record is mixed. While the labour-backed Socialist government that came to power in France in 1981 initially abandoned exchange-rate stability as a goal, by 1983 it was committed to a fixed currency peg (see Oatley 1997). In fact, during the inter-war period in Europe, left-wing governments tended to keep their currencies fixed to the gold standard longer than other governments (Simmons 1994). And looking across a broader range of countries, in which labour is the locally abundant factor and capital is scarce, the preferences of these broad classes of individuals when it comes to exchange rates becomes even more difficult to predict.

Perhaps one major reason why it is difficult to find compelling evidence to support simple class-based interpretations of exchange-rate politics is that individuals tend to see things very differently depending on the industries in which they are employed and invested. If we allow, as in previous discussions above, that factors of production are typically very specific to particular industries, we get a very different picture of the alignment of individual preferences on the exchange-rate issue. And the picture is also much clearer. Individuals employed or invested in sectors that invest or sell in foreign markets are likely to favour exchange-rate stability, since fluctuations in rates impose costs on their international transactions and because they have a relatively small economic stake in domestic (versus foreign) macroeconomic conditions. Those individuals associated with firms and banks that invest heavily in foreign markets, for example, and export-orientated sectors that sell a large proportion of their output abroad, should thus tend to support fixed exchange rates. On the other hand, owners and employees in import-competing industries and those producing non-traded services (for example, building, transportation, sales) whose incomes depend overwhelmingly on domestic economic conditions, are likely to favour flexible exchange rates that allow the government

more control over monetary policy. There is some compelling evidence supporting these predictions, especially in the debates over exchange-rate policy in the most advanced economies. In Europe in recent decades, for example, the strongest support for fixing exchange rates (and ultimately, for creating a common European currency) has come from the international banks, multinational firms in a diverse range of industries (including auto firms such as BMW and Mercedes), and from export-orientated sectors. The strongest opposition to fixed rates has tended to come from owners and labour unions associated with import-competing industries such as coal, steel, and textiles, especially in nations such as France and Italy that have battled relatively high rates of inflation (see Frieden 1994). In developing nations, recent studies have indicated that governments are more likely to float their currency when the import-competing manufacturing sector accounts for a large proportion of the local economy (Frieden et al. 2001).

Finally, when a government does decide to fix or stabilize its currency, it must also decide the level at which to set the exchange rate. Whether the currency should be 'stronger' (that is, take a higher value versus other currencies) or 'weaker' (a lower value) is a second, important dimension of exchange-rate policy. Even when the currency is floating, in fact, if it happens to move strongly in one direction or another, the issue can become a salient one, since the government may be called upon to intervene in an effort to raise or lower the exchange rate towards some new target. What is interesting in this regard is that the alignment of the various groups in terms of preferences for fixing versus floating the currency are not quite the same as the way they are positioned on the issue of the actual rate that should be set or targeted. A stronger currency will harm those in both export-orientated and import-competing industries, since it will make their products less attractive to consumers relative to the foreign alternatives. Individuals in these sectors should prefer a weaker currency. But a weaker currency will harm all others in the local economy by eroding their purchasing power when it comes to buying foreign goods and services. Owners and employees in non-traded sectors should prefer a stronger currency, as should any multinational firms or international banks that are investing abroad and purchasing foreign assets (Frieden 1994). In the real world of politics, in cases in which the level of a nation's exchange rate has in fact become a salient political issue, these types of coalitions do appear to emerge.

Devaluation of the US dollar became a major election issue in the 1890s, for example, with the rise of the Populist movement, supported predominantly by export-orientated farmers who demanded a break from the gold standard in order to reset the dollar exchange rate at a lower level. The Populists were opposed most strongly by banking and commercial interests in the north-eastern states, who favoured a strong dollar (see Frieden 1997).

KEY POINTS

- According to the Stolper–Samuelson theorem, trade benefits those who own the factors of production with which the economy is relatively well endowed, and hurts owners of scarce factors.

- In the alternative 'specific factors' model, individuals employed or invested in export industries are the ones who benefit from trade, while those who are attached to import-competing industries are disadvantaged.

- The leading research assumes that the specific factors approach is the most appropriate way to think about the effects of trade in the contemporary advanced economies.

- Immigration harms the real earnings of local workers with similar skill levels to those of the arriving workers, while benefiting everyone else in the host country.

- Inflows of foreign capital will hurt individuals who own capital in the local economy, while benefiting all local landowners and workers.

- Individuals attached to firms and banks that invest abroad or export a large proportion of their output are likely to favour a fixed exchange rate. On the other hand, owners and employees in import-competing industries and those producing non-traded services are likely to favour a flexible exchange rate.

- A stronger currency will harm those in both export-orientated *and* import-competing industries, while benefiting all others in the local economy.

BOX 4.4

The Politics of the Rising Dollar

Between 1980 and 1985, the US dollar rose by approximately 50 per cent in value against the Japanese yen and by roughly similar amounts against the German Deutschmark and the British pound. The rapid dollar appreciation placed immense strain on US producers of traded goods and services, and by 1985 the Reagan government was being lobbied strenuously by a large variety of groups asking for some kind of action to halt the rise (see Destler and Henning 1989). The strongest pressure came from groups in a broad collection of export-orientated sectors, including grain farmers, firms such as IBM and Motorola in the computer industry, and Caterpillar, a large exporter of construction equipment and machinery. The voices of these exporters were swelled by protests coming from firms in import-competing industries, including the major auto companies and the steel-makers. The initial reaction from the Reagan administration was to sit tight, and characterize the rise of the dollar as a sign that the rest of the world held the United States and its economy in high esteem. The government had set a course to restrain inflation when entering office in 1981, and had raised US interest rates considerably. Taking action to devalue the dollar would have thrown into substantial doubt this commitment to defeat inflation. After their initial pleas were rebuffed by the White House, however, many groups from the steel, auto, and textiles industries began demanding new forms of trade protection instead, bombarding Congress with calls for trade barriers that would make up for the competitive effects of the dollar appreciation. It was this threat of runaway protectionism in Congress that finally prompted the government to take action on the dollar. In 1985, the White House reached an agreement with the governments of Japan, Germany, Britain, and France, which became known as the **Plaza Accord** (a reference to the lavish New York hotel in which it was negotiated). This deal provided for a co-operative effort to manage a gradual depreciation of the dollar against the other currencies, with each government agreeing to alter its macroeconomic policies in such a way as to ease demand for the dollar compared with other currencies (for example, the Reagan government agreed to lower interest rates and to make a new effort to reduce the size of the US budget deficit). By giving up some control over macroeconomic policy, in co-ordination with other governments, the White House was able to reverse the rise of the dollar and ease the strain imposed on US producers of traded goods and services.

Institutions

Once we have specified the preferences of different individuals and groups on any particular issue we need to think about how much influence they will have over policy outcomes. This is where political institutions come in to play. Political institutions establish the rules by which policy is made, and thus how the policy preferences of different groups are weighed in the process that determines the policy outcome. It is appropriate here to start with the broadest types of rules first, and consider the formal mechanisms by which governments and representatives in legislative bodies are elected (or otherwise come to power). These broad features of the institutional environment have large effects on all types of policies. But then we can move on to discuss more specific aspects of the legislative process and administrative agencies that have implications for the formulation and implementation of trade, immigration, investment, and exchange-rate policies.

Elections and representation

Perhaps it is best to start with the observation that the general relationship between democratization and foreign economic policy-making is a matter that is still open to considerable theoretical and empirical doubt. Part of the puzzle is that there is a great deal of variation in the levels of economic openness we have observed among autocratic nations. In autocratic regimes, the orientation of policy will depend on the particular desires and motivations of the (non-elected) leadership, and there are different theoretical approaches to this issue. Non-elected governments could pursue trade and investment liberalization, on the one hand, if they calculate that this will increase their own power or wealth (for example, through taxation) by increasing national economic output. Such policies may be easier to adopt because autocratic leaders are more insulated than their democratic counterparts from the political demands made by any organized domestic groups that favour trade protection and limits on foreign investment (Haggard 1990). Perhaps this is an apt description of the state of affairs in China, as it has been opening its economy gradually to trade and investment since the 1980s, and non-democratic governments in Taiwan and South Korea pursued trade liberalization even more rapidly in the 1960s. On the other hand, autocratic governments may draw political support from small, powerful groups that favour trade protection. Many such governments appear to have used trade and investment barriers in ways that were aimed at consolidating their rule (Wintrobe 1998). The experience in Sub-Saharan African nations since the 1960s, and in Pakistan and Myanmar, seems to fit this mould. Without a detailed assessment of the particular groups upon which a particular authoritarian regime depends for political backing, it is quite difficult to make predictions about likely policy outcomes under non-democratic rule.

In formal democracies that hold real elections, the most fundamental set of political rules is the set that defines which individuals get to vote. If the franchise law gives more weight to one side in a policy contest compared to others, it can obviously have a large impact on policy outcomes. Where only those who own land can vote, for example, agricultural interests will be privileged in the policy-making process. If this landowning elite favours trade protection, as it did in Britain in the years before the Great Reform Act of 1832, then such a policy is almost certain to be held firmly in place. By shifting political power away from landowners and towards urban owners of capital and labour, extensions of the franchise had a major impact on all forms of economic policy during the late nineteenth and early twentieth centuries in Europe, America, and elsewhere. In England, the extension of voting power to the middle and working classes, achieved in the reforms of 1832 and 1867, had the effect of making free trade politically invincible—with a huge block of workers along with the urban business class supporting trade openness, and only a tiny fraction of the electorate (the traditional rural elites) against it, a government that endorsed tariffs or restrictions on investment would have been committing electoral suicide. In the United States and Australia, on the other hand, where labour and capital were in relatively scarce supply, the elimination of property qualifications for voting and the extension of suffrage had exactly the opposite effect, empowering a larger block of urban voters who favoured high tariffs. In general, extensions of the franchise to urban classes tend to produce more

open policies toward trade, immigration, and investment in labour and capital-abundant countries, but more closed or protectionist policies in labour- and capital-scarce economies.

The precise rules by which representatives are elected to national legislatures are the next critical feature of the institutional environment. Scholars have suggested that, in parliamentary systems in which legislative seats are apportioned among parties according to the proportion of votes they receive ('proportional representation'), narrowly organized groups have far less impact on policy-making in general than they do in electoral systems in which individual seats are decided by the plurality rule (see Rogowski 1987). Parliamentary systems with proportional representation tend to encourage the formation of strong, cohesive political parties which appeal to a national constituency and have less to gain in electoral terms by responding to localized and particularistic demands in marginal or contested districts (McGillivray 1997). Other types of systems, in contrast, tend to encourage intra-party competition among individual politicians and the development of a 'personal vote' in particular electoral districts, and are thus more conducive to interest-group lobbying. The implications for foreign economic policies are usually spelt out in very clear terms: we expect that proportional representation systems with strong political parties (for example, Sweden) will typically produce lower levels of trade protection and other restrictions than alternative types of electoral systems (for example, Britain, the United States) in which particular local and regional interests have a greater influence.

These conclusions about the impact of particularistic groups in different types of electoral systems rest upon a critical insight derived from theoretical work on collective action in trade politics: that there is a fundamental asymmetry between the lobbying pressure generated from groups seeking protectionist policies, and the lobbying pressure that comes from groups who oppose such restrictions. The main reason for this is that restrictions on imports and other types of exchange, when imposed one at a time, tend to have very uneven effects. As we

BOX 4.5

The Institutional Foundations of the Gold Standard

Why was the gold standard, the system of fixed exchange rates that appeared to work so well in bringing order and stability to the global economy between the 1880s and 1914, so difficult to re-establish in the 1920s? One very important reason has to do with the major changes in political institutions that took place in Western nations around the time of the First World War. The gold standard required that governments give up control of monetary policy in order to keep the value of their currencies fixed in terms of gold (and one another). In essence, macroeconomic policy was held hostage to exchange-rate policy, so that currency values were stable. This was especially difficult for small economies that happened to run large balance of payments deficits at the set rates of exchange. To maintain their exchange rates, they were forced to reduce the supply of their money in circulation and raise interest rates, thereby reducing economic activity at home and increasing unemployment. If they were already in the middle of an economic recession, this meant making the downturn even worse. Governments could only follow through with this type of commitment to a fixed exchange rate if the economic costs of recession—which fell predominantly upon workers who lost jobs and income, and small businesses and farmers driven into debt—did not have direct political consequences in terms of their ability to remain in office. This changed in many nations around the start of the twentieth century, when electoral laws were reformed, extending the franchise to larger proportions of the population (including workers who had previously been denied the right to vote in many places). Around the same time, labour organizations, including trade unions and labour parties, grew in political strength in almost all the Western economies, using strikes to push for political reforms while gaining significant electoral representation for the first time. Given these profound changes in the lie of the political land, the attempts to recreate the gold standard in the inter-war period appear to have been doomed from the outset. Governments elected by much broader segments of the population were increasingly unwilling to give up their ability to manage domestic economic conditions, especially during recessions, in order merely to maintain the gold parity. Eventually, after weathering several smaller crises, the system collapsed when governments began to abandon the gold standard completely after 1929 in response to the onset of the Great Depression.

know from the analysis of the specific factors model above, the benefits of a tariff on a particular good are concentrated on the owners of capital and labour engaged in that particular industry. If the tariff is substantial, these benefits are likely to be quite large as a share of the incomes of those individuals, and thus they will typically be willing to spend a good deal of their time and energy (and savings) lobbying to ensure they get the tariff they want. The stakes are very high for them. In contrast, the costs of the tariff are shared among all the owners of other types of specific factors in the economy; they are dispersed so broadly, in fact, that they tend to be quite small as fraction of the incomes of these individuals. Thus it is unlikely that those hurt by the new tariff will be prepared to devote resources to lobbying against the policy proposal. Collective political action will always be much easier to organize in the relatively small groups that benefit from a particular trade restriction than in the much larger groups (the rest of the economy) that are hurt by the restriction (see Olson 1965). Perhaps the best example of this logic is the extraordinary political power that has been demonstrated by the small, highly organized agricultural groups in Europe, the United States, and Japan since the 1950s. These groups, which together represent a tiny fraction of the population in each political system, have been able to win extremely high (if not prohibitive) rates of protection from imports and lavish subsidies (see Tyers and Anderson 1992).

Other aspects of electoral institutions may also play a role in shaping policy outcomes. In general, smaller electoral districts in plurality systems may be expected to increase the influence of sectoral or particularistic groups over elected representatives, and thus lead to higher levels of protection (Rogoswki 1987; Alt and Gilligan 1994). In larger districts, political representatives will be forced to balance the interests of a greater variety of industry groups when making decisions about policies, and will be less affected by the demands of any particular industry lobby, and a larger share of the costs of any tariff or restriction will be 'internalized' among voters within the district. From this perspective, upper chambers of parliaments, which typically allocate seats among representatives of much larger electoral districts than those in lower chambers, tend to be less inclined toward trade protection and other types of restrictive foreign economic policies. Meanwhile, in legislative chambers in which seats are defined along political—geographical lines without regard for population (for example, in the United States Senate, where each state receives two seats), agricultural, forestry, and mining interests in underpopulated areas typically gain a great deal more influence over policy-making than they can wield in chambers (for example, the United States House of Representatives) where legislative seats are defined based on the number of voters in each district.

We have generally been focusing on trade policies, since most of the past research on the effects of institutions has tended to concentrate on tariff levels. But recent studies also suggest that differences in electoral institutions can have a significant impact on exchange-rate policies. In particular, in plurality systems in which elections are all-or-nothing contests between the major parties, governments appear to be far less likely to fix exchange rates and give up control over monetary policy than governments in proportional representation systems (see Clark and Hallerberg 2000). It appears that the costs of having ceded control over monetary policy in plurality systems, should the government face an election contest during an economic slump, are much higher than elsewhere. This difference also appears to be more pronounced for governments in plurality systems, in which the timing of

elections is predetermined by law (Bernhard and Leblang 1999).

Legislatures and policy-making rules

The rules that govern the way national legislatures go about making laws can have profound effects on the way the preferences of individuals and groups are aggregated into different types of foreign economic policies. These rules determine the way new policies are proposed, considered, amended, and voted upon. They structure the interactions among different legislative and executive bodies, and establish which branches have what types of agenda setting and veto power over policy.

Most of the recent research on the impact of legislative institutions on foreign economic policies has been focused on American trade policy. The point of departure for many studies is the infamous Smoot–Hawley Tariff Act of 1930, which was such a disaster that it helped to inspire a fairly radical change in the rules by which the Congress has dealt with trade policy ever since. The core of the legislative problem, as many see it, is the possibility for 'log rolling' or vote-trading between protectionist interests. The benefits of a tariff or trade restriction can often go to an import-competing industry located almost entirely in one electoral district, with the costs borne generally by individuals across the rest of the economy. In such cases, lobbying pressure by these industries can generate a protectionist log roll when tariffs are being set by voting among members of a legislature: each member of the legislature will propose generous protective measures for industries in his or her own district without accounting for the costs they impose on individuals elsewhere. To gain support for these measures, each member will vote in favour of similar measures proposed by other legislators. If members can vote indefinitely on a sequence of such proposals, a policy that includes every new tariff can be the equilibrium outcome (supported by each legislator's belief that a vote against another's proposal would induce

MICHAEL J HISCOX

BOX 4.6

The Reciprocal Trade Agreements Act of 1934

In 1930, the US Congress passed the infamous Smoot–Hawley Tariff Act, which raised import duties on a vast array of manufactured and agricultural goods (some to over 200 per cent), and was dubbed the 'worst tariff bill in the nation's history' even before it was passed. Retaliation from other countries, in the form of higher tariffs, was swift and substantial, and the subsequent sharp decline in world trade and the collapse of the fragile international monetary system increased the depth and scope of the Great Depression. The 1930 tariff bill was widely regarded as a case of protectionist log-rolling run wild. The Senate alone made 1,253 amendments to the original House bill, and duties on over 20,000 items were altered (see Pastor 1980: 77–78). When the Democrats won control of the White House, and majorities in Congress, in 1932, they looked for a way to make a change. Rural interests still made up a large part of the Democrats' electoral base, especially in the south, and still strongly favoured trade and the party's traditional anti-tariff platform. Unilateral tariff reductions were politically sensitive in the middle of a recession, however, and were not popular at all among workers, who had thrown their support behind the Democrats in the 1932 campaign. Franklin D. Roosevelt's secretary of state, Cordell Hull, a long-time advocate of free trade,

instead designed new legislation that would permit the president to negotiate bilateral treaties with trading partners, to restart trade by making reciprocal reductions in import duties. Passed as the Reciprocal Trade Agreements Act in 1934, the legislation granted the president authority (for three years) to negotiate alterations of up to 50 per cent in the existing import duties. When that initial authority expired in 1937, Congress renewed it and continued to do so in the decades that followed. Beginning in 1974, the president's authority was expanded to cover negotiations over a range of **non-tariff barriers to trade**, although various procedural and monitoring provisions were also introduced to constrain executive behaviour, and the Congress maintained the power to approve or reject any trade agreement by vote (under the so-called 'fast-track' provision that prohibited amendments and set a firm time limit for a ratifying vote). The delegation of policy-making power to the executive branch, which can aggregate the costs and benefits of protection across the entire nation and bargain for reciprocal changes in the policies of other governments to open foreign markets to American exports, is credited with reorientating US trade policy away from protectionism in the decades since 1934 (see Destler 1995; Gilligan 1997).

others to retaliate by offering an amendment to withdraw protection from the defector's district). The result of such unchecked log-rolling is a vast array of protective measures, such that all individuals are far worse off than they were before the bill was passed (see Weingast *et al.* 1981).

According to conventional wisdom, the Smoot–Hawley tariff was just such a log-rolling disaster, and Congress reacted to it in a remarkably sensible way by redesigning the rules governing the way trade policy was made. Specifically, Congress delegated to the executive branch the authority to alter US trade policy by negotiating reciprocal trade agreements with other countries. This practice of delegating negotiating authority to the president has been continued since 1934. By delegating authority

over policy to the president, who would presumably set trade policy to benefit all individuals within the one, *national* electoral district, this innovation eliminated the spectre of protectionist log-rolling completely, and ensured that all the costs of trade protection were fully 'internalized' by a decision-maker accountable to all voters. In addition, by empowering the president to negotiate trade agreements that elicited reciprocal tariff reductions from other countries, the change helped to mobilize support for trade liberalization among export interests who could now expect improved sales abroad as a result of tariff reductions at home.

The lessons drawn from this case are almost certainly overstated, and the conventional account has some gaping inconsistencies. In particular, there appears to have been no learning at all on the part of members of Congress between 1930 and 1934: the congressional voting records indicate that, among the members voting on both bills, almost all those who voted for Smoot–Hawley in 1930 voted against the RTAA in 1934 (see Schnietz 1994). Moreover, it is not at all clear that protectionist log-rolls have been an otherwise unsolvable problem for tariff legislation in the US Congress (or elsewhere)—what of all the cases in which *liberalizing* bills were passed by legislatures in the absence of delegation? In the US Congress itself, the major acts passed by the Democrats when in control of government before the 1930s (the Wilson Tariff of 1894 and the Underwood Tariff of 1913) stand out in this regard. Examples also abound in the legislative histories of other Western democracies. It should not be a mystery as to why. In parliamentary systems, political parties play critical roles in controlling the legislative agenda. In proportional representation systems these parties compete for a share of the national vote, and so legislation designed to appease district-specific interests holds little appeal. Even in plurality rule systems, however, the majority party that forms a government typically imposes strict control over the policy agenda in a way that prevents such self-defeating log-rolls. Finally, the notion that presidents, simply by dint of having a large (national) constituency, must be champions of freer trade, is hopelessly ahistorical. Here again, we cannot ignore the critical role played by political parties. In the US case, the Republican base of support between the 1840s and 1940s was concentrated among manufacturing interests in the north-east and midwest states and was staunchly protectionist, and a long list of Republican presidents championed high tariffs in election campaigns and backed the most protectionist of Republican tariff bills in Congress (see Hiscox 1999). More generally, in all the Western democracies, political parties typically have very distinct core constituencies among the electorate, defined in regional or class terms, to whom they are principally accountable when designing

policies. Whether a government allows protectionist amendments during legislative deliberations of policy, and whether a president supports trade liberalization, will depend on their partisan affiliation and the preferences of their party's core electoral base.

Despite the distortions, the story of the RTAA does still hold some valuable lessons for thinking about ways in which legislative rules can affect foreign economic policies. The explicit institutional connection that the RTAA forged between tariff reductions at home and reciprocal reductions in tariffs abroad certainly played a role in generating increased support for trade policy reform among export-orientated industries, and thus made it easier for all policy-makers to support trade liberalization. This link is now more-or-less routine, of course, for policy-making in most Western governments, as a consequence of their membership commitments in the WTO. For nations outside the WTO, however, most of them being developing countries, where attempts to liberalize trade policy have a poor political track record, this does suggest that governments are more likely to succeed with trade reform if they can do so as part of a bilateral or regional free trade agreement with major trading partners.

The RTAA also offers a lesson about group access to lawmakers that is often overlooked. Up to 1934, congressional committee hearings were pivotal in shaping the trade legislation voted on in the US House and Senate. The hearings format, which assigned particular days for receiving testimony on the duties to be levied on different commodities, was especially convenient for industry group lobbying. This system was changed completely in 1934. After the RTAA, hearings were typically limited to general discussions about whether to extend the president's negotiating authority and, after 1974, whether to implement previously negotiated agreements (under 'fast-track' provisions that prohibited amendment). Closing off this very direct channel by which groups had been able for years to lobby for changes in duties on particular items may have had the most profound effect on trade policy-making in the United States. In general, *any* type of policy-making rule that provides routine access for organized groups to exert lobbying pressure to change particular features of legislation will make trade protection and other forms of restriction more likely—including open legislative hearings and 'commissions' or industry advisory panels set up within government agencies to gather opinions from producer and labour groups (see Alt and Gilligan 1994; Verdier 1994).

Legislative institutions can also influence other types of foreign economic policies. One line of work by scholars has been focusing on the general differences between multi-party coalition governments and single-party majority governments. Coalition governments appear to have less incentive than majority governments to alter their monetary policy prior to elections, to try to boost economic activity in an 'opportunistic' fashion, since voters find it difficult to assign blame or credit to any single party within the coalition. An implication seems to be that coalition governments are also much more likely than other types of government to adopt fixed exchange rates and give up control over monetary policy (see Bernhard and Leblang 1999).

Bureaucratic agencies

Lastly, there is the issue of how foreign economic policies are implemented or administered by the bureaucratic agencies of each government. The rules that are established to regulate these agencies, and the way they make decisions, can play a powerful part in shaping policy outcomes. Legislatures delegate the responsibility for implementing their laws to these agencies, establishing the rules by which they are to operate, the ways in which their performance is monitored and evaluated, and so on. Built into these relationships between the legislature and the bureaucracy, however, there is always some measure of 'slack'—that is, some room for bureaucrats to manoeuvre, free from legislative

interference. This bureaucratic independence can have important effects in terms of foreign economic policies.

When it comes to the implementation of trade policies, for example, there is often a real fear that the bureaucratic agencies that administer various aspects of trade laws may develop far too cosy a relationship with the sectors of the home economy that they are supposed to be regulating. This danger of bureaucratic 'capture' appears to be very real. In the US case, the Departments of Commerce and Agriculture are both regarded as unapologetic advocates of protection for their 'clients'—American business firms and farmers. Indeed, the International Trade Administration, located within the Department of Commerce, is renowned for having 'gone native'. Charged with making rulings on petitions from US companies claiming that foreign firms are dumping products below cost in the American market, the ITA finds in favour of local firms in around 99 per cent of cases (see Bovard 1991).

This problem is by no means unique to the American system. In Japan, the Ministry for International Trade and Industry (MITI), and the Ministry for Agriculture, Forestry, and Fisheries (MAFF), have long been known for their extremely close ties with Japanese industry, and the farming and fishing communities (see Okimoto 1988: 310). While MITI was for many years appded by Western observers as the model for a new kind of autonomous state bureaucracy, capable of targeting subsidies expertly to particular manufacturing industries that would excel in competition with foreign producers (Johnson 1982), comprehensive evidence from recent studies indicates that MITI in fact allocated support to favoured industries in a highly political and ineffective way, a situation much like that it bureaucracies elsewhere (see Beason and Weinstein 1993).

In general, extreme cases aside, the interplay between bureaucratic independence and accountability is complex. In some issue areas, greater independence is generally regarded as desirable. Central banking is perhaps the most important case. The general problem, which we have discussed briefly above, is often referred to as the time inconsistency of monetary policy. Governments have an incentive to allow an unexpected rise in inflation that boosts economic activity, especially when facing an election. But since private actors know this, any promises a government may make to keep inflation in check may not be considered credible. Even if the government has all the best intentions, private actors might nevertheless keep inflation expectations high. By delegating control over monetary policy to an independent central bank that is insulated from any political temptations to alter monetary policy, the government can beat the problem. Moreover, independent central banks also appear to play an important part in shaping currency policies. Recent studies have indicated that governments in countries with independent central banks are less likely to engage in electorally motivated manipulations of exchange rates (Clark and Reichert 1998). And a related claim is that governments that can commit credibly to low inflation by establishing an independent central bank are less likely to need to fix their exchange rate in order to gain anti-inflationary credibility. Central bank independence and fixed exchange rates, in other words, can function as policy substitutes (see Clark and Hallerberg 2000).

KEY POINTS

- Restrictions on the franchise can give more weight to one side relative to others in contests over foreign economic policies. Extensions of the franchise to urban classes tend to produce more open policies toward trade and investment in labour and capital-abundant countries, and more closed or protectionist policies in labour and capital-scarce economies.

- Collective action is easier to organize in the relatively small groups that benefit from a particular trade restriction than in the much larger groups that are hurt by the restriction, so the strongest lobbying pressure tends to come from protectionist groups.

- Proportional representation systems with strong political parties typically generate lower levels of trade protection and other restrictions than plurality rule systems, in which particular local and regional interests have a greater influence.

- Small electoral districts in plurality rule systems tend to increase the influence of sectoral or particularistic groups over elected representatives when compared to larger districts, and thus lead to higher levels of protection.

- In plurality rule systems, in which elections are all-or-nothing contests between the major parties, governments are less likely to fix exchange rates than governments in proportional representation systems.

- Whether a government allows protectionist log-rolling in a legislature, and whether a president supports trade liberalization, will depend on their partisan affiliation and the policy preferences of their party's core electoral constituency.

- An explicit institutional connection that links tariff reductions at home with reciprocal reductions in tariffs abroad (for example, a free-trade agreement), can generate much stronger support for trade policy reform among export-orientated industries.

- Rules that provide access for organized groups to exert lobbying pressure to change particular features of legislation make trade protection and other forms of restriction more likely.

- The delegation of policy-making authority to bureaucratic agencies or bodies independent from national legislatures may not produce policies less affected by lobbying from protectionist interests, since groups may gain privileged access to decision-makers in such agencies.

- The existence of an independent central bank makes it less likely that a government will choose to fix the exchange rate.

Conclusions, Extensions, and Complications

There is really no such thing as the 'national interest' when it comes to foreign economic policy—or rather, there is no single national interest; there are many. Different individuals have very different conceptions of what is best for the nation and, not coincidentally, best for themselves, when it comes to setting foreign economic policies. This chapter has attempted to outline the principal divisions that usually characterize domestic political battles over trade, immigration, investment, and exchange rates. These divisions, as we have seen, tend to fall along either class or industry lines. Owners of capital and workers are typically pitted against one another when it comes to restrictions on inflows of labour or capital, for example, but they tend to take the same position in each industry on trade and exchange-rate issues since the effects of policy can be very different for different sectors of the economy.

Once we know who wants what, the next task involves figuring out who gets what they want from the political process. This second step involves understanding how policies are decided in different countries, and thus how differences in political institutions affect economic policy choices. Our ultimate goal is to work out why governments in different countries often choose very different types of trade, immigration, investment, and exchange-rate policies. We might also hope to form some reasonably accurate predictions about what our governments are likely to do in the future. Understanding why governments make the choices they do, and predicting what they will do next, requires careful attention to the political pressures they face from domestic groups, and to the ways in which the preferences of these groups are aggregated into collective decisions by political institutions. But there are at least three additional complications to this simple analytical picture that we should discuss briefly here. The first is related to the knowledge or information that individuals have about the effects of different

policies, and about the preferences of others; the second extension involves allowing for linkages between the various policy issues, and between these issues and other non-economic policy concerns; and the third complication involves international bargaining, and the ways in which we might think about the connection between domestic politics and international politics.

Information and the role of ideas

Who gains and who loses? And who wins the political contest between those who gain and those who lose? Answering these questions in each issue area is at the heart of the standard political economy approach we have outlined above. In keeping with traditional assumptions, we have been taking it for granted that individuals know what they want, know what others want, and know what types of policies will have what kinds of effects. These are heroic assumptions. A great deal of the most recent research in both economics and political science has in fact tried to depart from this notion that people have full or complete information about their world, examining the effects of uncertainty, asymmetry in information among actors, and changes in knowledge that might be attributable to learning and the impact of new ideas. It is useful in this respect to distinguish between two basic types of information that individuals may be missing: people may be lacking knowledge about the effects of different policies on economic outcomes, or they may not have full knowledge about other people (including government leaders) and their preferences. We can discuss each of these informational problems separately.

What if we allow that individuals are not sure about the effects of different types of policies? It took us some time to disentangle the various effects of trade, immigration, investment, and exchange-rate policies above, with the help of several simplifying assumptions, so this does seem an important question to pose. This clearly provides a large window through which new ideas, in the form of new beliefs about cause-and-effect relationships between policies and outcomes, might have a large impact on policy-making. This is the view espoused by John Maynard Keynes (1936: 383) in his famous contention that 'the ideas of economists and political philosophers, both when they are right and when they are wrong, are more powerful than is commonly understood. Indeed the world is ruled by little else'.

Several prominent scholars have indeed argued that foreign economic policies have changed markedly in response to new ideas about these policies and their effects. The abandonment of mercantilist restrictions on trade and investment by most European governments in the nineteenth century has been attributed, in large measure, to the ideas of Adam Smith and David Ricardo and the development of classical trade theory (Kindleberger 1975; Bhagwati 1988). The multilateral liberalization of trade and investment among Western economies in the post-Second-World-War era, allowing governments considerable scope for managing their domestic economies to avoid recessions, has similarly been traced to the refinement of classical and neoclassical economic theories and the ideas of Keynes himself (Ruggie 1982; Goldstein 1993). More recently, the rush to liberalize trade by governments in developing nations has been attributed to a learning process and the discrediting of the idea that rapid development could be achieved by **import-substitution** policies (see Krueger 1995). Competing ideas about cause-and-effect relationships often appear in policy debates, and dominant ideas are frequently embedded within policy-making institutions as the foundations for rules followed by bureaucratic agencies (Goldstein 1993). Yet there remains much debate about the degree to which these types of ideas are independent of the interests that might be served by them. Max Weber's famous analogy compared ideas to 'switchmen' who determine the tracks along

which human behaviour, pushed by interests, travel (Weber 1913/1958). From a more sceptical perspective, one might suggest that the individuals who gain and lose the most from any economic policy, such as tariffs on trade, have all the knowledge they need about its effects, and need no new ideas from economists to help them out; the policies just reflect the wishes of those interested actors who have the most political clout, and the ideas that attract our attention are just the ones sprinkled like holy water over the new legislation (to borrow an equally memorable metaphor from Kindleberger (1975: 36). The relationship between ideas and interests is still very murky, and will remain so until we have a better understanding of where new ideas about policy come from, and what explains which ideas catch on and spread.

But by focusing only on the role of new ideas and how they might change knowledge about policies, we may be missing the bulk of the iceberg here when it comes to the impact of incomplete information. We noted in the discussions above that while foreign economic policies such as tariffs on imported goods generate real costs for a large set of owners and workers in all the other (non-protected) sectors of the economy, these costs are dispersed across such a large number of individuals that the 'per person' losses can be extremely small. Not only will it not pay for those affected to take political action to oppose the tariff in these cases, it may not even pay for them to spend any time or resources acquiring accurate information about the policy and its effects. Public opinion experts typically regard foreign economic policies as a particularly complex set of issues, about which survey respondents have very low levels of information (see Bauer *et al.* 1972: 81–84). Survey responses to questions about these issues tend to vary drastically with simple changes in question wording, making it very difficult to pinpoint where the public stands on any given policy question at any particular point in time (see Destler 1995: 180). One implication is that voters may be very susceptible to issue-framing or manipulation by political leaders and organized lobby groups whenever these issues become more prominent.

MICHAEL J HISCOX

BOX 4.7

The Rise of Free Trade in Europe

The publication of *The Wealth of Nations* by Adam Smith in 1776 stands out as an intellectual landmark in the history of thinking about international trade, pointing out the critical role that trade plays in encouraging specialization, and the resulting gains in efficiency and wealth. Smith adroitly punctured the old doctrine of **mercantilism**, which favoured expanding exports while restricting imports and hoarding gold, making it clear that national wealth is defined not by stocks of gold but by how much citizens can consume with the resources they have at their disposal. But the modern theory of international trade really began with the arrival of David Ricardo's *Principles of Political Economy and Taxation* in 1817. Ricardo demonstrated that trade is mutually beneficial for all countries, even a country that cannot produce anything more efficiently than other nations in terms of the costs of its inputs. As long as the costs of production are different in different nations, Ricardo's analysis showed that it must be true that, in terms of the opportunity costs of production (the value of

other things that might have been produced with the inputs used to make a given item), each nation will be better at producing some things than others, and thus there is a basis for specialization and exchange that will leave both countries better off. This 'law of comparative advantage', which Paul Samuelson has called the most beautiful law in economics, has had a profound impact on all scholarly and political debates about trade ever since. That the cause of free trade was taken up enthusiastically by the leading English political economists, including John Stuart Mill, all inspired by Ricardian theory, and that these ideas also spread rapidly throughout Europe during the nineteenth century, has led many scholars to suggest that the broad shift away from trade protectionism in Europe (which began in 1846 with the repeal of the Corn Laws that Ricardo himself had attacked) was a result in large measure of a profound change in the way leaders understood the economic effects of trade (see Kindleberger 1975; Bhagwati 1988).

Recent research on political communication and public opinion has highlighted this possibility (for example, Manheim 1991; Zaller 1992: 95). To the extent that this type of influence can be exercised, the politics of globalization may be regarded, at least to some degree, as a competition in issue framing among organized interests on different sides of the debate trying to sway public opinion to their side. This did appear to be an important dimension of the intense debate over NAFTA in the United States in 1993 (Holsti 1996: 52).

Another interesting implication of incomplete information among voters is that it may provide an explanation for why governments so often seem to do very inefficient things when setting foreign economic policies. Economists are fond of pointing out that if a government really wanted to redistribute income to particular groups of owners and employees, using restrictions on trade is a very inefficient way to go about it. It would be far better just to make a direct, lump-sum payment

to these individuals and avoid the inefficiencies generated by trade barriers that prop up uncompetitive industries. But if the costs to taxpayers of such direct payments are more visible (because they must appear, say, in the government's annual budget), they are more likely to generate a backlash among the voters on whom the burden falls. If this is true, it may make sense for a government to use trade policies to redistribute income to favoured groups, because these policies provide an effective disguise in a low-information environment (see Tullock 1983). From this perspective, the use of trade protection can be characterized as 'optimal obfuscation' (Magee *et al.* 1989).

Finally, what happens if we allow that individuals, even if they are fully informed about the effects of foreign economic policies, may nevertheless be uncertain about the motivations or intentions of the government managing them. One circumstance in which this type of incomplete information can become important is when setting exchange-rate policy, as we have discussed above. Since governments have an incentive to print money and allow a burst of inflation when facing an election, any promises they make to keep inflation in check may not be considered credible by private actors, who understand that the government has an incentive to bluff and portray itself as 'tougher' on inflation than it really is. The problem is that no one can be sure that the government values its low-inflation reputation enough (relative to how much it wants to gain re-election) to keep its pledge; even if the government had followed through with its promises, private actors might nevertheless keep inflation expectations high. If there is no independent central bank to which control of monetary policy can be ceded, governments in these circumstances are likely to be drawn more to fixing the exchange rate, especially in countries that have a history of chronic inflation. Fixing the value of the currency is a way for the government to signal to private actors that it is committed to keeping inflation under control by raising the potential costs to itself should it fail.

Another important context in which incomplete information about the government may play a key role in shaping policies is the case in which a government is attempting to reform trade policy in the face of stiff opposition from groups in import-competing industries. In such cases, since the government may indeed have an incentive to back down if it encounters a major political revolt, any promises it makes in advance to hold fast to the reforms may not be considered credible by the groups (who know very well that the government could just be trying to bluff its way through the painful reforms). Thus, even if the government does fully intend to stick with the reforms, it might have to weather a long and costly (and perhaps even violent) political protest. Again, tying its own hands in some clear and visible way can be an especially attractive policy option for a government in this situation, and by signing an international trade treaty with a major regional partner, it might be able to do the trick. This desire to make a credible commitment to trade reform is widely held to have been

one reason why the Mexican government initiated the negotiations that produced the NAFTA agreement in 1993, after two decades of failed efforts to lower trade barriers unilaterally (see Whalley 1999).

Combinations of policies and issue linkages

Up to this point we have been examining one type of foreign economic policy at a time. It is clear, however, that the effects of different policy instruments often depend on how *other* policies are set. In the basic Heckscher–Ohlin model, trade and factor movements are *substitutes* for one another—more of one type of international flow will generally mean less of another, and vice versa. If exports of labour-intensive products can move easily across a border between a labour-abundant economy (where wages are low) and a labour-scarce economy (where wages are high), this will tend to equalize labour costs over time, reducing the incentives for workers themselves to try to migrate between countries. If exports between the countries are blocked or impeded, more workers are likely to try to cross the border into the country that pays higher wages. When a dam is placed in front of flows in one channel it tends to divert flows into other channels.

This interaction among policies can become very interesting, because we know that while trade and factor flows are substitutable in general terms, they in fact have different types of effects on individuals. Individuals may thus have preferences for different combinations of policies. Perhaps the best example concerns the relationship between trade flows (and trade barriers) and direct investment. There is a great deal of evidence that firms engage in direct investment in markets as a way of 'jumping' trade barriers that would inhibit exports, and they even seem to reduce exports and invest more to stave off anticipated pressure for tariffs among local firms—a phenomenon known as 'quid pro quo foreign investment' (Bhagwati *et al.* 1987; Blonigen and Feenstra 1996). Local firms may be able to raise trade barriers, since they should have the lobbying support of their workers, whose jobs are endangered by high levels of imports, but they are less likely to win restrictions on inward direct investment by foreign firms, since workers in the industry will benefit from any new inflows of capital. Indeed, the best *policy combination* for local workers in an industry facing competition from a (relocatable) foreign producer is a high tariff *and* no restrictions on inward foreign investment. Local firms would prefer restrictions of *both* types of exchange, but would accept any restrictions rather than none at all if these are the politically feasible options. This political logic helps to explain the common pattern in policies towards the automobile industry in Europe and North America, where restrictions on imports were negotiated with Japanese auto firms but no restrictions were imposed to block the same firms from investing heavily in production facilities within both markets.

Exchange-rate policy can also be 'in play' at the same time as trade policy. Trade policy and exchange-rate policy are partially substitutable: a 1 per cent depreciation of the currency is equivalent to a 1 per cent across-the-board tariff on imports and a 1 per cent subsidy for all exports. But, clearly, the coalition that supports depreciation—those invested and employed in both import-competing and exporting industries—is different from the coalition that would support higher tariffs (import-competing interests). Exchange-rate policies tend to be more rigid than trade policies, in general, mainly because the credibility of monetary policy commitments is undermined by frequent shifts in policy. But when there is an opportunity for the government to alter the exchange rate, intense lobbying for protection by import-competing groups (or even just the threat of it), may induce export interests to help persuade the government to weaken the currency—an outcome that would ease the competitive pressure on producers threatened by imports, while not harming (benefiting, in fact) those engaged in export industries. This seems to have been the case in the United States in the early 1980s, as the value of the US dollar rose

dramatically. While the White House appeared to prefer to leave both its currency and trade policies unchanged, fearing a spate of protectionist legislation from Congress in response to lobbying by firms and unions in import-sensitive sectors, and hearing support for depreciation from export interests as well, it moved in 1985 to weaken the value of the dollar. Similarly, in many Latin-American nations in the 1980s and 1990s, governments attempting reforms aimed at lowering barriers to trade were able to render these changes more politically palatable to threatened sectors by devaluing exchange rates at the same time (see De Gregorio 2001).

Perhaps even more important, in some ways, than these connections between different foreign economic policies are the linkages that have been made with increasing frequency in recent policy debates between these policies and a variety of *non-economic* issues. Some of these linkages are not new. Trade and investment policies have always been connected in various ways to the issue of national security. Most governments place tight controls on trade in weapons and dangerous chemicals, for example, and restrictions on foreign investment in strategically important industries (such as, energy, airlines, and broadcasting) are also common. And governments have strong incentives to lower barriers to trade and investment more rapidly among alliance partners than with other nations in the international system, as the post-Second-World-War experience in Europe (and among the industrialized democracies more generally) makes clear (see Gowa 1994). All individuals within an economy tend to share similar concerns about national security, so this form of issue linkage tends to affect policy-making in a fairly straightforward way, generating more support among all citizens for policy options that contribute most clearly to national security. But foreign economic policies are now linked more regularly with a range of other non-economic issues, about which individuals tend to have more varied opinions. Most importantly, trade and investment are now frequently linked to discussions of environmental policy and to human rights issues in the political debates about globalization in Western democracies.

How do these issue linkages affect the analysis of the politics of trade and investment? The clearest impact is the involvement of a variety of organized environmental and human rights groups in recent debates over regional trade agreements and the WTO (see Destler and Balint 1999). The members of these groups care deeply about addressing environmental and human rights problems in their own countries and in other countries around the world; and they either believe that globalization is making these problems worse and thus should be restrained in some way, or they argue that trade and investment provide economic leverage which can and should be used to persuade governments in developing nations to improve environmental and labour standards and democratic institutions. The position taken by many of these groups is that all trade agreements, including the WTO itself, should include provisions for minimum environmental and labour standards that would be enforced (if necessary) by the imposition of trade sanctions. Many environmental groups have also lobbied for changes to the existing rules of the WTO, so that laws that discriminated against foreign products on environmental grounds (for example, import bans on tuna caught using nets that also endanger dolphins) would be permissible. But environmentalists and human rights activists have also expressed grave concerns about the behaviour of multinational firms in developing nations, with much of the focus being on whether these large corporations are moving production to areas in which they can pollute and otherwise damage the environment, or run 'sweatshop' factories in which they mistreat and underpay workers, avoiding the regulatory supervision that would prevent such behaviour in their home countries. The policies recommended by these groups, and in particular by human rights organizations worried by the lack of democratic institutions in countries such as China, typically involve a more proactive use of economic sanctions—that is, Western governments cutting off trade with, and investment to, such 'problem'

nations until their leaders make significant political reforms. Consumer boycotts aimed at particular corporations that are investing in such nations are usually warmly recommended too (although these types of consumer actions represent private market behaviour and are thus not a question of public policy).

One important general development has been the formation of what might be called 'Baptist and bootlegger' coalitions between some of these issue groups, and the business and labour organizations that have an economic stake in restricting international trade and/or investment. This type of coalition gets its name from American politics in the era of Prohibition, when strong support for the ban on alcohol sales came from Baptists, on moral grounds, and from bootleggers, who made large fortunes selling alcohol on the black market (see Yandle 1984). In recent debates over the NAFTA in the United States, for example, environmental groups such as the Sierra Club joined with labour unions in lobbying against the agreement, on the grounds that it did not contain provisions that would ensure a substantial improvement in environmental and labour standards in Mexico (see Destler and Balint 1999: 42–45). And recent 'anti-sweatshop' campaigns, organized by human rights groups and student activists, and targeting foreign investment and outsourcing by US apparel manufacturers to nations such as Vietnam and China, have been backed financially and supported enthusiastically by American textile unions and firms producing locally.

The concern among many analysts, especially among those who generally support international economic integration for its ability to raise living standards in all countries, is that these types of political coalitions may be hijacked by their protectionist members who support restrictions on international trade and investment *regardless* of whether they have any positive (or negative) long-term effects on environmental conditions or human rights standards. It would be far better, many argue, to pursue improvements in environmental and human rights standards by working towards separate international treaties dealing with those precise issues in a more direct way, perhaps by compensating developing nations for making costly improvements to their environmental and labour laws. Sanctions could severely limit economic growth in the very poorest developing countries, where governments are likely to resist making political concessions (especially democratic reforms that increase the risk that they will be toppled from power). The issues are complex, however, and the political problems difficult. The 'Baptists' are drawn to supporting economic sanctions rather than other policy instruments (for example, new international treaties, or foreign aid grants to nations that improve their environmental standards), because they have calculated that these alternatives are politically infeasible. With the support of the 'bootleggers' for restrictions on trade and investment, however, they might stand a greater chance of getting something done that will have beneficial effects.

The general point here is that our simple, one-issue-at-a-time approach to the analysis of foreign economic policies becomes much more complicated when we allow that different policy instruments are often up for grabs at the same time and have partially substitutable effects, and if take into account the fact that a variety of groups are often interested in using the tools of foreign economic policy to advance non-economic types of goals. Often it is the institutional context in which government decisions are made (many of the features of which we have discussed above) that determines which types of policy instruments are more adjustable than others, and which types of political coalitions are more viable than others. The most comprehensive and persuasive accounts of economic policy-making will take all these complexities into account.

International bargaining and domestic politics

Finally, recalling the discussion by Aggarwal and Dupont in the previous chapter, it is worth pausing here briefly to consider the ways in which the domestic politics of foreign economic policies may be translated into international-level bargaining over these same issues. What we really require here is a theoretical model of the policy-making process that takes into account all the incentives and constraints operating among actors at both domestic and international levels. This is the type of model that Putnam (1988) famously envisioned, using the metaphor of the two-level game. A government engaged in international economic negotiations in fact plays two different political 'games' at the same time, he suggested, with its actions constituting 'moves' that must be seen not only in the context of the demands made by individuals and groups in *domestic* politics, but also in view of the bargaining power it has when negotiating *international* agreements with other governments. Government leaders negotiate with other leaders at the international level over the terms of economic agreements, and in those negotiations the relative size and strength of the economy can make a tremendous difference to the terms that can be demanded. But the leaders must be attuned to the preferences of the domestic groups whose support they need to remain in office, and the set of international deals that would be ratified or supported by these groups at home.

To date, theoretical work along these lines has focused mainly on differences between the preferences of legislative and executive branches of government, and their different agenda-setting and vetoing powers, and how these features of domestic politics affect the outcomes of international negotiations and agreements (see Evans *et al.* 1993; Milner 1997*a*). Much of the attention has been directed to the so-called 'Schelling conjecture', which holds that a hawkish domestic constituency—represented in the simplest models as a legislature that prefers very little international co-operation—can in fact improve the bargaining power of the executive branch in its dealings with foreign counterparts (Schelling 1960: 28–29). Recent work has also focused on how executive–legislative divisions affect the credibility of governments during international negotiations (for example, Martin 2000) and whether international agreements are negotiated to allow for greater flexibility in cases when future changes in domestic political coalitions might lead to substantial shifts in the types of policies a government can implement (Downs and Rocke 1995).

While being full of insights about the effects of domestic political institutions on the prospects for international co-operation, this line of work has so far paid very little attention to the roles played by organized interests and voters in shaping legislative and executive preferences on particular policy issues. In fact, to date, standard political economy models of trade politics, emphasizing the role played by organized lobby groups in the formulation of policy, have not been linked at all to two-level game models of negotiations over trade and other economic agreements. Moreover, the existing work on two-level games tends to concentrate overwhelmingly on parameters that operate only on one level—domestic politics in the home nation. Features of the strategic relationship between nations, such as the economic and military asymmetries that might affect relative bargaining power, or common ties to alliances or international institutions that might affect incentives to co-operate, are largely ignored. We clearly need a better two-level mousetrap: a model that incorporates a fuller representation of organized interests and lobbying at the domestic level, while also allowing for the ways in which incentives and constraints are generated at the international level.

In practice, most international political economists work with partial theories that focus on one set of causal variables operating at one level. Some argue that the features of the international system, such as the distribution of economic power, and any specific nation's position within it, impose broad but important constraints on what governments can and cannot do when setting policies. Others, in keeping with the orientation of this chapter, argue that the prime focus of our attention should be placed on what is going on within nations—their particular sets of political institutions, and the preferences and lobbying activities of different group of individuals—since it is these things that primarily determine the policies chosen by governments. But, in principal, almost all scholars recognize that politics at both the domestic and international levels should be a feature of any complete analysis of foreign economic policy. Integrating theoretical insights about politics at these two levels is an extremely complex and challenging task that still remains, to a very large extent, undone.

KEY POINTS

- To understand the domestic origins of foreign economic policies, we need to perform two main tasks: first, to map the policy preferences of different groups in the domestic economy; and then to specify how political institutions affect the way that these preferences are aggregated into government decisions.

- Policy preferences depend mainly on the types of assets people own, and how the income earned from those assets is affected by different policies.

- Political institutions affect policy outcomes by defining who has a vote, how political representatives are elected, and how policy-making takes place in legislatures, and is delegated to presidents and government agencies.

- New ideas about cause-and-effect relationships appear to have had a large impact on foreign economic policies in different eras. The relationship between ideas and interests is far from clear, however, and we need a better understanding of where new ideas about policy come from, and what explains which ideas catch on and spread.

- Foreign economic policies involve a complex set of issues about which most voters have very low levels of information. As a result, the politics of globalization may be regarded to some degree as a competition in issue framing among organized interests.

MICHAEL J HISCOX

- If private actors have incomplete information about the degree to which the government is committed to policy reforms, the government may have an incentive to tie its own hands in some visible way (for example, by fixing the exchange rate, or signing a trade treaty) to signal its intentions in a credible way.

- Since the effects of a change in one type of foreign economic policy may depend on choices made about other types of policy, individuals may have preferences over different combinations of policies that are closely related (for example, tariffs and restrictions on inward investment induced by tariffs).

- Trade and investment policies are also linked to discussions of *non-economic* issues. One important development has been the formation of 'Baptist and bootlegger' coalitions between environmental and human rights groups concerned about globalization, and business and labour organizations that have an economic stake in restricting international trade and investment.

- Governments may be thought of as playing political games at two levels, their actions constituting moves that are both responses to demands made by groups in *domestic* politics, and responses to offers made by other governments in *international* negotiations.

- We need a better theory of two-level games that incorporates fuller representations of both domestic and international politics. In practice, most international political economists employ partial theories that focus only on variables operating at a single level.

QUESTIONS

1. If the economic case for trade liberalization is so strong, why is it that governments continue to impose barriers to trade and are engaged so frequently in trade disputes?

2. Trade theory does not imply that every individual within each nation will benefit from the lowering of trade barriers, just that aggregate benefits will exceed aggregate losses. Who stands to benefit most from trade liberalization in the advanced economies of Europe, Japan, and the United States, and who is most likely to be disadvantaged? What about the situation in developing nations with different types of factor endowments?

3. Can these different groups of individuals reach some kind of agreement so that trade liberalization can benefit everyone? What are the political obstacles to this type of agreement?

4. Is it inappropriate to think only, or primarily, in terms of economic gains and losses when evaluating the effects of increased international trade? How important are other types of concerns (for example, national security, income inequality, environmental hazards, human rights abuses) in the political debates that determine policy outcomes?

5. What types of electoral and policy-making institutions tend to mitigate the effects of lobbying by protectionist groups when it comes to the determination of trade policy? Are electoral systems based on proportional representation likely to generate less protection than plurality systems?

6. Do the economic effects of immigration shape the political struggles over changes in immigration law? Or do the politics of immigration reflect other types of cultural and social divisions within host countries?

7. What are the economic effects of foreign investment for the source country and for the host country? Does foreign investment generate a 'race to the bottom' in labour and environmental standards in developing countries? Does it inhibit democratic reform?

8. What economic and political changes during the twentieth century led to the abandonment of fixed exchange rates among the advanced economies? Why do many developing countries continue to fix their exchange rates?

 FURTHER READING

Trade

■ Destler, I. M. (1995), *American Trade Politics,* 3rd edn (Washington, DC: Institute for International Economics). This is required reading for anyone interested in how US trade policy is made. It provides a comprehensive analysis of American political institutions and policy-making.

■ Hayes, J. P. (1993), *Making Trade Policy in the European Community* (London: Macmillan). This book provides a thorough discussion of the processes of trade policy-making in the European Community.

■ Hiscox, M. J. (2002), *International Trade and Political Conflict* (Princeton, NJ: Princeton University Press). An analysis of historical changes in levels of factor specificity in several Western nations, relating these changes to shifts in political alignments in trade politics.

■ Krueger, A. O. (1995), *Trade Policies and Developing Nations* (Washington, DC: Brookings Institution). An engaging discussion of trade liberalization in developing nations in recent years.

■ Rogowski, R. (1989), *Commerce and Coalitions* (Princeton, NJ: Princeton University Press). A sweeping analysis of coalitions in trade politics in a variety of historical contexts, based on an application of the Stolper–Samuelson theorem.

Immigration

■ Borjas, G. J. (1999), *Heaven's Door: Immigration Policy and the American Economy* (Princeton, NJ: Princeton University Press). A provocative analysis of the effects of immigration in the United States in recent decades.

■ Fetzer, J. S. (2000), *Public Attitudes toward Immigration in the United States, France, and Germany* (Cambridge: Cambridge University Press). This book uses available survey data to compare public attitudes towards immigration in the United States, France, and Germany, and the determinants of anti-immigrant sentiments.

■ Tichenor, D. J. (2002), *Dividing Lines: The Politics of Immigration Control in America* (Princeton, NJ: Princeton University Press). A very impressive history of immigration politics in the United States.

Investment

■ Crystal, J. (2003), *Unwanted Company: Foreign Investment in American Industries* (Ithaca, NY: Cornell University Press). An excellent study of political debates about inward direct foreign investment in the United States.

■ Graham, E., and Krugman, P. R. (1995), *Foreign Direct Investment in the United States* (Washington, DC: Institute for International Economics). This book provides a comprehensive analysis of the economic and political effects of inward foreign investment.

■ Moran, T. (1998), *Foreign Direct Investment and Development* (Washington, DC: Institute for International Economics). An excellent study of the effects of direct foreign investment in developing nations.

Exchange rates

■ Frieden, J., Ghezzi, P., and Stein, E. (eds) (2001), *The Currency Game: Exchange Rate Politics in Latin America* (New York: Inter-American Development Bank). A very interesting collection of research on the politics of exchange-rate policies in Latin America.

■ Henning, R. C. (1994), *Currencies and Politics in the United States, Germany, and Japan* (Washington, DC: Institute for International Economics). This book provides a clear and detailed discussion of exchange-rate policy-making in the United States, Germany, and Japan.

■ Simmons, B. A. (1994), *Who Adjusts? Domestic Sources of Foreign Economic Policy During the Interwar Years* (Princeton, NJ: Princeton University Press). An impressive analysis of the political determinants of exchange-rate policies adopted by Western nations in the inter-war period.

Institutions

■ Gilligan, M. (1997), *Empowering Exporters: Reciprocity and Collective Action in Twentieth Century American Trade Policy* (Ann Arbor, MI: University of Michigan Press). A fine study of the importance of institutionalizing reciprocity in trade policy-making.

■ Hiscox, M. J. (1999), 'The Magic Bullet? The RTAA, Institutional Reform, and Trade Liberalization', *International Organization,* 53/4: 669–698. A critical review of research on the RTAA that emphasizes the role of political parties and their core constituencies in the politics institutional change.

■ Rogowski, R. (1987), 'Trade and the Variety of Democratic Institutions', *International Organization,* 41/2: 203–223. A classic analysis of the ways in which different types of electoral institutions affect trade policy outcomes in democracies.

■ Wintrobe, R. (1998), *The Political Economy of Dictatorship* (Cambridge: Cambridge University Press). An excellent analysis of policy-making in non-democratic regimes.

Extensions and complications

■ Elliott, K. Ann, and Freeman, R. (2003), *Can Labor Standards Improve under Globalization?* (Washington, DC: Institute for International Economics). This book provides a comprehensive review of the debates about whether trade and investment policies should be linked to agreements about improving labour standards in developing nations.

■ Goldstein, J., and Keohane, R. O. (eds) (1993), *Ideas and Foreign Policy: Beliefs, Institutions, and Political Change* (Ithaca, NY: Cornell University Press). An important collection of essays discussing the impact of new ideas on foreign policy outcomes.

■ Graham, E. (2000), *Fighting the Wrong Enemy: Anti-Global Activists and Multinational Enterprises* (Washington, DC: Institute for International Economics). A compelling analysis of the effects of direct foreign investment in developing nations that argues that criticisms made by environmental and human rights groups are misguided.

■ Irwin, D. (1996), *Against the Tide: An Intellectual History of Free Trade* (Princeton, NJ: Princeton University Press). A sweeping account of theoretical developments in economics that support the case for trade liberalization.

 WEB LINKS

● For regular research reports and briefs on policy issues:
www.iie.com   Institute for International Economics.

● For theoretical background on international economics and helpful beginner guides:
www.internationalecon.com   International Economics Study Center.
www.amosweb.com/gls   Amos World Economics Glossary.

● For data and analysis of public opinion on international economic issues:
http://pewglobal.org   The PEW Global Attitudes Project.
www.pipa.org   The Program on International Policy Attitudes (PIPA).

● For data on world trade, migration, and investment:
www.wto.org/english/res_e/statis_e/statis_e.htm   WTO's International Trade Statistics.
www.ilo.org/public/english/protection/migrant/ilmdb/ilmdb.htm   ILO's International Labour Migration Database.
www.unctad.org/Templates/Page.asp?intItemID=3204&lang=1   UNCTAD's World Investment Directory.

● For information and statistics on trade, immigration, investment, and exchange-rate policies:
http://cs.usm.my/untrains/trains.html   UNCTAD's TRAINS Database of Trade Control Measures.
www.wto.org/english/tratop_e/dda_e/tnc_e.htm   WTO's Negotiations Committee.
www.ustr.gov   United States Trade Representative (USTR).
http://europa.eu.int/comm/trade   European Union Trade Policy.
www.meti.go.jp/english/index.html   Japanese Trade Policy.
www.migrationpolicy.org   The Migration Policy Institute.
www.imf.org/external/np/tre/tad/exfin1.cfm   IMF's Country Finances and Exchange Rates.
www.federalreserve.gov   Federal Reserve Board.
www.bankofengland.co.uk   Bank of England.
www.ecb.int   European Union Central Bank.
www.boj.or.jp/en   Bank of Japan.

 Visit the Online Resource Centre that accompanies this book for more information:
www.oxfordtextbooks.co.uk/orc/ravenhill2e/

Appendix 4.1

BOX 4.8

The Theory of Comparative Advantage

The case for free trade was stated succinctly by Adam Smith. In *The Wealth of Nations*, he wrote: 'If a foreign country can supply us with a commodity cheaper than we ourselves can make it, better buy it of them with some part of the produce of our own industry, employed in a way in which we have some advantage' (Book IV, Section ii: 12). The idea here is simple and intuitive. If a country can produce some set of goods at lower cost than can a foreign country, and if the foreign country can produce some other set of goods at a lower cost, then clearly it would be best for the country to trade its relatively cheaper goods for the foreign economy's relatively cheaper goods. In this way both countries can gain from trade. This is the theory of trade according to **absolute advantage**.

David Ricardo, working in the early part of the nineteenth century, realized that absolute advantage was a limited case of a more general basis for international trade (the idea was originally stated by another economist, Robert Torrens, in *Essay on the External Corn Trade*, published in 1815, but most historians of economic thought believe that Ricardo reached his conclusions independently). Consider Table 4.1. Portugal can produce both cloth and wine more efficiently, that is, with less labour input than England (it has an absolute advantage in the production of both commodities). Ricardo argued that nonetheless it could still be mutually beneficial for both countries to specialize and trade.

The logic of comparative advantage rests on the *opportunity costs* of producing goods across countries; that is, the amount of one good that has to be given up to produce another good. In Table 4.1, producing a unit of wine in England requires the same amount of labour as required to produce two units of cloth. Production of an extra unit of wine means forgoing production of two units of cloth (that is, the opportunity cost of a unit of wine is two units of cloth). In Portugal, the labour required to produce a unit of wine would only produce 1.5 units of cloth (that is, the opportunity cost of a unit of wine is 1.5 units of cloth in Portugal).

To concentrate on wine production in Portugal requires giving up relatively less cloth output than would be the case in England. Similarly, if England produced only cloth, the amount of wine production forgone would be relatively smaller than if Portugal did so.

Portugal is thus relatively better at producing wine than is England: if Portugal concentrated on producing wine it would give up a smaller volume of cloth production than would England. Portugal is said to have a *comparative advantage* in the production of wine. England is relatively better at producing cloth than wine; so England is said to have a comparative advantage in the production of cloth.

Because relative or comparative costs differ, it can still be mutually advantageous for both countries to trade *even though Portugal has an absolute advantage in producing both commodities*. For international welfare to be maximized, Portugal should specialize in the product in which it is relatively most efficient; and England in the commodity in which it is relatively least inefficient.

Table 4.2 shows how trade might be advantageous. Costs of production are as set out in Table 4.1. In this example, England is assumed to have 270 person hours available for production. Before trade takes place, it produces and consumes eight units of cloth (requiring 120 person hours of labour input) and five units of wine (150 person hours). Portugal has fewer labour resources, with a total of 180 person hours of labour available for production. Before trade takes

Table 4.1 Comparative Costs of Production (Cost Per Unit in Person Hours)

Country	Cloth	Wine
England	15	30
Portugal	10	15

Table 4.2 Production Before and After Trade				
	Production before trade		Production after trade	
Country	Cloth	Wine	Cloth	Wine
England	8	5	18	0
Portugal	9	6	0	12
Total	**17**	**11**	**18**	**12**

place, it produces and consumes nine units of cloth (requiring 90 person hours of labour input) and six units of wine (90 person hours). Total production for the two economies combined is seventeen units of cloth and eleven units of wine.

If both countries now specialize, with Portugal producing only wine and England producing only cloth, and all their labour resources are devoted to the single product, England can produce (270 divided by 15) units of cloth and Portugal (180 divided by 15) units of wine. Total production by the two economies is eighteen units of cloth and twelve units of wine. Specialization according to comparative advantage and international trade, therefore, has enabled overall welfare to increase because total production has gone up by one unit of cloth and one unit of wine.

For trade to take place, the ratio of the price of the two goods must be lower than the domestic opportunity costs of production; that is, a bottle of wine will have to sell for somewhere between 1.5 and 2 bales of cloth. Note that the theory says nothing about distributional questions; that is, where in this range the price will settle, and thus who will gain most from trade.

The simple theory of comparative advantage makes a number of important assumptions:

- There are no transport costs.
- Costs are constant and there are no economies of scale.
- There are only two economies producing two goods.
- Traded goods are homogeneous (that is, identical as far as the consumer is concerned).
- Factors of production (labour and capital) are perfectly mobile internally but not internationally.
- There is full employment in both economies.
- There are no tariffs or other trade barriers.
- There is perfect knowledge, so that all buyers and sellers know where the cheapest goods can be found internationally.

Despite the lack of correspondence between the contemporary globalized economy and these assumptions, most economists believe that the fundamental principle that Ricardo identified still holds.

PART 2

Global Trade

5 The Evolution of the Global Trade Regime

GILBERT R WINHAM

 Chapter Contents

- Introduction
- Historical Antecedents: 1860 to 1945
- The ITO and the GATT: 1947 to 1948
- Multilateral Trade Negotiations: 1950s to 1980s
- The Uruguay Round and the WTO: 1986 to 1994
- The WTO in Action: 1995 and Beyond
- Conclusion

 Reader's Guide

The twentieth century witnessed a remarkable growth in international institutions, and nowhere was this growth greater than in the international trade system. Out of the ashes of a world economy torn by war and depression, a world trading regime was initiated at mid-century with the creation of the **General Agreement on Tariffs and Trade** (GATT) in 1947, which began with a few simple procedures and rules designed to promote the idea that if someone in one country can produce something that people in another country want to buy, they should have the right to sell it to them. From this simple beginning, the world trade regime developed by the end of the century into the most prominent example of co-operation between countries in the entire international system. This chapter reviews the history of this extraordinary development.

Introduction

Today, the global trade regime is a rules-based political system where the rules flowing from international agreements that seek to promote and stabilize economic exchanges between countries are ranged against the regulations of national governments that often seek to restrict those exchanges. The purpose of the international rules is to reduce the protectionism of national regulations, but even more, to reduce the uncertainty and unpredictability of international trade relations, and to promote stability. The task of this chapter will be to show how the global trade regime has been established through the actions of trading countries over the past 150 years, and how it became institutionalized in the World Trade Organization (WTO).

The global trade regime of the late twentieth and early twenty-first centuries is based on three components: trade, national regulations, and international agreements. Trade and national regulations have been a theme and counterpoint throughout much of history, in the sense that when national regulations receded, trade flourished; and when those regulations intensified, trade languished. To this combination can be added the third factor of international agreements, by which countries attempt to establish international rules that would restrict their own (and other countries') capacity to interrupt international trade through national regulation. Rules and regulations appear to be inherent in our highly ordered lives, and the irony is that in order to reduce regulation of one kind, it requires the intercession of rules of another kind. The important issue is where the rules or regulations come from, and whether their purpose is to reduce or expand the scope of our economic activity.

Trade, which is a staple of our modern global political economy, is also a historic, and even prehistoric, phenomenon. It was important to many ancient and medieval powers. Trade lay at the centre of state revenue and state power in ancient Athens; Ptolemaic Egypt, the Italian city states of Venice, Florence, and Genoa; and the German Hanseatic League. Nowhere was this clearer than in ancient Athens, which developed through commercial activities and at its height was totally dependent on trade. Athens exported silver and olive oil, and the boundaries of its trade have been charted over time by the shards of pottery urns that have been discovered throughout the Mediterranean region. In return, the Athenians were dependent on the import of grain, which was essential to maintain the population of Athens in an arid region.

In examining the global trade regime, trade is by necessity the starting point, but government is equally part of the story. This point has been observed by many writers, but perhaps was expressed most effectively by John Condliffe (1950: 27), as follows: 'The beginnings of trade are to be found in the enterprise of groups and individuals, but regulation and taxation of trade are almost as old as trade itself. In tracking history, if enterprise is the theme, regulation is the counterpoint. As soon as the track begins to be beaten out, established authority intervenes to control and levy tolls upon the traders.'

Early trade was a primitive exercise in economic enterprise. The means of regulating trade were equally primitive. The earliest means were tolls, exacted by local leaders for permission to pass through territory, or to trade, or simply for protection. From the earliest times, tolls were an expression of military control and political sovereignty, and if one controlled territory, one could exact tribute through tolls at will. This resulted in a great hindrance to trade, especially in Europe, which was divided into many small jurisdictions during the Middle Ages.

A more modern method of regulation than tolls was the tariff, or customs duty, which we now recognize as a percentage tax added to the price of imported goods. Tariffs are still with us today, but they are among the oldest functions of government. The purpose of early tariffs, whether on imports or exports, was to raise revenue. Tariffs were effective for this purpose, because, by the beginning of the eighteenth century, duties on imported goods had come to be the chief source of revenue in European countries. A further function of the tariff was to protect domestic producers from foreign competition.

Today, protectionism is the main purpose of the tariff. The revenue function is less important in developed countries, as governments have found other, more effective, means to raise revenues, although the tariff is still an important source of revenue in some developing countries. However, as if to demonstrate the ingenuity of government regulators, new forms of protection have arisen, collectively known as non-tariff measures (NTMs). These measures have now become more important than tariffs, the latter having been greatly reduced (again, mainly between developed countries) by successive trade agreements under the General Agreement on Tariffs and Trade (GATT).

The regulations that have restricted trade in recent decades have been the work of national governments. But those same governments have also reached international agreements with other governments attempting to constrain the extent to which domestic policies would restrict the free flow of international trade. These agreements started as simple undertakings between peoples as to how their commercial relations would be conducted, and trade agreements are almost as old as trade itself. For example, commercial treaties have been discovered between the kings of ancient Egypt and Babylonia, giving the parties the right to exact duties on the merchandise of traders or travellers. In more modern times, such treaties have been instrumental in establishing the rules whereby trade could be carried on between different political jurisdictions.

There has been a close relationship between trade and commercial treaties through history, to the extent that it accounts for much of the diplomatic practice between countries. An important watershed in this relationship occurred in the mid-nineteenth century with the Cobden–Chevalier (or Anglo-French) Treaty of 1860. This treaty initiated a brief period of liberalized trade between the United Kingdom and the Continent, which ended with the world depression of 1873–96. However, the treaty demonstrated that trade agreements could serve as an effective means of trade liberalization by alleviating some of the worst effects of competitive national regulation, and it set the stage for the deployment of trade negotiation in the twentieth century.

KEY POINTS

- The international trade regime is based on three components: trade, national regulations, and international agreements.

Historical Antecedents: 1860 to 1945

War and depression

The impact of government regulation on trade was well understood by the nineteenth century from the writings of Adam Smith and other political economists. Smith noted that, in addition to raising revenue, tariffs also had the effect of protecting domestic producers from foreign competition, something Smith and other reformers generally viewed with disfavour. As a political movement, however, the effort to curtail protectionist regulation did not begin until the Reform Act of 1932 in England. A campaign for free trade had begun among British merchants in the second quarter of the nineteenth century. The campaign was part of a broader effort of political reform in British society, and its eventual success resulted in part from the political realignment introduced by the Reform Act. The campaign was led by Richard Cobden, who demonstrated the importance of pragmatic leadership in promoting the ideal of free trade. In 1848, Britain repealed the Corn Laws, which provided high protection to agricultural products, and followed up this action with a series of administrative and diplomatic measures over the next two decades that put free trade into practice. Meanwhile, on the Continent, the French free trade movement had sought to convince the government of Louis Napoleon to reciprocate the British move towards free trade that was initiated by the repeal of the Corn Laws. No action was taken until the opportunity arose to incorporate a tariff negotiation in a commercial and political treaty with Great Britain. The Cobden–Chevalier treaty of 1860 was the result, which later helped to open the French market to British manufacturers (Rosecrance 1986).

The European system enjoyed a brief period of liberal commercial exchange that started in the 1830s and lasted until the 1870s. This period was dominated economically by Great Britain. The Napoleonic Wars of the early 1800s had left British manufacturing capabilities unscathed, and following the wars, Britain's economic strength allowed it to become the leading creditor country in the world. Britain provided aid and loans to European nations and had large exports of foreign investment, mainly to the United States and British colonies in Asia. In sum, the mid-century period of free trade essentially originated in the domestic politics of Britain and spread to the nations of Europe through the mechanism of international commercial treaties. The European commitment to free trade was considerably less enduring than the British, and it turned around quickly in the face of depression after 1870. For the British, however, free trade was the principal commercial policy of the nation until well after the First World War.

Protectionism reasserted itself in Europe as a straightforward response to hard times. As a result of a series of rapid technological improvements in the mid-1850s, the comparative advantage in grain growing shifted decisively to the New World, with the result that grain prices fell sharply in European markets. At the same time, a slump occurred in industrial production, which continued for over two decades in the form of low prices and low return on capital for manufactured products. International competition became severe, and in all countries there were strong pressures for protection against imports. One by one, national governments succumbed to the pressures, and reversed the period of relatively free trade that had been established prior to the 1850s. Austria-Hungary raised tariffs in 1876, and Italy followed in 1878. In 1879, Germany shifted to a protectionist policy and, because of its size in the European economy and its philosophy of nationalism and mercantilism, it set a protectionist tone for the overall system. France responded to German protectionism with restrictions of its own and, for its part, the United States continued the protectionism it had pursued throughout the nineteenth century. The United Kingdom, the Low Countries, and Switzerland, however, resisted the move toward higher tariffs, but by the end of the century, the UK was the only major nation practising free trade (Kindleberger 1951).

The depression that began in the 1870s also ushered in a lengthy period of protectionism that never really changed until after the Second World War. In the early part of the twentieth century, growing nationalism, and then war in 1914, exacerbated the protectionist trend that was already well established in response to the economic conditions of the late 1800s. The war broke up an imperfect but workable equilibrium between internal economic policies, trade, and payments that had existed under the gold standard of the nineteenth century. The war produced enormous dislocation that was even more serious in economic terms than the destruction that had occurred. The results were maladjustments to the free flow of labour, capital, and goods, which created impediments to economic activity that lasted well into the 1920s. But continued war planning also played an important role in the European mentality after 1919. In the realm of economic policy, war planning took the form of mercantilism, and later a bilateralism (that is, a focus on negotiating agreements with individual trade partners rather than through an international organization), inspired by Nazi Germany but copied by many other countries. Both mercantilism and bilateralism were designed to place the interests of the nation ahead of the wider community, and they inevitably took their toll on the economic performance of the overall system. The practice of both mercantilism and bilateralism, like war itself, was an expression of nationalism in economic policy.

The breakdown of the international economic system from war undoubtedly deepened the depression within national economies, and nations made efforts at the international level to repair the damage. Two such efforts stand out. The first was the World Economic Conference of 1927, and the associated Conference on Import and Export Prohibitions and Restrictions (Shonfield 1976). These meetings were aimed at countering the trend towards increased tariffs that was occurring in all countries during the 1920s. Countries initially agreed on a tariff truce and an agreement that would regulate quotas and other restrictions. However, the agreement failed to receive sufficient signatures to become binding, and the tariff truce was later discarded by individual country actions. The second effort was the World Economic Conference of 1933, at which time countries tried to achieve an international currency-stabilization agreement amid wildly fluctuating exchange rates that were perceived to be causing significant disruptions to international trade. This plan failed to attract the Americans and, in the wake of the collapsed conference, countries engaged in a period of competitive exchange-rate devaluations during the mid-1930s.

Reciprocal Trade Agreements Act of 1934

The United States had emerged from the First World War as the largest trading nation in the world; hence it was likely that domestic events affecting US trade capabilities would have a wide impact on commercial relations in the international system. This was the case with two events of the early 1930s: the Smoot–Hawley tariff of 1930, and the Reciprocal Trade Agreements Act of 1934 (Tasca 1938). The former was the culmination of a trend toward protectionism that had begun in the late nineteenth century, while the latter was the beginning of a trend toward liberalism that was interrupted by the Second World War but then continued into the present. These two events were major watersheds in commercial policy, and probably more important than the Second World War because they were economic events originating in the world economic system, rather than being the economic results of upheaval in the international political system.

The Smoot–Hawley Act of 1930 raised US duties to historic levels and increased the scope of tariff coverage as well. The Act was not a dramatic turnabout in protectionism, since US tariffs were already high, and all major trading nations were protectionist at that time. Rather, it represented a new level in the long movement by nations toward closing off their economies to foreign imports. In the wake of the Smoot–Hawley tariff and the retaliation by foreign countries that it precipitated, world trade fell by about two-thirds by the mid-1930s. The breakdown of trade after 1930 was alarming to Western governments, but even more alarming was the process that had led to that breakdown. The Smoot–Hawley Act was written in congressional committees that were essentially unable to master the detail that had become inherent in any major tariff legislation. Because of this economic illiteracy, and because of the general sympathy toward protectionism that had been created by the depression, Congress essentially extended protection to all those groups that demanded it. The spectacle was that of a gross excess of the democratic process and a loss of control over the economy by both the US president and the congressional leadership.

The breakdown of trade took its toll on public sympathy toward protectionism. The tariff became an issue in the presidential election of 1932, and was attacked by Democratic candidate Franklin D. Roosevelt as contributing to the depression. Following his election, Roosevelt appointed Cordell Hull as Secretary of State, a man committed to the view that free trade was an essential ingredient in world prosperity, and an even more important ingredient in international peace and stability. Hull and his officials began working with Congress to prepare new tariff legislation, and two years later the legislation was enacted under the title Reciprocal Trade Agreements Act (RTAA) of 1934 (see Hiscox, Box 4.6, page 116 in this volume).

The RTAA produced a revolution in US and even international trade policy. The central element of the RTAA was that it empowered the president to lower (or raise) tariffs up to 50 per cent from Smoot–Hawley levels in the course of trade negotiations with other countries. From the standpoint of American politics, the RTAA transferred tariff-setting policy to the presidency, which could organize itself bureaucratically for the task, and away from the Congress, which had ultimately prove to be incapable of managing the tariff or of discriminating between the many appeals brought by constituents for protection. This transfer substantially increased the control the government exercised over trade policy, and it has been an essential part of the US trade policy structure ever since 1934. From the standpoint of international politics, the RTAA was revolutionary in that it accepted implicitly that setting tariff rates could no longer be exclusively a unilateral policy by a nation state, but was rather a bilateral matter to be settled through negotiation. This action was reminiscent of the efforts by Michel Chevalier in the previous century to use commercial and political negotiation to reduce trade restrictions between France and Britain, and it began the changeover from a protectionist trade policy that had existed since the 1870s.

The US government pursued reciprocal trade agreements with other countries as far as economic circumstances after 1934 would allow. By 1939, the United States had concluded twenty-one agreements, which made reductions in about a thousand duties. All agreements were made on a most-favoured nation (MFN) or non-discriminatory basis, which slowed the negotiation because it engaged more parties, but also for the same reason extended the impact of the agreements more widely. The RTAA agreements were successful in increasing the flow of international trade, but the greatest value of the programme was that it provided a corpus of experience in trade liberalization that became integrated after the Second World War. The act of reaching bilateral agreements gave governments the opportunity to create mechanisms for liberalizing trade, which was demonstrated by the fact that most of the GATT articles drawn up in 1947 were taken from various agreements reached during the previous decade under the RTAA system. For example, the escape clause that was written into Article XIX of the GATT was drawn from an agreement the United States reached with Mexico in 1942.

The reciprocal trade programme was concurrent with a sea change in US and world public opinion regarding protectionism and free trade. In 1930, the passage of the Smoot–Hawley tariff took place in an environment favourable to protectionism, and within a legislative system that encouraged protectionist pressure groups to press their demands vigorously. This can be contrasted with the climate that existed in 1953–4, when the Republican Party under Dwight Eisenhower reversed its historic policy of protectionism by extending the RTAA of 1934. In the second case, public opinion was much more supportive of free trade, and there was relatively little effective protectionist pressure on the legislators, particularly from the more important economic interest groups in the country (Bauer *et al.* 1972). What appeared to have changed, not only in the United States but also elsewhere, was the principle of free trade versus protectionism, or more precisely, the expectations that people held as to which principle was just and would ordinarily prevail as a general rule. This change created a more favourable economic context for the major changes in the world trade regime that occurred after the Second World War.

KEY POINTS

- Organized efforts to establish freer trade in Europe began in the middle of the nineteenth century.

- A lengthy period of protectionism was initiated by the world depression that began in the 1870s, and then continued as a result of the world wars

  and depression of the first half of the twentieth century.

- Efforts to establish a liberal international trading system were begun with the US Reciprocal Trade Agreements Act of 1934.

The ITO and the GATT: 1947 to 1948

Post-war economic situation

The ascendancy of the United States in the early post-war period was immediately evident in the play of international policy-making. In terms of security policy, the United States took over the leadership of the Western alliance. The United States enjoyed a preponderant position in the formation of the United Nations and other post-war international organizations. Reconstruction aid to Europe through the Marshall Plan further demonstrated the primacy of the United States in the Western system. In addition, US economic hegemony could be demonstrated by figures representing three important areas of the international economic system, namely international monetary payments, trade, and foreign investment. In 1947, the United States held about 70 per cent of the monetary gold stock of the world. Even a decade later, this figure had not dropped below 59 per cent of the world's stock (Cooper 1968). There was an acute shortage of US dollars over this period, and the dollar itself began to serve as a reserve currency for international payments. Regarding trade, by 1950 the United States accounted for nearly 17 per cent of world trade,

and its share was about one and one-half times the share of the United Kingdom, the next leading nation (Krasner 1976). Through the decade of the 1950s, the United States increased its preponderance in world trade. By 1960, US trade was 20 per cent of overall world trade, over twice as large as that of the next leading nation (the UK), and roughly equal to the combined total of the three leading European economies, namely the UK, France, and West Germany. Finally, with regard to foreign investment, the United States went from an initial accumulated stock of foreign investment of $7 billion in 1946 to over $100 billion in 1973. The latter figure represented 51 per cent of total world foreign investment in that year (UN Commission on Transnational Corporations 1978). The second ranking nation in foreign investment in 1973 was the United Kingdom with 13.5 per cent, or about a quarter of the US total. In sum, all the major indicators of international economic performance demonstrate that the United States was in a unique position of leadership in the first two decades of the post-war period.

United States' leadership rested relatively easily on other Western nations because the security concerns of the Cold War with the Soviets encouraged those nations to be more willing to follow than they might otherwise have been. However, any system where one nation is dominant is likely to reflect the values of that nation, which was the case of the trade regime set up under the GATT after 1947. One American value that was carried forward to the international system was a relatively liberal pro-business, anti-government approach to international trade, which to the Europeans was problematic because of the uncertain circumstances facing European economies after the war, and their emphasis on maintaining low levels of unemployment. For the Americans, however, trade liberalization was an attractive goal in ideological terms, and it was also consistent with the US national interest, since the United States was favourably positioned to benefit from freer trade.

A second American value was that of multilateralism, intended to guarantee non-discrimination between all countries participating in the trade regime. The Americans blamed the collapse of international trade in that period on the 'closed' imperial trading blocs the Europeans created in the inter-war years, and saw in multilateralism a means of removing trade restrictions. However, the Europeans were much more guarded, fearing that their weaker economies would be unable to withstand the strain of multilateral trade liberalization. In the place of multilateralism, the Europeans promoted the virtues of regionalism, which later came to fruition in the forming of the institutions that led to the present-day European Union (EU). Yet another American value was a legal approach to international trade relations, complete with the conception of a code of international trade law backed up by a mechanism for settling disputes between parties. For their part, the Europeans were wary of a code approach to international trade relations, and sought instead to preserve their right to administrative discretion. They preferred to build a post-war trading system on practice rather than formal legal commitments (Gardner 1969).

The result of the different approaches taken by the United States and its allies is that the trade regime was, and has always been, based on compromise in the face of policy disagreements. Because of its predominant position, the US approach prevailed on most issues, but the rules that were negotiated were often riven with exceptions that weakened the legitimacy and effectiveness of the regime. It is important when assessing the trade regime to recall that it has always been based on a negotiated consensus, and that in the real world consensus is often only achieved through compromises that are unpalatable to the purists.

The rules of the GATT

Led by the United States, the Second World War allies attempted to create a new structure for the international system following the war. An essential part of this attempt was the Bretton Woods Conference of 1944, which established the International Bank for Reconstruction and Development (World Bank) and the International Monetary Fund (IMF). Along with these efforts in the development and monetary fields, the allies met in several conferences to establish the architecture of an international trade regime. To that end, countries concluded and signed an agreement to establish an International Trade Organization (ITO) in 1948, which was to complete the triad of functional organizations in the area of international economic relations. However, the US Congress failed to ratify the agreement, and without US involvement the ITO would have been irrelevant. In place of the ITO, countries relied on the General Agreement on Tariffs and Trade (GATT), established in 1947, to provide structure for the rapidly expanding trade system. The GATT itself was simply a contract embodying trade rules that were negotiated during a multilateral tariff negotiation in 1947. The GATT rules were partly a mechanism to ensure that countries that reduced protection by lowering tariffs did not reinstitute that protection through other measures. The GATT was never intended to function as an international organization. The fact that the GATT came to look and function like an international organization is the result of a largely unplanned and incremental accretion of political and legal powers. It was institution building by accident.

The GATT rules are contained in the thirty-five articles of the General Agreement (Jackson 1969). Perhaps the most important rule was that of non-discrimination, which is found in Articles I and III of the GATT. Article I is known as most-favoured nation principle (see Box 5.1). It required that any advantage—such as a lowered tariff—granted to another contracting party would immediately be accorded to all other contracting parties. This obligation—strongly promoted by the United States—attacked the practice of bilateral tariff preferences, which were commonly employed for political reasons before to the Second World War, and which compartmentalized and therefore reduced the flow of trade between nations. The United States prevailed on this matter, but not before it compromised with the Europeans on preferential trade arrangements for their colonies. Another aspect of non-discrimination was found in Article III, which obliged nations to treat foreign products—once they had been imported and duty paid—no less favourably than domestic products with respect to taxes and other requirements. In general, Article I ensured that a country could not discriminate externally, and Article III ensured it could not discriminate internally.

The principles of external and internal non-discrimination were not easy to establish in international trade. For example, in the 1930s, Article I non-discrimination, or most-favoured nation treatment, would have required a country such as Great Britain to give another country (even Nazi Germany) that did not discriminate against British trade the same tariff preferences it might have negotiated with a third country. This principle had the effect of elevating economics over politics in international relations, and was the subject of internal debate in Western countries in the years leading up to the Second World War. Similarly, Article III non-discrimination was also difficult for nations to accept, because it removed a whole range of policy tools (such as internal taxes or distribution requirements) that governments

BOX 5.1

Most-Favoured-Nation Principle (MFN)

The **most-favoured nation** principle was introduced into the trade agreements of the 1930s and incorporated as Article I of the General Agreement on Tariffs and Trade in 1947. It required GATT Contracting Parties to extend to all signatories the benefits of any agreement that it might reach with any other country (that is, the 'most-favoured nation') in the GATT. The GATT provided a forum, and a legal regime, within which countries were encouraged to negotiate and to reach agreements to lower tariffs on a reciprocal basis. Normally, a country (for example, Great Britain) would conclude such an agreement on a bilateral basis with the principal supplier of a good (for example, an agreement with Canada to lower the tariff on winter boots), but the resulting lowered tariff would be accorded to all countries exporting winter boots to Great Britain. In this example, it would be assumed that Canada might reciprocate by lowering its tariff on another good, of which Great Britain was the principal supplier to Canada.

The effect of the MFN principle was to eliminate discrimination between trade partners, as countries were in principle obliged to have one MFN tariff that applied to all other countries, and therefore were prohibited from applying different tariffs on the same product coming from different countries. Non-discrimination introduced the problem of **free riding** where a country might take unreciprocated benefits from a lowering of tariffs by other countries, but this was regarded as a lesser problem than that caused by overtly discriminatory tariff policies. The overall purpose of MFN and non-discrimination was to create a unified multilateral trading system, and to prevent the international trade system from degenerating into a balkanized system of regional preferences.

traditionally used to extend preferential treatment to domestic products.

Non-discrimination continues to be the cornerstone of the international trade system. Article I remains a basic building block of the GATT, and even though it has been somewhat compromised by preferential free trade agreements, nations negotiating those agreements have been careful to ensure that preference arrangements did not introduce new protectionism into the broader system. As for Article III, its relevance is demonstrated by the frequency with which it has been tested in GATT, and now World Trade Organization dispute settlement panels. An early example is the 1988 case on Canadian Liquor Board practices, where a panel found that discriminatory mark-up and listing practices by Canadian provincial liquor boards were inconsistent with Canada's obligations to its trading partners under Article III. This decision created pressure for reform of the Canadian practices.

A second important GATT rule was the prohibition in Article XI against quantitative and other non-tariff restrictions to trade (Dam 1970). The theory of the GATT was to delegitimize the use of protectionist measures other than tariffs, hence Article XI contained the stark obligation that 'no restrictions other than duties (that is, tariffs)' shall be maintained on the importation of any product. Article XI is increasingly regarded by trade lawyers as a key constraint on governments. For example, confrontations between trade and environmental concerns are a staple of contemporary trade policy, and Article XI obligations are the crux of this debate, as was illustrated in a 1991 GATT panel decision on tuna. At issue was environmental legislation in the United States which prevented the sale of tuna caught by methods that also kill dolphins, which served as the rationale for a ban on imports of tuna from Mexico. The United States lost the case when the GATT panel determined that the US restrictions violated that nation's obligations to Mexico under Article XI.

A third GATT rule deals with the methodology adopted by the GATT for reducing trade restrictions. This methodology was the sponsorship from time to time of tariff negotiations to be conducted 'on a reciprocal and mutually advantageous basis' and 'directed to the substantial reduction of tariffs' (Article XXVIII bis). The concept of reciprocity is the most interesting aspect of this methodology. Reciprocity can be seen as a normal aspect of negotiation in general, which in international trade has been promoted as a political imperative where nations give tariff reductions in order to get similar benefits from their partners, although economists often deride this concept, arguing that it is countries offering tariff reductions that make their economies more efficient and hence realize the benefit. Nevertheless, in the GATT's early history of trade negotiations, reciprocity was a guiding beacon as countries began the process of dismantling tariff protectionism. However, reciprocity as a concept ran into difficulties when developing countries acceded to the GATT. Because it is questionable whether equal treatment of unequal partners in trade negotiations could be considered reciprocal, numerous exceptions from full reciprocity were granted by industrialized GATT partners in favour of developing countries. For example, in various negotiations, an attempt was made to mitigate the obligations of GATT membership for developing countries through the concept of special and differential treatment. In the end, the efforts to water down GATT reciprocity for developing countries have produced very little in concrete terms, which demonstrates how difficult it is in international trade to depart from the notion of 'equal treatment under the law'. Nevertheless, demands for special treatment are a continuing aspect of the trade regime, as evidenced in the Doha trade negotiations (discussed later in this chapter).

Two other basic norms of the GATT are safeguards and the concept of 'commercial considerations'. Safeguards were based on the operational plan of the GATT framers that restrictive measures on trade would be converted to tariff protection, and then tariffs would be reduced through multilateral negotiations. In a situation where tariff reductions created an especially difficult political problem in any contracting party, the GATT also allowed (in Article XIX) for nations to backtrack on their commitments (that is, to raise tariffs) for a period of time to permit the orderly adjustment of domestic markets. The intent was to ensure that problems in specific industries did not compromise the general process of liberalization. The fact that the GATT has accommodated itself to protectionist pressures over the years has often been viewed positively by governments and commentators as an example of pragmatism and resilience.

The other rule of 'commercial considerations', or support for the values of the free market versus government interventionism, is implicit in the entire framework of the GATT. The term is mentioned specifically in Article XVII, where state-controlled enterprises are enjoined to act according to 'commercial considerations', and it is implicit in Article XVI, where the harmful effect of subsidies on efficient production is mentioned. Because the GATT represents commercial, free-market values, it has been a successful organization in a world that has recently moved in the same direction, and continues to move in that direction following the dissolution of international communism in the early 1990s.

In sum, the rules of the GATT provided a basis for governance in a narrow, but fundamentally important, sector of international relations. In any regime, or even government, the test of the regime is that the rules are understood, and that they guide behaviour. Without doubt, the rules of the GATT were known in the main, and they were usually followed by the contracting parties to the Agreement (Hudec 1975).

KEY POINTS

- Following the Second World War, the United States was a preponderant presence in the world economy, and took a leadership role in post-war planning.

- Trading nations established the General Agreement on Tariffs and Trade (GATT) in 1947, and attempted in 1948 to create an International Trade Organization (ITO), which failed to receive ratification by the US Congress.

- The GATT obliged importing countries not to discriminate in favour of products coming from one country over those from another, or in favour of domestic products over foreign products, once the latter had paid any duties required and entered the importing country.

- The principles and rules of the GATT provided a rudimentary basis for the regulation of international trade.

Multilateral Trade Negotiations: 1950s to 1980s

Post-war negotiations and the Kennedy Round

The main role of the GATT was to liberalize trade, and most decisions to that end were initiated in trade negotiations. The GATT was established to support the trade negotiations in 1947, and following that date the GATT sponsored multilateral negotiations in 1949 (Annecy), 1951 (Torquay), 1956 (Geneva), 1960–1 (the Dillon Round), and in 1963–7 (the Kennedy Round). Further negotiations were the Tokyo Round (1973–9), the Uruguay Round (1986–93), and the WTO Doha 'Round', initiated in January 2002, and continuing at the time of writing. Of these nine negotiations, the first four after 1947 took up some important institutional matters, such as the accession of new members, but they did not make significant progress in liberalizing trade. One reason is that the European countries relied heavily on non-tariff measures through the mid-1950s, and hence any tariff concessions given during GATT negotiations were not meaningful in trade terms. Furthermore, European recovery from the war did not occur as quickly as expected, as evidenced by the fact that European currencies were not made fully convertible until 1958, which made it difficult for these countries to increase their exposure to international competition. In practice, the United States was the preponderant actor in the early negotiations, and offered most of the tariff concessions.

The GATT incorporated the bilateral negotiation process established by the RTAA, and simply multilateralized it (Diebold 1952). However, this change was not accomplished in a single stroke. The early GATT tariff negotiations were multilateral in name, but the real action occurred bilaterally between nations that served as principal suppliers and principal consumers of each other's products. Bilateral agreements were then multilateralized automatically through the most-favoured nation principle. If a country were, say, to halve its tariff of 10 per cent on Country A's widgets following bilateral negotiations with A, it would be obliged to extend the new tariff of 5 per cent on all imports of widgets from any other GATT contracting party. Nations could, and often did, remain aloof from the bilateral negotiating process, while nevertheless taking advantage—as free riders—of reductions concluded by other nations. Over time, the emphasis in the GATT shifted from the negotiation of tariff reductions to the negotiation of legal codes of behaviour. The latter negotiations are more fully multilateral, and are carried out in a process reminiscent of domestic parliamentary legislation, with a structured committee process leading to decisions in broader forums.

The Kennedy Round of 1963–7 emerged as the first significant negotiation in GATT after the initial negotiation in 1947 (Preeg 1970). It led to an average tariff reduction among the participants of about 35 per cent, in sharp contrast to the reduction of less than 10 per cent on a much smaller volume of trade in the Dillon Round that preceded it, or even the 20 per cent reduction achieved in the

negotiation of 1947. The negotiation also produced an anti-dumping code designed to help standardize national policies in this difficult and contentious area, and an international grain agreement that established price ranges for wheat and provided for multilateral sharing of food aid to developing countries. The Kennedy Round was, moreover, the first GATT negotiation at which the nations of the European Community (EC) participated as a single unit, which was the first time Europe and America engaged in a major negotiation across the Atlantic on an apparent basis of equality and reciprocity. It is interesting to note the historical correlation between a successful outcome in trade negotiation and the increasing equality of the major actors in those negotiations, for it is a trend that continued through the Kennedy Round and on into the Tokyo Round of the 1970s.

Apart from the economic results of the Kennedy Round, there were important political results that flowed from the successful completion of this major negotiation. The negotiation of trade liberalization in GATT was always a continuing struggle between liberalizing and protectionist forces. Those governments favouring liberalization have used negotiation, especially multilateral negotiation, as the principal means to trade free from protectionist restrictions. Those favouring protectionism have been more ascendant, and more effective, between major trade negotiations. This increased the salience and importance of any given negotiation over time, because there would be an increasing number of policy issues riding on the outcome. Thus, the pressure at the Kennedy Round to reach an acceptable settlement was increased, and ensured that any deadlock would constitute a failure that would go beyond the issues at the table.

The upshot was that the Kennedy Round took on enormous importance as a symbol as it went along. It became a test of the national will of the major participants to continue the post-war trend towards trade liberalization. Even more important, it was a test of the willingness of nations to avoid a breakdown that would lead to increased protectionism. The main reason the Kennedy Round succeeded is

BOX 5.2

Dumping and Anti-Dumping Duties

Dumping in international trade is generally understood as selling a product to another country for less than its sale price in the exporting country. Dumping is defined more precisely in Article VI of the GATT as exporting below the 'normal value' of a product, and is determined through a comparison of the price of the product in both the exporter's and importer's markets, or through an analysis of the exporter's costs of producing the product versus what it sold for on export. Determining 'normal value' through an examination of production costs can be uncertain and can lead to high anti-dumping duties, especially in non-market economies, where prices may not have the same meaning as in market economies.

Dumping is 'condemned' by the GATT if it causes injury to a domestic industry producing a 'like product' in the importing country. In the event a product is dumped and causes injury, as determined by an anti-dumping investigation conducted by the government of the importing country, the importing country can impose an 'anti-dumping duty' (in other words, an additional tariff) equal to the margin of dumping, meaning the difference between the normal value of the product and its export price.

In plain terms, dumping amounts to underselling, which is acceptable competitive behaviour within countries, but which is generally considered objectionable in the politically sensitive terrain of international commerce. Anti-dumping actions are widely sought after by import-competing industries as a convenient means of protection against foreign competitors, especially since trade laws in most countries make it relatively easy to establish a case against foreign dumping. As a result, there has been a sharp increase in the incidence of anti-dumping actions by GATT and WTO Members since the 1980s. For example, worldwide anti-dumping initiations rose from around 150 a year in 1981 to 366 a year in 2001, before falling to about 200 by 2004 (Jones 2006). It is possible that the drop after 2001 resulted from a disinclination to initiate actions during the negotiation of the Doha Round. Developing countries have increased their own use of anti-dumping investigations, and between 1995 and 2005 seven of the ten heaviest users of anti-dumping actions were developing countries.

To sum up, anti-dumping duties can be viewed as a harassing and objectionable impediment to legitimate trade, and consequently countries have negotiated Anti-Dumping Codes in the Kennedy, Tokyo, and Uruguay Rounds designed to discipline the actions governments can take to protect domestic industries from foreign dumping. National legislation and international treaties on dumping and anti-dumping duties can be traced back to the beginning of the twentieth century, and these practices have been perhaps the most highly litigious and politicized area of the trade regime since its inception.

that governments feared what the implications of failure might mean for the international economic system, and because they wanted to avoid blame for causing such implications. In a strict sense, of course, it is clear that a deadlock in the Kennedy Round would have meant only that nations did not agree to reduce tariffs or other restrictions; this would have had no necessary consequences for increased protectionism. However, the situation was not framed in such terms. The political reality was that nations felt under great pressure to avoid a breakdown of a dialogue that had extended for five years, and of a settlement that would help to structure trading relations in the foreseeable

future. Among these general concerns, the positions that delegations took on individual tariffs or products ultimately became less important. Thus the main political result of the Kennedy Round was the achievement of the agreement itself, especially since the agreement was significant in trade terms.

Tokyo Round

At the close of the Kennedy Round in 1967, the GATT secretariat, led by Director-General Sir Eric Wyndham-White, sought to convince the major trading nations to extend liberalization into the area of **non-tariff barriers** (NTBs) to trade (Evans

1971). This initial effort was unsuccessful, but by the early 1970s chaos in the international monetary system and increasing use of non-tariff barriers in response to the surge of exports from Japan and the newly industrializing economies (NIEs) resurrected fears of trade protectionism and convinced national governments to begin a new negotiation in the GATT. This negotiation, named after the city in which it was initiated, started slowly because of the need to gather and classify enormous amounts of trade data with respect to NTBs. The negotiation was delayed further by the need for the United States to pass legislation authorizing the president to negotiate (an event that was not completed until January 1975), and by the US election of 1976. The negotiation effectively got under way in 1977, and comprehensive offers from delegations were in place by early 1978. Serious bargaining took place during the following year, and in April 1979 the final agreements were signed, subject to later ratification.

The agreements reached at the Tokyo Round were the most comprehensive and far-reaching results achieved in trade negotiations since the creation of the GATT (Winham 1986). The results fell into three categories: six legal codes (plus a sectoral code for trade in aircraft) that dealt with NTBs; tariff reductions; and a series of revisions of GATT articles primarily of interest to developing countries. The six codes updated and expanded aspects of the trade law of the GATT, and were the most important part of the Tokyo Round accords. These covered, respectively, customs valuation procedures, import licensing, technical standards for products, subsidies and countervailing duty measures, government procurement, and anti-dumping duty procedures. However, negotiations on a safeguards code failed.

The general thrust of the code negotiations was to effect a 'constitutional reform' of GATT law, and as well to improve the openness, certainty, and non-arbitrariness of the rules governing international trade. In some areas this was accomplished without appreciable controversy. In codes on customs valuation, import licensing, and technical barriers, nations proceeded from the widely shared philosophy that government regulations in these areas should not be used to provide protection for domestic producers, by design or otherwise. In other areas, agreement was more problematic. The attempted code on Article XIX safeguards encountered a determined insistence by the European Commission regarding the right to apply safeguards selectively on a targeted basis, rather than non-discriminatorily or across the board. Selectivity in particular was resisted by the developing countries, which would be the primary targets of this tactic. Also, the code on subsidies and countervailing duties triggered deeply-held disagreements between the United States and the Commission over the appropriateness of agricultural export subsidies in modern government practice, but in the end this disagreement was reconciled by limiting the actions taken on agriculture, and the code was signed.

The second category of results from the Tokyo Round was tariff reductions. To put these results in perspective, tariff negotiations were the main item of business in the six multilateral negotiations that were held under GATT auspices through the Kennedy Round of 1967. Tariffs were not the major focus of the Tokyo Round, yet the average reductions of about 35 per cent of industrial nations' tariffs achieved in this negotiation were comparable to the reductions of the Kennedy Round. The reductions covered more than $100 billion of imports, and were phased in over an eight-year period beginning in 1980 (Cline 1983).

A major controversy in the tariff negotiation was to arrive at a tariff-cutting formula for manufactured products. A similar controversy had occurred in the Kennedy Round, at which time nations settled on a linear approach (50 per cent cut across the board, less exceptions) supported mainly by the United States. In the Tokyo Round, proponents of a tariff-harmonizing formula carried the day, and nations agreed to table offers according to a compromise Swiss formula that generally required tariff cuts to be proportional to the size of the tariff. The final bargaining produced a number of exceptions to the general formula, particularly in industries where imports were already high, and 'sensitive' domestic interests were threatened. For example, in the United States, where the average tariff cut was 31 per cent, the duties for leather imports were reduced by only 4 per cent; for apparel, 15 per cent; for automobiles, 16 per cent; and tariffs for footwear and colour televisions were exempted from any cuts. Similar exceptions were made by other trading nations.

The third category of Tokyo Round results was a proposed series of revisions to GATT Articles known as the 'framework' agreements. Negotiations on this subject were initiated by Brazil, intending to clarify GATT obligations and ease those obligations for developing countries. The framework agreements covered subjects such as safeguard actions for development purposes (or infant industry promotion), trade measures taken to correct payments deficits, export controls, and deviations from most-favoured nation procedures for developing countries. One important accord in the framework package was the Understanding regarding Notification, Consultation, Dispute Settlement, and Surveillance, which required GATT members to notify trading partners of the trade measures they adopt, and thus to provide an early warning for all countries of actions that might affect their interests adversely. The framework agreements did not substantially rewrite GATT law to advantage developing countries, and as a result many of those countries felt the results were 'frustrating and incomplete' (*Multilateral Trade Negotiations* 1979: 34). However, the agreements did improve GATT language on matters related to developing countries, and therefore probably improved the capacity of the GATT legal machinery to mediate and reduce trade disputes.

The Tokyo Round underscored the extent to which multilateral negotiation had become a point of departure for managing the international trade system. In contrast with past GATT negotiations, which were largely limited to the reduction of tariffs, the Tokyo Round was a rule-making exercise of major proportions. Furthermore, the agreements of the Tokyo Round constituted legal rules that reached further into the nation state and impacted more deeply on individual human behaviour than was the case with most international agreements. The process of negotiating these rules was extraordinarily complex, and arguably the code negotiations of the Tokyo Round were the most advanced, in terms of bureaucratic complexity, of any multilateral negotiations occurring at that time. The greatest complexity lay in attempting to integrate the conflicting trade legislation of many nations into a co-ordinated set of international rules. In their efforts to mesh the rule-making apparatus of different countries into a single structure, the Tokyo Round negotiators faced problems that became commonplace a decade later as nations coped with the implications of an increasingly interdependent world.

> **KEY POINTS**
>
> - Multilateral trade negotiations were conducted in the GATT to reduce tariff protectionism on a reciprocal basis.
>
> - In the Tokyo Round (1973–9), countries focused on the more difficult task of reducing non-tariff measures that afforded protection in international trade. These measures were regulated through the negotiation of international codes of behaviour.
>
> - The Tokyo Round demonstrated the importance of multilateral negotiation to the management of the international trade system.

The Uruguay Round and the WTO: 1986 to 1994

Background

The next major effort to further establish the world trade regime was the Uruguay Round negotiation, which was launched at a GATT ministerial meeting in Punta del Este, Uruguay, in September 1986 (Croome 1995). The path to the Uruguay Round was difficult indeed. The previous GATT multilateral negotiation had made considerable progress in reducing protectionism from non-tariff barriers. Pressure began to build shortly after 1979 to expand the GATT regime to include new issues—such as services, investment, and intellectual property—in addition to the old issues that dealt with trade in goods. In particular, the United States argued that a new negotiation was necessary to make the GATT relevant to a changing world economy, and in 1982 a GATT ministerial meeting was convened to consider this possibility. The idea met sharp resistance, particularly from developing countries that were overwhelmed by the global debt crisis and mainly concerned to expand traditional exports to developed countries to service debt obligations to the International Monetary Fund, Western governments, and private banks. Led by India and Brazil, the developing countries insisted that they were not sufficiently developed to negotiate the new issues, such as services, on an equal footing with the developed countries. Moreover, developing countries held that the developed countries had evaded their obligations in some of the traditional goods, such as textiles or agricultural products, which were of particular importance to developing countries, and demanded further liberalization in these areas as a precondition to any new negotiations. The result was that the 1982 ministerial meeting was a failure for the proponents of new negotiations, although the meeting did establish important work programmes that generated the data needed for future negotiation.

The most dramatic part of the lead-up to the Uruguay Round negotiation came in the week-long special ministerial session at Punta del Este in September 1986 (Winham 1998a). At the eleventh hour, it was agreed between the Americans and the Indians that the session would launch negotiations on a range of issues, including services, but that negotiations on services would be undertaken in a separate structure from those on goods, which presumably would lessen the prospects that developed countries could force trade-offs between services and the traditional subjects in the negotiation. Once the breakthrough on services occurred, it was clear that the remaining issues did not warrent holding up the prospect for a new negotiation, and settlement quickly followed on investment and intellectual property, which had also been major sticking points between the developed and developing countries.

New issues

The agenda of the Uruguay Round comprised fifteen negotiating groups arranged initially in four principal categories: market access (including the critical areas of agriculture and textiles); reform of GATT rules; measures to strengthen the GATT as an institution; and the new issues, specifically services, investment, and intellectual property (Preeg 1995). The new issues were included in the negotiation in order to make the GATT more relevant to developments in the world economy, and to respond to strong pressures coming from industry in developed countries. By the late 1980s, services had come to account for well over half of the gross domestic product (GDP) of developed countries, and they were beginning to account for an increasing proportion of international trade. For the GATT, the incorporation of services was not a straightforward matter. Services are not goods, which had always been the focus of GATT rules, but rather are processes in which skills and knowledge are exchanged in order to meet a particular consumer need. They can include processes as widely differentiated as engineering consulting, financial **intermediation**, tourism, or legal advice. Services often require the movement of the factors of production (for example, the establishment of a bank branch in a foreign country to sell financial services), a condition that is constantly affected by changes in technology that decrease the barrier separating non-traded from traded services. For its part, the GATT had identified many services as 'non-traded goods', although this characterization was dropped and services became recognized as an integral part of the international economy. There are many obstacles that can prevent a free exchange of services between countries, but an important one is the reluctance of domestic authorities to grant foreign firms the right to establish and do business in their markets. Such a refusal may be motivated by protectionist impulses, but it may also be inspired—for example in the case of prudential banking legislation—by a desire to protect the consumer, who is often viewed as

being at a disadvantage with respect to the foreign service provider.

Because countries have different regulatory objectives and standards, the result is that the global services market is essentially protectionist. GATT principles required non-discrimination among trade partners, national treatment of foreign suppliers, and transparency in the process by which domestic rules are developed, but the provision of services often requires the opposite behaviour if the consumer is to be protected and provided with a reliable and quality service. Governments generally seek to provide consistent regulation over their own markets; again, arguably, this might require discrimination against trade partners that apply different standards from trade in services. Because services are processes, defining them is difficult unless a strict functional definition is employed. The stricter the definition, however, the greater the chance that discrimination will occur. Yet, without strict definitions, domestic regulation may more easily be circumvented.

BOX 5.3

Uruguay Round Agreements

The GATT Multilateral Trade Negotiation known as the Uruguay Round began in September 1986, effectively concluded in December 1993, and formally concluded with official signatures at the Marrakesh (Morocco) Ministerial Meeting in April 1994. The Uruguay Round produced a wide range of agreements integrated under a common legal system. What is usually thought of as the 'WTO system' is contained in the Marrakesh Agreement Establishing the World Trade Organization (WTO) and the Dispute Settlement Understanding (DSU). The WTO Agreement established the WTO as an international organization, and ensured that all the agreements negotiated at the Uruguay Round were accepted as a **single undertaking**, thus increasing the legal integration of the WTO trade regime. The dispute settlement system established by the DSU was also intended to apply to all areas of the Uruguay Round Agreements, hence it is an integral part of the architecture of the new WTO system.

The Uruguay Round Agreements comprise about sixty agreements totalling some 550 pages, covering subjects as widely diversified as agriculture, safeguards, trade in intellectual property, **rules of origin**, textiles and clothing, and technical barriers to trade. These agreements can be accessed on the WTO website www.wto.org under the title 'Legal Texts of the WTO Agreements'. In addition, the Uruguay Round Agreements also included the General Agreement on Tariffs and Trade 1994, which effectively incorporated the GATT of 1947 into the WTO system. There were some additional agreements interpreting various provisions of the GATT, such as the meaning of 'other duties and charges' in Article II, which covers tariff schedules, but there is historical and legal continuity from the basic rules and provisions of the GATT to the modern WTO trade regime.

The tasks for the negotiators at the Uruguay Round were to incorporate GATT principles of transparency, national treatment and reciprocity, as well as newer principles such as market access, into an area of trade that was conceptually dissimilar from trade in goods, the normal milieu of GATT principles and practice (Arup 2000). Given the paucity of information on trade in services, the first task was to develop a common database on which substantive decisions could later be made. Second, a code of principles (which later became known as the General Agreement on Trade in Services—GATS) would have to be negotiated to provide for a standard of treatment between countries of trade in services. Finally, the code of principles would have to be applied to specific sectors of services trade. To do this, negotiators needed to analyse existing measures that restricted trade in services in order to propose measures that would liberalize trade in specific services sectors.

The two other new issues on the Uruguay Round agenda were investment and intellectual property. Investment was included because by the 1980s it had become apparent that investment was interchangeable with trade, and, more important, that trade liberalization might be less valuable in stimulating international economic exchanges unless it is accompanied by the liberalization of investment regimes. However, investment has always attracted considerable regulation in importing countries because of the risk to sovereignty associated with high levels of foreign investment in sensitive industries. In the Uruguay Round, the negotiation of a multilateral investment agreement eventually proved to be an unreachable goal, and the agreement that was reached on **trade-related investment measures (TRIMs)** dealt with only a small proportion of the issues raised in the negotiation.

Trade-related aspects of intellectual property rights, better known as TRIPs, was the third of the new issues. Intellectual property rights grant state protection to producers of new ideas, but this protection was not well established in the international economy (Maskus 2000). Producers of high-tech products sought to internationalize the intellectual property protections they enjoyed in their home country, and producers' associations such as the Pharmaceuticals Manufacturers Association demanded constraints on generic industries that arguably did not recognize legitimate patents on drugs. Negotiations in the Uruguay Round began by addressing the problem of counterfeit goods in international trade, but developed countries—which asserted that inadequate protection of intellectual property rights was a serious non-tariff barrier to trade—quickly pressed for a broader negotiation over patents and copyrights. Developing countries, led by India and Brazil, viewed TRIPs protection as a potential barrier to trade in its own right, but they were more concerned over the monopolies effectively granted in developed countries for products such as pharmaceuticals, which they considered crucial to the public interest. The developing countries acquiesced on this issue because they felt their losses were compensated by gains elsewhere in the overall accord, and an agreement was concluded that set international standards for certain protections dealing with copyrights and patents (Winham 1998a). However, the controversy over the TRIPs Agreement continued as a mainstay of WTO politics, as developing countries saw intellectual property rights as a mechanism by which developed countries could maintain a competitive edge relative to countries that lacked a sophisticated technological infrastructure.

Developing countries

For most of the history of the GATT, the developing countries have been marginal players. The GATT itself was largely a creation of the United States and its Western allies, and focused mainly on trade rather than economic development, which was the central concern of the poorer countries of Africa, Asia, and South America. Above all, the GATT took aim at the high level of tariffs in the trading system, and promoted the reduction of these tariff levels in developing countries (see Figure 5.1). By comparison, in terms of trade policy, most

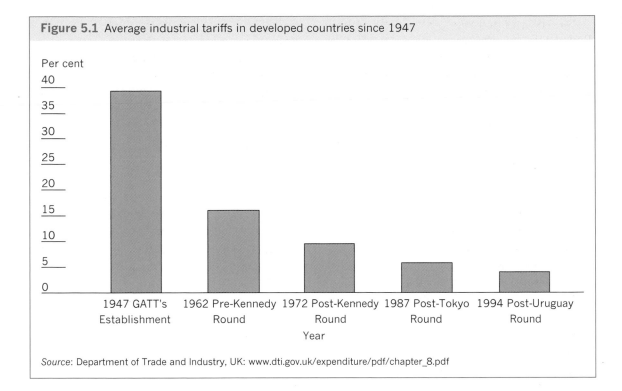

Figure 5.1 Average industrial tariffs in developed countries since 1947

Per cent

Source: Department of Trade and Industry, UK: www.dti.gov.uk/expenditure/pdf/chapter_8.pdf

developing countries pursued a policy of import substitution industrialization (ISI), which called for high protective tariffs to force consumers to purchase domestic-made products at the expense of imports. These policies encouraged developing-country governments to pursue trade policies of self-sufficiency, and to seek 'special and differential' benefits in GATT negotiations in lieu of accepting the multilateral rules of the GATT based on reciprocity. The upshot was that, as the GATT system matured, it became clear that one of the major threats to that system was its inability to be relevant to traders and governments in countries representing over two-thirds of the world's population. This threat was largely overcome in the Uruguay Round negotiation, for one of the results of the negotiation was that, for the first time, developing countries became fully integrated into the world trade regime.

The developing countries did not support the initiation of the Uruguay Round. Led by India and Brazil, they insisted that they were not sufficiently developed to negotiate the new issues such as services on an equal footing with the developed countries. Also, they argued that developed countries had not honoured their past commitment in traditional goods such as textiles or agriculture, and that further liberalization in these areas would be a precondition for any new negotiation. However, once developing countries relented and agreed to negotiate, they quickly engaged in all the issues before the negotiation. As the negotiation continued, it became clear that the capacity to determine the outcome of the Uruguay Round fell mainly to the two major trading powers: the United States and the European Union. At this point, a curious change took place: the major powers that had been so insistent on a new negotiation reached a deadlock, largely over agriculture, while the developing countries that had fought so hard against a new negotiation for most of the 1980s became the greatest advocates for its successful conclusion in the early

1990s. From 1991 until the conclusion of the in Uruguay Round December 1993, the developing countries kept the pressure on the majors to settle their differences, which was an important element in the multilateral agreement that was eventually reached.

The turnaround in the developing countries' position was one of the most interesting stories of the Uruguay Round (Winham 1998a). It occurred, first, because developing countries were advantaged by two negotiating principles that underlay the Uruguay Round; namely, consensus and the single undertaking. Single undertaking meant that all issues of the negotiation were treated as a single package, with no exceptions, unlike the Tokyo Round, where agreements were signed on a plurilateral (or pick and choose) basis, with the result that countries were subject to differing rights and obligations. Consensus—which was a traditional GATT principle—meant that multilateral agreement required the passive support (that is, no formal opposition) of all participants. These principles combined to increase the power of small and middle-sized powers at the Uruguay Round, which was demonstrated dramatically at the 1988 ministerial meeting in Montreal when five Latin-American countries withheld consensus from an interim package agreement because their concerns over agriculture were not being met by the major countries. This action emboldened the developing countries, and led them to take a greater interest in the overall negotiation.

Second, despite the reality that developing countries continued to be economically disadvantaged in comparison to developed countries, the agreements reached at the Uruguay Round were favourable to the interests of the former. Developing countries as a group benefited from agreements on agriculture, textiles, and clothing (and probably services), while they may have lost out on intellectual property and anti-dumping practices. Most important, however, developing countries were advantaged by the institutional arrangements resulting from the Uruguay Round Agreements, namely the strong dispute settlement mechanism and the creation of the World Trade Organization itself. On balance, these advantages encouraged the developing countries to support the Round.

Finally, and most important, the market-based economic reforms that took place in many developing countries in the 1980s encouraged their governments to look more favourably on the market-based principles and objectives of the GATT. That these changes were concurrent with pressures to liberalize economies from Western countries and international financial institutions is undeniable, but in the end the fall of communism and the obvious success of certain free market countries such as Singapore or Taiwan led to an internal policy revolution in many countries. For example, India suffered a severe financial crisis in 1991, following which it introduced reforms designed to deregulate the national economy and increase its economic efficiency. In the wake of these domestic reforms, India revised its negotiating strategy at the Uruguay Round from opposition to support for a multilateral agreement. In India and in many other developing countries, the impact of internal reform was to increase the congruence between domestic policies and the principles of the international trade regime.

The United States and the European Union

The structure of the contemporary international trade regime is centred mainly around the US–EU bilateral relationship (Bergsten 1999). However, this was not always the case. Until the early 1960s, the United States held a preponderant position in relation to other members of the GATT, and in multilateral negotiations it offered most of the concessions and expected little in return from other countries. This situation began to change in the Kennedy Round, when the six European Common Market countries negotiated as a single bloc. The change was largely completed by the Tokyo Round, when the European Community (now the European

Union) had expanded to include the United Kingdom, making the EC the largest trading entity in the international system.

Negotiations in the Tokyo Round and subsequently could be characterized as a pyramidal process. This means that agreements were usually initiated between the principal players, namely the United States and the European Union, and then presented successively to middle-sized and smaller parties to establish a multilateral consensus. Pyramidal negotiation operates when there is a wide disparity of power among negotiating parties, and in particular when the negotiating structure is bipolar. On the positive side, pyramidal negotiation places the onus for initiating agreement on the parties that have effective power to veto a multilateral agreement. A drawback, however, is that this negotiation structure leaves less scope for smaller powers involved in large multilateral negotiations to influence the outcome or to protect their particular interests. As a result, criticism from smaller actors, including in particular developing countries, is endemic in multilateral trade negotiations.

The negotiation over agriculture in the Uruguay Round offered a good example of pyramidal negotiation. At the outset of the negotiation, a group of approximately fourteen agricultural exporters from among the developed and developing countries formed under Australian leadership to promote the liberalization of global agricultural markets. Known as the Cairns Group, these countries played an important role in the early stages of the negotiation in bridging the differences between the United States and the European Union over agricultural trade. However, by January 1992, it became clear that the Uruguay Round was blocked, and the reason was the agricultural negotiation between the major players. Agricultural trade had long been a difficult problem for many countries in the GATT system, but in the Uruguay Round the inherent problems of agriculture was compounded because this issue pitted the interests of the United States and the European Union against one another. The US–EU differences stemmed mainly from the fact that, since the 1960s, Europe had established a protectionist policy under the Common Agricultural Policy (CAP), while the United States was moving towards a comparative advantage in agricultural exports. The Uruguay Round thus turned into a politicized contest between the major playesr, and for eighteen months the main activity of the multilateral negotiation was a series of bilateral encounters between US and EU officials. This blockage halted progress in areas other than agriculture, and even between other countries. The United States and the European Union eventually reached a resolution of their differences in the 'Blair House' accords on agriculture, but agriculture continued to be the major stumbling block to a general agreement until very late in the negotiation. This whole affair re-emphasized the importance of the major players in multilateral trade negotiation.

Results

The Uruguay Round agreements were concluded on 15 December 1993. In comparison to the results achieved in previous negotiations, they represented an enormous accomplishment for the world trading system (see Table 5.1). These agreements created the World Trade Organization, which represented institutional progress in that the WTO is a formally constituted international organization and not—as the GATT was—mainly a contract regarding trade rules between countries. The WTO had enormous symbolic importance for the world trade regime, but it also had practical significance as well. Internally, the WTO and the Uruguay Round agreements provided for clearer rules on trade, and reduced the fragmentation and inconsistency that had existed between various GATT-sponsored agreements. Externally, the WTO reinforced the role of trade in international economic relations, and it permitted trade concerns to be represented more fully in relations with the World Bank and International Monetary Fund.

Second, the various agreements reached at the Uruguay Round greatly expanded the rules of the international system of trade. New issues such as services were brought under multilateral rules for the first time, while old issues such as agriculture and textiles, which had long been essentially outside GATT disciplines were brought under multilateral rules, thereby beginning the lengthy process of reducing protectionism in two sectors that had for a long time resisted the progression towards a more liberal world trade regime (Paarlberg 1997). Third, the Uruguay Round agreements were accepted by the developing countries engaged in the negotiation, and represented the most far-reaching commitments those countries had made in the international trade regime. Effectively, they brought the developing countries into that regime. The Uruguay Round concluded at a time when many developing countries were undergoing substantial liberalization, and the confluence of change in the developing world and the deepening of the multilateral regime will engage trade more fully in the progress towards international development.

Finally, the Uruguay Round agreements represented a further step towards a system based on rules rather than power in international trade. The agreements advanced the rules-based nature of trade relations between countries, and thereby increased the economic security of smaller and middle-sized countries in their relations with larger powers. In particular, the agreements established a formal, integrated dispute settlement system to replace the largely *ad hoc* mechanism that had evolved under the GATT. The agreements created an obligation for countries to adjudicate an issue if a trading partner seeks this recourse. Conversely, countries are obligated not to use unilateral trade sanctions as an alternative to multilateral dispute settlement actions under the WTO. Both provisions were intended to increase the prospects that countries, regardless of their size and power, would be equal before the law in trade disputes.

KEY POINTS

- Developing countries resisted efforts by developed countries to establish a new GATT negotiation following the Tokyo Round.

- The Uruguay Round (1986–93) comprised a lengthy negotiating agenda, including new issues such as trade in services and trade-related intellectual property rights (TRIPs).

- The most difficult issue in the Uruguay Round was trade in agriculture, particularly between the major parties, the European Union and the United States.

- The Uruguay Round was an enormous accomplishment for the international trade system. International rules were established in most important areas of international trade, the World Trade Organization (WTO) was created, and a more effective dispute settlement system established. The developing countries became full participants in the WTO system.

Table 5.1 Results of GATT Negotiations: 1960–1994

Negotiation	No. of countries	Results
Dillon Round 1960–1	26	• Average tariff cut of 10% on $4.9 bn of trade
Kennedy Round 1963–7	62	• Average tariff cut of 35% on $40 bn of trade • Anti-dumping code
Tokyo Round 1973–9	102	• Average tariff cut of 35% on more than $100 bn of trade • Six codes dealing with non-tariff measures, plus aircraft code • Revision of GATT articles for developing countries

Table 5.1 (*continued*)

Negotiation	No. of countries	Results
Uruguay Round 1986–94	128	• Average tariff cut of 39% on $3.7 tr of trade • Twelve Agreements (including Agriculture, Textiles, Subsidies, Safeguards) • New issues: Agreements on Trade in Services (GATS) and trade related intellectual property (TRIPs) • Dispute Settlement Understanding (DSU) • Creation of WTO, new legal footing for the multilateral trade regime

The WTO in Action: 1995 and Beyond

The structure of the WTO

The WTO was created as part of the results of the Uruguay Round negotiations that concluded on 15 December 1993, and it came into existence on 1 January 1995. Also included in the Uruguay Round results were a series of agreements that established rules dealing with agriculture, services, textiles and clothing, intellectual property, as well as a number of other issues related to trade. These agreements advanced substantially the rules-based nature of the trade regime originally established under the GATT. As the late Professor Raymond Vernon (1995: 330) observed shortly after the conclusion of the Uruguay Round, 'The agreements, if taken at their face value, show promise of reshaping trade relationships throughout the world.' This statement surely reflects the stunning accomplishment of the negotiation, which was all the more remarkable given the low expectations held at the start of the round.

The WTO portion of the Uruguay Round agreements created an unusual international organization. Most international organizations have specified procedures for making decisions in the name of the collectivity, but instead the WTO continued many of the consensual practices of the GATT. Essentially, the WTO represented a contract between its members, the purpose of which was to establish trade rules and then to back up those rules with a powerful dispute settlement system. To understand the WTO, it is necessary to examine important legal elements drawn from the WTO Agreement and the Dispute Settlement Understanding (DSU).

At the outset, the WTO Agreement established explicitly a new international organization that was to provide symbolic visibility and permanence for international trade policy in the international system (Jackson 1998). The WTO was vested with legal personality, which the GATT did not have, and which placed the WTO on the same footing as other organizations such as the IMF or the World Bank. The WTO Agreement further stated that the WTO should be the 'common institutional framework' for trade relations among its members, and should 'facilitate the implementation' of the various

Uruguay Round Agreements. These provisions were important in that they centralized the governance of the trade system far more than had existed under the GATT. By comparison, the GATT in the 1990s was rapidly becoming a pot-pourri of decentralized separate agreements, which risked creating a watering down of the central obligations of the trade regime.

Second, the WTO Agreement provided that members would accept the WTO and the various other Agreements as a single piece, and would be obliged to bring their domestic laws into conformity with those Agreements. This commitment incorporated the well-known concept of 'single undertaking' that crystallized during the Uruguay Round negotiation. The single undertaking meant that countries were not free to pick and choose among the various agreements, as in the Tokyo Round, but were required to accept and implement the agreements as a package deal. This stratagem ensured that negotiators would make trade-offs in arriving at their final offers in the negotiation, and it also helped to clarify the obligations of members in the implementation stage that followed.

Third, the WTO Agreement provided for institutional structure and decision-making procedures for the new organization, which was more complex than the GATT had been to take into account the greater complexity of the subject matter in the Uruguay Round Agreements. On one point, however, the WTO continued the practice of the GATT, namely in the provision of decision making by consensus. The WTO Agreement in Article IX defined consensus as existing 'if no Member, present at the meeting when the decision is taken, formally objects to the proposed decision'. This procedure meant that the WTO would continue mainly as a contract organization that would not create obligations for individual countries beyond those it had accepted under the consensual decision-making practices of the WTO.

As for the DSU, it is first necessary to note that the Uruguay Round negotiators were aware they were creating a vast addition to international trade laws, and they further recognized a legal system needed to be backed up with judicial procedures for the laws to have any real impact. In practical terms, this meant that a WTO member embroiled in a dispute with another member should have a right to proceed to a judicial process, and that the result of that process should be (legally) binding on the parties. The DSU provided for this basic right, and its significance can be appreciated by the fact that similar rights are practically non-existent in international law.

The practice of dispute settlement was begun on a customary basis under the GATT, and certain procedures, such as the establishment of adjudicatory panels to hear cases, were well in place prior to the creation of the WTO. The WTO's DSU improved the system in a number of ways. First, whereas the GATT had required the consent of both parties for a panel to be established (thereby allowing the party complained against to quash the panel procedure), the DSU provides in Article 6 that: 'If the complaining party so requests, a panel shall be established'. Furthermore, for the panel decision to become legally binding (or 'adopted' by the Council, the plenary body of the GATT's Contracting Parties), the GATT required consensus of all parties, meaning that the party that lost the case would have to acquiesce if the report were to be adopted. This procedure was not as meaningless as it might seem, as dispute settlement was a valued concept under the GATT, and consensual adoptions were the normal outcome of disputed cases. Nevertheless, GATT practice was an example of weak law, which was strengthened under the DSU by the requirement that a panel report would be adopted unless members decided by consensus *not* to adopt the report. This meant that a winning party would have to oppose adoption if the report was to be rejected, which is unlikely; hence the DSU rules virtually provide that panel reports are automatically binding (Palmeter and Mavroidis 1999).

Second, the DSU strengthened the scope and mechanics of dispute settlement in the WTO. An Appellate Body was established to improve the consistency of legal decision-making. The coverage of dispute settlement was extended to all areas of the

Uruguay Round Agreements, which provides for an integrated legal system and removes the competition that previously existed between differing dispute settlement mechanisms. Finally, the DSU makes it obligatory for Members engaged in a dispute to use the WTO system and not resort to unilateral measures, as in the past, to settle the matter themselves. Taken in sum, the DSU represented an extraordinary step forward in the application of legal principles and methods in international law. That it would happen in the trade regime is an indicator of how much that regime has become governed by rules established in multilateral negotiations.

The WTO as an organization

The WTO is described most accurately as a formally contracted body of rules backed up by a judicial system and a minimum of political structure (Winham 1998b). The GATT, which was mainly a contract between parties, had provided for the possibility of joint organizational action by the 'Contracting Parties', but such actions were not emphasized in the General Agreement. By contrast, the WTO Agreement outlines a number of specific functions to be taken by the WTO as a collective body. These include: the implementation and administration of the Uruguay Round Agreements; maintenance of a forum for further negotiations; administration of the dispute settlement system; administration of the Trade Policy Review Mechanism (TPRM); and liaison with the World Bank and the IMF. With the exception of liaison with international financial institutions, these functions had first been established under the GATT on a customary basis.

The principal structures established to carry out the functions of the WTO are a Ministerial Conference meeting every two years (see Table 5.2); a General Council, which is a continuation of the Council of the GATT, and which can also meet as a Dispute Settlement Body and TPRM Review Body; and three councils in the area of goods, services, and intellectual property. Various other organs are mandated in the WTO Agreement, such

Table 5.2 WTO Ministerial Conferences

Singapore, 9–13 December 1996

Geneva, 18–20 May 1998

Seattle, 30 November–3 December 1999

Doha, 9–13 November 2001

Cancun, 10–14 September 2003

Hong Kong, 13–18 December 2005

Source: WTO
(www.wto.org/english/thewto_e/minist_e/minist_e.htm)

as the Committee on Trade and Development, and additional bodies can be created by the Ministerial Conference as it deems necessary.

The WTO Agreement provided for a secretariat, which in the GATT had developed on an informal and customary basis. The WTO secretariat is small compared to the tasks it is expected to perform, and it is certainly small in relation to other international economic organizations. For example, in 1996, the complete staff of the WTO numbered 513, whereas comparable figures for the World Bank and the International Monetary Fund were 6,781 and 2,577, respectively (Blackhurst 1998). This same research showed that the WTO personnel numbers were exceeded by some fifteen international organizations, including some, such as the UN Industrial Development Organization (1,758 individuals) and the World Intellectual Property Organization (630 individuals), that have a much lower profile than the WTO.

As noted previously, decision-making in the WTO is based on consensus, the practice that had developed by custom in the GATT. Consensus is not the same as unanimity, and it is clear that the legal definition in Article IX of the WTO Agreement, as well as past and contemporary practice, permits countries to abstain and therefore to allow decisions to go forward in cases where not all members are in agreement with the issue under consideration. Consistent with the requirement for consensus, most organs of the WTO are plenary, and all members are able to participate.

The tasks of the WTO are carried out by its professional staff, and by the vigorous involvement of the Geneva delegations of the WTO members, which allows the WTO to function with a small secretariat. The WTO is usually described as a 'member-driven' organization, meaning that the members and not the secretariat are mainly responsible for setting the agenda and carrying out the functions of the organization. In the important routine tasks of the organization—including judgements on waivers of obligations, initiation of disputes or complaints, accession of new members, or working parties on free trade areas—action can only be taken by officials from member governments. Research from 1997 indicates that, to cover this workload, there were some 97 members with representation in Geneva, with an average of about five professional officers per delegation (Blackhurst 1998). These officials, plus their back-up support in home capitals, slightly exceeded the manpower available in the WTO secretariat in the same year.

In addition to the principal structures of the WTO mentioned previously, there are over twenty-five committees and working groups, and a fluctuating number of working parties on accessions of new members, all of which in principle are plenary bodies. In addition, there are organs with limited membership, including the Textiles Monitoring Body, plurilateral committees, dispute settlement panels, and the Appellate Body. Additionally, multilateral trade negotiations occasionally create further structure and tasks, and during the Tokyo and Uruguay Rounds a parallel structure under a Trade Negotiations Committee was struck to service those negotiations. Finally, there is an informal and fluid structure of consultation groups designed to bring 'like-minded' members together to discuss issues of common concern. The work associated with the various organs of the WTO is carried out mainly by the Geneva delegations of the members, with assistance from the WTO secretariat. The frequency of meetings is large and growing, and countries with small delegations are hard-pressed to monitor, let alone direct, the activities of the organization. Indeed, many of the least developed countries have no representation in Geneva, and have little capacity to pursue their own interests independent of the positions taken by developing countries as a bloc.

One of the important tasks of the WTO is to monitor and research the trade policies of the members. An important element in this task is the Trade Policy Review Mechanism (TPRM) which was begun by the GATT in 1989, roughly midway through the negotiation of the Uruguay Round. The TPRM is simply a review of a member's trade policy regime, conducted in part by the member itself and by officials of the GATT/WTO secretariat. Major trading countries such as the United States can expect a review once every two years, but for smaller countries the rotation will be less frequent. The main purpose of a TPRM review is information dissemination and transparency, but the reviews are also a valuable tool to evaluate whether members are in full compliance with their obligations under various WTO Agreements. The TPRM reviews are an example of collective executive action in an organization that has very much played down the executive function in comparison to the rule-making and rule-adjudication functions. Depending on the development of the international trade system and the politics conducted within that regime, the executive function of the WTO could become a much more important factor in the future.

The politics of the WTO

It is common to describe the WTO as a 'rules-based' system. Like the GATT before it, the WTO consists mainly of a set of rules intended to promote trade between member countries, and in particular to provide for non-discrimination in trading relations. In any system of rules, a mechanism for handling disputes is a natural and logical extension of that system. In the GATT, a dispute settlement system developed by customary practice, but in the WTO it was mandated by international agreement in the form of the DSU, and included in the Uruguay Round Agreements. The DSU is a particularly powerful form of international dispute settlement, and the management of this system has created political controversy among the members of the WTO.

At the outset it should be noted that dispute settlement procedures have been used frequently in the WTO. World Trade Organization statistics (WTO 2000c) indicated that, in slightly more than five years of operation, there had been some 193 member complaints to the WTO on 151 distinct trade issues. By October 2003, total complaints numbered over 300. Approximately half of the complaints are settled or dropped in the consultation phase that precedes formal dispute settlement (Davey 2000). Once a case is formally engaged, it proceeds to a three-person panel comprising trade experts for a legal decision, and then, if requested, it will continue to the Appellate Body on appeal. Once a decision has been reached, the next issue is implementation. This is a problem the WTO accepted in moving to a legally binding dispute settlement system compared to the more diplomatic and political system that existed previously in the GATT, where countries could avoid a legal decision they could not live with. In the WTO, countries are legally obliged to accept and implement a negative dispute settlement decision, and it is possible for an injured party to take retaliatory action, even though such an action is counter-productive from the standpoint of liberalizing the trade, regime in that it erects further barriers to trade. But for the largest WTO members, it is usually impossible to oblige a powerful country—even through retaliatory sanctions—to implement an adverse decision that it is determined to ignore. This was particularly the situation with the *Hormones* and *Bananas* cases, two disputes that divided the United States and the European Union. The problem is that if major powers are able to circumvent the obligation to implement adverse panel decisions, the WTO dispute settlement system will quickly lose the moral authority to secure implementation from any countries. This could be a fatal blow to the WTO rules-based regime.

There are other problems with dispute settlement that have been raised by developing countries. One is the costs of litigation before WTO panels and the Appellate Body. There has been a tendency for disputes to grow in legal complexity, a problem that was already evident in the GATT in the late 1980s. There are now more agreements to consider, and the prospect of appeal to the WTO Appellate Body has increased the importance of factual evidence and precise legal argument. The complexity and costs are especially hard to manage for developing countries, which generally have small delegations in Geneva and therefore may be forced to choose between hiring expensive counsel or simply forgoing the opportunity to pursue a dispute settlement case. These difficulties can impel developing countries towards a defensive rather than an offensive posture in dispute settlement, and may reduce the market-opening possibilities that the dispute settlement system may hold for more affluent WTO members.

A second problem is what some countries have called the 'politicization' of the dispute settlement system. One issue is the tendency, in some countries that have lost WTO cases, for governments to come under political criticism for permitting unwarranted foreign interference in domestic policies. Such criticism inevitably forces government officials to take political acceptability (as well as WTO law) into account when deciding how to implement dispute settlement decisions. A second issue is the decision of the Appellate Body to accept *amicus curiae* briefs from environmental non-governmental organizations (NGOs) in the Shrimp–Turtle case between the United States and a number of developing countries. The Appellate Body took this action to address criticisms that by refusing to accept inputs from NGOs (such as, for example, the World Wildlife Fund or Greenpeace), the WTO dispute settlement system was undemocratic and not inclusive. However, the action of accepting legal briefs from NGOs undercut the concept of the WTO as an organization having nation states as members, especially when some poorer WTO members might not have the capability or financial resources to submit *amicus curiae* briefs themselves, even if they had the legal right to do it. Thus, in attempting to increase the democratic inclusiveness between developed country governments and the NGOs that are their domestic constituents, the democratic inclusiveness and juridical equality of the developing country members of the WTO is called into question.

In spite of such problems, dispute settlement is functioning reasonably well in the WTO, and indeed it is the cornerstone of the regime. Any system of rules requires a judicial function to interpret and apply the rules to specific cases, and the WTO system continues to serve the interests of the members. However, the rules are not always clear, and some judicial interpretation will be necessary to apply the rules to specific cases. As a result, panels and the Appellate Body will continue to face difficult decisions in which criticism is inevitable but outright condemnation is unlikely.

Negotiations

One of the major tasks of the WTO is to promote trade negotiations. This task is mandated in the WTO Agreement, which calls on the organization 'to provide a forum for negotiation' on matters arising under the Uruguay Round Agreements, and on further issues concerning the multilateral trade relations of the members. This mandate is more precise than that which existed under the GATT. However, the sponsorship of negotiations did arise by customary practice under the GATT, and in time those negotiations proved their value in terms of forwarding the agenda of trade liberalization. Hence, the WTO Agreement effectively codified GATT customary practice, and built negotiation of new issues into the organizational mission of the WTO.

The WTO moved quickly after 1995 to carry out its mandate to sponsor negotiations. In the area of trade in services, the Uruguay Round had concluded without commitments forthcoming from members in financial or telecommunications services. These became subjects of new negotiations, and by 1997 the WTO was able to announce major new agreements in both areas. The telecom agreement produced new liberalizing commitments from sixty-nine governments covering 90 per cent of global telecom revenues, while the financial services agreement included fifty-six scheduled offers from seventy countries (counting the EU as fifteen countries). Most important, the United States participated in both agreements, and dropped its previous refusal to apply concessions to all other participating countries on the basis of the most-favoured nation principle.

Further, in 1997, another negotiation concluded that was novel and not a continuation of the Uruguay Round. In March of that year, some forty governments concluded the WTO Ministerial Declaration on Trade in Information Technology Products (ITA) that freed trade on computer and telecommunications equipment. This agreement was concluded very quickly and it is significant because, together with the telecom agreement, it covers trade of a value equal to that of agriculture, automobiles, and textiles combined. These agreements represent the new economy in terms of commerce between nations, and it is clear that that commerce is now more liberalized than the commerce of the old economy.

In the areas of agriculture and trade in services, the Uruguay Round agreements had included a 'built-in agenda' that called for new multilateral negotiations to start in 2000. These negotiations got under way despite the failure of the Seattle Ministerial Conference in December 1999, which attempted to establish a mandate for a new round of negotiations in all areas. Thus, even allowing for the setback of Seattle, the WTO demonstrated it was capable of sponsoring new negotiations on a sectoral basis following the conclusion of the Uruguay Round. Over time, it appears that negotiation has become less an exceptional part of the GATT/WTO regime and more part of the normal business of multilateral trade relations. The WTO is moving towards a regime of 'permanent negotiation', in which the organization begins to look more like a typical national legislature and less like the occasional diplomatic encounters of international relations.

The WTO Agreement calls for a ministerial meeting every two years, and the Seattle meeting of

December 1999 provided an opportunity for some members to press for the commencement of a major new round of trade negotiations. As had been the case with the Uruguay Round, calls for a new negotiation occasioned a major rift in the multilateral trade regime. The European Union enthusiastically supported a new negotiation, and proposed a set of new issues including the controversial subjects of investment and competition policy. It was, however, less forthcoming on agricultural subsidies. For its part, the United States also favoured a new negotiation and proposed reductions in trade barriers in industrial goods, but it insisted on introducing trade sanctions to protect domestic policies related to labour and the environment. Developing countries feared these would be directed mainly at them. The United States also resisted tariff concessions on textiles, and was lukewarm towards negotiations on investment and competition policy. On agriculture, Washington continued its long-standing policy of making maximum demands on the European Union. Japan also supported a new negotiation, especially on new issues, but it was prepared to stonewall discussions on agriculture. Finally, the fifteen-nation Cairns group of agricultural exporters, including both developed and developing countries, continued the strong position they had initiated in the Uruguay Round against export subsidies on agricultural trade.

The developing countries were generally hostile to the idea of a new negotiation, largely on the grounds that there was unfinished business from the Uruguay Round, such as agricultural liberalization and implementation of the Uruguay Round Agreements; they argued that these had to be settled before the international trade community could undertake new initiatives. India took the lead in expressing these concerns, and elaborated what became known as the implementation issue. A central argument was that the Uruguay Round Agreements had been unfair to developing countries, in that those agreements obliged governments to carry out costly administrative reforms, or to participate in subsequent negotiations they were unprepared to tackle. Arguably, these obligations

were more easily borne by developed countries that were more affluent, or already had more elaborate government or administrative structures. Another argument in the implementation debate was that developed countries had drawn up, and then implemented, the Uruguay Round Agreements in a way that denied to developing countries the benefits supposedly forthcoming from those agreements. This argument was buoyed up by the belief in developing countries that they had accepted greater liberalization of their own markets than was the case in developed countries, with the result that they did not receive the export access for their products, especially agriculture and textiles, that they had imagined. In sum, India made the case that the developing countries had received a bad deal from the Uruguay Round, and that, before any new negotiation could begin, some effort should be made to redress the inequities of the previous negotiation.

The Seattle Ministerial Conference was thus compromised by the conflicting positions of the various WTO members (Odell 2002). To this was added a bitter fight over the selection of the WTO director-general, which took place over the six months prior to Seattle and compromised the preparations normally required for success in any major ministerial meeting. The meeting itself in Seattle was also compromised by street protests from groups opposed to the WTO and to globalization, and even by mismanagement of the negotiating agenda at the meeting itself. These factors combined to make the Seattle Ministerial Conference a spectacular failure. Ministers left Seattle without agreeing to launch a new round, and the collapse was so complete that no communiqué was produced promising the usual efforts at co-operation in the future.

Members were alarmed at the failure at Seattle, and recognized it as a test of the success of the WTO itself. Following the Seattle meeting, work continued at the technical level to bridge the many gaps between WTO members. It was recognized that the two-year cycle of ministerial meetings provides a stern test for the political viability of the organization, and members were determined to resolve as many problems as possible before the next meeting in the autumn of 2001.

Gradually, the major participants introduced concessions into their negotiating positions. The European Union reduced its expectations for new rules on investment and competition policy, and the USA dropped its contentious demands on labour rights and the environment. There was also some promise of movement in agriculture, which has traditionally been the sticking point in GATT negotiations. Coupled with the increased flexibility shown by the participants, the WTO secretariat itself was better organized to mediate political differences and to manage the enormous detail associated with a large multilateral trade negotiation.

By September 2001, the most extreme positions had been modified and the parties had achieved a single negotiating text, which is the *sine qua non* for success in multilateral negotiation. By this time, it was clear that the major issues for the WTO membership were those of particular importance to the developing countries, especially implementation and agriculture, as well as a concern that had suddenly arisen on the world stage—the access to medicines needed to combat disease in poorer countries. Developing countries were fearful that the Intellectual Property Agreement would prevent access to cheaper generic drugs to fight AIDS and other diseases that poorer societies were pray to, and they demanded a modification of the TRIPs Agreement to permit discretion to override drug patents in the event of a national health emergency. Developed countries were generally unwilling to forgo concessions that had been achieved in the Uruguay Round, and the issue festered for several years while the AIDS epidemic gathered momentum, particularly in Africa. The severity of the AIDS crisis brought moral pressure to bear on developed country governments and the pharmaceutical industry that had supported strong patent rights in the Uruguay Round.

The ministerial conference was held in Doha, Qatar, in November 2001. The conference agenda was pre-negotiated and well prepared, as, in comparison to the Seattle draft declaration that had

402 pairs of square brackets in the text (which indicate disagreement), the draft declaration for the Doha meeting had only thirteen pairs of brackets remaining for ministerial decisions (Odell 2002). The Doha draft reflected the continuing effort at compromise that had characterized the discussions since September. However, the TRIPs/health issue remained outstanding, and it was important enough that it threatened to cause the meeting to break down in disagreement. The stakes were high: for the developed countries, the TRIPs agreement represented an important security against the misappropriation, and even theft, of intellectual property, but for the developing countries, access to lower-cost generic medicines could easily be translated into lives saved or lost in the fight against AIDS and other diseases. An end to this impasse was eventually reached through an agreement to extend the date by ten years, until 2016, for least developed countries to provide patents on pharmaccuticals, and by a formal affirmation that 'the TRIPs agreement does not and should not prevent Members from taking measures to protect public health'. The latter statement only reiterated rights that were already contained in the TRIPs agreement itself, but it was accepted by developing countries because it created a presumption that WTO members would be able to exercise their rights to procure generic medicines, and more important, that other members (particularly the USA) would be unlikely to take dispute settlement actions against members that exercised those rights.

The resolution of the TRIPs/health issue ensured the success of the Doha meeting, although it would take another twenty-one months to eliminate the final obstacles to cheaper drug imports (WTO 2003b). Other issues were settled at Doha, particularly the question of implementation, where the parties agreed to roll much of this agenda into the forthcoming negotiation. With the success of the Doha meeting, the WTO members formally initiated a new multilateral negotiation, with a deadline of December 2004. The agenda comprised twelve wide-ranging issues, the focus of the negotiation was development, and in keeping with this focus the members eschewed the term 'Round' in favour of the title Doha Development Agenda (DDA). The DDA began in January 2002.

In its short history, the WTO suffered a serious setback in the Seattle Ministerial Conference, and then rebounded to launch a new multilateral negotiation in the Doha Ministerial Conference. The latter meeting laid out an agenda for the negotiation, and the negotiation went forward, but it was met with frequent delays and progress was slow. The first major deadline for the DDA was the ministerial meeting in Cancun, Mexico, in September 2003, at which time the Declaration from the meeting was to take the form of an updated agenda and progress report on the DDA. In Cancun, the WTO members were unable to reach consensus on a Ministerial Declaration. Once again, the WTO met with failure.

The goal at Cancun was to reach an interim agreement on the outstanding problems of the negotiation sufficient to advance the work of the DDA. This goal came to nothing when the Mexican foreign minister chairing the conference exercised his discretion and abruptly called a halt to the negotiation. The issues on which the negotiation broke down were investment and competition policy, which were pressed for by the European Union and Japan, but opposed vigorously by a group of, mainly African, developing countries. However, behind these issues was the far greater problem of agriculture, where, again, developing countries were intent to register their displeasure at the agricultural subsidy practices of the United States and the European Union. For example, four West African producers of cotton demanded a sectoral initiative to eliminate cotton subsidies in countries such as the USA, the EU, and China, but they received a response suggesting that African countries should diversify their production, a message they interpreted as telling them to stop growing cotton. This response inflamed the Africans, and added to the antipathy that threatened to spiral out of control at the conference.

The Doha Round, the ninth multilateral negotiation to be held under the GATT/WTO regime,

was originally scheduled to conclude no later than January 2005. This deadline was made impossible to achieve by the impasse that occurred between developed and developing countries at the Cancun meeting in September 2003. Following this setback, delegates managed to get the negotiation back on the rails with a new approach to the Doha Work Programme adopted in the 'July Package' by the WTO General Council on 1 August 2004. The July Package extended the Doha Round deadline beyond January 2005, and established December 2005 for the next Ministerial Conference in Hong Kong. Most importantly, it singled out the subjects of agriculture (subsidies and tariffs), non-agricultural market access—NAMA (mainly, industrial tariffs), and, to a lesser degree trade in services, for priority attention in the negotiation. Additionally, the July Package reaffirmed the importance of a sectoral negotiation on cotton, and agreed to pursue the matter in the negotiations on agriculture.

The negotiation slowed in early 2005, with developing countries pressing developed countries, mainly regarding agriculture, while the latter insisted they could not take unilateral action on agriculture without receiving reciprocal concessions on industrial tariffs and services from developing countries. In the Hong Kong Ministerial Conference in December 2005, gruelling negotiations kept the Round alive, but they failed to produce the specific numbers or formulas needed to move to the next level of bargaining over tariffs and subsidies. The Meeting produced an agreement to eliminate agricultural subsidies by the year 2013, but beyond that its major accomplishment was to set a deadline of 30 April 2006 for the tabling of full modalities (that is, the numbers inserted into tariff and subsidy-cutting formulas) in agriculture and NAMA. The WTO director general, Pascal Lamy, claimed this action had put the troubled Doha Round 'back on track'.

Negotiators failed to solve the problem of modalities by the 30 April deadline, however, and they failed in subsequent meetings over the following months. By most accounts, the major blockage occurred over agriculture, with the European Union unwilling to make substantial reductions on agricultural tariffs, and the United States unprepared to offer significant concessions on agricultural subsidies. Then, too, developing countries as a group were disinclined to make much movement on industrial tariffs or services. By 2007, a profound malaise had enveloped the negotiation. Although there is no fixed termination date for the negotiation, the legislation (formally known as Trade Promotion Authority) authorizing US officials to conclude a trade agreement without Congressional amendments expires in July 2007, after which foreign countries would probably refuse to negotiate with the United States. Unless the legislation were to be renewed—an unlikely prospect—the Doha Round would effectively end in mid-2007.

Beneath the difficulties of the Doha Round lay a subtle change in the politics of the WTO. The GATT was the creation of developed countries, and up to the Uruguay Round the developing countries were largely passive bystanders in the evolution of the international trade regime. This changed with the creation of the WTO, and this change has since accelerated, particularly with the accession of China to full WTO membership (WTO 2001*b*). At the Cancun Ministerial Conference, a group of developing countries formed a coalition, known generally as the G20 countries, that succeeded in polarizing much of the debate into a North–South struggle. The basis for this polarization was the firm belief of the G20 that the benefits of the trade regime have not been proportioned equitably between developed and developing countries, especially in terms of the results of the Uruguay Round Agreements. This is a belief that is increasingly given some credence by observers of international economics, and will have to be addressed by the organization in the future if progress is to be achieved in the international trade regime ('Special Report', *Economist*, 20 September 2003).

KEY POINTS

- The WTO is a rules-based international organization that operates on the basis of consensus. Members are legally bound to act in way that are consistent with the rules they have negotiated, as interpreted by the dispute settlement mechanism.

- The work of the WTO is carried out by a series of committees supported by a small international secretariat. The dispute settlement mechanism has been especially active.

- The WTO has promoted further negotiated agreements in financial and telecommunications services, and in trade in information technology products.

- The WTO Agreement calls for a Ministerial Conference every two years. In December 1999, in Seattle, Washington State, USA, some members sought support to commence a new multilateral negotiation, but the meeting concluded without agreement. In November 2001, in Doha, Qatar, following lengthy pre-negotiations between developed and developing countries, WTO Ministers agreed to initiate a new negotiation with a deadline of December 2004.

Conclusion

The start of the Doha negotiation was a reaffirmation of the direction the world trade regime has taken since the middle of the twentieth century.

The focus of the regime has been to create rules whereby countries can exchange goods and services with a minimum of interference from national governments, and the means to accomplish that task has been to reach agreements through international negotiation. Such agreements are an important form of regulation, or system management, in the international economy. Trade has always been regulated, but in the past that regulation has mainly been done unilaterally by national governments, and has always posed a potential threat to trade and the stability of the international economy, as events of the 1930s amply demonstrated. Today, the regulation of trade is carried out as much through the negotiation of trade agreements as through the actions of domestic agencies, the purpose being to replace inward-looking national regulation with a broader conception of international rules. There is a need to keep the trade system moving in a liberal direction consistent with an open international society, because the alternatives to an open society—witnessed in the inter-war period in the twentieth century–were so damaging to the interests of all countries.

The GATT, and now the WTO, are central features of the international trade system. Through negotiations in these institutions, analogous to law-making in domestic parliaments, countries have been able to establish a rules-based regime for regulating international trade. The negotiation process is critically important to the success of the WTO, but it is a fickle and sometimes fragile process. When it is successful, the rules of the regime are advanced, and all countries can be said to benefit from the greater stability and predictability that comes from a regime based on rules rather than on the play of power politics. But the negotiation process is not always successful, and just as an absence of consensus occasionally paralyses the legislative agenda in domestic parliaments, the absence of consensus also stops the WTO from dealing with problems that many members think need to be addressed. If there is a major difference between domestic parliaments and the WTO, it is that an impasse in the former rarely calls into question the survival of the institution, whereas when an impasse occurs in the WTO, there is always the fear that the organization will be eclipsed, and that countries will use other means, including unilateral actions, to resolve the problems they face in the trade system. Thus an analogy is often made between the WTO and a bicycle: both need to maintain forward momentum in order to remain stable.

As it looks to the future, the greatest challenge facing the WTO will be to incorporate the developing countries fully into a liberal international trade regime. Included in the Preamble to the WTO Agreement is a statement expressing the need that developing countries should 'secure a share in the growth in international trade commensurate with the needs of their economic development'. The Cancun Meeting was a political wake-up call that the developing countries will use their negotiating power to realize their aspirations in the Doha negotiation and beyond. Since the 1950s the GATT and WTO have endured despite many challenges, but the task of implementing a global and inclusive trade regime will be the most imposing test of all.

KEY POINTS

- A Ministerial Conference in September 2003, in Cancun, Mexico, failed to find consensus on a Declaration designed to advance the work of the Doha negotiation.

- The greatest future challenge to the WTO is to find consensus between the developed and developing members of the organization.

? QUESTIONS

1. What are the basic components of the international trade regime? Give examples.

2. What was the effect of the US Reciprocal Trade Agreements Act of 1934?

3. What does non-discrimination mean in international trade; and how is it put into effect by the rules of the GATT?

4. Compare the results of the Kennedy and Tokyo Rounds of GATT multilateral trade negotiations.

5. What was the role of the developing countries in the Uruguay Round negotiation; and why was it historically significant?

6. What were the challenges encountered in negotiating rules for trade in services in the Uruguay Round negotiation?

7. How does the WTO differ from the GATT?

8. What is the WTO Dispute Settlement Understanding (DSU), why is it necessary, and what are some of the difficulties with its operations?

9. What are the challenges for the WTO in conducting the multilateral trade negotiation known as the Doha Development Agenda?

FURTHER READING

■ **Bhagwati, J. (1988),** *Protectionism* **(Cambridge, MA: MIT Press).** A short but incisive review of the history, ideology and practice of the trade policy of protectionism.

■ —— **(1991),** *The World Trading System at Risk* **(Princeton, NJ: Princeton University Press).** An analysis of the challenges to the trading system that the Uruguay Round negotiation was intended to counter.

■ **Condliffe, J. B. (1950),** *The Commerce of Nations* **(New York: W. W. Norton).** A penetrating history of international trade that makes use of the memorable concept of the contest between enterprise and regulation.

■ **Croome, J. (1995),** *Reshaping the World Trading System: A History of the Uruguay Round* **(Geneva: World Trade Organization).** An official history of the Uruguay Round noted for its detail and accuracy.

■ **Jackson, J. H. (1998),** *The World Trade Organization: Constitution and Jurisprudence* **(London: Pinter).** An analysis of the WTO legal regime by a foremost scholar of international trade law.

■ **Jones, V. C. (2006) 'WTO: Antidumping Issues in the Doha Development Agenda', CRS Report for Congress (Washington, DC: Congressional Research Service, Library of Congress).** An up-to-date and informative review of anti-dumping practices.

■ **Ostry, S. (1997),** *The Post-Cold War Trading System: Who's on First* **(Chicago: University of Chicago Press).** A masterful history of international trade from 1945 onwards that blends economics, politics, and law into a rounded analysis of the subject.

■ **Preeg, E. H. (1995),** *Traders in a Brave New World: The Uruguay Round and the Future of the International Trading System* **(Chicago: University of Chicago Press).** A well-organized review of the major events of the negotiation that created the current international trade regime.

■ Rosecrance, R. (1986), *The Rise of the Trading State: Commerce and Conquest in the Modern World* **(New York: Basic Books).** A comprehensive treatment of the history of trading relations.

■ Winham, G. R. (1992), *The Evolution of International Trade Agreements* **(Toronto: University of Toronto Press).** A review of trade agreements from antiquity to the mid-Uruguay Round, based on the 1991 Bissell Lectures at the University of Toronto.

■ WTO Secretariat (2000), *From GATT to the WTO: The Multilateral Trading System in the New Millennium* **(Geneva: World Trade Organization).** A collection of authoritative papers by noted experts on international trade and trade policy.

 ## WEB LINKS

● The main link for international trade is the WTO link: **www.wto.org.**
Other useful links are national ministries of international trade that can be found via Google, such as **www.ustr.gov** (United States) or **www.international.gc.camenu.asp** (Canada).

 Visit the Online Resource Centre that accompanies this book for more information: www.oxfordtextbooks.co.uk/orc/ravenhill2e/

6 Regionalism

JOHN RAVENHILL

Chapter Contents

- Introduction
- Why Regionalism?
- The Rush to Regionalism
- The Political Economy of Regionalism
- The Economic Consequences of Regional Integration
- Regionalism and the WTO: Stepping Stone or Stumbling Block?

Reader's Guide

The number of regional trade agreements has grown rapidly since the World Trade Organization (WTO) came into existence in 1995. Close to half of world trade is now conducted within these preferential trade arrangements, the most significant exception to the WTO's principle of non-discrimination. Governments have often entered regional economic agreements motivated primarily by political rather than economic considerations. Nonetheless, they may prefer trade liberalization on a regional rather than a global basis for several economic reasons. This chapter reviews the political economy of regionalism: why regional trade agreements are established, which actors are likely to support regional rather than global trade liberalization, the effects that regionalism has had on the trade and welfare of members and non-members, and the relationship between liberalization at regional and global levels.

Introduction

When the Japanese prime minister, Junichiro Koizumi, and his Singaporean counterpart, Goh Chok Tong, signed a bilateral trade agreement in January 2002, Japan departed from the rapidly depleting ranks of WTO members that were not parties to a discriminatory trade arrangement. By the end of 2006, of the WTO's 150 members only one, Mongolia, was not a party to one or more regional trading agreements (RTAs). These take various forms, ranging, in scope of co-operation, from free trade areas to economic unions (see Box 6.1).

RTAs are the most important exception that the WTO permits to the principle that countries should not discriminate in their treatment of other members. Parties to regional arrangements are obliged to notify the WTO of the details of their agreements; the Committee on Regional Trade Agreements has responsibility for ensuring that the agreements comply with the WTO's provisions (for agreements involving only developing economies, the responsibility lies with the Committee on Trade and Development). World Trade Organization data reflect the explosion in the number of regional arrangements that has occurred since the early 1990s. Throughout its entire existence, from 1948 to 1994, the General Agreement on Tariffs and Trade (GATT) received 124 notifications of regional trade agreements, of which only sixty-five were still in force when it was replaced by the WTO. Between 1995 and March 2007, the WTO received notification of a further 227 agreements (WTO 2007; also see Figure 6.1). In addition, the WTO estimated that, at the latter date, a further seventy RTAs were operational but had yet to be notified to it. This growth in regionalism has led to a marked increase in the share of world trade conducted within regional trade agreements, now accounting for roughly a-half of world trade (but note that not all trade between regional partners benefits from treatment better than that offered to non-members— the most-favoured

nation tariff may be zero; or companies may decide not to complete the paperwork required to comply with rules of origin (see Box 6.5 on page 193)).

Three sets of rules in the WTO permit the creation of RTAs:

- Article xxiv of the GATT lays down conditions for the establishment and operation of free-trade agreements and customs unions covering trade in goods.

- the Enabling Clause (formally, the 1979 Decision on Differential and More Favourable Treatment, Reciprocity and Fuller Participation of Developing Countries) permits regional agreements among developing countries regarding trade in goods.

- Article v of the General Agreement on Trade in Services (GATS) establishes conditions that permit liberalization of trade in services among regional partners.

At the end of 2006, of the 214 RTAs in force, 147 came under the auspices of Article xxiv, 45 were under GATS Article v (the most rapidly growing category of agreement), and 22 under the Enabling Clause (WTO 2006b). The last of these categories includes what could become the world's largest preferential market, the China–ASEAN Free Trade Area.

Why do governments choose to pursue their foreign economic policy objectives through regionalism rather than through other strategies? What explains the recent growth in regionalism? What economic and political interests are driving integration at the regional level? What impact do regional agreements have on the economies and political systems of participants? And what are the consequences of the growth of regionalism for the global trading system? These are the principal questions this chapter addresses (our focus is on trade rather than the recent growth in regional collaboration on finance). But first, we turn to

BOX 6.1

A Hierarchy of Regional Economic Arrangements

Regional integration arrangements are usually perceived as a hierarchy that runs from free trade areas, through customs unions and **common markets**, to economic unions. The terminology of 'hierarchy' is used because each level incorporates all the provisions of the lower level of integration. This does not imply that particular regional arrangements will necessarily progress from a lower to a higher level of integration. Nor is it the case that regional partnerships inevitably begin at the lowest level and then move to 'deeper' integration: some arrangements, for example, have been established as customs unions.

A free trade area exists when countries remove tariffs and **non-tariff barriers** to the free movement of goods and services between them. Governments, meanwhile, are free to choose how they treat goods and services imported from non-regional-partner states. Membership in one free trade area therefore does not prevent a country from establishing or joining other free trade areas: Mexico, for example, is a party to agreements with more than thirty countries. Because free trade areas impose relatively few constraints on national decision-making autonomy, they are the easiest of the regional arrangements to negotiate. More than 90 per cent of regional partnerships take the form of free trade areas. Examples include NAFTA, the Japan–Singapore Economic Partnership Agreement, and the Baltic Free Trade Area.

A customs union goes beyond the removal of barriers to trade within the region to adopt a common set of policies towards imports from countries outside the region. This includes agreement on a common level of tariffs (often referred to as a common external tariff) on all extra-regional imports. Such agreements inevitably cost governments autonomy in their foreign economic policies (joint institutions are usually required to negotiate and administer the common external trade policies). They will also have distributive effects, depending on the level at which the common external tariff is set for various items. Consequently,

customs unions are usually more difficult to negotiate than are free trade areas. The relatively small number of customs unions includes the Andean Community, CARICOM, MERCOSUR, and the Southern African Customs Union. Many have experienced difficulties in negotiating a common external tariff. Even in the European Union, individual states maintained different tariffs on some products for more than thirty years after its formation. MERCOSUR's negotiation of a common external tariff took fifteen years longer than anticipated, it applied to only three-quarters of total products, and even then was not accepted by two of its associate members, Bolivia and Peru.

A *common market* includes a customs union as well as allowing for free movement of labour and capital within the regional partnership. Such free flows of factors of production inevitably require governments to collaborate in additional policy areas to ensure comparable treatment in all countries within the common market. Few governments historically have been willing to accept the loss of policy-making autonomy that occurs in a common market. The Andean Community, CARICOM, the COMESA (Common Market for Eastern and Southern Africa) grouping, and MERCOSUR have committed themselves to work for the establishment of a common market, but it is too early to judge whether their aspirations will be realized.

An *economic union* includes a common market plus the adoption of a common currency and/or the harmonization of monetary, fiscal, and social policies. Only the European Union has reached this level of economic integration.

Many of the free trade agreements signed in recent years also include provisions for 'deeper' integration, the most common of which relate to the removal of restrictions on investment flows. But even though these are elements often found in common markets, these free trade areas do not aspire to the creation of a common external tariff or to the free flow of labour within the regional grouping.

matters of definition: what do we mean by regionalism?

Regionalism refers to a formal process of intergovernmental collaboration between two or more states. It should be distinguished from *regionalization*, which refers to the growth of economic interdependence within a given geographical area.

One of the few issues on which writers on regionalism agree is that there is no such thing as

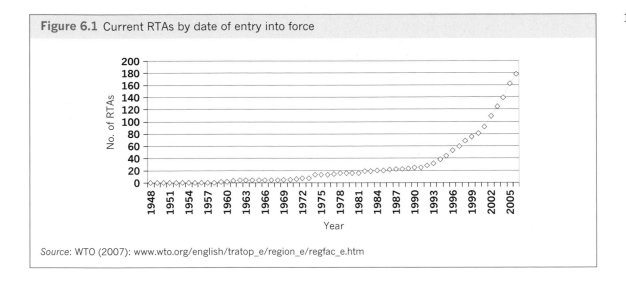

Figure 6.1 Current RTAs by date of entry into force

Source: WTO (2007): www.wto.org/english/tratop_e/region_e/regfac_e.htm

a 'natural' region. Regions are social constructions whose members define their boundaries. Consider, for example, the European Union: in its successive incarnations—European Economic Community, European Community, and, now, the European Union (EU)—its membership has risen from its six founders to the total at the time of writing of twenty-seven. And debates over EU membership for Turkey show that no consensus exists on either geographical or cultural criteria that could be used to distinguish 'European' from 'non-European'.

For most of the post-Second-World-War period, the concept of regional economic integration has generally been associated with an arrangement between three or more geographically contiguous states. Again, the EU provides an excellent example, but consider also East African Cooperation (Kenya, Tanzania, and Uganda), and the Andean Community of Nations (Bolivia, Colombia, Ecuador, and Peru). In recent years, however, a large number of preferential trade agreements have been signed that involve only two parties (for example, China–Hong Kong), and sometimes these bilateral agreements link parties that are not geographically contiguous (for example, Korea and Chile). Because non-global agreements are subject to the scrutiny of the WTO's Committee on Regional Trade Agreements, however, they are also

frequently labelled 'regional'. The appropriateness of such terminology is questionable (some commentators suggest that, because many of the recent agreements are not regional in the conventional geographical sense and do not free all trade between the parties, they are better termed 'preferential' rather than 'regional' or 'free' trade agreements). But it is not just the terminology that is problematical: the arguments of the large body of theoretical work on regional integration, which was developed with groupings involving multiple members from the same geographical region in mind, may not be applicable to arrangements that involve only two parties, or those that involve states that are not geographical neighbours.

Table 6.1 demonstrates the complexity of the current configuration of 'regional' arrangements—essentially all strategies for trade liberalization that fall between unilateral action at the one extreme and negotiations at the global level in the WTO at the other. Bilateral agreements can occur either between neighbours or between countries that are far removed from one another. Regionalism, as conventionally understood, is a *minilateral* relationship—that is, one that involves more than two countries, on a geographically concentrated basis—for example, the North American Free Trade Agreement (NAFTA) or the ASEAN Free

Table 6.1 Example of the Geographical Scope of Trade Liberalization Strategies

Unilateral	Bilateral		Minilateral			Global
	Geographically concentrated	Geographically dispersed	Geographically concentrated	Geographically dispersed		
	Bilateral within region	**Bilateral transregional**	**Regionalism**	**Trans-regionalism**	**Inter–regionalism**	
Trade liberalization in SE Asia, Australia, and NZ in 1980s and 1990s	Australia–New Zealand CER	Singapore–USA	NAFTA	APEC[a]	EU–Mercosur CER–AFTA	GATT/WTO

[a]Unlike the other RTAs discussed in this chapter, APEC is not a discriminatory arrangement; its members have pledged to reduce their trade barriers on imports from all sources
Source: Adapted from Aggarwal (2001: 238)

Trade Area (AFTA) (Table 6.5, on page 204, lists the principal minilateral regional trade groupings). In recent years, however, two other forms of minilateral groupings have emerged among members that are geographically dispersed. *Transregional* groupings link individual countries located in different parts of the world. A good example is the Asia-Pacific Economic Cooperation (APEC) grouping, whose membership comprises twenty-one countries from the Americas, Asia, Oceania, and Europe (Russia). Many of the recently negotiated bilateral RTAs—for example, USA–Jordan, Singapore–New Zealand—link countries from different geographical areas. *Interregional* arrangements join two established minilateral economic arrangements, as between the European Union and MERCOSUR (the Common Market of the Smith, comprising Argentina, Brazil, Paraguay, and Uruguay), and ASEAN and the Australia–New Zealand Closer Economic Relations Trade Agreement (ANZCERTA). By the end of 2006, more than twenty-five transregional and interregional agreements were operational.

Why Regionalism?

Economists assert that an economy's welfare can be maximized, other than in very exceptional circumstances, if governments lower trade barriers on a non-discriminatory basis (either through unilateral action or through negotiations at the global level that adhere to the WTO's principle of non-discrimination). Regional trade agreements, on the other hand, can reduce global welfare by distorting the allocation of resources, and may even lead to welfare losses for their members (see Box 6.2). Moreover, from the political scientist's perspective, it is usually more efficient to negotiate

BOX 6.2

The Costs and Benefits of Preferential Trade Agreements: Trade Diversion and Trade Creation

Jacob Viner (1950) was the first author to present a systematic assessment of the economic costs and benefits of regional economic integration, and to demonstrate, contrary to the then conventional wisdom, that a selective removal of tariffs might not be welfare enhancing. He argued that increased trade between parties to a regional arrangement can occur through two mechanisms. **Trade creation** occurs when imports from a regional partner displace goods that have been produced domestically at higher cost, which can no longer compete once the tariffs on imports from the regional partner are removed. **Trade diversion** occurs when imports from a regional partner displace those that originated outside the regional arrangement, the displacement occurring because the extra-regional imports are no longer price-competitive when the tariffs on trade within the region are removed. Consider, for example, a hypothetical example of what might happen with the implementation of the North American Free Trade Agreement (see Table 6.2 below). Let us assume that Indonesia was the lowest-cost source of imported cotton T-shirts for the United States. Before the implementation of NAFTA, when all countries faced the same level of tariffs on their exports to the US market, its T-shirts were preferred to the higher-cost products of Mexican firms. Assume that the tariff on T-shirts was 10 per cent, and the cost of manufacturing and delivering an Indonesian T-shirt to the USA was $5, while that for a Mexican T-shirt was $5.40. Adding the 10 per cent tariff to the costs of manufacturing and delivery, the price paid by the importer before NAFTA would be $5.50 for an Indonesian shirt and $5.94 for a Mexican shirt.

Following the implementation of NAFTA, however, the tariff on imported T-shirts from Mexico is removed.

For the importer, the Mexican T-shirt is now the least expensive ($5.40) because it is no longer subject to tariffs, while the Indonesian product will still face a 10 per cent tariff and still cost the importer $5.50. Assuming that the importer chooses the lowest-cost product, imports will be switched after the regional scheme comes into effect from the lowest-cost producer (Indonesia) to Mexico, a relatively expensive producer, which now benefits from zero tariffs in the US market.

Several consequences follow from this trade *diversion*. The consumer in the USA *may* gain because the cost to the importer of purchasing a T-shirt falls from $5.50 to $5.40 (although the producer/wholesaler/retailer may be able to capture some or all of this gain). The US government, however, loses the tariff revenue (50 cents for each imported T-shirt) that it previously derived from taxing Indonesian T-shirt imports (the new imports from Mexico not being subject to tax). For the US economy as whole, therefore, the potential gain to consumers is significantly exceeded by the loss of tariff revenue (which is, of course, a form of taxation income for the government). Considered again from the perspective of the US economy, real resources are wasted because more money is being spent ($5.40 compared with $5.00) for each imported T-shirt. And, unless exceptional circumstances prevail, the Indonesian economy will also suffer a welfare loss because of the decline in export revenue it experiences (and with the loss of the US market, it may also have to lower the price of its T-shirt exports to compete in other markets).

If trade diversion outweighs trade creation, then the net effect of a regional scheme on its members' welfare can be negative.

Table 6.2 The Potential for Trade Diversion after the Removal of Tariffs on Intra-Regional Trade (US $)

	Cost of production	Tariff cost pre-NAFTA	Cost to importer pre-NAFTA	Tariff post-NAFTA	Cost to importer post-NAFTA
Indonesia	5.00	0.50 (10%)	5.50	0.50(10%)	5.50
Mexico	5.40	0.54 (10%)	5.94	Zero	5.40

a single agreement with a large number of states than to undertake a series of negotiations with individual states or with small groupings (because it both economizes on the resources needed for negotiations and increases the opportunities for trade-offs in reaching a package deal).

Why, then, has regionalism not only been attractive to governments throughout the post-war period but has apparently become increasingly so since the 1980s? Governments usually have multiple motives when entering an arrangement as complex as a regional partnership: it would be naïve to expect to find a single factor that explains governments' actions across all regional agreements. Moreover, governments often enter regional economic agreements primarily for political rather than economic reasons.

Political motivations for entering regional trade agreements

Economic co-operation and confidence building

Regionalism frequently involves the use of economic means for political ends: the improvement of inter-state relations and/or the enhancement of security within a region. In international relationships that have a history of conflict, or where no tradition of partnership exists, co-operation on economic matters can be a core element in a process of confidence building.

The origins of post-war European economic integration provide an excellent example. The European Coal and Steel Community (ECSC), created by the 1951 Treaty of Paris, was the first of the institutions of what was to evolve eventually into the European Union. The ECSC, founded by France, West Germany, Italy, Belgium, the Netherlands, and Luxembourg, pooled the coal and steel resources of its members by providing a unified market for these commodities (perceived as being critical to any military capacity); it also created a unified labour market in this sector. The underlying objective was to manage the rebuilding of Germany's post-war economy and to integrate it with those of

its neighbours, thereby helping to restore confidence among countries whose conflicts had embroiled the world in two major wars.

In a similar fashion, the Association of South-East Asian Nations (ASEAN) was founded in 1967 to promote economic co-operation in an attempt to build confidence and avoid conflict in a region that was the site of armed struggles in the Cold War era. Two of its founding members, Indonesia and Malaysia, had engaged in armed conflict in the period 1963–6 as the Indonesian government of President Sukarno attempted to destabilize the newly independent Malaysia. Over the years, ASEAN membership expanded and the organization successfully used co-operation on economic matters to overcome deep-seated inter-state rivalries and suspicion. In 1998, one of the visions of ASEAN's founders was realized when its membership was expanded to include all ten of the countries of South-East Asia (including Vietnam and Cambodia that had in the previous quarter of a century been at war with other ASEAN states and with one another).

In some cases, regional economic integration has been stimulated by a desire to enhance the security of regional partners against threats emanating from *outside* the membership of the regional arrangement. The Southern African Development Coordination Conference (SADCC), for example, was founded in 1980 in an attempt to reduce members' dependence on South Africa during the apartheid era.

Regional economic co-operation and the 'new security agenda'

Offers by industrialized countries in recent years to extend regional economic co-operation to their less developed neighbours have frequently been encouraged by concerns about 'non-traditional' security threats emanating from less developed partners. Such threats include environmental damage, illegal migration, organized crime, drug smuggling, and international terrorism. Regional co-operation may help to address these issues directly (for example, though NAFTA's provisions on the environment); or, as proponents hope, indirectly by promoting economic development and thereby ameliorating the conditions that were perceived as fostering the security threats. Concerns about new security threats played a part in European enthusiasm for new agreements with Mediterranean states, and in US interest in extending NAFTA to other Western Hemisphere countries.

Regionalism as a bargaining tool

Many of the regional economic agreements that developing countries established from the 1950s to the 1970s were motivated by a desire to enhance their bargaining power with transnational corporations and with trading partners. They were often inspired by the work of the UN's Economic Commission for Latin America, and its principal theorist, Raul Prebisch, whose ideas were taken up subsequently by writers from the dependency school. Prebisch (1963, 1970) argued that regional integration was essential in order to provide a sufficiently large market to enable the efficient local production of goods that had previously been imported. Moreover, a regional partnership would enhance bargaining power with external actors if the partners negotiated with one voice. One approach, as in the Andean Pact (founded in 1969 by Bolivia, Chile [which withdrew in 1976], Colombia, Ecuador, and Peru) was to adopt a system of region-wide industrial licensing. The intention was to prevent TNCs from gaining concessions by playing off governments of the region against one another, and to use the 'carrot' of access to a larger regional market to extract concessions from potential investors.

Less developed countries (LDCs) have also used regional partnerships as a way of gaining more aid from donor countries and organizations. Over the years, various governments and international organizations have encouraged regional economic integration among developing countries, and have set aside some of their aid budgets to promote regional projects. The European Union has been a particularly enthusiastic supporter of regionalism in other parts of the world, providing both financial assistance and technical support.

Moreover, a World Bank (2000: 20) study notes that, by pooling their diplomatic resources in a regional arrangement, LDCs are sometimes able to achieve greater prominence in international relations, to negotiate agreements that would not be available if they had acted individually, and to ensure the election of their representatives to key positions in international organizations. The best example of a successful pursuit of this strategy, the Bank suggests, is CARICOM, the Caribbean Community and Common Market.

But it is not just developing countries that have perceived regional economic partnerships as a means for enhancing their bargaining power. The Japanese Ministry of Economy, Trade and Industry, for example, in advocating participation in discriminatory regional arrangements, pointed to the possibility that, by facilitating partnerships with like-minded countries, they could increase Japan's leverage within the WTO (METI 2000). The foundation (in 1989) of APEC was linked to perceptions that it could help to pressure the European Union into trade concessions during GATT's Uruguay Round of trade negotiations (Ravenhill 2001). And some authors have suggested that the negotiation of the Treaty of Rome, which established the European Economic Community in 1957, was motivated at least in part by European countries' desires to increase their leverage against the United States in the upcoming GATT talks (Milward 1984, 1992).

Regionalism as a mechanism for locking-in reforms

Regional trade agreements can enhance the credibility of domestic economic reforms and thereby increase the attractiveness of economies to potential foreign investors (Rodrik 1989). Such considerations have become more important in an increasingly integrated global economy, where countries are competing to stake their claims as preferred partners in global production networks (see Thun, Chapter 11 in this volume).

Commitments made within a regional forum can be more attractive to potential investors than those made in global institutions, for several reasons.

Countries' compliance with their commitments is likely to be scrutinized more closely within a regional grouping: the numbers of partners to be monitored is smaller than within the WTO with its 150 members, and any breaking of commitments is more likely to have a direct impact on regional partners and lead to swift retaliation. Some regional arrangements provide for regional institutions to monitor the implementation of agreements. Moreover, repeated interactions with a small number of partners within regional arrangements may make governments more concerned about their reputations (their credibility as collaborators) than they would be within more diffuse multilateral forums (Fernandez and Portes 1998).

Regional arrangements may be particularly effective in enhancing the credibility of commitments when LDCs enter partnerships with an industrialized country as, for example, in Mexico's participation in NAFTA (Haggard 1997). And the possibility that the policy coverage of the RTA may be more comprehensive than agreements at the global level—embracing, for example, rules on competition policy and on the treatment of foreign investment—further enhances the potential of regional arrangements as a device for signalling to potential foreign investors the seriousness of a government's commitment to reform.

Regionalism to satisfy domestic political constituencies

Often, the choice of trade policies faced by governments is not between liberalization at the global level and liberalization at the regional level, but between a regional agreement and unilateral liberalization. In contrast to a unilateral lowering of tariffs, which is usually politically difficult for governments because domestic groups believe that the government is giving something away (tariff protection) and not receiving anything in return from other countries, a regional trade agreement provides a means for a government to ensure that it receives concessions (reciprocity) from its partners in return for those *it* has offered. And, in so far as a regional agreement makes it easier politically for

governments to undertake liberalization, and therefore enhances such activities, it may be beneficial not just for regional partners but also for the wider international community.

Ease of negotiating and implementing agreements

The larger the number of states, the more likely it is that they will have a greater diversity of interests that will complicate negotiations. Moreover, the larger the number of members, the more difficult it is to monitor behaviour and to enforce sanctions in the event of non-compliance (Oye 1985; Keohane 1984). A regional agreement with a limited number of partners might be easier to negotiate and implement than one at the global level. This logic is particularly applicable to bilateral trade agreements.

On the other hand, numerous cases exist of large numbers of governments successfully concluding international agreements (within, for example, the United Nations on issues ranging from arms control to the environment, to human rights (see, for example, Osherenko and Young 1993: 12)). Kahler (1992) has argued persuasively that success in solving the numbers problem depends on institutional design (a problem the WTO has yet to address effectively). Mechanisms for discussing issues and voting procedures can be adapted to counter the problems of numbers and diversity. A larger number of participants may bring the potential for greater gains and more opportunities for trade-offs among the parties.

In short, the international relations literature is inconclusive on the relationship between the number of participants and the successful negotiation and implementation of agreements. There are plenty of cases where regional negotiations have failed to produce agreements or have taken a very long time to complete (for example, a free trade agreement between Japan and Korea was proposed in 1998 but negotiations had not been concluded successfully by 2007). Of greater importance to shaping state action, however, are the perceptions that governments hold on this issue. And there is little doubt that many *believe* that regional agreements are easier to negotiate than those at the global level, given the numbers and diversity of WTO membership. The failure of the WTO ministerial meetings in Seattle in 1999 and Cancun in 2003 reinforced these beliefs.

Economic motivations for regionalism

Here we can distinguish between two possibilities: (*a*) where governments, for economic reasons, prefer a regional economic agreement to unilateral liberalization, or to a non-discriminatory multilateral agreement; and (*b*) where they prefer a regional agreement to the status quo.

Economic reasons for choosing regionalism over multilateralism

Regionalism enables continued protection of sectors that would not survive in global competition

Even though mainstream economic theory suggests that welfare gains will be maximized when trade liberalization occurs on a non-discriminatory basis, governments may nonetheless prefer a regional (discriminatory) trade agreement. This alternative is attractive, for example, when they (and interest groups, such as manufacturers' or farmers' associations, which almost certainly will be actively lobbying the government) believe that domestic producers will be successful in competition with regional partners and will benefit from the larger (protected) market that a regional scheme creates, but that they would not survive competition from producers located outside the region. Added to this is the possibility (discussed in more detail later in this chapter) that governments will be able to exclude 'politically sensitive' non-competitive domestic sectors completely from the trade liberalization measures negotiated within a regional agreement, whereas such exclusion would be more difficult at the global level.

A more benign variant of this argument is that a reform-minded government may seek to enter a regional agreement as a way gradually to expose inefficient domestic producers to international competition, with the expectation that competition from regional partners will generate reforms that will eventually enable the sector to be exposed to full international competition. In this scenario, regionalism is a stepping stone to broader liberalization.

Regionalism provides opportunities for 'deeper integration'

Regionalism may be more attractive than a multilateral treaty to pro-liberalization governments, because it enables agreement on issues that would not be possible in the WTO, where membership is more diverse. Since the early 1990s, a number of governments—such as those of the United States, Singapore, Chile, and Australia, which have been seeking to raise the tempo of trade liberalization—have turned to regional agreements in an attempt to promote 'deeper integration'. This concept refers to co-operation that goes beyond the traditional liberalization menu of removing tariff and non-tariff barriers. It may include, for example, agreements on the environment, on the treatment of foreign direct investment (FDI), on domestic competition (anti-trust) policies, on intellectual property rights, and on labour standards. The North American Free Trade Agreement (NAFTA) was one of the first free-trade agreements to incorporate provisions on many of these matters. As trade liberalization within the WTO reduced the significance of border barriers, so matters of 'deeper integration' have grown in importance as governments seek to establish a level playing field with their partners.

A regional approach may facilitate reaching agreement on these politically sensitive issues if the partner states share certain characteristics—for example, similar levels of economic development. Regional agreements, especially bilateral free trade areas, may also enable more powerful states to bring their weight to bear more effectively on weaker parties, for whom the price of gaining security of access to a larger market may be to accept undertakings on issues of 'deeper integration', such as their treatment of foreign investment, and so on (on this issue of unequal bargaining power in regional agreements, see Helleiner 1996, and Perroni and Whalley 1994).

Economic reasons for preferring regionalism to unilateralism or the status quo

Larger markets and increased foreign investment

Governments may not have the option of choosing between a regional agreement and an agreement at the global level: the latter may simply not be available at the time. The choice that governments face is to stick with the status quo, to liberalize on a unilateral basis, or to seek a regional agreement. Besides the political advantages, noted above, that a regional agreement often has over unilateral action, economic advantages may also come into play. Co-ordinated liberalization on a regional basis broadens the geographical scope of liberalization and may also enable a widening of the product coverage of the agreement, thereby increasing the potential economic gains.

Compared with the status quo, a regional economic agreement can confer two principal economic benefits. First, it provides a larger 'home' market for domestic industries, possibly enabling them to produce more efficiently because of economies of scale (Box 6.3). How significant an advantage is gained from regionalism will depend on the number of partner economies and their relative size: a firm in a large economy is unlikely to make significant gains in economies of scale if the regional partnership is with only a couple of much smaller economies.

Second, regionalism can increase the attractiveness of an economy to potential investors. Companies previously supplying the separate national markets through exports from outside the region may now find that the unified regional market is of sufficient size to make local production (and hence foreign investment into the region) attractive. Gains from FDI may be particularly significant when a less developed country enters into a regional partnership with one or more industrialized economies. Companies may be able to take advantage of the relatively low-cost labour in the less developed country to supply the whole of the regional market from factories established there. The best example here is the dramatic increase that occurred in foreign direct investment into Mexico following the signing of NAFTA in 1994. Inflows of FDI to Mexico, which averaged $8 billion a year in the period 1990–5, rose to $14 billion in 1997 and $24 billion in 2001 (UNCTAD 2002c: 304, Annex table B.1). Some evidence also exists of similar effects elsewhere; for example, FDI inflows to ASEAN increased after it negotiated its free trade area (UNCTAD 2003: 47, box II.5).

BOX 6.3

Economies of Scale

In modern manufacturing, which often depends on the use of expensive machinery and on very large investments in research and development (R&D), large-scale production often enables firms to produce at a lower average cost per unit. These *economies of scale* can result not only from a more efficient use of machinery and of labour, but also because specialist managers and workers can be employed, savings can be made in borrowing on the financial markets (which generally charge higher rates of interest to smaller borrowers), raw materials can be purchased more cheaply when bought in bulk, and advertising costs are spread across a higher volume of output.

A related concept is *economies of scope*. These occur when firms are able to spread various costs (including, for example, R&D, accounting, marketing) across various products, which may (although not necessarily) be related (for example, production of calculators and of LCD screens for laptop computers).

A related strategy is for governments to attempt to establish their economies as regional hubs. For a number of activities, companies will wish to establish only one office in a geographical area (it might, for example, be a central office responsible for procurement, or for providing management services to all of the company's regional subsidiaries). One of the reasons why some governments appear to have chosen to negotiate multiple regional trade agreements is that this strategy enhances their prospects of attracting companies' 'regional' headquarters as the economy becomes a 'hub' for multiple regional 'spokes'. Singapore, an active proponent of regional trade agreements, is a good example—it has a larger number of regional corporate headquarters than any other developing economy. Regional hubs may also be attractive to subsidiaries of multinational enterprises seeking to take advantage of the preferential access the RTAs provide to third-country markets. For example, US subsidiaries operating in Singapore enjoy duty-free access to the Japanese market for their products (subject to meeting the rules of origin in Singapore's economic partnership agreement with Japan), something not always available to them if they exported to Japan from their home base in the USA.

> **KEY POINTS**
>
> - Governments often enter regional trade agreements for political reasons.
>
> - These include: enhancing security; improving their international bargaining positions; signalling to potential investors the seriousness of their commitment to reforms; to satisfy domestic constituencies' demands for 'reciprocity'; and because they perceive regional agreements are easier to negotiate than those within the WTO.
>
> - Economic motivations for regionalism include access to a larger 'domestic' market; possibilities for attracting additional foreign direct investment (FDI); the possibility of engaging in 'deeper integration'; and the opportunity afforded to continue to protect politically sensitive, globally uncompetitive industries.

The Rush to Regionalism

The rush to regionalism that began in the mid-1990s is the second major wave of RTAs since the Second World War: the first occurred in the early 1960s, largely in response to the 1957 establishment of the European Economic Community (regionalism, however, has a much longer history, dating back several centuries: the previous peak in regional activity occurred in the inter-war period, when industrialized countries responded to the Great Depression by attempting to form closed trading blocs with less developed countries; in the case of European countries, this was with their colonies).

Many of the agreements negotiated in the 1960s linked less developed countries together. In Africa, the growth of regionalism followed former European colonies gaining their independence in the late 1950s and early 1960s. As in Latin America, the other continent where regionalism took off in this period, the principal objectives of the regional agreements were to promote local import-substituting industrialization, and to enhance the bargaining power of participants *vis-à-vis* external actors (in Asia, few regional economic partnerships, with the exception of ASEAN, emerged, not least because of Cold War conflicts that divided countries in this part of the world). In marked contrast with the most recent wave of regionalism, the agreements among less developed countries in the 1960s aimed to restrict imports from outside the region (in other words, they deliberately sought trade diversion—

see Box 6.2 on page 177—and to control foreign investors).

The landscape of inter-state relations in Latin America, and particularly in Africa, soon became littered with the debris of failed regional arrangements. One reason was that few of the parties to regional arrangements were significant economic partners for one another. This was particularly so in Africa, where the economies had been shaped in the colonial era to produce primary commodity exports for the European market. The share of intra-regional trade (that is, trade with regional partners) in countries' overall trade was often less than 5 per cent. A consequence was that liberalization of trade on a regional basis in itself brought the participants few immediate benefits.

Moreover, liberalization of trade within a region often exacerbated existing inequalities among the partner states. Where companies had a choice of a single country location to serve the unified and protected regional market, they usually preferred the city where infrastructure was most developed. Industries therefore tended to cluster around 'growth poles' and shunned the more poorly-resourced towns and cities in the least developed parts of the region. The less developed countries in a regional partnership frequently found that they faced significant costs from trade diversion as imports from outside the region were replaced by relatively high-cost production from their partner states. They also lost tariff revenue, on which many less developed economies depended heavily as a source of government funding (the loss occurring both because of the removal of intra-regional tariffs, and from the diversion of imports from outside the region to goods sourced from regional partners).

Some regional arrangements (including ASEAN and the Andean Pact) attempted to address the problems caused by this unbalanced growth by pursuing a policy of industrial licensing: the location of new industrial plants would be agreed by governments and allocated across different parts of the region to ensure that the less developed countries gained a share of the benefits from integration. But such an approach was politically unpopular with the governments of the more developed partners. They perceived the losses in investment forgone and the generally negative responses from foreign partners as exceeding any gains they made from collaboration with their less developed regional partners.

Arguments about the distribution of benefits from regionalism led to the collapse of many of the schemes established in the 1960s, and to a heightening of tensions between regional partners. Contrary to the idea that regionalism might improve inter-state security, disputes over the distribution of benefits from regional partnerships contributed in some instances to the onset of armed conflicts between former regional partners—for example, the 'soccer war' between former Central American Common Market members Honduras and El Salvador in 1969, and hostilities between former East African Community members Uganda and Tanzania in 1979.

The new regionalism

The failure of many regional trade agreements among less developed countries in the 1970s (Figure 6.1 on page 175 shows how few schemes from the 1960s and 1970s are still in force at the time of writing) occurred at a time when there was a considerable degree of pessimism about the prospects for the European Community. There, integration had proceeded more slowly than many had anticipated, and progress was punctuated by increasingly acrimonious disputes among the member governments. By the middle of the 1970s, when worldwide economic conditions were more turbulent than at any time since 1945 because of the Organization of Petroleum Exporting Countries-induced oil price rises and subsequent recession, regional integration no longer appeared to be a viable solution to the problems of interdependence that governments faced. To political leaders and academics alike, regional integration appeared to be increasingly obsolescent—the terminology the intellectual father of European integration studies, Ernst B. Haas (1975), applied at the time to theories of integration.

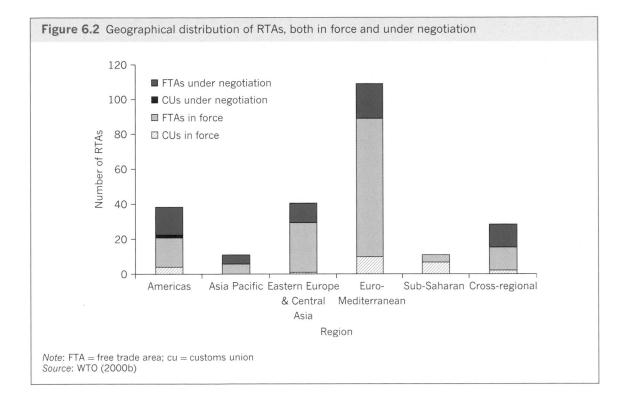

Figure 6.2 Geographical distribution of RTAs, both in force and under negotiation

Note: FTA = free trade area; cu = customs union
Source: WTO (2000b)

Two factors were to change the global context to make it far more favourable to regionalism in the 1990s. The first was the end of the Cold War. Regional economic agreements, like other aspects of international economic relations, are, in Aggarwal's (1985) terminology, 'nested' within the overall security context. A dramatic change in the security context opened up new possibilities for partnerships among countries that had previously been on opposite sides of the Cold War divide. In Europe, the disintegration of the former Soviet Union and the 1991 break-up of COMECON, the Council of Mutual Economic Assistance (founded in 1949 by the Soviet Union as an alternative to the assistance that the USA was providing Western Europe through the **Marshall Plan**, its membership expanded to include Czechoslovakia, East Germany, Poland, Hungary, Romania, Bulgaria, Mongolia, and Albania), opened the way for East European countries to enter into economic agreements with the European Union (and, for some,

eventual membership in the EU), and required new arrangements to be established amongst their former members if economic co-operation was to be sustained. Georgia, for example, signed six free-trade agreements with other former Soviet republics in the 1990s (see Figure 6.2).

The concentration of new regional agreements in Europe in the 1990s underlines the importance of East European fragmentation for the growth in the number of regional trade agreements (the enlargement of the EU in 2004 and 2007 subsequently made many of these treaties redundant). In Asia too, the end of the Cold War broke down the barriers that had previously prevented regional economic integration. In 1991, China joined the APEC grouping, which included its former Cold War foes Japan, the USA, and South Korea. In 2001, demonstrating the enormous improvement of relations that had occurred in East Asia over the previous decade, China began to negotiate a free trade agreement with ASEAN.

The second contextual factor was the growth in global interdependence, and the ascendancy of neo-liberal ideas in Western governments and in the international financial institutions. The growing integration of markets—for goods, services, and finance—placed increasing pressure on governments to pursue market-friendly policies. Potential foreign investors quickly voted with their feet when faced by governments attempting to impose conditions on them: indeed, from the early 1980s onwards, the balance of bargaining power between investors and governments shifted dramatically, so that investors were increasingly able to demand concessions from host governments on issues such as taxation, rather than accepting restrictions on their activities. Similarly, financial markets were quick to punish governments that were perceived to be inward-looking or inclined towards interventionist measures.

In this new context, the regional arrangements that developed were often designed to enhance states' participation in the global economy, to signal their openness to foreign investment, and to seek access to the markets of industrialized countries. Unlike the arrangements from the 1960s and 1970s, the new regionalism frequently involved partnerships between industrialized and less developed economies—that is, they were often North–South rather than South–South in orientation. The North American Free Trade Agreement is the most prominent example; meanwhile, many less developed economies sought free trade agreements with the European Union, and by the early years of the twenty-first century, Japan had begun to negotiate free trade agreements with less developed economies in South-East Asia and Latin America.

It was not just less developed countries that responded to the increased market integration by seeking regional economic partnerships. The decision by European member states to deepen integration and to complete the implementation of a single internal market (brought into being by the Single European Act, signed in 1986), has been interpreted widely as an attempt to strengthen the capacity of European companies to compete in the

new global market place (Sandholtz and Zysman 1989; Schirm 2002).

Table 6.3 illustrates a number of the factors contributing to the explosive growth in regionalism in the 1990s. Transition economies (the former Soviet bloc countries) were involved in more than half of all RTAs signed in the 1990s (including forty that only involved other transition economies). Reflecting the desire of Southern countries to seek alliances with Northern partners, there was also a dramatic jump in the number of RTAs linking developed with developing countries in the 1990s. In contrast, only six of the more than 120 agreements initiated between 1990 and 2002 linked two or more developed economies.

A variety of other factors also contributed to the growth of regionalism in the 1990s.

Frustration with the difficulties of negotiating global agreements

The GATT began as a relatively small international institution dominated by Western industrial countries (see Winham, Chapter 5 in this volume). As more countries joined the GATT, so the difficulties of reaching agreement were intensified among an increasingly diverse group on an agenda that was becoming more complex. The consequence was that it took much longer to bring successive rounds of GATT talks to a conclusion.

When the Uruguay Round of GATT negotiations stalled over issues relating to trade in agricultural products, governments turned to regional agreements both as a substitute for a global agreement and as a means of increasing pressure on other countries to attempt to persuade them to make concessions in global talks. Similar considerations applied a decade later when the WTO prepared to launch a new round of global trade negotiations: membership of the WTO was approaching 150 economies and the agenda was even more complex. The 'debacle in Seattle'—the failure of the WTO's ministerial meeting in December 1999—convinced many governments (including some that previously

Table 6.3 Notified RTAs in Goods by the Date of Entry into Force and Type of Partners (as of January 2003)

	Developed–Developed	Developed–Developing	Developed–Transition	Developing–Developing	Developing–Transition	Transition–Transition	Total
1958–1964	2	0	0	1	0	0	3
1965–1969	0	0	0	0	1	0	1
1970–1974	5	1	0	2	0	0	8
1975–1979	0	3	0	1	0	0	4
1980–1984	2	1	0	2	0	0	5
1985–1989	1	1	0	2	0	0	4
1990–1994	3	3	4	5	1	5	21
1995–1999	3	7	0	4	2	16	32
2000–2002	0	11	4	8	2	5	30
2003–2005	2	9	0	4	2	16	33
Total	**18**	**36**	**8**	**29**	**8**	**42**	**141**

Note: Developed countries include Canada, the United States, EU, EFTA, Japan, Australia, and New Zealand; transition countries include the former Soviet Union, Eastern and Central Europe, the Baltic States, and the Balkans; the remaining countries are (self-) classified as developing
Source: Crawford and Florentino (2005); table 1

had been hostile towards RTAs—for example, Japan; see METI 2000), that negotiation of a new global agreement would not bring early results and that they should therefore look to RTAs if they wished to advance their trade agendas. The failure of the Cancun WTO ministerial meeting in September 2003 and the suspension of the Doha Round negotiations in July 2006 reinforced these beliefs.

Bandwagoning and balancing: 'contagion' effects

The fact that post-war regional integration has come in two waves points both to the likelihood that common responses have occurred across various parts of the globe to the same stimuli (especially to increased economic interdependence), and to the possibility that regionalism in one part of the world triggers regionalism elsewhere through 'demonstration', 'emulation', or 'contagion' effects.

The establishment of the European Common Market in 1957, with its apparently positive impacts both on inter-state relations and on the economies of its members, inspired a wave of imitations among less developed countries. Similarly, the completion of the single internal market in the EU in 1992 and the establishment of NAFTA in 1994 led governments elsewhere to take a keener interest in becoming participants in regional agreements. The Japanese government report cited above, for example, presented a detailed review of academic studies of existing regional arrangements, concluding that they generally had a positive effect on the welfare of member states. For many governments, therefore, the new interest in regionalism was primarily a defensive response to developments elsewhere. And some governments that were already party to regional arrangements sought new ones in an attempt to reduce their dependence on existing regional partners. Mexico, for example, began negotiations for free trade arrangements with the European Union and Japan as a means of reducing its heavy reliance on its NAFTA partners.

It was not just governments, however, that were prompted into action by regionalism elsewhere. The essence of preferential trade agreements is that they are discriminatory: non-members do not share the benefits they provide. Companies located in non-member countries therefore find that RTAs place them at a competitive disadvantage. They have an incentive to lobby their governments either to bandwagon by joining existing regional arrangements where such possibilities exist, or to negotiate a treaty that provides them with equivalent access to markets. For example, following the implementation of NAFTA and the signature of the Mexico–EU Free Trade Agreement, Japanese manufacturers found themselves at a disadvantage in competing in the Mexican market. Whereas their American and European counterparts enjoyed duty-free access to Mexico, Japanese companies faced tariffs averaging 16 per cent. The main business grouping, the Japan Federation of Economic Organizations—*Keidanren*, lobbied the government to sign a free trade agreement with Mexico that would give Japanese companies equivalent access to that enjoyed by their competitors (Ravenhill 2003).

The proliferation of preferential trade agreements across the globe, with the potential competitive disadvantages they bring for non-participants, increases the incentives for governments either to join existing agreements or to seek similar arrangements for their own exporters (Baldwin 1997; Oye 1992).

The change in the US attitude towards preferential agreements

The United States government was the strongest supporter of a non-discriminatory multilateral approach to trade in the negotiations that led to the creation of GATT at the end of the Second World War. Not only had the USA been a victim of the discriminatory colonial trading blocs that the European powers had created in the inter-war period, but it also believed that their closing off of international trade had made a significant contribution to the global recession of the 1930s. It was largely through US insistence that non-discrimination was enshrined as the cornerstone of the post-war global trade regime.

Washington was, however, willing to tolerate regional trading groupings that discriminated against its exports where it believed that these helped to achieve its political objectives through, for example, facilitating reconciliation between former enemies and strengthening the economies of the participants so that they would be less susceptible to the perceived communist threat. Security concerns trumped economic principles. The primary example was the European Economic Community (EEC). Washington had encouraged European recipients of Marshall Plan assistance (see Box 6.4), to co-ordinate their plans. It put pressure on France to accommodate the rebuilding of Germany's industry and to devise a mechanism that would allay French concerns (which ultimately became the Schuman Plan for the European Coal and Steel Community). The US government supported the formation of the EEC in 1957 even though it was obvious that the new Community, like the ECSC, would not be fully compatible with GATT requirements for regional agreements, and would discriminate against US exports. At the same time, it exerted pressure on the Europeans not to introduce any provisions that would increase discrimination against US economic interests. Its support for European integration was also accompanied by American initiatives in the GATT for new rounds of global negotiations, with the objective of reducing overall tariff levels and thus the discrimination its exporters would face in the European market (the 'Kennedy Round', 1963–7, was the response to the EEC's creation, and the 'Tokyo Round', 1973–9, the response to the first enlargement of the Community when Denmark, Ireland, and the United Kingdom were admitted in 1973).

Washington's attitude towards regional economic agreements among less developed countries

BOX 6.4

The Marshall Plan

Under the Marshall Plan, the US government provided $11.8 billion in grants and a further $1.5 billion in loans to assist in the rebuilding of European economies (and, in some cases, those of their colonies) in the years 1948–52. The United Kingdom received the largest volume of grants ($2.8 billion) followed by France ($2.5 billion), Italy ($1.4 billion), and West Germany ($1.2 billion). The Plan was an outgrowth of Washington's concerns about the perceived growth of Soviet influence in Europe. Funds were used for purposes such as purchasing new machinery for factories, providing technical assistance to enable Europeans to become familiar with new technologies, and the rebuilding of roads, railways, and ports. The bilateral assistance provided to Europe under the Marshall Plan far exceeded the funds available from the **International Bank for Reconstruction and Development** (World Bank). The Organization for European Economic Co-operation (which subsequently evolved into the Organization for Economic Co-operation and Development (OECD)) was created to manage the Marshall Plan aid.

was more ambivalent. Although it appreciated the possibility that regionalism might improve the security of the participants, its enthusiasm was tempered because of the anti-import and pro-interventionist frameworks that figured prominently in many of the regional schemes among less developing countries in the 1960s. Its support for regional economic integration among Latin-American countries was therefore at best lukewarm. And, in other parts of the world, especially Asia, Washington opposed any movement towards a regional agreement from which it would be excluded.

The US attitude towards regional economic agreements changed in the early 1980s as it despaired of the slow progress in global trade liberalization and bristled at the growing trade distortions generated by the European Community's Common Agricultural Policy (CAP). United States' trade representative, William Brock, announced in 1982 that Washington was willing to enter into regional trade agreements. Negotiation of a free trade agreement with Israel followed quickly. The USA also launched the Caribbean Basin Initiative, a programme of trade preferences for the island states of the region. Far more significant, however, was Washington's positive response to a Canadian proposal for negotiation of a free trade agreement. In one sense this was not a dramatic departure in American trade policy. Washington had offered such an agreement

to Canada on several occasions over the previous century, only to be rebuffed by a Canadian government concerned about maintaining its economic independence. Nonetheless, the signature of the Canada–US Free Trade Agreement in 1988 sent a dramatic signal to other members of the international community. This was reinforced in the following years when the first Bush administration indicated its willingness to construct a 'hub and spokes' framework that would link the USA in a series of free trade agreements with partners in Central and Latin America, Oceania, and East Asia.

The new approach to trade policy in the early 1990s was stated succinctly by Lawrence Summers, who became under-secretary of the Treasury for International Affairs in the first Clinton administration: that there should be a 'presumption in favor of all the lateral reductions in trade barriers, whether they be multi, uni, tri, plurilateral' (quoted in Frankel 1997: 5). In other words, the policy was one of 'anything goes' in trade policy as long as it contributed to trade liberalization, there no longer being a presumption that discriminatory regional agreements would be barriers to liberalization at the global level.

With the United States itself in the second half of the 1990s actively pursuing regionalism through NAFTA and advocating its extension into a Free Trade Area of the Americas, it would have been difficult for Washington to maintain its opposition to regionalism in other parts of the world. The change in attitude was particularly important in facilitating the development of preferential trade arrangements in East Asia. Whereas Washington had vigorously opposed a proposal from Malaysian prime minister, Mahathir Mohamad, in the early 1990s for the creation of an East Asian Economic Group, which would have excluded the countries of North America and Oceania that were members of the rival APEC grouping, by the late 1990s it acquiesced in the creation of an equivalent grouping (ASEAN Plus Three—the ten ASEAN members plus China, Japan, and South Korea), and in numerous East Asian moves to negotiate bilateral free trade arrangements.

Making existing preferential trade arrangements compatible with WTO requirements

Some of the new free trade areas came into being because industrialized countries perceived that they needed to make their trade agreements with less developed countries compatible with the WTO's regulations. Here, the European Union has again been the most important actor.

The European Union had previously constructed a network of preferential trade arrangements with the countries of the southern Mediterranean and with the ACP grouping, comprising over seventy countries in Africa, the Caribbean, and the Pacific, many of which had formerly been European colonies. These agreements had been negotiated in contexts entirely different from that prevailing in the second half of the 1990s. The arrangements with the ACP grouping were codified in the Lomé Conventions, the first of which had come into effect in 1975 at the height of the demands from less developed economies for the creation of a **New International Economic Order**. Reflecting a context in which industrialized countries were responsive to the demands from less developed economies for special treatment, the Conventions offered duty-free access to the European market for most ACP exports, without obliging the ACP countries to provide similar preferential treatment to European exports: in other words, they were non-reciprocal arrangements. (Treaties with southern Mediterranean countries, signed in 1975–7, offered similar duty-free access to the European market: the Mediterranean countries committed themselves to lower their tariffs on imports from the European Community but the timetable for this process was not specified).

Besides their general trade provisions, the Lomé Conventions also included special arrangements for specific products, including bananas, beef, rum, and sugar, on which some countries' export earnings were heavily dependent. These typically enabled their sale in European markets at prices much higher than those prevailing elsewhere. In some instances, they rested on a segmentation of the European market, with, for example, exports of ACP bananas being subject to different treatment in the United Kingdom and in France than they received in Germany and the Netherlands. The European Union in fact operated three different tariff regimes for bananas even though, as a common market, it had supposedly adopted a common external tariff. The new commitment to realizing a single internal market in the EU in 1992 made it impossible to maintain this arrangement for ACP bananas.

In an attempt to preserve the special position of ACP bananas, the European Union introduced an interventionist system of import licensing that discriminated against bananas coming from non-ACP countries (primarily Central and Latin America). Several of these producing countries challenged the new EU banana regime in the GATT; they were supported by the US government, which had been lobbied by the two giant US agribusiness firms, Dole and Chiquita, which handled most of the trade in Central- and Latin-American bananas. The outcome of the lengthy and convoluted dispute, which spanned the period during which the WTO took over from the GATT, and which at one stage threatened to trigger a 'trade war' between the United States and the European Union, was that a WTO Dispute Settlement Panel found that the European provisions on bananas contravened several of its articles. The Europeans eventually backed down, committing themselves to introduce arrangements that were compatible with their WTO obligations (Ravenhill 2004).

The dispute illustrated how the WTO makes it possible for less developed countries to initiate a successful challenge against an aspect of the trade policies of an economic superpower—in this case the EU. It also demonstrated the significance of the changed arrangements for dispute settlement with the transition from the GATT to the WTO: unlike the situation under the GATT, when countries simply ignored dispute settlement judgements they did not like, the EU had no viable alternative but to conform to the WTO's requirements. More important than the specifics of the banana dispute itself are the implications of the WTO's judgement for rules governing the relations between industrialized and less developed economies.

In finding that the EU's banana regime contravened several of its provisions, the WTO rejected European arguments that the trade arrangements with the ACP were legitimized by WTO rules on RTAs and on special treatment for less developed economies. The WTO found that the Lomé Convention did not conform to its rules for regional trade arrangements because the ACP countries were not required to remove their tariffs on European imports (under the requirements of Article xxiv, all parties to a regional economic agreement must liberalize 'substantially all trade' between them). Moreover, the Convention did not conform to the

rules on preferences for less developed economies because it gave special treatment to one group (the ACP) but not to other economies at similar levels of development. These rulings left the EU with only one other avenue for seeking WTO legitimacy for the Convention: to apply under Article ix of the WTO for a special waiver from the most-favoured nation rule. But the requirements for such a waiver are more stringent under the WTO than they were in the GATT, the waiver is only for a fixed term, and would not prevent WTO members from subsequently challenging specific elements of the arrangements. In other words, a waiver would have provided little assurance to the ACP states that the provisions would not be disrupted in the future.

Faced with this dilemma, the EU decided that the only means through which it could provide long-term trade security for the ACP would be to abandon its previous approach and to negotiate arrangements that were compatible with WTO rules on regional trade agreements (Article xxiv). It proposed to do this by concluding a series of economic partnership agreements with groupings of ACP countries, to be negotiated by the end of 2007. A similar decision had been made earlier regarding the trade agreements with the countries of the southern Mediterranean: in its Barcelona Declaration of 1995, the EU stated its intention to negotiate WTO-compatible free trade agreements with these countries. These have subsequently been concluded with Tunisia (1995), Israel (1995), Morocco (1996), Jordan (1997), Egypt (1999), Algeria (2001), and Lebanon (2002).

KEY POINTS

- The regional trade agreements of the 1960s and 1970s aimed to promote regional industrialization behind tariff walls.

- They often broke down because of disagreements over the distribution of benefits and costs from regional co-operation.

- The new regionalism differs from the previous wave in that participating countries are typically using

agreements to increase their integration into the world economy.

- Its origins lie in the end of the Cold War, the perceived success of RTAs elsewhere; frustrations with the pace of trade liberalization at the global level; a desire to make existing preferential trade relations compatible with WTO rules; and a change in US attitudes towards regionalism.

The Political Economy of Regionalism

Private sector interests

Previous sections of this chapter have identified several reasons why governments and private sector actors might wish to pursue regional economic integration. It is straightforward, for example, to suggest that, when companies face high tariffs in markets where their competitors' products enter duty free because of the existence of free trade arrangements, they will lobby their governments to obtain similar arrangements. But other than for these defensive reasons, when might companies support the establishment of a regional free trade area rather than choose either continued protectionism or non-discriminatory liberalization?

To address this question requires a starting point that is far removed from the assumptions of trade theory as developed in neoclassical economics (which assumes constant returns to scale and immobile factors of production; that is, unit costs of production are the same regardless of the size of the production run, and factors of production—for example, capital—will not move across national boundaries). In particular, it rests on the possibility that companies will be able to produce more efficiently for a regional rather than a domestic market, because they are able to capture economies of scale, on the increasing mobility of capital, and on observations regarding the geographical distribution of subsidiaries of transnational corporations.

The economies of scale argument assumes that regional integration is able to provide firms with the minimum market size required for them to capture scale economies, whereas the domestic market alone is too small for this to happen. But why would firms not prefer multilateral liberalization so as to gain access to even larger global markets? The reason is that a regional agreement will provide an opportunity to retain tariff and other barriers against competitors from outside the region. The logic is that of strategic trade theory, one component of which asserts that it is possible for governments to provide an advantage to their domestic companies if they offer a protected domestic market that enables them to realize economies of scale (Krugman 1990; for an application of the argument to the regional level, see Milner 1997b; and Chase 2003, 2005).

The other departure from conventional trade theory rests on an acknowledgement that contemporary manufacturing often involves conducting various stages of production in different geographical locations to take advantage of local characteristics such as relatively low-cost labour or a concentration of product- or industry-specific skills. From the 1980s onwards, United States and European firms, facing intense competition in their domestic market from imports from East Asia, established subsidiaries in relatively low-labour-cost neighbouring countries, from which they sourced components (see the discussion in Thun, Chapter 11 in this volume). The establishment of regional free trade areas facilitates this corporate strategy (and here it is appropriate to remember the North–South architecture of many of the new regional arrangements of the 1990s—for example, trade agreements between the European Union and Eastern European and Mediterranean countries, NAFTA, and the Caribbean Basin Initiative). Moreover, the rules of origin, in NAFTA for example, that allow components sourced from US companies to be counted towards requirements that goods must meet if they are to be deemed to have been manufactured in Mexico, serve as a protectionist device that provides further advantage to US-based corporations (for further discussion, see Cox 2000).

Even though transnational corporations (TNCs) disperse their activities to capitalize on local characteristics, their production and sales are frequently concentrated within one geographical region. This geographical concentration of activities is likely to cause many TNCs to put their efforts into lobbying for regional trading agreements rather than for liberalization at the global level, because their principal interest is in removing barriers to trade between those countries in which their manufacturing plants are located. This concentration on the regional level is encouraged by the better prospects there, compared with the global level of pursuing the 'deeper integration' that multinational enterprises (MNEs) need for efficient integration of their production networks—for example, agreements on the treatment that foreign investment will receive, protection of intellectual property rights, and facilitation of the movement of skilled workers and management.

Economies of scale and regionalization of production may both incline companies towards lobbying for regional trade agreements, but their impact on the attitudes of labour is likely to be more ambiguous. On the one hand, the possibility of gaining larger market share, longer production runs, and higher profits through the realization of economies of scale offers the prospect to labour of additional employment, higher wages and so on. On the other hand, the opportunity that the negotiation of a free trade area provides companies to regionalize their production will be likely to worry labour unions in relatively high-wage countries that will fear that labour-intensive stages of production will be moved to those parts of the region with lower labour costs. It was not surprising, therefore, that companies with regionalized production networks lobbied in favour of NAFTA whereas labour unions (together with American firms that produced solely within

---

BOX 6.5

Rules of Origin

Countries that enter into a free trade agreement are inevitably concerned that non-members should not exploit the benefits they provide to their partners. In particular, they fear that because free trade areas (unlike customs unions) do not have a common external tariff, non-members will send goods into the free trade area through the country with the lowest tariff, and then use the free trade provisions of the grouping to access other members' markets. This *trade deflection* will lead to a loss of tariff revenue for the economies with higher tariffs, and possibly to greater competition for their domestic producers.

Consider, for example, the following hypothetical situation. Assume that Mexico has a 5 per cent tariff on cameras, whereas Canada and the United States both have a 12 per cent tariff. If they were able to take advantage of the introduction of free trade under NAFTA, Japanese camera manufacturers would export their cameras to Mexico and supply Canada and the United States from these exports. Both the Canadian and US governments would lose tariff revenue that they would otherwise collect on imports of Japanese cameras. And Japanese cameras (now subject to a lower tariff) would become more competitive

than they otherwise would have been with cameras produced in Canada and the United States.

To prevent free trade areas from causing trade deflection of this type, their members typically adopt what are called rules of origin. These are intended to ensure that goods will only benefit from the provisions of the free trade agreement if they can be considered to have 'originated'—that is, to have been produced—in the partner country. Goods that are merely passing through the partner country or, for example, have been re-stamped as 'Made in Mexico', will not qualify for duty-free access to other members' markets. Determining where a product has originated has become increasingly difficult in an integrated global economy, with goods often being assembled from components manufactured in several countries.

Rules of origin typically take one or more of the following forms:

(a) *A value-added criterion.* This specifies that a particular percentage of the value of the export must have been generated within the partner country. For example, to qualify as a local product for the purposes of NAFTA, 62.5 per cent of the value of an automobile must have been generated locally.

(b) *A change of tariff heading criterion.* The World Customs Organization has developed a 'Harmonized System Nomenclature' of tariff headings that classifies all products according to their degree of processing, ranging from raw materials through semi-processed products to finished manufactures. Under this criterion, a good is considered to have been produced domestically if a change in tariff heading results from the local processing/manufacture.

(c) *A specific processing criterion.* This stipulates that particular stages in the production of the export must have been undertaken locally. For example, cloth may only be considered a local product if weaving has been undertaken locally.

(d) *A specific components criterion.* This establishes that particular parts of the finished good must have been manufactured locally for it to qualify for duty-free treatment. In NAFTA, colour television sets are considered to be local products only if their picture tubes have been manufactured locally. Usually, rules of origin allow for 'cumulation', so that components sourced from partner countries are counted as if they had been produced domestically (so that, for example, a colour TV manufactured in Mexico containing a picture tube manufactured in the USA would be classed as a local product for NAFTA rules of origin purposes).

As is evident from these examples, rules of origin are usually product-specific and can be very complex.

Specification of the rules of origin often constitutes the bulk of the agreements that establish free trade areas. Those for NAFTA, for example, run to close to 200 pages of small print. They require detailed, complex negotiations. The complexity of rules of origin is often viewed as a barrier to developing economies' participation in international trade, especially when they have to cope with multiple sets of rules that govern trade with different partners.

The negotiation of rules of origin, moreover, whose product-specific provisions often appear to be arbitrary, offers an opportunity for domestic interests to attempt to seek protection from the effects of regional trade liberalization. Setting a high value-added criterion may make it impossible for rival producers in partner countries to qualify for duty-free access to the domestic market. And the requirement that a specific component be produced locally may increase the discrimination against non-members and exclude them from the enlarged regional market. For example, Schiff and Winters (2003: 80) cite the example of tomato ketchup. Under the 1988 Canada–US Free Trade Agreement (CUSFTA), ketchup produced from imported tomato paste qualified as a local product and received duty-free treatment. When the CUSFTA was converted into NAFTA, however, the new rules of origin stated that ketchup would be considered a local product only if it contained tomato paste manufactured within NAFTA. The result was *trade diversion* from Chile to Mexico: whereas Chile accounted for more than 80 per cent of US imports of tomato paste before NAFTA, after the introduction of the NAFTA rules of origin Chile's share dropped to 5 per cent, while Mexico's share rose to 75 per cent.

---

the USA for the domestic market) expressed their concern that the agreement would generate, in the words of H. Ross Perot, a 'giant sucking sound' as US jobs were lost to Mexico (Chase 2003).

The politics of regional deepening: neo-functionalist and intergovernmental explanations

As indicated in Box 6.1 on page 174, governments that enter regional agreements involving more than the creation of a free trade area inevitably have to

agree to establish institutions that 'pool their sovereignty' on policies that have to be determined at the regional level—for example, the determination of common external tariffs and other common foreign economic policies in customs unions. The deeper the integration—that is, the broader the scope of policy issues on which members agree to co-operate—the greater will be the number of policy areas on which regional institutions will have to be given competence (unless members agree to a policy of mutual recognition whereby they accept policies/standards in other member countries as if they were their own).

Political scientists have long been fascinated by the question of whether, once a regional arrangement has been established, it generates its own momentum towards not only closer economic ties but also closer political integration. The vast majority of regional economic agreements take the form of free trade areas, which, because they do not require setting a common external tariff, provide little stimulus for the establishment of a regional institution to co-ordinate policies. Most free trade areas do provide a process for the resolution of disputes between the parties over the interpretation and/or implementation of the free trade area's rules, but this is usually managed by secretariats within the governments of the member countries. For example, although there is a NAFTA secretariat, which administers the dispute resolution procedures created by the agreement, this is a 'virtual' secretariat comprised of three sections located within the respective national governments. Very limited scope is available to such national agencies to act to promote deeper regional integration: indeed, the very lack of the creation of any alternative source of authority at the regional level is one of the attractions of free trade areas to many national governments. Even in those free trade areas where member governments have agreed to create a central secretariat, as in ASEAN, they often deliberately keep such institutions weak so that they do not develop as challengers to national governments.

With deeper integration, the scope for regional institutions to act autonomously may increase. The best example is the European Union, the only regional agreement that has fully implemented a common market and moved beyond this to form an economic union. It has by far the most complex of governance arrangements of any regional grouping. As Helen Wallace (2000: 44) suggests, 'much of what makes the EU so interesting . . . is the density of institutions and the evidence of institutional creativity. EU institutions provide both opportunities and constraints, and they serve to channel and to structure the behaviour of political actors from the participating countries'.

The principal political organs at the regional level are a supranational secretariat, the European Commission ('supranational' because it is autonomous from the governments of the member states and its officials have the responsibility of promoting the interests of the EU as a whole rather than those of specific members), an institution comprised of ministers from the national governments (the Council of Ministers), the European Parliament (directly elected since 1979 by voters in the member states), and the European Court of Justice (which is charged with interpreting the various EU treaties that member states have signed). The EU treaties now extend far beyond the liberalization of internal trade and the establishment of common foreign economic policies to include competition policies, environmental policies, common foreign and security policies, justice and home affairs, and regional development. The European Union and its member states now constitute a complex web of multilevel governance, with authority for making and implementing policies on various issues being split between institutions at the regional, national, and, in some cases, the subnational level (for further discussion, see Bomberg and Stubb 2003; and Wallace and Wallace 2000).

Most of the theorizing in international relations on regionalism has concentrated on the European experience. The early years of European integration inspired the development of neo-functionalist analysis (Haas 1958; Lindberg 1963). This approach suggested how a regional grouping could generate a momentum of its own that would lead to a deepening of co-operation. The logic was that co-operation in one area of economic activity would produce pressures for co-operation in other areas as the costs of pursuing uncoordinated policies became increasingly evident to member states and private-sector actors, a process that the *neo-functionalist* theorists termed 'spillover'. Entrepreneurial leadership by regional institutions could intensify the pressures for further co-operation.

In the European Union, the European Commission has the power to take initiatives in the various areas where the members have agreed that the EU has competence; it thus has the capacity to shape agendas and to push for further co-operation at the European level. The European Court of Justice's responsibility for interpreting the treaties and for adjudicating disputes between member states affords it an opportunity that extends into the realm of policy-making; over the last quarter of the twentieth century some of its judgements significantly extended the scope of European competence.

One element of neo-functional theorizing was to emphasize the significance of the unintended consequences of previous actions and decisions. For example, member states did not anticipate the important role that the Court of Justice would come to play in extending the scope of integration when they created a body that was intended to arbitrate disputes on the implementation of treaties. For theorists in the neo-functionalist tradition, the logic of spillover and the creative leadership provided by regional institutions can provide the integration process with a dynamic of its own (Sandholtz and Stone Sweet 1998 provide a recent example of theorizing from this perspective).

The neo-functionalist approach has been challenged consistently by scholars who assert that national states have primacy in the integration process. Stanley Hoffmann (1966) pioneered this challenge; the economic historian Alan Milward (1992) subsequently developed the theme that integration in Europe is best interpreted as a strategy pursued by national states to strengthen their own positions. Andrew Moravcsik (1998) presents the most theoretically sophisticated articulation of this 'liberal intergovernmental' argument, suggesting that the major steps forward in European integration were driven not by the European Commission or the Court of Justice, but by member governments responding in a rational way to domestic economic interests. Key decisions on integration reflect bargains struck among member states; the most significant European institution therefore is not the supranational Commission but rather the intergovernmental Council of Ministers. For writers in this tradition, to the extent that member states delegate authority to community institutions, such moves are 'calculated, rational, and circumscribed' (Bomberg and Stubb 2003: 11).

In this hotly contested debate, as is often the case in international relations theorizing, authors writing from one perspective have been reluctant to acknowledge that the arguments of the competing school have any legitimacy. Because the EU embraces such a wide array of activities, and the competencies of its various actors and the balance of power between them have evolved over time, it is possible for both sides to this debate to find compelling examples that support their case. Rather than perceiving this issue as a dichotomy of government preferences versus the actions of supranational institutions, it would be more helpful to focus on the interaction between these two. Sandholtz (1993) has argued persuasively that state preferences themselves are not formed in a vacuum: membership of the EU itself has become an important influence on how governments define their interests.

To date, the failure of those other regional schemes that aspire to become common markets to realize their aspirations inevitably limits to the European context debates about the role that supranational institutions can play in driving integration forward. Meanwhile, it is too early to tell whether the neo-functional logic of spillover will apply to some of the more significant free trade areas, most notably NAFTA, that were established in the 1990s.

- Corporations may prefer regionalism to global trade liberalization if it enables them to capture economies of scale while avoiding exposure to global competition.

- Regionalism may be particularly attractive to companies that seek 'deeper integration' to facilitate the operation of regional production networks (through, for example, provisions to safeguard investments).

- Unskilled labour in industrialized economies is likely to oppose regional integration if this includes less developed economies with significantly lower labour costs.

- Because most RTAs are free trade areas, they requiring little pooling of sovereignty and afford little scope for the emergence of sources of power at the regional level that rival national governments.

- In the EU, evidence from different sectors at different periods of time supports arguments from both the intergovernmental and the neo-functionalist perspectives.

The Economic Consequences of Regional Integration

The discussion of trade diversion in Box 6.2 on page 177 reminds us that no assumption can be made that regional trade agreements will necessarily enhance the welfare of their participants. It is not straightforward to estimate the effect that RTAs have had on members' trade and their welfare more generally because the impact of many other variables has to be taken into consideration.

Regional agreements and members' trade

That the share of world trade conducted within RTAs has risen, as noted at the beginning of this chapter, reflects both an increase in the number of RTAs and an increase in the share of the total trade that members of RTAs conduct with one another. Table 6.4 shows for the major minilateral RTAs how the share of intra-regional trade in members' total trade evolved in the last quarter of the twentieth century.

The share of intra-regional trade in the total trade of members of some regional agreements rose dramatically: most notable here were NAFTA, CARICOM, and MERCOSUR. In contrast, ASEAN states were little more important as trading partners for one another in 2005 than they had been thirty-five years before, despite implementing a free trade agreement in the interim. The record of many African RTAs was mixed: SADC was notably successful in increasing intra-regional trade, a reflection of the reintegration of the post-apartheid South Africa into the regional economy.

Simple statistics of this type, however, do not tell us whether the RTA itself has been a significant influence on trade among the member economies. Multiple factors other than the existence of a regional trade agreement can influence the volume of trade between any two countries. Among the most important of these are the size of the two economies, the levels of per capita income, the geographical distance between the two countries (and hence the transportation costs in trading), whether or not they share a common boundary, and whether or not their populations speak the same language. Such factors have to be built into any model that attempts to isolate the impact of the regional agreement itself on trade. Jeffrey Frankel (1997) has undertaken the most comprehensive modelling of this type. He finds that after allowing for the various factors identified above, regional trade agreements have had a (statistically significant) positive impact on the trade between their members. This positive effect is particularly pronounced for agreements among less developed economies, including ASEAN and MERCOSUR, but trade among EU member states was also 65 per cent above the level that would otherwise have been expected in the absence of a regional trade agreement. These results echo those in several other studies. The evidence points strongly to preferential trade agreements having caused changes in patterns of international trade.

These results in themselves, however, do not distinguish between trade creation and trade diversion effects, and thus tell us little about the welfare effects of the regional trade agreements.

Again, isolating the causes of the increased trade is no easy task. The new preferences created for regional partners have to be viewed in the context of other changes in the participants' trade policies, including, for example, any reduction of their tariffs towards non-members of the regional agreement (as occurred in the 1980s and 1990s, both through unilateral liberalization and through implementation of GATT/WTO agreements).

A major study by the World Bank (2000) finds that although the ratio of intra-regional trade to gross domestic product (GDP) increased in all regional groupings reviewed, so too did the ratio of trade with extra-regional partners to GDP. In other words, not only did trade with regional partners grow in economic importance but so too did trade with countries outside the region. Consequently, the Bank concluded, while studies suggest that some trade diversion occurred in the EU, European Free Trade Association, and NAFTA, 'the picture is sufficiently mixed that it is not

Table 6.4 Changes in the share of intra-regional trade in selected RTAs, 1970–2005

	1970	1980	1985	1990	1995	2000	2005
EU (1957)	59.5	60.8	59.2	65.9	62.4	65.7	65.7
NAFTA (1994)	36.0	33.6	43.9	41.4	41.5	46.4	42.9
CACM (1961)	26.0	24.4	14.4	15.4	21.7	13.7	n.a.
Andean Group (1988)	1.8	3.8	3.2	4.2	7.5	8.2	9.4
CARICOM (1973)	4.2	5.3	6.3	8.1	12.1	14.6	n.a.
MERCOSUR (1991)	9.4	11.6	5.5	8.9	19.2	20.4	15.7
ECOWAS (1975)	2.9	9.6	5.1	8.0	9.0	9.6	n.a.
SADC (1992)	4.2	0.4	1.4	3.1	10.6	11.9	n.a.
ASEAN/AFTA (1992)	22.4	17.4	18.6	19.0	22.0	23.8	24.6
GCC (1981)	4.6	3.0	4.9	8.0	6.8	5.0	n.a.

Note: Figures in parentheses refer to year in which the RTA came into force
Source: WTO (2003c; table 1B.11); updated with author's calculations from data in WTO 2006a; Appendix table A3: www.wto.org/english/res_e/statis_e/its2006_e/its06_appendix_e.htm

possible to conclude that trade diversion has been a major problem' (World Bank 2000: 48), a finding consistent with Frankel's (1997) comprehensive study (see also Krueger 1999).

That RTAs may distort members' trade patterns to only a limited extent is consistent with the lowering of MFN tariffs (and thus the preferential margins enjoyed by partner countries) that has occurred since the 1980s. In Canada, half of all MFN tariff lines are duty free; while in the United States, the figure is 35 per cent. As noted in the previous chapter, the average tariff level in industrialized countries on imports of manufactured goods is less than 5 per cent. A similar trend towards tariff reduction is also evident in most less developed countries, with an inevitable consequence for the preferential margins that RTAs create. In ASEAN, for example, in roughly two-thirds of the tariff lines, MFN and preferential tariffs are identical. For many of the others, the preferential margin is so small in the most developed economies (Singapore and Malaysia) that few companies have found it worthwhile to meet the rules of origin requirements and file the necessary paperwork: less than 5 per cent of all intra-ASEAN trade takes advantage of preferential tariffs. Not only do many RTAs create few advantages for partners for many exports, they also seldom help in the most heavily protected areas: when 'sensitive' sectors are protected by high MFN tariffs, governments frequently also exempt them altogether from the regional agreement or minimize the liberalization provided.

Scale economies and competition effects

Regional trade agreements affect the welfare of their participants through impacts beyond those on trade itself. One argument made in support of RTAs is that they will lead to increased investment flows for participants. As noted earlier, inflows of foreign direct investment into Mexico increased substantially after the signature of NAFTA. Similarly, the establishment of the European Community and

the subsequent deepening of European integration through the completion of the single internal market led to substantial increases in foreign direct investment in the EU, both intra-regionally—that is, from one member state to another, and from external countries (Motta and Norman 1996).

The other means through which RTAs are often assumed to improve the welfare of participating countries is by increasing the size of the 'home' market. As noted earlier, this can be particularly important for firms dependent on access to a market larger than that available within one country to achieve economies of scale. Moreover, regionalism may generate increased competition for domestic companies, thereby forcing them to become more efficient. Again, estimating these effects requires complex economic modelling with often 'heroic' assumptions. Although the computer simulations reach dramatically different conclusions depending on the assumptions they use, the most frequent finding is that regional integration produces only a very limited positive aggregate effect on the economies of participants (on the Asia-Pacific region, for example, see Scollay and Gilbert 2001). Critics suggest that these findings reflect the inability of the models to capture the 'dynamic' effects of regional integration, those that develop over time as companies benefit from scale economies and other efficiencies. Others, however, argue that the majority of benefits from regionalism come from the beneficial effects of companies responding to increased competition rather than from realizing economies of scale, and that these competitive benefits can be achieved more effectively through non-discriminatory liberalization that exposes domestic companies to worldwide competition (Schiff and Winters 2003: 51–52).

In short, the verdict on the economic effects of regional trade arrangements is mixed and frequently inconclusive. Economic models suggest that there is little evidence that RTAs have generated significant trade diversion. They do appear to have been associated with increased inflows of foreign direct investment. Yet their overall effects on the economic welfare of participants, if positive, have been of limited magnitude. And in the most sophisticated of regional schemes, the European Union, welfare benefits arising from improved competitiveness in manufacturing have been offset at least partially by the welfare losses caused by the EU's Common Agricultural Policy.

KEY POINTS

- Although considerable complexity is involved in attempting to isolate the economic effects of RTAs, evidence suggests that they have led to more trade among members than would otherwise be the case.

- RTAs do appear to have encouraged increased investment in member states.

- Economic simulations suggest that RTAs have had little aggregate effect on members' economic welfare.

- Little evidence exists that RTAs have produced significant trade diversion.

Regionalism and the WTO: Stepping Stone or Stumbling Block?

The advent of the new regionalism has been accompanied by a lively debate about its relationship to trade liberalization at the global level. Will regional trade agreements facilitate or obstruct global trade liberalization or, in Bhagwati's (1991) terminology, are regional agreements stepping stones or stumbling blocks?

Several arguments suggest how regional agreements might facilitate global negotiations:

1. Global negotiations involving regional groupings reduce the number of actors involved;

2. Reaching agreement on issues of deeper integration will be easier within regional groupings; these agreements can serve as models for global treaties;

3. Regional agreements can enhance the competitiveness of domestic industries, paving the way for full liberalization;

4. Regional agreements improve the financial position of export-orientated interests, thereby providing them with the means and incentive to lobby governments for broader liberalization.

5. When regional agreements provide companies from some countries with preferential access to a foreign market, their competitors in other countries will lobby their governments to sign agreements that will provide them with equivalent access. This attempt 'to level the playing field' will produce what Baldwin (1997, 2006) has called a 'domino' effect in regionalism.

The intuitively attractive argument that regional groupings simplify global negotiations by reducing the number of parties is counteracted by the difficulties that regional groupings often have in reaching a common position (witness the European Union on agricultural issues in global negotiations). Moreover, once a regional grouping has reached internal agreement on its own position, it may have little flexibility in bargaining with other actors. And there is no assurance that the common position adopted by a regional grouping will not be more restrictive than that held by a majority of its member states: in other words, the regional grouping can end up throwing its combined weight behind policies that might not have been supported by a majority of its members had they acted individually in the global negotiations. The recent proliferation of regional trade arrangements, many of which have overlapping memberships, suggests further complications should negotiations occur between 'regions' rather than between individual countries.

Until recently, little evidence existed to support arguments that agreement on contentious issues or on matters of 'deeper' integration could be reached more easily at the regional level. The European Union, for example, has found it very difficult to liberalize the most politically sensitive areas of trade, especially in agriculture. In the OECD's words, 'regionalism has often failed to crack the hardest nuts' (2002: 20). And few regional agreements had moved beyond the basics of removing tariffs. Nonetheless, the recent wave of regionalism has provided greater encouragement for the argument that deeper integration on issues such as investment and the environment is accomplished more easily through negotiations among a limited sub-set of countries (for further discussion, see OECD 2002). Developments at the regional level on these issues, however, have yet to be translated into global agreements, so the idea that regional agreements will subsequently have a positive influence on global negotiations has yet to be substantiated.

The argument that regional agreements will enable industries to become internationally competitive, and therefore that an RTA will ease the path towards non-discriminatory liberalization, assumes that the level of competition at the regional level will be similar to that in the global market place, to which firms will be able to graduate. An alternative proposition is also intuitively plausible: that the regional market will be of sufficient size to enable firms to realize economies of scale, and that they will prefer to operate with the comfort provided by the external tariff of the regional grouping rather than be exposed to enhanced competition. Companies content with operating in the regional market may be strengthened financially through regional integration, and therefore may have an incentive to lobby against extending trade liberalization beyond the region.

Critics who see regional agreements as stumbling blocks in the path of global liberalization assert that:

- They magnify the influence of power disparities in international trade relations, enabling larger economies to impose their will on smaller partners, thus gaining advantages through rules of origin that would not be achieved if liberalization occurred on a global basis, and thereby enhancing popular resentment in smaller, less developed economies against trade liberalization.

- They lead to a diversion of scarce bureaucratic resources and political leadership away from global trade negotiations and towards those at the regional level.

- They give rise to what Bhagwati (1995) has termed a 'spaghetti bowl' effect of numerous, criss-crossing preferential arrangements with a multiplicity of tariff rates and different rules of origin. The complexity of regulations provides opportunities for special pleading by interest groups and generally increases the costs of engaging in international trade. With countries being members of several RTAs, each with its own set of rules, companies face difficult decisions on where to establish subsidiaries and where to source their inputs (OECD 2002: 18).

- They provide exporters with the access to markets that they desire, thereby removing their incentive to lobby the government either for further liberalization at the global level, or for a further opening up of their domestic markets.

- They enable governments to exempt sensitive political sectors from liberalization, thereby energizing protectionist forces and strengthening political resistance against liberalization at the global level.

The exemption of sensitive sectors from liberalization rests on the possibility that regional arrangements will not be comprehensive in their product coverage because members are able to exploit the ambiguity of the WTO's rules on RTAs

JOHN RAVENHILL

(Box 6.6 below summarizes these rules). For the WTO to regard regional trade agreements as legitimate, average duties at the regional level must not be higher than those imposed by individual members before the agreement, and the arrangements must cover 'substantially all the trade' between the parties. The first of these obligations is ambiguous because it does not take into account rules of origin and non-tariff barriers; moreover, a substantial gap often exists between the tariff levels that countries have committed to in the WTO (so-called 'bound' rates) and the actual tariffs (usually lower) they have applied. In entering a regional agreement, countries can therefore keep the regional tariffs below their bound levels while in fact imposing higher rates than they previously applied to non-members.

The ambiguities of the second obligation—the requirement that RTAs should cover substantially all trade—are of even greater import, because they have enabled countries to exclude politically sensitive sectors from regional agreements. The European Union, for example, did not include most of Mexico's and South Africa's agricultural exports in the free trade agreements it signed with these countries. Similarly, the Japanese government excluded the few agricultural products that Singapore exported to it from its free trade agreement with the island state.

The political significance is that free trade agreements that provide partial liberalization can give exporters what they want (access to foreign markets) while enabling governments to avoid tackling the problem of inefficient domestic industries. The result is a process of 'liberalization without political pain'. The continued protection that uncompetitive domestic industries enjoy by being exempted from regional liberalization may encourage them to lobby against any liberalization, whether at the regional or the global level. Meanwhile, the wider the network of preferential trade agreements, the less of an incentive will domestic exporters have for lobbying for liberalization at the global level (Ravenhill 2006b). Take Mexico as the current extreme example. It has more than thirty preferential trade agreements with partners on all continents that account collectively for more than 60 per cent of global GDP and more than 97 per cent of its exports (the vast majority, of course, going to the United States). The signing of RTAs has substantially reduced the incentive for Mexican exporters to expend resources in lobbying for global liberalization. Some observers have suggested that the difficulties in negotiating the Doha Round have been exacerbated by its becoming an 'agriculture' round because manufacturing and service interests, having obtained export market access through RTAs, showed little interest in lobbying for liberalization at the global level (in contrast to the Uruguay Round).

The evidence

The sometimes contradictory arguments on the relationship between regional trade agreements and global trade liberalization rest on intuitively plausible hypotheses, but ones that are not easy to test. Moreover, the relatively brief period for which many of the new regional agreements have been operating makes it difficult to reach conclusions about their effects (and generalization is hazardous

BOX 6.6

The World Trade Organization and Preferential Trade Agreements

Article XXIV of the GATT lays down the criteria that regional arrangements must meet to be regarded as legitimate by the WTO. Members' customs duties under the new agreement must not 'on the whole' be higher or more restrictive than those previously imposed by the individual countries. The preferential agreement, according to Article XXIV.8, must also eliminate duties and other restrictions on 'substantially all the trade' between participants.

These provisions have generated enormous controversy over the years. In particular, members have failed to reach agreement on defining and applying the phrase 'substantially all the trade'. The WTO notes 'there exists neither an agreed definition of the percentage of trade to be covered by a WTO-consistent agreement nor common criteria against which the exclusion of a particular sector from the agreement could be assessed'. The European Union, a pioneer in negotiating preferential trade agreements, has argued that the Article XXIV.8 requirement has both a quantitative and a qualitative element, with at least 90 per cent of the trade between parties being covered and no major sector excluded. But other members have contested this interpretation, which raises its own problems of definition: how is the 90 per cent of trade to be measured (does it refer only to existing trade, or to that which might take place should restrictions be removed)? And how does one define a 'major' sector? An agreed interpretation of Article XXIV.8 is one of the items on the agenda in the current Doha Round of multilateral negotiations.

The lack of agreement on Article XXIV.8 has stymied the work of the WTO's Committee on Regional Trade Agreements, created in February 1996 to examine preferential trade agreements and their implications for the multilateral trading system. Members have been unable to agree that any of the large number of PTAs notified to the Committee since 1996 is fully compatible with the relevant rules. Lack of consensus has prevented the Committee from finalizing its other reports. The WTO's record on this matter is similar to that of the GATT, which was able to agree on the compatibility with Article XXIV of only four of the more than fifty RTAs submitted to it for consideration. Political considerations have dominated decision-making on this issue. Nowhere was this more evident than when a GATT Working Party considered whether the Treaty of Rome, which established the EEC in 1957, met the requirements for RTAs. Faced with a threat by the Europeans to quit GATT should their integration arrangements be found to be incompatible with the full requirements of Article XXIV (which they clearly were), the GATT Working Party failed to reach consensus in its deliberations. Ultimately, contracting parties' desire (as much for security as for economic reasons) for integration in Europe to proceed outweighed their concerns about the legality of the agreements. Subsequently, GATT and the WTO have simply failed to pass judgement on the vast majority of RTAs they have examined, including CUSTA and NAFTA (one of the rare exceptions was GATT's approval in 1994 of the customs union between the Czech and Slovak Republics, rendered obsolete when both parties joined the EU in 2004).

The rules relating to the establishment of preferential trading arrangements among less developed economies under the 'Enabling Clause' are even less restrictive than those under Article XXIV. They make no reference to coverage of trade, the complete elimination of duties or to a timetable for implementation. They require only that the regional agreement does not constitute a barrier to most-favoured nation trade reductions or cause 'undue difficulties' for other members. RTAs notified to the GATT/WTO under the Enabling Clause include AFTA and MERCOSUR.

As part of the Doha Round negotiations, WTO members agreed on a new 'transparency mechanism' for regional trade agreements. Members negotiating regional agreements will be obliged to provide early notification of an RTA to the WTO: the WTO Secretariat will have a new role in preparing a factual presentation on the agreement for consideration by the Committee on Regional Trade Agreements or the Committee on Trade and Development. How effective this new scrutiny of agreements will be remains to be seen.

when the agreements themselves differ so markedly in their scope and content).

Two pieces of evidence support those who believe that regional trading agreements have not been barriers to liberalization at the global level. The first is the successful conclusion of the Uruguay Round of GATT negotiations which, as documented in the previous chapter, produced major steps forward in liberalization at the global level (although most of the Uruguay Round's negotiations took place *before* many of the agreements that are part of the new wave of regionalism came into being). The second is that members of many of the regional trade agreements, particularly those in Latin America, have lowered their barriers to non-member states more rapidly than did countries that were not members of regional agreements (Foroutan 1998). Although it is impossible to demonstrate a causal relationship here, the logic is straightforward: lowering barriers to non-members at the same time as entering a preferential trade arrangement reduces the risk of welfare loss through trade diversion. Critics of the new regionalism, however, point to evidence that after joining regional arrangements, Israel, Mexico, and MERCOSUR members, when they encountered economic difficulties, all raised their tariffs against non-members but exempted their regional partners.

Like so many other issues relating to the new regionalism, the link between RTAs and global liberalization remains inconclusive. Whether or not the current Doha Round of global

---

Table 6.5 Membership of Minilateral Regional Trading Agreements

AFTA	ASEAN Free Trade Area www.aseansec.org/12025.htm	Brunei Darussalam, Cambodia, Indonesia, Laos, Malaysia, Myanmar, Philippines, Singapore, Thailand, Vietnam
APEC	Asia-Pacific Economic Cooperation www.apecsec.org.sg	Australia, Brunei Darussalam, Canada, Chile, China, Hong Kong, Indonesia, Japan, Korea, Malaysia, Mexico, New Zealand, Papua New Guinea, Peru, Philippines, Russia, Singapore, Chinese Taipei (Taiwan), Thailand, United States, Vietnam
BAFTA	Baltic Free-Trade Area	Estonia, Latvia, Lithuania
BANGKOK	Bangkok Agreement www.unescap.org/tid/mtg/concession.asp	Bangladesh, China, India, Republic of Korea, Laos, Sri Lanka
CAN	Andean Community www.comunidadandina.org	Bolivia, Colombia, Ecuador, Peru
CARICOM	Caribbean Community and Common Market www.caricom.org	Antigua & Barbuda, Bahamas, Barbados, Belize, Dominica, Grenada, Guyana, Haiti, Jamaica, Monserrat, Trinidad & Tobago, St Kitts & Nevis, St Lucia, St Vincent & the Grenadines, Suriname
CACM	Central American Common Market www.sice.oas.org/trade/camertoc.asp	Costa Rica, El Salvador, Guatemala, Honduras, Nicaragua
CEFTA	Central European Free Trade Agreement	Albania, Bosnia and Herzegovina, Bulgaria, Croatia, Czech Republic, Hungary, Kosovo, Macedonia, Moldova, Montenegro, Poland, Romania, Serbia, Slovak Republic, Slovenia
CEMAC	Economic and Monetary Community of Central Africa www.cemac.cf	Cameroon, Central African Republic, Chad, Congo, Equatorial Guinea, Gabon
CER	Closer Economic Relations Trade Agreement www.dfat.gov.au/geo/ new_zealand/anz_cer/anz_cer.html	Australia, New Zealand
CIS	Commonwealth of Independent States www.cis.minsk.by	Azerbaijan, Armenia, Belarus, Georgia, Kazakhstan, Kyrgyz Republic, Moldova, Russian Federation, Tajikistan, Turkmenistan, Ukraine, Uzbekistan

Table 6.5 (*continued*)

COMESA	Common Market for Eastern and Southern Africa www.comesa.int	Angola, Burundi, Comoros, Democratic Republic of Congo, Djibouti, Egypt, Eritrea, Ethiopia, Kenya, Libya, Madagascar, Malawi, Mauritius, Rwanda, Seychelles, Sudan, Swaziland, Uganda, Zambia, Zimbabwe
EAC	East African Community	Kenya, Tanzania, Uganda
EAEC	Eurasian Economic Community	Belarus, Kazakhstan, Kyrgyz Republic, Russian Federation, Tajikistan, Uzbekistan
ECO	Economic Cooperation Organization www.ecosecretariat.org/	Afghanistan, Azerbaijan, Iran, Kazakhstan, Kyrgyz Republic, Pakistan, Tajikistan, Turkey, Turkmenistan, Uzbekistan
EEA	European Economic Area http://ec.europa.eu/comm/external_relations/eea/index.htm	EC, Iceland, Liechtenstein, Norway
EFTA	European Free Trade Association www.efta.int	Iceland, Liechtenstein, Norway, Switzerland
EU	European Union europa.eu	Austria, Belgium, Bulgaria, Cyprus, Czech Republic, Denmark, Estonia, Finland, France, Germany, Greece, Hungary, Ireland, Italy, Latvia, Lithuania, Luxembourg, Malta, Netherlands, Poland, Portugal, Romania, Slovakia, Slovenia, Spain, Sweden, United Kingdom
GCC	Gulf Cooperation Council www.gcc-sg.org/	Bahrain, Kuwait, Oman, Qatar, Saudi Arabia, United Arab Emirates
GSTP	General System of Trade Preferences Among Developing Countries www.g77.org/gstp/	Algeria, Argentina, Bangladesh, Benin, Bolivia, Brazil, Cameroon, Chile, Colombia, Cuba, Democratic People's Republic of Korea, Ecuador, Egypt, Ghana, Guinea, Guyana, India, Indonesia, Islamic Republic of Iran, Iraq, Libya, Malaysia, Mercosur, Mexico, Morocco, Mozambique, Myanmar, Nicaragua, Nigeria, Pakistan, Peru, Philippines, Republic of Korea, Romania, Singapore, Sri Lanka, Sudan, Thailand, Trinidad and Tobago, Tunisia, United Republic of Tanzania, Venezuela, Vietnam, Yugoslavia, Zimbabwe
LAIA	Latin American Integration Association www.aladi.org	Argentina, Bolivia, Brazil, Chile, Colombia, Cuba, Ecuador, Mexico, Paraguay, Peru, Uruguay, Venezuela
MERCOSUR	Southern Common Market www.mercosur.org.uy	Argentina, Brazil, Paraguay, Uruguay
MSG	Melanesian Spearhead Group	Fiji, Papua New Guinea, Solomon Islands, Vanuatu

(*continued overleaf*)

Table 6.5 (*continued*)

NAFTA	North American Free Trade Agreement www.nafta-sec-alena.org	Canada, Mexico, United States
PTN	Protocol relating to Trade Negotiations among Developing Countries	Bangladesh, Brazil, Chile, Egypt, Israel, Mexico, Pakistan, Paraguay, Peru, Philippines, Republic of Korea, Romania, Tunisia, Turkey, Uruguay
SAPTA	South Asian Preferential Trade Arrangement www.saarc-sec.org/main.php? t = 2.1.5	Bangladesh, Bhutan, India, Maldives, Nepal, Pakistan, Sri Lanka
SPARTECA	South Pacific Regional Trade and Economic Cooperation Agreement	Australia, New Zealand, Cook Islands, Fiji, Kiribati, Marshall Islands, Micronesia, Nauru, Niue, Papua New Guinea, Solomon Islands, Tonga, Tuvalu, Vanuatu, Western Samoa
TRIPARTITE	Tripartite Agreement	Egypt, India, Yugoslavia
UEMOA/ WAE MU	West African Economic and Monetary Union www.uemoa.int	Benin, Burkina Faso, Ivory Coast, Guinea Bissau, Mali, Niger, Senegal, Togo

trade negotiations is brought to a successful conclusion within a reasonable time frame will be a significant pointer to the validity of the contending arguments about the relationship between regionalism and the broader trade regime.

KEY POINTS

- A lively debate among writers on RTAs has produced several plausible arguments suggesting that regionalism can facilitate or hinder trade liberalization at the global level.

- The new regionalism is of such recent origin that the evidence regarding its effects remains inconclusive.

- The success of the Uruguay Round refuted the popular arguments in the late 1980s that the world economy was about to fragment into three rival trading blocs. But the results of the Doha Round will be a more significant indicator of the effects of the new regionalism on liberalization at the global level.

? QUESTIONS

1. How does the 'new regionalism' differ from that of the 1960s and 1970s?

2. For what economic reasons might governments prefer trade liberalization at the regional rather than the global level?

3. What political benefits might membership of a regional agreement bring?

4. What are the likely sources of domestic political opposition to regionalism?

5. Why might companies lobby for liberalization at the regional rather than the global level?

6. What is 'deeper' integration?

7. What were the sources of the failure of many of the regional trade agreements of the 1960s and 1970s?

8. Why did the United States government change its mind in the early 1980s on the desirability of regional trade agreements?

9. How does trade creation differ from trade diversion?

10. Why are rules of origin regarded as a protectionist device?

11. What evidence is there that regional integration has had a positive impact on the economies of participating economies? And what has been its impact on non-members?

12. For what reasons might regionalism assist or impede trade liberalization at the global level?

 FURTHER READING

General

■ **Bhagwati, J., and Panagariya, A. (eds) (1996), The** *Economics of Preferential Trade Agreements* **(Washington, DC: AEI Press).** An accessible overview of arguments by economists against regionalism.

■ **Crawford, J.-A., and Florentino, R. V. (2005), 'The Changing Landscape of Regional Trade Agreements', WTO Discussion Paper 8 (Geneva: World Trade Organization), www.wto.org/english/ res_e/booksp_e/discussion_papers8_e.pdf.** A comprehensive assessment of recent RTAs by two members of the WTO Secretariat.

■ **Fawcett, L., and Hurrell, A. (eds) (1995),** *Regionalism in World Politics: Regional Organization and International Order* **(Oxford: Oxford University Press).** An initial exploration of the new regionalism with overviews and case studies.

■ **Frankel, J. A. (1997),** *Regional Trading Blocs in the World Economic System* **(Washington, DC: Institute for International Economics).** The most comprehensive examination of the effects of regional trade agreements.

■ **Haas, E. B. (1975),** *The Obsolescence of Regional Integration Theory* **(Berkeley, Calif.: Institute of International Studies, University of California).** A reconsideration of the relevance of early integration theory.

■ **Mansfield, E. D., and Milner, H. V. (eds) (1997),** *The Political Economy of Regionalism* **(New York: Columbia University Press).** A recent collection of articles from a political economy perspective on regionalism in general, it includes case studies of the principal geographical regions.

■ **Moravcsik, A. (1998),** *The Choice for Europe: Social Purpose and State Power from Messina to Maastricht* **(Ithaca, NY: Cornell University Press).** The most sophisticated statement of the liberal intergovernmental approach to regionalism.

■ **World Bank (2000),** *Trade Blocs* **(New York: Oxford University Press).** A review of the evidence on the economic and political effects of regionalism and their relevance to less developed economies.

Africa

■ **Bach, D. (ed.) (1999),** *Regionalisation in Africa: Integration & Disintegration* **(Bloomington, Ind.: Indiana University Press).** A collection examining the relationship between regionalism, regionalization, and state disintegration in Africa.

The Americas

■ **Cameron, M. A., and Tomlin, B. W. (2000),** *The Making of* **NAFTA:** *How the Deal was Done* **(Ithaca, NY: Cornell University Press).** Analyses the negotiating process leading up to the signing of the NAFTA treaty.

■ **Hufbauer, G. C., and Schott, J. J. (1993), NAFTA:** *An Assessment* **(Washington, DC: Institute for International Economics).** An early review of the terms of the NAFTA treaty.

■ **Roett, R. (ed.) (1999),** *Mercosur: Regional Integration,* **World Markets (Boulder, Colo.: Lynne Rienner).** A collection of articles on integration among MERCOSUR members and their relations with the global economy.

Asia-Pacific

■ **Aggarwal, V. K., and Morrison, C. E. (eds) (1998),** *Asia-Pacific Crossroads: Regime Creation and the Future of APEC* **(New York: St. Martin's Press).** A collection of articles on the foundation of APEC, the objectives of its founders, and its early impact.

■ **Aggarwal, V. K., and Urata S. (eds) (2006),** *Bilateral Trade Agreements in the Asia-Pacific: Origins, Evolution, and Implications* **(London: Routledge).** Reviews the recent spate of bilateral agreements in the Asia-Pacific region.

■ **Ravenhill, J. (2001), APEC** *and the Construction of Asia-Pacific Regionalism* **(Cambridge: Cambridge University Press).** Applies the theoretical literature on regionalism to APEC's foundation and operating principles.

Europe

■ **Bomberg, E. E., and Stubb, A. C. G. (2003),** *The European Union: How Does It Work?* **(Oxford: Oxford University Press).** An up-to-date introductory text on the EU.

■ **Milward, A. S. (1992),** *The European Rescue of the Nation-State* **(London: Routledge).** A historical review of European integration from an intergovernmental perspective.

■ **Wallace, H., and Wallace, W. (eds) (2000),** *Policy-Making in the European Union,* **4th edn (Oxford: Oxford University Press).** The most comprehensive and theoretically sophisticated overview of the various dimensions of EU integration.

Table 6.5 (see page 204) lists addresses for the websites maintained by most regional trade agreements.

www.wto.org/english/tratop_e/region_e/region_e.htm The WTO website's gateway to the organization's material on regional trade agreements.

 Visit the Online Resource Centre that accompanies this book for more information:
www.oxfordtextbooks.co.uk/orc/ravenhill2e/

PART 3

Global Finance

7

The Evolution of the International Monetary and Financial System

ERIC HELLEINER

➔ **Chapter Contents**

- Introduction
- The Fate of a Previous Globally Integrated Financial and Monetary Order
- The Bretton Woods Order
- The Crisis of the Early 1970s
- From Floating Exchange Rates to Monetary Unions
- The Dollar's Declining Global Role?
- The Globalization of Financial Markets
- Conclusion

✔ **Reader's Guide**

The international monetary and financial system plays a central role in the global political economy. Since the late nineteenth century, the nature of this system has undergone several transformations in response to changing political and economic conditions at both domestic and international levels. The most dramatic change was the collapse of the integrated pre-1914 international monetary and financial regime during the inter-war years. The second transformation took place after the Second World War, when the **Bretton Woods** order was put in place. Since the early 1970s, another period of change has been under way as various features of the Bretton Woods order have unravelled: the **gold exchange standard**, the **adjustable peg** exchange-rate regime, the US dollar's global role, and the commitment to **capital controls**. These various changes have important political consequences for the key issue of who gets what, when, and how in the global political economy.

Introduction

It is often said that money makes the world go around. In this age of globalization, the saying appears more relevant than ever. International flows of money today dwarf the cross-border trade of goods. And the influence of these flows seems only to be enhanced by their unique speed and global reach.

If money is so influential, it is fitting that it should have a prominent place in the study of global political economy, and that scholarly research on the political economy of international monetary and financial issues has grown very rapidly in recent years. While perspectives vary enormously within this literature, scholars working in this field share the belief that the study of money and finance must embrace a wider lens than that adopted by most economists.

Economists are trained to view money and finance primarily as economic phenomena. From their standpoint, money serves as a medium of exchange, a unit of account, and a store of value, while financial activity allocates credit within the economy. Both of these functions are critical to large-scale economic life, since they facilitate commerce, savings, and investment.

These descriptions of the economic role of money and finance are certainly accurate, but they are also limiting. Money and finance, after all, serve many political purposes as well (not to mention social and cultural ones). In all modern societies, control over the issuing and management of money and credit has been a key source of power, and the subject of intense political struggles. The organization and functioning of monetary and financial systems are thus rarely determined by a narrow economic logic of maximizing efficiency. They also reflect various political rationales relating to the

pursuit of power, ideas, and interests (Kirshner 2003).

The interrelationship between politics and systems of money and finance is particularly apparent at the international level, where no single political authority exists. What money should be used to facilitate international economic transactions and how should it be managed? What should be the nature of the relationship between national currencies be? How should credit be created and allocated at the international level? The answers to these questions have profoundly important implications for politics, not just within countries but also between them. It should not surprise us, then, that they provoke domestic and international political struggles, often of an intense kind.

This chapter highlights this point by providing an overview of the evolution of the international monetary and financial system since the late nineteenth century. The first section examines how changing political circumstances, both internationally and domestically, during the inter-war years undermined the stability of the globally integrated financial and monetary order of the pre-1914 era. The next section describes how a new international monetary and financial system—the Bretton Woods order—was created in 1944 for the post-war period, with a number of distinct features. The following four sections analyse the causes and consequences of the unravelling of various features of that order since the early 1970s: the gold exchange standard, the adjustable peg exchange-rate regime, the US dollar's prominent global role, and the commitment to capital controls. In the next chapter, Louis Pauly addresses another feature of the contemporary international financial order: its vulnerability to crises.

The Fate of a Previous Globally Integrated Financial and Monetary Order

Debates about contemporary economic globalization often note that this trend had an important precedent in the late nineteenth and early twentieth centuries. This is certainly true in the monetary and financial sector (see McGrew, Chapter 9, and Hay, Chapter 10 in this volume). Cross-border flows of money increased dramatically in this earlier period and, according to some criteria, even surpassed those in the current era in significance for national economies. Some of these flows involved short-term capital movements that responded primarily to interest rate differentials between financial centres around the world. Others involved long-term capital exports from the leading European powers to international locations. The United Kingdom, in particular, exported enormous amounts of long-term capital after 1870, sums that were much larger as a percentage of its national income than any creditor country is exporting today (James 2001: 12).

These capital flows were facilitated by the emergence of an international monetary regime that was also highly integrated, indeed much more so than in the current period. By 1914, the currencies of most independent countries and colonized regions around the world were linked to the same **gold standard** (see Box 7.1). The result was a fixed exchange-rate regime with an almost global reach. Indeed, some European countries went even further, to create regional 'monetary unions' in which the currencies of the member countries could circulate in each others' territory. Two such unions were created: the Latin Monetary Union (LMU) in 1865 (involving France, Switzerland, Belgium, and Italy) and the Scandinavian Monetary Union (SMU) in 1873 (involving Sweden and Denmark, plus Norway after 1875). A high-level international conference was held in 1867 to consider the possibility of a worldwide 'monetary union' of

---

BOX 7.1

The Theory of the Adjustment Process under the International Gold Standard

In theory, the international gold standard was a self-regulating international monetary order. External imbalances would be corrected automatically by domestic wage and price adjustments, according to a process famously described by David Hume: the 'price–specie flow mechanism'. If a country experienced a balance of payments deficit, Hume noted, gold exports should depress domestic wages and prices in such a way that the country's international competitive position—and thus its trade position—would be improved. Hume's model assumed that most domestic money was gold coins, but the domestic monetary system of most countries on the gold standard during the late nineteenth and early twentieth centuries was dominated by fiduciary money in the form of bank notes and bank deposits. In this

context, the monetary authority that issued notes and regulated the banking system had to stimulate the automatic adjustments of the gold standard by following proper 'rules of the game'. In the event of a trade deficit, it was expected to tighten monetary conditions by curtailing the issue of notes and raising interest rates. The latter was designed not just to induce deflationary pressures (by increasing the cost of borrowing) but also to attract short-term capital flows to help finance the payments imbalance while the underlying macroeconomic adjustment process was taking place. In practice, however, historians of the pre-1914 gold standard note that governments did not follow these 'rules of the game' as closely and consistently as the theory of the gold standard anticipated (Eichengreen 1985).

this kind. As the scramble for colonies intensified after 1870, many imperial powers often encouraged the circulation of their currencies in the newly acquired colonies during this period (Helleiner 2003; chs 6, 8). These currency unions and imperial currency blocs were designed to make economic transactions within each union or bloc easier to conduct.

The end of globalization

What can we learn from this era in our efforts to understand the political foundations of international money and finance? Perhaps the most interesting lesson is that this globally integrated financial and monetary order did not last. In the contemporary period, globalization is sometimes said to be irreversible. A study of the fate of this earlier globalization trend, however, reminds us to be more cautious. In particular, it highlights the importance of the *political* basis of international money and finance.

The first signs of disintegration came during the First World War, when cross-border financial flows diminished dramatically and many countries abandoned the gold standard in favour of floating currencies. After the war ended, there was a concerted effort—led by the United Kingdom and the United States—to restore the pre-1914 international monetary and financial order, and this initiative was initially quite successful. Many countries did restore the gold standard during the 1920s, and international capital flows—both short-term and long-term—also resumed on a very large scale by the late 1920s (Pauly 1997: ch. 3).

But this success was short-lived. In the early 1930s, a major international financial crisis triggered the collapse of both international lending and the international gold standard. This development signalled what Harold James (2001) has called 'the end of globalization'. The international monetary and financial system broke up into a series of relatively closed currency blocs.

Within each bloc, currencies were usually fixed *vis-à-vis* each other, and some international lending resumed. But between the blocs, currencies were often inconvertible and their value fluctuated considerably for much of the decade. International flows of capital between the blocs were also limited, and often regulated tightly by new capital control regimes.

Hegemonic stability theory

What explains this dramatic change in the nature of the international monetary and financial regime? A prominent explanation within international political economy (IPE) scholarship has been that the transformation was related to a change in the distribution of power among states within the international monetary and financial arena (see, for example, Kindleberger 1973). According to this hegemonic stability theory, the pre-1914 international financial and monetary regime remained stable as long as it was sustained by British hegemonic leadership. Before the First World War, the United Kingdom's currency, sterling, was seen to be 'as good as gold' and it was used around the globe as a world currency. Britain was also the largest creditor to the world and London's financial markets held a pre-eminent place in global finance. The United Kingdom's capital exports helped to finance global payments imbalances and they were usefully counter-cyclical; that is, foreign lending expanded when the UK entered a recession, thus compensating foreign countries for the decline in sales to the UK. During international financial crises, the Bank of England is also said to have played a leadership role in stabilizing markets through lender-of-last-resort activities.

However, after the First World War, the United Kingdom lost its ability to perform its leadership role in stabilizing the global monetary and financial order. The United States replaced it as the lead creditor to the world economy, and the US dollar emerged as the strongest and most trustworthy world currency. New York also began to rival London's position as the key international financial centre. In these new circumstances, the United States might have taken on the kind of leadership role that the United Kingdom had played before the war. But it proved unwilling to do so because of isolationist sentiments and domestic political conflicts between internationally orientated and more domestically focused economic interests. The resulting leadership vacuum is blamed for the instability and eventual breakdown of the gold standard and integrated financial order during the inter-war period.

Hegemonic stability theorists criticize several aspects of US behaviour during the 1920s and early 1930s. Its capital exports during the 1920s were pro-cyclical; they expanded rapidly when the US economy was booming in the mid-to-late 1920s, but then came to a sudden stop in 1928, just as the growth of the US economy was slowing down. The collapse of US lending generated balance of payments crises for many foreign countries that had relied on US loans to cover their external payments deficits. The United States then exacerbated these countries' difficulties by raising tariffs against imports with the passage of the 1930 Smoot–Hawley Act. As confidence in international financial markets collapsed in the early 1930s, the USA also refused to take on the role of international lender-of-last-resort, or even to cancel the war debts that were compounding the crisis.

Changing domestic political conditions

This interpretation of the evolution of the international monetary and financial system from the pre-1914 period and into the inter-war period is not universally accepted (see, for example, Calleo 1976; Eichengreen 1992; Simmons 1994). One line of criticism has been that it overstates the significance of UK leadership in sustaining the pre-1914 monetary and financial order. The distribution of financial and monetary power in that era is said to have been more pluralistic than hegemonic, with stability being maintained by co-operation between leading central banks rather than unilateral UK leadership. Even more important is the argument that the transformation of the international financial and monetary system was generated more by a change in the distribution of power *within* many states than between them.

According to this latter perspective, the stability of the pre-1914 international monetary and financial order was dependent on a very specific domestic political context. In that era, elite-dominated governments were strongly committed to the classical liberal idea that domestic monetary and fiscal policy should be geared to the external goal of maintaining the convertibility of the national currency into gold. When national currencies came under downward pressure in response to capital outflows or trade deficits, monetary and fiscal authorities usually responded by tightening monetary conditions and cutting spending. These moves were designed partly to induce deflationary pressures, which improved the country's international competitive position, and thus its trade balance. Equally important, they were aimed at restoring the confidence of financial market actors and encouraging short-term capital inflows (see Box 7.1). Indeed, the very fact that governments were so committed to these policies, and to the maintenance of their currency's peg to gold, ensured that short-term capital movements were highly 'stabilizing' and 'equilibrating' in this period.

The strength of governments' commitments to these policies, however, rested on a particular domestic political order. Deflationary pressures could be very painful for some domestic groups, particularly the poor, whose wages were forced downwards (or who experienced unemployment if wages did not fall). The poor also often bore the brunt of the burden when government spending was cut. These policies were politically viable only because many low-income citizens had little voice in the political arena. In most countries, the electoral franchise remained narrow before 1914. In many countries, central banks were not even public bodies in this period, and in colonial or peripheral regions, monetary authorities were often controlled by foreign interests.

After the First World War, the domestic political order was transformed in many independent states. The electoral franchise was widened, the power of labour grew, and there was increasing support for more interventionist economic policies. In this context, it was hardly surprising to find new demands for monetary and fiscal policies to respond to domestic needs rather than to the goal of maintaining external convertibility of the currency into gold, and the confidence of foreign investors. Governments began to run fiscal deficits, and central banks came under new public pressure to gear interest rates to address domestic unemployment.

It was these new domestic circumstances—rather than declining UK power—that many believe played the key role in undermining the stability of the integrated international and monetary system during the inter-war period. As governments ceased to play by the 'rules of the game', the 'self-regulating' character of the gold standard began to break down (see Box 7.1). Short-term international financial flows also became more volatile and speculative, as investors no longer had confidence in governments' commitment to maintain fixed rates and balanced budgets. Faced with these new domestic pressures, central banks also found it more difficult to co-operate in ways that promoted international monetary and financial stability.

In the context of the international financial crisis of 1931 and the Great Depression, many governments then chose simply to abandon the gold standard in order to escape its discipline. At the time, the collapse of international lending and export markets, as well as speculative capital flight, had left many countries with enormous balance of payments deficits. If they stayed on the gold standard, these deficits would be addressed by deflationary policies designed to press wages and prices downwards. A depreciation of the national currency provided a quicker, less painful, manner of adjusting the country's wages and prices *vis-à-vis* those in foreign countries in order to boost exports and curtail imports.

A floating exchange rate also provided greater policy autonomy to pursue expansionary monetary policies that could address pressing domestic economic needs. While on the gold standard, a government wishing to bolster economic growth by lowering interest rates would experience capital flight and an outflow of gold and would be forced to reverse the policy in order to restore the stability of the currency. With a floating exchange rate, the government could simply let the exchange rate depreciate. The exchange rate would adjust to the changing level of domestic prices and wages instead of the other way around. This depreciation would also reinforce the expansionary intent of the initial policy, since exports would be bolstered and imports discouraged. More generally, it is worth noting that a floating exchange rate was also attractive to many governments in the early 1930s because it could insulate the country from monetary instability abroad, particularly from the deflationary pressures emanating from the USA at this time.

In addition to abandoning the gold standard, many governments during the 1930s turned to capital controls to reinforce their national policy autonomy. With this move, they insulated themselves from the disciplining power of speculative cross-border financial movements. If, for example, a government wanted to bolster domestic economic growth by lowering interest rates or engaging in deficit spending, it no longer had to worry about capital flight. For this reason, it was natural to find John Maynard Keynes, the leading advocate of such domestically-orientated, activist macroeconomic management, emerge as one of the strongest supporters of capital controls in the early 1930s. As Keynes put it, 'let finance be primarily national' (Keynes 1933: 758).

KEY POINTS

- In the late nineteenth and early twentieth centuries, a highly integrated global financial and monetary order existed. By the early 1930s, it had collapsed, and was replaced by a fragmented order organized around closed economic blocs and floating exchange rates.

- Some believe the reason for the breakdown of the pre-1914 order was the absence of a state acting as a hegemonic leader to perform such roles as the

provision of stable international lending, the maintenance of an open market for foreign goods, and the stabilization of financial markets during crises.

- Others argue that the pre-1914 order was brought down more by a domestic political transformation across much of the world, associated with expansion of the electoral franchise, the growing power of labour, and the new prominence of supporters of interventionist economic policies.

The Bretton Woods Order

If an integrated international monetary and financial order was to be rebuilt, it would need to be compatible with the new priority placed on domestic policy autonomy. An opportunity to create such an order finally arose in the early 1940s, when US and UK policy-makers began to plan the organization of the post-war international monetary and financial system.

Embedded liberalism

At the time, it was clear that the United States would emerge from the war as the dominant economic power, and US policy-makers were determined to play a leadership role in building and sustaining a more liberal and multilateral international economic order than the one that had existed during the 1930s. The closed economic blocs and economic instability of the previous decade were thought to have contributed to the Great Depression and the Second World War. But US policy-makers did not want to see a return to the classical liberal international economic order of the pre-1930s period. Instead, they hoped to find a way to reconcile liberal **multilateralism** with the new domestically orientated priorities to combat unemployment and promote social welfare that had emerged with the New Deal.

This objective to create what Ruggie (1982) has called an 'embedded liberal' international economic order was shared by Keynes, who had emerged as the policy-maker in charge of UK planning for the post-war world economy during the early 1940s. He worked with his American counterpart, Harry Dexter White, to produce the blueprint for the post-war international monetary and financial order that was soon endorsed by forty-four countries at the 1944 Bretton Woods conference (Van Dormael 1978; Gardner 1980).

At first sight, the blueprint seemed to signal a return to a pre-1930s world. Signatories to the Bretton Woods agreements agreed to declare a par value of their currency in relation to the gold content of the US dollar in 1944. At the time, the US dollar was convertible into gold at a rate of $35 per ounce. By pegging their currencies in this way, countries appeared to be establishing an international gold standard—or, to be more precise, a 'gold exchange' standard or 'gold-dollar' standard. And at one level, the objectives underlying the Bretton Woods agreements were indeed similar to those of the gold standard. The Bretton Woods architects sought to re-establish a world of international currency stability. Floating exchange rates were associated with beggar-thy-neighbour competitive devaluations,

ERIC HELLEINER

speculative financial flows, and the general break-down of international economic integration.

A different kind of gold standard

But several other features of the Bretton Woods agreements made clear that this commitment did not signal a return to the kind of gold standard of the 1920s or the pre-1914 period. First, countries were given the option of adjusting their countries' par value whenever their country was in 'funda-mental disequilibrium'. This was to be, in other words, a kind of 'adjustable peg' system, in which countries could substitute exchange-rate devalu-ations for harsh domestic deflations when they experienced sustained balance of payments deficits. Currency realignments of up to 10 per cent from the initial parity were to be approved automatically, while larger ones required the permission of the newly created International Monetary Fund (IMF). Even in the latter case, the priority given to domestic policy autonomy was made clear; the Articles of the Agreement of the IMF noted that the Fund 'shall not object to a proposed change because of the domestic social or political policies of the member proposing the change' (Article iv-5).

Second, although countries agreed to make their currencies convertible for current account transac-tions (that is, trade payments), they were given the right to control all capital movements. This provi-sion was not intended to stop all private financial flows. Those that were 'equilibrating' and designed for productive investment were still welcomed. But the Bretton Woods architects inserted this provi-sion because they worried about how speculative and disequilibrating flows could disrupt both stable exchange rates and national political autonomy. Regarding the latter, Keynes and White sought to protect governments from capital flight that was initiated for 'political reasons' or with the goal of evading domestic taxes or the 'burdens of social legislation' (quoted in Helleiner 1994: 34). Capital controls could also enable governments to pursue macroeconomic planning through an independent interest rate policy. As Keynes (1980: 149) put it,

'In my view the whole management of the domestic economy depends upon being free to have the ap-propriate rate of interest without reference to rates prevailing elsewhere in the world. Capital control is a corollary to this.'

The Bretton Woods architects also established two public international financial institutions: the International Bank for Reconstruction and De-velopment (IBRD) (known as the World Bank) and the IMF. At a broad level, these institu-tions—particularly the IMF—were given the task of promoting global monetary and financial co-operation. More specifically, they were to assume some aspects of international lending that had previously been left to private markets. The IBRD was designed to provide long-term loans for re-construction and development after the war, a task that the private markets were not trusted to perform well. The IMF was to provide short-term loans to help countries finance their temporary balance of payments deficits, a function that was designed explicitly to reinforce those countries' policy autonomy and challenge the kind of external discipline that private speculative financial flows and the gold standard had imposed before the 1930s (see Box 7.2).

For the first decade and a half after the Second World War, the Bretton Woods system, it has been said, was in 'virtual cold storage' (Skidelsky 2003: 125). It is certainly true that the IMF and IBRD played very limited roles during this period, and that European countries did not make their cur-rencies convertible until 1958 (the Bretton Woods agreements had allowed for a 'transition' period of no specified length, during which countries could keep currencies inconvertible). At the same time, however, most governments outside the Soviet or-bit were committed to the other principles outlined at Bretton Woods: namely, the maintenance of an adjustable-peg exchange-rate regime; the gold exchange standard; and the control of capital move-ments. Moreover, although the IMF and World Bank were sidelined, other bodies—particularly the US government, but also regional institutions such as the European Payments Union—acted in

BOX 7.2

How Does the IMF Work?

While the World Bank can borrow from the private markets to fund its lending, the IMF's capacity to lend comes primarily from the contributions of member governments. On joining the IMF, all member governments pay a 'quota' to the institution that largely reflects their relative size within the world economy. The amount of money they can borrow from the Fund is then determined by their quota size. Quotas also play a very significant role in determining voting shares within the Fund. All countries are allocated 250 'basic votes', but the bulk of their voting share is determined by their quota size. At the time of the founding of the IMF, 'basic votes' made up 11 per cent of total votes, but this figure has fallen to approximately 2 per cent at the time of writing because of the entrance of new members and quota increases.

Quotas are reviewed at least every five years, and the relative share of various countries has changed over time in response to these reviews. The US quota share, for example, has fallen from more than 30 per cent of the total votes in 1944 to roughly 17 per cent today, while the shares of countries such as Japan, Germany, and Saudi Arabia have increased considerably. The most recent adjustment of quotas took place in September 2006, when an agreement was reached to provide four countries, whose existing shares were particularly out of line with their growing economic significance, with quota increases: namely, China, South Korea, Mexico, and Turkey.

The IMF is governed by its Board of Governors, which meets annually. Day-to-day decision-making, however, is delegated to the Executive Board, which meets several times a week. The Executive Board started with only twelve executive directors, with the five largest country contributors being assigned a single seat and other members being represented by 'constituency' groups. Today, the number of executive directors has risen to twenty-four and, in addition to the five largest contributors, single-country constituencies have been created for Saudi Arabia, China, and Russia.

the ways that Keynes and White had hoped the Bretton Woods institutions would. Public international lending was provided for temporary balance of payments support, as well as for reconstruction and development. United States policy-makers also promoted 'embedded liberal' ideals when they were engaged in monetary and financing advisory roles around the world (Helleiner 1994: ch. 3; 2003: ch. 9).

During the heyday of the Bretton Woods order, from the late 1950s until 1971, the IMF and IBRD were assigned a more marginal role in the system than Keynes and White had hoped for.

But governments remain committed to the other key features of the order. What, then, became of the Bretton Woods order? In some respects, it seems to be still alive. Currencies remain convertible, and the IMF and IBRD still exist (although their purpose has been altered, as described below). In the following sections, however, I explore the causes and consequences of the unravelling of the other features of the Bretton Woods regime since the early 1970s: the gold exchange standard; the adjustable-peg exchange-rate system, the US dollar's prominent global role, and the commitment to capital controls.

KEY POINTS

- The Bretton Woods conference in 1944 created a new international monetary and financial order that was inspired by an 'embedded liberal' ideology and backed by US leadership.

- Governments joining this order committed themselves to currency convertibility for current account payments; a gold exchange standard; an adjustable-peg exchange-rate regime, an acceptance of capital controls, and support for the IMF and World Bank.

- Many of the features of the Bretton Woods order were in place between 1945 and 1958, but this order reached its heyday between 1958 and 1971.

The Crisis of the Early 1970s

The breakdown of the gold exchange standard

The Bretton Woods system is usually said to have begun to collapse during the early 1970s, when both the gold exchange standard and the adjustable-peg exchange-rate system broke down. The former was brought to a swift end in August 1971, when the United States suddenly suspended the convertibility of the US dollar into gold. Since other currencies had been tied to gold only via the US dollar, this move signalled the end of gold's role as a standard for other currencies as well. This breakdown had in fact been predicted as far back as 1960, when Robert Triffin (1960) had highlighted the inherent instability of the gold exchange standard. In a system where the dollar was the central reserve currency, he argued that international **liquidity** could be expanded only when the United States provided the world with more dollars by running a balance of payments deficit. But the more it did so, the more it risked undermining confidence in the dollar's convertibility into gold.

One potential solution to the **Triffin dilemma** was to create a new international currency whose supply would not be tied to the balance of payments condition of any one country. Keynes had in fact proposed such a currency—which he called 'bancor'—during the negotiations leading up to the Bretton Woods conference. In 1965, the United States began to support the idea that the IMF could issue such a currency as a means of supplementing the dollar's role as a reserve currency, and **Special Drawing Rights** (SDR) were finally created for this purpose in 1969. The SDR was not a currency that individuals could use; it could be used only by national monetary authorities as a reserve asset for settling inter-country payments imbalances (and subject to certain conditions). Despite its potential, IMF members have never been willing to issue

significant quantities of SDR to enable this currency to play much of a role in the global monetary system.

During the 1960s, and in particular after the mid-1960s, Triffin's predictions were increasingly borne out. US currency abroad did grow considerably larger than the amount of gold the US government held to back it up. In one sense, the situation was beneficial to the United States: the country was able to finance growing external deficits associated with the Vietnam War and its domestic Great Society programme (which produced rising imports) simply by printing dollars. Indeed, the United States was doing much more than providing the world with needed international liquidity by the late 1960s; it was actively exporting inflation by flooding the world with dollars. In another sense, however, the country was becoming increasingly vulnerable to a confidence crisis. If all holders of dollars suddenly decided to convert the US currency into gold, the USA would not be able to meet the demand. Another cost to the USA was the fact that the dollar's fixed value in gold was undermining the international competitiveness of US-based firms. If other countries had been willing to revalue their currencies, this competitiveness problem could have been addressed, but foreign governments resisted adjusting the value of their currencies in this way.

A crisis of confidence in the dollar's convertibility into gold was initially postponed when some key foreign allies—notably Germany and Japan—agreed not to convert their reserves into gold (sometimes as part of an explicit trade-off for US security protection: Zimmerman 2002). But other countries that were critical of US foreign policy in this period—France in particular—refused to adopt this practice, seeing it as a reinforcement of American hegemony (Kirshner 1995: 192–203). Private speculators also increasingly targeted the US dollar, especially after sterling was devalued in 1967. When speculative pressures against the dollar reached a peak in 1971, the United States was forced to make a decision: it could either cut back the printing of dollars, or simply end the currency's convertibility into gold.

The US decision to take the latter course reflected its desire to free itself from the constraint on its policies that gold convertibility imposed (Gowa 1983). In the eyes of many observers, this decision also signalled an end to the kind of 'benevolent' hegemonic leadership US policy-makers had practised in the international monetary and financial realm since the 1940s. Some attributed this change in US policy to the fact that the United States was losing its hegemonic status in the international monetary and financial realm. From this perspective, the breakdown of the gold exchange standard provided further evidence to support the hegemonic stability theory that a stable integrated international monetary and financial order requires a hegemonic power. Others, however, suggested that US hegemonic power remained substantial in world money and finance, but what had changed was the United States' interest in leadership. Faced with new domestic and international priorities, US policy-makers chose to exploit their position as the dominant power in this realm of the global economy to serve these ends. To support the thesis that the United States remained an important global monetary power, scholars pointed to the fact that the US dollar remained the unchallenged dominant world currency after 1971 (for example, Strange 1986; Calleo 1976)—a point to which we shall return below.

The collapse of the adjustable-peg exchange-rate regime

The second feature of the Bretton Woods monetary order that broke down in the early 1970s was the adjustable-peg system. This development took place in 1973, when governments allowed the world's major currencies to float in value *vis-à-vis* one other. The new floating exchange-rate system was formalized in 1976, when the IMF's Articles of Agreement were amended to legalize floating

exchange rates, and to declare that each country now had the responsibility for determining the par value of its currency.

The end of the adjustable-peg system was triggered partly by the growing size of speculative international financial flows—a phenomenon explained in a later section—which complicated governments' efforts to defend their currency pegs. Equally important, however, was the fact that influential policy-makers began to re-evaluate the merits of floating exchange rates. We have already seen how the Bretton Woods architects took a very negative view of the experience of floating exchange rates before the Second World War. Indeed, the drawbacks of floating exchange rates were deemed to be so obvious that there had been very few serious defences of them at the time. By the early 1970s, however, floating exchange rates had attracted a number of prominent advocates, particularly in the United States (Odell 1982).

These advocates argued that floating exchange rates could play a very useful role in facilitating smooth adjustments to external imbalances in a world where governments were no longer willing to accept the discipline of the gold standard. Under the Bretton Woods system, the idea of using exchange-rate changes for this purpose had, of course, already been endorsed; governments could adjust their currency's peg when the country was in 'fundamental disequilibrium'. But, in practice, governments had been reluctant to make these changes because exchange-rate adjustments often generated political controversy, both at home and abroad. Governments usually made these adjustments only when large-scale speculative financial movements left them no option. The result had been a rather rigid and crisis-prone exchange-rate system, in which countries often resorted instead to international economic controls, particularly on capital flows, to address imbalances. A floating exchange-rate system would allow external imbalances to be addressed more smoothly and continuously, and without so much resort to controls.

It was also argued that floating exchange rates had unfairly been given a bad name during the 1930s.

Advocates argued that floating exchange rates need not necessarily be associated with either competitive devaluations or with a retreat from international economic integration, as they had been in the 1930s. Their role in encouraging destabilizing speculative financial flows during the 1930s was also questioned. Financial movements in that decade, it was argued, had been volatile, not because of floating exchange rates but because they were responding properly to the highly unstable underlying economic conditions of the time (for example, Friedman 1953).

KEY POINTS

- The initial signs of the unravelling of the Bretton Woods system are usually dated to the early 1970s, when the gold exchange standard and the adjustable-peg exchange-rate system collapsed.

- In 1971, the United States ended the gold convertibility of its currency, and, by extension, that of all other currencies. The US decision reflected its desire to free itself from the growing constraint on its policies that gold convertibility was imposing.

- The adjustable-peg exchange-rate regime of Bretton Woods was replaced in 1973 by a system of floating exchange rates between the currencies of the leading economic powers. The change was caused by heightened capital mobility and by a reconsideration of the merits of floating exchange rates among leading policy-makers, particularly in the United States.

From Floating Exchange Rates to Monetary Unions

Has the floating exchange-rate system performed in the ways that its advocates had hoped? The proponents of floating exchange rates were certainly correct that this exchange rate regime has not discouraged the growth of international trade and investment to any significant degree. Indeed, by enabling governments to avoid using trade restrictions and capital controls, floating exchange rates may have helped to accelerate international economic integration. Floating exchange rates have undoubtedly also often played an important part in facilitating adjustments to international economic imbalances. But critics have argued that their useful role in this respect should not be overstated.

Some have echoed the argument made in the 1930s, that floating exchange rates have encouraged destabilizing speculative financial flows because of the uncertain international monetary environment they create. These flows, in turn, are said to generate further volatility and misalignments in currency values. One of the best-known advocates of this view is Susan Strange (1986), who suggests that floating exchange rates have encouraged a kind of 'casino capitalism', in which speculators have come increasingly to dominate foreign exchange markets. From her standpoint, the consequences have been devastating:

> The great difference between an ordinary casino which you can go into or stay away from, and the global casino of high finance, is that in the latter all of us are involuntarily engaged in the day's play. A currency change can halve the value of a farmer's crop before he harvests it, or drive an exporter out of business ... From school-leavers to pensioners, what goes on in the casino in the office blocks of the big financial centres is apt to have sudden, unpredictable and avoidable consequences for individual lives. The financial casino has everyone playing the game of Snakes and Ladders. (Strange, 1986: 2)

It is certainly true that currency trading has grown very dramatically since the early 1970s; the size of daily foreign exchange trading increased from $15 billion in 1973 to almost $1,900 billion by 2004 (Gilpin 2001: 261; BIS 2005). The latter figure dwarfs the size of trading that would be necessary simply to service regular international trade and investment flows. As cross-border financial flows have grown dramatically, it is also accurate that exchange rates have sometimes been subject to considerable short-term volatility and longer-term misalignments. In these circumstances, a floating exchange rate has often been the source of, rather than the means of adjusting to, external economic imbalances.

International exchange-rate management: the Plaza to the Louvre

One of the more dramatic episodes of a longer-term misalignment involved the appreciation of the US dollar in the early-to-mid-1980s. This currency movement was not responding to a US current account surplus; indeed, the country experienced a growing current account deficit at the time. Instead, the dollar's appreciation was caused by very large inflows of foreign capital, attracted by the country's high interest rates and rapid economic expansion after 1982. The appreciation proved to be very disruptive; it exacerbated the US current account deficit and generated widespread protectionist sentiments within the USA by 1984–5.

This episode led the USA and other major industrial countries to consider briefly a move towards more managed exchange rates. In September 1985, the G5 (the United States, the United Kingdom, the Federal Republic of Germany, France, and Japan) signed the Plaza Accord which committed these countries to work together to encourage the US dollar to depreciate against the currencies of its major trading partners. After the dollar had fallen almost 50 per cent *vis-à-vis* the yen and Deutschmark by February 1987, they then announced the Louvre

Accord, which established target ranges for the major currencies to be reached through closer macroeconomic policy co-ordination (Henning 1987; Funabashi 1988; Webb 1995).

This enthusiasm for a more managed exchange-rate system between the world's major currencies proved to be short-lived. The three leading economic powers—the United States, Germany, and Japan—were not prepared to accept the kinds of serious constraints on their macroeconomic policy autonomy that were required to make such a system effective. Many policy-makers in Germany and Japan also argued that the US interest in macroeconomic policy co-ordination seemed designed primarily to reduce its own external deficit by encouraging changes in macroeconomic policy abroad rather than at home. This complaint had been heard once before, during the late 1970s, when the US policy-makers last pressed Germany and Japan to co-ordinate macroeconomic policies. In both instances, US policy-makers sought to address their country's external payments deficit by pressing Germany and Japan to revalue their currencies and pursue more expansionary domestic economic policies. These moves would enable the United States to curtail its deficit without a domestic contraction by boosting US exports.

United States' pressure in these two cases was applied not just through formal negotiations but also informally by 'talking down the dollar'. The latter encouraged financial traders to speculate against the dollar, leaving the German and Japanese governments with two options. They could defend the US currency through dollar purchases, thereby preserving the competitiveness of domestic industry *vis-à-vis* the important US market as well as the value of their dollar-denominated assets. In the end, however, these purchases would probably produce the other result that the USA wanted: an expanding domestic monetary supply in Japan and Germany caused by the increased purchase of dollars. Alternatively, if they accepted the dollar's depreciation, pressure for domestic expansionary policies would still come from another source—domestic industry and labour that was hurt by the country's loss of competitiveness *vis-à-vis* the United States. The effectiveness of this 'dollar weapon' rested on the US dollar's key currency status and the fact that the US market remained such an important one for Japanese and German businesses in this period. It was a strategy that met with some success for the USA in both instances, although it also left the USA vulnerable to a crisis of confidence in the dollar at some key moments (Henning 1987).

The IMF and exchange rate management

Arguments for exchange rate management among the leading powers have emerged at other moments, most recently *vis-à-vis* China's large trade surpluses. In this most recent episode, US policy-makers, in particular, have pressed the IMF to take a more assertive stance in pressing the Chinese government to allow its currency to appreciate. These demands have generated new interest in the IMF's mandate in this area.

When it was created in 1944, one of the central purposes of the Fund was to oversee its adjustable-peg exchange rate regime. When that regime broke down in the early 1970s, many questioned the IMF's future. The outbreak of the international debt crisis in the early 1980s soon gave the Fund a new life as an institution focused on crisis management *vis-à-vis* poorer countries (see Pauly, Chapter 8 in this volume). But the Fund was also reborn in a second fashion after the early 1970s. In an effort to maintain some semblance of multilateral rules over the new floating exchange rate system, the IMF was given a new mandate in 1976—under Article IV in the Second Amendment to its Articles of Agreement—to 'exercise firm surveillance over the exchange rate policies of members' (quoted in Pauly 1997: 105).

The IMF's 'surveillance' activities have since become an important part of its overall operations. With individual member governments, the Fund engages in 'Article IV consultations' in which it offers advice about various aspects of their economic policies. It has also moved recently to boost its surveillance role beyond the bilateral context by creating 'multilateral consultations' in which systematically important countries can have a forum to discuss and debate specific issues of global economic significance.

The first such multilateral consultation—involving China, the Euro area, Japan, the USA, and Saudi Arabia—was announced in 2006 with a focus on global imbalances. Some have hoped that this kind of initiative might allow the IMF to take an active role in reinvigorating the kind of multilateral exchange rate management that characterized the Plaza to Louvre period. With its near universal membership, the IMF may be better suited than other bodies, such as the G7 or OECD, to launch this kind of initiative.

But sceptics argue that the IMF's ability to influence the decision-making of these powerful governments is likely to be very limited. Even in the bilateral context, the Fund's advice has generally had a significant impact only when backed up by the promise of loans. None of these governments is a borrower from the Fund. Without the financial 'carrots' of its loans, the IMF's power is limited and each of these governments faces enormous incentives to maintain control over exchange rates, given their significance to national economic life.

The creation of the euro

Although efforts to stabilize the relationship between the values of the world's major currencies have been limited since the early 1970s, some governments have moved to create stable monetary relations in smaller regional contexts. The most elaborate initiative of this kind has taken place in Europe. At the time of the breakdown of the Bretton Woods exchange-rate system, a number of the countries of the European Community (EC) attempted to stabilize exchange rates among themselves. These initial efforts were followed by the creation of the European Monetary System in 1979, which established a kind of 'mini-Bretton Woods' adjustable-peg regime in which capital controls were still widely used and financial support was provided to protect each country's currency peg *vis-à-vis* other European currencies. Then, with the Maastricht Treaty in 1991, most members of European Union went one step further to commit to a full monetary union: this was created in 1999.

The long-standing resistance of many European governments to floating exchange rates within Europe has been driven partly by worries that exchange-rate volatility and misalignments would disrupt their efforts to build a closer economic community. Exchange-rate instability was deemed to be disruptive not only to private commerce but also to the complicated system of regional public payments within the European's Community Common Agricultural Policy. But why go so far as to abandon national currencies altogether in 1999?

One answer is that the adjustable peg system of the EMS became unsustainable after European governments committed themselves to abolish capital controls in 1988. The latter decision left European currency pegs vulnerable to increasingly powerful speculative financial flows, a fact demonstrated vividly in the 1992–3 European currency crisis. At that moment, European governments faced an important choice. If they sought to preserve financial liberalization and exchange-rate stability, they would have to give up their commitment to domestic monetary policy autonomy. Open macroeconomic theory teaches us that it is not possible to achieve all three of these objectives simultaneously (see Box 7.3). If they agreed to abandon monetary policy autonomy within this 'impossible trinity', a logical next step was simply to create a monetary union that eliminated the possibility of future intra-regional exchange-rate crises altogether.

This choice was also made easier by the growing prominence of neo-liberal thought within European monetary policy-making circles (McNamara 1998). Neo-liberals were disillusioned with the kinds of activist national monetary policies that became popular in the age of embedded liberalism. This sentiment emerged partly out of experiences of inflation, and partly from the rational expectations revolution in the discipline of economics. The

---

BOX 7.3

The 'Impossible Trinity' of Open Macroeconomics

Economists have pointed out that national governments face an inevitable trade-off between the three policy goals of exchange-rate stability, national monetary policy autonomy, and capital mobility. It is only ever possible for governments to realize two of these goals at the same time. If, for example, a national government wants to preserve capital mobility and a fixed exchange rate, it must abandon an independent monetary policy. The reason is straightforward. An independent expansionary monetary policy in an environment of capital mobility will trigger capital outflows—and downward pressure on the national currency—as domestic interest rates fall. In this context, it will be possible to maintain the fixed exchange rate only by pushing interest rates back up and thereby abandoning the initial monetary policy goal. If, however, the government chooses to maintain the expansionary policy, it will need either to introduce capital controls or to embrace a floating exchange rate, thereby sacrificing one of the other goals within the 'impossible trinity'.

Historically, during the era of the gold standard, governments embraced fixed exchange rates and capital mobility, while abandoning national monetary policy autonomy. During the Bretton Woods order, national policy autonomy and fixed (although adjustable) exchange rates were prioritized, while capital mobility was deemed to be less important. Since the early 1970s, the leading powers have sacrificed a global regime of fixed exchange rates in order to prioritize capital mobility and preserve a degree of monetary policy autonomy. Many governments within this system, however, have embraced fixed rates at the regional or bilateral level by using capital controls or by abandoning national policy autonomy.

latter undermined a key idea that had sustained support for activist monetary policies: the Keynesian notion that there was a long-term trade-off between inflation and unemployment. By highlighting how experiences of inflation over time may encourage people to adjust their expectations, this new economic analysis suggested that activist monetary management could simply produce 'stagflation'—that is, a combination of high unemployment and high inflation. The appearance of stagflation during the 1970s seemed to vindicate this view. If people began to anticipate higher and higher levels of inflation, this analysis suggested that they would adjust their wage demands and pricing decisions accordingly, creating an upward inflationary spiral. To break these inflationary expectations, authorities would have to re-establish their credibility and reputation for producing stable money by a strong commitment to price stability. The perceived need for this kind of credibility and reputation has also been reinforced by the disciplining power of international capital markets (see, for example, Andrews and Willett 1997).

Neo-liberal monetary thinking played an important role in generating support for European Monetary Union (EMU). By eliminating a key macroeconomic rationale for wanting a national currency in the first place (that is, the commitment to activist national monetary management), it made policy-makers less resistant to the idea of abandoning these monetary structures. Indeed, many policy-makers saw the currency union as a better way to achieve price stability than by maintaining a national currency, because the union appeared to allow them to 'import' the German central bank's anti-inflationary monetary policy. Like the German Bundesbank, the new European central bank was given a strict mandate to pursue price stability as its primary goal. In addition, some neo-liberals have applauded the fact that EMU, by eliminating the possibility of national devaluations, might encourage greater price and wage flexibility within national economies as workers and firms are forced to confront the impact of external economic 'shocks' in a more direct fashion.

Because of this basis of support for EMU, many on the political left have been wary of the project. They worry that it might produce domestic de-regulation, cutbacks to the welfare state, and new constraints on states' abilities to address unemployment and other social and economic problems. The resultant costs, they suggest, will be borne disproportionately by vulnerable groups such as the poor and women (Gill 1998; B. Young 2002). Interestingly, however, there have also been many social democrats and unions across Europe—groups usually less friendly to neo-liberal thinking—who have been supportive of the drive to monetary union (Josselin 2001; Notermans 2001). Because it can protect a country from speculative currency attacks, some have seen EMU as creating a more stable macroeconomic environment in which progressive supply-side reforms could be undertaken to promote equity, growth, and employment. In some countries, adopting the euro has also been seen as a way to lower domestic interest rates by reducing risk premiums that the markets were imposing, a result that has actually improved governments' budgetary positions and prevented cuts to the welfare state. Some social democrats and unions have also hoped that EMU might eventually help to dilute the monetary influence of the neo-liberal Bundesbank across Europe, and encourage co-ordinated EU-wide expansionary fiscal policies. In addition, some social democrats and unions have seen EMU as an opportunity to reinvigorate national corporatist social pacts in which co-operative wage bargaining, employment friendly taxation schemes, and other social protection measures can assume a key role in the process of adjusting to external economic shocks.

The EMU project also had a broader political meaning. In addition to challenging US power (see below), the creation of the euro has been seen as an important symbol of the process of fostering ever-closer European co-operation. Many analysts also argue that the decision to create the euro was linked to a broader political deal between Germany and other European countries at the time of the Maastricht Treaty. Many European countries—especially France—had become increasingly frustrated by the domination of the European monetary system by the German Bundesbank, and they pressed for EMU as a way to dilute its influence. Germany is said to have accepted EMU when it came to be seen as a trade-off for European (and especially French) support for German reunification in 1989 (see, for example, Kaltenthaler 1998).

Currency unions elsewhere?

The European experiment in creating a currency union has triggered talk of a similar move in some other regions. Is this likely to happen? Economists try to help address this question by analysing whether each region resembles an 'optimum currency area' (see Box 7.4). In practice, though, this kind of economic analysis has had little predictive power in the European context, or elsewhere. One of the longest-standing monetary unions in the world is the CFA franc zone involving many former French colonies in west and central Africa, and its member countries do not come close to resembling an 'optimum currency area'. Like EMU, that monetary union was formed and has been sustained

by certain political conditions. Particularly important in that case have been the power and political interests of France in the colonial and post-colonial context (Stasavage 2003).

Another region where interest in monetary union has grown is the Americas. Beginning in 1999, many policy-makers in that region began to debate the idea of creating a currency union that would be based on the US dollar. Two countries—Ecuador and El Salvador—went beyond talk to action and introduced the US dollar as their national currency, in 2000 and 2001, respectively. The new interest in dollarization across Latin America was partly a product of the ascendancy of neo-liberal monetary ideas there. As in Europe, many neo-liberals in the region saw the abandonment of the national currency as a way of importing price stability; in this case, from the US Federal Reserve. Advocates of dollarization have also argued that it will help to insulate countries from speculative financial flows, and will attract stable long-term foreign investment.

The dollarization debate also emerged from a context where many Latin-American countries have experienced a kind of informal, partial dollarization since the 1970s. Local residents have often turned to the US dollar as a store of value, a unit of account,

---

BOX 7.4

Monetary Unions and the Theory of Optimum Currency Areas

The theory of optimum currency areas was first developed by the Nobel-prize-winning economist Robert Mundell (1961) to evaluate the pros and cons of forming a monetary union among a selected group of countries. While assuming the union will produce microeconomic benefits in the form of lower **transaction costs** for cross-border commerce, the theory focuses its analytical attention on the potential macroeconomic costs associated with abandoning the exchange rate as a tool of macroeconomic adjustment. If these costs are low, the region is said to approximate more closely an 'optimum currency area' that should be encouraged to create a monetary union.

To evaluate how significant these costs are in each regional context, the theory examines a number of

criteria. If selected countries experience similar external shocks, for example, the theory notes that they are more likely to be good candidates for monetary union, since they will each have less of a need for an independent exchange rate. Even if they experience asymmetric shocks, the macroeconomic costs of abandoning national exchange rates may still be low if wages and price are very flexible within each country, if labour is highly mobile between countries, or if there are mechanisms for transferring fiscal payments among the countries. Each of these conditions would enable adjustments to be made to external shocks in the absence of an exchange rate.

and even a medium of exchange, as a way to insulate themselves from domestic monetary and political uncertainty. The option has been made easier by the broader liberalization and deregulation of Latin-American financial systems in this period. Since informal dollarization has already eroded national monetary sovereignty considerably, it has lessened resistance to the idea of formal dollarization.

Formal dollarization also has many opponents in Latin America. Critics highlight that countries that dollarize are giving up key tools—domestic monetary policy and the exchange rate—with which their governments can manage their domestic economies. The potential costs, they argue, have been well highlighted in Argentina's recent experience. Between 1991 and 2001, Argentina managed its national currency on a 'currency board' basis, which tied the value of the currency tightly to the US dollar. When the country began to experience growing current account deficits after the mid-1990s, the only way it could correct the problem—while retaining this monetary regime—was to undergo a costly deflation. This deflation produced high unemployment and dramatic cuts to government spending, and contributed to the country's massive financial crisis of 2001–2.

Critics also point out that, while European countries are joining a monetary union in which they have some say, the adoption of the US dollar would leave Latin-American countries as monetary dependencies. United States policy-makers have begun to debate what kind of support they might provide to countries that adopt the US dollar, and their answer to date has been 'very little'. They have made it clear that dollarized countries would not be offered any role in the decision-making of the US Federal Reserve, and that Fed officials have no intention of taking the concerns of dollarized countries into account when they set US monetary policy. United States policy-makers are not even willing to consider providing lender-of-last-resort support to institutions in dollarized countries. The only support they have discussed seriously is the sharing of the seigniorage revenue that the United States would earn from the dollar's circulation in Latin-American countries that formally dollarize (see Box 7.5). Even this idea, however, was not able to pick up enough support to be endorsed by US Congress or US financial officials when it was debated in 1999–2000. As Cohen (2002) puts it, US policy-makers seem to prefer a policy of 'passive neutrality' on the question of dollarization in Latin America. In his view, the only scenario in which US policy-makers might become much more supportive is if the euro began to pose a serious challenge to the dollar's international position.

BOX 7.5

What is 'Seigniorage'?

Seigniorage is usually defined as the difference between the nominal value of money and its cost of production. This difference is a kind of 'profit' for the issuer of money. In medieval Europe, this source of revenue was often very important for ruling authorities. They could earn it either openly by adding a 'seigniorage' charge (above the normal mint charge that offset the cost of minting) when producing metallic coin, or more secretly by debasing their coin through a reduction of its weight or its 'fineness' (by increasing the proportion of non-precious alloy). If the surreptitious strategy were to be detected by the public, its effectiveness would be undermined, as people would either not accept the coins or accept them only at a discount. In more modern times, metallic coins no longer dominate the monetary system, and governments now earn seigniorage also through the issuing of paper currency as well as indirectly through their regulation of the creation of bank deposit money. National monetary authorities earn seigniorage not just from the use of the money they issue by citizens within their borders; the international use of their currency will augment the seigniorage revenue they earn even further.

The Dollar's Declining Global Role?

Cohen's (2002) observation raises the question of the US dollar's future role as a world currency. When US policy-makers ended the dollar's convertibility into gold in 1971, some predicted that the US currency's role as the dominant world currency would be challenged, since the dollar was no longer 'as good as gold'. In fact, the dollar's central global role has endured. It has continued to be the currency of choice for denominating international trade across most of the world, and has remained the most common currency held by many governments in foreign exchange reserves. In the private international financial markets that have grown dramatically in recent years (for reasons explained below), the US dollar has also been used more than any other currency as a store of value and for denominating transactions since the early 1970s (Cohen 1998: ch. 5). The US dollar has even been used to an increasing degree by market actors within many countries—not just in Latin America but elsewhere too—as a unit of account, a store of value, and even a medium of exchange since the 1980s (Cohen 1998).

In some respects, the US dollar's enduring central global position is a product of inertia. There are many 'network externalities' that reinforce the continued use of existing currencies, both within

countries and at the international level, even when those currencies demonstrate considerable instability (Cohen 1998). Some foreign governments have also continued to hold their reserves in US dollars and denominated their international trade in dollars because of economic and political ties with the USA (see, for example, Gilpin 1987; Spiro 1999). Perhaps most important in explaining the dollar's enduring global role, however, has been the fact that US financial markets, particularly the short-term markets, have remained among the most liquid, large and deep in the world. This has made the holding and use of US dollars particularly attractive to private actors and foreign governments. The two other leading economies—Japan and West Germany—have not cultivated liquid deregulated short-term money markets that rivalled those of the USA, in which yen-denominated or Deutschmark-denominated assets could be held.

Emerging challenges to the dollar's dominant position

Only very recently has the dollar's position as the dominant world currency begun to be challenged seriously. One challenge has come from the creation of the euro in Europe. Some European policy-makers have supported the euro's creation for this reason: they have seen it as a tool to bolster Europe's power in the global political economy (Henning 1998: 563–565). In outlining the official rationale for monetary union in its 'One Market, One Money' report, the European Commission (1990: 194, 191), for example, praised how the euro would bring greater 'symmetry' to the global monetary order, and force the United States to become 'more conscious of the limits of independent policy-making'.

What kind of a challenge will the euro pose to the US dollar? In 1990, the European Commission (1990: 182) predicted that the euro would be a particularly attractive international currency because it would be backed by a conservative central bank dedicated to price stability, and because it would be able to be held in unified European money markets that would be 'the largest in the world'. At the time of writing, however, the euro's challenge to the dollar has proved to be less significant than this prediction. One reason has been that European financial markets remain highly decentralized and, in the words of Fred Bergsten (1997: 88), there is 'no central government borrower like the US Treasury to provide a fulcrum for the market'. Cohen (2003) also argues that the euro's international use is held back by uncertainties regarding the governance structure, and thus the broader political credibility of the whole initiative.

The European Commission (1990: 183) noted a second way in which the euro's creation might threaten the dollar. It observed that, with no more intra-EC foreign exchange intervention necessary, an estimated $230 billion of the total $400 billion of foreign exchange reserves of EC member states would no longer be needed, the majority of which was held in dollars. If these excess reserves were suddenly sold, Pauly (1992: 108) has predicted, the result would be 'destabilizing in the extreme' for the dollar. Again, however, European governments have so far shown little interest in provoking this kind of monetary confrontation with the United States.

More generally, it is also worth noting that the creation of a common European central bank might encourage Europe to present a more unified voice in international monetary politics. European Union countries could, for example, unify their voting stances in the IMF, where they already hold a larger collective voting share than the United States.

The other challenge to the dollar's role comes from Japan, where policy-makers have recently become much more interested in promoting the international use of the yen, especially in the East Asian region (Grimes 2003). Despite Japan's emergence as the world's leading creditor in the 1980s, the yen was used very little at the international level throughout that decade. Even the Japanese themselves relied heavily on the US dollar in their international transactions in both trade and finance. Indeed, the bulk of their assets held abroad remained in this foreign currency, a quite unprecedented and vulnerable situation for the world's largest creditor.

The East Asian financial crisis of 1997–8 encouraged many Japanese policy-makers to want to promote the yen's international role, especially in the East Asian region, where Japan's trade and investment was growing rapidly. The crisis highlighted Japan's limited financial power in the region, and East Asia's reliance on the US dollar. To cultivate the yen's international role, the Japanese government has begun to pursue various initiatives such as fostering a more attractive short-term money market in Japan and encouraging the growth of yen-denominated lending from Japan.

The internationalization of the yen, however, has been held back by problems in the Japanese financial system, and by resistance from countries such as China to the idea of Japanese regional monetary leadership (Katada 2002). In the face of this latter resistance, some officials in Japan and elsewhere in the region have begun to suggest that East Asian monetary co-operation might be fostered more effectively on the basis not of the yen but of an Asian Currency Unit (ACU). Modelled on the European Currency Unit (ECU) that was a precursor to the euro, the ACU could reduce the influence of the dollar by acting as a unit of exchange whose value was determined by the weighed average of a basket of the region's currencies. Although the finance ministers of ASEAN, China, South Korea, and Japan agreed to research the idea at a May 2006 meeting, the prospect of this initiative leading to a fully-fledged East Asian monetary union any time soon is considered remote by most observers.

Consequences of the dollar's declining role?

If the dollar's dominant global position is in fact challenged in the coming years, what will be the consequences? To begin with, the United States will lose some benefits it has derived from the currency's status. In addition to the international prestige that comes from issuing a dominant world currency, the US dollar's use abroad has produced extra 'seigniorage' revenue for the US government, as noted above (see Box 7.5 on page 230). The pre-eminence of the dollar as a world currency has also enhanced the USA's ability to finance its external deficits. In addition, we have seen already how it has helped to persuade foreign governments to help correct these US deficits by adjusting their macroeconomic policies. The USA may thus feel its policy autonomy more constrained as the dollar's global role diminishes.

The erosion of the dollar's central global position will also have consequences for the world as a whole. In particular, it raises the question of whether the international monetary system will be more or less stable without a dominant monetary power. Drawing on the inter-war experience, some have predicted that increasing global monetary instability lies ahead. But others have suggested the opposite. David Calleo (1987: ch. 8) has long argued that a world monetary order based on more 'pluralistic' or 'balance of power' principles may be more likely to produce stability over time than one based on hegemony. A hegemonic power, in his view, is inevitably tempted to exploit its dominant position over time to serve its own interests rather than the interests of the stability of the system. Interestingly, European Commission president, Jacques Delors, advanced a similar argument in defending the EMU in 1993; in his words, the creation of the euro would make the EU 'strong enough to force the United States and Japan to play by rules which would ensure much greater monetary stability around the world' (quoted in Henning 1998: 565).

KEY POINTS

- The US dollar continued to be a dominant global currency after it ceased to be convertible into gold in 1971. This was in large part a result of the unique attractiveness of US financial markets.

- Recently, the US dollar's global role is beginning to be challenged by the euro and the yen, although these challenges should not be overstated.

- These challenges will impose new constraints on US policy-making, but their wider systemic implications for global monetary stability are hard to predict.

The Globalization of Financial Markets

The final feature of the Bretton Woods regime that has broken down since the early 1970s involves a trend that has already been mentioned a number of times: the globalization of private financial markets.

Recall that the Bretton Woods architects endorsed an international financial order in which governments could control cross-border private financial flows, and public international institutions would be assigned a key role in allocating short-term and long-term credit at the international level. Today, this world appears to be turned upside down. Enormous sums of private capital flow around the world quite freely on a twenty-four-hour basis. And the size of these flows dwarfs the lending activities of the IMF and World Bank (whose loans have become focused exclusively on poor countries).

Explaining financial globalization

How did we get from there to here? The growth of global telecommunications networks has enabled money to be moved around the world much more easily than in the past. A number of market developments have also been significant. The dramatic expansion of international trade and multinational corporate activity from the 1960s onwards, for example, generated some of the growing demand for private international financial services. The 1973 oil price rise also provided a big boost to the globalization of finance, when private banks took on the role of recycling the new wealth of oil-producing countries. Private actors were also encouraged to diversify their assets internationally by the increasingly volatile currency environment after the breakdown of the Bretton Woods exchange-rate system in the early 1970s. The risks and costs of international financial activity were also lowered throughout this period by various market innovations such as the creation of currency futures, options, and swaps.

In addition to these technological and market developments, the globalization of finance has been a product of political choices and state decisions (Helleiner 1994). In particular, it has been encouraged by the fact that states liberalized the tight capital controls they employed in the early post-war years. The first step in this direction took place when the British government encouraged the growth of the 'euro-market' in London during the 1960s. In this financial market, the British government allowed international financial activity in foreign currencies—primarily US dollars in the early years—to

be conducted on an unregulated basis. After the mid-1970s, the globalization of finance was encouraged further when many governments dismantled their capital control regimes, which had been in place throughout the post-war period. The United States and United Kingdom led the way, abolishing their national capital controls in 1974 and 1979, respectively. They were soon followed by other advanced industrial countries. Indeed, by the 1990s, an almost fully liberal pattern of financial relations had emerged among advanced industrial states, giving market actors a degree of freedom in cross-border financial activity unparalleled since the 1920s.

Poorer countries have generally been less willing to abolish capital controls altogether. But an increasing number have done so, and others have liberalized their existing controls in various ways in this period. Many small poorer states—particularly in the Caribbean—have also played a central role in fostering financial globalization by offering their territories as a regulation-free environment for international financial activity. Places such as the Cayman Islands have emerged as very significant international banking centres in the world (Palan 2003).

Why have states largely abandoned the restrictive Bretton Woods financial regime? The growing influence of neo-liberal ideology among financial policy-makers played a part. As we saw in the last section, neo-liberals were less sympathetic to the Bretton Woods idea that national policy autonomy needed to be protected. Where Keynes and White had endorsed the use of capital controls for this purpose, many neo-liberals have applauded the fact that international financial markets might impose an external discipline on governments pursuing policies that were not 'sound' from a neo-liberal standpoint. Neo-liberals have also criticized the role that capital controls might play in interfering with market freedoms and preventing the efficient allocation of capital internationally.

The liberalization of capital controls has also been seen by some policy-makers as a kind of competitive strategy to attract mobile financial business and capital to their national territory (Cerny 1994).

The British support for the euro markets and their decision to abolish capital controls in 1979 were both designed to help rebuild London's status as a leading international financial centre in this way. The US support for financial liberalization (both at home and abroad) was also designed to bolster New York's international financial position as well as to attract foreign capital to the uniquely deep and liquid US financial markets in ways that could help finance US trade and budget deficits. The smaller, offshore financial centres have also seen the hosting of an international financial centre as a development strategy that could provide employment and some limited government revenue (from such things as licenses and fees). Once governments such as these had begun to liberalize and deregulate their financial systems, many other governments also felt competitive pressure to emulate their decisions in order to prevent mobile domestic capital and financial business from migrating abroad. As their country's firms became increasingly transnational and had access to foreign financial markets, policy-makers also recognized that national capital controls could only be enforced in very rigid ways that would be costly to the national economy (Goodman and Pauly 1993).

Implications of financial globalization for national policy autonomy

What have been the implications of the globalization of finance? One set of implications is addressed in the next chapter: the vulnerability of global financial markets to financial crises. A second set of implications relates to the concerns of the Bretton Woods negotiators. As noted above, they worried that a liberal international financial order would undermine their efforts to create a stable exchange-rate system and to protect the autonomy of national policy. We have already seen how financial globalization has indeed complicated the task of maintaining fixed exchange rates. But what about its implications for the autonomy of national policy?

This question has generated much debate in the field of IPE. Some have argued that financial globalization has severely undermined the autonomy of national policy, since it gives investors a powerful 'exit' option to exercise against governments that stray too far from their preferences. Like Keynes and White, proponents of this view argue that this discipline is felt particularly strongly by governments that pursue policies disliked by wealthy asset holders, such as large budget deficits, high taxation, expansionary macroeconomic policies that risk inflation, or more generally policies that reflect left-of-centre political values (Gill and Law 1989; McKenzie and Lee 1991; Kurzer 1993; Cerny 1994; Sinclair 1994; Harmes 1998). These new constraints—what Thomas Friedman (2000) calls the 'Golden Straightjacket'—are said to help explain why governments across the world have shifted away from these kinds of policies since the 1970s.

Southern governments are seen to be especially vulnerable to the discipline of global financial markets. This is partly because their financial systems are so small relative to the enormous size of global financial flows. It is also because investors tend to be more skittish about the security of their assets in contexts where economic and political instability is higher and there is a prospect of defaults. The 1994 Mexican peso crisis and the 1997–8 East Asian financial crisis are cited to show how entire countries' economic prospects can be devastated overnight by a sudden loss of confidence in international financial markets. More generally, Southern countries have also suffered from the fact that their wealthy citizens have taken advantage of the new global markets to park their assets in safer Northern financial markets. During debt crises, the size of this 'flight capital' from many debtor countries has often equalled or surpassed that of the country's external debts. In other words, these countries were often creditors to the world economy at the very moment that their governments were managing a severe debt crisis; if this flight capital could be repatriated, these countries would have experienced no debt crisis and associated loss of policy autonomy (Lissakers 1991).

Other scholars suggest that these arguments about the declining policy autonomy of national governments are overstated. We have seen already how macroeconomic theory suggests that states can retain a high degree of monetary policy autonomy in an atmosphere of capital mobility if they are willing to allow the exchange rate to fluctuate (see Box 7.3 on page 227). Ton Notermans (2000), for example, has highlighted how European governments such as Sweden and Norway succeeded in pursuing expansionary monetary policies throughout the 1970s and 1980s by retaining a floating exchange rate. Indeed, from Notermans' perspective, these governments eventually abandoned expansionary macroeconomic policies not because of the external constraint of financial globalization but because of a growing inability to contain inflation domestically as tripartite collective bargaining structures unravelled and domestic financial innovation undermined traditional monetary tools.

Michael Loriaux (1991) puts forward a similar analysis of the well-known experience of Mitterrand socialist government in France in the early 1980s. When this government abandoned its unilateral Keynesian expansion in 1983, many scholars pointed to the experience as a confirmation of the new constraints imposed by financial globalization. But Loriaux suggests that the constraint was a more domestic one. In the new atmosphere of floating exchange rates after 1973, he shows how the French government was increasingly unable to pursue expansionary policies because the inflationary consequences of a devaluation could not easily be contained. This inability to contain inflation stemmed from the existence of an 'overdraft economy', which resulted from the structure of the French domestic financial system. From this perspective, the French state lost control over its macroeconomic policy not because of financial globalization but because its domestic financial system was ill-suited to the macroeconomic imperatives of the new world of floating exchange rates. Ironically, as Loriaux points out, the financial deregulation and liberalization programme launched by the Mitterrand government after 1983

had the effect of increasing rather than decreasing the ability of the state to control monetary policy. It enabled the state to regain control over monetary policy by eliminating the overdraft economy that had been fostered by the old financial system.

The importance of exchange-rate policy in providing a degree of macroeconomic autonomy has also been highlighted in the case of capital flight from Latin-American countries. Jonathan Crystal (1994) argues that much of the capital flight experienced by Latin-American countries in the 1970s and 1980s could have been avoided through the use of different exchange-rate policies. He demonstrates that countries maintaining overvalued exchange rates have suffered much more serious capital flight than those that have not, and shows how government decisions to maintain overvalued exchange rates reflected domestic political constraints rather than the influence of global financial markets.

Other authors suggest that the disciplining effect of global finance on governments with high levels of government spending, high taxation, or a more general left-of-centre political orientation has been exaggerated (see the discussion in Hay, Chapter 10 in this volume). Garrett (1995) has highlighted how many OECD governments have been able to use borrowing in international capital markets in the last two decades to finance increased government spending (see also Swank 2002). In the 1970s, and again during much of the 1990s, countries in Latin America and East Asia also found that global financial markets offered funds that enhanced their fiscal autonomy in the short term. That these borrowing experiences often ended up in debt crises that undermined policy autonomy was a product of a number of factors often unrelated to financial globalization, such as unexpected sudden shocks to the world economy and particular patterns in the use of the borrowed funds. More generally, in a detailed study of the preferences of international financial market actors, Mosley (2003) found that these actors were concerned primarily with overall national inflation rates and aggregate levels of fiscal deficits; they did not worry about governments' overall level of spending, taxation, or their political orientation when considering investment decisions (although this result was less true when they considered investments in Southern countries).

Many poor countries have also found their policy autonomy boosted by an aspect of the financial globalization trend that has received less attention from IPE scholars: flows of remittances from rich to poor countries. These flows have been growing rapidly in recent years, and they are generally much more stable than the lending of rich-country investors. Indeed, they are sometimes even counter-cyclical; that is, they increase when the recipient country is undergoing difficult economic times (see, for example, Kapur and McHale 2003).

Finally, those who think that the power of global financial markets over nation states has been overstated often point to the fact that states retain the ability to reimpose capital controls when their policy autonomy is threatened. The decision of the Malaysian government to adopt this strategy during the East Asian financial crisis provides one such example (Beeson 2000). Another prominent case has been Chile, which has used controls on speculative capital inflows in order to manage its relationship with the global financial system more effectively (Soederberg 2002). These examples are cited to support the broader point that powerful global financial markets ultimately rest on political foundations that are established by nation states (Pauly 1997).

Distributive and environmental implications of financial globalization

Scholars of international political economy have also been interested in some other implications of financial globalization that attracted less attention at Bretton Woods, one of these being its distributive impact within countries. Neo-Marxist scholars have argued that financial globalization has bolstered the power of an emerging, internationally mobile capitalist class, while eroding that of labour. The emerging transnational capital class has gained 'structural power' through its new ability to exit—or simply to threaten to exit—domestic political settings. This power has been used to reinforce neo-liberal ideology and a kind of 'internationalization of the state' which serves the interests of this new class (Gill and Law 1989).

Jeffrey Frieden (1991) has also highlighted new political divisions that have emerged within the business sector. While transnational corporations and owners of financial assets and services have gained from financial globalization, businesses that are more nationally based have often not. In a world of heightened capital mobility, he argues, these two groups are in fact increasingly at loggerheads over policy choices within the 'impossible trinity'. The former generally prefer exchange-rate stability because of their involvement in international trade and finance, even if this involves a cost of abandoning monetary policy autonomy. Those in the non-tradable sector are inclined to defend monetary policy autonomy even if this involves accepting a floating exchange rate.

Some scholars have also analysed the gendered implications of financial globalization (Singh and Zammit 2000; van Staveren 2002). To the extent that global financial integration has been associated with the retrenchment of the welfare state, the costs have often been borne more by women than men. Cutbacks to government spending in areas such as health, education, public transportation, and other social services frequently have the effect of increasing the role played in these areas by the unpaid sector of the economy, a sector traditionally dominated by women. When countries experience international financial crises, other aspects of the burden of adjustment can also be strongly gendered. During the Asian financial crisis, incomes in the informal sectors—where women are heavily represented—fell particularly sharply, and job cuts in the formal private sector often fell more heavily on women. Aslanbeigui and Summerfield (2000: 87, 91) also note how 'across the region, migrant workers, the majority of whom were women, were expelled from host countries' and they quote the World Bank's observation that 'child labour, prostitution and domestic violence' increased during the crisis. Other analysts have also highlighted how even global financial markets themselves are made up overwhelmingly of male traders and they operate with a culture and discourse that is hyper-masculinized (McDowell 1997; De Goede 2000).

A final issue that received little attention at the time of the Bretton Woods conference concerns the environmental implications of global financial markets. Scholarship on this topic has been fairly limited within the field of IPE to date, but some interesting themes have been put forward by those who have addressed it. In particular, a number of analysts have suggested that speculative and volatile international financial flows reward instant economic results and short-term thinking in ways that greatly complicate the kind of long-term planning that is required for the promotion of environmental values. During the East Asian financial crisis, for example, governments scrapped environmental programmes and there was an intensification of deforestation, mining, and other economic activities that put pressure on natural ecosystems (Durbin and Welch 2002). Even two analysts working with the World Business Council on Sustainable Development acknowledge that 'it is clear that the globalization of investment flows is speeding the destruction of natural forests' (Schmidheiny and Zorraquin 1996: 10). International investors, they note, push firms to harvest

an entire forest for a short-term windfall profit rather than manage the forest in a sustainable fashion over the long term. They conclude: 'sustainable development is concerned with the importance of the future. Financial markets discount the future routinely and heavily' (Schmidheiny and Zorraquin 1996: 8). On the other hand, the short-termism of global financial markets should not be overstated, because one powerful actor in global finance—the global insurance sector—does have a longer-term perspective that has led it to play a key role in lobbying for action on climate change in order to reduce the risk of future claims in this area (Paterson 2001).

KEY POINTS

- The globalization of financial markets has been driven not just by technological and market pressures but also by the decisions of states to liberalize capital controls that had been popular in the early post-war years.

- A hotly contested subject among IPE scholars concerns the question of whether, and to what extent, global financial markets have eroded the policy autonomy of national governments.

- Financial globalization has also had important distributive consequences along class, sectoral, and gender lines. Its environmental implications may also be significant, but they require more detailed study.

Conclusion

The international monetary and financial system has undergone three important transformations since the late nineteenth century, in response to changing economic and political conditions. During the inter-war years, the global integrated monetary and financial order of the pre-1914 period broke down. At the Bretton Woods conference of 1944, a new order was built on 'embedded liberal'

principles. Since the early 1970s, the third change has been under way as a number of the features of the Bretton Woods system have unravelled.

In some respects, the emerging international monetary and financial system is reminiscent of the pre-1914 world. The commitment to a liberal and integrated global financial order is similar, as is the interest in regional monetary unions (although these unions today are a more ambitious kind than the Latin Monetary Union and Scandinavian Monetary Union). Like their counterparts in that earlier era, many contemporary policy-makers are also committed to the idea that the principal goal of monetary policy should be to maintain price stability. At the same time, however, the absence of a gold standard today, and the commitment of many governments to floating exchange rates, mark a sharp difference from the pre-1914 period. This contrast reflects the enduring commitment of many governments to the idea that first emerged during the inter-war period, that exchange-rate adjustments can play a useful role in bolstering policy autonomy and facilitating balance of payments adjustments. The beginnings of a decline in the dollar's dominant position and the growing interest in large regional currency zones have also led some to draw parallels to the inter-war years.

Each of these transformations in the nature of the international monetary and financial system has had important consequences for the key question of who gets what, when, and how in the global political economy. Monetary and financial systems—at both the domestic and international levels—serve not just economic functions. They also have implications for various political projects relating to the pursuit of power, ideas, and interests. For this reason, the study of money and finance cannot be left only to economists, who have traditionally dominated scholarship in this area. It also needs the attention of students of international political economy who have an interest in these wider political issues.

QUESTIONS

1. Does historical experience suggest that a hegemonic leader is necessary for a stable international monetary and financial system to exist?

2. For how much longer will the US dollar remain the world's key currency?

3. Has the floating exchange-rate system created a kind of 'casino capitalism' which is creating an increasingly unstable global political economy? Should the leading powers attempt to stabilize the relationship between the values of the major currencies?

4. Has the creation of the euro been a positive move for Europeans? Should other regions emulate the European example, and are they likely to do so?

5. To what extent has financial globalization undermined the power and policy autonomy of national governments? Is financial globalization irreversible?

6. How important has financial globalization been in influencing class, sectoral, and gender relations within countries? What are its environmental consequences?

FURTHER READING

■ **Andrews, D. (ed.) (2006),** *International Monetary Power* **(Ithaca, NY: Cornell University Press).** A collection of essays concerning the relationship between state power and international money.

■ **Cohen, B. (1998),** *The Geography of Money* **(Ithaca, NY: Cornell University Press).** An analysis of the ways in which national currencies are being challenged in the current age by one of the pioneers of the field of the political economy of international money.

■ **Cohen, B. (2004), The** *Future of Money* **(Princeton, NJ: Princeton University Press).** A kind of sequel to his *The Geography of Money*, which addresses key policy questions relating to the changing nature of money in the contemporary world.

■ **Eichengreen, B. (1992),** *Golden Fetters: The Gold Standard and the Great Depression: 1919–1939* **(Oxford: Oxford University Press).** An analysis of international monetary and financial relations during the inter-war years.

■ **Gallarotti, G. (1995),** *The Anatomy of an International Monetary Regime* **(New York: Oxford University Press).** A survey of the political economy of the international gold standard.

■ **Germain, R. (1997),** *The International Organization of Credit* **(Cambridge: Cambridge University Press).** An analysis of the evolution of the international financial system since the early modern age.

■ **Henning, C. R. (1994),** *Currencies and Politics in the United States, Germany and Japan* **(Washington, DC: Institute for International Economics).** An analysis of the politics of exchange-rate policy-making in the three leading economic powers.

■ **Kirshner, J. (1995),** *Currency and Coercion: The Political Economy of International Monetary Power* **(Princeton, NJ: Princeton University Press).** An analysis of how monetary relations are used as an instrument of state power.

■ **——(ed.) (2002),** *Monetary Orders* **(Ithaca, NY: Cornell University Press).** An edited collection that highlights the political foundations of national and international monetary systems.

■ **Pauly, L. (1997),** *Who Elected the Bankers? Surveillance and Control in the World Economy* **(Ithaca, NY: Cornell University Press).** A study of the evolution of global financial and monetary governance throughout the twentieth century.

■ **Porter, T. (2006)** *Globalization and Finance* **(Oxford: Polity Press).** An overview of the politics and governance of global financial markets.

■ **Strange, S. (1998),** *Mad Money: When Markets Outgrow Government* **(Ann Arbor, MI: University of Michigan Press).** A survey and critique of the contemporary international monetary and financial system.

 WEB LINKS

● **www.attac.org** The website of a leading international lobby group pressing for global financial reform.

● **www.bis.org** The website of the Bank for International Settlements. The Bank is the 'central bankers' bank' and it provides detailed analyses of international monetary and financial developments.

● **www.eurodad.org** The website of a leading non-governmental organization based in Europe that addresses international financial issues relating to poorer countries.

● **www.imf.org** The website of the International Monetary Fund.

 Visit the Online Resource Centre that accompanies this book for more information: www.oxfordtextbooks.co.uk/orc/ravenhill2e/

8 The Political Economy of Global Financial Crises

LOUIS W PAULY

Chapter Contents

- Introduction
- National Politics and International Markets
- The Nature and Variety of International Financial Crises
- The Changing Global Context
- Crisis Prevention
- Crisis Management
- Dilemmas of Global Governance

Reader's Guide

Since the early 1970s, the world economy has been participating in an experiment involving, on the one hand, the opening and deepening of financial markets and, on the other, the dispersion of the political authority required to regulate truly global markets. The resulting governance dilemmas are nowhere clearer than in the circumstances surrounding financial crises capable of expanding across national borders. This chapter explores the political economy of crisis prevention and crisis management in the evolving world system. It pays particular attention to the challenges confronting emerging-market countries in recent years.

Introduction

As in the immediate post-1945 period, promoting a deepening of interdependence among the economies of the world continues to be a strategic objective of the United States and its main allies. During the 1970s, efforts accelerated to extend this logic from real economies, where tangible goods and services are produced, to financial markets. Financial booms and busts have always characterized modern capitalism, but from the 1970s crises in financial markets began to spill more readily across national borders.

The collapse of the Bretton Woods exchange-rate system in the early 1970s occurred at the same time as a broadening movement towards opening and liberalizing capital markets around the world. Although economists still argue over the precise effects this movement has had on the efficiency of real economies, its most obvious negative effect has been to make it easier for intermittent financial shocks to spread misery beyond the localities where they originated. For this reason, policy-makers in the leading states in the system have engaged in simultaneously competitive and co-operative efforts to enhance financial market efficiency and safety. Deregulation has gone hand in hand with increased prudential supervision and efforts to encourage better risk management by private financial intermediaries.

Financial panics nevertheless recur, and now spread rapidly across both functional and geographical borders. In the parlance of bankers and investors, markets still periodically become illiquid as financial assets cannot be sold without incurring massive losses in value. In 1997 and 1998, for example, this is precisely what happened, as panic spread from stock to bond to banking markets, and from East Asia to Russia, Latin America, and eventually to Wall Street. The system itself seemed threatened as both bankers and investors lost the confidence necessary to make the very acts of lending and buying bonds and stocks conceivable.

Looming over economic policy-makers around the world was the spectre of the terrible decade spanning the US stock market collapse in 1929 and the start of the Second World War in 1939, when global economic depression brought widespread unemployment and political extremism, especially—but not exclusively—in Germany and Japan. As the crisis of the late 1990s worsened, anyone observing closely the faces of the world's leading finance ministers and central bank governors, anyone listening carefully to their verbal attempts to calm international markets, anyone monitoring what they did as crisis managers would have been justified in wondering whether a similarly catastrophic period lay just ahead.

After the Second World War, most countries were cautious about moving back to the kind of financial openness characteristic of the British-led world economy in the pre-1914 period. Over time, this sense of caution dissipated and capital market liberalization came back into vogue. In the face of the crisis of the late 1990s, however, some countries responded by reimposing draconian capital controls, while the United States took the highly unusual action of effectively bailing out not a money-centre clearing bank, as it had done before when faced with the serious risk of contagion in its core payments system, but a prominent investment fund engaged in highly sophisticated speculation. When the panic was still gaining momentum, one of the world's leading currency speculators offered a surprising diagnosis: 'Financial markets are inherently unstable; left to their own devices, they are liable to break down. More important, many social values are not properly represented by market forces' (Soros 1997*b*; see also Soros 1997*a* and 1998). After the crisis had passed, not only radical critics of capitalism raised now-obvious questions. In the words of the former chief economist of the World Bank and chairman of the US President's Council of Economic Advisers,

'While money should be flowing from the rich to the poor and risk from the poor to the rich, the global financial system is accomplishing neither. With poor countries left to bear the brunt of risk, crises have become a way of life—with more than a hundred crises in the last three decades' (Stiglitz 2006: 246).

The preceding chapter set out the broad context for understanding the changing monetary dimension of our contemporary global economy. This chapter looks in depth at the political economy of its recurring financial crises. For students of international relations and international economics, such moments in time are worth considerable attention. They open a unique window on the fragile political structures that continue to underpin globalizing markets. Those markets promise prosperity and peaceful interaction among the world's still-distinctive societies, but they cannot and do not in themselves ensure such outcomes. In this regard, the early chapters of this book drew attention to the importance of collaboration among the political authorities leading that system. International financial crises demonstrate both the continuing importance of such collaboration and the continuing difficulty of achieving it. They also raise larger questions about the political implications of deeper monetary and financial integration.

National Politics and International Markets

It is the real economy that matters. Only when something goes wrong with the underlying financing do most of us become aware of its importance. This distinction reflects a vital insight. The prices of most financial assets and liabilities fluctuate continuously, and every such price movement is meaningful to someone, somewhere. But financial gyrations only matter visibly to the lives of most people when they suddenly change and have a direct effect on the fundamental mechanisms through which jobs are created or destroyed, and goods and services are produced (the 'real' economy). In the democratic systems currently lying at the heart of an integrating global economy, financial market ups and downs can be constructive. When they facilitate innovation, production, and exchange, adjustments in the prices of financial claims are helpful to the real economy and can serve to stabilize the underlying political order. Their specific political effects can be important (see Hiscox, Chapter 4 in this volume), but they tend to be invisible to most producers and consumers. Economic benefits and costs are distributed and redistributed as financial prices move, but the process usually occurs in such a way that no particular group or groups with overwhelming political power become aggrieved enough to seek fundamental systemic change.

Turbulence in financial markets can also be destructive, however, and then its political effects tend to be very obvious and very negative. When panic feeds on itself and spreads the psychology of fear, the confidence of savers, investors, producers, and consumers is undercut. Crisis conditions can engender spiralling declines in disposable incomes and life prospects. When they impose costs deemed to be unbearable by the politically weak, the local effects can be traumatic for all concerned. But when they impose costs deemed to be unbearable by the politically strong and mobilized, they can retard economic progress significantly and destabilize political order. In recent years, countries as disparate as Argentina and Indonesia tragically exemplified this negative syndrome and rekindled memories of past systemic disasters (see Box 8.1).

The globalizing political economy gradually and intentionally built up in the wake of depression and

LOUIS W PAULY

BOX 8.1

The Policy Challenges of Financial Openness: The Case of Argentina

Blessed with abundant natural resources, diversified industries, and a well-educated labour force, Argentina might have become a regional beacon of prosperity during the twentieth century. Instead, political crises, bad luck, and economic policy mistakes plagued the country. After decades of troubles, hyperinflation struck in 1989. In April 1991, the government embarked on a bold policy experiment to reverse the economy's course. The Convertibility Plan rigidly pegged the value of the peso to the US dollar and by doing so constrained the ability of the central bank to print money. Simultaneously, the government announced a wide range of structural reforms to make the economy more flexible, competitive, and open. Initially, the plan achieved dramatic results. Inflation fell, international capital flowed in, and the economy grew by an average of 6 per cent through 1997. Late in 1998, however, a surprisingly severe recession began, and its effects were compounded by the unusual turbulence then being experienced in global financial markets. What happened next is still the subject of great controversy and debate, both inside Argentina and abroad.

As capital inflows dried up, some say the government did not react quickly enough with domestic policy adjustments. Others point to large loans from the IMF inadequately conditioned on such adjustments, and to a currency devaluation by Brazil that undercut Argentina's export competitiveness. Still others blame the panic then gripping private foreign lenders and investors for reasons that had little to do with Argentina itself (the aftermath of the Asian financial crises of 1997–8). In any event, in the middle of 2001, capital flew out of the country and the confidence of domestic as well as foreign investors collapsed. Bank runs, the suspension of IMF loans, and severe political and social unrest ensued. In December 2001, the country partially defaulted on

its international debts; the next month it abandoned its currency peg, and as the peso's value plummeted, the value of its debt, now largely denominated in US dollars, exploded. During 2002, the economy contracted by 20 per cent and unemployment rose to between 20 and 25 per cent of the workforce.

In retrospect, it became clear that either the currency regime should have been abandoned during more halcyon days in 1996 or 1997, or that its continuation should have been supported by tighter **fiscal policies**, a reduction in international borrowing, and lower labour costs. At the time, neither course of action had any domestic political traction, and international creditors, including the IMF, proved willing to ignore the logic that would later seem so obvious. Even so, according to a key IMF staffer, in 1998 'a crisis might have been avoided with good luck—for example, had the dollar depreciated against the euro, had Brazil not been forced to devalue, or had international capital markets not deteriorated—but Argentina's luck ran out' (Allen 2003: 131; also see Mussa 2002, and IMF 2003a).

In the end, to the consternation of the IMF and its other creditors, a new government defaulted on much of its external debt. By 2004, a bounce in local and international economies and a distinct lack of solidarity among Argentina's external creditors provided the policy space necessary to cut debt and debt-servicing loads significantly, and to rekindle domestic production. By then, however, most people in Argentina were much poorer than they had been a decade earlier, and disquieting signals had been sent to the rest of the developing world regarding the wisdom of globalization. Policy mistakes remained as easy to make as ever, financial openness made them deadly, and when crises occurred, the rules of the game were uncertain and manipulable (Blustein 2005).

world war in the mid-twentieth century rested on the assumption that it would eventually draw a widening circle of shared prosperity. But recurrent financial crises cast doubt on such an assumption. They raise a host of political challenges for national policy-makers trying to secure the economic and social

benefits promised by economic openness while minimizing associated social and political costs.

International economic interdependence formed a core element in the strategy of systemic stabilization and development designed mainly by the United States and the United Kingdom in the wake of the Second World War. The central idea of reconstructing a world based on open-market principles was not new, but its early architects deliberately tried to limit the extent to which the initial version of the strategy involved the banking industry. Who could forget the disappointed dreams of liberals earlier in the century? In 1912, the British intellectual, Norman Angell, had famously opined:

> Commercial interdependence, which is the special mark of banking as it is the mark of no other profession or trade in quite the same degree . . . is surely doing a great deal to demonstrate that morality after all is not founded upon self-sacrifice, but enlightened self-interest . . . And such a clearer understanding is bound to improve, not merely the relationship of one group to another, but the relationship of all men to other men, to create a consciousness which must make for more efficient human co-operation, a better human society. (Keegan 1998: 12)

Alas, Angell was to be proven wrong, two years later, when the interdependence of bankers did nothing to prevent the coming of a catastrophic war, and even more decisively two decades later, when the decisions of their national overseers helped to plunge the world into an even deeper abyss.

The initial post-1945 political consensus reconceived the idea of what was desirable in commercial interdependence to exclude financial activity that was not trade related. In time, as we shall see, Angell's view once again became the common wisdom, albeit with a twist born of repeated financial crises and repeated reminders that the machinery of global capitalism required attentive political oversight. As John Ruggie put it, international market forces were embedded in domestic political economies that rendered market regulation and programmes aimed at guaranteeing minimum levels of social welfare legitimate (Ruggie 1982, 1998).

In the aftermath of the Second World War, the advanced industrial democracies leading the system built significant welfare states in one form or another. In effect, national and local governments took responsibility for the security of their citizens,

and they defined it more broadly than ever before to include not only physical safety but also a minimum standard of living. The economic turmoil associated with financial crises had in earlier days been considered to be beyond the responsibility of governments. Now, economic stability, social security, and non-inflationary growth in disposable incomes were considered to be not only legitimate but also necessary policy objectives for which governments could and should be held to account.

Years of depression and war left another related legacy. Whereas the 1930s had been characterized by various measures that closed national economies off from one another, after 1945 the leading democratic welfare states sought increasingly to achieve core political objectives through freer but still managed economic interaction. Fearing the kind of cross-border financial contagion experienced in the previous decade, however, they initially sought to limit that interaction to trade and financial flows required to facilitate trade. Gradually, international capital flows in the form of foreign direct investment (FDI) became easier as well. National financial markets, nevertheless, were kept distinctly separate. Nationally licensed banks and other financial intermediaries were typically viewed as constituting the 'commanding heights' of economies that governments were now deliberately trying to steer. They were closely regulated, and international capital movements not directly related to trade or permissible foreign direct investment remained limited.

As Eric Helleiner describes in the preceding chapter, these arrangements began to break down in the 1960s. The changing preferences of those same national governments lay behind a series of explicit and implicit policy choices that cumulatively pushed the system back towards one characterized by freer international capital movements. In democratic countries, the changing interests of key constituents shifted the ground on which policy was made. Certainly, multinational corporations and large banks sought new sources of profit in more open markets, but a widening range of citizens also gradually became convinced of the virtues of diversifying their investments internationally.

Governments themselves, moreover, came increasingly to consider external markets as attractive places to sell their bonds. They also believed that loosening the regulation of the non-domestic activities of financial institutions had the potential to generate jobs, prestige, and wealth. Benefits aside, leading governments also became convinced over time that the costs of attempting to maintain a relatively closed international financial system were increasing. Openness to capital flows through private markets came to be perceived broadly as both necessary and sufficient for generating prosperity in the long run. In deference to those markets, public-sector flows, whether in the form of overseas development assistance or facilities extended through multilateral organizations such as the World Bank and International Monetary Fund, were intentionally kept limited.

We return below to the changing conditions that allowed large-scale international capital flows, and to their consequences. It is important first to underline the fact that policies after 1945 that were intended to separate national financial markets had by the opening of the 1970s clearly shifted in the direction of liberalization. By the 1980s, a similar shift was under way in much of the developing world. Even as such fundamental policy reorientations gathered steam, however, episodes of financial crisis reminded policy-makers and market participants continually of certain historical lessons.

Stable, well-functioning financial markets required stable, well-functioning regulatory authority beneath them. Market actors needed clear operating rules. **Property rights** had to be established and adjudicated when conflicts arose. Predictable procedures had to be in place to handle inevitable bankruptcies. Someone had to provide the degree of insurance necessary to limit the chance that specific debt defaults could cause the kind of cascading panics commonly witnessed in earlier times. Some agency had to be entrusted with the responsibility and endowed with the capability to act as **lender of last resort**. Finally, and in light of the risk that the very existence of such ultimate insurance facilities might tempt potential beneficiaries to act

imprudently, a risk that economists call **moral hazard**, this last-resort lending function had to be linked with the prudential supervision of financial intermediaries by competent and legitimate authorities.

After the experience of the 1930s, when financial contagion spread around the world, all advanced industrial states applied such lessons within their national markets. Some gave the bulk of regulatory and supervisory responsibilities to their central banks, while some split responsibilities between central banks and other official agencies. Most initiated some kind of deposit insurance scheme to ameliorate the risk of domestic bank runs, and they all tried to leave as much scope as domestic circumstances would allow for self-discipline by market actors themselves. They nevertheless established back-up procedures to deal with emergencies. When no one else would lend sufficiently to financial institutions whose survival was deemed vital to larger national interests, some arm of the state was endowed with the capacity and the mandate to do so. Across the developing world, one challenge confronted repeatedly in recent decades has been to create similar facilities. When they cannot meet that challenge, and in particular when financial distress threatens global order, the International Monetary Fund is now available to perform similar functions. Since the Fund's underlying authority is of a limited and delegated nature, however, there are a myriad of economic and political controversies associated with its interventions.

National polities can certainly establish national regulators to govern national financial markets. When they fail to do so, it is appropriate to inquire into the reasons for internal weaknesses, or whether external political pressures exacerbate those weaknesses. But when those markets become ever more open, and ever more integrated, how can the authority to regulate them become fully transnational? All the functions listed above still have to be fully met in a world potentially characterized by deeply integrated financial markets. What is missing, of course, is global polity capable of sustaining policy instruments analogous to those that have been established at the national level.

Therein lies the central political dilemma posed by the contemporary move towards broader financial openness. Moments of crisis focus an analytical spotlight on that very dilemma.

KEY POINTS

- Financial markets have always been prone to bouts of instability.
- During the twentieth century, leading states built up national regulatory and supervisory systems to limit the dangers of financial crises.
- Cross-national regulatory co-ordination became necessary after international capital movements accelerated in the 1970s, but remained difficult to sustain and expand politically.

The Nature and Variety of International Financial Crises

Financial crises start with sharp breaks in the prices of key financial instruments. The expectations of market participants suddenly change. Shocks course through markets, and participants seek rapidly to adjust their positions. Most commonly, the holders of financial claims rush to make them liquid and mobile. They sell assets they expect to depreciate in value, and buy assets they expect to rise in value. As in any market where demand rapidly shrinks and supply rapidly expands, the prices of unwanted assets plummet. Those forced to sell lose extravagantly, while sudden opportunities are presented to shrewd risk-takers able and willing to buy and hold until calm returns. Behind such radical breaks in financial markets that can seem abstract to all parties except the most obvious winners and losers, institutions in the business of financial intermediation can fail, vast wealth can evaporate, and cascading human tragedies can follow in train.

Contemporary crises

Over the post-1945 period, the consequences of crisis moments have varied in their severity and scope. The moments that particularly interest us here are those defined most often by plummeting prices in the value of a nation's banking assets at the core of its payments system (referred to as a banking crisis) and/or in the value of its currency relative to other currencies (referred to as a currency crisis). When creditors are exposed to these kinds of shocks in a country's main financial markets, their reactions can generate crises that spill over national borders. Capital flight out of one market translates into capital inflow into others. Excessive price declines in one asset class translate into excessive price increases in another. The failure of foreign subsidiaries can lead to the failure of parent institutions. A crisis-induced run on a particular nation's currency translates into the rapid relative appreciation of the currencies of trading partners. The pain of importers in one country is shared by exporters in another. Under conditions of deepening interdependence, in short, financial crises can be contagious.

The classic definition of a crisis revolves around the notion of a 'turning point'. Serious international financial crises mark crucial turning points, not simply for national or regional economies where they arise, but for the system as a whole. The most dangerous times for the system have occurred when banking crises and currency crises have coincided and threatened the real economies of leading states. From a systemic point of view, the most helpful responses aim at limiting real economic damage, preventing recurrences, and establishing better methods for managing the distribution of associated costs when such prevention fails. The most damaging responses are those that threaten the legitimacy of the post-1945 international consensus and push national economies back toward autarky. Believers in *laissez-faire* doctrines counsel policy passivity when financial crises occur; they assert that markets will correct themselves, and that official intervention delays necessary economic adjustments. There is good empirical evidence to support such a belief. Nevertheless, policy-makers in states confronted by deep financial crises have for many decades been extremely reluctant to take their advice. Students of political economy must understand why.

Indebtedness, uncertainty, and shocks

Capitalist economies rest on foundations of debt. Borrowing and lending fuel economic growth. In principle, the aggregate financial claims created by the interaction of consumers, producers, savers, and investors in an economy are eminently supportable as long as expected future incomes exceed expected future debt repayments. The same logic applies when once-separated economies become more integrated. Fundamentally, this involves the integration of markets for information.

Since we cannot know the future, expectations of future income flows are always uncertain. When the extent of such uncertainty can be estimated with any degree of precision, it becomes appropriate to speak of risks. Risks can be assessed, mitigated, and managed. Indeed, this is precisely what banks do when they accept deposits from savers, pool the proceeds, and make loans to borrowers. Through such activities, financial claims are generated, priced, and

exchanged. The different time horizons of savers and borrowers are 'mediated'. In the absence of financial intermediaries, the ability of a particular firm, or of a particular country, to invest would be limited to the amount that firm or country could save out of its own resources at any given moment, or out of the resources of others with whom it was itself in direct contact.

Specific financial claims (assets from the point of view of creditors, liabilities from the point of view of debtors) become insupportable all the time. Mistakes are made, misjudgements occur, market conditions change unexpectedly. In the wake of such 'shocks', the expectations of investors shift and a rush to liquidate assets ensues. Debtors and creditors, especially creditors late through the exit door, suffer reductions in their wealth and restraints on their future economic prospects. When national markets are open, insupportable claims multiply and the system as a whole feels the pain. Exchange rates cannot hold, financial asset prices tumble, and a generalized crisis can arise. Credit dries up, investors put their resources into low-risk/low-return instruments, and debtors default.

The history of capitalism is replete with such events, as well as with the efforts of national policy-makers to ameliorate their consequences in the real economy. As Charles Kindleberger put it in the title of a famous book, manias, panics, and crashes seem to be inherent in the market-based system that evolved over time (Kindleberger 1978). Indeed, few close observers deny that modern financial markets are fragile (Lamfalussy 2000). Nevertheless, few participants are prepared to concede that they must necessarily be unstable, or that better alternative non-market mechanisms for broadly-based resource redistribution in complex economic and social systems are feasible. The massive human failures associated with planned economies in the twentieth century are not easy to forget. The policy challenge taken seriously since the 1970s, therefore, has been to mitigate financial market fragility and work incrementally to render an interdependent, market-based system more stable as a whole. Deeper political questions concerning the distributive justice of such a system, especially for those on its margins, have moved up only very recently on the list of associated policy priorities.

Contemporary history highlights two crucial facts when financial markets cross legal and political borders: the probability of crisis increases as information becomes less readily accessible for all market participants, and the problem becomes particularly acute for developing countries. In Barry Eichengreen's words, 'Sharp changes in asset prices—sometimes so sharp as to threaten the stability of the financial system and the economy... are likely to be especially pervasive in developing countries, where the information and contracting environment is least advanced' (Eichengreen 2002: 4).

Deepening financial linkages bring with them unavoidable problems, the solutions to which require collective action. Information asymmetries combine with the political independence of participants to pose problems beyond the capacities of individual states to resolve. Only some kind of collaborative regulation can give participants confidence that those markets will work in the long run to the benefit of all. Early in the twenty-first century, co-operative regulatory structures remained fragile in themselves. Clearly, participants have an interest in working together to ensure systemic stability. But they are also motivated to compete with one another and to care more about local than distant demands for distributive justice. In the structure of contemporary financial markets, the information asymmetries analysed by economists and the power asymmetries analysed by political scientists overlap.

Incidence of international financial crises

Economic historians commonly depict the period 1870 to 1914 as the first to witness the rapid expansion of cross-border financial markets (Flandreau and Zumer 2004). Although few countries were involved, by some measures the scale of international

financial intermediation far exceeded anything that has developed since then. A golden age for only some, the purchase and sale of financial claims to foreigners boomed, albeit only at certain points during this period. So too did defaults, especially around 1875, and again when the world began marching towards what became known as the Great War. In an era when the values of the main currencies were meant to be pegged firmly to one another (recall the discussion in the previous chapter of the gold standard, which itself never worked perfectly), such defaults often translated into bank failures. After 1919, the incidence of banking crises escalated, but so too did currency crises when re-pegged exchange rates would not hold. The disastrous decade that begain in 1929 was characterized by the dreadful coincidence and global explosion of banking and currency crises (Kindleberger 1973). Figure 8.1 summarizes graphically the frequency of such crises since the emergence of industrial capitalism.

Currency crises continued to plague the system that eventually emerged from the ashes of the Second World War. Efforts by the United States and its victorious allies to ensure internal financial stability did succeed in reducing the incidence of banking crises. But even after 1945 recurrent currency crises strained efforts to restore a stable exchange-rate system reminiscent of the pre-1914 gold standard era. Those efforts failed decisively in the early 1970s, when the link between the world's leading currency and the price of gold was broken decisively. After 1973, banking crises once again became a fact of international economic life; so too did their coincidence with currency crises. As Figure 8.2 shows, such linked crises were especially frequent in the markets of newly industrializing countries.

From the standpoint of governments committed to helping their domestic markets 'emerge' and grow through international interaction, necessary financial resources may be gathered from four main sources: domestic savings, foreign governments, foreign investors, and foreign creditors. A

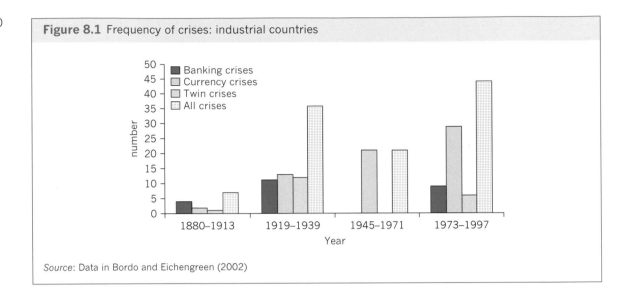

Figure 8.1 Frequency of crises: industrial countries

Source: Data in Bordo and Eichengreen (2002)

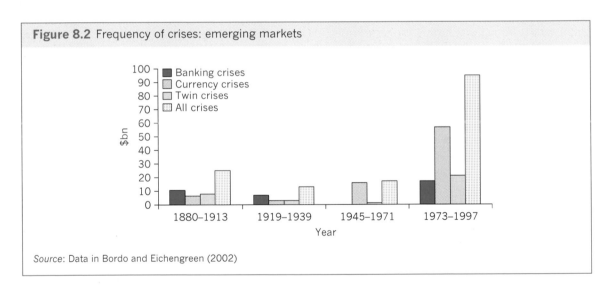

Figure 8.2 Frequency of crises: emerging markets

Source: Data in Bordo and Eichengreen (2002)

rapidly increasing reliance in recent decades on the last of these sources surely had much to do with political preferences. In any event, the dependence on foreign creditors is well established. So too are attendant banking and currency crises. Their repeated occurrence was presaged by the earlier experience of industrial countries themselves.

KEY POINTS

- The most damaging financial crises occur when banking systems and currency markets come under pressure simultaneously.
- In recent years, such crises have occurred with most frequency in emerging-market countries.

The Changing Global Context

From the 1940s to the 1970s, currency crises involving advanced industrial states repeatedly stimed the system and often forced adjustments in exchange-rate pegs. Banking crises certainly did occur in individual countries, but overall restrictions on international capital movements tended to keep their effects localized. In the aftermath of the abandonment of the pegged-rate system among the major currencies and the non-coincidental loosening of capital controls, however, the industrial countries confronted the first great banking crisis of the new era. In 1974, the failure of a German bank, Bankhaus I. D. Herstatt, to honour its foreign exchange contracts had knock-on effects globally, which ultimately caused even the Franklin National Bank of New York to fail as well (Spero 1980). Long memories recalled the collapse of the Credit-Anstalt Bank in Austria in 1931 and the contagion it spread through world markets (Schubert 1992). The post-1945 international economic system as a whole, however, did not revert to depression, and lessons for avoiding systemic crises were certainly learned in the years after the Bretton Woods exchange-rate system collapsed. We shall return to them later in the chapter.

In the 1980s, coincident banking and currency crises in emerging markets raised the most pressing concerns for the system. Fuelling the emergence of these markets, especially in such regions as Central and South America and East Asia, were rising international capital flows. Banks based in advanced industrial countries rapidly expanded their international lending operations throughout the 1970s, multinational corporations diversified their investment activities, and gradually individual investors in the richer countries expanded their appetites and capacities for buying bonds and other financial instruments issued by governments and firms in developing countries. Some associated capital flows were trade-related, some investment-related,

and some simply reflected the kinds of financial speculation inherent in a capitalist system now becoming more global.

Movement toward financial openness in developing countries

From the 1970s onwards, but most prominently in the late 1980s and early 1990s, industrial countries and countries aspiring to that advanced status moved collectively, not only towards increased openness in their trade-related current accounts but also in their investment-related capital accounts. In essence, they rendered more interdependent an ever-wider range of their still nationally regulated financial markets, and opened themselves up to less regulated financial markets now imaginatively labelled 'off-shore' (Palan 2003). Until the crisis years of the late 1990s, rising volumes of capital flowed through these markets to developing countries that were deemed creditworthy. Figures 8.3, 8.4, and 8.5 depict this change over time, as well as the dramatic reversal after 1997.

The explosion of international financial intermediation after the 1980s, and the rising incidence of financial crises with cross-border effect were obviously related. For policy makers, the relevant questions were what they have always been: when real economic growth rates were sought in excess of those capable of being generated by domestic savings, how were the benefits and costs of financial openness to be distributed?

Opportunities and costs of openness

In principle, inward flows of privately owned capital make it possible for real economies to grow more rapidly than if they rely solely on domestic resources. In practice, the extra costs associated with crisis-induced capital outflows, bank bailouts,

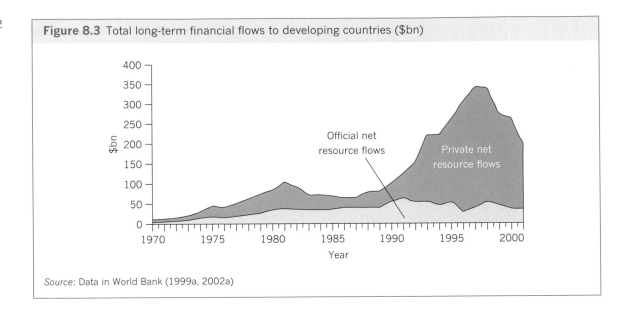

Figure 8.3 Total long-term financial flows to developing countries ($bn)

Source: Data in World Bank (1999a, 2002a)

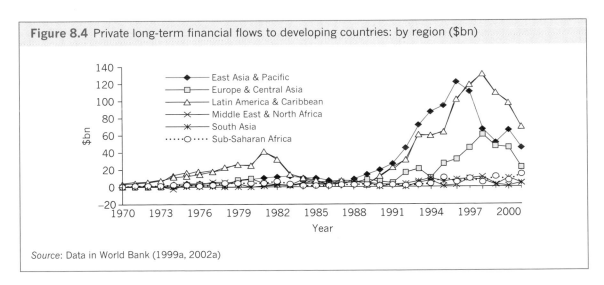

Figure 8.4 Private long-term financial flows to developing countries: by region ($bn)

Source: Data in World Bank (1999a, 2002a)

and the lost confidence of investors occasionally threatens to undermine real economies, set back the process of industrialization, and disrupt underlying political and social orders. Figure 8.6 offers an indication of the historical costs of currency crises in terms of lost economic output.

Behind such statistical measures lies a human story repeated time after time in recent history. The costs of financial crises often include unemployment, increasing taxes, personal despair and hopelessness, family breakdown, and rising crime rates. In emerging markets, their public face can culminate in deepening poverty, *coups d'état*, and military dictatorship. Who would deny that it is best to avoid such outcomes? But their very possibility is inherent in the macro-policy choices both leading states and those aspiring to their level of prosperity made in the post-1945 period. With the

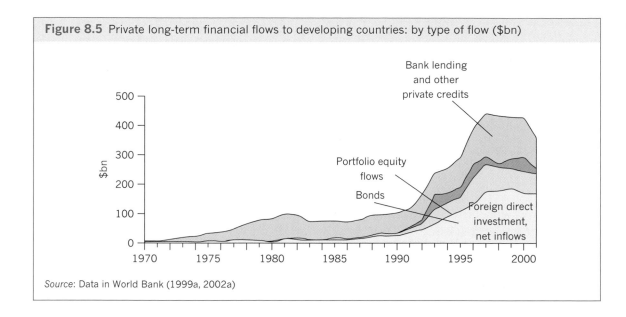

Figure 8.5 Private long-term financial flows to developing countries: by type of flow ($bn)

Source: Data in World Bank (1999a, 2002a)

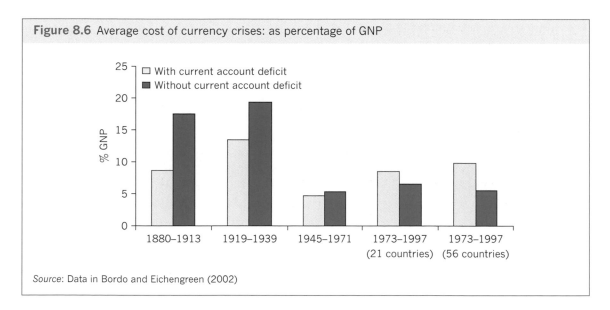

Figure 8.6 Average cost of currency crises: as percentage of GNP

Source: Data in Bordo and Eichengreen (2002)

final collapse in 1989 of the only alternative system once attractive to some—that of state socialism and central planning—financial openness apparently marked the only feasible road to the future. To be sure, nevertheless, all but the most dependent states retained the ability to determine the speed with which they went down that road, and all but the weakest retained levers of power sufficient to influence the internal distribution of the benefits and costs incurred by doing so.

National policy reform, international system consequences

In essence, by the 1980s it had become clear that states constituting the international economy had moved away collectively from one set of policy trade-offs and towards another. Immediately after the Second World War, they sought to reconcile their newfound desire for exchange-rate stability with their interest in maintaining independent monetary policies. Both as a matter of logic and of policy, they therefore had to tolerate limits on inward and outward capital flows—the 'unholy trinity' idea discussed by Helleiner in Chapter 7 in this volume (Mundell 1963). Four decades later, their priorities had changed. Now, capital mobility and monetary autonomy were privileged, and they were willing to tolerate floating exchange rates as well as a degree of volatility in their expanding financial markets (Obstfeld and Taylor 2004).

In the 1970s, certainly, some developing countries sought to limit the future role of privately owned international capital, and they demanded a new international economic order, which would have greatly expanded state interference in international markets (Krasner 1985). By the 1980s, most of them had abandoned such a quest, a phenomenon referred to by one close observer as a 'silent revolution' (Boughton 2001). Few, however, joined the leading states in embracing a clearer trade-off between financial openness, monetary independence, and exchange-rate stability. In the latter regard, the painful earlier experience of leading states in attempting to hold on to exchange-rate pegs would be repeated. So too would be the experience of bank failures.

Over time, exchange rates measure the relative price levels across economies that are linked together by trade and investment. They can, however, also gyrate wildly in the face of speculative pressures or unanticipated economic or political shocks. As real economies become more open to trade and foreign investment, such volatility can be difficult to manage, both economically and politically. In the short run, exporters, importers, and investors may be able to hedge their foreign exposures, but this is costly and becomes more problematic as time horizons expand. Standard, if still disputed, economic theory suggests that the way to ameliorate excessive currency volatility is to co-ordinate a range of

national monetary and fiscal policies. Industrialized economies demonstrated only intermittent interest in doing so after the move to floating exchange rates, despite rhetorical expressions to the contrary at successive high-profile meetings of the G7/8 and other collaborative bodies (Baker 2006). They have instead left it to financial markets to attempt to impose whatever level of fiscal and monetary discipline was necessary to stabilize the system as a whole. In practice, the stronger the country—that is, the more it was capable of generating and retaining its own domestic savings and/or the more it was capable of attracting foreign capital flows despite its pursuit of fiscal and monetary policies that might, in principle, be expected to have the opposite consequence—the lower such disciplinary effects turned out to be. In any event, through such macro-policy choices, industrialized economies constructed a system that relied on the possibility of sharp reversals in capital flows to force on themselves and others that modicum of co-ordination required for economic interdependence to deepen.

To be sure, as Helleiner noted in the previous chapter, some states sought to restore a degree of exchange-rate stability for themselves by limiting their own monetary independence within regional or bilateral arrangements. The member states of the Economic and Monetary Union in Europe took such a collective choice to its limit. But even they subsequently gave priority to financial openness and regional monetary autonomy over the stability of the exchange rate between the euro and other major currencies. By the 1980s, again, the system as a whole was relying increasingly on open financial markets to encourage the cross-border adjustments entailed by international economic interaction.

In other words, having moved to an international economic system based on flexible exchange rates among the major currencies, industrialized economies found that financial market liberalization represented a less politically costly alternative than any other for the management of economic interdependence. They did not forswear capital controls under any circumstances. But there gradually emerged a normative preference against anything other than temporary measures to limit international capital movements (Abdelal 2007).

Throughout the 1980s and early 1990s, despite prominent banking and currency crises in Mexico and other emerging markets, newly industrializing and many developing countries moved towards liberalization of their capital accounts. As official sources of development assistance dwindled relative to other capital flows, the implicit systemic promise was that emerging markets could attract the capital that they needed through ever more open private capital markets.

Nevertheless, even at the time of writing, capital flows continue to encounter friction at national borders. It is risky and not cost-free to move money outside the national market where it originates. In other words, there has yet to arise a truly global financial market characterized by perfect capital mobility (see the discussion in Hay's Chapter 10 in this volume). Despite a general trend towards capital market liberalization, no binding international treaty on financial flows analogous to that governing trade flows ever emerged to codify an underlying political understanding on the trade-offs implied by financial openness. The closest multilateral instrument was the OECD Code of Liberalization of Capital Movements, which is limited in its membership, scope, and capacity to encourage compliance. Also never rising above the level of commonly shared understanding was the idea that private markets on their own would provide adequate financing for development if countries simply maintained sound macroeconomic policies. As the decade of the 1990s progressed, that very idea was to be sorely tested.

The Asian financial crises of the late 1990s highlighted the reasons why states did not codify their tacit agreement to move towards financial openness after the Bretton Woods system broke down, and why policy makers in some developing countries came once again to doubt that a new system dominated by private firms and financiers based in rich countries would ultimately serve their interests. Before the crises hit, some prominent voices were advocating an explicit amendment of the Articles of Agreement of the International Monetary Fund to extend the Fund's jurisdiction (and by implication, an underlying preference for openness) from short-term balance-of-payments issues to long-term policies governing inward and outward capital movements. After Malaysia summarily reinstated capital controls in response to its own crisis, and Chile experimented throughout the 1990s with sophisticated measures to restrain the inflow of short-term capital, debate on the proposition ceased. At the same time, a new chapter in a long-running policy debate on how best to deal with currency and banking crises opened. It is worth reviewing in some detail the chain of events set off by developments in Thailand, as they demonstrated vividly the risks associated with financial openness (see Box 8.2).

Political sovereignty and economic interdependence

During periods of euphoria in financial markets, participants tend to forget historical lessons. When a fund manager is sitting on a portfolio earning 5 per cent per annum, it is difficult to watch colleagues earning 150 per cent. Watching too long may even cost that manager his or her job. But only the most ideological of participants in global markets choose to ignore the past entirely. The governments of industrialized economies have surely not suffered from collective amnesia in the contemporary period.

The reluctance of these governments to embrace unambiguously the principle that capital had an inviolable legal right to cross borders, and their evident reluctance to designate clearly an international overseer for markets now ever more tightly linked together, is telling. The architects of the post-1973 order could not easily balance emergent market facts with political realities. They could not lodge ultimate political authority over international capital markets at the level where it logically belongs. No international agency has been authorized to regulate or supervise international capital

BOX 8.2

The Global Financial Panic of the Late 1990s

In the mid-1990s, interest rates fell and stock markets boomed in North America and Western Europe. Banks and portfolio investors, including rapidly expanding mutual funds and so-called 'hedge' funds that pooled the capital of institutional and wealthy investors, increasingly looked abroad for higher returns. But with those higher returns came higher risks.

At the same time, Japanese banks, confronting stagnant demand in a slumping home market, sought the higher earnings promised in neighbouring countries. Both public sector and private sector borrowers in emerging markets suddenly found new and ready sources of funds, and they borrowed heavily. Since interest rates were especially low on short-term debt, they were confident that they would be able to refinance their obligations easily when they came due.

In Thailand, much of this new debt was denominated in the local currency, the baht, which the Thai government valued at a pegged, not floating, rate. By buying Thai securities or making loans denominated in Thai baht, investors and creditors, in essence, bet that the baht would hold its value at least until they had a chance to sell their investments or have their loans repaid. Early in 1997, however, Japanese banks, which then held about half of the country's foreign debt, began to lose confidence in the ability of Thailand to defend its exchange rate. They sought to reduce their exposures there as well as in a number of neighbouring countries, where they also held large portfolios of short-term loans. Their pull-back prompted a regional liquidity crunch. Other creditors and investors, both domestic and foreign, fearing losses as local currencies came under pressure, headed for the exits. Fears of a devaluation of the Thai baht became self-fulfilling, while other Asian nations, whose industries competed to sell similar goods to the same foreign markets, needed to defend their competitive edges by allowing their own currencies to depreciate.

Capital suddenly flew out of South Korea, Indonesia, and Malaysia, a phenomenon now exacerbated by the panicked reactions of hedge fund investors back in North America and Europe. Just as a bank hit by a run of depositors is forced to raise case hurriedly by calling in loans, these hedge funds had to meet demands for withdrawals by liquidating their assets. As their Thai assets declined in redeemable value, they withdrew what they could as quickly as possible from their Korean, Malaysian, Indonesian, and even Hong Kong and Singapore portfolios. The overall result was as predictable as it was painful. **Liquidity** dried up across the region, and the solvency of local institutions recently considered sound was called into question.

The government of Malaysia tried to stem the panic by doing what foreign investors had come to consider unthinkable; it risked its future ability to re-enter global markets by imposing capital controls to forbid the repatriation of what its prime minister labelled the immoral gains of speculators. Others took the more conventional route of calling in the IMF to provide emergency funding as a stop-gap measure until the panic subsided. Borrowing from the Fund and other multilateral agencies came, as usual, with conditions attached, but in this situation the terms were particularly controversial. Whereas borrowing countries saw themselves struggling against a short-term problem, the Fund began to insist on more fundamental kinds of reform designed to make East Asian markets, including financial markets, more open and transparent. Talk of neo-imperialism by Western powers became commonplace as national incomes fell across the region, imports declined, and a cut-throat competition to maintain export industries ensued.

In the middle of the East Asian debacle, Russia's post-1991 experiment with frontier capitalism crashed into a wall of unsustainable foreign debt. In retrospect, it certainly seems that many foreign investors had unwisely discounted the possibility that Russia's new class of tycoons would take careful measures to spirit their own capital out of the country. By the summer of 1998, even a massive IMF loan could not bolster confidence in the value of the rouble. It also could not attract back private Russian capital invested in safe Western investments, nor could it sustain the confidence of the American and European investors in 'emerging market' funds that had recently and aggressively bought what turned out to be extremely risky securities backed by the Russian government. When the government defaulted in August and devalued the rouble, seismic shocks were immediately felt at the core of the world's financial system. Stock markets plummeted around the world. Fearing that other emerging markets would follow Russia, panicked financiers pulled vast amounts of capital out of Mexico, Brazil, Argentina, and elsewhere.

In September, Long-Term Capital Management (LTCM), a particularly prominent and highly leveraged American hedge fund with little direct exposure in emerging markets, found its previously extremely successful investment strategies wrecked as the crisis spread unexpectedly from Asia to Russia (Lowenstein 2001). While the consensus view among American financial market regulators would ordinarily have been to let such an entity bear the brunt of its mistakes, and even to fail, panic had by then gripped Wall Street itself. The Federal Reserve encouraged a consortium of LTCM's creditors to take over the firm's books, gradually unwind its bad bets, and replace its management. No one doubted that the full faith and credit of the US government would be available if required, but in the end this more limited emergency operation succeeded, and calm gradually returned to the markets of industrial countries. It would take longer for confidence to be restored in emerging markets. When it was, many countries, especially in Asia, began building up their own monetary reserves and creating regional mechanisms for emergency financing that promised to attenuate the future influence of US-led institutions such as the IMF.

flows—not the International Monetary Fund, not the World Bank, and not the Bank for International Settlements. None has been provided with the resources necessary to act as true lender-of-last-resort. States have instead opted to allow the financial institutions they themselves continue to license and supervise to expand their international operations on the understanding that national regulators would co-ordinate their supervisory policies and emergency practices informally to the necessary extent. In times of confidence-withering crises, who would ultimately be responsible for bailing out financial institutions confronting the prospect of collapse? In the wake of actual financial crises in the decades following the breakdown of the Bretton Woods exchange-rate system, the answer became increasingly clear. The basic operating principle remains 'home country control' (Kapstein 1994). Lender-of-last-resort facilities remain under the exclusive purview of individual states themselves. At most, pre-emptive or precautionary credit can be made available by states collectively, perhaps through treaty-based intergovernmental organizations such as the International Monetary Fund, perhaps through less formal regional understandings and bilateral reserve-swapping arrangements (Henning 2002). But no state has shown itself willing to delegate ultimate financial responsibility to any supranational institution.

Perhaps there was a moment in time, just after the Second World War, when one could sense a window opening on a world where states would delegate a coherent piece of their monetary, if not fiscal, sovereignty to a technical agency with a binding, enforceable mandate. By 1973, however, it was difficult to argue with the proposition that the final abandonment of the Bretton Woods exchange-rate system indicated that the co-ordination of national fiscal and monetary policies could only be voluntary and would probably be episodic. How, then, could a reliable foundation for globalizing capitalism be constructed? If deeper financial interdependence remained a collective goal even as fiscal and monetary sovereignty remained sacrosanct, as it apparently did, then those same states confronted the logically alternative necessity of co-ordinating their more technical policies and instruments governing financial markets. From the Mexican debt crisis of 1981 to the Asian crisis of 1997, the actions of states individually and collectively indicated clearly that they understood this logic. That their progress was not smooth or always far-sighted should surprise no one familiar with the way most policies are constructed in democracies, the form of government shared in the states that built the world economy after 1973. The co-ordination of national policies is difficult in the best of times. The prospect of future systemic gains is, in truth, not often a successful motivator (see Aggarwal and Dupont, Chapter 3 in this volume). As an empirical proposition demonstrated time and again since 1973, the prospect of imminent national and systemic losses seems a much more reliable motivator of necessary policy co-ordination (Aggarwal 1996).

Financial crises and the reactions of governmental authorities define the key dynamic. In short, the policy domain for serious collective action in the post-1973 era has necessarily taken in a broadening range of measures required for reducing but never entirely eliminating the chance that future cross-border financial crises will occur. At the same time, each new crisis, now including those in emerging markets, has led to the construction of new collaborative techniques for handling emergencies made inevitable by the persistent reluctance of state authorities to give up their political independence

entirely. Outside of the idiosyncratic regional context of Europe, where the establishment of the Eurozone suggests more ambitious political objectives, these efforts may be summarized under the rubrics of crisis prevention and crisis management.

KEY POINTS

- Financial crises generated policy innovations inside industrial states, and the pattern is repeating itself in many emerging-market nations.

- Sovereignty remains an important value in a globalizing economy.

- Collaborative efforts, often through international institutions, can assist developing countries as they open their financial markets.

Crisis Prevention

No modern financial market exists for long without common standards understood by all participants. At the most basic level, financial information must be expressed in an understandable form. Accounting, auditing, and licensing rules form the bedrock. In all but the most limited local markets, or in all but the most libertarian utopias, such rules have not been generated spontaneously. Some actor must provide the collective goods of standard setting, adjudication, reform, and, ultimately, enforcement. Even illegal markets, if they are to persist, require someone to provide those minimal requirements. In legal markets, by definition, such collective goods are provided by the final maker of binding laws. To be sure, ultimate authorities can and do delegate the responsibility to define and promote technical standards in many of the world's financial markets. But all contemporary markets that are legal rest on standards and enforcement procedures associated with governmental authority in

one form or another. Even central banks that we now conventionally label 'independent', such as the European Central Bank, derive their authority from constitutional arrangements or inter-state treaties.

Defining and defending public interests

Moments of financial crisis have tested this reasoning, even in recent times. International financial crises expose jurisdictional ambiguities and overlaps. But they are typically followed by new preventive measures, supported directly or indirectly by political authorities. They have not, however, yet been followed by the establishment of an unambiguous global standard setter or a global agency capable of final enforcement. The frontier of markets integrating themselves across political and legal boundaries therefore remains characterized in the final analysis by intergovernmental bodies charged with negotiating common cross-border understandings on appropriate standards and their enforcement (Bryant 2003). This is not to suggest that organizations created by private sector actors have been absent. For example, standard-setting bodies set up by accounting and other types of firms or private associations are increasingly common. In the United States, the United Kingdom, and elsewhere, governments have often been willing to let market participants attempt to reach agreement among themselves on best practices. When such attempts fail and markets are threatened with disruption, however, governments and central banks come out of the shadows.

Contemplating the ever-present possibility that a bank it regulated could fail and thereby compromise the financial system as a whole (called systemic risk), governments retained the ability either to dip into national treasuries to save it, or to allow it to be liquidated in an orderly fashion. As banks expanded their international operations, regulators had necessarily to begin working with their foreign counterparts on common standards for prudential supervision and common approaches to the management of emergencies. Just as a common military defence among allies entails negotiating common understandings on burden sharing, so international bank regulation also rests on the negotiation of such standards.

But regulated banks often bear the costs associated with prudential supervision. Over time, other kinds of financial intermediaries, such as investment funds and trust companies, found ways to provide analogous services more cheaply. With the emergence of lightly regulated non-bank financial institutions in domestic and international markets in the 1960s and 1970s, the same logic of international collaboration on standard-setting and enforcement spread beyond the banking sector. The provision of insurance, stock underwriting and sales, and pooled investing services had by the 1990s clearly become global businesses. To some extent, most firms in these businesses remained supervised in some sense in their home markets,

but the governmental agencies licensing and overseeing them often expressly tried to limit their own responsibility for bailing them out in an emergency. That is, their licensing authorities attempted to limit the risk that those firms would make imprudent judgements and take excessive risks in the knowledge that they would not be allowed to fail. As in the banking sector, though, setting standards, defining enforcement responsibilities, and preventing official liabilities became more complicated as functional and geographic barriers were allowed to erode throughout the post-1970s era. Drawing a clear dividing line between public interests and private risks would rarely be a straightforward task any more.

Cross-national co-ordination on regulatory policies

Well into the 1980s, the main arenas within which financial regulators sought to co-ordinate their standard-setting and enforcement activities were easy to identify. Bilateral negotiations between national regulators and central banks were nothing new. After the fallout from the Herstatt failure spread globally through foreign exchange markets, such interaction became multilateralized through a central bankers' club organized under the institutional auspices of the Bank for International Settlements (see Box 8.3 on page 261). The Basel Committee on Banking Supervision technically reports to the governors of the world's leading central banks (the so-called G10, which in fact now includes more than ten members), but it continues to be the key standard-setting forum for the largest financial institutions operating across national borders, institutions that still typically have a bank at the core of complicated conglomerate structures. The prevention of future international financial crises defines the core mandate of the Basel Committee. This has led it to experiment with protocols for minimum standards for back-up capital reserves to be held by banks, and to work with other national and regional bodies to bolster the transparency and effectiveness of prudential supervision beyond the narrowly defined banking sector. In 2006, the most extensive and detailed effort to ensure capital adequacy came in an accord commonly dubbed Basel II. Under its terms, international lenders were encouraged to bring sophisticated risk-management techniques into the core of their internal decision-making procedures. The fact that this seemed to provide a new source of competitive advantage for the largest money-centre banks was not the only controversy engendered by the new accord, and work immediately began on 'Basel III'. Over time, the work of the Basel Committee has come to be complemented and supplemented by other formal or informal intergovernmental bodies. It has also, quite intentionally, stimulated voluntary efforts by private-sector groups such as the Washington-based Institute of International Finance to foster greater prudence and self-discipline by financial intermediaries.

To the extent it can be labelled a coherent strategy, the efforts of leading states to prevent systemic financial collapse in recent decades have obviously been characterized by incremental institution building. They have favoured technical policy co-ordination to the extent necessary to ensure the deepening integration of stable, not risk-free, financial markets but not necessarily beyond that. Their success in systemic crisis prevention must be assessed against the counterfactual standard suggested in the famous Sherlock Holmes story that turns on the dog that did not bark.

In such a light, it would be hard to argue that the main architects of today's international capital markets have not made progress. In various national and regional crises, from the Herstatt crisis to the Mexican and Latin American debt crises of the 1980s, and the Asian and Russian crises of the 1990s, systemic meltdown did not occur. Despite near misses, when expectations of disaster at the core of the system were perceived by policy-makers to be on the verge of self-fulfilment, it seems unlikely that blind, dumb luck accounts entirely for the persistence of the larger strategic idea of deepening international financial interdependence. A cynic might contend that stabilizing the core of the system—the

New York–London–Frankfurt–Paris–Tokyo international payments, settlement, and investment nexus—is part of an implicit project that drains financial resources from the rest of the world. Such a view was certainly suggested by the pull-back of private capital from emerging markets after the Asian crisis. That flow soon reversed itself in the most promising markets, and contemporary work programmes of the Basel Committee, the IMF, the World Bank, and other international organizations can be interpreted more generously as embodying the attempts of leading states to extend the project of global financial market construction safely beyond the core. Real resources were certainly being put into efforts to help establish reliable supervisory standards and instruments in a widening range of developing countries, often through expanding technical assistance by international organizations. Future market facts will ultimately tell the tale, for capital should in theory flow reliably over the long term from capital-rich areas of the world, where returns should be relatively low, to capital-poor areas, where returns should be relatively high. In the aggregate, that was simply not happening in the early years of the twenty-first century.

Broader policy context

Note, again, a fundamentally related policy arena where leading states have invested considerable rhetorical energy, and occasionally expended serious political capital—namely the arena of macroeconomic policy. It is widely accepted, and for good reason, that sound fiscal and monetary policies in the states at the core of the world economy are required for international financial integration to proceed in a constructive manner Steady, sustainable growth in real economies, low inflation, and spreading prosperity defines an objective much like motherhood. Everyone favours it, no one objects to it, and the principles supporting it are impeccable. The relevant political question, however, has remained the same since 1973. How can co-operative efforts to achieve fiscal and monetary stability be encouraged in the absence of some overarching agreement on an economic constraint, such as could theoretically be provided by a binding commitment to stable exchange rates? After 1973, leading states conceded that such a commitment could not be maintained; the most they could agree upon was a commitment to 'a stable system of exchange rates' facilitated by 'firm surveillance' by the International Monetary Fund (James 1995, 1996; Pauly 1997). (In the 1990s, the member states of the Economic and Monetary Union in Europe went further among themselves by constructing a common currency and a common monetary policy, but, significantly, not a common fiscal policy.)

Beyond technical measures designed to prevent crises in markets assumed to be functioning more smoothly over time, nothing could guarantee 'sound' monetary and fiscal policies in industrialized economies. A system conducive to mutually beneficial financial interdependence tending in the direction of deeper and deeper cross-border integration continues to rest on the self-discipline and voluntary policy co-ordination of the states themselves. Properly functioning financial markets can,

at most, send signals that might encourage such self-discipline. As in the past, those markets are shaped by collective perceptions of the ability of states to manage their debt burdens (Flandreau and Zumer 2004). Fiscal and current account deficits that cannot easily be financed internally will have to be financed externally at higher and higher real interest rates, which will eventually force adjustment.

This was the essence of what came to be called the **Washington Consensus** during the 1990s: national authorities should design their policies in such a way as to stimulate develop and growth without excessive price inflation, to balance their fiscal accounts over a cycle, to keep external accounts within readily financeable bounds, to deepen their internal financial markets, and to open their markets for goods and services, and eventually for all forms of private capital investment. Despite the scepticism elicited by each new financial crisis, it remains in place and informs the work of an ever-widening array of intergovernmental and private sector forums, where the standard-setting, crisis prevention, and surveillance work embodied in the post-1973 IMF can be complemented (Cutler *et al.* 1999) (see Box 8.3).

BOX 8.3

Institutions for Collaboration on International Financial Policies and Practices

International Monetary Fund Designed at the Bretton Woods Conference, July 1944. (For details on its subsequent evolution, see this chapter and Helleiner, Chapter 7 in this volume.)

International Bank for Reconstruction and Development (World Bank) Also created originally at Bretton Woods (see Wade, Chapter 12, and Thomas, Chapter 13, in this volume.)

Bank for International Settlements Established in 1930 to oversee Germany's war reparation payments. After the Second World War, this Basel, Switzerland-based institution assisted European governments in their monetary and financial interactions. After the 1960s, its role in facilitating a multilateral payments system in Europe made it an obvious venue for intensifying dialogue among central bankers, now

including the United States and other non-European countries, on a broad range of regulatory and supervisory issues. Today, the BIS provides a meeting venue and secretariat for several collaborative committees, including the Basel Committee of Banking Supervision that promotes common understandings on risk management and capital adequacy for banks operating internationally.

International Organization of Securities Commissions With a secretariat based in Montreal, Canada, IOSCO sponsors conferences and other linkages among the regulators of national stock and other securities markets. Designed to facilitate the sharing of information and best practices, it developed during the 1970s as buyers and sellers of securities increasingly moved their funds across national borders.

International Association of Insurance Supervisors Established in 1992 to encourage co-operation among regulators and supervisors of insurance companies. Since 1998, its secretariat has been housed in Basel, Switzerland, where it receives technical assistance from the BIS.

International Accounting Standards Board and **International Federation of Accountants** Private sector bodies organized by professional accounting associations to encourage international standardization of accounting principles and auditing practices. Activities intensified during the 1970s; came to prominence in the 1990s after a series of accounting scandals in the United States and other major markets.

United Nations Various UN commissions, agencies, and departments, such as the Department of Economic and Social Affairs in the New York-based secretariat, have mandates to review international financial developments and seek to promote understanding among member states on issues of equity and efficiency in the global economy. In the 1970s, the UN was a primary venue for debate on demands from developing countries for a 'New International Economic Order'. More recently, its focus has shifted to ensure the availability of adequate financing for developing countries and to promote internationally agreed Millennium Development Goals for poverty reduction and sustainable development (the 'Monterrey Consensus').

G7/G8 Dating back to informal meetings of European finance ministers after the collapse of the Bretton Woods exchange-rate arrangements, regular annual meetings of financial officials and heads of government now occur under this rubric. Originally five, then seven—including the United States, France, the United Kingdom Germany, Japan, Canada, and Italy—now routinely includes Russia and representatives from the European Union. Meetings often involve the confidential sharing of information on financial and economic policies. Personal relationships developed and reinforced by this contact are often seen to be useful when it comes to co-ordinating national policies rapidly in the face of international financial crises. There is no secretariat.

Organization for Economic Co-operation and Development Evolved out of post-Second World War efforts to facilitate the use of **Marshall Plan** resources. Often now considered a think-tank for industrial countries contemplating various forms of economic policy co-ordination.

Financial Action Task Force Initiated at the 1989 summit meeting of the G7 to examine measures to combat money laundering. A small secretariat based in the OECD, but not technically part of that organization, co-ordinates national efforts. Its mandate was expanded after 11 September 2001, and the Task Force now co-ordinates a range of work programmes designed to disrupt international networks involved in the financing of terrorism.

Joint Forum on Financial Conglomerates An effort spawned after 1996 by the Basel Committee of Bank Supervisors, IOSCO, and IAIS to promote common understandings on the regulation of private financial institutions increasingly bringing banking, securities underwriting, and insurance activities under one corporate roof.

Financial Stability Forum Following the international financial crises of the late 1990s, the G7 finance ministers and central bank governors sought to bring together national financial regulators from a wide range of countries hosting important international financial centres, together with international organizations involved in financial policy matters. The FSF began meeting in April 1999; it has a small secretariat based at the BIS.

World Trade Organization Having grown out of the **General Agreement on Tariffs and Trade**, under which national trade policies have been liberalized on a multilateral basis ever since 1948, the WTO now has growing responsibilities for trade in various services, including a widening range of financial services (see Winham, Chapter 5 in this volume).

Regional Development Banks With local mandates akin to the global development mandate of the World Bank, these multilateral organizations are now involved in providing technical advice for financial market deepening, regulation, and supervision in Africa, Latin America, East Asia, Eastern Europe, and Central Europe.

Chiang Mai Initiative In the wake of the Asian financial crisis of 1997—8, East Asian states began discussions aimed at facilitating greater regional monetary co-operation. Beginning in 1999, a series of bilateral reserve-swapping facilities began to be arranged. Under crisis conditions, usable reserves would thereby be bolstered and deployed to defend exchange rates and stabilize financial markets. Most country-to-country agreements did not aim entirely to avoid extra-regional engagement, for large drawings were typically conditioned on the existence of adjustment programmes supervised by the IMF. The Initiative, however, is commonly viewed as reflecting residual distrust of the systemic leadership of the United States and weakening international solidarity.

Capital controls

The Washington Consensus notwithstanding, political economists remind us that one other policy instrument remains in the arsenal of states seeking to prevent financial crises from spilling over into their markets: the unilateral instrument of capital controls. In a world of globalizing finance, intentionally constructed by national authorities, circumstances can and do arise where the perceived costs of ideological consistency exceed the perceived benefits. In the post-1973 system, capital controls were, with good empirical evidence, depicted as increasingly ineffective. For industrialized countries, they were indeed obsolescent, if never entirely obsolete (Goodman and Pauly 1993). They became more difficult to enforce, easier to evade, disruptive to long-term investment, and susceptible to political corruption. Nevertheless, individual states continue to experiment with more sophisticated measures to manage their currencies, attract desired capital flows (like loans and investments facilitating production and trade), and discourage unwanted flows (like speculative purchases of currencies in the expectation of quick gains).

Emerging markets tend to be governed by systems still incapable of the more subtle forms of capital-influencing policies. In the late 1990s, even observers inclined to see all overt capital controls as apostasy and to predict long-term deleterious effects from the undermining of investor confidence, paid careful attention to tax policies adopted by Chile on short-term capital inflows designed to moderate speculative activity. Malaysia went even further by intervening (temporarily) in old-fashioned ways to impede outflows. Controversial as such policies were, and remain, in the short term they can provide breathing space for policy-makers in national systems not yet capable of meeting the prudential, risk-management, and crisis-prevention standards of advanced industrialized countries (Kaplan and Rodrik 2002; Haggard 2000). Still, it did not take long for internal pressures against the retention of such capital controls to build in Chile and Malaysia after crisis conditions eased, nor did external political pressures for re-engagement with globalizing markets let up (Santiso 2006). Given a systemic environment that continues to incline in the direction of expanding the scope for private-sector financing of principal processes of economic adjustment, development, and growth, maintaining a realistic distinction between 'bad' speculation and 'good' investment becomes more difficult all the time. Like advanced industrial states before them, emerging-market states in more halcyon times are focusing less on designing better capital controls and more on appropriately sequencing policy and regulatory reforms. The crises of recent years gave policy-makers and analysts alike a new appreciation of the importance of timing in the opening of financial markets and of the need to adapt general prescriptions to local circumstances.

KEY POINTS

- Since the collapse of the Bretton Woods exchange-rate regime, governments have attempted to co-operate more intensively to prevent financial crises.

- Fundamental macroeconomic policy choices usually condition the flow of capital across national borders, but capital flight can sometimes occur unexpectedly.

- Policy co-ordination to reduce the chances that a localized financial crisis will spread has often involved talk about joint moves in fiscal and monetary policy-making, but more substantive movement to render global markets more stable has occurred in the area of technical collaboration on regulatory and supervisory policies.

Crisis Management

Debt rescheduling and restructuring

When the financial obligations of a business firm become unsustainable given available resources, the classic question is whether the underlying problem is one of illiquidity or insolvency. The distinction is rarely clear-cut in practice, and one problem can easily slide into the other. In the typical case of illiquidity, creditors or investors in the firm might judge that a short-term loan or capital injection will get it past a payments crisis and enable it to find solid footing once again. In the case of insolvency, they would judge that it is no longer a going concern, and that further lending would be worse than useless. One of two options might then be chosen. The firm could be taken over by its creditors and its balance sheet reorganized in an attempt to re-create some kind of viable business, or the firm's assets could be liquidated to retire as many of its liabilities as possible before finally closing its doors. In advanced capitalist systems, national bankruptcy laws exist to guide these procedures, and courts are often required to make the ultimate decisions. If Schumpeter was right and processes of creative destruction are the essence of modern capitalism, national governments use bankruptcy to clear their economic systems and enable those processes to repeat themselves. In the end, they no longer send failed entrepreneurs to debtors' prison but instead give them another chance.

Countries facing financial crises in an interdependent system are in a somewhat analogous position to a firm unable to meet its obligations. Aggregate debts become unsustainable, creditors demand repayment, and the resources available to settle accounts deteriorate in value. The national balance sheet requires adjustment. Crisis conditions may be generated by government overspending, by excessive imports, or by the building up of private-sector debt that cannot be financed domestically.

Any of these situations might motivate the government to increase the rate of production of its monetary printing press. Inflation would normally be the consequence, and if the fundamental problem is one of temporary illiquidity this might provide the necessary space for internal adjustments to occur. If much of a country's debt is owed to foreigners and is denominated in foreign currency, however, such a policy may quickly deepen the problem and easily turn it into one akin to the insolvency of a business firm. Inflation in the local currency by definition pushes up the value of foreign currency liabilities. Expecting further declines in the purchasing power of the local currency, domestic as well as foreign creditors and investors rush to preserve their capital, and even to get it out of the country. A deteriorating real exchange rate makes debt repayment more costly, imported goods required to facilitate revenue-generating production become more expensive, creditors and investors in future production lose confidence. The debtor government can default on its loans, or try to allow private firms under its purview to default with impunity, but then it risks cutting its economy off from future capital inflows that have no domestic substitute. The country becomes caught in the downward, vicious economic syndrome of deflation and depression. The situation in Argentina in 2001 provided a vivid example few emerging-market nations found attractive.

Obviously missing in such a scenario is a mechanism for the orderly bankruptcy of a national economy. Absent is a lender-of-last-resort, internationally agreed liquidation procedures, and a final court to replace managers and supervise the forced adjustment of the national balance sheet. This is, of course, no accident. In the conceptual extreme, the sovereignty of a state implies the absolute right both to resort to war and to default on debts. As a classic realist might argue, the ability in practice to claim such a right is in the final analysis a function of the raw power a state has in its possession to enforce its decision. In the real world, the sovereignty of particular states is compromised all the time (Krasner 1999). Unilateral defaults, payment moratoria, or standstills can be, and often are, declared by debtors. On the other hand, national assets can sometimes be seized unilaterally by aggrieved creditors.

The architects of the post-1945 system deemed financial crisis and economic uncertainty to be the handmaidens of war. At Bretton Woods, therefore, they took the first steps in designing mechanisms that would limit the extent to which sovereign participants in the system would find themselves pushed to default on their debts. Time and again, from 1945 up to the present day, the main creditor states and the private financial institutions they license and regulate found themselves designing and redesigning substitutes for gunboat diplomacy, namely programmes that provide certain debtor states with the functional equivalent of last-resort lending facilities or of debt-restructuring services loosely analogous to those found in domestic bankruptcy courts. Ad hoc debt reschedulings and restructurings have been common since the 1980s. International banks as well as official agencies providing export credits informally organized themselves into negotiating groups (the so-called London Club and Paris Club, respectively) to manage such arrangements. Frequently, however, the threat of default has drawn attention from the creditor governments themselves.

The rise of emerging markets and their special needs

In the early post-war decades, the main economic imbalances capable of derailing the system as a whole occurred in industrial countries. They typically manifested themselves as currency crises (often when governments sought to defend the par value of their currencies while running substantial trade deficits), so it was no coincidence that the International Monetary Fund was usually enlisted either to help resolve them or retroactively to bless new currency pegs or unorthodox financial arrangements. Ever since the 1980s, as noted above, the main crises capable of derailing the system have occurred in emerging markets, and, more often than not, the IMF has found itself at the centre of efforts to chart that middle path between financial anarchy and global governance. Many other institutions have also been involved in one way or another, but at moments of systemic crisis the main creditor states have shown a repeated inclination to work with and through the IMF and a small group of central banks.

The immediate objective of the IMF at such moments of crisis is to help break the psychology of fear and mistrust among its members and in the markets. Its ultimate mission, however, is to assist in stabilizing the financial underpinnings necessary for real national economies to become more deeply interdependent and more reliably prosperous through expanded trade. That the IMF was not dissolved after 1973 reflected much more than bureaucratic inertia. Most importantly, the Fund's balance of payments financing facilities, which had grown over time in both size and flexibility, as well as its ability to attach policy conditions to the use of such facilities, proved to be extremely convenient to its major member states. This was demonstrated whenever an industrial state confronted financial problems capable of disrupting the international economic system or of seriously disturbing regional political stability. During the 1970s and 1980s, such situations arose mainly in the industrializing world, and in particular in Latin America. After 1989, countries in transition from socialism became a focal point and, in the late 1990s, countries as diverse as Indonesia, Russia, and South Korea turned to the Fund for assistance.

In such cases, Fund officials demonstrated to their masters the usefulness of having an arbiter available, one that could at least provide surveillance over the key economic policies of members capable of generating external effects. Also proving itself useful was the Fund's legitimating role as a forum, wherein all member states were represented and had the right to voice opinions and vote on policies. Most importantly, however, the Fund proved handy when financing packages were required by members facing either routine or chronic balance of payments problems.

In retrospect, it is not surprising that the Fund evolved into the central crisis manager for emerging markets in a system that moved over time from one based on the interdependence of national exchange-rate policies and underlying macroeconomic choices, towards one involving the deepening interaction of trade, investment, and financial policies. In this context, the leading states in the system confronted three basic choices every time one country or another found that it could not pay its bills to external customers or service its debts to external creditors:

1. They could do nothing, and risk the crisis spilling over to other countries and perhaps also into their own domestic systems.

2. They could intervene directly by providing adequate financing from their own resources to the troubled country, and work directly with it to address the fundamental causes of the problem.

3. Or they could do the same indirectly, collectively, and more cheaply through the Fund and other collaborative institutions.

In practice, the third option often proved to be the least unattractive of the three, except for cases involving the weakest and most isolated developing countries. For countries whose periodic debt problems were widely perceived as being capable of seriously disrupting the system as a whole, the option of doing nothing, and of thereby letting markets attempt to force necessary adjustments, seldom seemed wise to policy-makers charged with making such a decision. Moreover, the option of exposing their own taxpayers to the unmediated hazards of crisis resolution has typically proved itself to be almost as unpalatable as bearing the political costs of unilaterally trying to impose conditions on recalcitrant debtors. The third option therefore nearly

always found a sufficient number of advocates, in both creditor and debtor countries.

Institutional responses to emerging market crises

Against a changing global financial environment, the International Monetary Fund often eclipses other institutional competitors, an ability that many observers attribute to its close connections with the finance ministries of industrialized economies and, in particular, of the United States. In the best-case scenarios, the Fund can use its own limited resources to permit adjustment to occur gradually; it has the potential to encourage better policies and better risk management in the future by imposing policy conditions that are politically tolerable to members in crisis; it can work with private banks, investment funds, and bondholders to co-ordinate the creditor side of debt restructurings; and it can provide a technical repository for lessons learned in crisis management. In the worst-case scenarios, such as when Russia defaulted in the mid-1990s, and when Argentina did the same at the start of the next decade, the Fund can take on the politically important function of the scapegoat.

The IMF's crisis management role became more obvious as capital account liberalization became a clearer collective policy objective at the international level. In the late 1990s, the challenges this posed for developing countries clarified themselves. Economic development along capitalist lines required sophisticated management; sound, confidence-inducing macroeconomic policy frameworks; and the rational ordering of processes through which real economies were opened to external financial markets. States with shallow tax systems, weak legal systems, poor regulatory structures, and fragile financial systems are likely also to be desperate for capital inflows. Such states tend also to face domestic political constituencies supportive of fixed exchange-rate regimes. Many such states now found themselves pushed and pulled to open their capital markets and make it easier for external creditors to move into them. As some discovered to their regret, however, this implied that foreign banks, and increasingly foreign financial investors with shorter time horizons, could also more easily move out. They discovered too that such movements could be triggered not only by any objectively reasonable loss of confidence by those investors in the integrity of domestic financial institutions or in the value of the national currency; they could be triggered by confidence-sapping shocks originating far away.

John Maynard Keynes once famously drew a telling analogy between the psychology at the heart of financial markets and the classic beauty contest, where one wisely bets not on the contestant one deems most attractive but rather on the contestant one thinks others will consider the most attractive. How much more difficult must it be for developing countries dependent on volatile capital inflows to anticipate the whims of foreign investors, especially if they lack adequate monetary reserves and the wherewithal for sophisticated exchange-rate management? In any case, aside from easy-to-write but hard-to-follow prescriptions for sound macroeconomic policies and deepening internal capital markets, recent developments suggest few alternative sources of financing to accelerate development and growth. According to IMF data, net private capital flows to all emerging-market countries averaged $130 billion per year between 1990 and 1997 and $79 billion per year during the crisis years of 1998 to 2002. In 2005, however, they totalled $254 billion, of which $212 billion came in the form of foreign direct investment. By way of comparison, official flows (aid and other governmental funds) averaged $21 billion between 1990 and 1997, $8 billion between 1998 and 2002, and in fact reversed themselves in 2005, when $139 billion flowed out of emerging-market governments to advanced industrial countries (BIS 2006: 43, table III.4).

A new global architecture?

Key policy debates, not surprisingly, now revolve around the theory and practice of crisis management in emerging markets and around reducing the exposure of the most needy countries to excessively volatile capital flows (Tirole 2002; Eichengreen 2003; Roubini and Setser 2004). After the East Asian crisis, such debates filled library shelves with a myriad proposals for a new global financial architecture.

Beyond the preventive measures discussed in the previous section, proposals for crisis management are conventionally grouped into three main categories: the unilateral, the multilateral, and the supranational (Eichengreen 2002: chs. 3 and 4; Bryant 2003: chs. 8–10). In the first category, both conservative believers in the virtues of unfettered markets and the defenders of absolute sovereignty in developing countries join in a common cause. Crises, when they occur, are to be managed by unlucky or unwise external investors taking their share of losses, and by debtor governments reverting to defaults and/or capital controls with attendant risks to their future access to external financing. In less extreme circumstances, private creditors and debtors would be left to their own devices to work out debt restructuring arrangements and to encourage reforms in national exchange-rate regimes.

At the other end of the spectrum, various proposals envisage the construction of global institutions that would come closer to serving as the functional equivalents of domestic emergency-lending, bankruptcy, and liquidation arrangements. Two successive deputy managing directors of the IMF made such proposals, one for the Fund to be legally empowered to play the role of lender-of-last-resort and the next for the Fund to serve as a kind of ultimate bankruptcy court by overseeing a Sovereign Debt Restructuring Mechanism (Fischer 2000; Krueger 2002; Goodhart and Illing 2002). Similar ideas had previously stimulated serious policy debates. Even in the aftermath of the Asian and Argentinian crises, neither proved politically robust. The seriousness with which they were now proposed, however, proved adequate to move both the US Treasury and international financiers to embrace the voluntary inclusion of 'collective action clauses' in future emerging-market bond issues. Such clauses are designed to encourage co-operation among bondholders in future situations requiring debt restructuring. By specifying in advance, for example, how defaults would be handled, the clauses would in principle discourage individual bondholders from holding out for full repayment when others were prepared to compromise and share any losses (Blustein 2005). In any event, such an approach proved politically acceptable and was widely seen to represent the middle position on the spectrum imagined above, albeit with courts, not state executives or international organizations, playing the key role in future debt workouts.

In the years following the Asian and Argentinian crises, zealots advocating capital controls, supranational regulation, or radically free markets quickly receded from public view. The economic and political costs of their favourite proposals may be presumed to have become clear to those charged with decision-making responsibilities in creditor and debtor countries (Isard 2005). Until the next systemic threat arose, the most practical steps looked likely to evolve on the complicated intermediate terrain, where leading states and their most powerful constituents would continue to press the cause of globalizing private finance. Industrializing states, most obviously in East Asia, would seek to limit associated risks by building up regional arrangements and (arguably) excessive levels of national monetary reserves. Certain very poor countries would have their debts forgiven in the context of new allotments of foreign aid. And chastened multilateral institutions such as the IMF and the World Bank would continue to search for stable political balances among their diverse memberships sufficient to support reforms in their policies and internal governing structures (Truman 2006; Woods 2006). Whether such efforts will prove adequate, especially for the developing world, remains a pressing but open question best addressed against the background of what alternatives would be both economically and politically feasible.

KEY POINTS

- International financial crises are usually more difficult to manage than domestic ones because of jurisdictional ambiguities.

- Some basic level of co-ordination is required in crisis management.

- For emerging markets, the IMF has often taken a lead role in attempting to resolve crises.

- Policy debates continue on effective mechanisms for the restructuring of unsustainable debt in some developing nations.

Dilemmas of Global Governance

Globalizing financial markets remain fundamentally a political experiment at an early stage. Although once rejected as impracticable and excessively risky, since the 1970s the true architects of the international political economy—the United States, its key allies in the industrial world, and the most powerful domestic constituencies within them—have demonstrated little serious interest in advancing any alternative experiment. Ever more open financial markets might not ultimately succeed in generating a more stable, more prosperous, and fairer world order. But no other plan was on offer in the early twenty-first century. There was, however, a grudging recognition that private finance moving by under its own steam would not be likely to provide adequate resources in the foreseeable future to the world's least developed countries. For this reason, proposals proliferated for significant increases in foreign aid budgets and for massive debt write-offs (see Thomas, Chapter 13 in this volume). Although some progress was recorded in this regard in the aftermath of the crisis years of the late 1990s, follow-through remained limited and tentative. Leaders and legislators in the world's major capitals clearly continue to hope that more open private financial markets will provide most of the external financial resources required by countries aspiring to prosperity in a global economy.

Nevertheless, few with any historical memory believe that those markets could build a better world automatically. Few policy-makers or close observers argued with any conviction that the global economic governance necessitated by financial openness would establish itself. One critical issue comes down to leadership in a system rendered more complicated, not only by the increased sophistication of markets but also by the contemporary dispersion of regulatory authority. Another is linked to evaluations of economic fairness in a system that continues to favour development strategies that have the perverse effect of allowing net capital in the aggregate to flow from poor to rich countries.

A sense that reliable and just political leadership at the global level will turn out to be impracticable in the long run may lie deep in the consciousness of those attempting to build regional bulwarks as the experiment in economic and financial globalization continues (see Ravenhill, Chapter 6 in this volume). Still, the persistent reliance by policy-makers on multilateral institutions when they confront collective problems, such as those associated with financial crisis prevention and in particular crisis management, suggests that the post-1945 ideal of systemic collaboration remains alive. Students of political economy are left to contemplate the conditions under which increasingly interdependent states and more open societies can govern themselves with an enlightened sense of their mutual interests.

? QUESTIONS

1. What causes financial crises?
2. Why are certain crises contagious?
3. What special risks are associated with international finance, and how have regulators tried to keep pace with the risks inherent in international finance?
4. What alternatives to private financial markets exist for countries aspiring to development and economic prosperity?
5. What measures have been proposed for the prevention of financial crises?
6. How should international financial crises be managed more effectively?
7. What are the political limits on more effective crisis management?
8. What are the implications of current global crisis prevention and management systems for questions of distributive justice, both for the system as a whole and for specific countries?

FURTHER READING

■ Abdelal, R. (2007), *Capital Rules: The Construction of Global Finance* (Cambridge, MA: Harvard University Press). An insightful analysis of the normative foundations of contemporary international capital markets.

■ Baker, A. (2006), *The Group of Seven: Finance Ministries, Central Banks and Global Financial Governance* (London New York: Routledge). An in-depth examination of the history and current debates surrounding this exclusive forum of leading states now closely identified with 'decentralized globalization'.

■ Blustein, P. (2001), *The Chastening: Inside the Crisis that Rocked the Global System and Humbled the IMF* (New York: Public Affairs). An engaging, fast-paced account of the financial disturbances of the late 1990s. The author interviewed many of the major financiers, government officials, and political leaders involved; he weaves together a fascinating and disquieting tale.

■ ——(2005), *And the Money Kept Rolling In (And Out): Wall Street, the IMF, and the Bankrupting of Argentina* (New York: Public Affairs). The sequel, on the multi-faceted debacle of the biggest sovereign default to date.

■ Bryant, R. (2003), *Turbulent Waters: Cross-Border Finance and International Governance* (Washington, DC: Brookings Institution). A balanced exploration of the history and contemporary character of global finance by a leading economist attentive to the realities of national and international politics.

■ Eichengreen, B. (2003), *Capital Flows and Crises* (Cambridge, MA: MIT Press). A prolific economist provides a highly readable account of the causes and consequences of international financial crises.

■ Flandreau, M., and Zumer, F. (2004), *The Making of Global Finance, 1880–1913* (Paris: OECD Development Centre). An excellent and nuanced study of the development of international capital markets in the first era of financial globalization, with clear and provocative lessons drawn for developing countries today.

■ Goodhart, C., and Illing, G. (eds) (2002), *Financial Crises, Contagion, and the Lender of Last Resort* (Oxford: Oxford University Press). An enlightening assessment of the strengths and weaknesses of institutions and practices at the global level aiming to govern interdependent financial markets.

■ Haggard, S. (ed.) (2000), *The Political Economy of the Asian Financial Crisis* (Washington, DC: Institute for International Economics). A solid, comparative examination of the political factors at work within the emerging markets implicated most directly in the financial turmoil of the 1990s.

■ Isard, P. (2005), *Globalization and the International Financial System* (Cambridge: Cambridge University Press). An analysis by an IMF economist, with a useful discussion of practical remedies for the dilemmas faced by policy-makers in developing countries.

■ James, H. (1996), *International Monetary Cooperation Since Bretton Woods* (Washington, DC: International Monetary Fund). An accessible account of how the monetary dimension of the world economy evolved in the post-1945 era, by an outstanding economic historian.

■ Kindleberger, C. P. (1978), *Manias, Panics, and Crashes: A History of Financial Crises* (New York: Basic Books). A path-breaking orientation to the fragile financial underpinnings of modern capitalism.

■ Lowenstein, R. (2001), *When Genius Failed: The Rise and Fall of Long-Term Capital Management* **(London: Fourth Estate).** A well-told tale of greed, hubris, and moral hazard in contemporary capital markets.

■ Obstfeld, M., and Taylor, A. (2004), *Global Capital Markets: Integration, Crisis, and Growth* **(Cambridge: Cambridge University Press).** A detailed history of international capital mobility since the late-nineteenth century, by two prominent economists.

■ Pauly, L. W. (1997), *Who Elected the Bankers? Surveillance and Control in the World Economy* **(Ithaca, NY: Cornell University Press).** An examination of the development of the IMF and its principal role in the wake of twentieth-century financial crises.

■ Roubini, N., and Setser, B. (2004), *Bailouts or Bail-Ins? Responding to Financial Crises in Emerging Markets* **(Washington, DC: Institute for International Economics).** An overview of the complicated political and economic issues associated with sovereign debt restructuring, including a very good bibliography and glossary.

■ Santiso, J. (2006), *Latin America's Political Economy of the Possible* **(Cambridge, MA: MIT Press).** The chief economist of the OECD Development Centre provides an elegant assessment of contemporary changes in a region wracked by financial shocks over many decades.

■ Stiglitz, J. E. (2002), *Globalization and its Discontents* **(New York: W. W. Norton).**

■ ——(2006), *Making Globalization Work* **(New York: W. W. Norton).** Provocative critiques of the reactions of governments and international organizations to the economic disasters befalling much of the developing world in recent years, by the former chief economist of the World Bank.

■ Strange, S. (1998), *Mad Money: When Markets Outgrow Governments* **(Ann Arbor, MI: University of Michigan Press).** The late, great international political economist provides a rousing and contentious introduction to the policy and technical innovations that increased dramatically the volume and volatility of global financial flows.

■ Tirole, J. (2002), *Financial Crises, Liquidity, and the International Monetary System* **(Princeton, NJ: Princeton University Press).** A challenging analysis of crucial differences between finance within a country and finance that crosses national borders.

■ Truman, E. (2006), 'A Strategy for International Monetary Fund Reform', *Policy Analyses in International Economics* **77 (Washington, DC: Institute for International Economics).** An in-depth analysis by a former senior US Federal Reserve official of contemporary challenges and options for adaptation of the key multilateral instrument for crisis prevention and management in emerging markets.

■ Woods, N. (2006), *The Globalizers: The IMF, the World Bank and Their Borrowers* **(Ithaca, NY: Cornell University Press).** A constructively critical assessment of the policies of the Bretton Woods twins and their internal governance procedures.

WEB LINKS

● **www.imf.org/** International Monetary Fund.

● **www.worldbank.org/** The World Bank Group.

● **www.un.org/esa/desa/** United Nations, Department of Economic and Social Affairs.

- **www.bis.org/**   Bank for International Settlements.
- **www.oecd.org/**   Organization for Economic Cooperation and Development.
- **www.g7.utoronto.ca/**   G7/G8 Information Centre.
- **www.iif.com/**   The Institute of International Finance.

 Visit the Online Resource Centre that accompanies this book for more information:
www.oxfordtextbooks.co.uk/orc/ravenhill2e/

PART 4

Globalization and Its Consequences

9

The Logics of Economic Globalization

ANTHONY MCGREW

Chapter Contents

- Introduction
- A Global Economy? 'Embedded Globalization' and the Rescaling of Economic Activity
- The Logics of Economic Globalization
- The Second Age of Globalization: Another Extraordinary Episode?
- The Prospects for Economic Globalization: Why Politics Still Matters

Reader's Guide

In 1987, Robert Gilpin's *The Political Economy of International Relations* was published, a defining event in the coming of age of international political economy as a discrete field of academic enquiry. Less than two decades later, Gilpin issued a second edition, retitled as *Global Political Economy*, reflecting, as noted in the book's preface, the fundamental changes that had taken place in the nature of the international economic order in the intervening period. The most significant change, he observes, is 'the globalization of the world economy' (Gilpin 2001: 3). However, the extent, significance, and consequences of this globalization remain hotly contested in academia and beyond. Indeed, the very concept of globalization is the subject of controversy, not to mention its questionable validity as both a description and an explanation of the dynamics of the contemporary world economic order.

Engaging with these controversies, this chapter argues that economic globalization—understood simply as the widening, deepening, and speeding up of worldwide interconnectedness—aptly describes, even if by itself it cannot explain, the emergence today of a singular global political economy. Acknowledging that globalization is neither inevitable nor irresistible, the analysis presents a systematic specification of its causes or logics: the principal task of this chapter. It elucidates the principal accounts of globalization, offering some critical judgements on which, if any, provide a convincing explanation of 'the globalization of the world economy'. By concentrating on the causes of globalization, the analysis does not address the matter of its presumed effects or consequences—for example, on state sovereignty, patterns of inequality, or social democracy—which are the subject in particular of Chapter 10 in this volume. Instead, the discussion emphasizes the distinctive features of contemporary economic globalization and the continuing role of politics—both local and global—in shaping its future trajectories. In short, the chapter addresses three questions:

1. What is economic globalization, and what are its principal features?
2. How does theory help us to explain contemporary economic globalization?
3. Is economic globalization today all that new?

Introduction

In the aftermath of the cataclysmic attacks on the United States on 11 September 2001, obituaries for globalization were numerous. These momentous events, according to John Gray, heralded a new epoch in world affairs: 'The era of globalisation is over' (Naím 2002). In similar vein, John Reston Saul proclaimed 'the end of globalism', and Justin Rosenberg concluded 'the "age of globalization" is unexpectedly over' (Rosenberg 2005: 2; Saul 2005). Measured in terms of flows within the circuits of the world economy, economic globalization appeared to stall. As subsequent discussion will show, this slowing was a very temporary hiatus, as patterns of global economic exchange have subsequently intensified. The obituaries for economic globalization have proved to be somewhat premature. Indeed, the current 'second age of globalization' (the first age being the *belle époque* of 1870–1914) is evidently far more resilient and socially embedded than many (even its most ardent advocates) have acknowledged. As the annual *Foreign Policy* Globalization Index has noted: 'The resilience of globalization indicates that it is a phenomenon that runs deeper than the political crises of the day' (Kearney and *Foreign Policy* Globalization Index 2005: 53).

For students of global political economy, the really puzzling question is why economic globalization has proved to be so resilient and so enduring since the 1980s despite a series of major shocks—from 9/11, to the East Asian crisis of 1997, the Iraq war of 2003, and the tsunami of 2004? One response to this question, which is developed in this chapter, is that economic globalization is much more 'socially and institutionally embedded' than its many advocates or critics have presumed (James 2001). This is not to suggest that it is either inevitable or irresistible, but rather to acknowledge the ways—structurally, institutionally and ideationally—in which economic

globalization constitutes the dominant (but not the sole) tendency in the contemporary world economy. This second age of globalization is perhaps best described as an age of 'embedded globalization'.

Among those of a more sceptical persuasion, the notion of embedded globalization seems to be at odds with the 'war' on global terrorism, heightened nationalism and protectionism, the reassertion of geopolitics, US military hegemony, the power of states, and the strengthening of border controls. This new climate of fear and insecurity, in other words, suggests globalization is more an ideological than a material fact: a social construction of the world that conceals the real forces shaping the global political economy, whether geopolitics or capitalist imperialism (see the discussion in Hay, Chapter 10 in this volume). By contrast, for those of a more globalist persuasion, the fact that patterns of world-wide economic interaction have proved to be so resilient in the context of such a seriously inhospitable environment seems incontrovertible evidence of 'really existing globalization' (Kearney and *Foreign Policy* Globalization Index 2006). What is at issue here, at least in part, are differing understandings of, and evidence for, globalizing tendencies.

Since it is such a 'slippery' and overused concept within the social sciences, and has a colloquial life outside the academic world, it is hardly surprising that globalization should engender intense debate—not to mention plain confusion. No generally accepted definition exists. It is crucial to establish from the outset, therefore, how the concept is framed within the global political economy literature. Accordingly, the first section of the chapter will address three interrelated questions, namely:

1. What is globalization?

2. Is there substantive evidence of the globalization of economic activity?

3. To what extent is globalization the principal tendency within the contemporary world economy?

Following this analysis, the second section will identify and analyse the principal causes and the dominant theories of globalization. In doing so, it will draw an important distinction between what Rosenberg (2000) refers to as 'theories of globalization' and 'globalization theory'. Section three will draw on the discussion of causes to explore the notion of embedded globalization through a comparison of its first 'golden age' (1870–1914) with the current epoch—the second age of globalization. In the concluding section, the discussion will relate the analysis of causes to an exploration of the centrality of politics and governance—both local and global—to the social embeddedness of contemporary economic globalization.

A Global Economy? 'Embedded Globalization' and the Rescaling of Economic Activity

Within the wider political economy literature, globalization per se is synonymous with a process of intensifying worldwide economic integration. Thus, for example, P. Hirst and G. Thompson assert that 'We can only begin to assess the issue of globalization if we have some relatively clear and rigorous model of what a global economy would be like' (Hirst and Thompson 2003: 99). This economism—that globalization can be understood solely, or even primarily, as an economic phenomenon and is therefore to be analysed in relation to a perfectly integrated global market—contrasts with the broader understanding of the concept in the social science literatures (see Box 9.1). Here, globalization tends to be conceived as a multidimensional, rather than a singular, process—evident across the cultural, political, ecological, military, and social domains—which is both open-ended, in so far as it discloses no historically determinate or fixed outcome, and complex, in that it is associated with patterns of transworld integration and fragmentation (Held *et al.* 1999; Keohane and Nye 2003). Underlying these different conceptions are significant methodological disagreements about how complex historical and social phenomena, such as globalization, are best analysed (Rosenberg 1995). This lack of agreement suggests the need for some caution in two significant respects: either in privileging the economic automatically in any systematic analysis of globalization, but more especially in drawing general conclusions about globalization as a social process, solely from an analysis of the economic sphere. Economizing globalization, in other words, is a *categorical* mistake. That said, few discussions of globalization can, or do, ignore its economic foundations.

Conceptually, globalization is often elided with notions of liberalization, internationalization, universalization, Westernization, or modernization (Scholte 2000). However, as Scholte argues, none of these terms alone capture its distinctive attributes or qualities. Within the global political economy literature, economic globalization is generally specified in reasonably precise terms as 'the emergence and operation of a single, worldwide economy' (Grieco and Ikenberry 2003: 207). It is measured by reference to the growing intensity, extensity, and velocity of worldwide economic interactions and interconnectedness, from trade, through production and finance, to migration. In this regard it is conceived as a *process*, rather than a fixed outcome or condition, in so far as it refers to a *historical*

BOX 9.1

Globalization

Globalization is variously defined in the literature as:

1. 'The intensification of worldwide social relations which link distant localities in such a way that local happenings are shaped by events occurring many miles away and vice versa' (Giddens 1990: 21).

2. 'The integration of the world economy' (Gilpin 2001: 364).

3. 'De-territorialization—or . . . the growth of supra-territorial relations between people' (Scholte 2000: 46).

4. '[A] global economy . . . in which distinct national economies and, therefore, domestic strategies of national economic management are increasingly irrelevant' (Hirst and Thompson 1999).

5. '[T]he international integration of markets in goods, services, and capital' (Garrett 2000*a*).

---

tendency towards heightened levels of worldwide economic interconnectedness. Indeed, there is a substantive conceptual difference between the notion of a globalizing world economy, in Gilpin's terms (2001) and a fully or partially *globalized world economy* which implies a fixed state or condition of economic integration.

This distinction between process and condition (that is 'becoming' and 'being') is emphasized by Keohane and Nye, who differentiate between globalization—as a historical process—and globalism—the resulting condition at any particular historical moment (Keohane and Nye 2003). The implication is that, since globalization is neither an inevitable nor a secular tendency, it is associated, at particular historical moments, with thicker or thinner forms of globalism. Translated into the language of global political economy, globalization can be associated with deeper or shallower forms of worldwide economic integration.

Understood as a process, economic globalization also implies an evolving *transformation* or qualitative shift in the organization and dynamics of the world economy. Quite simply, cumulative patterns and networks of trans-border economic activity over time dissolve the separation of the world into discrete national economic units. This process makes the distinction between the domestic and world economy increasingly problematic to

sustain—for academics and policy-makers alike. In other words, globalization generates emergent or systemic properties such that the world economy increasingly begins to operate as a singular system (Sayer 2000). This structural shift may be evident in, among other things, the formation of global markets, production networks (see Thun, Chapter 11 in this volume), a global division of labour, and business competition, together with worldwide systems of economic regulation and management that range from the World Trade Organization to the International Accounting Standards Board.

Underlying these shifts in the scale of economic organization are contemporary informatics technologies and infrastructures of communication and transportation. These have facilitated new forms and possibilities of virtual real-time worldwide economic organization and co-ordination. In the process, distance and time are being substantially reconfigured such that, for example, economic and other shocks in one region of the world can rapidly diffuse around the globe, often with serious local consequences (see, for example, Pauly, Chapter 8 in this volume). Although geography still matters very much, it is nevertheless the case that globalization is associated with a process of *time-space compression* —literally a shrinking world—in which the sources of even very localized economic developments, from interest rate changes to corporate restructuring, may be traced to economic conditions or agents in markets on other continents.

However, a single worldwide economy is not necessarily coextensive with a universal or planetary economy. More specifically, 'worldwide' is generally taken to refer to *interregional or intercontinental* patterns of economic exchange and enmeshment. Accordingly, globalization is best conceived as embodying a *rescaling* of economic space manifested in the intensification of inter- or supraregional and multicontinental networks and flows of economic activity (Brenner 1999). In this respect it is one (albeit significant) historical tendency operating within the world economy, just as regionalization, nationalization and localization can be identified as other tendencies—whether as complementary or competing tendencies remains subject to substantial theoretical and empirical disagreement. As a principal tendency, globalization denotes a relative *denationalization* of economic relations as significant aspects of economic life become organized increasingly on an interregional or multicontinental scale transcending bounded national economic space (Held *et al.* 1999; Keohane and Nye 2003). This rescaling, however, is not experienced uniformly across every region or economy, since globalization is also recognizably an uneven *process*. Differential patterns of enmeshment in, or marginalization from, the worldwide economy define its 'variable geometry' (Castells 2000). Such unevenness generates a distinctive geography of inclusion and exclusion such that the notion of a worldwide or global economy is less (geographically and socially) inclusive than that of a universal or planetary economic order. The implications of this distinction, as will become clear, are highly significant for empirical assessments of economic globalization.

Having established this general conception of economic globalization, its relevance and centrality describing, understanding, and explaining the world economic order can be ex- Two interrelated questions will be

- Is there substantive evidence of the globalization of economic activity?
- Is actually existing globalization the dominant tendency within the contemporary world economy?

Within the existing literature, as noted previously, there are broadly two sets of responses to these questions: the globalist and the sceptical. In short, whereas globalists consider that world economic trends disclose unprecedented levels of global economic exchange, such that there can be little doubt either of the existence of a singular worldwide economy or globalization as its principal tendency, the sceptics remain much less convinced. They conclude not only that globalization is highly exaggerated, but also that contrary tendencies, from growing regionalism to intensifying geo-economic competition, are creating a more segmented and fragmented world economy. Of course, these two categories—globalists and sceptics—are a heuristic device for simplifying the nature and sources of the underlying disagreement, thereby concealing considerable differences within each camp, or common ground between them. Yet on the critical issue of whether globalization is an actually existing or dominant historical tendency, they differ profoundly. The reasons for this will become clearer through an examination of historical trends in respect of the principal economic factors in the world economy: namely trade, finance, production, and labour.

Trade

It is the confluence of secular trends and patterns of world trade, capital flows, transnational production, and migration that for globalists affirms the validity of the globalization tendency. As Samir Amin concludes, while economic globalization is nothing new, it has 'undeniably taken a qualitative step forward during the recent period' (1997: 31). For most of the post-war period, world trade has grown much faster than world output, and significantly so since the beginning of the 1990s (Irwin

2002; WTO 2006c). World exports, measured as a proportion of world output, were three times greater in 1998 than in 1950; the WTO estimates this ratio stood at 29 per cent in 2001 and was about 27 per cent in 2005, in comparison with 17 per cent in 1990 and 12.5 per cent in 1970 (WTO 2001a, 2006a). Despite 9/11 and the subsequent downturn in the world economy, world trade measured as a proportion of world output remains at levels well in excess of the high points of 1990s globalization (Kearney and *Foreign Policy* Globalization Index 2003; WTO 2003a; 2006a). World merchandise trade exceeded $10 trillion in 2005 ($10159 bn), almost sixty-five times the value of world trade in 1963 ($157bn), and services trade stood at $2415 bn (compared to $365bn in 1980, an almost 700 per cent increase) (WTO 2006c).

Trade now involves a larger number of countries and sectors than at any time in the recent past, while developing economies now account for a growing share of world export markets (increasing from 19.2 per cent in 1970 to 32.1 per cent in 2005). They have become especially important players in trade in manufactures, and even in the services sector (Held *et al.* 1999; WTO 2002, 2006b; UNCTAD 2005: 11). Trade has also become increasingly important to many economies, in particular to developing states, as evidenced by the growing share of national GDP accounted for by exports. Over the post-war period, the ratio of exports to GDP for all countries increased from 5.5 per cent in 1950 to 17.2 per cent in 1998, and for many of the major OECD and developing states it more than doubled (Kaplinsky 2005; table 1.1). Trade now reaches deeper than ever before into more sectors of many national economies as an expanded array of goods have become tradable.

Of course, world trade remains highly concentrated, both geographically—OECD countries account for the largest proportion of world merchandise trade (some 65 per cent), and a small number of East Asian countries' for the bulk of developing countries' exports; and sectorally—in 2005, manufacturing constituted 58 per cent of total world trade (in value terms), fuels 13.9 per cent, services 20 per cent, and agriculture only 6.7 per cent (Held *et al.* 1999; UNCTAD 2005: 133; WTO 2006a). This concentration is hardly surprising, given that OECD countries account for the largest share of world economic output and are by far the largest economic units. Yet, since the 1990s, this dominance has become more diluted (the developed economies' market share of world merchandise exports eroded from 75 per cent in 1970 to 64.8 per cent in 2003) with the emergence of new trading powers (such as Brazil, Russia, India, and China—the so-called 'BRIC' economies) resulting from structural changes in the world economy associated with a new global division of labour (changes in countries' trade specialization in the world economy) and the intensification of worldwide competition through trade (UNCTAD 2005: 133).

Patterns of trade have altered significantly since the 1960s and particularly so in the past few years. A new geography of trade is emerging that reflects the changing location of manufacturing production as East Asia and other **newly industrializing economies** (NIEs) take on the role as the world's factories. At the same time, most OECD economies have increased their trade in services significantly and these now account for almost a quarter of their exports (WTO 2006a). Falling costs of transportation, the communications revolution, liberalization, and the growth of **transnational corporations** have all contributed to a new global division of labour. As noted above, developing economies, in particular the NIEs in East Asia, have increased their share of world merchandise trade; and the composition of their exports has also altered dramatically. This restructuring is evident in the current pattern of developing country exports, in which fuels account for 18 per cent (by value), commodites 12.7 per cent, and manufactures 68.1 per cent, compared to 38.8 per cent, 26 per cent, and 31.4 per cent, respectively, in 1980 (UNCTAD 2005: 91).

In just over a quarter of a century, the share of manufactures in developing countries' exports has more than doubled. This shift has also been accompanied in recent years by a significant expansion in trade between developing economies (South–South trade) which has also almost doubled, from 22.9 per cent to 40.9 per cent of their total exports. However, this South–South trade is highly concentrated among East Asian economies, which accounted for some two-thirds of its total in 2003 (UNCTAD 2005). Even so, the NIEs are becoming increasingly important engines of global trade, such that some have argued 'the South is gradually moving from the periphery of global trade to the centre'. A recent World Bank report similarly observes that 'growth in the global economy will be powered increasingly by developing countries' (UNCTAD 2004b: 1; World Bank 2006: xiii). In just over three decades, China has evolved from being a negligible force in global trade to the world's third-largest exporter in 2005, and is expected to be in second place in 2007 (World Bank 2006; WTO 2006a).

These structural shifts constitute a new pattern of specialization (or division of labour) within the world economy, which is also associated with an intensification of economic competition. In 2003, 40 per cent of manufactured imports into the OECD economies were produced in developing economies, compared with 12 per cent in 1973 (World Bank 2006: xix). In the manufacturing sector, and also increasingly within the services sectors, the expansion of trade increases competitive pressures on domestic businesses, in both the North and the South. It is not just that OECD economies confront cheaper imports from the world's new manufacturing zones, in East Asia or Latin America, or lower-cost services from India and South Africa, but that competition among and between the OECD economies and developing economies has also intensified as production and markets become globalized.

Lower-cost imports impose greater price competition, while the dominance of intra-industry trade (trade in similar products or services) between OECD economies brings domestic business and labour into direct competition with their foreign counterparts. This development has significant distributional consequences for employment and wage levels within countries, although decomposing

its effects is a complicated matter such that its implications for labour remain hotly contested (Lawrence 1996b). Seeking competitive advantage is articulated either through more efficient domestic production methods or the fragmentation of production—that is, 'slicing up the value chain' or outsourcing production such that firms draw on worldwide networks of suppliers that produce where greatest economies of scale or efficiency gains can be realized (see Thun, Chapter 11 in this volume). Through such mechanisms, productive and competitive forces become globalized whilst economies in different regions become more tightly integrated. One recent study suggests that intra-industry and inter-firm trade accounted for at least 30 per cent of the growth of world trade in the period 1970–90 (Hummels 2001). Global trade is associated increasingly with the consolidation of a new global division of labour between North and South, which is associated with an intensification of global economic competition.

In so far as dense trade flows occur between the major regions of the world economy—namely the Asia-Pacific; the North American Free Trade Agreement (NAFTA); and European Union (EU) cores—global markets in goods and services might be assumed to exist. The most obvious examples of such markets are those in key primary commodities, such as oil or wheat, which set benchmark world prices. But global markets are far from the textbook notion of the perfectly integrated market. Despite the dramatic trade liberalization since the 1960s, in which formal tariffs have become negligible (average world tariff rates almost halved from 15 per cent to 8 per cent between the 1970s and 1990s), significant non-tariff barriers to trade remain, while distance, history and culture still continue to influence patterns of world trade (Centre for Economic Policy Reform 2002). Such factors make the scale and continuing annual growth of trade—some 13 per cent in 2005 and averaging 10 per cent over the whole period 2000–5—all the more remarkable (WTO 2006a: 3). However, much trade is conducted regionally, leading to the suggestion that the dominant tendency is one of regionalization rather than globalization (Chortareas and Pelagidis 2004: 20). This is particularly evident in the significant growth of regionalism (see Ravenhill, Chapter 6 in this volume) over recent decades. Yet, as R. E. Baldwin concludes in an exhaustive study of contemporary regional trading arrangements, there are good theoretical and empirical reasons to believe that 'multilateral and regional liberalisation [have] proceeded in tandem since 1947' (Baldwin 2006: 1487). Moreover, the increasing fragmentation of production creates significant pressures for competitive liberalization and makes it difficult to sustain any effective trade bloc 'when part of your wall encompasses the enemy camp' (Baldwin 2006: 1495). Despite regionalism, there is also evidence of a tendency for price differentials for traded goods to narrow, as might be expected in a global market place (IMF 2002: 122). Studies suggest that distance is no longer as crucial a determinant of patterns of world trade as in the past (Coe *et al.* 2002). Nor too does regionalism appear to be producing a segmentation of the world economy into separate regional markets. Although patterns of regional trade present a complex picture, *intra-regional* trade as a proportion of world merchandise trade, at an estimated 36 per cent, was lower in 2001 than it was throughout the 1990s (WTO 2001*a*: 6). As Table 6.4 (Ravenhill, Chapter 6 in this volume) indicates, the evidence does not demonstrate a secular trend towards the regional segmentation of the world economy. On the contrary, it is rather inconclusive, since in the case of both the European Union and Japan *inter*regional trade rose between 1990 and 2000, but remained constant for NAFTA, while the growth of *intra*regional trade outpaced the growth of interregional trade in several regions during the same period. Since 2000, the pattern is similarly inconclusive except in the case of NAFTA (UNCTAD 2004*a*; WTO 2005). These macro-regional trends also conceal the relative strategic importance to many economies of specific commodities in interregional compared to intra-regional trade (for example, oil). In a world of fragmented production, intimate connections exist between intra-regional and interregional trade activity, but these are often obscured in aggregate trade data. For example, the growth of regional trade among East Asian economies reflects principally trade in intermediate products that are then assembled (now predominantly in China) for export as finished goods to OECD markets in Europe and the USA (UNCTAD 2005: 136–138).

Of course, formally, under WTO rules, which at the time of writing have acquired almost universal reach, regionalism is required to be compatible with the multilateral trade order (see Ravenhill, Chapter 6 in this volume). This institutionalization of global rule-making and adjudication in trade matters marks a seminal development in the political construction of a truly global trade system. Through its very existence and functioning, the WTO defines a global regulatory framework that effectively constitutes the normative and legal foundations of global markets and their operation. In this respect, global markets are not just spontaneous constructions, but partly the product of the regulatory activities of multilateral bodies such as the WTO, not to mention the expanding role of transnational private merchant law (the new *lex mercatoria*) (Gill 1995; Cutler 2003). To this extent, trade globalization is not simply about trends in world trade but also about the critical importance of global and transnational trade authorities in the *constitution* of global markets.

Finance

Until comparatively recently, international finance was considered to be principally an adjunct to trade, a necessary mechanism enabling the international exchange of goods and services (Eichengreen 1996; Germain 1997). This direct association between finance and trade began to dissolve in the nineteenth century. By the twenty-first century it has become irrelevant, or at best marginal. Daily turnover on foreign exchange markets more than doubled from $590 billion in 1989 to $1,210 billion in 2001 and to an astonishing $1,880 billion in 2004 (compared to daily world exports of approximately $33 billion in 2005) (*BIS Quarterly Review* 2001;

Grieco and Ikenberry 2003: 214; BIS 2005: 5). As a multiple of world merchandise trade, annual foreign exchange turnover in 1973 was around twice the value of world trade, but by 2004 was more than sixty times greater (Held and McGrew 2002: 48). This activity, facilitated by instantaneous global communications, is conducted around the clock between the world's major financial centres on each continent. A worldwide foreign exchange market exists that determines the value of traded currencies, influencing the level of key financial variables such as national interest rates, and enabling the rapid movement of capital around the globe.

Following the significant liberalization of national financial markets since the 1980s, the level and geographical scope of global capital flows has also expanded enormously. By comparison with trade, which exhibited a compound growth rate of almost 10 per cent over the period 1964–2001, trans-border financial flows grew at a compound rate of almost 19 per cent (Bryant 2003: 141). To put this in context, Bryant calculates for the period 1964–2001 that, if the growth of international bonds—a form of securitized international lending/borrowing measured here in terms of stocks, not flows—had been at an equivalent level to the growth rate of all OECD economies, stocks of international bonds would be valued at some $776 billion, only 11 per cent of the actual $7.2 trillion in 2001 (Bryant 2003: 142). Similar patterns are evident for all other types of trans-border capital flows, from international issues of shares—which expanded from $8bn in the 1980s to a peak of $300bn in 2000, and subsequently surpassed in 2005 ($307.5bn); to cross-border trading in derivatives—which grew (measured in gross value) from $618.3bn in 1986 to $4,224bn in 2001 and more than doubled to $10,605bn in 2005 (equivalent to the annual value of world merchandise trade); and trans-border bank lending—which increased tenfold from $2,095bn in 1983 to $27,272bn in 2005 (Held *et al.* 1999: ch. 4; BIS 2003; Bryant 2003: 140; *BIS Quarterly Review* 2005; BIS 2005, 2006).

As with trade, the bulk of capital flows (some 66 per cent) is accounted for by the major OECD economies. While these interregional flows have intensified—64 per cent of trans-border investments in stock markets is intercontinental—this transnationalization is not replicated everywhere (IMF 2003*b*). Trans-border financial flows are highly uneven, such that while most emerging market economies have acquired increasing access to world financial markets, many of the poorest economies remain subject to, rather than active participants in, the operations of these markets (*BIS Quarterly Review* 2005). Capital flows to developing states have fluctuated considerably since the 1970s, peaking in the mid-1990s prior to the East Asian crash and subsequently falling back, although by 2006 they had rebounded to the previous peak of 1997 (IMF 2003*b*; World Bank 2006: 15). The distribution of these flows is concentrated significantly among the principal emerging market economies of Latin America, East Asia, and the European transition economies. Geography and history still exert an influence on capital flows although there is much less evidence of regionalization (Thompson 2006). Of course, this is not to conclude that the dynamics and volatilities of trans-border financial activities have no bearing on those on the world's periphery, for few economies can insulate themselves against the consequences of financial contagion in a real-time global financial system (Desai 2003).

Despite the unevenness of trans-border capital flows, the evidence suggests that since the 1980s there has been a significant integration of financial markets (Taylor 1996; Lane and Milesi-Ferretti 2003; Obstfeld and Taylor 2004). Financial integration is a matter of degree, or a tendency, expressed in relative measurements of greater or lesser intensity. It is assessed by a variety of measures (including stocks and flows of capital; asset and interest rate price convergence, synchronization of stock markets; and national business cycles) with the consequence that 'In attacking the problem of measuring [global] market integration, economists have no universally recognized criteria to turn to' (Obstfeld and Taylor 2004: 47). Not to mention the problem that different measures often lead to different conclusions. Not surprisingly, this has produced a considerable debate as to the scale and economic significance of financial globalization assessed in relation to tendencies towards the convergence, deepening, and institutionalization of worldwide financial activity, performance, and regulation (Watson 2001; Obstfeld and Taylor 2004).

Obstfeld and Taylor's (1998, 2003, 2004) econometric studies, among others, identify a narrowing of interest-rate differentials between the major OECD economies after 1960 (they returned to their pre-1914 levels), as might be expected under conditions of high capital mobility and openness (Obstfeld and Taylor 1998, 2003, 2004; Fujii and Chinn 2001; Goldberg et al. 2003). Although short of complete convergence, international differentials remain comparable to those within most national economies (for a given financial asset) while they persist for much more limited periods than in the past, an outcome that might be expected in the context of 24-hour global financial trading (Fujii and Chinn 2001; Goldberg et al. 2003; Obstfeld and Taylor 2004). In contrast, Feldstein and Horioka's classic study (1980) concluded that levels of national savings and national investment appeared to be highly correlated (see Hay, Chapter 10 in this volume), indicating significant barriers to financial integration (Feldstein and Horioka 1980). This finding has also been confirmed by other studies such that in much of the orthodox literature it is regarded as a 'stylized but very robust fact' (Obstfeld and Taylor 2004: 62).

For orthodox economists, these findings present something of a puzzle in so far as the relative ease of global capital mobility should theoretically imply low (rather than the observed *high*) correlations between domestic savings and domestic investment. Accordingly, the Feldstein–Horioka puzzle has attracted much attention as a measure of global financial mobility and integration. A broad range of recent studies have 'solved' the puzzle, in that they provide significant empirical evidence that the savings–investment correlation appears

to have weakened since the 1990s—a period of intense trans-border capital flows (Coakley et al. 1998; Abbott and Vita 2003; Banerjee and Zanghieri 2003; Coakley et al. 2004; Giannone and Lenza 2004). Other studies have questioned the methodological and theoretical robustness of the Feldstein–Horioka puzzle, rather than the empirical findings, as a measure of capital mobility and integration (Baxter and Crucini 1993; Taylor 1996; Hoffmann 1998). These suggest that the observed correlations—probably a product of the theoretical assumptions and econometric modelling—are not inconsistent with high capital mobility, and as such are an imperfect measure of global financial integration.

Other measures, such as the stock of foreign assets as a proportion of world GDP, indicate a much less ambiguous conclusion in so far as this increased from 6 per cent in 1960 to 25 per cent in 1980, and to 92 per cent in 2000 (Obstfeld and Taylor 2004: 55). Similarly, flows of capital as a share of GDP have grown since the 1960s, although they have not necessarily returned to the levels of the *belle époque* (Obstfeld and Taylor 2004: 60). Furthermore, there is considerable evidence that capital controls—legal restrictions on capital flows—have declined significantly since the 1970s for OECD states, and the 1980s for most developing economies (and were associated with the shift to a floating exchange rate regime) (Obstfeld and Taylor 2004: 165). Bryant accordingly concludes in his study of global finance that 'the analogy of nearly autonomous national savings [and investment] reservoirs is no longer appropriate' (Bryant 2003: 152). Capital is by no means perfectly mobile in so far as global financial markets are imperfect. Even so, the dominant tendency has nevertheless been in the direction of greater, rather than lesser, (uneven) financial integration.

Tendencies towards financial integration have also been accompanied by processes of financial deepening (measured in terms of contagion effects, or the synchronization of financial markets and national business cycles) (Obstfeld and Taylor 2004). Finance pervades the operation and management of all modern economies, representing for many—to borrow Hilferding's (1910/1981) vocabulary—a new epoch of 'finance capitalism'. To the extent that national financial systems are increasingly integrated (in real time) with global capital markets, the consequences of financial developments or volatility abroad is magnified and diffused rapidly at home. For example, on 27 August 1998, the stock markets on every continent fell significantly in reaction to the spread of currency crises from Asia to Russia and Latin America (Desai 2003: 198). Irrespective of contagion effects in crises, the evidence suggests that major stock markets and stock market returns have become increasingly synchronized since the 1970s (Longin and Solnik 1995; Bekaert *et al.* 2005).

This synchrony in financial market movements across the globe is not uniform, since local conditions do make a difference; moreover, it is more evident at times of crisis. Nevertheless, it denotes the heightened significance of global financial conditions for domestic financial stability, and vice versa (Eichengreen 2002). Indeed, M. Bordo, in a study of business cycles over the last 120 years, points to evidence of a 'secular trend towards increased synchronization' (Bordo and Helbling 2003: 42). This process of financial deepening arises out of the interaction between the greater 'financialization' of national economies and its overlapping with global financial activity. Evidence of this is to be found during the 1990s, for example, in increased foreign holdings of national public debt—in the Eurozone an increase from 16 to 30 per cent, and in the United States from 19 per cent to in excess of 35 per cent at the time of writing—not to mention increased foreign holdings of shares, private financial assets, and the almost doubling of the ratio of foreign assets to national GDP for most OECD economies (Held *et al.* 1999; IMF 2002; Mosley 2003). In 2005, foreigners owned some 50 per cent of the total stock of US Treasury Bonds, enabling the USA to maintain both lower interest rates than would otherwise be the case, and to fund its historic twin deficits (fiscal and balance of payments) (Warnock and Warnock 2006: 1–4). Furthermore, although many studies

have pointed to the 'home bias' effect, which refers to investors' preference for domestic assets, such that the international diversification of investment portfolios appears to be relatively low (in the US, foreign equities constitute around 12 per cent of total holdings) recent studies have qualified these findings (Thompson 2006). Cai and Warnock, for example, demonstrate that this finding in part is a product of how home bias is measured, especially a failure to distinguish the kinds of domestic assets purchased (Cai and Warnock 2006). When such distinctions are made, they 'nearly eliminate the home bias puzzle' (Cai and Warnock 2006: 3).

Associated with this financial deepening is a process of institutionalization as the organization and infrastructures of transborder finance become regularized and systematized through the activities of (public and private) global agencies and networks. This institutionalization is evident in the enormous expansion of multinational banking—for example, HSBC, 'the world's local bank'—as well as the surveillance and global standard-setting activities of the IMF, BIS, and the multiplicity of official and private transborder networks, from the Financial Action Task Force to the International Accounting Standards Board (see Pauly, Chapter 8 in this volume). It is through the operation of these institutions that the essential infrastructure of global financial markets is developed and extended, from the SWIFT global financial inter-bank payments system to mechanisms for managing sovereign 'bankruptcy'. In the process, the global or interregional integration of financial markets is reinforced.

Production

Although data on transborder capital flows include foreign direct investment (FDI), political economists usually focus separately on FDI, since it denotes effectively the globalization of production (see Thun, Chapter 11 in this volume). Outsourcing production around the world is now widespread in the most dynamic industrial sectors. Indeed, both investment in overseas production facilities

(FDI) and production fragmentation (that is, the outsourcing of production to foreign independent third parties integrated within transnational production chains or networks), have increased dramatically since the 1970s (UNCTAD 2002c; 2006b). Driving and dominating this process is the transnational corporation (TNC). By comparison with the recent past (say, 1990), transnational production rather than trade has become the principal means of servicing foreign markets. Transnational corporations account (at the time of writing) for more than 25 per cent of world production, 80 per cent of world industrial output, approximately 40 per cent of world merchandise trade, and 10 per cent of world GDP (compared to 7 per cent of world GDP in 1990) (Gilpin 2001: 289; UNCTAD 2001, 2003, 2006b). They have become important determinants of the location and organization of production and services in the world economy, especially within the most advanced and dynamic economic sectors, integrating and reordering business activity between and within the world's three principal economic regions and their associated hinterlands. These developments are characterized by, among other factors: an increased scale and scope; processes of transnational economic restructuring; and the consolidation of a new global division of labour.

Since the 1970s flows of FDI have not only become more geographically diffuse, but also much more intense (Dunning 2000; UNCTAD 2001; for further discussion, see Thun, Chapter 11 in this volume). At the start of the twenty-first century, total world (inward) FDI reached a new peak of $1,409.6bn, almost four times the level of 1995 and over six times that of a decade earlier (UNCTAD 2001: 3; 2006b). After 2001, FDI flows initially declined dramatically, with the slowdown in the world economy, but have subsequently increased to just over $916bn in 2005 compared to an average of $548bn in 1994–9 (UNCTAD 2003: 2; 2006b: 2). FDI at the time of writing is well over ten times that of 1982, and has grown at rates well in excess of that of two decades earlier, in the process outstripping world GDP growth, exports and capital investment (UNCTAD 2006b: 7). With this has come a mergers

and acquisition boom, as the pressures for global corporate consolidation intensifies, exceeding previous historic highs in 2000 with deals to the total value of a record $3,900 billion (*Financial Times*, 21 December 2006: 1). Furthermore, significant flows (more than $10bn) reach more than fifty countries (including twenty-four developing economies) compared to seventeen (and seven LDCs), respectively, in 1985 (UNCTAD 2001: 4).

As UNCTAD notes, the 'trend towards integration on ever larger geographical scales is relatively new. Supply chains have extended to new areas of the globe and integrated formerly distinct regional production activities' (UNCTAD 2002c: 13). This reflects a variety of factors including proximity to new markets and technological shifts in the capacity to organize and manage production at a distance (Dicken 2003). But it is no longer simply manufacturing production that is on the move, but increasingly, with the digitization of information and communications advances, the provision of services, such as call centres, information processing, and legal and banking services (Held *et al.* 1999: ch. 5; UNCTAD 2001: 6).

Widely diffused as it is, both flows and stocks of FDI nevertheless remain concentrated among and within the major OECD economies (see Thun, Chapter 11 in this volume). Moreover, official FDI flows significantly understate actual levels of foreign investment, since some estimates indicate it finances only 25 per cent of the total of such productive investment abroad (Held *et al.* 1999: 237). While some FDI reaches every continent, it remains highly uneven in its dispersion—but this is changing. In 2000, OECD economies were the destination for some 80 per cent of FDI (inflows), the source of 88 per cent of FDI (outflows), 86 per cent of the world stock of (outward or exported) FDI, and 67 per cent of the world stock of (inward) FDI (UNCTAD 2006b: 7). However as M. Obstfeld and A. M. Taylor observe 'this trend may have turned, with FDI to poorer countries increasing in magnitude, and, importantly, reaching a more widely dispersed group of recipient countries' (Obstfeld and Taylor 2004: 83). Recent years have witnessed a significant change in the pattern of inward and outward FDI flows—with almost a doubling of the share accounted for by developing economies (inward from 17.5 per cent in 1990 to 36 per cent in 2005; and outward 6.9 per cent and 12.3 per cent, respectively)—and in FDI stocks (inward from 20.7 per cent in 1990 to 27.2 per cent in 2005; and outward 8.3 per cent to 11.9 per cent, respectively) (UNCTAD 2006b: 2, 7). This exceeds quite significantly the average shares of FDI invested in or by developing countries throughout the 1990s. Developing economies, particularly in East Asia, are both an increasingly significant destination for, as well as source of, FDI. These trends disclose a concentration of investment within and between the European Union, the United States, and Japan as the largest economies; and between these economies and the NIEs of Asia, (to a lesser extent) Latin America, and the East European transition economies. This concentration has been conceived variously as triadization or regionalization, but this misrepresents the complex matrix of intra-regional and interregional flows of FDI and networks of production (Dunning 2000; Dicken 2003). It is the very clustering of FDI around the three major economic regions combined with the intensity of interregional flows that reinforces the dynamic of global productive integration.

In linking the dynamics of economies, FDI is also associated with processes of economic restructuring. Although the notion of 'footloose capital' is very much a cliché, the consequences of the mobility of capital are evident in structural changes across many OECD economies and the rise of NIEs in Asia and Latin America (Rowthorn and Wells 1987; Castells 1996; Kapstein 2000; Hoogvelt 2001; Dicken 2003). There is much debate both about the significance of the deindustrialization of OECD economies in recent decades and its causes (Piore and Sabel 1984; Krugman 1994; Wood 1994; Lawrence 1996b; Rodrik 1997; Burtless et al. 1998; Schwartz 2001). Although the impact of globalization, as opposed to technological change, on the decline of manufacturing employment in many OECD economies is disputed,

there is general agreement that capital mobility and, increasingly, outsourcing nevertheless play a significant role in their continuous economic transformation. De-industrialization in these economies is linked directly with the industrialization of many developing economies as production is shifted to lower-cost locations, both through expanded FDI but increasingly through outsourcing arrangements (which require no capital input)(Rowthorn and Wells 1987; Wood 1994; Lawrence 1996b; Rodrik 1997; Munck 2002; UNCTAD 2002c; 2006; Dicken 2003). This is not to argue that the mobility of productive capital is unconstrained, since it is not. Proximity to local markets, institutional factors, and productivity calculations limit the potential for industrial capital to relocate abroad, either rapidly or at all. Nevertheless, over time the cumulative impact of such mobility, along with the expansion of trade, has contributed to major structural changes in the world economy.

Among the most obvious of these structural changes is the evolution and consolidation of a new worldwide division of labour. A significant shift has occurred in the location of manufacturing production, from OECD economies outwards to NIEs in East Asia, Latin America, and other parts of the developing world (Gilpin 2001: 140). Some estimates suggest that between 1977 and 1999 alone, some 3 million US manufacturing jobs were lost as production relocated abroad, but with the contraction in employment almost four times greater than the expansion of employment in developing regions (Harrison and McMillan 2006: 40–41). To a more limited extent, a similar trend is evident in the services sector, most notably in back-office functions, customer services, data and information processing, and so on (WTO 2001a; 2006b). At the same time, the raw material sector has declined, measured as a proportion of world FDI and trade, such that many developing economies have entered, or seek to enter, the manufacturing business. As a result of these shifts, the geography of world economic activity has been transformed in recent years, with important consequences for the distribution of productive power and wealth, and ultimately for the politics of global economic relations (Gilpin 2001; Crafts and Venables 2003). This is patently evident with the rise of China, India, and Brazil as key players in the global political economy.

A second, and related, structural change, has been the intensification of transnational and interregional competition for market share, technological advantage, and rapid product innovation. Such competition is no longer necessarily best conceived as occurring simply between self-contained national economic units, but rather increasingly between firms and businesses in different regions of the globe, in so far as the new geography of world economic activity links distant markets through the operations of giant **multinational corporations** (MNCs) and interregional production networks (Gilpin 2001: 180–182). Economic and corporate competition becomes globalized, since it transcends regions, biting deeper into national economies and magnifying the consequences of local conditions and differences (Held *et al.* 1999, ch. 5). Domestic competition between supermarket chains for agricultural produce, for example, turns farmers both at home and abroad into direct competitors. Given the existence of instantaneous communications, it is not only the scope but also the rapidity with which global competition evolves that contributes significantly to its intensity (Harvey 1989; Castells 1996).

A third significant change is in the nature of production processes, particularly in manufacturing but also in services, which is not captured effectively by flows or stocks of FDI. Outsourcing, or the cross-border fragmentation of production, is increasingly a key means by which production in many sectors is located and re-located abroad to realize efficiency and competitive gains (although it tends to be concentrated in the low-valued-added segments of the production cycle or service provision) (Dicken 2003; Kaplinsky 2005). Since it requires minimal capital investment or ownership, but rather involves collaborative or contractual relationships between producers and a range of suppliers, it is increasingly open to a much wider range of economic agents, from small publishing houses

to major transnation[...] relies on complex tran[...] within and between regio[...] such that, paradoxically, it [...] tegration of productive proce[...] creasing geographical fragment[...] (Gereffi and Korzeniewicz 1994[...] reliance on production chains pres[...] to orthodox conceptions of the worl[...] as constituted by discrete national econo[...] spaces, since it suggests a better depiction (although messier but perhaps more accurate) of a networked global economy—what, in the context of trade, Baldwin (2006) refers to as the spaghetti or noodle bowl analogy (Castells 2000; Brenner 2004; Sassen 2006).

Labour migration

In comparison to capital and goods, labour is relatively immobile. That said, labour flows (especially unskilled) are geographically extensive and, in terms of direction, reflect an almost mirror image of capital flows in so far as they have become primarily South *to* North (Held *et al.* 1999; Castles and Miller 2002; Chiswick and Hatton 2003). As an International Organization for Migration report noted, 'no country remains untouched by international migration' (IOM 2005: 381). Outward flows of people are predominantly a developing-country phenomenon and, despite greater restrictions, they are, surprisingly, on a scale of the mass migrations of the early twentieth century (Chiswick and Hatton 2003: 74). Though complex in origin and destination, interregional (as opposed to intra-regional) migration expanded enormously over the period 1950–2000 (Chiswick and Hatton 2003). In 2005, migrants totalled around 190 million of the world's population, more than twice the level of 1970 (at 82.5 million), making up some 3 per cent of the global workforce, but 9 per cent of the workforce in the developed world (Freeman 2006: 2). Inward migration is somewhat concentrated, in that 75 per cent of migrants were domiciled in just twenty-three

70, and only twenty-eight countries (IOM 2005: 382). Furthermore, migration tends to be an increasingly urban phenomenon, in so far as migrants concentrate in major urban areas (for example, 23 per cent of Parisians, 28 per cent of Londoners and 30 per cent of the population of Abidjan (West Africa) were born abroad) where there are more employment opportunities. Today, 50 per cent are female whereas in the past migrants were overwhelmingly male (Freeman 2006: 4–5). Skilled labour migration from South to North is also on the increase, linked to skills gaps and demographic trends in the North. Significantly too, the huge expansion of temporary workers moving between world regions, facilitated by low-cost transport infrastructures, is additional to these official figures, and is of growing importance to certain sectors (for example, in construction and agriculture) within many developed economies (for example, in the USA, the UK and even in South Africa, which annually hosts 100,000 guest workers) (Freeman 2006: 8).

These developments reflect tendencies towards the integration of distant labour markets (Silver 2003). Such tendencies might be expected to produce some convergence in wage rates (both within the North, and between it and the South) most particularly for the skilled, but overall a growing divergence between rates for skilled and unskilled workers, given the preponderance of the latter among migrants and within the South. There is some evidence to confirm such trends, although the causal role of migration—as opposed to other factors such as trade, technology, or capital mobility—is debated (Galbraith 2002; Firebaugh 2003; Lindert and Williamson 2003). One incontrovertible trend, however, is the growing scale and importance of remittances by migrants, which quadrupled between 1990 and 2004, and which for many labour-exporting countries in the South has become 'an increasingly important source of foreign exchange' (UNCTAD 2006a: 100). According to UNCTAD estimates, the level of migrants' remittances in 1990 was about 50 per cent of total official aid flows, or on a similar scale to FDI flows

from North to South. Today, it far exceeds the value of aid flows, and for many countries also exceeds flows of FDI (for example, remittances to India in 2005 totalled $20.5bn, compared to inward FDI of $11.9bn) (UNCTAD 2006a: 100). Migration is of growing significance to the globalization of labour markets and economic activity more generally.

Globalization: the dominant tendency?

Significant disagreement exists within the existing literature as to whether the above trends point to the integration of the world economy or to its growing segmentation or implosion. Although there is fairly widespread and general agreement among students of global political economy that, in the period since 1945—and in particular since the 1980s—there has been a remarkable intensification of trans-border economic activity, this development lends itself to divergent interpretations (Gordon 1988; O'Brien 1992; Castells 1996; Dicken 2003; Held et al. 1999; Hirst and Thompson 1999; Gilpin 2001; Hoogvelt 2001—for further discussion, see Hay, Chapter 10 in this volume). Whatever the scale and significance of economic globalization, it is, as the references to regionalization and segmentation suggest, by no means the sole tendency operating within the contemporary world economy. Those of a more sceptical persuasion pay greater attention to these other trends contesting the idea that globalization is the principal or dominant tendency shaping the world economy at the start of the twenty-first century (see Box 9.2). In doing so, they mount a rigorous challenge to the very concept of globalization as either a useful description or an explanation of the current period. Two significant arguments dominate this sceptical analysis. The first concerns the real limits to global economic integration; and the second the exaggerated nature of contemporary economic globalization, particularly in relation to the powerful tendency towards regionalization.

BOX 9.2

Sceptical Argument

1. Globalization is exaggerated and far from historic- ally unprecedented.

2. The world economy was much more integrated and open during the *belle époque* of 1870–1914, when interest rates, commodity prices, and wages showed significant signs of convergence.

3. Regionalization and triadization, not globalization, are the dominant tendencies in the contemporary world economy.

4. Globalization is an ideology that serves the in- terests of particular social and political forces.

Studies of the significant impacts of history, geo- graphy, borders, culture, and politics on worldwide economic integration suggest that the present phase of economic globalization has not overcome the fundamental barriers of distance, national borders, and market segmentation (Feldstein and Horioka 1980; Gordon 1988; Boyer and Drache 1996; Burt- less *et al*. 1998; Garrett 1998*a*; Weiss 1998; Rieger and Leibfried 2003). Gravity models of interna- tional trade (a form of regression analysis) which take into account geographic distance, demonstrate an almost exponential decline in trade activity as the distance between trading partners increases (Car- rere and Schiff 2004; Thompson 2006). Moreover, border and home bias effects (which measure economic divergence between countries and the tendency of investors or consumers to buy do- mestic assets/goods, respectively) do not appear to be diminishing. For example, there appears to be very little evidence of a significant trend towards international financial diversification. The implic- ation is that, if globalization was the dominant tendency today, much higher levels of trade and financial flows might be expected, as well as much greater economic convergence, than presently exists (Thompson 2006). Globalization in these respects is therefore considerably overstated.

Furthermore, the sceptics suggest, a more crit- ical interrogation of international economic trends since the 1970s attests to increasing segmentation rather than integration of the world economy (Ruig- rok and Tulder 1995; Berger and Dore 1996; Boyer

and Drache 1996; Hirst and Thompson 1999; Hay 2000; Rugman 2000). As argued by Hay (Chapter 10 in this volume), the dominant patterns in the world economy over recent years have been the increasing regionalization and triadization of economic activ- ity. This is evident not just in trade flow patterns but has also been reinforced by the recent huge expansion in the numbers of preferential trade agreements (agreements between groups of states, each of which give preferential access to the oth- ers' markets) covering an increasing proportion of world trade (Crawford and Florentino 2005; Raven- hill, Chapter 6 in this volume). This segmentation of the world economy along regional lines, and the continuing dominance of OECD economies, accounts for the absence of the substantive global economic convergence that might be expected un- der conditions of globalization. It might therefore be concluded convincingly that regionalization or seg- mentation, rather than globalization, of the world economy is the dominant tendency today, or, as G. Thompson concludes, that the system is 'one poised between "globalization" and supranational "regionalization"' (Hay 2000; Thompson 2006).

Few would dispute that there are limits to glob- alization. Economic globalization here is conceived as a much more complex process than simply a jug- gernaut of world economic unification, in which distance and borders, along with the weight of his- tory and ties of culture, are effectively annihilated in the construction of a single global economic space. As noted above, it is associated with processes of both global economic integration and fragmentation, inclusion and exclusion, and convergence and divergence. National and local economies, to varying degrees, are embedded in global economic networks and systems while, to varying degrees, national and local factors mediate their impact. Distance, borders, and national differences do still matter—but perhaps not quite to the extent that some sceptics assert. Recent studies of the border effect on economic interactions suggest it is much less significant than earlier studies have claimed—with only either moderate or negligible impacts on trade flows (Anderson and van Wincoop 2001; Gorodnichenko and Tesar 2005). Moreover, as noted previously, the evidence does not suggest that there exists a significant home bias in financial markets (the Feldstein–Horioka puzzle) or portfolio investment (see page 287). Indeed, the evidence points to the fact that the savings–investment and home bias puzzles, if not solved, are today significantly less puzzling than they were in the 1980s (Baxter and Crucini 1993; Anderson and van Wincoop 2001). Even the most advanced national economies are not as perfectly integrated as orthodox economic theory suggests should be the case, since subregional and sectoral divergences continue to matter. In this respect, indicative limits to globalization are not incompatible with the notion of the world economy as being imperfectly, rather than perfectly, integrated.

Since few economies (apart from Myanmar and North Korea) are completely isolated, autarky—the pursuit of national self-sufficiency as an economic strategy—appears defunct since national economic fortunes cannot be decoupled entirely from the dynamics of the world economy. This is evident in the manner and speed with which regional crises or slowdowns in world economic activity have a wide and rapid impact across the globe (Bordo and Helbling 2003; Pauly, Chapter 8 in this volume). Furthermore, as the earlier discussion noted, interregional flows of trade, capital, and migrants have increased significantly over recent decades. As one leading economic historian has put it—since 1950, 'Interrelations between the different parts of the world economy have greatly

intensified' (Maddison 2001: 125). This is not to argue that regionalization and concentration of economic activity are not occurring, but rather to conclude that they are not the dominant trends shaping the world economy. Neither are they necessarily incompatible with economic globalization, since in several respects they reinforce it (Schirm 2002). As Baldwin argues, in a world of fragmented production, the political economy of regionalism produces an inherent tendency towards trade globalism (Baldwin 2006). Regionalization can magnify the consequences of interregional economic integration (and vice versa). The concentration of interregional flows within the OECD triad is principally evidence of the unevenness of economic globalization rather than triadization or regionalization per se. That globalization has not measured up to the ideal of neoclassical economic theory, which posits a perfectly integrated world market (of price and income convergence), is readily explicable to theorists of imperfect markets/competition and of institutional economics (Gilpin 2001). Except for the most ardent advocates of neo-liberal economics, few would argue that economic globalization can be assessed solely by measures of economic convergence, because the most pronounced phase of global economic convergence, as economic historians note, was the inter-war period, paradoxically a period of unprecedented deglobalization, when economies rapidly converged, but towards economic collapse (Dowrick and DeLong 2003).

As G. Garrett remarks, 'No matter how many different numbers are presented . . . the growth of international economic activity in the past 30 years remains staggering' (Garrett 2000a: 947). A global economy is in the making, constituted by, and through, the infrastructures and dynamics of economic globalization. This process of economic integration, however, is highly uneven to the extent that it is associated with both economic convergence and divergence, as different economies/subregions/sectors are integrated differentially into this world economic order. Globalization is the dominant, but not the sole, tendency in the world economy, while regionalization (or segmentation) is a complementary rather than competing tendency. Economic globalization today, as in the past, is marked by patterns of both economic convergence and divergence or, in the language of classical Marxism, 'uneven (world) development'. This complexity is not captured by most orthodox economic treatments of globalization, which equate it solely with global economic convergence. Recent political and economic crises—from 9/11 to the Iraq War—have not undermined globalization, which appears to be more socially and institutionally embedded than many sceptics assumed. This conclusion, however, does not imply any necessary or particular kinds of consequences of globalization for the state, economic development, or global politics. Such matters remain open and require separate investigation and theorization (see Chapters 10–14 in this volume). Having established globalization as a 'really existing condition', the focus logically turns to the cardinal question;

namely, what forces are driving this further 'extraordinary episode' in the history of the world economy?

KEY POINTS

- Globalization is not a singular process, but its economic dimension is critical.

- Economic globalization defines the principal trend in the contemporary global economy.

- It is associated with growing but uneven worldwide economic integration.

- Regionalization and segmentation are not necessarily incompatible with economic globalization.

- Economic globalization has not diminished as a consequence of recent global political and economic crises, suggesting that it is much more institutionally embedded than many sceptics have assumed.

The Logics of Economic Globalization

Identifying the causes of economic globalization is a difficult and tricky intellectual task. Difficult because there are multiple dynamics at work, and tricky because the very notion of causation raises some thorny philosophical questions. Casting the latter aside for the moment, it is important to be clear about what is being explained here: in other words, it is necessary to identify whether the focus is on the *general* determinants of economic globalization, or the determinants of the *current* phase of economic globalization. Explaining one is not quite the same as explaining the other (Robertson 2003). Given the story so far, the focus will be primarily, but not exclusively, upon the latter. The complexity of contemporary economic globalization is such that the search for a single, determinate logic is likely to prove unsuccessful since 'in explaining

social change no single and sovereign mechanism can be specified' (Giddens 1984: 243).

In crude terms, the literature distinguishes between thick or thin conceptions of causation. In its thickest sense, causality implies determination in so far as causes are considered both necessary and/or sufficient to bring about an event or given social phenomenon (Mellor 1995: 6). Thus technology, it is often argued, is the cause of globalization, because technology is sufficient to bring it about, and globalization could not have occurred in its absence. Thinner conceptions of causation refer to dispositions, in the sense of the conditions, tendencies, or factors that make given events or social phenomena more rather than less likely or probable (McCullagh 1998: 173). So the liberalization of national economies, following the political revolution of neo-liberalism in the 1980s, can be viewed as a cause of economic globalization to the extent that it made it more, rather than less, probable, and thereby not simply a historical accident or arbitrary development. The thinnest conceptions of causation emphasize the contingency of history—that it could readily be otherwise—in that globalization is the product of the coincidence of unique circumstances and the specific interventions of social agents. However, since many complex social phenomena, such as economic globalization, involve a multiplicity of causes, few theories of globalization develop either a rigidly determinist or contingent explanatory account. Before examining these theories in some detail, it will be helpful to analyse the principal logics of globalization.

Principal logics

Explanations of economic globalization tend to focus on three interrelated factors or social forces; namely; *technics* (technological change and social organization); *economics* (markets and capitalism); and *politics* (ideas, interests, and institutions). Since they are so closely interrelated, the principal methodological problem for analysts lies in unbundling the causal mechanisms involved (Garrett 2000*a*). Distinguishing them analytically is the first step. This will be followed in a subsequent section by an exploration of how some of the principal theories combine and configure these three causal logics in their explanatory accounts of contemporary economic globalization.

Technics is central to any account of globalization, since it is a truism that, without modern communications infrastructures in particular, a worldwide economy would not be possible. All writers refer to the transformation in communications and transport technologies and the way in which this has 'shrunk the globe'. 'Action at a distance' increasingly transcends national borders, not to mention continents, so that time and space are compressed. In this process, the distinction between domestic economic activity and

global economic activity becomes less easy to sustain as global markets evolve. Rather than the liberalization of national economies driving globalization, it can be argued that technological change drives liberalization, especially in the financial sector (Garrett 2000*a*). Modern communication technology not only provides the infrastructure of a real-time global economy but also facilitates new forms of transnational and global economic organization, from production through to regulation.

This informatics revolution has underwritten not only the infrastructure of an evolving global economy but also, according to Dicken and others, a 'global shift' (Dicken 2003). This is expressed in the combined move towards service-based or post-industrial economies within the advanced core of the world economy, and the associated rise of industrial economies in the developing world. To paraphrase Giddens, 'technology is inherently globalizing' in so far as contemporary economic globalization is conceived as a product of the second industrial revolution—the logic of the informatics age.

Crucial as technology is to any account of economic globalization, so too is its specifically *economic* logic. This is discussed in two distinct sets of literature: that of orthodox economics, which explains globalization in terms of market dynamics; and that of radical political economy, which explains it in terms of the imperatives of capitalism. In the case of the former, globalization is considered to be a direct consequence of market competition whether, as in the case of trade, in terms of the operation of comparative or strategic advantage, or in relation to transnational production in terms of imperfect competition or the product cycle (Dunning 1993; Gilpin 2001).

The structure and functioning of markets is conceived as being central to understanding the competitive dynamics that lead inevitably to the globalization of economic activity. Drawing on both neoclassical and new economic theories, the principal concern is identifying the specifically economic logic—understood in terms of the pursuit of profit, wealth, and market position—which explains the process of global economic integration and the location or distribution of economic activity (see Box 9.3). By contrast, radical political economy draws on the Marxist tradition that locates economic globalization in the expansionary and universalizing logic of modern capitalism. This expansionary logic is a product of capitalism's structural contradictions—the tendency for overproduction combined with the relative impoverishment of workers—and its insatiable requirement for capital accumulation; that is, profit. Economic globalization is driven by the continual search among the corporate sector for new markets, cheaper labour, and new sources of profitability; a process facilitated and encouraged by governments and the agencies of global economic governance as they work to reproduce the very system on which their political legitimacy partly depends (Callinicos 2003). In short, the specifically economic logic of globalization arises from both the dynamics of markets and the dynamics of capitalism.

Politics—shorthand here for ideas, interests, and institutions—constitutes the third logic of economic globalization. Almost all accounts of contemporary globalization make reference to the rise and dominance of neo-liberal ideology throughout the OECD world, along with its associated policies of liberalization, deregulation, and privatization. If technology provides the physical infrastructure of economic globalization, it is the significant movement towards 'market-driven politics' (Leys 2001)—greater emphasis on *laissez-faire* capitalism—that provides its ideological infrastructure.

Irrespective of the party holding office, the dominant political trend since the 1970s in OECD states has been towards the liberalization of national economies and the easing of restrictions on capital mobility. This has enabled—some might argue, driven—the creation of more integrated global markets and the globalization of production. Governments, or rather states, have been central to the process of economic globalization. They have been instrumental in establishing the necessary national political conditions and policies—not to mention vital regional and global institutions, agreements, and policies—essential to its advancement. Promoted and advocated by a powerful configuration of domestic and transnational coalitions and lobbies, economic globalization is very much a political construction or project. It depends on a particular configuration of social and political forces, both national and transnational, to sustain or accelerate

---

BOX 9.3

Economic Theory and Globalization

1. Neoclassical theory explains globalization in terms of **comparative advantage**, market forces, and economic convergence.

2. Free trade involves economies trading what they have a comparative advantage or efficiency in producing, thus in theory maximizing both national and global welfare.

3. Market forces and global competition ensure that similar goods and services are produced efficiently and at a minimum cost.

4. Market convergence ensures that prices and interest rates in a globalizing economy become increasing equalized or differences increasingly narrowed.

5. New trade theory, locational theory, and the theory of imperfect competition explain why perfectly competitive global markets do not exist, and why market segmentation (differences and lack of complete convergence) occurs even in a globalizing world economy.

its momentum against the background of an established but rising anti-globalization political backlash.

Central to the politics of the current globalization project is the hegemonic power and role of the United States, as the world's sole hyper-power. To the extent that a liberal world economic order, as Gilpin (2001) and others argue, is a by-product of US global dominance, then shifts in US strategic interests and domestic politics will have significant consequences for economic globalization. On the other hand, to the extent that the relative economic power of the United States has been eroded in recent years, the politics of globalization has become far more complex, not to say shaped, by the interplay between the principal global economic players—states, international organizations, and transnational corporations—as well as the agencies of transnational civil society. In sum, contemporary economic globalization has an underlying political logic in so far as it is the product of political ideology; national or international public policy; and the interests and interactions between states, global institutions, and national and transnational social forces.

In different measure and combination, these three logics—technics, economics, and politics—inform the principal theories of globalization to be found in the existing literature. All theories, to differing degrees, draw upon these three logics in identifying the causal mechanisms of contemporary economic globalization. How they do so is explored in the following section.

Principal theories

As Rosenberg (2000) observes, there are many theories of globalization—its causes and dynamics—but little substantive globalization theory. This distinction is important in that it suggests that any notional globalization theory must be parasitic upon, if not entirely subservient to, the 'grand theories' of social science. To date, no discrete or singular globalization theory—which seeks to provide a

coherent and systematic account of its causes, consequences, and developmental trajectory—can be said to exist. Nor is there any singular theory of globalization, only a proliferation of schools and analyses. Accordingly, the emphasis here will be on identifying distinctive theories of globalization, with subsequent elaboration and critical examination of their principal formulations.

Few convincing accounts of economic globalization, given its complexity, locate its origins in a single causal logic. However, existing theories do make judgements both about the relative significance or configuration of different causal logics, in effect privileging some over others in their explanatory narratives. Along the continuum from thicker to thinner forms of causal explanation, accounts vary according to whether they give preference to the structural, the conjunctural, or the contingent sources of economic globalization.

Broadly speaking, structural explanations are thick causal accounts because they tend towards the deterministic: they highlight the imperatives or developmental logic of social and economic systems. Thus, structuralist accounts of economic globalization explain it in terms of the imperatives or drivers of technological advance and/or capital accumulation. Globalization is considered almost an *inevitable* consequence of either modern technologically advanced societies—recall Giddens' dictum that 'modernity is inherently globalizing'—or the expansionary imperatives of capitalism. While structuralist accounts can answer the why and how questions of globalization—why it came about, and how—they are less valuable in explaining its specific historical form (what kind?) or timing (why now?) (see Table 9.1).

In contrast, conjunctural explanations are much better at explaining its timing and its form as well as its more historically specific causes. Conjunctural accounts, which are causally thinner than structural explanations, pay more attention to the confluence of particular historical circumstances, trends, and events, which together combine to produce a given social phenomenon at a specific point in time and in a given form. As McCullagh (1998: 178)

Table 9.1 Economic Globalization: Types of Theory

	Causal mechanism	Primary concepts
Structural	Imperatives of domestic and international systems	Imperatives Inevitability Determinate
Conjunctural	Emergent properties of confluence of separate logics and circumstances	Conditional Tendencies Dispositions
Constructivist	Ideas and discourses as constitutive	Contingent Incidental Indeterminate

summarizes it, 'the cause of an event is a conjunction of things which together have a tendency to produce a certain kind of outcome'. Thus, contemporary economic globalization can be understood as a consequence of a multiplicity of tendencies (technological, economic and so on) interacting with particular historical conditions and policies (for example, the end of the Cold War) to produce its distinctive (neo-liberal) form. Rather than stressing the inevitability of globalization, conjunctural explanations stress its conditionality.

Finally, accounts that stress the contingency of economic globalization emphasize its causal indeterminacy—the absence of a fully specified causal mechanism. Although such explanations may be less relevant to answering the 'why' question, they are particularly pertinent to addressing 'how, when and what' type questions. As such, these might be considered very thin, rather than thick, causal accounts of economic globalization because they stress its almost *incidental* or *arbitrary* (rather than inevitable or conditional) origins. Attention therefore tends to be focused much more on the role of ideas—economic globalization as an idea or prevailing discourse—rather than seeking to identify specific causal connections within the empirical evidence of economic trends (Schirato and Webb 2003: 21; see also Hay, Chapter 10 in this volume). Accordingly, it can be argued that understanding the social or discursive construction of economic globalization is just as—some would say, more—important as

identifying underlying causal patterns in the empirical data.

Structural theories of economic globalization can be distinguished in respect of how far they privilege domestic or global structures. Those that emphasize the primacy of domestic structures locate the sources of economic globalization in the nature and dynamics of modern societies. Since the nineteenth-century French philosopher Claude Saint-Simon wrote of the universalizing logic of industrial societies, the primacy of technology as the motor of globalization has figured prominently in the political economy literature. This thesis is to be found, in more nuanced and less deterministic formulations in the work of Ohmae (1990), Strange (1998b), Rosecrance (1999), and Garrett (2000a), among others.

Technology is privileged in such explanations, not simply because it has shrunk the globe but also because it is often conceived as the principal dynamic of social change in advanced societies. Just as the technological revolution of industrialism transformed European agricultural societies, so today the information revolution is transforming the nature of production and social organization. In this 'virtualization' process, to borrow Rosecrance's (1999) label, borders no longer define the boundaries of national economic space, while distance becomes a less significant or costly barrier, although not entirely irrelevant, to the organization of production and economic activity. Moreover, this technological revolution enables firms and national economies, irrespective almost of geographic location, to exploit their comparative economic advantage and specialize further in the production and trading of those goods and services at which they are most efficient. Technological change, in other words, brings in its wake both economic and political change in the form of globalized markets and the liberalization of economies. Since continual technological innovation is a structural (recursive) feature of modern (and modernizing) societies, then economic globalization, notwithstanding its cyclical fluctuations, is an inevitable feature of the contemporary global political economy.

That technology is a necessary requirement of economic globalization is not doubted, but for Marxist theorists (historical materalists) it is by no means a sufficient explanation. It is the capitalist form of the economy that is the crucial explanatory factor, not technology, which is subservient to the dynamics of capitalist accumulation and competition. Wood (2003: 14–15) summarizes this argument well: 'Capitalism . . . is driven by certain systemic imperatives, the imperatives of competition, profit-maximization and accumulation . . . globalization is their result rather than their cause.' The sources of globalization are therefore located in the necessary requirement of capitalism constantly to acquire new markets and to produce more efficiently in order to sustain levels of profitability and reproduce itself. Cultivating global markets and producing abroad to maximize profits and corporate efficiency are the consequence of the structural imperatives and contradictions of capitalist economies rather than technological innovation per se.

Moreover, these expansionary tendencies are shaped by intensifying economic competition and the resulting concentration of economic power in huge national and transnational corporations that can readily exploit new technologies and economies of scale to produce more efficiently and compete more effectively, both at home and abroad. Liberalization and the rolling back of the state, reinforced by the disciplines of global institutions such as the WTO and IMF, are conceived ultimately as

responses to these developments rather than their author. Such accounts do not deny the importance of political agency or the strategic action of states and other social forces, but rather assert that in the very last event these are of only partial relevance in explaining economic globalization (though they are highly relevant to understanding the particular form it takes; for example, Empire in the nineteenth century versus Corporate globalization in the twentieth).

In so far as the main engines of capitalist globalization are located in a small number of OECD economies, there is some disagreement as to whether the contemporary period is best described as a renewed phase of capitalist imperialism, a distinctly new form of globalized capitalism system, or a historically-novel, global capitalist empire (Hardt and Negri 2000; Callinicos 2003; Gill 2003; Wood 2003). Irrespective of how it is characterized, the principal logic of contemporary economic globalization is located, in Marxist theory, firmly with the imperatives of capitalist development.

Beyond these domestic-level explanations, other structural theories give priority to international or global system-level structures. Within all the major schools of theory in global political economy—realist, liberal, and Marxist—frequent emphasis is placed on the role of hegemony—or the dominance or pre-eminence of a single power or superpower—in creating and maintaining the conditions for an open world economy, and so economic globalization. In effect, the hierarchical structure of power relations in the global political economy creates the necessary conditions for economic globalization. Despite their otherwise radically different theoretical positions, R. Gilpin, G. J. Ikenberry, and I. Wallerstein all assert that hegemony is an essential condition for the development and perpetuation of a globalizing world economy (Wallerstein 1983; Gilpin 1987; Ikenberry 2001). Without a hegemonic power capable of establishing a stable and managed world order, through both persuasion and coercion, economic globalization would be little more than an ideal. It is hegemony that makes an open world economy possible. That said, it is also an essential precondition of economic globalization that the hegemonic power is a liberal-capitalist power and thus has a material interest in creating and sustaining a liberal world economic order as opposed to a world empire. In this respect, hegemonic theory is entirely compatible with domestic level structural accounts, which consider economic globalization as a consequence of the imperatives of capitalist accumulation and market forces. However, to the extent that the hegemonic power becomes predatory or unilateralist, the necessary conditions for economic globalization will be eroded.

By contrast, the relative decline of the hegemon, as Keohane (1984) suggests, may have little impact, to the extent that globalization becomes institutionally embedded. Under current conditions, the reassertion of US hegemony is likely to hamper, if not undermine, economic globalization if Washington pursues a unilateralist or predatory agenda; or will reinvigorate it if it seeks to advance the further liberalization of the world economy. Of course, theory also points to the limits, contradictions, and ultimate erosion of hegemonic power, suggesting that economic globalization has to be understood primarily as a historical phenomenon (Gilpin 1981).

Whereas structural theories explain economic globalization as a path-dependent outcome of systemic—whether domestic or international—imperatives, by contrast *conjunctural* accounts are rooted in a more context-dependent analysis. This is not to suggest that structural forces or tendencies are ignored—on the contrary, they form the context of any historical analysis—but rather they are combined with a greater attention to the unique configuration of political, social, national and global conditions that precipitated contemporary economic globalization. There is also a greater recognition of the role of strategic action by governments or other key agencies, and the interaction between social forces, political institutions, and ideas in advancing or constraining processes of global economic integration. Rather than an inevitability, economic globalization is understood as being 'rooted in history and

shaped by particular political, social and cultural conditions . . . a conjunctural correlation of forces that are subject to reversal' (Petras and Veltmeyer 2001: 46). Among the most comprehensive studies in this context is Castells's three-volume study of the rise of 'global informational capitalism' (Castells 1996, 1997, 1998).

Castells sets out to explain the most recent phase of economic globalization, which he dates to the 1980s, rather than to produce a generalizable account of economic globalization per se. Castells identifies the principal sources of this new *belle époque* in the profound restructuring of the major capitalist economies, itself a response to the economic and political crises of the 1970s (Castells 2000). This period was characterized by historic shifts in the technological, economic, and political spheres that, while insufficient in themselves to forge a new epoch of globalization, in conjunction they provided the vital conditions in which it could flourish. Just as two atoms of hydrogen combine with one atom of oxygen to produce a new substance called water, so, by analogy, the specific configuration and conjunction of developments in these three spheres—technics, economics, and politics—gave rise to the current epoch of globalization. In other words, globalization emerged out of—in more technical language, is an emergent property of—the particular confluence of historical conditions in the technological, economic, and political domains (Sayer 2000: 12). What, then, were these significant developments?

According to Castells, they were, respectively, the information technology revolution; capitalist restructuring; and the political hegemony of the neo-liberal project (Castells 2000: Prologue). Tracing these developments to the dissipation, in the 1970s, of the post-war system of managed capitalism, Castells identifies in the informatics revolution of the 1980s a new production paradigm that facilitated a process of global economic restructuring. Overseas manufacturing production became more technically feasible as well as economically necessary. Production began shifting abroad while the major economies became increasingly service-based (post-industrial) or, in Castells' language, 'informational'. This deindustrialization in the core economies was accompanied by industrialization in its hinterlands. However, as Castells argues, this 'Restructuring of business firms, and the new information technologies, while being at the source of globalizing trends, could not have evolved, by themselves, toward a networked global economy without policies of de-regulation, privatization, and the liberalization of trade and investment' (Castells 2000: 147).

Politics, but more specifically the advocacy and implementation of neo-liberal (market-enhancing) ideas, policies, and institutional (both national and global) reforms, played a significant role in this process to the extent that he argues 'The decisive agents in setting up a new global economy were governments, and, in particular, the governments of the wealthiest countries, the G7, and their ancillary institutions' (Castells 2000: 137). The advance of this political project was also greatly assisted by the collapse of communism and thus any feasible political alternative to the capitalist model of development. For Castells, the emergence of a historically unique 'global informational capitalism' that has 'the institutional, organizational, and technological capacity to work as a unit in real time, or in chosen time, on a planetary scale' can be traced to the specific historical conjuncture of technological, economic, and political circumstances of the 1980s (Castells 2000: 104).

Castells' analysis of globalization is among the most comprehensive and sophisticated. However, as with other conjunctural accounts (Scholte 2000; Gill 2003), it is vulnerable to the criticism that in advocating an essentially multicausal account, it simply avoids specifying a coherent or convincing causal mechanism. In simpler language, since almost every key factor is regarded as a cause of globalization, by definition, nothing in particular can be said to be its specific cause. To critics, conjunctural accounts do not so much explain—that is, identify a causal mechanism or mechanisms—so much as provide a rich description of economic globalization.

This judgement is a little harsh because it presumes a strongly scientific or positivistic model of causation identified with some determinate causal mechanism. By contrast, historical or interpretative models of causation readily acknowledge such causal complexity (McCullagh 1998; Sayer 2000; Benton and Craib 2001). Nevertheless, a more fundamental problem is that conjunctural analyses fail to accept, although they imply, the essential indeterminacy or contingency of complex social phenomena, such as globalization, and thus cannot really claim adequately to explain it (Wendt 1998).

Economic globalization refers both to a process of growing material interconnectedness as well as to the 'idea' or consciousnesses of that process. Obviously, the two are interrelated but in quite complex ways. *Social constructivist* analyses are far more interested in the idea of economic globalization, and why it has become such a pervasive discourse or way of talking and theorizing about the world economy. Although they do not discount the relevance of globalization's material manifestations—in terms of flows of trade and investment—social constructivists are far more interested in its ideational or discursive construction. In this respect they argue, to paraphrase A. Wendt, that globalization is what states and others make of it, rather than a preordained or objective condition, and as such is a largely contingent phenomenon (Wendt 1992).

Rather than seeking to identify the causal mechanisms that generate globalization, constructivists seek to explore how widely-shared ideas or discourses of economic globalization are constitutive of—that is, make real or give intersubjective meaning to—the very process itself; for example, the popular discourse or idea of globalization as an inevitable or irresistible juggernaut of social change (see Box 9.4). In simple terms, there can be no economic globalization without the idea or discourse of economic globalization. This is not to argue that globalization is simply a product of the collective imagination. On the contrary, it is largely to acknowledge that in naming or identifying these material trends in the world economy as a process of 'economic globalization', that very process becomes

BOX 9.4

Causal and Constitutive Theory

1. Causal theories refer to explanations that identify specific or general causal mechanisms which can be said to be both necessary and/or sufficient to produce the social effects or social phenomenon that is the object of analysis.

2. Constitutive theories refer to explanations that demonstrate how ideas, values, and beliefs or discourses about the world construct 'reality' and thus

constitute, in part, the very social phenomenon under investigation.

3. An intense debate exists as to whether causal and constitutive theories are different or similar kinds of explanations and, thus, whether in effect reasons can be considered, in the strictest sense, to be causes.

---

socially or discursively constructed and is thus given intersubjective meaning. Social constructivism, therefore, has an important bearing upon how globalization is interpreted and understood, both within the academy and beyond. Accordingly, to make sense of globalization it is first necessary to deconstruct or unpack the dominant ideas or discourses that inform how it is generally interpreted or conceived, and the extent to which such ideas or discourses reflect or misconstrue contemporary world economic trends.

As Petras and Veltmeyer (2001: 11) observe, 'Globalization is both a description and a prescription, and as such, it serves as both an explanation . . . and an ideology that currently dominates thinking, policy making and political practice.' Those studies that have drawn on the insights of this kind of social constructivist methodology generally tend to conclude that the genesis and diffusion of the 'idea of economic globalization' is more important to understanding and explaining the contemporary economic condition than is a rigorous assessment of the actual empirical trends (Hay and Watson 1998; Rosamond 2001; Schmidt 2002; Hay, Chapter 10 in this volume). For the constructivists, the evidence is less important than the fact that to the extent that states, social forces, and international agencies perceive and understand the world principally within the discourse of globalization, they reproduce and perpetuate it to a large extent irrespective of what the

empirical evidence discloses. There are also very good reasons why they do so, and in this context political interest and motivations—the power of political agency—becomes of critical importance. Irrespective of the objective existence of globalization, it is incontrovertible that the *idea* of economic globalization plays a crucial role in co-ordinating, communicating, and legitimating a range of diverse political projects, from the politics of the Third Way to the politics of the New Right (Schmidt 2002). Economic globalization, in such accounts, is therefore distinguished by its essential *contingency* more so than its inevitability. It is as much, if not more of, an ideational, rather than material, phenomenon. As such it is not so much determined by collective ideas but rather constituted by, and through, them, with significant consequences for the politics of globalization (see Hay, Chapter 10 in this volume).

Making sense of the logics of economic globalization

How are these different accounts of the causes of economic globalization to be reconciled? Do these distinctive types of theory offer competing or complementary explanations? Is a 'grand theory' of economic globalization attainable? Such questions flow naturally from an examination of the theoretical pluralism that is the hallmark of global political economy. If there is no singular theory of globalization this is partly, but not exclusively, a consequence of the fact that there is no universally accepted set of criteria—or epistemology—against which the validity of theories of global political economy can be judged. This does not mean that rational judgements cannot be made as to which theories present a more or less convincing account of globalization, but simply that such judgements cannot in any meaningful sense establish their 'truth'—or its true causes. Quite simply, the problem is that, as within the social sciences more generally, an appeal to the evidence or the 'facts' of globalization largely proves inconclusive, since the 'facts' are often compatible with competing theories. That is, theories are underdetermined. Thus, for example, the evidence discussed in the first part of this chapter supports theories that identify both technology and politics as the principal cause of globalization. Accordingly, rather than seeking the unattainable grail of objective truth, a more productive approach may be to explore whether or how these three distinctive types of theory might be conjoined and so contribute to a more comprehensive understanding and explanation of the logics of economic globalization (see Table 9.2).

In a very interesting article, Eric Helleiner (1997) seeks to realize precisely that goal. Drawing on the scholarship of Fernand Braudel, a renowned social historian, Helleiner concludes that to understand and explain economic globalization as a historical and social process it is necessary to adopt and combine different temporal perspectives. These distinct temporal perspectives reflect the different pace of historical time: from the *longue durée* of centuries over which change can appear to have a glacial momentum, shaped as it is by deeper social structures and recurrent patterns of socio-economic organization, through the *epochal*, or conjunctural in which the pattern of socio-economic change over several decades seems to prefigure the emergence of a new era or social formation, to *l'histoire événementielle*, or contemporaneous, in which social agents—from individuals to governments—are daily engaged in reacting to, or in seeking to shape, events and circumstances as they perceive and interpret them.

As Helleiner (1997: 95) suggests, these 'three temporal perspectives are useful not just in describing economic globalization, but also in understanding and explaining it'.

A direct correspondence may be observed between these temporal perspectives and the three types of theory elaborated in the preceding section: the *longue durée* is associated with structural accounts; the epochal with the conjunctural; and the contemporaneous with constructivism.

As Gilpin (2001: 364) observes, 'globalization has been taking place for centuries'. Understood as a process of secular historical development, economic globalization might therefore best be explained through the medium of structural theories that locate its causes in the dynamics of enduring systems or recurrent patterns of socio-economic organization. Thus economic globalization can be understood as an intrinsic feature of the modern age: of modern societies and the modern international state system or, to use a grand term, modernity. Conceived from a temporal vantage point of the *longue durée*, economic globalization appears as a chronic or persistent—although by no means linear—historical trend that, as Helleiner (1997: 95) comments, 'also makes it seem an almost irreversible one'. To understand and explain economic globalization therefore, requires some account of the deeply embedded structures of the global political economy—capitalism, industrialism, hegemony and so on—which are its underlying drivers. At one level, such accounts are essential, since, while they cannot explain its specific historical features or rhythms, they do offer insights into why economic globalization has been a recurring feature of the global political economy for many centuries.

In contrast, particular historical epochs of intensifying global economic integration, like that of today, are better explained by conjunctural theories. Such theories seek principally to account for the cyclical and historical rhythms of economic globalization: how and why it accelerates or contracts at different historical moments, and the specific configuration it takes—from empire to global markets.

Table 9.2 Economic Globalization Summary: Types of Theories and Forms of Explanation

	Principal methodological focus	Causal mechanisms	Focus	Indicative account of globalization
Structural	Focus on organizing principles of domestic and international systems Holistic analysis Emphasis on dynamics or 'laws' of the social totality	Tends towards (economic, technological or political) determinism Emphasis on inevitability, irresistible forces Path-dependent outcomes	Why and How questions	Ohmae (1990)/Rosecrance (1999)—technics primary causal logic Woods (2003)—imperatives of capitalism Gilpin (1987)/Wallerstein (1983)—political imperatives of hegemony—globalization as Americanization
Conjunctural	Unique configuration of social forces and historical circumstances Political decisions and agency	Emphasis on tendencies and conditional factors Confluence of events and circumstances Emergent properties	How, When and What form	Castells (1990, 1997, 1998, 2000)—global informational capitalism product of conjuncture of technics, economics and political developments in 1980s
Constructivist	Role of ideas crucial in shaping how agents view and act on the world Discourse of globalization—globe talk—constructs the way the world is understood and acted on by social agents Discourse of economic globalization constitutes it rather than simply mirrors it	Constitutive rather than causal explanation—globalization is made real through discourse Emphasis on motivations, interests, ideas and political agency	When and What form	Schmidt (2002)—how the discourse of globalization came to play the crucial role in co-ordinating, communicating, and legitimating European government economic strategies in the 1990s

In doing so, such accounts emphasize discontinuity, rather than continuity (as in structural accounts) with the past. Thus the entire debate about whether contemporary globalization is unprecedented by comparison with the *belle époque* is indicative of an epochal or conjunctural perspective. Understood from such a perspective, the origins of contemporary economic globalization are to be located in a particular conjuncture of factors and forces within a specific historical context. This provides a different frame of reference from the structural, as it suggests that economic globalization is 'also a clearly reversible process' because the conjuncture of forces that hold it together at any given moment may (or will) eventually dissipate (Helleiner 1997: 95). Conjunctural accounts thereby complement structural theories because they provide an explanation of globalization's episodic and discontinuous evolutionary pattern, offering specific insights into what drives it forward (or backwards) at particular moments in history.

Finally, from a contemporaneous perspective, Helleiner notes that economic globalization 'often appears as a political weapon used and promoted by certain groups' as 'a project in which the local is increasingly "globalized" . . . in an active and deliberate way' (Helleiner 1997: 96). Constructivist explanations that emphasize motivations, strategic actions, and the political struggles over globalization offer significant insights into its contemporaneity. Such accounts complement both structural and conjunctural theories because they can explain how and why economic globalization comes to be constructed through the multiplicity of actions of, and interactions between, individual and collective (political and economic) subjects or agents, from consumers to corporations, and protestors to politicians. From this contemporaneous perspective, economic globalization appears decidedly contingent or fluid. Constructivism privileges the explanation of the motives, interests, ideas, and institutions that are constitutive of such action. In providing this, constructivist theories of economic globalization—which emphasize its essential contingency—function to correct those marked tendencies in structural and conjunctural accounts that play down the significance of social agency—ideas, motivations, and choices. In doing so, the former very much complements the latter.

For much the same reason that economic globalization is considered causally complex, necessitating a multi-causal analysis, so too, following Helleiner (1997: 102), must it also be conceived as a 'layered' historical process; that is, 'taking place at several different historical speeds'. Accordingly, understanding and explaining the current phase of economic globalization requires a causal analysis that is not only sensitive to its multiple logics—technics, economics, and politics—but also to its multiple speeds—the *longue durée*, epochal, and contempraneous. No single theory, or account, of economic globalization meets, or is ever likely to meet, such demanding requirements (Rosenberg 2000). This should not induce academic despondency, because, as has been argued, by drawing on philosophically compatible structural, conjunctural, and constructivist accounts a more systematic and layered analysis of economic globalization is entirely feasible, even if this falls short of the explanatory properties of an ideal globalization theory.

KEY POINTS

- Economic globalization is conceived as having three logics: technics, economics, and politics.

- There are three main types of theory associated with economic globalization: structural, conjunctural, and constructivist.

- These can be distinguished in terms of their distinctive causal terms: imperatives, tendencies, and contingency.

- Understanding globalization as a historical process involves examining it in terms of three speeds of social change: the *longue durée*, the epochal, and the contemporaneous.

● The three theories of globalization correspond with each of these three speeds, explaining economic globalization from a different temporal perspective.

● The three theories of economic globalization are therefore in principal complementary, producing a layered explanation from its structured to its contingent origins.

The Second Age of Globalization: Another Extraordinary Episode?

Remarking on a previous epoch of global economic transformation, John Maynard Keynes wrote of 'an extraordinary episode in the economic progress of man', in which 'the internationalization of . . . economic and social life . . . was nearly complete' (quoted in Grieco and Ikenberry 2003: 206). Many of his liberal contemporaries, such as Norman Angell, associated (what later became known as) this *belle époque* (1870–1914) with the emergence of a new world order in which war was becoming increasingly unthinkable (McGrew 2002). The guns of August 1914 brutally suppressed such liberal idealism. This first age of liberal, or more accurately, imperial, global economic integration has acquired totemic status in the current debates about globalization. For those of a sceptical persuasion, it is the gold standard against which the many empirical claims concerning contemporary economic integration can be debunked (Hirst and Thompson 1999). By contrast, for those persuaded that the world is at present in the grip of the second age of globalization, it has become the benchmark against which to validate its historically unprecedented features. This has given rise to a voluminous literature of comparative economic history, dissecting and contrasting the two great ages of globalization in the search for conclusive—or rather, elusive—evidence as to which can lay claim to being the more 'globalized' (see Table 9.3). The

real significance of this enterprise, however, is more political than historical. Because the critical issue is not the comparative scale of globalization so much as what the comparison discloses about the limits to, or scope for, national politics under conditions of global economic integration. Or as M. Bordo, B. Eichengreen, and D. A. Irwin put it, 'why globalization a century ago did not create the same dilemmas as now' (Bordo *et al.* 1999).

For Gilpin, 'although globalization had become the defining feature of the international economy at the beginning of the twenty-first century' the current world economy, in comparison with the *belle époque*, remains considerably less globalized and integrated (Gilpin 2001: 3). This is a view shared with other economic historians (for example, O'Rourke and Williamson 1999). The implication is that, far from being unprecedented, economic globalization today is essentially a return to the developmental trajectory of the world economy inaugurated by the birth of the industrial age. In their study of global finance, Obstfeld and Taylor identify a more differentiated picture in which, on some measures (gross capital flows and stocks of foreign capital), globalization is considerably greater today, on others it has converged with pre-1914 levels (interest rate differentials, national savings and investment correlations), and on yet others still it is below that of the pre-1914 era (flows of capital to the South and

Table 9.3 Epochal Shifts in Globalization Since 1820

Epoch	Intercontinental commodity market integration		Migration and world labour markets		Integration of world capital markets What happened to integration (Feldstein–Horioka Slope Coefficient)
	Change in price gaps between continents	Why they changed	How migrant shares changed in receiving countries	Why they changed	
1820–1914	Price gaps cut by 81%	72% because of cheaper transport; 28% because of pre-1870 tariff cuts	Migrant shares rise	Passenger transport costs slashed, push and pull (immigration policies remain neutral)	60% progress from complete segmentation towards market integration
1914–50	Gaps double in width, return to 1870 level	New trade barriers only	Migrant shares fall	Restrictive immigration policies	Reversion to complete market segmentation
1950–2000, especially since 1970	Price gaps cut by 76%, now lower than in 1914	74% because of policies freeing trade; 26% because of cheaper transport	Migrant shares rise	Transport costs drop, push and pull again (no net change in immigration policies)	60% progress from complete segmentation towards market integration
Overall 1820–2000	Price gaps cut by 92%	18% because of trade policies; 82% because of cheaper transport	No clear change in US migrant shares, but rises elsewhere	Policy restrictions, offsetting transport improvements	60% progress from complete segmentation towards market integration

Source: Lindert and Williamson (2003)

net capital flows) (Obstfeld and Taylor 2004). In contrast, for Gilpin (2002), and O'Rourke and Williamson (1999) among others, the world economy still has some way to go in order to achieve the comprehensive levels of global capital, trade, commodity and labour market integration of the pre-1914 era (O'Rourke and Williamson 1999; Gilpin 2002). As O'Rourke and Williamson (1999: 2, 14) emphasize,

"By 1914, there was hardly a village or town anywhere on the globe whose prices were not influenced by distant foreign markets, whose infrastructure was not financed by foreign capital, whose engineering, manufacturing, and even business skills were not imported from abroad, or whose labour markets were not influenced by the absence of those who had emigrated or by the presence of strangers who had immigrated "

and

"involved the most extensive wage and living standard convergence the Atlantic economy has ever seen "

Indeed, Hoogvelt describes the current era as one of the implosion of global economic activity as it has become increasingly concentrated in the OECD and a handful of NIEs by comparison with the age of empire (Hoogvelt 2001). The implication is that the significance of the second age of economic globalization is considerably exaggerated and thus its consequences have been significantly overstated, particularly with respect to national politics and the continuing centrality of state power to the proper functioning of the world economy ((Hirst and Thompson 1999; see also Hay, Chapter 10 in this volume). This, in some respects, has become the orthodox view.

As many economic historians acknowledge, however, whether economic globalization is greater today than in the *belle époque* cannot be determined definitively (Obstfeld and Taylor 2003). As a point of comparison with the present, it is perhaps more relevant to compare the similarities and differences, mainly qualitative, between the two ages (see Table 9.3). Many recent studies suggest

that levels of global economic integration are today comparable, if not more so, on most measures to the period of the *belle époque* (Geyer and Bright 1995; Bordo *et al.* 1999; Lindert and Williamson 2001; Maddison 2001; Taylor 2002). As Bordo *et al.* conclude, 'the globalization of commodity and financial markets is historically unprecedented' (1999: 56). In particular, while financial integration 'measured in terms of net flows as a percentage of GDP is quite similar in the post-1975 and pre-1914 periods, gross flows are greater today' while the correlation between domestic savings and investment (the Feldstein–Horioka puzzle) is now at 'the levels of the pre-1914 period' (Bordo *et al.* 1998: 17, 3). Table 9.3 demonstrates that the world economy of the twenty-first century evidences very similar levels of integration, while Dowrick and DeLong, two leading economic historians, conclude that 'It is hard to argue today that there is any dimension . . . save that of mass migration in which we today are less "globalized" than our predecessors at the end of-World War I' (2003: 191).

That said, economic globalization today displays some profound *qualitative* differences from that of the pre-1914 era. Most notable are real-time world financial markets; the breadth and depth of trade and financial cross-border activity; the speed of economic exchange; the scale of gross economic flows of goods, and short-term as opposed to long-term capital; the institutionalization of economic relations at an interregional level through global and regional organizations, MNCs, and transnational regulatory bodies; and, finally, the fact that twenty-first-century globalization is experienced much more unevenly than in the *belle époque* (Geyer and Bright 1995; Deibert 1997; Held *et al.* 1999; Garrett 2000*a*; Scholte 2000; Obstfeld and Taylor 2004). Bordo *et al.* note too that 'while net [capital] flows as a percentage of GNP a century ago may have been comparable to those of the present day, the breadth of international capital market integration is greater today' (Bordo *et al.* 1998: 26). Both the sources and destinations of capital flows today are far more diversified than in the pre-1914 era, while 'gross asset and liability positions were very close to net positions before 1914, in contrast to today where most major industrial countries are both major creditors and debtors'(Wilkins 2003; Bordo 2005: 10). In terms of economic structure, there are profound differences in relation to the global division of labour. The first age of globalization involved de-industrialization on the periphery and industrialization in the core, while the second age has entailed the reverse. The current phase of economic globalization undoubtedly displays many unique attributes—from the scale of short-term capital flows to transnational production—and a 'secular trend towards increased synchronization' of national business cycles. Combined, these trends produce novel political and economic dilemmas for governments (Eichengreen 1996; Rodrik 1997; Bordo and Helbling 2003: 431).

As Garrett concludes, 'global market integration is qualitatively different and deeper today' (Garrett 2000a).

What, then, is to be made of economic globalization today? If not historically unprecedented, it is certainly more than comparable to that of the *belle époque*—although today it is uniquely configured and constituted. As a consequence, 'Globalization today raises new issues of governance not just because it is conjoined with . . . [democratic political systems] . . . but because the economic phenomenon itself is different: integration is deeper and broader than a hundred years ago' (Bordo *et al.* 1999: 3–4). Some of the implications of this for the politics and governance of globalization is the focus of subsequent chapters (especially Hay, Chapter 10 in this volume).

The Prospects for Economic Globalization: Why Politics Still Matters

If today's second age of globalization is more than comparable to the *belle époque*, what does this imply for its effective governance? Drawing on the preceding analysis it is possible to sketch out three broad arguments about the politics and governance of economic globalization. These are necessarily truncated and oversimplified rehearsals of the more substantive debates discussed in subsequent chapters (see, in particular, Hay, Chapter 10 in this volume).

As noted above, the perspective of the *longue durée* is associated with structural theories of economic globalization that in turn tend to presume its inevitability, if not inexorability. Governance and politics—whether at a global, national, or local level—are thereby conceived as being highly constrained by the limits and opportunities for active intervention imposed by the operation of global markets, capitalist imperatives, and US hegemony.

Operating within these parameters, the role of politics and governance is principally functional: to stabilize the global political economy and provide it with some legitimacy, particularly in times of crisis. Beyond these parameters, they have a limited impact, especially in 'taming' or resisting globalization, so that political institutions tend to be regarded as largely epiphenomenal—that is, having a symbolic but not a transformative function. Of course, only in its most hyperglobalist or deterministic formulations is the room for politics defined so narrowly (Greider 1997). In sum, globalization conceived as the result of technological, capitalist, or hegemonic imperatives induces a sensitivity to the limits to politics consonant with the reproduction of the global political economy in its current capitalist form: the future trajectory of economic globalization is unlikely to be altered fundamentally by the ebb and flow of current political developments.

In contrast, epochal perspectives, and their associated conjunctural analyses, tend to give particular weight to politics and governance in co-ordinating and managing the global political economy. In key respects, the politics of the major states and the institutions of global economic governance are conceived as playing a critical role in forging and managing economic globalization. As Castells (2000: 147) argues, economic globalization and the globalized economy to which it gave rise were 'politically constituted'. Politics, in other words, provides the ideological, institutional, and motivational resin that bonded together the conjuncture of circumstances and the correlation of social forces that facilitated and fuelled the current epoch of economic globalization. However, once unleashed, the dynamics of economic globalization cannot readily be controlled, and the politics and governance of the global political economy is transformed into a contest between the very powerful technological, economic, and social forces driving globalization forward and the much weaker (but arguably more numerous) social forces contesting its logic. As Castells (2000: 147) concludes, any 'decoupling from the global economy implies a staggering cost: the devastation of the economy in the short-term, and the closing of access to sources of growth'. Under these conditions, politics is a critical (though not necessarily the determining) factor in shaping the future trajectory of economic globalization. In particular, political choices are constrained. In other words, the future trajectory of globalization, notwithstanding major war or economic collapse, will be shaped through the interaction between its political and its economic logics: that is, in the vortex of politics and markets. In this respect a *political economy* reading of globalization is thereby all but essential.

Finally, a contemporaneous perspective that focuses on the immediate context encourages an emphasis on the contingency of economic globalization and thus its essential political malleability. In so far as globalization is what politicians and social forces make of it, then its future trajectory is connected to the struggle over its discursive construction: the struggle for globalization's soul (Dryzek 2006). Competing discourses of globality are readily apparent, from the post-Washington consensus, the clash of globalizations and the global war on terror, to the discourse of global justice and global governance, and the de-globalization discourse of the anti-capitalist movement. To the extent that the discourse of the war on terror acquires hegemony, the politics and governance of globalization will be transformed from a major focus of public and academic attention into a largely incidental matter. For many, this may be a comforting thought—an authentic obituary for globalization—but for many it will simply represent the substitution of one hegemonic social construction of the global political economy by another, which is distinguished only by its entirely more alarming and incoherent logic (Mann 2003).

The future trajectory of economic globalization is wholly speculative. That it is so is both a source of intellectual despair and a huge relief. Despair, since it reaffirms the explanatory weakness of existing theories, and relief because it confirms that the future remains to be made, even if not within conditions of human choosing, to paraphrase Karl Marx. As such, the politics and governance of globalization will undoubtedly play a significant role in the making of the twenty-first-century global political economy, one hopes for the better, but quite possibly for the worse.

QUESTIONS

1. What are the principal causes of globalization?

2. Is economic globalization a product of technology or of capitalism, or both?

3. 'Technics made globalization.' Discuss.

4. In what sense, if any, do constructivist theories provide a convincing account of the origins of economic globalization?

5. Which is the more convincing: the globalist or the sceptical analysis of economic globalization?

6. Outline the globalist case and critically evaluate it with reference to the historical evidence.

7. Why does it matter if the world economy was more economically integrated in the *belle époque*?

8. How does Braudel's analysis help us to understand the logics of economic globalization?

9. Critically assess the argument that economic globalization is simply a political project.

10. 'Economic globalization is much more limited than many realize' (Gilpin 2001). Critically assess this proposition with reference to contemporary global economic trends.

FURTHER READING

■ **Amin, S. (1997),** *Capitalism in the Age of Globalization* **(London: Zed Books).** A useful overview of contemporary Marxist thinking about globalization, its driving forces and consequences for states.

■ **Castells, M. (2000),** *The Rise of the Network Society* **(Oxford: Blackwell).** This is now a contemporary classic account of the political economy of globalization, comprehensive in its analysis of the new global informational capitalism.

■ **Dicken, P. (2003),** *Global Shift: Transforming the World Economy,* **4th edn (London: Sage).** This is an excellent introduction and comprehensive account of the new global division of labour and the globalization of production in the world economy.

■ **Garrett, G. (2000), 'The Causes of Globalization',** *Comparative Political Studies,* **33/6: 945–991.** A really interesting and thorough exploration of the causal dynamics of globalization written from a rather orthodox political economy position, but nevertheless critical of much of the contemporary sceptical analysis.

■ **Giddens, A. (1990), The** *Consequences of Modernity* **(Cambridge: Polity Press).** A classic statement of the rootedness of globalization in the long-term historical processes of modernization or modernity. It is less a political economy than a historical sociological account of globalization which takes it seriously as a transformative force.

■ **Gilpin, R. (2001),** *Global Political Economy* **(Princeton, NJ: Princeton University Press).** A more sceptical view of economic globalization which, although taking it seriously, conceives it as an expression of Americanization or American hegemony.

■ **Held, D., and McGrew, A. (2007),** *Globalization/Anti-globalization* **(Cambridge: Polity Press).** A comprehensive examination of the academic and political controversies surrounding globalization.

■ **Hirst, P., and Thompson, G. (1999),** *Globalization in Question* **(Cambridge: Polity Press).** An excellent and sober critique of the hyperglobalist arguments, it is thoroughly sceptical about the globalization thesis, viewing it as a return to the *belle époque* and heavily shaped by states.

■ Robertson, R. (2003), *The Three Waves of Globalization: A History of Developing Global Consciousness* (London: Zed Books). A very good account of globalization as a long-term historical process driven by a combination of economic and political factors.

■ Rosenberg, J. (2000), *The Follies of Globalization Theory* (London: Verso). A very erudite and rigorous critique of the globalization literature which, although sceptical about its wilder claims, considers that globalization can only be understood from a historical materialist perspective.

■ Scholte, J. A. (2005), *Globalization: A Critical Introduction*, 2nd edn (Basingstoke: Palgrave). An excellent introduction to the globalization debate, from its causes to its consequences for the global political economy, from within a critical political economy perspective.

■ Wood, E. M. (2003), *Empire of Capital* (London: Verso). A novel reworking of the classical Marxist account of imperialism which takes globalization seriously as a new phase of capitalist development accompanied by a unique form of empire.

 WEB LINKS

● **www.isn.ethz.ch/linkslib** Good links to security and global economy nexus.

● **www.wto.org** Official WTO site with useful material about its policies and data on world trade.

● **www.theglobalsite.ac.uk** Good site for the globalization debate and related links.

● **www.tradeobservatory.org** Unofficial site operated by NGOs critical of the WTO and economic globalization.

● **www.polity.co.uk/global** Good site for the globalization debate and many good links.

● **www.rgemonitor.com** Excellent site for whole range of material on global economy and economic globalization.

● **www.indiana.edu/~ipe/ipesection** Good site for general material on IPE.

● **www.nber.org** Excellent studies of economic globalization in NBER Working Paper series.

 Visit the Online Resource Centre that accompanies this book for more information: www.oxfordtextbooks.co.uk/orc/ravenhill2e/

10 Globalization's Impact on States

COLIN HAY

 Reader's Guide

There is no topic more controversial in the field of global political economy than the impact of globalization on the accountability, autonomy, capacity, and sovereignty of the nation state. Arguably, the democratic character of governance in contemporary societies is at stake in such debates. This chapter reviews the extensive controversy that surrounds such questions, focusing attention on the principal mechanisms in and through which globalization is seen to have an impact on the nation state, and the empirical evidence that might either substantiate or question the existence of such mechanisms. It provides a detailed assessment of the case for and against the globalization thesis, examining the extent to which global economic integration might be seen to restrict the parameters of domestic political autonomy. It concludes by considering the complex and sometimes paradoxical relationship between globalization, democracy, and the nation state.

Introduction

It is over thirty years since Charles Kindleberger boldly proclaimed that 'the nation-state is just about through as an economic unit' (1969: 207). Since then, we have witnessed a remarkable profusion of apocalyptic predictions of the demise of the nation state. In such accounts, globalization is invariably cast in the role of prosecutor, judge, jury, and executioner. Yet despite such doom-laden prognoses, government expenditure continues to account for a significant and, in many cases, rising, share of gross domestic product (GDP), while the nation state remains the principal focus of political identification, and the principal locus of political debate and contestation in an interdependent world. Given this seeming paradox it is perhaps not surprising that the question of the impact of globalization on the development of the state has become a subject of considerable interest and intense controversy. Opinions range widely.

Though perhaps less influential than it once was, the view that globalization is in the process of, or has already, precipitated a terminal crisis of the nation state is still widespread. Others see such apocalyptic claims as being wild and unfounded extrapolations from anecdotal evidence. Proponents of such a view, they suggest, confuse a crisis of the *form* of the nation state for a crisis of the nation state per se. Yet others see globalization as a process driven by states that has, in many cases, served to strengthen, and certainly to increase, the significance of state intervention for economic performance. Still others question the role of globalization in such dynamics, suggesting either that globalization—though real—has little to do with the developmental trajectory of the nation state, or that the claim that we have witnessed a systematic process of globalization is itself mythical. Finally, there are those who suggest that the very *idea* of globalization as a harsh and non-negotiable economic constraint has itself exerted a powerful influence in confining the political

ambitions of elected officials to those consistent with the pervasive neo-liberal orthodoxy. It is this, rather than globalization per se, they suggest, that has given rise to the impression of a waning of the nation state's autonomy, capacity, and sovereignty.

Much more than academic pride is at stake in such debates. For whether or not we see globalization as restricting the parameters of political choice domestically, and whether or not we see the nation state as having a present or, indeed, a future, will have a very significant bearing on the space for political autonomy we perceive there to be. This, in turn, has significant consequences for the extent to which we might legitimately hold elected officials accountable for their conduct in office. Given the significance of the issues with which we are dealing, it is important to proceed with a certain degree of caution.

We should perhaps be wary of accepting uncritically, as many have, that globalization leaves states (and the governments that give effect to state power) with no alternative other than to capitulate to the demands and desires of mobile investors. To do so is effectively to deny the possibility of the democratic governance of economic processes in contemporary societies, certainly at the national level. In other words, there is a certain danger that, in accepting over-hastily an influential conception of the inevitable demise of the nation state's capacity and autonomy, we provide a convenient alibi for politicians keen to justify otherwise unpalatable social and economic reforms by appeal to the harsh economic realities of a global age. Perhaps our politicians deserve such an alibi; perhaps the constraints of the global economy are so exacting and all-pervasive as to warrant the appeal to such a 'logic of no alternative'; and perhaps these are valid and defensible conclusions. The crucial point for now is that we cannot allow ourselves to accept at face value such claims without detailed consideration—both theoretical and empirical—of the arguments for and *against* such a view.

Though space does not permit a fully comprehensive exploration of the relevant issues, it is my aim in what follows to survey the existing literature in this area and, in doing so, to provide a basis for such an assessment. It is important to emphasize at the outset, however, that there is no agreed or emerging consensus on globalization's impact on the state. Commentators are divided and are likely to remain so. As we shall see, this is, at least in part, because of the rather slippery nature of the term globalization itself, which has come to mean a range of rather different things to a range of different analysts.

The chapter is in four sections. In the first, I seek to establish a few necessary preliminaries, distinguishing in particular between the politics of globalization and the globalization of politics. In the second, I identify the principal mechanisms in and through which globalization is seen to have an impact on the nation state, before turning, in the third section, to the empirical evidence that might either substantiate or question the existence of such mechanisms. In the final section, and by way of a conclusion, I consider the complex and sometimes paradoxical relationship between globalization, democracy, and the nation state, looking both at the impact of globalization on states, and the state's impact on globalization.

The Globalization of Politics and the Politics of Globalization

It is crucial at the outset that we distinguish between the globalization of politics and the politics of globalization. This is particularly important given the tendency, especially prevalent amongst international/global political economists, to talk about globalization as if it were a transparent, self-sustaining, and purely economic dynamic (on the dangers of such 'economism', see also Teivainen 2002). It is a key contention of this chapter that globalization is not a tendency that is furthered, or indeed countered, in the *absence of political actors*. As such, it has a politics that must be a central ingredient of any adequate account of its development.

By the *globalization of politics,* I refer to the displacement of political capacities and responsibilities from the national and/or regional levels to the genuinely global level, through the development of institutions of global governance (such as the IMF and the World Bank).

By the *politics of globalization,* I refer to the politics of the process of globalization itself, to the political drivers of globalization, and to the consequences of such a process for political conflict, practice, and the distribution of political responsibility.

Whether, and to what extent, we observe a globalization of politics is a matter of empirical judgement. It is likely to relate, among other things, to our evaluation of the extent and significance of genuinely global institutions of governance, the relative significance of regional institutions, and the degree to which the emergence of global institutions might be seen to give rise to a politics independent of, and irreducible to, that between discrete nation states or regions. Yet whatever specific judgement we reach—and opinion again varies considerably (compare, for example, Buzan *et al.* 1998; Krasner 1999; Archibugi 2003)—we must acknowledge that if globalization exists at all, and even if it is confined exclusively to the economic and cultural spheres, it has a politics. While we may well deny the globalization of politics, then, unless we deny globalization itself, we cannot deny the *politics* of globalization. It is with the latter that this chapter is principally concerned.

More specifically, I shall focus on three analytically separable, but nonetheless interconnected, dimensions of the politics of globalization:

1. The implications and consequences of globalization (whether economic, political, or cultural) for the capacity and autonomy of the nation state.

2. The interpretation of the opportunities and constraints associated with globalization and the consequent appeal, in political contexts, to the language of globalization (often, as we shall see, to justify social and economic reforms).

3. The role of political actors, particularly state actors, in the political 'authoring' of globalization and the processes that either sustain or impede its development.

The first of these might be seen as the *structural* dimension, relating as it does to the constraints and opportunities of the external environment for domestic political actors. The second relates to the *ideational* dimension and, more specifically, to the ways in which political actors understand the constraints and opportunities that the external environment presents to them. The third relates to the *intentional*, *strategic*, or *agential* dimension—to the role of political actors in the creation and re-creation of the very external environment in which they find themselves. Together they suggest an approach to the questions of the impact of globalization on the state, and the state's impact on globalization, in which political actors are always present, in which the ideas they hold about their environment shape their political conduct, and in which they are never free of the constraints (and opportunities) of the environment they have created (for a further elaboration, see Hay 2002*b*: 253–260).

Such a perspective is applied, in the pages that follow, to a series of more substantive issues and controversies. These might together be taken to comprise an agenda for a consideration of the politics of globalization (see Box 10.1).

Each set of issues, as we shall see, reveals a separate and distinct politics of globalization. By drawing attention to the multifaceted politics of globalization in this way, my aim is to contribute

---

BOX 10.1

The Politics of Globalization: Key Controversies

- The extent to which globalization might be seen to diminish the autonomy and 'perforate' the sovereignty of the nation state (on 'perforated sovereignty' see Duchacek 1990; Jessop 2002).

- The extent to which globalization might be seen to establish powerful tendencies towards global political convergence and homogenization.

- The extent to which it is right to identify a globalization of political problems—the proliferation of issues that require a response in the form of concerted global action.

- The extent to which we can point to a parallel globalization of political solutions and the corresponding

emergence of more-or-less dedicated institutions, mechanisms, and processes of *global governance*.

- The extent to which we can identify the global diffusion of 'best practice' policy solutions (or potential solutions) and/or policy models in the form of the transfer of ideas about 'good' practice between nations (whether by choice or imposition).

- The extent to which globalization might be seen to promote the development of a global polity or *cosmopolis* capable of transcending the state (see, for example, Archibugi 2003; Zolo 1997).

to the attempt to restore political (and one might hope, democratic) scrutiny and accountability to processes more conventionally seen as economic

and inexorable—and, consequently, as not subject to political deliberation (see, more generally, Hay 2002*a*).

KEY POINTS

- The impact of globalization on the autonomy, capacity, and sovereignty of the nation state is much disputed.

- It is important to distinguish between the politics of globalization (the political drivers of the process of globalization) and the globalization of politics (the displacement of political responsibilities and capacities from the level of the nation state through the emergence of institutions and processes of global governance). Globalization has a politics whether or not politics has become globalized.

- It is equally important to distinguish between and to acknowledge the structural, ideational, and strategic dimensions of the process of globalization. The first of these relates to the constraints and opportunities presented by globalization; the second to the way in which those structural factors are understood; and the third to the role of political actors in 'authoring' the process of globalization itself.

Globalization and the Crisis of the Nation State

If we are to assess the impact (if any) of globalization on the viability of the nation state, we must first identify the principal mechanisms in and through which globalization is held, in conventional accounts, to limit the capacity, autonomy, and sovereignty of the nation state. Before doing so, however, it is perhaps important to emphasize that most strong variants of the globalization thesis—which present the nation state as a casualty of globalization—tend to do so without pointing directly or explicitly to the mechanism or mechanisms involved (see, for example, Ohmae 1990, 1995; Reich 1992). At best, it seems, they treat the existence of such mechanisms as being self-evident. What we tend to see, instead, is what Andreas Busch (2000: 34) refers to as 'casual empiricism'—the anecdotal appeal to, and extrapolation from, single pieces of evidence which appear to confirm the general tenor of the argument being advanced.

At times, however, casual empiricism gives way to 'casual theoreticism'. Here, tangential reference is made to the increased bargaining power and/or mobility of capital in an era of globalization. In doing so, 'hyperglobalists' appeal, whether they are aware of it or not, to mechanisms derived from neoclassical open economy macroeconomic models (for reviews of the relevant literature, see Obstfeld and Rogoff 1996; Rødseth 2000; Ugur 2001). This is an important point, and gives a first clue as to the character of the hyperglobalization thesis. Because it serves to indicate that, for such authors, it is *economic* globalization that is the principal factor limiting the capacity and autonomy of the state in the contemporary context. In short, economic globalization gives mobile international investors the upper hand over domestic political authorities.

Without going into any technical detail, it is useful to examine further such open economic macroeconomics models. In particular, it is important that we:

1. Establish the assumptions on which such models are predicated;

2. Assess the plausibility of such assumptions; and

3. Consider the sensitivity of the conclusions derived from such assumptions (for the viability or otherwise of the nation state) to modifications in the initial premisses from which they are derived.

The hyperglobalization thesis

Arguably, the key factor determining the inevitability of state retrenchment for hyperglobalists is the heightened mobility of capital. The logic to which they appeal is, in fact, very similar to that elaborated by Adam Smith in 1776.

❝ The . . . proprietor of stock is properly a citizen of the world, and is not necessarily attached to any particular country. He would be apt to abandon the country in which he is exposed to a vexatious inquisition, in order to be assessed a burdensome tax, and would remove his stock to some country where he could either carry on his business or enjoy his fortune at his ease. A tax that tended to drive away stock from a particular country, would so far tend to dry up every source of revenue, both to the sovereign and to the society. Not only the profits of stock, but the rent of land and the wages of labour, would necessarily be more or less diminished by its removal. ❞ (Smith 1776/1976: 848–849; cited in Swank 2002: 245)

Updated and restated in more familiar terms, the argument goes something like this: In closed national economies, such as those which (supposedly) characterized the early post-war period, capital is essentially immobile and national in character; it has no 'exit' option. In such an environment, governments can impose punitive taxation regimes on unwilling and relatively impotent national capitals with little cost to the domestic economy (apart from the tendency for capitalists to hoard rather than to reinvest their profits). With open economy conditions, such as are conventionally held to characterize the contemporary era, this is no longer the case. Capital may now exit from national economic environments at minimal cost (indeed, in most neoclassical inspired models, at zero cost).

Accordingly, by playing off the regulatory regimes of different economies against one another, capital can ensure for itself the highest rate of return on its investment. *Ceteris paribus,* capital will exit high-taxation regimes for low-taxation ones, comprehensive welfare states for residual states, highly regulated labour markets for flexible ones, and economies characterized by strict environmental regulations and high union density for those characterized by lax environmental standards and low union density. The clear prediction would be that capital will seek out the high growth regimes of, for example, newly industrialized countries (NICs) (like Malaysia, for example) unencumbered by a powerful environmental lobby, burdensome welfare traditions, rigid labour market institutions, and correspondingly higher rates of taxation.

The process pits one national economy against another in an increasingly intense competitive struggle. States effectively must clamber over one another in an ever more frenzied attempt to produce a more favourable investment environment than their competitors to attract mobile ('footloose') foreign direct investors. Yet this is not a one-shot game—and an early influx of foreign direct investment (FDI) only increases the dependence of the state on its continued 'locational competitiveness'. If investment is to be retained in such an environment, states must strive constantly to improve the investment opportunities they can offer relative to their competitors. Any failure to do so would only precipitate a haemorrhaging of invested funds, labour shedding, and, in turn, an economic crisis. A neo-Darwinian survival of the fittest effectively guarantees that states must internalize the preferences of capital, offering ever-more attractive investment incentives, ever-more flexible labour markets, and ever-less restrictive environmental regulations, if they are not to be emptied of investment, economic activity, and employment. Big government, if not perhaps the state itself, is rendered increasingly anachronistic—a guarantor not of the interests of citizens or even of consumers, but a sure means to disinvestment and economic crisis.

Little wonder, then, that the hyperglobalization thesis tends to predict 'social dumping', 'competitive deregulation', and a race to the bottom in terms of social and environmental standards, a process lubricated by the 'deregulatory arbitrage' of footloose and fancy-free transnational corporations.

The policy implications of such an account are painfully clear. As globalization serves to establish competitive selection mechanisms within the international economy, there is little choice but to cast all regulatory impediments to the efficient operation of the market on the bonfire of welfare institutions, regulatory controls, and labour market rigidities.

Plausible, familiar, and compelling though such a logic may well appear, it serves us well to isolate the assumptions on which it is predicated. Because, as we shall see, it is these, rather than any inexorable process of globalization, that ultimately cause the crisis of the nation state. They are principally five-fold, and each can be challenged on both theoretical and empirical grounds (see Box 10.2).

Each of these premises is at best dubious, at worst demonstrably false. Such assumptions, it should perhaps be noted, are not justified in neo-classical economics in terms of their accuracy, but because they are convenient and make possible abstract quasi-mathematical modelling. That defence, whatever one thinks of it, is simply not available to proponents of the hyperglobalization thesis, whose borrowings from neoclassical economics rarely extend past the assumptions to the algebra.

Consider each assumption in turn. While it may seem entirely appropriate to attribute to capital the sole motive of seeking the greatest return on its investment, the political and economic history of capital provides little or no support for the notion that capital is blessed either with complete information or even with a relatively clear and consistent conception of what is its own best interest. Moreover, as the political economy of the advanced capitalist democracies demonstrates well, capital has a history of resisting social and economic reforms that it has later come both to rely on and actively to defend (see, for example, Swenson 2000).

BOX 10.2

Core Assumptions of the 'Hyperglobalization' Thesis

1. That capital invests where it can secure the greatest net return on that investment, and is possessed of perfect information of the means by which to do so.

2. That markets for goods and services are fully integrated globally, and consequently national economies must prove themselves to be competitive internationally if economic growth is to be sustained.

3. That capital enjoys perfect mobility and the cost of 'exit' (disinvestment) is zero.

4. That capital will invariably secure the greatest return on its investment by minimizing its labour costs in flexible labour markets and by relocating its productive activities to economies with the lowest rates of corporate taxation.

5. That the welfare state (and the taxation receipts out of which it is funded) represent nothing other than lost capital to mobile asset holders and have no positive externalities for the competitiveness and productivity of the national economy.

The second assumption is, again, a convenient fiction, used in neoclassical macroeconomics to make possible the modelling of an open economy. Few, if any, economists would defend the claim that markets for goods or services are fully integrated or clear instantly. Indeed, the degree of integration of such markets is an empirical question and, as such, an issue to which we shall return in the next section.

If the first two assumptions are problematic, then the third is demonstrably false, at least with respect to certain types of capital. Because, however mobile portfolio capital may appear in a digital economy, the same is simply not the case for capital invested in infrastructure, machinery, and personnel. Consider inward FDI. Once attracted to a particular locality, foreign direct investors acquire a range of non-recuperable or sunk costs—such as their investment in physical infrastructure, plant, and machinery. Consequently, their exit options become seriously depleted. While it is entirely 'rational' for foreign direct investors to proclaim loudly their mobility, exit is perhaps most effective as a threat.

What this in turn suggests is that predictions of the haemorrhaging of invested capital from generous welfare states are almost certainly misplaced. A combination of exit threats and concerns arising from the hyperglobalization thesis about the *likelihood* of exit may well have had an independent effect on the trajectory of fiscal and labour market reform. But there would seem to be no a priori reason to hold generous welfare state and high corporate taxation burdens as being incompatible with the attraction and retention of FDI. As we shall see in greater detail in the next section, this is precisely what we find from the empirical record. Not only have the most generous welfare states consistently proved the most attractive locations for inward foreign direct investors (Locke and Kochan 1985; Swank 2002), but volumes of foreign direct investment (expressed as a share of GDP) are in fact found to be positively correlated with levels of corporate taxation, union density, labour costs, and the degree of regulation of the labour market (Dunning 1988; Cooke and Noble 1998; Traxler and Woitech

2000; Wilensky 2002: 654–655). As Duane Swank notes, 'contrary to the claims of the international capital mobility thesis . . . the general fiscal capacity of democratic governments to fund a variety of levels and mixes of social protection and services may be relatively resilient in the face of internationalisation of markets' (2002: 276). Here it is perhaps instructive to note that despite a marked tendency for direct corporate taxation to fall in recent years in line with the predictions of such neoclassically inspired models, the overall burden of taxation on firms has in fact remained remarkably constant, rising marginally since the mid-1980s (Kiser and Laing 2001; Steinmo 2003).

No less problematic are assumptions four and five—that capital can only compete in a more intensely competitive environment on the basis of productivity gains secured through tax reductions and cost shedding (through rationalization, downsizing, and the flexibilization of labour) and that the welfare state is, for business, merely a drain on profits. Such assumptions reflect a narrowly Anglo–US conception of competitiveness—and, as we shall see presently, are difficult to reconcile with the empirical evidence. Though ever more influential, the hyperglobalization thesis extrapolates wildly and inappropriately from labour-intensive sectors of the international economy in which competitiveness is conventionally enhanced in this way to the global economy more generally. It fails to appreciate that foreign direct investors in capital-intensive sectors of the international economy are attracted to locations such as the Northern European economies neither for the flexibility of their labour markets nor for the cheapness of the wage and non-wage labour costs that they impose, but rather for the access they provide to a highly skilled, reliable, and innovative labour force. High wages and high non-wage labour costs (in the form of payroll taxes) would seem to be a price many multinational corporations regard as worth paying for a dynamic and highly skilled workforce.

At this point, it might be objected that the above paragraphs relate principally to the investment behaviour of foreign direct investors and not to financial market actors. This is a valid point. Indeed, although the hyperglobalization thesis has rather more to say about the former, it has much to say about the latter too.

Its assumptions about finance capital and financial markets are similar to those about productive/invested capital and markets in goods and services. Yet the small differences are significant. Referring again to Box 10.2, the first assumption applies equally to invested and investment capital, and is equally problematic. Yet whether it is accurate or not arguably matters rather less in the case of portfolio capital. For such investors do not need to act rationally or with perfect information in order to inflict considerable damage on the currencies against which they may be tempted to speculate, and the stocks and shares they may be tempted to dump—as the influential literature on 'irrational exuberance' and 'herding instincts' in financial markets makes very clear (see, for example, Schiller 2001). Assumption two also applies equally to financial markets and to those in goods and services (see Pauly, Chapter 8 in this volume). All are assumed to be global and perfectly integrated. This may seem like a more plausible assumption to make of financial markets but, as we shall see in the next section, as an empirical claim it is not easily reconciled with the available evidence. Assumption three, though problematic for productive/invested capital, as already discussed, again seems more plausible for portfolio investors. Stocks and shares can certainly be traded, and assets swapped from one denomination to another, in the flickering of a cursor. Yet whether this *potential* is reflected in the actual behaviour of financial markets is, again, an empirical question and the subject of some debate. This, too, is discussed further in the next section. Assumptions four and five are not directly relevant to finance capital, but they can be adapted to financial actors. Hyperglobalists tend to assume that portfolio investors have a clear interest in, and preference for, strong and stable currencies backed both by implacable independent central banks with hawkish anti-inflationary credentials and governments wedded in theory and in practice to fiscal moderation

and prudence. Any departure from this new financial orthodoxy, it is assumed, will precipitate a flurry of speculation against the currency and a haemorrhaging of investment from assets denominated in that currency. Governments provoke the wrath of the financial markets at their peril. This, again, is an intuitively plausible proposition that would seem to be borne out by a series of high-profile speculative flurries against 'rogue' governments. It is, however, an empirical claim and, as we shall see later, one that a growing body of scholarship reveals to be considerably at odds with the empirical evidence.

As the above paragraphs perhaps serve to indicate, the theoretical case against the hyperglobalization thesis is strongest with respect to the assumptions made about productive/invested capital. Its assumptions about investment/portfolio capital, if perhaps overly simplistic, are, on the face of it, more plausible. Yet they give rise to a series of substantive claims and predictions that have prompted an important empirical challenge to the thesis. This provides the principal focus for the next section. Before turning to such issues, however, it is important that we first consider the implications of the hyperglobalization thesis for the question of convergence, prior to examining an alternative and rather more political account of the origins of the contemporary crisis of the nation state.

Convergence, dual convergence, or divergence?

The hyperglobalization thesis predicts a simple convergence among previously distinct 'models' or 'varieties' of capitalism—on an Anglo–US or liberal ideal type—driven by attempts to enhance labour market flexibility, welfare retrenchment, and the intensification of tax competition. This can be represented schematically (see Figure 10.1).

Globalization is the driving force, unleashing as it does an intense competitive struggle between contending models of capitalism. It exposes all economies (here, A–E) to common pressures which, in turn, produce common outcomes. Since liberal models of

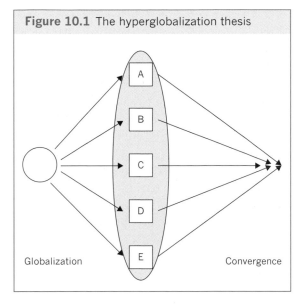

Figure 10.1 The hyperglobalization thesis

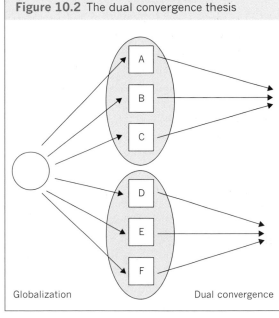

Figure 10.2 The dual convergence thesis

capitalism best approximate the preferences of mobile capital for open markets, low-taxation regimes, and light regulation, they establish themselves rapidly as the model to be emulated. Convergence on this Anglo–US ideal type is held to be rapid, lubricated by capital's exit from more highly regulated regimes.

Globalization (perfect capital mobility and perfect competition under open economy conditions) generates common pressure (inputs); states and/or political-economic regimes have no independent mediating role (no insitutional effects); hence convergence on best practice assuming complete information, rational action, and Darwinian competition—in short, *common inputs produce common outputs*.

Globalization produces a variety of common pressures to which competing models of capitalism are differentially exposed; this exposure tends to promote a dual process of convergence, accentuating the difference between liberal market economies and co-ordinated market economies—in short, *globalization generates common pressures; and these are refracted institutionally to produce a dual convergence* (see Figure 10.2).

Influential though this simple convergence thesis is, it is not as unquestioned as it once was. An

alternative and increasingly influential account points to a rather more complex process of 'dual' or 'co-convergence', again driven by globalization (see above).

In this contending account, more attention is paid to the role of institutional factors in mediating the state's response to globalization. Models of capitalism are differentiated by virtue of the rather different institutions they embody. In the now conventional classification, *liberal market economies* (such as the USA and the UK) and *co-ordinated market economies* (such as Germany, Sweden, and the Netherlands) are contrasted (Hall and Soskice 2001).

The competitive pressures unleashed by globalization may make similar demands of these institutions (such as balanced budgets, flexible labour markets, and the control of inflation), but these can be delivered in different ways in different institutional domains. Consequently, the 'varieties of capitalism' approach, as it has come to be known, predicts not a simple or singular process of convergence on the liberal (or Anglo–US) model, but rather a complex or dual convergence in which capitalist polities cluster more closely around the liberal and co-ordinated ideal types (Hall and Soskice 2001; see also Garrett 1998*b*, 2000*b*; Kitschelt *et al.* 1999; Iversen, Pontusson, and Soskice 2000).

In its sensitivity to institutional variations among different models of capitalism, and in its recognition that common external pressures need not translate into common outcomes, the 'varieties of capitalism' approach represents a considerable advance on the hyperglobalization thesis. Yet in a number of significant respects it, too, is problematic (see also Blyth 2003; Goodin 2003; Watson 2003; Hay 2004):

1. It may, unwittingly, borrow too much from the hyperglobalization thesis in presenting globalization as the principal agent of convergence (paying insufficient attention to the often regional character of processes of economic integration and/or to the differential exposure of economies to globalization, for example).

2. In drawing a rigid and rather static distinction between liberal and co-ordinated market economies, it is not perhaps as sensitive to institutional diversity as it might be (see also Crouch and Streeck 1997).

3. It makes a series of empirical predictions/claims about dual convergence which are, at best, contestable—as we shall see in the following section.

Global problems, national solutions?

Thus far we have tended to focus exclusively upon mechanisms identifying *economic* globalization as the key determinant of the contemporary crisis of the nation state. Yet arguably altogether more plausible is a rather more political mechanism. Strictly speaking, this does not so much point to the diminished capacity and sovereignty of the state in an era of globalization as to the globalization of the problems with which the nation state is confronted—and its inability to deal with such

problems. Indeed, it points to the more general lack of the political capacity to deal with genuinely global problems and risks that result from the continued ascendancy of the nation state as a political unit.

The classic example here is the problem of high-consequence global environmental risks (Beck 1992; Giddens 1990). This is well expressed in the so-called tragedy of the commons first identified by Garrett Hardin (1968). Hardin provides an intuitively plausible and all too compelling model of the seemingly intractable problem of environmental degradation in contemporary societies. The systematic exploitation and pollution of the environment, it is argued, is set to continue, since individual corporations and states, despite a clear collective interest, choose not to impose on themselves the costs of unilateral environmental action. Their logic is entirely rational, though potentially catastrophic in its cumulative consequences. Such actors know that environmental regulation is costly and, particularly in an open international economy, a burden on competitiveness. Accordingly, in the absence of an international agency capable of enforcing the compliance of all states and all corporations, the anticipation of free riding is sufficient to ensure that corporations and states do not burden themselves with additional costs and taxes. The long-term effects for the environment are all too obvious, preventing as they do a global solution to a genuinely global problem (see the discussion in Dauvergne, Chapter 14 in this volume).

The extent to which the narrowly perceived self-interest of states and governments can subvert the development of effective mechanisms and institutions of global governance is well evidenced by the Bush administration's withdrawal from the 1997 Kyoto Protocol (committing signatories to staged reductions in greenhouse gas emissions); and, for its critics, by the fact that such a protocol, even if fully implemented, would serve to reduce only slightly the pace of an ongoing process of environmental degradation.

This is a most important example, and a number of broader implications might be drawn from it (see Box 10.3).

BOX 10.3

The Implications of the 'Tragedy of the Commons'

1. The tragedy of the commons is, effectively, a modern-day morality tale. It is indicative of a more general disparity between the need for and supply of effective institutions and mechanisms of global governance. For while it is easy to point to genuinely global problems requiring for their resolution co-ordinated global responses, it is far more difficult to find examples of the latter.

2. As this perhaps suggests, the tragedy of the commons is not really a story of the crisis of the nation state at all. Because it is the continued capacity of many (if perhaps not all) states to behave unilaterally and to veto international agreements that preclude the appropriate globally co-ordinated collective response. In other words, political globalization (effective and authoritative institutions of global governance) is impeded by the retention of the nation state's sovereignty. This is less a crisis of the nation state, then, than a crisis produced by the resilience of the nation state.

3. While the proliferation of genuinely global political problems does point to the incapacity of a system of sovereign states to deal with the challenges it now faces, it does not indicate any particular incapacity of states to deal with the problems and issues with which they have always dealt. This is, then, less of a story of a loss of capacity than of the proliferation of issues with which the nation state has never had the capacity to deal effectively.

4. Finally, and rather perversely, the disparity between the need for and supply of global solutions to global problems is merely exacerbated by economic globalization, as this has served to drive states, at pain of economic crisis, to elevate considerations of competitiveness over all other concerns, including environmental protection. There is a clear and obvious danger that the narrow pursuit of short-term economic advantage will come at the long-term price of a looming environmental, economic, and political catastrophe.

KEY POINTS

- Many of the strongest versions of the globalization thesis fail to specify the mechanism by which globalization might be seen to limit the capacity, autonomy, and sovereignty of the nation state.

- Nonetheless, a variety of such mechanisms have been posited. These are principally economic in character and often rely on stylized assumptions about the behaviour of capital drawn from open-economy neoclassical economics. These assumptions can be questioned both theoretically and empirically.

- The hyperglobalization thesis predicts a simple convergence between 'models of capitalism' under conditions of (economic) globalization; the more recent 'varieties of capitalism' perspective predicts a more complex process of dual convergence. There are theoretical problems with both sets of predictions.

- The nation state has always suffered from a limited capacity to deal with genuinely global problems; and such problems are proliferating. The 'tragedy of the commons' provides a compelling model of the consequences of this lack of capacity, pointing to the need for effective and democratic institutions of global governance.

Globalization and State Retrenchment: The Evidence Assessed

As suggested in the previous section, the hyperglobalization thesis tends to present a theoretical, indeed largely hypothetical, argument for the contemporary crisis of the nation state. If its assumptions are accepted, then the predicted crisis of the nation state is little more than a logical inference. Yet, as we have seen, there may be good theoretical grounds for challenging some of these assumptions, and with them the claimed inevitability of the state's loss of capacity, autonomy, sovereignty, and legitimacy. In the end, however, these are empirical questions—and it is to the empirical evidence itself that we must turn if we are to assess the validity of the hyperglobalization thesis, and to assess the impact, if any, of globalization on states. It is to this task that we now turn. We begin first by considering the dependent variable.

The dependent variable: state retrenchment

It is perhaps appropriate to begin with the simplest data which address most directly the contemporary condition of the state. If the state were to experience a potentially terminal crisis, we might expect to see clear evidence of systematic state retrenchment. Moreover, we would expect this to be most pronounced in highly open economies whose public spending had traditionally accounted for a high proportion of GDP. Table 10.1 presents data on government expenditure expressed as a proportion of GDP for a number of developed countries from the 1960s, conventionally the point of departure for political economies of globalization.

The evidence itself is fairly unequivocal. These, for the most part extremely open and developed economies, show little sign of systematic retrenchment of state expenditure in the so-called era of globalization. There is certainly some evidence

since the 1980s of a decline in the proportion of GDP devoted to public spending. Though invariably greatest where unemployment has fallen the most, this is consistent to some extent with the predictions of the hyperglobalization thesis. Yet what is perhaps more important is that in every case the size of the state (as expressed as a share of GDP) has increased considerably over the period, peaking in most cases in the early to mid-1990s.

Of course, state expenditure is not the only means of gauging quantitatively the role of the state. Figure 10.3 presents time-series data on the proportion of the total workforce employed directly by the state since the 1960s.

Again, the evidence is unequivocal. This period, the much-vaunted era of globalization, has witnessed the development of the largest states the world has ever seen, and there is little evidence of this trend being reversed.

It would certainly seem that globalization is compatible with a far higher level of state expenditure than the hyperglobalization thesis would seem to imply. This presents something of a paradox: a widely accepted conception of state crisis and retrenchment which seems to stand in some tension to the available empirical evidence. There are at least four potential solutions to this conundrum, each with rather different implications:

1. That the conventional wisdom on the subject is indeed correct, that 'big government' represents an ultimately unsustainable drain on competitiveness in an era of globalization, but that the institutional form of the state has become so entrenched and embedded as to make its reform and retrenchment an incremental process upon which we are now only slowly embarking. (Though perhaps the most plausible defence of the 'crisis of the

Table 10.1 Government Expenditure as a Share of GDP

	AUL	AUS	BEL	CAN	DEN	FIN	FRA	GER	IRE
1960	22.1	32.1	34.6	28.9	24.6	26.6	34.6	32.0	28.0
1965	25.6	37.9	36.5	29.1	29.6	30.8	38.4	36.3	33.1
1970	25.5	39.2	42.1	35.7	40.2	30.5	38.9	37.6	39.6
1975	32.4	46.2	51.3	40.7	47.5	38.4	43.5	47.1	46.5
1980	34.1	48.5	58.7	41.5	56.2	39.4	46.2	46.9	50.8
1985	38.5	51.7	62.3	47.1	59.3	45.0	52.2	47.5	54.8
1990	37.7	49.4	55.3	47.8	58.6	46.8	49.9	45.7	41.4
1996	35.9	51.6	52.9	44.7	63.6	1.0	55.0	49.1	42.0
2000	32.9	46.9	46.8	41.1	51.1	43.7	47.5	44.5	35.0
2005	32.9	45.0	47.3	39.5	51.2	45.8	49.8	46.2	37.5
Net growth[a] (%)	49	46	35	45	108	64	37	39	25
Growth to peak (%)	74	61	80	65	158	129	59	53	96
Decline from peak (%)	15	13	24	16	19	25	9	6	26

	ITA	JAP	NTL	NOR	NZL	SWE	SWZ	UK	USA
1960	30.1	18.3	33.7	32.0	26.9	31.1	17.2	32.6	27.2
1965	34.3	18.6	38.7	34.2	–	36.0	19.7	36.4	27.2
1970	34.2	19.3	45.5	41.0	–	43.7	21.3	39.3	31.6
1975	43.2	27.3	55.9	46.6	–	49	28.7	46.9	34.6
1980	45.6	32.7	62.5	49.4	38.1	65.7	29.7	44.6	33.6
1985	50.8	32.7	59.7	45.6	–	64.3	31.0	46.2	36.4
1990	53.6	32.3	57.5	54.9	41.3	60.8	30.9	42.3	36.6
1996	52.7	35.9	49.2	49.2	34.0	59.1	39.4	43.0	32.4
2000	44.1	31.9	41.7	39.4	36.4	52.2	33.9	37.7	34.2
2005	46.4	30.9	45.7	42.8	34.7	52.0	36.4	44.7	36.6
Net growth[a] (%)	47	74	24	23	35	68	94	16	20
Growth to peak (%)	69	96	85	72	[54]	111	129	44	35
Decline from peak (%)	13	14	27	22	[16]	21	8	5	0

Notes: AUL = Australia; AUS = Austria; BEL = Belgium; CAN = Canada; DEN = Denmark; FIN = Finland; GER = Germany; IRE = Ireland; ITA = Italy; JAP = Japan; NTL = Netherlands; NOR = Norway; NZL = New Zealand; SWE = Sweden; SWZ = Switzerland; UK = United Kingdom; USA = United States
[a]Net growth here refers to the percentage increase in the share of GDP devoted to government expenditure
Source: Calculated from OECD, *Economic Outlook*, various years

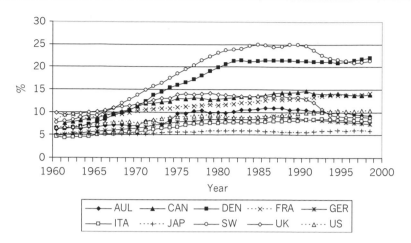

Figure 10.3 Government employment: as a share of total employment

Notes: AUL = Australia; BEL = Belgium; CAN = Canada; DEN = Denmark; FIN = Finland; GER = Germany; ITA = Italy; JPN = Japan; NOR = Norway; UK = United Kingdom; USA = United States
Source: Calculated from Huber *et al.* (2004)

nation state' thesis, this argument is rarely made in the existing literature. It might, however, draw inspiration from the work of historical institutionalists, who have pointed consistently to the inertial nature of complex institutions like the state; see, especially, Pierson 1994, 1996).

2. That the conventional wisdom, though somewhat overstated, is basically correct, since the aggregate empirical evidence in fact masks the real degree of retrenchment. Once we control for demographic and other 'welfare inflationary' pressures (such as higher levels of unemployment and the near exponential growth in health care costs since the 1960s), observed state expenditure is in fact substantially below what we would anticipate, were consistent level of generosity and coverage to have been maintained (Esping-Andersen 1996*a*, 1996*b*; Rhodes 1996, 1997; Barr 1998). We have not witnessed, nor should we expect to witness, a terminal crisis of the nation state, but we have already experienced a significant process of state retrenchment driven by globalization.

3. That while the aggregate evidence may indeed mask the real degree of retrenchment that has occurred, the conventional wisdom is still wrong, since there is no a priori reason to hold globalization responsible for such retrenchment and/or no consistent evidence of a historically unprecedented process of globalization in recent years (Hirst and Thompson 1999; Wilensky 2002).

4. That, in expecting globalization to precipitate a terminal crisis of the state, the conventional wisdom is simply inaccurate. Far from representing a drain on competitiveness, the state is the very condition of competitiveness in an increasingly competitive international/global market (Weiss 1998). Globalization does not discriminate principally between states on the size of their expenditure but on their effectiveness in promoting and sustaining international competitiveness. Consequently, while we might expect to see convergence on

best practice between states, we should not expect to see a withering of the state itself (Cerny 1995, 1997).

As these arguments already indicate, there are a number of ways of rehabilitating an albeit somewhat 'respecified' variant of the globalization thesis in the light of the above evidence. We probably can reject the notion that globalization has precipitated a terminal crisis of the nation state. Yet the evidence considered so far is by no means incompatible with the claim that globalization circumscribes the parameters of domestic political choice and is the principal determinant of the state's developmental trajectory. If we are to assess that claim, then we need to turn our attention from the dependent variable (the extent of state retrenchment) to the independent variable (the process of globalization itself). Before doing so, however, it is important that we first consider one remaining aspect of the dependent variable—the question of convergence.

The dependent variable: convergence or dual convergence

Having originally placed their emphasis on the crisis and transcendence of the nation state as a political unit responsible for regulating an economic jurisdiction (Ohmae 1990, 1995), proponents of the hyperglobalization thesis now more frequently cast institutional and policy convergence as the dependent variable (Teeple 1995; Gray 1998; Parker 1998). Globalization remains the independent variable and is depicted as a stable equilibrium and as an entirely non-negotiable external economic imperative that exposes all economies within the global system to near identical pressures and challenges. In a highly competitive environment in which only the fittest survive, successful adaptation will rapidly be emulated, resulting in a powerful tendency to convergence.

As we have seen, the institutional sensitivity of the 'varieties of capitalism' approach appeals to a similar logic (and an identical independent variable),

in predicting a rather different outcome—a more complex process of dual convergence around liberal and co-ordinated market economic models.

To what extent are these contending predictions borne out by the empirical evidence? Since we might consider convergence with respect to any number of potential dependent variables, this is a somewhat contentious issue to which we cannot hope to do full justice here. Space prevents an exhaustive survey. Nonetheless, we would once again expect the convergence or co-convergence theses to be most relevant to the most developed and most open economies in the world system. Moreover, given that welfare expenditure is described most frequently in the globalization literature as the kind of unnecessary indulgence that can no longer be afforded in an era of heightened competition among nations, we might expect to find the strongest evidence of convergence or co-convergence among European welfare states.

Yet the evidence simply does not bear out that expectation (see also Hay 2003). Limits of space allow us to consider only social transfer payments (expressed as a percentage of GDP). These are, in essence, a measure of basic welfare expenditure. For ease of comparison they are here standardized at 100 for 1960. Precisely because these are standardized measures, they are bound to show an initial divergence. Yet, the convergence thesis would lead us to expect initial divergence to be checked considerably by the 1980s and 1990s. It would predict, in short, an oval-shaped distribution. And the co-convergence thesis would predict the emergence of two clusters—one grouped around Germany, the other around the United Kingdom.

Neither prediction is borne out by the evidence (see Figure 10.4). Instead, consistent paths are mapped out from the 1960s, which social models continue to follow for the most part to the present day. The wide initial variance in growth rates is sustained over time. This is not a story of systematic welfare retrenchment, nor is it a story of the diminishing distinctiveness of regime types—which seem, if anything, to be reinforced over time. Indeed, it is the Nordic welfare states that have grown

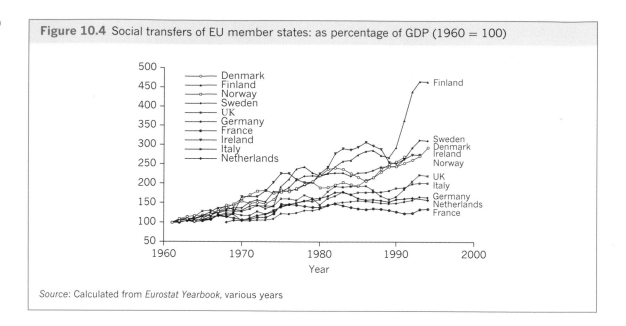

Figure 10.4 Social transfers of EU member states: as percentage of GDP (1960 = 100)

Source: Calculated from *Eurostat Yearbook*, various years

the most. Under globalization, it would seem, the most generous welfare states have thrived.

Second, we might consider the raw unstandardized data itself—that is, social transfers expressed as a share of GDP. To aid the analysis, European welfare regimes are grouped here in terms of the conventional threefold classification. The *Nordic* regime type refers to Sweden, Denmark, Finland, and Norway; the *conservative* regime type refers to Germany, the Netherlands, Italy, and France; and the *liberal* regime type to the United Kingdom and Ireland.

What the raw data reveals is that it is only relatively recently that the distinctiveness of the Nordic social democratic regime type has emerged. This is the most generous in terms of welfare provision and, one might expect, the most exposed as a consequence of globalization. Again, it seems, the evidence is in some tension with the predictions of the existing literature (see Figure 10.5), because, far from being associated with welfare retrenchment the period of (supposedly) most intensive globalization (the 1980s to the present day) has been associated with the emergence and consolidation—not the retrenchment—of the most generous welfare states the world has ever known.

Finally, we might also note that the standard deviation (a measure of dispersion about the mean) for social transfers rises over time, indicating divergence rather than convergence.

Of course, we cannot infer from such evidence that globalization is not an agent of convergence or co-convergence, merely that the evidence considered here is not consistent with such a claim. It is also important to note that, even were this a valid inference to draw, it would be wrong to conclude from this that globalization has no impact on the nation state. Because, if globalization serves, as some have suggested, to increase the sensitivity of economic performance to the *quality* of public policy (see, for example, Weiss 1998), then there is no particular reason to expect either a crisis of the state or convergence. Moreover, if, as is widely assumed, globalization generates common pressures for neo-liberalization, and this has been more enthusiastically embraced in regimes already characterized by their liberalism, we might expect to see at least an initial period of divergence.

But what evidence is there of an historically unprecedented phase of globalization capable of generating such pressures? We turn now to the independent variable.

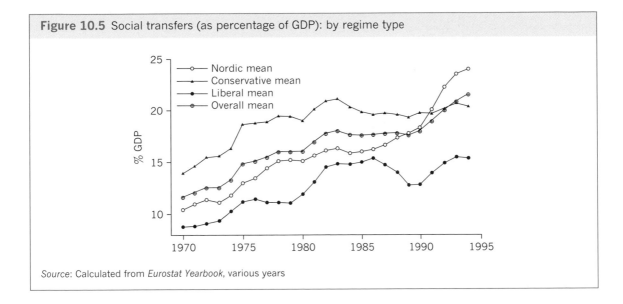

Figure 10.5 Social transfers (as percentage of GDP): by regime type

Source: Calculated from *Eurostat Yearbook*, various years

The independent variable: globalization

As already noted, proponents of the hyperglobal-ization thesis have rarely felt the need to defend the intuitively plausible claim that we live in a fully integrated global economy. Casual and anecdotal appeals to supporting evidence largely exhaust the empirical content of this literature. Yet, in recent years, a more rigorous and systematically evidential assessment of patterns of economic integration has emerged, and its authors have invariably drawn a rather different set of conclusions. Thus, on the basis of an exhaustive (if not uncontroversial) assessment of the empirical evidence, sceptics such as Paul Hirst and Grahame Thompson (1999) conclude that globalization is, in fact, a rather inaccurate description of existing patterns of international economic integration and cannot credibly explain the development of the state in recent years (for an important critical response to their work see Held *et al.* 1999).

The principal claims of this literature are sum-marized in Box 10.4 and discussed in more detail in the following pages.

The comparative history of global economic integration

It is conventional, as already noted, to date the current era of globalization from the 1960s. And it is certainly the case that if we plot economic data from the early 1960s to the present we see clear evidence of an almost exponential increase in trade and capital flows (expressed as shares of global GDP). Yet, it would be wrong to infer from this the development of an unprecedented integration of the global economy, without first considering the history of economic integration.

If we do that, then what becomes very clear is the sensitivity of the conclusions drawn by proponents of the globalization thesis to their preferred start date. If we extend the time frame, choosing as a starting point the late nineteenth or early twen-tieth century, a rather different picture emerges. Consider, first, economic openness from the per-spective of the significance of trade in national output (the value of imports plus exports expressed as a share of GDP).

As Hirst and Thompson note, 'apart from the dramatic differences in the openness to trade of

---

BOX 10.4

The Empirical Case against the Globalization Thesis

1. Although the period since the 1960s has seen the growing openness of national economies (such that imports plus exports are equivalent to a growing proportion of GDP), there is still some considerable way to go before pre-First-World-War figures are likely to be exceeded (Bairoch 1996; Hirst and Thompson 1999).

2. There continues to be a positive and, indeed, strengthening relationship between public spending (as a share of GDP) and economic openness (Cameron 1978; Katzenstein 1985; Rodrik 1996, 1997; Garrett 1998b).

3. There is no inverse relationship, as might be expected, between the volume of inward foreign direct investment and levels of corporate taxation, environmental and labour market regulations, generosity of welfare benefits or state expenditure as a share of GDP (Dunning 1988; Cooke and Noble 1998; Traxler and Woitech 2000; Wilensky 2002).

4. Trade and international flows of capital (such as FDI) tend to be extremely concentrated within the core 'triad' (of Europe, North America, and Pacific Asia) providing evidence of regionalization and 'triadization', but hardly of globalization (Petrella 1996; Frankel 1997; Hirst and Thompson 1999).

5. The pace of economic integration is higher *within* regions (such as Europe, North America, or Pacific Asia) than it is *between* regions, suggesting that regionalization rather than globalization is the overriding dynamic in the process of international economic integration (Frankel 1997; Kleinknecht and ter Wengel 1998; Hay 2004; Ravenhill, Chapter 6 in this volume).

6. Financial integration has failed to produce the anticipated convergence in interest rates one would expect from a fully integrated global capital market (Zevin 1992; Hirst and Thompson 1999).

7. Financial integration has failed to produce the anticipated divergence between rates of domestic savings and rates of domestic investment that one would expect in a fully integrated global capital market—the so-called **Feldstein–Horioka puzzle** (Feldstein and Horioka 1980; see also Epstein 1996: 212–215; Watson 2001).

8. Though the liberalization of financial markets has certainly increased the speed, severity, and significance of investors' reactions to government policy, capital market participants appear to be far less discriminating or well-informed in their political risk assessment than is conventionally assumed (Swank 2002; Mosley 2003). Consequently, policy-makers may retain rather more autonomy than has been widely accepted.

---

different economies demonstrated by these figures . . . the startling feature is that trade to GDP ratios were consistently higher in 1913 than they were in 1973 . . . Even in 1995 . . . the US was the only country that was considerably more open than it was in 1913' (1999: 27). True, the composition of trade in, say, 1913, is likely to be remarkably different from that in 1973 or 1995, reflective in the case of the United Kingdom, the Netherlands, and France by a strongly colonial dimension in the pre-First World War period. Nonetheless, in inviting a closer examination of the character, and not just the quantity, of trade, Hirst and Thompson provide a powerful challenge to the conventional literature. It should, however, be noted that, since

1995, levels of world economic integration have indeed surpassed those experienced during the latter half of the nineteenth century.

The data with respect to capital flows reveal a similar pattern. Between 1870 and 1914, international capital flows between the G7 economies averaged some 4 per cent of GDP, peaking at around 6 per cent in 1914. Between 1914 and 1970, they declined to 1.5 per cent of GDP. Since 1970 they have charted a consistent upward trajectory, rising to 3 per cent of GDP by the early 1990s. Yet they still have a long way to go to reach the figures of the pre-First World War period (Lewis 1981; Turner 1981; Bairoch 1996: 184; Hirst and Thompson 1999: 28, figure 2.4; See Figure 10.6).

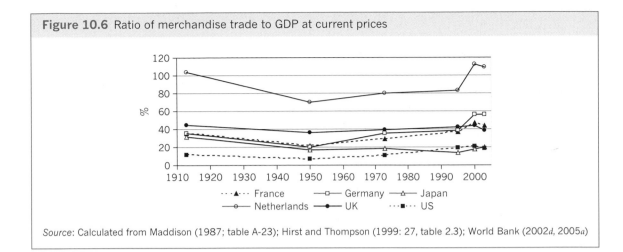

Figure 10.6 Ratio of merchandise trade to GDP at current prices

Source: Calculated from Maddison (1987; table A-23); Hirst and Thompson (1999: 27, table 2.3); World Bank (2002*d*, 2005*a*)

In quantitative, if not perhaps in qualitative, terms, the current period is not unprecedented or, indeed, unsurpassed.

In sum, then, whilst from the mid-1970s there has been an increasing trend towards financial and trade integration, economic openness was greater in the pre-First World War years than in the 1990s.

'Stateness' and openness

Arguably more significant, and certainly less contested, are recent attempts to reproduce and update David Cameron's (1978) path-breaking study of the covariance of economic openness and public expenditure. Such findings are particularly damaging to the globalization orthodoxy that predicts a strong inverse correlation between 'stateness' and openness—high levels of state expenditure (expressed as a proportion of GDP) *should* suppress the globalization of the domestic economy.

What Cameron demonstrated in a now famous paper published in the *American Political Science Review* in 1978 was a strong positive correlation between trade openness and social protection, funded through taxation. In other words, international economic integration seemed to go hand in hand with comprehensive social provision. Moreover, openness was also positively correlated with social

democratic tenure, union power, and the degree of regulation of the labour market.

More damaging still to the orthodox globalization thesis has been more recent research in this vein by, among others, Peter Katzenstein (1985), Dani Rodrik (1996, 1997), and Geoffrey Garrett (1998*b*). What these authors demonstrate is that the strength of the correlation between openness and government expenditure in OECD countries has only grown in subsequent decades. For proponents of the hyperglobalization thesis, this takes some explaining. Yet for Dani Rodrik it is easily explained:

> What should we make of this? I will argue that the puzzle is solved by considering the importance of social insurance and the role of government in providing cover against external risk. Societies that expose themselves to greater amounts of external risk demand (and receive) a larger government role as shelter from the vicissitudes of global markets. In the context of the advanced industrial economies specifically, this translates into more generous social programmes. Hence the conclusion that the social welfare state is the flip side of the open economy! (Rodrik, 1997:53)

Rodrik's is, of course, not the only possible explanation. Equally plausible is that high levels of state expenditure are a result of success in international markets—a consequence rather than a condition of the globalization of the domestic economy. Yet, whichever way round it is, economic openness would seem to be far more compatible with state expenditure than is conventionally assumed.

The determinants of inward foreign direct investment

As we saw in an earlier section, orthodox accounts of globalization tend to make a series of clear and more or less plausible assumptions about the preferences and interests of mobile investors. Such assumptions, as was shown, are directly responsible for the influential thesis that states enhance their locational competitiveness to foreign direct investors by offering targeted investment incentives, eliminating labour market rigidities, reducing the burden of corporate taxation, and ensuring that environmental regulations are not overly restrictive. Alter the assumptions, and a rather different set of inferences (and consequent policy implications) follow.

Recent scholarship, which examines the *revealed* preferences of foreign direct investors as exhibited in actual investment decisions (rather than making a priori assumptions about such preferences), challenges the globalization orthodoxy in important respects. Particularly notable here is the work of W. N. Cooke and D. S. Noble (1998) on the geographical distribution of foreign direct investment from the United States. This work contains a number of significant findings, each troubling to proponents of the hyperglobalization thesis:

1. It is direct market access and/or proximity to market that is the single greatest determinant of investment location. Inward direct investors value, above all else, geographical proximity to a substantial and affluent market. Consequently, the greatest single predictor of the volume of inward investment is total income within a 1,000-kilometre radius of the investment site.

2. Once access and proximity to market are controlled for, educational attainment/skill level is the most critical factor in determining the attractiveness of an industrial relations regime. Yet the effect is complex and not as anticipated. As Cooke and Noble note, 'with respect to investments in low-skill-low-wage countries, the evidence indicates that US multinational corporations have sought to match lower work force education with the limited labour skill requirements of operations that get located in low-skill-low-wage countries . . . [A]cross low-wage-low-skill countries US multinationals invest more in locations with the lowest levels of education' (1998: 596). This much is consistent with the hyperglobalization thesis. Yet, 'in contrast, it appears that, in matching the high labour skills requirements of operations located in high-skill-high-wage countries, US multinationals invest more in countries with both higher average education levels and higher hourly compensation costs' (1998: 596). This reveals a globally segmented market for inward investment, in which only developing countries are compelled to compete in terms of labour costs. Investors, it would seem, are perfectly prepared to pay the price of the highly trained and appropriately skilled workforce that (some) developed economies are capable of providing.

3. Moreover, and in seeming confirmation of this, it is not just the quantity (duration or level of attainment) of education that is important. Though it is difficult to gauge empirically, the evidence strongly supports the thesis that it is the *quality* and not the *cost* of skilled labour that is the key determinant of investment behaviour. Again, it would seem, cost (direct or indirect) is no impediment to investment if the anticipated return provides adequate compensation for that cost. Thus, skill and productivity differences between economies make a significant and additional difference in attracting inward investment. Comparing the United Kingdom and Germany, Cooke and Noble explain,

'both have comparable average years of education . . . but substantially different average hourly compensation costs . . . Germany's unmeasured skill base has garnered about $2.3 billion more in US FDI per industry than has the UK's unmeasured skill base . . . high-skill-high-wage countries that further enhance skill levels can attract significant additional US foreign direct investment' (1998: 602).

4. The conclusion is clear: 'countries need not encourage . . . wage restraint, since high hourly compensation costs do not reduce . . . foreign direct investment, provided these costs are matched by higher skills and productivity' (1998: 602).

This, and other similar evidence (see, for example Dunning 1988; Traxler and Woitech 2000; Swank 2002; Wilensky 2002) seriously challenge both the assumptions on which the hyperglobalization thesis is predicated and the predictions it makes about exit from highly regulated labour market regimes with generous welfare states funded out of taxation receipts.

Globalization or 'triadization'

In the highly contentious political economy of globalization, perhaps no issue is more controversial than the geographical character of the process of international economic integration that we have witnessed since the 1960s. It is, in particular, the challenge posed to the conventional wisdom by the recent work of arch globalization sceptics, Paul Hirst and Grahame Thompson (1996, 1999), that has provided the central focus of attention and controversy (see also Petrella 1996: 77–81; Allen and Thompson 1997; and, for a flavour of the critical responses, Perraton *et al.* 1997; Held and McGrew 2002: 38–57).

Hirst and Thompson, along with a growing crescendo of 'sceptics', have questioned the extent to which the term globalization characterizes accurately both the pattern of economic integration

within the international political economy today, or the trajectory of relations of economic integration and interdependence since the 1960s. Rather than a process of globalization, they suggest, a process of 'triadization' is, and has been, under way (1996: 2, 63–67). By triadization they refer to the selective and uneven process of deepening economic integration between the 'triad' economies; and by the 'triad' economies they refer to North America, South-East Asia, and Europe. In short, some economies are more 'globalized' than others, and this must ultimately lead us to challenge the appropriateness of the appellation 'globalization', as a significant and rising proportion of international economic activity is conducted within and between the triad economies. This is true of trade, foreign direct investment, and finance. For Hirst and Thompson, then, the developmental path of the international economy is characterized far more accurately by pointing to the effects of two separate processes:

1. A more general process of intra-regional economic integration or 'regionalization' (discussed in more detail later in this chapter); and

2. A more specific process of interregional economic integration drawing the triad economies into an ever-denser web of complex interdependencies.

The appeal, and indeed much of the novelty, of Hirst and Thompson's work when first published was its reliance on a substantial body of empirical evidence. Before their contribution, the innumerable empirical assertions made in the literature on globalization were largely unsubstantiated, or defended only in a loose and anecdotal sense. Indeed, Hirst and Thompson's iconoclastic claim was that such assertions simply could not be defended evidentially. In doing so, they pointed to the far from global character of flows of trade, investment, and finance. Space does not permit a detailed exploration of this evidence. Suffice it to note that, between 1991 and 1996, over 60 per cent of all flows of FDI were conducted within and between the triad economies and, in 1995, over 75 per cent of the accumulated stock of FDI was located within the same triad bloc (Hirst and Thompson 1999: 71; see also Brewer and Young 1998: 58–60). Between 1980 and 1991 the figures were almost identical (Hirst and Thompson 1996: 68). The triadic concentration in the accumulated stock of outward FDI is even more pronounced (see Figure 10.7) The more recent trends show a sizeable growth in inbound FDI destined for the less developed economies. Yet this is largely a result of the opening up of the Chinese economy.

Moreover, in 1996, despite accounting for only 14.5 per cent of the world's population, these economies accounted for some two-thirds of global

exports (Hirst and Thompson 1999: 73). This figure is only marginally lower than that for 1992 (70 per cent). Yet it is significantly greater than for either 1990 (64 per cent), 1980 (55 per cent), or 1970 (61 per cent) (Hirst and Thompson 1996: 69; Petrella 1996: 79). Finally, as Riccardo Petrella notes, 'during the 1980s, the triad accounted for around four-fifths of all international capital flows . . . [while] the developing countries' share fell from 25 per cent in the 1970s to 19 per cent' (1996: 77).

How much damage this does to the globalization thesis depends, to a large extent, on what one takes that thesis to be. Indeed, arguably, the debate is largely semantic (see also Scholte 2000: 14–20). Sceptics such as Hirst and Thompson and Petrella adopt a rather more exacting definition of globalization, it seems, than many of the hyperglobalization theorists. If, to count as evidence of globalization, processes either have to be genuinely global in scope or operative in unleashing such dynamics, then globalization characterizes poorly the condition and trajectory of the international economy. If, on the other hand, globalization means little more than economic openness (as witnessed by greater volumes of trade, investment, and financial flows as a share of global GDP) then globalization is certainly under way but it is unlikely to have the effects so frequently attributed to it. This is the challenge the sceptics present—one, it would seem, that is largely borne out by the empirical evidence.

Globalization or regionalization

Hirst and Thompson's (1996) emphasis, particularly in the first edition of *Globalization in Question*, is on the process of 'triadization', and hence upon a series of interregional processes of economic integration linking North America, East Asia, and Europe. Yet, as indicated above, this rests on the prior identification of a more general tendency towards regionalization (within, and indeed beyond, the triad economies). In fact, in the second edition of *Globalization in Question*, the significance of triadization is played down somewhat as, on the basis of a re-examination and updating of

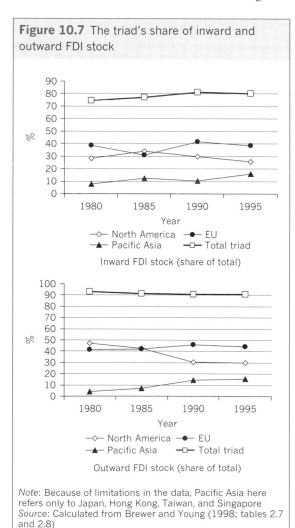

Figure 10.7 The triad's share of inward and outward FDI stock

Inward FDI stock (share of total)

Outward FDI stock (share of total)

Note: Because of limitations in the data, Pacific Asia here refers only to Japan, Hong Kong, Taiwan, and Singapore
Source: Calculated from Brewer and Young (1998; tables 2.7 and 2.8)

the available evidence, regionalization now emerges as the pervasive tendency within the international economy (Hirst and Thompson 1999: especially 99–103). Here, again, Hirst and Thompson's work provides a powerful statement of a developing consensus among sceptical voices.

Yet it is the work of Jeffrey Frankel that is perhaps the most comprehensive on the question of regionalization (see, especially, Frankel 1997, 1998). On the basis of a detailed examination of the empirical record, he demonstrates that, with respect to trade, any tendency to globalization or even *inter*regional economic integration has been swamped by the rapid growth in *intra*-regional integration. A result largely of the growth of preferential trading arrangements at the regional level, intra-regional trade accounts for an ever-growing share of global economic activity, suggesting once again that globalization is in fact an increasingly inaccurate characterization of both the process of economic integration and the resulting pattern of economic interdependencies (see Figure 10.8, and Ravenhill, Chapter 6 in this volume, Table 6.3).

Such findings have been replicated for FDI flows to and from Europe (Kleinknecht and ter Wengel 1998; Hay 2004). While this provides strong evidence of regionalization, it does not exhaust the case against the globalization thesis. Arguably rather more discriminating empirically is data on the regional concentration of trade. As Frankel explains,

'to obtain a usable measure of regional concentration, we need to adjust the intraregional trade share by a measure of each group's importance in world trade' (1997: 25–26). This is achieved by dividing each regional grouping's trade share (as shown in Figure 10.8) by that region's share of total world trade. The resulting index of intra-regional concentration again reveals a pervasive regionalization tendency, because, in a globalizing world we would expect the value of such intra-regional concentration ratios to fall consistently over time. As Figure 10.9 makes very clear, with

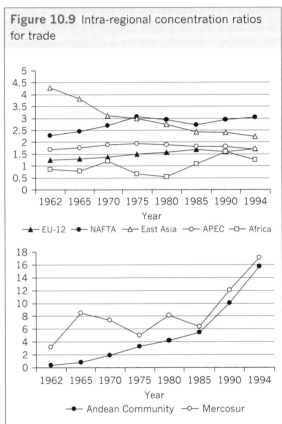

Figure 10.9 Intra-regional concentration ratios for trade

Notes: EU-12 = Belgium (and Luxembourg), Denmark, France, Germany, Greece, Ireland, Italy, Netherlands, Portugal, Spain and United Kingdom; NAFTA = USA, Canada and Mexico; East Asia = ASEAN-6 (Brunei, Indonesia, Malaysia, Philippines, Singapore and Thailand) plus China, Hong Kong, Japan, Korea and Taiwan; Mercosur = Argentina, Brazil, Paraguay and Uruguay; APEC = East Asia-11 plus NAFTA-3 plus Australia, Chile, New Zealand and Papua New Guinea; Andean Community = Bolivia, Columbia, Ecuador, Peru and Venezuela
Source: Calculated from Frankel (1997: table 2.3)

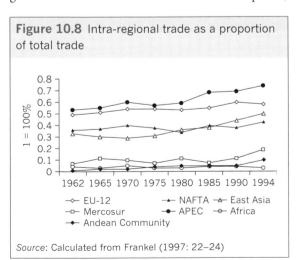

Figure 10.8 Intra-regional trade as a proportion of total trade

Source: Calculated from Frankel (1997: 22–24)

Conclusions

What are we to make of this? The overall picture that emerges is rather more complex than that described at the start of the chapter. While the economic processes usually labelled globalization have led to a greater degree of economic integration than at any point in the post-war period, current levels of economic interdependence are neither unprecedented historically nor perhaps as genuinely 'global' as is invariably assumed.

The impact of such processes on the capacity, autonomy, and sovereignty of the state is also complex. For while there is certainly some evidence of state retrenchment in recent years, especially once one controls for the higher demands placed on welfare states by demographic change and higher rates of unemployment, there would seem to be no clear evidence that globalization is the driver of this retrenchment. Indeed, the evidence reviewed in the previous section would suggest strongly that the constraints imposed on domestic political autonomy by heightened levels of economic integration (with respect to trade, foreign direct investment, or finance) have been grossly exaggerated. Yet this does not mean that globalization has had no impact on the nation state—merely that we need to be extremely cautious in attributing state retrenchment today to globalization.

Rather more plausible, and, sadly, overlooked in much of the existing literature, is the impact of *ideas* about globalization. If it is conceded that policy-makers increasingly view the world they face through a series of assumptions about globalization, then their conduct in office is likely to be shaped significantly by those assumptions. Arguably, then, the idea of globalization may be more influential in shaping the developmental trajectory of the nation state today than the *reality* of globalization (see Box 10.6).

BOX 10.6

The Role of Ideas about Globalization: Tax Competition between States

Consider tax competition between states. The hyperglobalization thesis suggests that, in a globalized context characterized by the heightened mobility of capital, vicious competition between states will serve to drive down the level of corporate taxation. Accordingly, any failure on the part of a state to render its corporate taxation levels competitive in comparative terms, through tax cuts, will result in a punitive depreciation in net revenue as capital exercises its mobility to exit. If governments believe the thesis to be true, or find it to their advantage to present it as true, they will act in a manner consistent with its predictions, thereby contributing to an aggregate depreciation in corporate taxation—whether they are right to do so or not.

To elaborate, were we to envisage a (hypothetical) scenario in which the hyperglobalization thesis was accurate, the free mobility of capital would indeed serve to establish tax competition between fiscal authorities seeking to retain existing investment levels while enticing mobile foreign direct investors to relocate. The price of any attempt to buck the trend is immediate capital flight, with consequent effects on budget revenue. In such a scenario, any rational administration aware (or assuming itself to be aware) of the mobility of capital will cut corporate taxes with the effect that no exit will be observed (Scenario 1 in Figure 10.10). Any administration foolish enough to discount or test the mobility of capital by retaining high levels of corporate taxation will be rudely awakened from its state of blissful ignorance or stubborn scepticism by a rapid exodus of capital (Scenario 2). In a world of perfect capital mobility, then, the learning curve is likely to prove very steep indeed.

Yet, were we to assume instead that we inhabit a world in which the mobility of capital is much exaggerated, and in which capital has a clear vested interest in threatening exit, the scenario unfolds rather differently. Here, fiscal authorities lulled into accepting the hyperglobalization thesis by the (ultimately hollow) exit threats of capital will cut rates of corporate tax, (falsely) attributing the lack of capital flight to their competitive taxation regime (Scenario 3). Yet, were they to resist this logic by calling capital's bluff, they might retain substantial taxation receipts without fear of capital flight (Scenario 4). The crucial point, however, is that while politicians believe the hyperglobalization thesis—and act on it—we cannot differentiate between Scenario 1 (in which the thesis is true) and Scenario 3 (in which it is false). Though in Scenario 1, globalization is a genuine constraint on political autonomy, and in Scenario 2 it is merely a social construction, the outcomes are the same. As this demonstrates, in the end (at least in this scenario), it is ideas about globalization rather than globalization per se that affects political and economic outcomes. [This makes the role of international institutions in the dissemination of ideas about globalization especially significant].

Source: Adapted from Hay (2002*b*: 202–204).

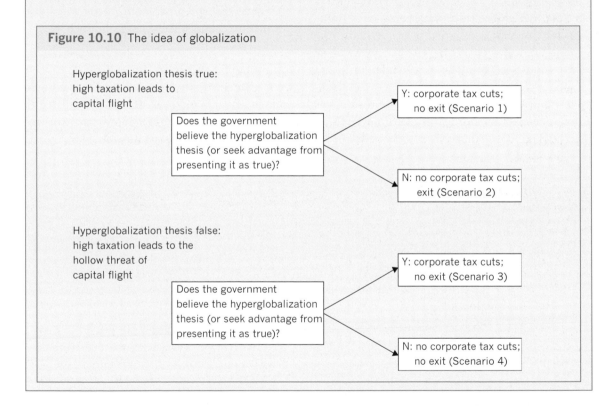

Figure 10.10 The idea of globalization

Hyperglobalization thesis true: high taxation leads to capital flight

Does the government believe the hyperglobalization thesis (or seek advantage from presenting it as true)?

Y: corporate tax cuts; no exit (Scenario 1)

N: no corporate tax cuts; exit (Scenario 2)

Hyperglobalization thesis false: high taxation leads to the hollow threat of capital flight

Does the government believe the hyperglobalization thesis (or seek advantage from presenting it as true)?

Y: corporate tax cuts; no exit (Scenario 3)

N: no corporate tax cuts; no exit (Scenario 4)

This raises an important point about democratic legitimacy and accountability today. It is all very well to argue that state autonomy remains essentially intact in an era of globalization, but if such autonomy is perceived to have been eroded by all credible candidates for political office, then such autonomy is purely hypothetical. While globalization might not have narrowed the field of democratic choice itself, the idea of globalization might well have done so—as parties across the political spectrum converge on a set of prudent economic and social policies designed to appease footloose multinational investors. Arguably, this has much to do with the widespread contemporary disaffection with liberal democratic regimes (see, for example, Pharr and Putnam 2000). Democracy is no less a casualty in such a scenario. This makes the public scrutiny of influential assumptions and ideas about globalization a most urgent political priority. It establishes once again the phenomenal importance of the ongoing controversy that surrounds the question of globalization's impact on the state.

One final point might also be noted. While there is in fact little evidence for the thesis that the nation state's capacity and autonomy has been eroded significantly by virtue of globalization, it is nonetheless the case that globalization poses a series of problems for the nation state that it has never had the capacity to deal with. We have seen, and are likely to continue to see, a proliferation of interlinked and genuinely global political, economic, and, above all, environmental problems requiring, for their resolution, effective institutions of global governance. This final point is perhaps the most troubling of all.

It is certainly tempting to dismiss globalization as a myth, or as a process with minimal impact on the historical capacities of the state. Yet the problem of the lack of the political capacity to deal with urgent global problems in an effective and democratic way remains. The challenges we face are essentially twofold:

1. To find ways of designing effective and democratic institutions of global governance capable of commanding political support and legitimacy; and

2. To find ways of passing responsibility, and indeed sovereignty, from a system of nation states that still provides the focus of political identification and citizenship to such institutions.

At the point at which we prove ourselves capable of responding to both of these challenges, we might legitimately begin to speak of a transcendence (if not perhaps a crisis) of the nation state. But that point is still a very, very long way off.

? QUESTIONS

1. Is there, or has there been, a crisis of the nation state?

2. What is meant by the globalization of politics, and has it occurred?

3. What mechanisms can be pointed to suggesting a clear link between globalization and state retrenchment?

4. What are the key assumptions of the hyperglobalization thesis? Are they plausible?

5. Is globalization an agent of convergence, dual convergence, divergence, or continued diversity?

6. How does the model of the 'tragedy of the commons' illuminate the problem of global governance?

7. Assess the evidence on whether state retrenchment has taken place.

8. What impact has globalization had on the development of the nation state?

9. Are the constraints on the autonomy and capacity of the nation state arising from globalization largely real or imagined?

FURTHER READING

■ **Cerny, P. G. (1997), 'Paradoxes of the Competition State: The Dynamics of Political Globaliza-tion',** *Government and Opposition,* **32/2: 251–274.** The clearest exposition of the highly influential 'competition state' thesis.

■ **Garrett, G. (2000), 'Shrinking States? Globalization and National Autonomy', in N. Woods (ed.),** *The Political Economy of Globalization* **(Basingstoke: Palgrave).** A clear and comprehensive survey of the existing literature and supporting evidence by an influential commentator.

■ **Hirst, P., and Thompson, G. (1999),** *Globalization in Question,* **2nd edn (Cambridge: Polity Press).** The definitive statement of the case against the globalization orthodoxy.

■ **Jessop, B. (2002),** *The Future of the Capitalist State* **(Cambridge: Polity Press).** The product of almost two decades of scholarship, this is perhaps the most important single work on the condition of the state today. Though dense and at times difficult, it rewards close reading.

■ **Mosley, L. (2003),** *Global Capital and National Governments* **(Cambridge: Cambridge University Press).** An exceptionally important recent addition to the existing literature, and a comprehensive reappraisal of the conventional wisdom about the domestic political constraints issuing from financial markets.

■ **Ohmae, K. (1996),** *The End of the Nation State: The Rise of Regional Economies* **(New York: Free Press).** Though widely discredited, still the core exponent and defender of the hyperglobalization thesis.

■ **Weiss, L. (1998),** *The Myth of the Powerless State: Governing the Economy in a Global Era* **(Cambridge: Polity Press).** A clear and accessible defence of the continued centrality and importance of the nation state in an era of globalization.

WEB LINKS

www.europa.eu provides a fantastic range of official papers, press releases and supporting data from the European Commission on EU member states.

www.oecd.org provides online access to a superb data archive of OECD member states.

www.imf.org provides online access to policy documents and supporting data from the IMF.

www.theglobalsite.ac.uk/globalization access to a large number of otherwise unpublished working papers on globalization and much else besides.

www.statewatch.org rather quirky but nonetheless interesting site which claims to monitor the activities of state-like bodies in Europe with a view to protecting civil liberties.

Visit the Online Resource Centre that accompanies this book for more information:
www.oxfordtextbooks.co.uk/orc/ravenhill2e/

11 The Globalization of Production

ERIC THUN

Chapter Contents

- Introduction
- The Rise of Global Production
- Global Value Chains: Governance and Location
- China As the World's Factory
- Conclusion

Reader's Guide

Although companies have been investing abroad for centuries, the current era of globalization has created an unprecedented range of possibilities for global firms to reorganize and relocate their activities. This chapter analyses how advances in transportation and technology allow a firm to divide up a **global value chain**—the sequence of activities that lead to the production of a particular good or service—and how these decisions create new opportunities and challenges for both companies and the societies within which they operate. The first section of the chapter reviews the rise of global production and the forces that have led to dramatic increases in **foreign direct investment** (FDI) and outsourcing. The central questions for any firm involved in global production involve how to govern the value chain and where to locate different activities. The second section provides a framework for understanding these issues and the implications of the various choices. The third section applies these concepts to the case of East Asia.

Introduction

Multinational corporations (MNCs) are the most public face of globalization. Defined as firms that have operations in two or more countries, MNCs are a source of hope and promise to those who seek to harness the power of economic globalization for purposes of development, and a source of fear and opposition to those who view globalization as a threat to national sovereignty. MNCs are pervasive. In 2005, there were some 77,000 parent companies, with over 770,000 affiliates. These affiliates produced an estimated $4.5 trillion in value-added, and employed some 62 million workers (UNCTAD 2006b: 9–10). The share of international production in world output, as measured by the share of value-added of foreign firms in world **gross domestic product** (GDP), increased from 7 per cent in 1990 to 10 per cent in 2005 (UNCTAD 2006b: 10). MNCs are also very tangible. They are not anonymous buyers and sellers engaged in arm's-length trade. Through FDI, they own assets and employ people in foreign countries. They are the companies behind the most powerful global brands. To populations that are being buffeted by the invisible forces of globalization, MNCs serve as very visible symbols of forces they cannot control.

Foreign investment on the part of MNCs, however, is only the tip of the iceberg that is the globalization of production. Firms such as Nike and Gap do not own the foreign factories that make their products; they use contractors who work to their specifications. Nike has slightly more than 20,000 direct employees, but its products are manufactured by more than 500,000 workers in over 700 factories in 51 countries (Locke 2003: 6). Gap bought 1 billion units of clothing in 2004, from 700 suppliers, and these suppliers owned and operated 3,000 factories in 50 countries, but Gap does not own a single factory abroad. These firms control global value chains—the sequence of activities through which technology is combined with material and

labour inputs, and then assembled, marketed, and distributed (Gereffi *et al.* 2005: 79)—and while they wield tremendous power, it is not the result of ownership arising from FDI. Similarly, electronic giants such as Apple, Dell and Hewlett-Packard rely on specialized manufacturing firms to make their products, and focus primarily on design, marketing, distribution, and service.

Global value chains are important determinants of who gets what, when, and how in the global economy. There are two sides to the global production coin. From the perspective of 'home' countries—where the headquarters of multinational firms are located—the key question is what will be left behind when production moves abroad. Because outward investment from the home economy of a multinational will potentially be moving jobs, technology, and profits beyond national borders, it creates fears of a 'hollowing out' effect. Will outward investment and outsourcing lead to an inexorable flow of jobs, technology, and profits to lower-cost countries? Will the competition for high value-added activities lead to a convergence of economic models? From the perspective of 'host' countries—the destinations of FDI and outsourcing—the question is whether they will be able to capture the high value-added activities, or whether they will be trapped into a dependent relationship with multinational firms in which they are limited to low value-added activities. Will the foreign firms contribute to the long-term development of the local economy, or will they inhibit the development of local firms? Will the foreign firms adhere to the social, political, and environmental standards of the local society, or will they behave in an imperialistic manner and/or engage in practices that would not be allowed in their home societies?

In both cases, the questions revolve around the distribution of resources, the bargaining leverage of the states that 'host' foreign investment, and the power of multinational firms to determine who gets which part of global production, and how this influences employment, the locus of knowledge and innovation, and the creation of profits in the world economy. This chapter will analyse how advances in transportation and technology have created new opportunities to divide up a value chain, how this creates new possibilities for global firms to reorganize and relocate the various activities that they engage in, and the opportunities and challenges these changes create for both home and host states and societies.

The Rise of Global Production

There is nothing new about foreign investment or international production. In the sixteenth century, chartered trading companies established foreign production facilities for much the same reasons as firms did centuries later—internalization within the firm was a means of economizing on frequent transactions that inherently had to occur in a particular location, whether in order to access particular raw materials or markets. The Dutch East India Company, for example, established a saltpetre plant in Bengal in 1641, a print works for textiles ten years later, and employed 4,000 silk spinners by 1717. In an era when the full cycle of activity (export, transport, and sale of goods from home to foreign markets, import, transport, and sale of goods from foreign to home markets) could take anywhere from eighteen to thirty months to complete, hierarchical co-ordination within the firm allowed a trading company to equate supply and demand more effectively (Carlos and Nicholas 1988: 403, 407).

In the nineteenth century, the Industrial Revolution spurred demand for raw materials, and companies sought to own and manage their sources of raw materials in order to reduce risk. For manufacturing companies, the result was vertical investments upstream and downstream, and a hub-and-spoke model of international production: raw materials were imported from the periphery, manufacturing took place at home, and finished goods were then distributed globally. In response to rising protectionism in the early twentieth century, firms began to make horizontal investments abroad: manufacturing capabilities were duplicated in foreign markets that were increasingly sheltered behind tariff barriers (Palmisano 2006: 128). In the 1920s and 1930s, for example, American companies such as General Motors, Ford, Firestone, Nabisco, General Foods, Hoover, ITT, and Honeywell rapidly increased the numbers of their manufacturing facilities in Europe. These were multinationals in the form that would dominate the global economy for much of the twentieth century. Certain activities, such as research and development, were concentrated in their headquarters, but other capabilities were duplicated in operations around the world. These companies pursued a multi-market strategy.

Numbers and trends

International production is not new, but its magnitude and the degree of fragmentation in global value chains is new. To an unprecedented degree, firms are able to break up their value chains and locate each discrete activity according to competitive advantage rather than geographical convenience. How can we measure the growth of global production?

One relatively straightforward indicator is the increase in FDI. Between 1982 and 2005, according to the United Nations Conference on Trade and Development (UNCTAD) *World Investment Report*, the value of FDI inflows (in current prices) increased from $59 billion to $916 billion (UNCTAD 2006*b*: 9). The ratio of world FDI inflows to global gross domestic capital formation (a measure of domestic investment) increased from 2 per cent in 1980 to 9.4 per cent in 2005 (UNCTAD 2000: xv–xvi, 2006*b*: 307). Two trends are important to note about these massive flows. First, they are highly concentrated. Developed economies received 59 per cent of inward FDI in 2005, and the top five of these economies received almost 50 per cent of global flows (UNCTAD 2006*b*: xvii, 4). The United Kingdom was the top recipient in 2005, for example (with a total inflow of $165 billion), and the European Union (EU) accounted for almost half of the world total (UNCTAD 2006*b*: xvii). The major sources of FDI are also frequently the major destinations.

Second, and a related point, mergers and acquisitions (M&As) between existing firms rather than greenfield (new) investment are the dominant form of foreign investment. In 2005, cross-border M&As reached a value of $716 billion, and 141 of these were mega deals of over $1 billion (UNCTAD 2006*b*: 13). These deals reflect the desire of firms to achieve the scale and scope to operate in what are increasingly global markets. Just as the development of technology, regulatory changes, and new modes of finance led to a wave of corporate M&As in the United States at the end of the nineteenth century, as firms shifted from a regional to a national focus, the same factors are now leading to a global focus (UNCTAD 1999: xx). Increasing regional integration and the introduction of a single currency in the EU, for example, have created a wave of M&A activity in Europe, and horizontal acquisitions between firms in the same industry (which, in terms of value, represented 70 per cent of M&A activity at the end of the 1990s) represent the quickest route to global scale and scope for firms seeking to access new markets and complementary capabilities (UNCTAD 1999: xix–xx). In short, the majority of FDI is the consolidation of corporate activity—large corporations being taken over by even larger corporations—in what is increasingly a global market for firms.

FDI has also become dramatically more important for developing countries. A developing country seeking external capital investment has four choices: official flows (from international development agencies and governments), commercial bank loans, portfolio flows (from institutional investors such as pension funds, insurance companies, and mutual funds), and FDI. Until the early 1990s, official flows were the dominant source of capital for developing countries, often in the form of loans that were made on concessional terms, but over the course of the 1990s there was a dramatic shift from public to private capital flows. This was partly the result of budgetary difficulties in developed countries, which led to a cutback in foreign aid, but it also reflected an ideological shift towards market-based approaches to public policy. By 2005, official flows to the developing world had largely dried up, and over half of the total resource flow to the developing world consisted of FDI ($334 billion). As is the case in the developed world, these flows tend to be concentrated: Brazil, China, Hong Kong, Mexico, and Singapore have been the five top FDI destinations in the developing world for virtually every year since 1996. In 2005, these five countries accounted for 48 per cent of the total flow to the developing world (UNCTAD 2006*b*: 4–5). Attracting FDI is important for developing countries, not just because it is the most stable form of foreign capital that is available, but as will be explained in greater detail below, because it is thought to have the potential to bring a package of benefits, including technology, managerial skills, and access to new markets.

Although FDI represents a critical element of global production, it only measures global production that takes place under foreign ownership, and neglects the outsourcing of production. Simply defined, outsourcing is the reallocation of a particular task from within one firm to another, and the two are usually separated by having different ownership (Sako 2006: 503). There is overlap between the two categories—an American firm that uses a Korean manufacturer located in China is both outsourcing (from the perspective, of the US firm) and reliant on FDI (from the perspective of the Korean firm)—but the distinction is important from an analytical perspective, because it points to the wide variety of governance forms in global value chains. And outsourcing need not necessarily be accompanied by any trans-border flows of capital—firms may be linked simply by 'arm's length' purchase arrangements, or the relationship may involve, for example, the transfer of expertise from purchaser to supplier.

Unfortunately, it is very difficult to determine the value of outsourcing transactions from general trade data. One possible measure (albeit with a regional bias) is the growth of trade in intermediate goods (components that are neither raw materials nor finished products). In Asia, for example, between 1985 and 1996, the value of all parts and component imports increased by 6 per cent, and accounted for 25 per cent of all manufactured imports by 1996. Trade in telecommunications components increased from 3 billion in 1985 to 41 billion in 1996 (when components accounted for 72 per cent of imports in the product group), and the increase in trade in electronic components was only slightly less dramatic (Ng and Yeats 1999: 10). A second measure (albeit with a sectoral bias) is the dramatic rise of specialist contract manufacturers. Electronic manufacturing services (EMS) firms, for example, receive designs for a broad spectrum of electronic products from brand-name firms, import or manufacture components, assemble the products, and then export the finished goods. The industry grew from nothing in the early 1980s—when IBM began to look for key suppliers for its personal computers in 1981—to $170 billion in revenue in 2005. Many of these companies have themselves become significant foreign investors. Flextronics—an example of one of the five largest firms in the sector—has manufacturing operations in thirty countries on five continents, employs over 50,000 people in China alone, and has revenues in excess of $15 billion. Flextronics and its competitors make 100 per cent of desktop computer motherboards, 83 per cent of laptop computers, and 33 per cent of cell phones, according to industry estimates

(figures from Deagon 2006). Similarly, in the auto industry, the largest supply firms are now almost as large as the assembly firms they serve. In order to save on development costs, take advantage of supplier knowledge, and maximize economies of scale, auto assembly firms outsource the design and manufacture of entire modules of a car to large supply firms. In 1992, there were only twenty-eight US auto supply firms with annual sales between $1 billion and $5 billion, and five companies with sales higher than $5 billion. In 1998, these numbers were forty-seven and thirteen, respectively (Veloso 2006: 16). Although not quite as dramatic as in the electronics industry, the outsourcing of manufacturing was a dominant trend in the auto industry during the 1990s.

Why now?

Politics has played a key role in the expansion of global production. The liberalization of trade was a critical prerequisite for the globalization of production. When trade barriers are high, a multinational firm will invest in production facilities abroad in order to access foreign markets, but it will hesitate to relocate portions of the value chain that must be integrated with other global activities—the fragmentation of value chains requires low tariff barriers. As Gibert Winham argues in Chapter 5 of this book, the trade regime is the most prominent example of global co-operation in the post-Second World-War era. Chastened by the breakdown of the global economy during the inter-war period, the United States began a return to liberalism with the passage of the Reciprocal Trade Agreements Act of 1934. After the Second World War, the trend of increased economic liberalism continued with each successive round of the General Agreement on Tariffs and Trade (GATT), and the result was the rapid expansion of world trade. World exports increased by close to 8 per cent per annum between 1950 and 1973, and by 5 per cent for the subsequent twenty-five-year period (Ravenhill, Chapter 1 in this volume).

The move towards a liberal trade regime at the international level had a corollary at the domestic level—a general trend towards market-based policies—and this expanded the range of options for global production. As Anthony McGrew explains in Chapter 9 of this book, the neo-liberal ideology associated with liberalization, deregulation, and privatization provided the normative infrastructure for economic globalization. In OECD states, governments across the political spectrum were instrumental in liberalizing national economies, and creating the policy and institutional frameworks that have enabled the growth of global trade and production.

Governments in the developing world used the expansion of global trade as an engine of growth. No region benefited more than East Asia. Scholars debate the extent to which economic growth in economies such as Korea and Taiwan was the result of government-led industrial policies (Amsden 1989; Wade 1990) as opposed to market-conforming policies (World Bank 1993), but reliance on export markets was clear in all these cases. Taiwan, for example, pioneered the use of export-processing zones—industrial parks where foreign firms could enjoy preferential trade and investment policies so long as their output was intended for export markets—at the same time as Japanese manufacturers were forcing American firms to reduce their costs by moving labour-intensive activities offshore. With the encouragement of the Taiwanese government and the United States Agency for International Development, General Instruments began manufacturing in Taiwan in 1964, and was followed over the next two years by twenty-four other American firms (Wade 1990: 94). This was in many important respects the beginning of the global manufacturing model that would dominate East Asia in the 1970s and 1980—firms from high-wage economies began to break apart their value chains and locate the manufacturing of each component according to competitive advantage. As the neo-liberal reforms took hold in China, Eastern Europe, India, and Latin America over the decades that followed, the scope of global manufacturing increased in turn.

At the same time as political changes were opening countries up to trade and investment, technology was extending the geographical reach of business, and making possible new forms of business organization. In many respects, this is an old story writ large. In the latter half of the nineteenth century, technology transformed the organization of business in the United States. As Alfred Chandler (1977: 75–80) has described, the spread of iron, coal, and machinery created the possibility of large-scale production in the United States, and the invention of the telegraph and expansion of railways created the means of communication and transportation that would allow these businesses to extend their geographical reach. These changes led to the emergence of the modern hierarchical corporation. Just as the telegraph and the railway allowed firms in the latter half of the nineteenth century to adopt a national rather than regional orientation, the improvement in transportation and technology in the latter half of the twentieth century allowed firms to adopt a global perspective. These changes led to the fragmentation of the value chain.

The first set of changes involved new forms of transportation. An obvious development was the introduction of commercial jet services in the 1950s. Less obvious, but probably even more important for world commerce, was the introduction of standardized shipping containers. Prior to the introduction of standardized steel and aluminum containers in the late 1950s, the process of loading and unloading cargo at the point of origin, at ports along the way, and at the destination was time-consuming and fraught with the possibility of loss and damage. Containers dramatically reduced the friction of transportation in global economy. Marc Levinson (2006: 7) provides a compelling illustration: a 35-ton container of coffee-makers in Malaysia can be loaded into a container at the factory door, taken to a port and loaded on to a ship, and then transported the 9,000 miles to Los Angeles in sixteen days. A day later, the container will be on a unit train to Chicago. If the train were to carry the capacity load of one of the new mega container ships—which can carry over 8,000 six-metre-long containers—it would stretch over 37 kilometres. Once in Chicago, the container of coffee-makers is transferred immediately to a flatbed lorry headed to Cincinnati, the distribution centre for the retailer. The process is not only inexpensive—in this case, less than the price of a single first-class air ticket from Malaysia to the USA—it is completely automated and the transfers at each juncture in the journey are seamless; human hands will not touch the contents of the container between the factory and the destination. In the late 1950s and early 1960s, transport costs were often a higher barrier to trade than were import tariffs (as high as 25 per cent of the cost of some products, according to one study) and the result was that globalization of production was not a cost-effective strategy (Levinson 2006: 9). At the time of writing, when 90 per cent of world trade is transported in shipping containers, transport in many industries is a marginal part of a company's overall cost structure. From the perspective of transport cost, it almost does not matter if a firm is doing business with a factory on the other side of town or the other side of the world.

If container shipping reduced the hurdle of transport costs, the digital revolution and the shift to modularity made it possible to separate the activities of the value chain and scatter them across the globe. The electronics industry has been at the cutting edge of the modular revolution (Baldwin and Clark 2000). Until the 1960s, the designs of the different parts of a computer system were highly interdependent, and consequently, when any new product was introduced, the design process would have to begin again from the start to ensure that all the component parts were compatible. The result was time-consuming and expensive, because teams of engineers within a single company had to work together on each component; outsourcing was not possible, because the connections between different parts of the product design were complex and varied in arbitrary and non-obvious ways (Baldwin and Clark 2000: 171). Like craftsmen putting together a custom-built piece of furniture, the engineers had

to work together, relying not on codified rules to piece together a machine but on tacit knowledge (information that cannot be written or coded in a set of instructions, but must be imparted by people working together).

The solution, introduced by IBM in the autumn of 1961, was to conceive of a family of computers—the System/360—that would include machines of different sizes and uses, but all of which would share the same instruction set and peripherals. A central office mandated the design rules that would determine how the different modules of the machine would interact with each other, and this allowed different teams of engineers to work independently on the aspects of each module that did not affect other modules. The shift to modularity increased the speed of the design process (because teams worked simultaneously), increased the rate of innovation (because teams could try any number of approaches so long as they adhered to the design rules for interacting with other modules), and created the flexibility needed to meet a variety of customer needs. Paradoxically, these advances also led to the end of IBM's dominance of the industry, because outside companies could perform the same role as internal company divisions, so long as they knew the design rules—easily specified as computer code—that would make their product compatible with an IBM machine (Baldwin and Clark 1997: 85). As a result, we now take it for granted that we can download photographs from a Canon camera to a Dell computer in order to print them on an HP printer. In other industries, the interfaces between modules are not always as easy to specify, but there is also a trend towards increasing modularity. As was pointed out in the previous section, auto assembly firms have been shifting responsibilities to their suppliers to as great an extent as possible. A Volkswagen truck factory in Brazil has taken this approach to the extreme. VW established the architecture of the production process and the interfaces that connect modules, but all the manufacturing is done by suppliers (Baldwin and Clark 1997: 87).

BOX 11.1

Modular Production

In the classic work on modularity, Baldwin and Clark (1997, 2000) define a modular system as one that 'is composed of units (or modules) that are designed independently but still function as an integrated whole' (1997: 86). The structural elements of a module are connected powerfully to each other and relatively weakly to elements in other modules of the same system (2000: 63). Every product that consists of multiple modules will have an *architecture* that specifies what modules are part of the system and what the function of each will be; *interfaces* that describe in detail how the modules will interact, connect, and communicate; and *standards* for testing the extent to which a module conforms to the design rules (1997: 86). Sako (2003) specifies how modularity fulfils different roles across the lifecycle of a product. In the design phase, the principle purpose of modularity is to reduce the lead-time of the design process, and the cost of design and development. In the manufacturing phase, the objective is to increase operational efficiency by allowing the mixing and matching of standardized components, thus allowing for both the benefits of scale efficiencies and greater customization and variety. Finally, when the product is being used, consumers want a product that is easy to use, compatible with other products, easily upgraded, and easily and inexpensively maintained. The objectives of the different phases are not always compatible. The core concern of product designers, for example, will be to ensure that the design of each module is independent of other modules, and this may lead to tight **interdependencies** within the module. When the consumer has to make a repair, however, rather than being able to replace an individual component, he or she may find that an entire (and expensive)

module must be replaced rather than an individual component.

Modularity does not lead inevitably to outsourcing, but it creates the possibility—it is difficult to outsource or separate the component parts of an integral product. Prior to the rise of mass production, for example, automobiles were made by craftsmen, and each vehicle had to be made in its entirety in a workshop because the component parts had to custom fit to each other. The workers were skilled in the principles of mechanical design and experienced with the materials with which they worked. As Womack *et al.* (1990) explain, production of the cars depended on the tacit knowledge of these craftsmen, and it was difficult to codify this knowledge reliably in a way that would make it readily accessible to outside firms; there was no standard gauging system, and machine tools at this point could not cut hardened steel. Because the craftsmen fitted each piece together individually, no two vehicles were exactly alike. The core innovation of Henry Ford was the development of a system that used a standard gauge and pre-hardened metal that would not warp during the manufacturing process, previously the major obstacle to standardizing the size of parts (Womack *et al.* 1990: 22–27). The introduction of interchangeable parts with standard interfaces made it possible for an auto firm to replace skilled craftsmen with unskilled assembly-line workers, and to outsource production of components. The benefits of outsourcing to a supply firm can be numerous: the supplier will be a specialist in the production of a particular component, it will be able to capture greater economies of scale (since it supplies many firms), and it will give the assembler greater flexibility to concentrate on other parts of the production process.

The ability to codify design information in digital form, particularly when combined with new forms of telecommunication to transmit this information, was a key enabler of globalization. As Suzanne Berger (2006: 76) explains, new software in the 1990s increased the ability of a wide variety of firms to digitize instructions and thus codify the interfaces within a product. This created new options with respect to location. Once engineers are

able to specify the 'hand-off' between two different modules within a product utilizing software, there is no longer any inherent reason why designers and production staff have to be located within the same facility. The design firm transmits the design specifications electronically to the production facility, and as long as the production facility meets the appropriate standards, it can be located anywhere. The ability to codify design information does not

to access the immobile resources of a particular place. A similar emphasis on the advantages inherent in a particular location is at the core of Michael Porter's (1990) concept of a firm's 'home base'. The home base consists of factors of production (and particularly specialized factors such as educational systems, technology and innovation systems, and infrastructure); demand conditions (the quality and quantity of the home market); related and supporting industries that are internationally competitive; and the national circumstances and context that influence the strategy, structure, and competitive practices of local firms. The interaction of these four attributes (what Porter calls the 'diamond of national advantage') leads to the creation of geographically concentrated clusters of competitive strengths that are mutually reinforcing. One of the greatest advantages of a multinational firm, according to Porter (1990: 60), is that it has the advantage of being able to combine the strengths of its own home base with other locations in its global network; at every stage of the value chain, a global firm can decide where to locate activities, to maximize the benefits of its global reach. If global value chains are the means of connecting a network of far-flung capabilities, the key then becomes a case of understanding why certain locations will vary in their ability to develop particular capabilities.

The traditional approach of comparative political economy has been to focus on the nation state, and to explain economic outcomes as a result of the relationship between domestic state institutions, patterns of industrial policy, and social actors. Successive generations of this approach analysed how national institutional structures responded to the challenges of economic adjustment in the advanced capitalist world (Katzenstein 1978, 1985; Schmitter and Lehbruch 1979; Zysman 1984). The most recent approach in this tradition has focused on systematic differences in the way that national economies are organized (Hall and Soskice 2001). Firms must co-ordinate activities with a range of economic actors—investors, other firms (suppliers and clients), the organizations that represent workers, and their own employees (in particular)—and firms that operate in liberal market economies will have very different characteristics and strengths from firms that operate in co-ordinated market economies (see Hays, Chapter 10 in this volume). This 'varieties of capitalism' approach assumes that 'the most important institutional structures—notably systems of labor market regulation, of education and training, and of corporate governance—depend on the presence of regulatory regimes that are the preserve of the nation-state' (Hall and Soskice 2001: 4). The result is a stark departure from the traditional perspective of economics on comparative advantage because the advantages of a particular location are not endowed by nature, but are the result of a complex constellation of interrelated institutions. Firms in a liberal market economy, for example, may have an advantage in activities that emphasize radical innovation; firms in a co-ordinated market economy may have an advantage in activities that require incremental innovation and manufacturing excellence. The key point from the perspective of global production is that multinational firms have the potential to access the advantages of all systems, and in doing so they can compensate for weaknesses at home.

Although national institutions are clearly important in shaping general patterns of economic co-ordination within an economy, an exclusive focus on the nation state as the unit of analysis can obscure as much as it reveals. There is increasing evidence that, as Anwar Shah and Theresa Thompson (2002: 5) of the World Bank put it, 'nation-states are too small to tackle large things in life and too large to address small things'. National governments do not have the same degree of autonomy to shape their national economies as they did in the past. As Colin Hay explains (Chapter 10 of this book), the extent to which globalization forces states to converge on a single economic model is the subject of fierce debate. While the resilience of distinct 'varieties' of capitalism is debated, few would question that nation states are increasingly aware of the international constraints on their economic policies. National governments that do not take into account international capital markets and foreign investors before making policy changes, for example, do so at their peril. At the same time as national governments are operating under greater constraints, decentralization—the process of devolving political, fiscal, and administrative powers to subnational units of government (Burki *et al.* 1999)—has been one of the dominant economic and political trends since the 1980s. This move towards decentralization started in advanced industrial nations, where free-market policy reforms were accompanied by a 'devolution revolution' that transferred authority and resources from central to local governments, and the approach was transferred to the developing world by the World Bank and development NGOs (Snyder 2001: 93).

The importance of regional economies is certainly not surprising to multinational firms that are seeking to access the best capabilities across the globe. If a firm wants to access high-tech capabilities in the United States, for example, the most capable firms are not scattered at random: they are clustered in places such as Silicon Valley in California; Route 128 outside Boston; or the Research Triangle in North Carolina. Why are national economic systems composed of disparate regional economies (Marshall 1920; Nadvi and Schmitz 1998)? One set of explanations focuses on the ability of firms in an industrial cluster to minimize transaction costs and maximize their share of specialized labour markets. For firms interested in design and technology, it is easier to identify new technologies and market trends; the flow of personnel between firms helps to disseminate knowledge; there is better access to highly specialized types of labour; and there may be better access to capital and other key inputs in a technology cluster (McKendrick *et al.* 2000: 46). For firms involved with manufacturing and operations, there are also benefits to agglomeration, although they are slightly different. Firms will benefit from lower transport costs and reduced transport times; greater economies of scale; a greater ability to increase production rapidly; specialized pools of labour; better ability to monitor and co-ordinate with suppliers; and a greater ability to monitor and imitate the competition (McKendrick *et al.* 2000: 46). A second (and not competing) set of explanations focuses on the political and economic characteristics of a particular region. In an era in which decentralization is a dominant political and economic trend, increasingly it is local institutions that help firms overcome the co-ordination problems of development (Thun 2006). The patterns of association in a region, types of intergroup relations, political representation, and forms of economic governance (both in the present and in the past) create different opportunities and constraints for economic actors, and these differences help to explain divergent economic outcomes within a single national economy (Locke 1995; Herrigel 1996).

KEY POINTS

- The activities within global value chains can be governed by a range of mechanisms, including market co-ordination, various forms of network co-ordination, and hierarchical co-ordination. The form of value chain governance is a key determinant of how power and profits are distributed among the key actors within the value chain.

- According to Dunning's eclectic paradigm, firms will engage in FDI when there are firm-specific advantages, location-specific advantages, and advantages of internalization.

- Gereffi *et al.* argue that the organization of a global value chain will vary according to the complexity of inter-firm transactions, the degree to which this complexity can be codified, and the extent to which the suppliers have the capabilities needed to meet the requirements of the buyers.

- When considering where to locate different parts of the value chain, firms must consider the cost of production and the competitive strengths and weaknesses of both nations and regions.

ERIC THUN

China As the World's Factory

There is no better place to analyse the trends in global production than China; the rise of China as an economic power has corresponded with the globalization of manufacturing. In the three decades since China began to make the transition to a market economy, the country has come to dominate world manufacturing, and the impact of this manufacturing juggernaut is difficult to ignore. China has a significant impact on the global prices of the inputs it sucks in to fuel its economic growth (even to the extent that manhole covers and highway railings disappear from countries on the other side of the world when Chinese commodity prices create the incentive for thieves to sell scrap metal) and the global price of the outputs it manufactures.

The impact of China on global manufacturing is difficult to overstate. From the perspective of economies that compete with it, the situation is often portrayed as grim. In 2006, the United States recorded a trade deficit of $232.5 billion with China—historically, the largest imbalance with a single trading partner—and when factories close in the United States and workers lose their jobs, China is an obvious target of political wrath.

From the perspective of multinational firms, however, the situation is very different. Although it is not the common understanding of the term, China is the 'world's factory' in the sense that much of the world's factories are operating in China; the impressive numbers that China chalks up in the global economy are thus as much a testament to foreign companies that have invested in manufacturing operations in China as they are an indication of the strength of Chinese-owned companies. The country is one of the leading destinations for global FDI. It consistently attracts over $50 billion of foreign investment a year, and in 2006 received $63 billion in FDI (*China Economic Quarterly*, 11/1, 2007: 4; for reasons why Chinese FDI figures may be considerably overstated

in official statistics, see Ravenhill 2006*a*: 661). These foreign-invested factories play a key role in Chinese manufacturing: over half of all Chinese exports are from foreign-invested factories, and over 80 per cent of technology-intensive exports are from foreign-invested factories (Rosen 2003: 22). Multinational firms benefit from Chinese production both when they invest in manufacturing facilities and when they outsource production to factories that produce in China (both foreign- and Chinese-owned). Consumers benefit from the low price of manufactured goods that are exported from China.

Location and global production

The patterns of foreign investment in China reflect the complex interaction of the multiple levels of location within which a multinational firm operates—the regional, the national, and the local—and the efforts of both firms and governments to balance concerns of efficiency, equity, and sovereignty.

First, and most obviously, the investment flows have led to the integration of national economies in the region. In fact, it is more accurate to speak of China as a *regional production base* than a national production base. When China began to reform its economy at the end of the 1970s, a development approach that emphasized foreign investment had the benefit of allowing the leadership to avoid the ideologically sensitive issue of whether to allow private-sector investment within China, and it created the opportunity for China to acquire technical and managerial skills rapidly from foreign firms. Special economic zones were located initially in the mainland provinces that were across from Taiwan and Hong Kong—the primary sources of investment during the 1980s—and as preferential policies were gradually expanded to include the entire coastal region of China, Japan and Korea became important sources of investment as well. These countries did not transfer entire industries to China; they transferred the labour-intensive activities to China, and the subsidiaries established then imported higher value-added components from their home country.

The extent of regional integration is reflected in a dramatic increase in intra-industry trade. Between 1990 and 2005, for example, the percentage of the electronics trade between Japan and China that consisted of components increased from slightly over 10 per cent in 1990 to almost 60 per cent in 2005 (METI 2006: 25). It is estimated that two-thirds of the inputs for China's processing activities come from Hong Kong, Japan, Korea, and Taiwan (Ravenhill 2006a: 670). At the end of 2003, according to Chinese statistics, there were a total of 28,401 Japanese-invested firms operating in China, and 27,128 Korean-invested firms. (see METI 2004: 3). In short, the United States trade deficit is with East Asia as a whole rather than with China: the high wage economies export components to China for final assembly, and then the finished goods are exported to the United States. In 2003, China had a large trade surplus with the United States (about $125 billion), but an almost equally large deficit with its Asian trading partners (about $99 billion) (Hufbauer and Wong 2004: 3). In trade statistics, a good that is shipped from China to the United States appears as an import from China even though

the value added in China may be as little as 20–40 per cent (Ravenhill 2006a: 669).

The formation of these regional networks is driven by high costs at home, and facilitated by advances in technology. The production process in a garment factory, for example, is distinctly low-tech and labour-intensive—a factory consists of rows of women sitting at sewing machines—but the linkages between different parts of the garment value chain can be very high-tech, and these linkages create the opportunity to manage offshore production networks more effectively. Until the early 1980s, for example, textiles and garments were Taiwan's number one export (Gee and Kuo 1997: 52). During the 1980s, however, the rising cost of labour in Taiwan and a strengthening currency decreased Taiwan's competitiveness, and led Taiwanese firms either to upgrade into higher value-added activities or to move production overseas. Taiwan's apparel and accessory exports peaked in 1987 (at $5 billion), and then began a rapid decline as firms moved manufacturing to low-cost regions such as China (Gereffi and Pan 1994: 130–131). The result is what Gereffi and Pan call a triangular manufacturing system: a foreign buyer places orders with a Taiwanese firm with which it has had a long-term relationship; this firm then issues the manufacturing orders with offshore factories (that it either owns or contracts); and the final goods are then shipped to the foreign buyer (Gereffi and Pan 1994: 127).

BOX 11.2

Triangular Manufacturing

Are companies always looking for low-cost labour? Not necessarily. The garment and apparel sector is a classic example of a labour-intensive industry, but actual decisions on where to locate production involves complex calculations of labour costs, quotas, and proximity to market. TW Industries, a Taiwanese garment manufacturer, is a typical example of a triangular manufacturing network (a pseudonym has been used to protect the confidentiality of an actual firm; the example is from Thun 2000). Its major customer

is Gap, and because the two firms have a long history of working together, Gap continued to maintain its relationship with TW even after most Taiwanese garment manufacturing had relocated to less expensive regions. TW maintains its headquarters and one factory in Taiwan, and has a network of factories in China, Indonesia, and Cambodia.

The production process at TW begins when Gap uses a computer-assisted design system to send the master garment patterns via the internet to TW headquarters. The local factory, although high-cost, is maintained to make samples—the workers are highly dependable and turnaround is quicker—and these samples are sent back to Gap via express mail. When the sample is approved, the headquarters must decide where to locate the production run. First, the cost of production is obviously important. In addition to the Taiwanese factory, TW has factories in China, Indonesia, and Cambodia, and wages vary considerably. The monthly wages for a worker are $800 per month in Taiwan, $100 in a coastal province of China, $30–$40 in Indonesia, and $50–$60 in Cambodia. The cost of production is a combination of labour cost and productivity, of course, and the latter varies as well. Using the Taiwan productivity rate as an index of 100, China is a 95, Indonesia 40–45, and Cambodia 55–60. Second, politics plays a key role in location decision. Prior to the elimination of the **Multifibre Arrangement** in 2005, TW had to be sure to locate production in countries that had the quotas necessary for the final markets. Even after these quotas were eliminated, TW seeks to have a geographical distribution of production facilities in order to protect itself from the risk of new tariffs and quotas. Finally, the proximity to market is critical. Because clothing is influenced by fashion and trends, it can be extraordinarily time-sensitive. Much like a fruit or vegetable that will lose its value as it ages on a grocer's shelves, a piece of clothing that is yesterday's fashion must be marked down dramatically in price. As a result, speed to market is absolutely critical: saving a few cents on labour costs is a pyrrhic victory if it causes a firm to miss a trend and the product ends up in a discount outlet rather than a department store display case. The calculation will vary by product: it continues to make sense to produce high-fashion items in high-cost areas such as New York or Los Angeles; relatively fashionable items will be produced in regions where they can get to market quickly (Mexico and low-cost regions of Europe are only hours away from major markets); and relatively stable items (such as men's tee shirts and underwear) will be produced wherever costs are lowest.

Managing the technology of the production network is of critical importance. Given the fashion-sensitive nature of much of the business, retailers want to keep inventories low. In fact, the ideal would be to have a factory behind the store, because this would allow the retailer to make each item of clothing as it is purchased. It would be possible to expand production when it became apparent that an item was becoming popular, and stop production of items that were not selling—discounting would never be needed. Obviously, this is not possible, but retailers try to use information technology to keep their inventories low and their supply chains as 'lean' as possible. The objective of lean retailing is to reduce the risk of selling a perishable good by continuously adjusting the supply of products offered to consumers at retail outlets so as to match the actual level of market demand (Abernathy *et al.* 1999: 55). Bar code and scanning technology will track sales at a retail store, for example, and this information will be sent to a distant factory at the close of business. The factory will not only manufacture the new clothing, but will place it on hangers, complete with price tags, and then air freight it back to the retail store. In some cases, the buyer is able to use specialized software systems and the internet to track the progress of an order through each stage of the production process.

The increasingly high-tech nature of the industry creates opportunities for Taiwanese firms because the emphasis of the global network shifts from achieving cost reductions through savings on labour costs (a primary weakness of the Taiwanese at home) to more effective management of the production network and the consequent ability to match supply to market demand more effectively (a potential strength of Taiwanese firms *vis-à-vis* companies with lower labour costs).

At the same time that East Asia is emerging as a regional economy with manufacturing networks that cross national borders, *local economic clusters* are extraordinarily important in China. The factories of particular townships and villages will often specialize in a particular product, and then dominate world markets. For example, 80 per cent of the world's metallic-shell lighters come from the city of Wenzhou in Zhejiang province. Not far away, in the town of Qiaotou, 700 family-run factories produce 15 billion buttons and 200 million metres of zippers a year—again, they are the world leaders (*China News Digest* 2006; Watts 2005). Qingxi Township in the southern city of Dongguan specializes in PC production, and has become so important in the production of monitors, motherboards, keyboards, and PC boxes that the deputy director of IBM Asia remarked that 'If there is a traffic jam between Dongguan and Hong Kong [where the port is located], 70 per cent of the world's computer market will be affected' (Enright *et al.* 2005: 62). Similar clusters can be found for bicycles, domestic appliances, furniture, plastic flowers, air-conditioners, and shoes—virtually any product imaginable.

The formation of these clusters is partly the result of a natural tendency on the part of firms to seek agglomeration economies, but government policy also played a key role. Over the course of the reform period in China, the central government gave increasing autonomy to local governments to shape their own economic policies, and gave them fiscal incentives to do so successfully (Oi 1992). The slate with which local governments had to work, however, was not a clean one: the economic history, the structure of government institutions, and the types of firms in a region created different sets of possibilities for different places. Small and entrepreneurial firms in Zhejiang province benefited from a local government that supported (or at least did not obstruct) private-sector firms and the lack of competing state-owned enterprises (Whiting 2001). Firms in capital and technology-intensive industries in Shanghai benefited from a local government that invested heavily in firm development and guided the process of technology transfer from foreign-invested enterprises. Light industrial firms in Guangdong province took advantage of local policies that favoured exporting and foreign investment from ethnic Chinese networks. In a decentralized economy environment, the role of local policy is as important as national policy in shaping the framework of opportunities and constraints within which firms must operate.

The competitive pressures that lead to regional integration in East Asia, and the opportunity to access world-class and inexpensive manufacturing capabilities in the various industrial clusters of China creates strong pressure on the *national 'varieties of capitalism'* of multinational firms that invest in China. As Hay points out in Chapter 10, there is no topic in the field of global political

economy that is more controversial than whether global capital, trade, and investment flows are leading towards a convergence of national institutions. This debate has a corollary in the literature on global production: when multinational firms and their suppliers move abroad, do they preserve certain characteristics of their home county? The characteristics of Japanese production networks, for example, are commonly perceived to be relatively closed when compared to American production networks—a result of the preferential trade relationships and cross-shareholding within Japanese corporate groups and long-term relationships between management and labour—and these characteristics have been seen as surprisingly durable when transferred abroad. The overseas subsidiaries of Japanese companies are less likely to employ local managers, less likely to rely on local sourcing (except when Japanese affiliates were located in the local economy), and less likely to transfer R&D activities to overseas affiliates (Encarnation 1999; Ernst and Ravenhill 2000; Solis 2003). According to this viewpoint, 'firms involved in global competition begin their lives under very different legal, social and political environments and histories . . . [and] while firms from different nations may eventually converge on some best practice, convergence may not happen quickly or automatically' (McKendrick *et al.* 2000: 9; see also Borrus and Zysman 1997). The durability of national foundations leads to unique corporate strategies, and alternate strategies lead to variation in the form of the production networks that bind regions together.

In China, both the durability of national approaches to investment and the intense pressures on these approaches are visible in the patterns of Japanese investment. When a Japanese firm begins to manufacture in China, for example, there has always been a strong tendency to continue to rely on the same Japanese suppliers. In some cases these will be suppliers that are part of the same industrial grouping, but it will also be Japanese suppliers that have had long-term relationships with the company in Japan. During the 1990s, the bulk of Japanese investment in China followed a predictable pattern:

the objective of Japanese firms was to lower costs, and, in keeping with the concept of a regional hierarchy, production was moved to China but core components and design continued to come from Japanese firms. Because the focus of these firms was on export markets, the drive to lower costs could not be at the expense of quality, and it was easier to maintain quality standards while using tried-and-true suppliers. Dalian, a city in north-eastern China, was a popular investment site because it was close to Japan and relatively easy to find workers there with Japanese-language skills. Within a decade, however, a distinct shift had began to emerge, as investment trends moved towards the greater Shanghai region in eastern China, and the Guangdong region of southern China. In a 2002 survey of Japanese firms with investments in China, 81 per cent of the firms in eastern China and 80 per cent of the firms in southern China had plans for expansion, compared to 46 per cent in north-eastern China (Marugami *et al.* 2003: 24). The 2004 survey indicated that only 13 per cent of Japanese firms in north-eastern China had plans for expansion, while the percentages for eastern and southern China were just under 70 per cent and 50 per cent respectively (although 64 per cent of Japanese electronics firms had plans to increase investments in southern China) (Marugami *et al.* 2005: 30, 32).

Why has the location of Japanese investments in China been shifting towards eastern and southern China? There are both push and pull elements to the shift. The push stems from competitive pressures and the consequent need to cut costs. First, Japanese investments in China are focused increasingly on access to the growing domestic marketplace—79 per cent of firms listed this as their primary motivation for increasing investment in 2002 (Marugami *et al.* 2003: 28). It is the world's largest market for telecommunication devices (wired and wireless) and one of the largest markets for digital consumer and computing devices (Ernst 2006). In this increasingly sophisticated market, it is often Chinese firms that are the key competitors, and they place tremendous cost pressure on foreign competitors. 'In terms of low-end products', commented one

Japanese manager, 'many Chinese companies sell them without taking into account profit margins. We can't compete with that' (Marugami *et al.* 2003: 39). (Chinese state-owned enterprises often focus on market share rather than profit levels, because they receive preferential access to capital from the government-dominated banking system.)

Second, the Japanese firms have to compete with multinational firms that are offshoring large parts of their manufacturing to low-cost producers in China, often at the expense of the small and medium-sized enterprises (SMEs) that have traditionally served as suppliers at home. The speed with which American firms have abandoned manufacturing in order to focus on product definition and design, software, and high-end services (Borrus and Zysman 1997; Sturgeon 2002) is perhaps not surprising given the characteristics of a liberal market economy, but Korea, which has retained a focus on manufacturing, has been equally ruthless in opening up its manufacturing networks to non-Korean firms. In 2004, Korea had close to 3 million SMEs—these firms employing the vast majority of workers in the manufacturing sector—and 86 per cent of these firms were sub-contractors to large firms (*Hankyoreh 21*, 9 June 2004). According to a survey conducted by the Federation of Small and Medium-Sized Enterprises in Korea, the large firms demanded price cuts of 5–10 per cent annually, and there was seldom a choice—the large firms simply demanded the price cuts (*Hankyoreh 21*, 9 June 2004). The options open to the SMEs are limited: they often do not have the technical ability to upgrade into new product areas, and if they move to China in an effort to cut costs, they have difficulty competing with Chinese firms. Firms such as Samsung, LG, and Hyundai have the classic firm-specific advantages (that is, brands, technology, and/or scale) that can be exploited when they move offshore, but their suppliers are not so fortunate. Although a political desire for balanced economic development and fear of a 'hollowing-out' of the Korean economy led to pressure on the large firms to support the country's SMEs, there are limits to this benevolence. 'In an environment in which we compete with global firms', commented a member of the Samsung Electronics purchasing team, 'it is meaningless to distinguish between domestic and foreign supply firms' (*Maeil Kyongjae* 2005). LG Electronics has been even more aggressive than Samsung, and has built up R&D capabilities in China partly in order to facilitate the development of local Chinese suppliers. Not surprisingly, given that they compete in the same environment as the Korean firms, Japanese firms find themselves under the same pressure to cut ties to higher-cost suppliers from home.

The primary reason Japanese investments in China are being pulled toward eastern and southern China is because these are the regions with the strongest component firms. As the director of the Japanese trade office in Dalian explained, it was no longer enough for Japanese firms simply to seek out low-cost labour and ready access to Japan; they were now being forced by competitive pressures to invest in the locations with the most capable component firms, and, in southern and eastern China, there are not only a wealth of Chinese component firms, but also Taiwanese and Korean firms (Yabuchi 2000: 1). Even as wages rise in southern China, the benefits of the local industrial clusters endure. In some cities in southern China, wages increased as much as 50 per cent over the previous three years, the president of a Canon factory in Zhuhai commented in early 2007, but because labour contributes only 5 per cent of the total cost of final assembly for a product such as a digital camera, they will not relocate: 'We could go from China to Vietnam to India and then to Africa [in search of lower wages]. But that would be a slash-and-burn approach. In reality, it's not like that' (Pilling and Mitchell 2007: 7).

The industrial clusters of China represent a particularly pure version of globalization of production—they consist not of local firms that have developed slowly over time, but are composed primarily of highly competitive foreign firms that have co-located in China and feed off of each other's strengths—and this puts pressure on ties that were formed in the less competitive context of the home country. The large Japanese firms have slowly been opening up their networks to take advantage of the world-class capabilities that are available in China, and this puts pressure on Japanese SMEs. In the past, a parent company was forced to maintain a certain level of business with its sub-contractors, and a 'treacherous' act could hinder its business with other firms, but overseas expansion to regions with highly capable supply firms creates new capabilities (JSBRI 2003: 187). According to a 2001 survey of Japanese SMEs, the parent company strategy that was having the most negative impact on their own operations was overseas expansion (JSBRI 2003: 187). The extent to which Japanese production networks open to non-Japanese firms varies both by firm and industry, and they continue to be far more closed than other national networks, but the trend is an important one. As Dieter Ernst argues (2006: 183), it signals the end of an unequal division of labour in East Asia, one in which the higher value-added activities and technology remain in Japan, and only the labour-intensive activities move offshore, the beginning of a complex process of 'hybridization' of national production networks (Ernst and Ravenhill 2000: 242).

It is worth noting that it is not only less competitive firms that lose out in this process, but also less competitive countries in the developing world. China contains the potent combination of a large market, low-cost labour, and a highly developed supply sector, and for many countries, this is a difficult combination with which to compete.

Governance and upgrading

The quantity of FDI that flows into China might make it the envy of the developing world, but it is increasingly a point of controversy within the country. Although advocates of openness argue that foreign investment would ultimately increase self-reliance, as Chinese firms gained technology and managerial capabilities, sceptics claim that Chinese firms have found it difficult to capture the gains from their participation in global production networks. In the wake of the rapid increase in inward FDI flows in the mid-1990s, the *Economic Daily*

(*Jingji Ribao*), an authoritative economic paper in China, ran a series of articles that were highly critical of the impact that foreign investment was having on Chinese firms. Openness was not inherently bad, the commentary argued, 'but looking across the countries of the world, [we see] that opening up definitely cannot be without certain principles and certain limits'. It is important to 'pay attention to protecting national industries', the paper concluded (Fewsmith 2001: 173–174). Academics have argued similarly that discrimination against entrepreneurial private-sector firms in China and in favour of foreign firms and inefficient state-owned enterprises has handicapped the development of Chinese companies. Yasheng Huang and Tarun Khanna point to Wal-Mart shelves sagging with Chinese-made goods, and make the point that relatively few products with the 'Made in China' label are made by indigenous Chinese firms. 'That is because China's export-led manufacturing boom is largely a creation of FDI . . .', they argue. 'During the last 20 years, the Chinese economy has taken off, but few local firms have followed, leaving the country's private sector with no world-class companies to rival the big multinationals' (Huang and Khanna 2003: 74).

To what extent have Chinese firms benefited from foreign investment and integration with global production networks? The automotive industry is a good test case because it is a sector that the Chinese government targeted for development in the early 1980s, and FDI has been the primary means of promoting it. The barriers to entry in the industry are also high for a developing country. The high cost of product development in the industry and the rapid advance of technology create strong incentives for assembly firms to share development costs with global suppliers. The assemblers group products around common underbody platforms, outsource the design and production of large modules of the car to global suppliers, and then rely on these firms to supply the modules wherever in the world they decide to assemble the vehicles. Global platforms spread the costs of development more widely by creating greater economies of scale for

each model, and outsourcing passes a good portion of the design burden for individual modules on to the supply firms. These same characteristics, however, make it very difficult for a local supply firm to become an upper-tier supplier in the network of a multinational firm (Humphrey and Memedovic 2003). Tier one global suppliers (for example, firms such as Bosch, Denso, and Visteon) are often as large and powerful as their customers, and they must be able to co-operate on the design of new models with the assemblers.

The intention of the Chinese government in forming joint ventures with multinational auto firms was clear—FDI would allow the domestic auto firms to gain access to technology and managerial skills—and because of the large potential of the domestic marketplace it was also clear that China had an enviable amount of leverage over multinational firms: foreign firms were not allowed to have a majority stake in an assembly joint venture (JV), they were often pressured to transfer large amounts of technology to their China projects, and until China joined the World Trade Organization they were forced to rapidly increase the percentage of components that were sourced from within China.

Despite these advantages, none of the Chinese partners in these JV projects has emerged as a major auto manufacturer in its own right. Not only do the JVs still dominate automobile production in China, but the only two Chinese firms that were in the top ten auto producers in 2006 were independent firms (Chery and Geely) that had never formed joint ventures with foreign firms. The failure of the Chinese partners in JV projects to develop capabilities independent of their foreign partner would seem to support those who argue that foreign investment is not the most effective way to develop strong indigenous firms, or, at the very least, indicate that capturing the gains of foreign investment cannot be taken for granted.

But state policy clearly does matter. Local governments were generally the key actors in formulating the policy environment for firms in the auto sectors, and they pursued a variety of approaches (Thun

2006). Shanghai adapted the policies of a local developmental state. The municipal bureaucracy compensated for underdeveloped capital markets by taking charge of the process of capital accumulation and investment in supplier development. Municipal officials also co-ordinated the process of technology transfer to local firms, controlled their relationships with the assembly plants carefully to ensure that they received a steady stream of orders, and monitored their development. These supply firms grew in both size and capabilities, and began to expand outside Shanghai. Other regions, such as Beijing and Guangzhou, took a more market-based approach. The small supply firms received little help in their search for investment capital, technology, and customers. Few firms were able to capture economies of scale, and, unable to raise volume, they were also unable to lower costs. Most became bankrupt. In contrast to Shanghai, where the Chinese partner in the joint venture is currently investing in developing an independent line of vehicles, the joint ventures in Beijing and Guangzhou are completely dominated by their foreign firms (primarily from Japan and Korea), and the Chinese partners have no aspirations to develop independent capabilities.

The recent success of independent firms is also not necessarily a repudiation of the JV strategy that dominated the industry for so long. In many respects, the new, independent firms are building on the base that the JVs created in China. Part of this strategy involves the strategic use of the supplier capabilities that the joint venture projects have developed, particularly in the greater Shanghai region. This involves the utilization not only of suppliers having a range of technical capabilities that the independent assemblers do not, but also designers who were trained at the JV projects and then created their own design firms. Part of this strategy involves luring Chinese engineers with long experience on the JV projects to work for a genuinely *Chinese* firm. The joint ventures served as a training ground for the auto sector and created a range of possibilities that did not exist prior to their formation. In short, the benefits of FDI do not necessarily flow directly to the Chinese partners at the JVs, but they nevertheless increase the local capabilities of the sector overall.

KEY POINTS

- Since the early 1980s, China has become a manufacturing powerhouse, and one of the world's leading destinations for FDI.

- China is a regional production base in the sense that a large proportion of its exports involve the processing trade: China imports higher-value goods from its more advanced neighbours, assembles these components into finished goods, and then exports these goods to final markets.

- Both the intensity of competition within China and the presence of highly capable supply firms from many countries has led to the weakening of national production networks.

Conclusion

Firms have long been a product of their immediate geography. They have always been shaped strongly by the regulatory and legal institutions of the states within which they are formed, the inputs available to them (human capital, raw materials, and components), and the nature of the markets within which they compete. The intensity of these constraints has varied over time, however. As early as the seventeenth century, firms were looking to distant countries for raw materials not available at home. In the early twentieth century, they began to relocate (and replicate) manufacturing activities in major foreign markets in order to escape protectionist trade barriers. Foreign production has been commonplace for centuries. What is new in the current era of globalization is that geographical dispersion no longer precludes global integration. Firms are able to break up their value chain in ways that were not previously possible, make a decision about where each particular activity should be located, and then integrate these far-flung activities with advanced technologies.

The globalization of production creates opportunities and challenges for both developing and developed economies. From the perspective of developing economies, the massive flows of foreign investment and the increased willingness of multinational firms to outsource production has create a range of opportunities that were not previously present. Under the right circumstances, multinational firms are willing to take offshore not only the labour-intensive activities that have traditionally gone to the developing world, but also the higher value-added activities. There are two significant caveats, however. First, the flows of FDI are highly concentrated (and multinational firms often display a strongly herd-like mentality). Countries with seemingly ideal investment climates can find themselves, through no fault of their own, without any investment. They might be too small; there might be a shortage of supporting industries and suppliers; they might not be easily accessible; or they might be located in what is otherwise a rough and dangerous neighbourhood. This problem is particularly harsh, of course, because private investment flows have largely replaced official sources of investment capital. In this environment, the poorest countries may easily find themselves worse off than in the past. Second, in those cases that are blessed with high rates of inward FDI, the gains for the domestic economy are far from guaranteed. Few countries are in as favourable a position as China to cope with the challenges of FDI, and yet even China continues to struggle with maximizing the benefits of foreign investment for indigenous firms. Indigenous Chinese firms often find themselves locked in a downward competitive spiral: because they usually compete in areas with low barriers to entry, competition is intense and profit margins thin, and

they often have little to invest in research and development. State policy is critical, particularly the support that is given to local firms, but it must be more nuanced than in the past—investment that flows in can just as easily flow out when host governments impose conditions that are too onerous. Rather than strong-arming multinational firms into transferring technology and utilizing local suppliers, it is far more effective (and more difficult) to create a policy environment that will support the development of the capabilities that multinational firms are seeking in their supply base.

From the perspective of developed economies, the globalization of production allows firms to choose à la carte from a global menu of production sites. No longer constrained by the limitation of having to conduct all activities in one particular geographical setting, the parts of the value chain can be broken up and located separately, according to the competitive needs of any particular activity. This allows a firm to compensate for weaknesses in their home base without completely abandoning it. Although the hope is always that the higher value-added activities will remain at home, the danger is that the outflow will be too great and a hollowed-out economy will be left behind. In the case of the regional production networks of East Asia, the fears of hollowing-out in the advanced economies that surround China have not yet been realized. Quite the contrary, in fact—the combination of the growing Chinese market and the increase of imports of high value-added components into China has been an economic engine for the region. The gains, however, are not evenly distributed. It is the small and medium-sized enterprises in an economy that have the most difficulty in adjusting, and these are often the firms that provide the bulk of employment at home. Trading relationships that appear to be mutually beneficial in the aggregate can mask significant dislocation and, as in the developing countries, public policy must focus on increasing the capacity of smaller firms to take advantage of the potential gains of globalization. In the absence of balanced growth, the possibility of a backlash against globalization is all too real.

KEY POINTS

- The rise of global production creates new opportunities for developing countries, but also real risks: first, for those that are unable to attract FDI; and second, for those able to attract FDI but unable to maximize the benefits for indigenous firms.

- Similarly, in developed economies, the gains from globalization are not evenly distributed, and in the absence of effective public policy this imbalance creates the possibility of a backlash against globalization.

 QUESTIONS

1. What have been the drivers of the globalization of production since the 1980s?

2. Why do multinational firms invest in equity stakes in foreign operations rather than form trading relationships with foreign firms?

3. What is modularity, and how does it increase the opportunities for global production?

4. How does the governance of a global value chain affect the prospects for upgrading in a developing country?

5. What factors does a firm need to consider when deciding where to locate production facilities?

6. What are the benefits of industrial clusters, and why do they form?

7. Why has China emerged as the world's factory, and what are the implications of this trend?

8. From the perspective of a developing country, is a heavy reliance on FDI good or bad?

9. From the perspective of an advanced capitalist economy, is the offshoring of production good or bad?

 FURTHER READING

■ **Abernathy, F. H., Dunlop, J. T., Hammond, J. H., and Weil, D. (1999),** *A Stitch in Time: Lean Retailing and the Transformation of Manufacturing* **(Oxford: Oxford University Press).** A detailed and fascinating account of how information technology has transformed retailing in the clothing industry.

■ **Baldwin, C. Y., and Clark, K. B. (1997), 'Managing in an Age of Modularity',** *Harvard Business Review,* **75/5: 84–93.** A classic account of how modularity creates new possibilities for structuring industrial sectors.

■ **Berger, S. (2006),** *How We Compete: What Companies Around the World Are Doing to Make it in Today's Global Economy* **(New York: Currency Doubleday).** A highly readable and knowledgeable analysis of how different companies and countries are coping with the challenges created by the globalization of production.

■ **Dunning, J. H. (1981),** *International Production and the Multinational Enterprise* **(London: Allen & Unwin).** A classic work on FDI.

ERIC THUN

■ Gereffi, G., Humphrey, J., and Sturgeon, T. (2005), 'The Governance of Global Value Chains', *Review of International Political Economy*, 12/1: 78–104. This article provides a framework for analysing the structure of global value chains.

■ Kaplinsky, R. (2005), *Globalization, Poverty and Inequality: Between a Rock and a Hard Place* (Cambridge: Polity Press). This book provides a cogent analysis of why many countries have difficulty in capturing the benefits of globalization.

■ Levinson, M. (2006), *How the Shipping Container Made the World Smaller and the World Economy Bigger* (Princeton, NJ: Princeton University Press). A fascinating account of how something as simple as a shipping container transformed the global economy.

■ McKendrick, D. G., Doner, R. F., and Haggard, S. (2000), *From Silicon Valley to Singapore: Location and Competitive Advantage in the Hard Disk Drive Industry* (Stanford, Califs: Stanford University Press). A detailed academic study of how decisions about location helped US firms to dominate the global hard disk drive industry.

■ Palmisano, S. J. (2006), 'The Globally Integrated Enterprise', *Foreign Affairs*, 85/3: 127–136. A concise account of the new model of global firm from the CEO of IBM.

■ United Nations Conference on Trade and Development (2006), *World Investment Report 2006: FDI from Developing and Transition Economies: Implications for Development* (New York Geneva: United Nations). The annual UNCTAD report on investment flows.

 WEB LINKS

● The primary source of data on global investment flows is the United Nations Conference on Trade and Development (UNCTAD). Its publications are available at **www.unctad.org**. For academic research on global value chains in a variety of industries and countries, see **www.ids.ac.uk/ids/global/index.html** and **www.globalvaluechains.org/**.

 Visit the Online Resource Centre that accompanies this book for more information:
www.oxfordtextbooks.co.uk/orc/ravenhill2e/

12 Globalization, Growth, Poverty, Inequality, Resentment, and Imperialism

ROBERT HUNTER WADE

Chapter Contents

Reader's Guide

The head of a Chinese family recently said to a BBC interviewer, 'You in the West all have washing machines and refrigerators and TVs. Why shouldn't we Chinese have the same?' This chapter moves towards an answer to his question, but with reference to the whole human race. It does so by assessing the free market argument, also known as the globalization or the neo-liberal argument, which promises substantial gains in living standards for ordinary people provided the world community sticks largely to free market policies.

The world has experienced a significant move towards free market policies since the 1980s; economic integration across borders has increased; a very large part of the world has started to function as a single economy. What have been the associated trends in growth, poverty and income inequality?

The neo-liberal argument reads the evidence as positive: falling poverty and global inequality, rising standards of living for ordinary people, and erosion of patron–client dependency. Globalization thus brings 'mutual benefit'. The interests of rich countries and poor countries, dominant classes and subordinate classes, are broadly aligned in favour of free markets, contrary to the standard 'conflicting interests' assumption of the left. The divides between North and South, core and periphery, and rich and poor are lags in the catch-up of the poor world to the prosperity of the rich world, not structural segmentations of world markets.

The global economic multilaterals (GEMs) such as the World Trade Organization (WTO), the World Bank, the International Monetary Fund (IMF), the Asian Development Bank, are rightly mandated to implement the **Washington Consensus** to free up trade and investment across borders, deregulate markets, and harmonize national regulations, to give economic actors a global 'level playing field' undistorted by state restrictions. The gains will be at risk if countries start to backslide on policy liberalization.

A lot is at stake. Here I summarize some doubts about the reality of neo-liberal-globalization's positive impacts on growth, poverty and inequality. I suggest that the world economy organized in this way may contain forces analogous to gravity, holding low-income countries down; and others, analogous to magnetic levitation, holding a small number of high-income countries up (comprising around 15 per cent of the world's population). At the end I discuss the political economy of statistics such as the poverty headcount, and suggest why we should be alarmed by the evidence and concerned to secure changes in world trade rules and the agendas of powerful development agencies.

" The problem today is not that there is too much globalization, but that there is far too little. " (Martin Wolf 2004*a*: xvii)

Introduction

Climate change, species extinction, resource depletion, and nuclear proliferation—these are by now well-recognized threats to the future of human civilization as we know it. Less familiar is the threat that the world economy over the twenty-first century will function in a relatively 'exclusionary' way, and that the caravan of people and countries will lengthen as the income gap between leaders and laggards grows. If so, our collective ability to manage existential crises such as climate change and nuclear proliferation will be impaired. Managing them requires a substantially higher level of co-operation than exists at present, yet co-operation fails when some parties consider the game to be stacked against them.

Data on the future is sadly lacking, but we can get some traction by understanding the past. There is general agreement on three points: (1) average living conditions have improved in most of the world since the 1950s, by much more than in the previous half century; (2) within countries, after-tax income distribution was fairly constant from the 1950s to the 1970s (tracking changes in income distribution was like watching grass grow, one economist said), but it became substantially more unequal during the 1980s, 1990s and into the 2000s in most countries for which data is available; and (3) between countries, the global expansion of capitalism since the eighteenth century has been accompanied by a steep rise in income inequality (some scholars say the Great Divergence started in the sixteenth century). Inequality between countries is now substantially greater than inequality within countries.

The dispute is about trends in between-country distribution and world distribution since about 1980. Many influential voices say that the world has finally turned a corner towards convergence rather than divergence, towards more equality and less poverty; that the world caravan is shortening as

the laggards begin to catch up. According to Martin Wolf, the celebrated economic columnist for the *Financial Times* and author of *Why Globalization Works* (2004*a*), 'The evidence strongly suggests that . . . inequality among households across the globe is . . . falling. There is also little doubt that not just the proportion of the world's population in extreme poverty, but the absolute numbers are falling' (2004*b*). Wolf bases his conclusion on statistics and research supplied by the World Bank, the IMF and related organizations.

Wolf and others understand these good trends as the result of the world economy becoming substantially more globalized (markets more integrated) after 1980 than before; and understand the acceleration of globalization as being the result of the worldwide shift towards free market (or neo-liberal) policies, and away from state 'intervention'. Neo-liberalism became 'global policy' around 1980, in the wake of the breakdown of the **Bretton Woods** economic architecture in the early 1970s, and has remained global policy ever since. 'Global policy' is policy that is developed and advocated by global actors, who play an advocacy role in multiple states and transnational forums. Examples of global policy actors include the World Bank, the IMF, and the WTO, as well as powerful national agencies such as the US Treasury and UK Treasury. Living standards will continue to improve provided developing countries stick to a neo-liberal agenda (also known in the context of developing countries as the Washington Consensus agenda; see Wade 2007*a*).

The underlying theory comes from Adam Smith. Harvard professor Gregory Mankiw, the author of a leading economics textbook and former chairman of the President's Council of Economic Advisers, recently reminded readers of the *Wall Street Journal* that 'Adam Smith was right when he said that "Little else is required to carry a state to the highest degree of opulence from the lowest barbarism but peace, easy taxes and a tolerable administration of justice'" (*Wall Street Journal*, 3 January 2006).

However, other (less influential) voices cast doubt on both the trends and the theory. They say that, far from the circle of prosperity widening, the opposite is happening: the gap between rich and poor is widening fast, and economic globaliz-ation is to blame. As US union leader, Jay Mazur, put it (2000: 80) '[G]lobalization has dramatically increased inequality between and within nations.'

Each side tends to conduct the debate as if its case was overwhelming, and only an intellectually deficient or dishonest person could see merit in the other's case. Wolf raised the temperature by claiming that the 'anti-globalization' argument con-stitutes 'the big lie'—a phrase usually reserved for a technique of Nazi propaganda. He warned of 'the en-emies [of globalization] mustering both outside and inside the gates' (*Financial Times*, 8 February 2000;

Wolf 2004*a*: 4). On the other hand, critics of neo-liberalism accuse its champions of putting thumbs on the scale so as confirm the prior conclusion that a 'power-less' process of globalization brings benefits to just about all participants through the automatic working of markets, provided states do not get in the way; which obscures the way that dominant industrial-financial states drive the policy side of globalization so as to tip the playing field in favour of themselves, their firms, their citizen-consumers, and above all, the tiny fraction that draws its income from owning and managing capital.

Who is right? A simple question, but nearly everything about the answer is contested: the defin-itions of 'poverty', 'inequality', and 'globalization', the statistical techniques, the trends, and the caus-ality from globalization to growth, poverty and inequality (Brune and Garrett 2005).

World Income Distribution

Figure 12.1 shows the distribution of world popu-lation by average country income. Here, incomes are measured at **purchasing power parity** (PPP) ex-change rates rather than current market exchange rates (see Box 12.1 on page 380). Notice the 'twin peaks' and the 'missing middle'. One peak contains the 70 per cent of the world's population living in countries whose **gross domestic product** (GDP) per capita is below PPP$5,000. The other peak is the 14 per cent who live in countries with a GDP per capita above PPP$20,000—the rich world. Only 4 per cent live in the missing middle, in coun-tries with average incomes between PPP$8,000 and PPP$20,000. Talk of the 'middle-income' countries can be misleading, as it suggests, wrongly, that they are 'mid-way' between the low-income and high-income countries. In fact, the middle-income countries fall towards the low end.

The distribution of the world's population by the income of individuals (based on household sur-veys) is much more skewed towards the tail than the distribution by countries' average income. The world average income is PPP$3,500, and 75 per cent of the world's population has an income of less than the average. Slightly more than 40 per cent lives on less than PPP$1,000 a year ($2.73 a day). Only 10 per cent has more than about PPP$10,000 a year.

The number of hours of work needed for an adult male entry-level employee of McDonald's to earn the equivalent of one Big Mac can be used as a more tangible index of 'economic hardship'. In the 'core' zone of Western Europe, North Amer-ica, and Japan, the figure is (as at early 2000s) in the range of 0.25 to 0.6 hours; in the middle-income countries such as South Korea and Malay-sia, 1.5 hours; in low-income China, 2.2 hours;

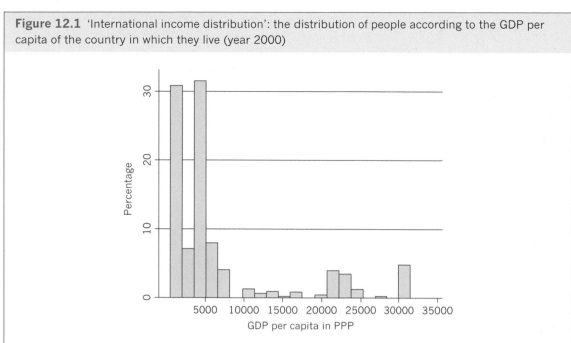

Figure 12.1 'International income distribution': the distribution of people according to the GDP per capita of the country in which they live (year 2000)

Notes: GDP = gross domestic product; PPP = purchasing power party; GDP shown in 1995 international dollars.
Source: Milanovic (2005: 129)

lower-income India, nearly 3 hours; in even-lower-income Pakistan, 3.5 hours. (Remember that a job in McDonald's is well up the prestige ranking in low-income countries; most people work in less desirable jobs.)

Our interest is not only in the shape of world income distribution and its movement over time, but also in the political economy arrangements behind it. A feudal society might throw up an income distribution with a similar shape as Figure 12.1 (a large peak of bonded labourers, a small peak of lords and knights, a scattering of artisans and merchants in between). On the other hand, a world economy with the financial stabilization framework of the Bretton Woods kind might today throw up a rather differently shaped income distribution; similarly for a world polity with three major poles rather than one.

Growth and Distribution

The growth rate of world GDP per capita fell by almost half between 1960–78 and 1979–2000, from 2.7 per cent to 1.5 per cent (Milanovic 2005: 34). A majority of the world's countries (56 per cent) experienced negative growth of GDP per person during the period 1980–98. Wolf presents a table (2004*a*; table 8.1) which shows the sharp slowdown in growth of GDP per head between 1950–73 and

1973–98 in every one of the world's seven regions except 'Asia (excluding Japan)'. Strangely, he makes no comment on the generalized slowdown, or its significance for his argument that 'globalization works'.

For the OECD as a whole, and for the USA, Europe, and Japan separately, the rate of growth per head fell in every decade from 1960–73, 1973–79, 1979–90, and 1990–2004. The fall in 1990–2004 is especially telling, because by this time the 1980s policies of squeezing inflation, deregulating, privatizing, liberalizing trade and capital movements had worked themselves through into macroeconomic stabilization and free markets; yet the promised upturn in economic growth did not appear.

Since 2000, the growth rate of world output has risen to 2.3 per cent for 2001–3 and higher for 2003–6. Some commentators say the rise is a long-delayed pay-off from 25 years of liberalization, and will continue for a long time in the future ('the end of history'). The rise may also be a cyclical swing from a long period of low growth, amplified by unsustainable consumption by American consumers drawing on Japanese, German and Chinese trade surpluses, and the wealth created by asset bubbles in equities and housing.

The world growth trend conceals large regional variations. Sub-Saharan Africa's economic performance has been dire; its average real income today is below the level of the 1980s, despite most states having implemented Washington Consensus-type **structural adjustment programme** for many years. Latin America's economic performance has been poor; its average income being about the same as during the 1980s, notwithstanding its generally diligent adoption of Washington Consensus policies. Eastern Europe's has also been very poor. On the other hand, South Asia's has improved since the 1990s from a very low base. China's excelled through the 1980s and 1990s, also from a very low base. The rest of (non-Japan) East and South-East Asia has grown fast from a higher base, apart from the severe crisis of 1997–9. Some of Asia's fast growth, however, is no more than the result of recording in the 'formal' sector previously unrecorded activity in the 'informal' and household sectors, as in the case of a man who divorces his wife and then employs a housekeeper.

Figure 12.2 shows these trends in the form of the ratio of average regional income to that of the high-income 'core'. The ratios for Latin Americn, Eastern Europe, and Sub-Saharan Africa fell after 1980; China and 'Asia minus China and India' rose, but even by 2001 they had reached only around 15 per cent of the North's (in PPP dollars). This is far from a picture of catch-up growth. Much of the caravan is falling even further behind.

Weighting the regional averages by regional population, we get a '1:3:2' world. There are roughly 1 billion people in the high-income countries; 3 billion in countries where growth rates have been substantially faster than in the high-income countries over the past two decades, though starting from very low-income levels and remaining at very low-income levels; and 2 billion where growth rates have been lower than in the high-income countries—some of these being in middle-income countries, and others in low-income countries. The large majority of developing countries are in the non-catch-up category. Less than 1 in 10 developing countries (with more than 1 million people) sustained real GDP per capita growth of even 3 per cent or more between 1960 and 2000.

The brutal fact is that, after decades of self-conscious development and market liberalization, the average income for the South is still only around 15 per cent of that of the North in purchasing power parity terms, and more like 5 per cent in foreign exchange rate terms (see below). Also, growth in the South is typically much more erratic than in a typical developed country, with periods of relatively fast growth followed by deeper and longer recessions.

Of the increase in world consumption over the 1990s, the majority accrued to those already in the top 10 per cent of world income distribution, the fast growth of countries with 3 billion people notwithstanding. Figure 12.3 shows (top half) the proportion of the world's population living at each consumption level, and (bottom half) the share

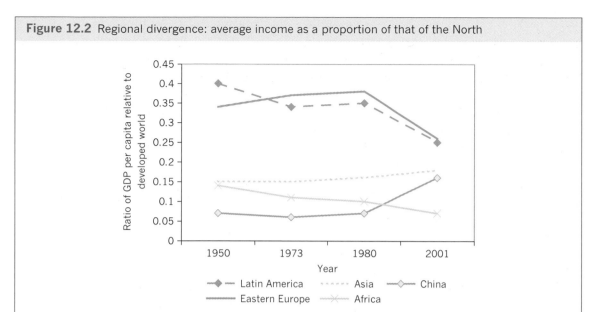

Figure 12.2 Regional divergence: average income as a proportion of that of the North

Note: Ratios in PPP values for income per capita, in 1990 Geary–Khamis dollars; 1 'Asia' does not include China, India or Japan
Source: UN (2006)

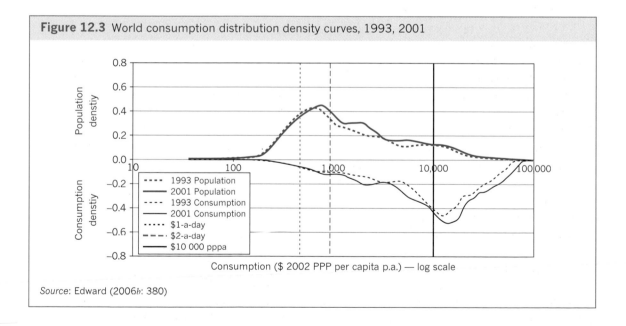

Figure 12.3 World consumption distribution density curves, 1993, 2001

Source: Edward (2006*b*: 380)

of world consumption accruing to each level. The dotted lines indicate 1993, the solid lines 2001. The area under the 1993 curves equals unity, while the area under the 2001 curves is larger in proportion to the increase in population and consumption between 1993 and 2001. Between these years, some 50 per cent to 60 per cent of the increase in world consumption accrued to those living on more than

PPP$10,000 in 1993—around 10 per cent of the world's population; of this 10 per cent, four-fifths lived in the high-income countries and most of the rest in Latin America. The remaining 40–50 per cent of the increase in world consumption accrued mainly to those living in 1993 on around PPP$3,000–6,000, of whom the majority were in the burgeoning middle class of China. Hardly any of the increase accrued to those on less than PPP$1,000 a year ($2.73 a day). Most of the latter lived in South Asia, Africa, and China.

In short, the 'Matthew Effect' is operating with a vengeance, 'To him that hath shall be given, to him that hath not shall not be given'. No surprise, then, that the North is receiving an influx of legal and illegal immigrants as communications improve, for the quickest way for the average Southerner to multiply their consumption many times is to hop across a border into the North, and there are many borders to choose from. Low-skilled workers can expect even bigger relative gains than high-skilled ones. The best-paid bus drivers in the world get thirty times the real wage of the worst-paid, while the best-paid computer programmers get 'only' ten times the salery of the lowest-paid, according to International Labour Organization (ILO) statistics.

BOX 12.1

Purchasing Power Parity

Among the cognoscenti, 'purchasing power parity' (PPP) is a hotly contested subject, but few who use the numbers know of the controversies and sources of error. The phrase refers to a method of taking countries' GDPs (physical quantities multiplied by prices in national currencies) and revaluing the given physical quantities using common standard international prices, to enable real comparisons between countries. The method responds to the fact that measures of relative incomes in different countries expressed in a common denominator currency such as the US dollar determined on the basis of market exchange rates do not accurately reflect purchasing power. This is because exchange rates vary daily, sometimes significantly, whereas the underlying structure of production, incomes and expenditures remains relatively stable. Exchange-rate conversions also do not take account of the fact that the price levels between countries are very different. PPP theory rests on the 'law of one price': the idea that competitive markets will equalize the price of identical traded goods in different countries when prices are expressed in the same currency, and transportation and transactions costs are excluded. It recognizes the fact that there is no free flowing substitution between traded and non-traded goods and services, and that national price level differences reflect the relative cost of the latter to the former. If exchange rates were to represent local purchasing power, then a dollar would buy the same amount of goods in all countries.

The calculation of PPPs is based on extensive price surveys in a large sample of countries, coupled with assumptions about the comparability of goods and services across countries (for example, 'shoes', 'textile weaving machinery', 'housing units'). The value of the collection of items making up the value of GDP in domestic prices is recalculated using 'international prices'. This makes it possible to derive the comparable real volume—a 'quantum' expressed on a standard value basis—of all the goods and services measured by each country's GDP.

Because the price of services, and thus of non-traded goods, is lower in poor countries, the main effect of PPP adjustments to national income data is to raise the income of poor countries relative to richer ones. For example, Turkey's average income at market exchange rates (FX dollars) was 10 per cent of the EU-15's in the early 2000s, and 24 per cent in PPP dollars. Sub-Saharan Africa's was 2 per cent in FX dollars and 7 per cent in PPP dollars.

The calculations are detailed and complex, involving hundreds of thousands of pair-wise price calculations. While there is a framework and a set of procedures for collecting these price and expenditure data locally, the core compilation has to be done centrally and not by national statistical agencies. The main source of the data on country prices is the International Comparison Project (ICP), launched in 1968 at the initiative of the UN Statistical Office and the Department of

Economics at the University of Pennsylvania, financed by the World Bank and the Ford Foundation; hence the name of the series—the Penn World Tables (PWT). In 1975, Eurostat began to produce PPPs for EU countries, as a way of determining financial contributions to the organization more fairly and to settle country disbursements. In 1980, the OECD expanded the work to cover all OECD countries, plus countries of Eastern and Central Europe. Around 1980, the UN Statistical Office took over the task of compiling global estimates and the work of co-ordinating the collection of international price data. But in the UN, the price collection effort soon languished, the head of the Statistical Office not wishing to use his budget for the work. The World Bank provided technical and financial support to the UN during this time, and took over responsibility for co-ordinating the global exercise in the early 1990s. In the mid-1990s, the World Bank (and the OECD) started to issue their own PPP numbers, using another method of aggregation (EKS), different from the one used by PWT (Geary-Khamis—G–K). There

are now two main series of global PPP data—PWT and the World Bank's. The series show some differences between countries' PPP-adjusted GDPs; and often more substantial differences in estimates of GDP components, such as private consumption, government consumption, and the like. The PWT numbers are used more frequently by academics than the World Bank's, in part because the PWT data provide more details on more countries for longer periods.

Dowrick and Akmal (2005) show that the Penn World Tables contain a systematic bias towards underestimating world income inequality, because of its use of a 'rich country' price structure to re-value GDP in poor countries (arising from the use of the G–K formula that gives greater weight to those prices involved in the largest number of transactions). They urge that the term 'purchasing power parity' be used only in a generic way, with additional specification of whether the numbers come from the PWT or sources based on a different method of making the PPP adjustment. More on this later.

KEY POINTS

- At the time of writing, the average income for the South is still only around 15 per cent of that of the North (in PPP terms). This is after five decades of self-conscious development and two and a half decades of concerted market liberalization.

- There has been a major growth slowdown during the age of intensified globalization—post-Bretton Woods, since around 1980—as compared with the previous two or three decades. The rate of growth of world GDP per person fell by almost half between 1960–78 and 1979–2000. For the OECD countries, output per capita grew more slowly in the period 1990–2004 than in previous decades back to 1960, despite macroeconomic stability and very liberal markets. This and other similar evidence gives the globalization argument a bloody nose.

- Growth rates varied substantially between regions. African countries performed particularly poorly;

also, from a higher starting point, did many Latin-American and central and East European countries. In contrast, East Asia's growth rates were the highest in the world, but from a low base.

- Between 50 per cent and 60 per cent of the increase in world consumption between 1993 and 2001 accrued to those with incomes of PPP$10,000 or more, constituting about 10 per cent of the world's population, four-fifths of whom live in the high-income countries. Only a tiny proportion of the increase accrued to those on PPP$1,000 or less.

- The upswing in world and developing country growth rates in the first few years of the twenty-first century may be a turning point; but more likely results from unsustainable imbalances in the world economy, such as the running-up of consumer debt in the USA, and gigantic trade surpluses in Japan, Germany and China.

Now to poverty and inequality. We have to ask about how the statistics are generated, as different methods produce different results. Economics is far from a neutral natural science 'telling it like it is'.

● ROBERT HUNTER WADE

Poverty

Understood as a lack of well-being, poverty should be treated as a multidimensional phenomenon, including income, hunger, disease, lack of shelter, lack of water and sanitation, and social exclusion. Let us duck these complexities and stick to an income, expenditure or consumption measure. The standard international extreme poverty (or 'destitution') line is PPP\$1 a day, and the extreme poverty headcount is the number of people in the world living on less than this amount. PPP\$2 a day is also used as a less frugal, 'ordinary poverty' line. The World Bank is the main source of the poverty numbers.

Table 12.1 summarizes the world poverty trends according to the World Bank. The number of people in destitution (under \$1 a day) fell by some 25 per cent between 1981 and 2001, and the proportion of the world population fell by almost half. This is good news.

The bad news is that the number living on less than \$2 a day increased, implying a big bunching between \$1 and \$2 a day; though the proportion of the world's population living on less than \$2 a day fell. More bad news comes from the fact that the fall in the number living on less than \$1 a day is entirely because of China. Take China out and the number in extreme poverty increased.

World Bank publications virtually always present the poverty numbers 'without a doubt'. Yet comparison of World Bank sources shows inconsistencies. In 1999, the Bank's high profile *World Development Report* said the poverty headcount was rising: 'The absolute number of those living on \$1-a-day or less continues to increase. The world-wide total rose from 1.2 billion in 1987 to 1.5 billion today' (World Bank 1999c: 25). In 2002, a high-profile report said, 'The number of people subsisting on less than \$1 per day rose steadily for nearly two centuries, but in the past 20 years it has . . . fallen by as much as 200 million, even as the world's population has risen by about 1.6 billion' (World Bank 2002b: 3). In 2004, the two Bank experts in charge of the poverty numbers said, 'By the frugal \$1 per day standard there were 1.1 billion poor people in 2001—almost 400 million fewer than 20 years earlier' (Chen and Ravallion 2004: 141).

Let us see how the poverty numbers are put together (see Reddy and Pogge 2002, 2003; Chen and Ravallion 2004; Edward 2006a). To find the world extreme poverty headcount, the World Bank first defines an international extreme poverty line for a given base year by using PPP conversion factors to convert the purchasing power of an average of the official national poverty lines of a set of low-income countries into the US dollar amount needed to have the same notional purchasing power in the United States in the same year. In its first global poverty estimation this procedure yielded a conveniently understandable US\$1 a day for the base year of

Table 12.1 Key World Poverty Numbers				
	1981		**2001**	
Severity	**Number (bn)**	**Percentage of world pop.**	**Number**	**Percentage of world pop.**
\$1 a day	1.5	33	1.1	18
\$2 a day	2.4	53	2.7	44

Source: World Bank PovcalNet (www.iresearch.worldbank.org/PovcalNet/jsp/index.jsp)

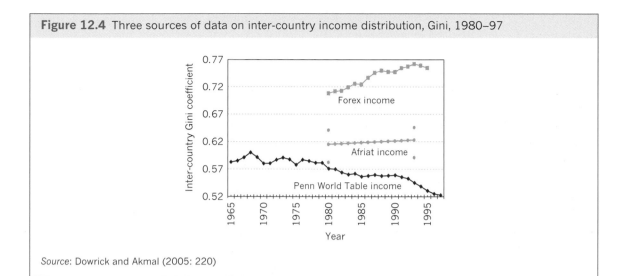

Figure 12.4 Three sources of data on inter-country income distribution, Gini, 1980–97

Source: Dowrick and Akmal (2005: 220)

1985. Then the Bank uses PPP conversion factors to estimate the amount of local currency, country by country, needed to have the same purchasing power in the same year as in the US base case. (So, by this method, Rs.10 may have the same purchasing power over a standard basket of goods and services in India in 1985 as $1 in the United States in the same year.) This gives an international extreme poverty line equivalent to US$1 per day, expressed in domestic currency (Rs.10 per day in the Indian example).

From household surveys, the Bank then estimates the number of people in the country living on less than this international extreme poverty line in the base year. It sums the country totals to discover the world total. It then uses national consumer price indices to keep real purchasing power constant over time, and adjusts the international extreme poverty line for each country upwards with inflation. The less frugal $2-a-day international poverty line is derived simply by doubling the destitution line, about as arbitrary a standard as can be imagined.

Large margin of error

The margin of error is large, for several reasons. First, the poverty headcount is very sensitive to the precise level of the international poverty lines. Figure 12.3 shows that the population–consumption curve is steep at the point of intersection of the $1-a-day line, meaning that small shifts in the line make large changes in the number of people below it. Recent research on China suggests that a 10 per cent increase in the line brings a roughly 20 per cent increase in the poverty headcount.

Second, the poverty headcount is very sensitive to the reliability of household surveys of income and expenditure. Some countries survey income, while others survey expenditure, and merging the results is not straightforward. The available surveys are of widely varying quality, and many do not follow a standard template. A study in India suggests that switching from the standard 30-day reporting period (asking people their expenditure over the previous 30 days) to a 7-day period magically cuts the number of poor in half, because the shorter recall period yields higher reported income or expenditure. The point is not that household surveys are less reliable than other possible sources (for example, national income accounts); but that they do contain large amounts of error.

Third, by far the two most important countries for the overall trend, China and India, have PPP-adjusted income figures that contain even more guesswork than for most other big countries. The government of China declined to participate in all the rounds of the International Comparison Project (see Box 12.1); so the PPP revaluations for China are based on econometric regressions rather than real data. The government of India declined to participate after the round of 1985. The lack of reliable price surveys for countries accounting for over a third of the world's population—hence the lack of reliable evidence on the purchasing power of even average incomes, let alone the income of the poor—compromises any statement about levels and trends in world poverty.

Note that other key world variables are also subject to large but unquantified margins of error. The absolute income per capita of the poorest countries is implausibly close to the survival minimum, which probably reflects substantial undercounting of agricultural, informal and black activities. The per capita income of the richest countries may be mis-stated, because of deficiencies in measuring inflation and quality improvements. Even as apparently solid a number as world population growth is uncertain. The World Bank's World Development Indicators for 2000 revised downwards the rate of growth of world population in 1980–90 by 40 per cent, and for 1990–9 by 13 per cent, which must be one of the biggest revisions to a major world statistic ever made. Yet the Bank made no comment on it. Most of the existing studies of world growth, poverty and inequality are based on the unrevised numbers, at cost to their reliability (Svedberg 2003).

Downward bias

Still other sources of error bias the poverty numbers downwards, making the number of poor people seem lower than it is; and the bias probably increases over time, making the trend look rosier than it is, for at least three reasons.

First, the Bank's international extreme poverty line underestimates the income or expenditure needed for an individual (or household) to avoid periods of food–clothing–shelter–water consumption too low to maintain health. And it avoids completely the problem that basic needs include unpriced public goods such as clean water and basic health care. The Bank's line refers to an 'average consumption' bundle, not to a basket of goods and services that makes sense for measuring poverty (though '$1 a day' does have intuitive appeal to a Western audience being asked to support aid). Suppose it costs Rs.30 to buy an equivalent bundle of food in India (defined in terms of calories and micro-nutrients) as can be bought in the USA with $1; and that it costs Rs.3 to buy an equivalent bundle of services (haircuts, massages) as $1 in the United States (Pogge and Reddy 2003). Current methods of calculating purchasing power parity, based on an *average* consumption bundle of food, services and other things, may yield a PPP exchange rate of, say, PPP US$1 = Rs.10, meaning that Rs.10 in India buys the equivalent average consumption bundle (food, services, etc.) as $1 in the United States. But this is misleading, because the poor person, spending most of his/her income on food, can buy with Rs.10 only a third of the food purchasable with $1 in the United States. To take the international extreme poverty line for India as Rs.10 therefore biases the number of poor downwards.

We have no way of knowing what proportion of food–clothing–shelter–water needs the Bank's international poverty line captures. But we can be fairly sure that if the Bank had used a basic needs poverty line rather than its present artificial one (an average of the national poverty lines of a somewhat arbitrary set of low-income countries) the number of the absolute poor would rise, because the national poverty lines equivalent to a global basic needs poverty line would probably rise, perhaps by 25–40 per cent (Reddy and Pogge's estimate, the range reflecting calculations based on PPP conversion factors for 1985 and 1993, and for 'all-food' and 'bread-and-cereals' indices).

A 30–40 per cent increase in a basic-needs-based international poverty line would, for the reason mentioned earlier, increase the world total of people in extreme poverty by a large fraction—probably at least 30–40 per cent. A recent study for Latin America shows that national extreme poverty rates, using poverty lines derived from calorific and demographic characteristics, may be more than twice as high as those based on the World Bank's $1-a-day line. For example, the World Bank estimated Brazil's extreme poverty rate (using its international extreme poverty line) at 5 per cent; while the Economic Commission for Latin America (ECLA), using a calories-and-demography poverty line, estimated the rate at 14 per cent. Similarly, Bolivia's extreme poverty rate according to the World Bank line was 11 per cent, but according to the ECLA line, 23 per cent; Chile, 4 per cent 8 per cent; Colombia, 11 per cent 24 per cent; and Mexico, 18 per cent 21 per cent (ECLA 2001: 51).

In view of the difficulties of defining a worldwide basic needs package, we could define a 'life expectancy poverty line' based on the pronounced kink in the relationship between individual income and individual life expectancy at around $3 a day and 72–74 years. Income increases above $3 a day bring only small gains in life expectancy; increases for those on less than $3 a day bring substantial gains. Switching to this life expectancy poverty line increases the world poverty headcount very substantially (Edward 2006b).

In short, we can be reasonably confident that switching from the Bank's rather arbitrary international extreme poverty line to one reflecting either the purchasing power necessary to achieve elementary human capabilities, or life expectancy close to potential, would raise substantially the number of people living in poverty in any given year.

Second, future 'updating' of the international poverty line will continue to lower the true numbers artificially. Worldwide average consumption patterns are shifting towards services whose prices relative to food and shelter are lower in poor than in rich countries, giving the false impression that the cost of the basic consumption goods required by the poor is falling. As Indians become wealthier and consume more services relative to food, a rupee appears to buy more than it used to; and so the PPP value of Indian incomes goes up. But poor Indians continue to spend most of their income on food, and for them the purchasing power of rupees has not increased. Part of the apparent fall in the number of people below a poverty line defined in PPP-adjusted rupees is therefore a statistical illusion. This effect is amplified by the widespread removal of price controls on 'necessities', and the lowering of tariffs on luxuries.

All these problems have to be resolved in one way or another in any estimate of world poverty, whoever it is made by. But the fact that the World Bank is effectively the monopoly provider introduces a further complication. The number of poor people is politically sensitive. The Bank's many critics (on both the right and the left) like to use poverty numbers as one of many pointers to the conclusion that it has accomplished 'precious little', in the words of former US Treasury Secretary O'Neill. The chairman of a taskforce established by the US Congress to report on multilateral economic organizations (Meltzer 2001) described the fall in the proportion of the world's population in extreme poverty from 28 per cent in 1987 to 24 per cent in 1998 as a 'modest' decline, the better to hammer the Bank. This provides a rationale for the USA to control the Bank, as in the statement by the head of the US Agency for International Development, 'Whether the US way of doing things drives some multilateral institutions, I think it should, because, frankly, a lot of the multilateral institutions don't have a good track record' (Wade 2004b: 391). When responding to criticism from powerful member states, the Bank plays up the fall in the poverty numbers to show it is doing a good job and deserving of support. When trying to enlist support for a bold initiative (such as the Comprehensive Development Framework) the Bank may play up the increase in poverty to show that it is needed even more.

ROBERT HUNTER WADE

- The good news is that, according to World Bank figures, the number of people living in extreme poverty (less than PPP$1 a day) fell by 25 per cent between 1981 and 2001; and the proportion of the world's population living in extreme poverty fell by almost half, from 33 per cent to 18 per cent. The bad news is that if China is excluded the number increased. And the number living on between $1 and $2 a day increased so much that the world total living on less than $2 a day increased. Even according to World Bank figures, not far short of half of the world's population is living on an income of less than PPP$2 a day.

- Despite the authoritative voice with which the World Bank delivers the poverty numbers, examination of how the numbers are constructed suggests that they have a large margin of error or indeterminacy; they probably contain a downwards bias; and probably make the trend look better than it is. They may be significantly different from the numbers that would result from the use of PPP conversion factors based more closely on the real costs of living of the poor (defined in terms of income needed to buy enough calories, micro-nutrients and other necessities in order not to be poor, or in order to enjoy life expectancy at the kink in the income–life expectancy curve).

- On the other hand, it is quite plausible that the *proportion* of the world's population living in extreme poverty, and ordinary poverty, has fallen. For one thing, household surveys are more likely to miss the rich than the poor, so their results may overstate the *proportion* of the population in poverty. For another, for all the problems with Chinese and Indian PPP income figures, we know enough about trends in other variables—including life expectancy, heights, and other non-income measures—to be confident that their poverty headcounts have indeed fallen dramatically since the 1980s. Moreover, the magnitude of world population increase over this period is so large that the Bank's poverty numbers would have to be *huge* underestimates for the world poverty rate not to have fallen. Any more precise statement about the number of the world's people living in extreme poverty and the change over time rests on quicksand.

- The sense of being on quicksand is not confined to the poverty numbers. The World Bank's World Development Indicators in 2000 revised downwards world population growth in the 1980s by 40 per cent, and in the 1990s by 13 per cent with no explanation.

Inequality

The world poverty headcount could move in one direction while world income inequality moves in another. The neo-liberal argument says they have both moved together: the world poverty headcount has fallen since the late 1970s, and world income inequality has also fellan. But in the past several years world income distribution has become a hot topic of debate in international economics and in sociology (hotter than world poverty). Disagreement about the inequality trends should not be surprising, given the collage of economic performance by region. Different measures emphasize different parts of the collage.

Much of the debate is mathematical, far removed from people's experience of inequality, and focuses less on the 'facts' than on the measures. It turns out that the only valid short answer to the question, 'What is the trend of world income distribution?', is, 'It depends on which combination out of many plausible combinations of measures and samples we choose.' Whereas we could get better data on the poor to the extent that the

BOX 12.2

The Gini Coefficient

Income inequality is usually measured through surveys of household income. Households are then ranked from lowest to highest on the basis of income, and divided into equal population groups, typically fifths (quintiles), or tenths (deciles). The share of income received by each population group is then compared with the share the population group would receive if all households received an equal share of the income.

The Gini coefficient is a number between zero and one that measures the degree of inequality in the distribution of income in a given society. The coefficient would be zero for a society in which each member received exactly the same income; and it would be 1.0 for a country in which one member received all the income and the rest nothing.

In practice, coefficient values range from around 0.25 for historically egalitarian countries such as Bulgaria, Finland, Hungary, Japan, and Sweden, to around 0.6 for countries with highly skewed distributions of income including Brazil, Central African Republic, Chile, Guatemala, Nicaragua, and Sierra Leone. In the United States, the growth of inequality since the 1970s is reflected in an increase in the Gini coefficient from 0.35 in the 1970s to 0.40 in the 1990s.

For further information on measuring inequality, see the World Income Inequality Database page at www.wider.unu.edu/wiid/wiid.htm#FullVersion.

poverty headcount would command general agreement, there is no best measure of world income inequality. Different measures measure different phenomena, and are useful for answering different questions.

The choices include: (1) alternative measures of income—GDP per person converted to US dollars using market exchange rates (FX dollars) or GDP per capita adjusted for differences in purchasing power across countries (PPP dollars); (2) alternative sources of PPP conversion factors—Penn World Tables or World Bank or Angus Maddison, or still others; (3) alternative weightings of countries—each country weighted by population or as one unit; (4) alternative measures of distribution—including the Gini, Theil or some other average coefficient (see Box 12.2), or gap or polarization measures such as the ratio of the average income of the top decile of world population to that of the bottom decile, or average income of one region to that of another; (5) alternative sources of incomes data—national income accounts or household surveys, and alternative ways of combining household surveys of income with surveys of expenditure; or (6) alternative samples of countries and periods.

Population-weighted between-country distribution

One set of choices produces the desired neo-liberal answer. It is inter-country (between-country) income distribution; and uses per capita incomes, PPP/PWT dollars, population weights, and the Gini coefficient. Measured in this way, international inequality increased over the 1960s and 1970s and then began to fall slightly around 1980, indicating declining income inequality. This is the good news: it suggests that the centuries old trend to divergence has reversed.

But the reversal of trend depends entirely on one giant case—China. Take China out and inter-country income inequality continued to rise after 1980. So, even using the combination of measures most favourable to the neo-liberal case, falling income inequality between countries is a function of China's fast growth since the early 1980s, not a *generalized* tendency of the world system.

The other bad news is that the result also depends on the use of the Penn World Tables method of calculating PPPs. As noted in Box 12.1 on page 380, Dowrick and Akmal show that the PWT method systematically understates the magnitude of inequality, and overstates its fall. The bias comes through the use of an average international price structure for re-valuing countries' GDPs, which results from weighting the countries' observed price structures by the relative expenditure at those prices; this means that the average international price structure reflects the price structures of *rich* countries—and so values services (for example, domestic services, haircuts) much more highly in poor countries, inflating the purchasing power of poor countries' currencies. (This is known as the Geary–Khamis method of aggregation.) When this bias is removed (for example, by switching from Geary–Khamis to the Afriat method), Dowrick and Akmal find that 'true [sic] inequality was stable or increasing slightly ... over the 1980s and 90s' (2005: 226). More exactly, three out of their four measures of inequality applied to Afriat-aggregated data show an increase, one shows constancy, but *none shows a decline*—even when China is included (see Figure 12.4 on page 383). That the trend towards falling inequality is reversed by switching from Geary-Khamis PPPs to Afriat PPPs underlines the fragility of the conclusion that world income inequality is falling. Indeed, a further bias towards rich country prices—hence toward exaggerating poor countries' incomes and their convergence with rich countries—comes from the self-selection of the countries that participate in the (statistically difficult) International Comparison Project. The participating countries tend to be statistically more advanced, and able to handle the complexities; which also tend to be the richer countries. China's and India's non-participation, noted earlier, is part of a wider selection bias.

In any case, this measure—average country incomes weighted by population—is interesting only as an approximation to income distribution among all the world's people or households, regardless of which country they live in. We would not be interested in measuring income inequality in the United States by calculating the average income for each state weighted by population if we had data for all US households.

World income distribution (between- and within-country)

Studies that attempt to measure income distribution among all the world's people show widely varying results, depending on things such as the measure of inequality, the sample of countries, the time period, and the sources of data. But several serious studies, measuring both between- and within-country distributions with different samples and time periods, and different measures of inequality, find that world income inequality has increased over a period since the 1970s/1980s (Dikhanov and Ward 2003; Dowrick and Akmal 2005; Milanovic 2005). Milanovic, for example, found a significant increase between 1988 and 1993, a smaller fall to 1998, and an increase to 2002, taking the Gini coefficient back up to the level of 1993. Across the body of studies the increase is small, but the consistency of the finding gives confidence that world income distribution (between- and within-country) has *not* become more equal, contrary to neo-liberal expectations.

Wage rate inequality

More doubts are cast on the reality of convergence or falling inequality by trends in industrial wage inequality within countries. Wage data has the great advantage over income data that pay is a much less ambiguous variable; it has been collected systematically by the United Nations since the early 1960s; and it gives many more observation points for each country than any data set on incomes. It is a useful way to get at the impacts of changes in trade policy and trade flows, or of manufacturing innovation and the like. The disadvantage of pay data, of course, is that it treats only a small part of the economy of many developing countries, and provides a proxy only for incomes and expenditure. But in fact it is not as limited as it might seem, because what is happening to pay rates in formal-sector activity reflects larger trends, including income differences between countries, and income differences *within* countries (since the pay of unskilled, entry-port jobs in the formal sector is closely related to the opportunity cost of time in the informal or agricultural sector).

Pay inequality within a large sample of rich and poor countries was stable from the early 1960s to the early 1970s, then declined till about 1980–2, then increased sharply from 1980–2 to the time of writing. The years 1980–2 are a turning point towards greater inequality in industrial pay worldwide. The countries within continents tend to show closely correlated movements in pay dispersions, suggesting macro forces at work. These findings are awkward to reconcile with neo-liberal expectations of the impact of globalization (James K. Galbraith and associates present several analyses of pay dispersions at http://utip.gov.utexas.edu).

Polarization or relative gap measures

Measures of inequality are measures of dispersion across the whole of the distribution. They can mislead by obscuring what is happening to major components, and by giving more weight to what is happening in the middle than at the extremes. If China's median income fell towards India's, 'world inequality' would be reduced by the smaller gap between each Chinese and each Indian, but increased by the bigger gap between each Chinese and those above. Simple 'gap' or 'polarization' measures can be more illuminating because they do not have this trade-off. They measure the income shortfall between a given country, region or other aggregate, and a comparator. We saw one such measure earlier—the ratios of regional income to the North's (see Figure 12.3 on page 379). We might also take the income of the top decile of the world's population over that of the bottom decile, or some variant.

Most such measures show widening gaps. For example, with countries grouped into deciles by their PPP GDP per capita, the ratio between top and bottom deciles almost doubled during the 1960–2000 period, from 19 to 1, to 37 to 1 (Milanovic 2005: 53). The polarization would be even more dramatic if we took the top 1 per cent's

income over the median or over the bottom 10 per cent's.

Unweighted between-country distribution

Yet another often-used measure is inter-country distribution without population weights, each country being treated as one unit (that is, China weighted the same as Uganda, say). Of course, we should not weight countries equally if we are interested simply in relative well-being. But we should weight them equally—treat each country as analogous to a laboratory test observation—if we are interested in growth theory and the growth impacts of public policies, resource endowments, and so on. We might, for example, arrange (unweighted) countries by the openness of their trade regime, and see whether more open countries have better economic performance.

Whatever our motivating question, the trend is clear: the Gini for unweighted inter-country income distribution held fairly steady from the mid-1960s to the early 1980s (having increased before then), and increased sharply after the early 1980s. Is the increase in inequality caused only by the collapse of Africa? No. With Africa excluded, the Gini fell from the mid-1960s to the early 1980s, and increased steeply after that. With countries grouped into deciles by GDP per capita, the growth rate of the bottom six deciles over 1978–2000 was either negative or approximately nil, while the growth rate of the top three deciles was substantially positive (1.9 per cent a year or more; see Milanovic 2005: 53). A study by the Economic Commission for Latin America concludes that there is 'no doubt as to the existence of a definite trend towards distributive inequality worldwide, both across and within countries' (ECLA 2002: 85).

Market exchange rate incomes

The inequality and polarization measures considered so far have all used PPP incomes. Economists tend to insist that the question, 'What is

Table 12.2 Intercountry Income Distribution, PPP$ and FX$, Gini Coefficient

Incomes	1965	1980	1995	2001
PPP	0.575	0.6	0.55	0.525
FX	0.7	0.725	0.75	0.725

Note: Afriat-PPP values are in between the values in this table

Source: Korzeniewicz and Moran (2006; figure 1), based on Penn World Tables data

happening to world income distribution?', should be answered only with PPP incomes, not FX incomes. However, sociologists who work on these issues tend to use FX incomes. Population-weighted FX income inequality increased unambiguously from the 1970s to the late 1990s, when it started to fall, thanks to China. As noted earlier, the PPP adjustment makes for better news by raising the incomes of poorer countries and poorer people substantially relative to FX incomes, and by slowing down or even reversing the trend towards widening inequality and widening gaps (see Table 12.2).

It is true that FX-based income comparisons suffer from all the ways in which official exchange rates do not reflect the 'real' economy: distortions in the official rates, exclusion of goods and services that are not traded, and sudden changes in the official exchange rate driven by capital movements rather than by trade movements. In principle, PPP adjustment is better for questions about relative domestic purchasing power or, more generally, access to material welfare.

But these are not the only questions for which we may be interested in income and its distribution. We may *also* be interested in income distribution as a proxy for the relative purchasing power of residents of different countries over goods and services produced in *other* countries. If we are interested in any of the questions about the impacts of one state, economy or region on others—including

the capacity of developing countries to repay their debts, to import capital goods, to participate in international organizations, and the incentive for people in one country to migrate to another country—we should use FX incomes. FX incomes are a better proxy for relative power and influence, a subject more comfortable for sociologists than economists.

For example, the reason why many poor small countries are hardly represented in multilateral negotiations that concern them directly is that they cannot afford the cost of hotels, offices, and salaries in places like Washington, DC, or Geneva, which must be paid not in PPP dollars but in hard currency bought with their own currency at market exchange rates. Similar reasons apply to why they cannot afford to pay the foreign exchange costs of living up to many of their international commitments—hiring foreign experts to help them exercise control over their banking sectors so that they can implement their part of the anti-money-laundering regime, for example. International organizations such as the World Bank and the IMF, which calculate voting shares partly on the basis of FX incomes, are not exactly pressing to switch to PPP incomes—which would cut the power advantage of the rich countries substantially.

The second main reason to reject the economists' claim concerns the weakness of the PPP numbers. The price data on which the numbers are based is spotty and almost completely absent for many important countries. Recall that China has never had a systematic price survey in line with the International Comparison Project's criteria; and India last had one in 1985. For these and other important countries, the PPP numbers are obtained mainly by extrapolation. Even for the sampled countries, the numbers are collected intermittently, rather than continuously, making statements of trends in PPP incomes across time problematic. Most of the results of the 1993–6 round had still not been made available by the mid-2000s.

The spotty and out-of-date quality of the data reflects the institutional weakness of the International

Comparison project, which through the 1990s was on the verge of collapse. While housed in the UN Statistical Office it received little support from senior officials and UN member states. They argued that it entailed a huge additional burden of work on participating governments and their statistical bureaux, and provided data of interest mainly to academics rather than policy-makers. Since the early 1990s, when the World Bank took it on, it has been carried forward by a few World Bank officials and consultants, still plagued by shortages of funding, managerial support, and data (Korzeniewicz *et al.* 2004). It was not able to supervise seriously the countries' data collection for the 1993–6 round, and the resulting non-comparability is part of the reason why data collected in 1993–6 had not been made available by the mid-2000s.

Moreover, there is no agreed methodology for deriving the conversion factors (see Box 12.1 on page 380). Plausibly constructed PPP incomes for China differ by a factor of two, and similarly for countries of the former Soviet Union before the 1990s. So, if incomes converted via market exchange rates do not give an accurate measure of relative purchasing power, then neither do the PPP numbers. Our confidence in the trends in PPP income distribution should be limited by the certainty of uncertainty.

The absolute income gap

The standard measures of inequality and gaps refer to relative incomes, not absolute incomes. To see why this is misleading, take two countries, Country A with per capita income of $30,000 (for example the USA; Denmark) and Country B with per capita income of $1,000 (for example the Philippines; Syria). Their relative income is 30:1 and the absolute gap is $29,000. If A's per capita income increases by 1 per cent to $30,300 and B's also increases by 1 per cent to $1,010 the relative gap remains constant. But the absolute gap increases from $29,000 to $29,290. If B jumped to 6 per cent growth while A continued at 1 per cent, the absolute gap would widen until year 35, and B would not catch up until year 70. If B grew at 4 per cent and A grew at 2 per cent, the

absolute gap would widen for 140 years and catch-up would take the best part of two centuries. Even this last scenario is optimistic, because, as noted earlier, less than one in ten developing countries (with more than 1 million people) sustained real GDP per capita growth of 3 per cent or more from 1960 to 2000.

No one questions that world absolute income gaps have been increasing fast—as between, for example, the average income of the top 10 per cent of world income recipients (countries and individuals) and that of the bottom 10 per cent, and between the top 10 per cent and the intermediate 60 per cent. China and India are reducing the absolute gap with the faltering middle-income states such as Mexico, Brazil, Russia, and Argentina, but not with the countries of North America, Western Europe, and Japan. If, as some evidence suggests, people commonly think about inequality in absolute rather than relative terms—those at the lower end feel more resentful and more inclined to migrate as absolute gaps increase, even as relative incomes become more equal—our answer to the question, 'What is happening to income inequality?' should not be blind to absolute gaps.

Country mobility

Which way do countries move in the income hierarchy? Table 12.3 shows two state mobility matrices, for 1960–78 and 1978–2000. They divide countries into four income categories (in PPP$ per person). The 'rich' category includes the Western European, North American, and Japanese core. The 'contenders' are countries whose incomes are two-thirds or more that of the poorest rich country (Portugal or Greece, say). The 'Third World' comprises countries with incomes between one-third and two-thirds that of the comparator. The rest are 'Fourth World'.

The majority of states, unsurprisingly, remained in the same income category. But stability was concentrated at the extremes: at the top, few states fell into a lower income category; at the bottom, virtually no states rose into a higher category. The

Table 12.3 State Mobility Matrices, 1960–78 and 1978–2000 (Percentages)

	Rich	Contenders	Third World	Fourth World	Total
1960–78					
Rich	73	20	7	0	100 (41)
Contenders	14	32	36	18	100 (22)
Third World	0	5	59	36	100 (39)
Fourth World	0	0	0	100	100 (25)
1978–2000					
Rich	82	12	6	0	100 (34)
Contenders	13	6	69	13	100 (16)
Third World	3	6	28	64	100 (36)
Fourth World	0	0	5	95	100 (44)

Source: Milanovic (2005; table 7.3)

middle two categories showed plenty of movement; most of it down. Two-thirds of the states in the 'contender' and the 'Third World' categories in 1978 had fallen into a lower category by 2000. Much the same exercise has been done with ten income categories and FX per capita income, yielding a similarly strong finding of downward country mobility except at the top (Ikeda 2004).

These movements invite the analogy between forces of the world economy and those of the physical universe: an analogue to gravity is hindering upward mobility, and an analogue to magnetic levitation is holding the rich economies up. Brazil is a case in point. For eleven years through the 1960s and early 1970s it was the 'miracle' economy, on course to be the first sizeable developing country to enter the ranks of the developed countries. Then it crashed, and has remained in roughly the same position in the world income and technology hierarchy ever since.

Case Studies

China and India

With 38 per cent of the world's population, China and India shape world trends. They have grown very fast over the past fifteen years (India) to twenty-five years (China), if the figures are taken at face value. China's average PPP income rose from 0.3 per cent of the world average in 1990 to 0.45 per cent in 1998, or 15 percentage points in only eight years.

We can be sure that China's and India's fast growth has reduced world poverty and inequality by more than would have been the case had they grown more slowly, and that world income distribution has become less bimodal as the bottom bulge moves out towards the 'missing middle'. About any stronger conclusion we have to be cautious. First, recall that China and India's PPP numbers are even more unreliable than those for the average developing country. Moreover, officials in China's National Bureau of Statistics are under strong pressure to 'toe the line' on key numbers. In October 2006, the Commissioner of the National Bureau of Statistics was arrested for 'corruption' and 'severe violation of (party) discipline' just after he announced a substantial upwards revision to GNP per capita and the growth rate. The top organs of the state had promised the US government that they would take steps to slow down China's growth, as an alternative to revaluing the yuan. Insiders consider the Commissioner's arrest to be punishment for politically incorrect revisions to official statistics.

Second, the surge of inequality within China and India partly offsets the reduction in world income inequality that comes from their relatively fast growth—though careful calculations of the relative strength of the two contrary effects have not yet been made. With respect to India, Deaton (2002) agrees that inequality in India has been increasing 'in recent years', and that consumption by the poor does not rise as fast as average consumption. Glittering shopping malls and mobile phone connections growing at the rate of 5 million a month coexist with a rate of child malnutrition twice that of Africa, and high child (especially female) mortality. The rich buy their way out of reliance on most public services, including water and electricity supply. New poverties are being created by dispossession and rising population density on limited land. On the other hand, it is also true that wealth and dignities are being created at the bottom; but slowly.

As for China, no other country has had its combination of very fast average growth and very fast rise of inequality since the early 1980s. Inequality is now higher than before the communists won the civil war in 1949, and higher than in the USA, Russia, and Japan. Inequality between regions is probably higher than in any other sizeable country. The ratio of the average income of the richest to poorest province (Guangdong to Guizhou) rose to 4.8 by 1993, and remained at 4.8 in 1998–2001 (current yuan). The corresponding figure for India in the late 1990s was 4.2, and the United States, 1.9.

The widening gaps between a sliver of 'mega-haves', a fraction of 'haves', and a great mass of 'have-nots' poses a serious threat to social cohesion in both India and China.

Elsewhere in East/South-East Asia inequality has risen in about three-quarters of the economies since the mid-1990s, a striking finding against the experience up to the late 1980s of fast growth and low inequality (lower than in most industrialized countries).

The United States and other anglophone political economies

All the countries of English settlement have experienced big increases in after-tax income inequality since the 1970s/1980s (Canada is an arguable exception). In the United States, the ratio of after-tax incomes 10 per cent from the top to 10 per cent from the bottom jumped from 4.7 around 1980 to 5.4 around 2000, maintaining the USA as the most unequal 'old' OECD country. The gains have accrued mainly at the very top. The highest-earning 1 per cent of Americans doubled their share of aggregate income from 8 per cent in 1980 to over 16 per cent in 2004, and the top 0.1 per cent (about 150,000 taxpayers) tripled their share, from 2 per cent in 1980 to 7 per cent in 2004. The top 0.01 per cent gained a nearly sixfold increase, from a little more than 0.5 per cent in 1980 to around 3 per cent in 2004 (*Economist*, 17 June 2006: 25–28). On the other hand, the typical worker earns only 10 per cent more in real terms than his counterpart twenty-five years ago, though productivity has risen much faster. Before 1980, the share of the very top had fallen continuously from a peak in 1929, through the Depression, the New Deal, the Second World War, and the post-war social compromise, flattening out around 1970. Initiated by Reaganomics and the larger post-Bretton Woods architecture, the continuous concentration of income at the very top going on for the past quarter century has pushed the United States back up to the top-inequality of the late nineteenth and early twentieth centuries, the era of the 'robber barons', the Great Gatsby, and labour unrest. Today, the affluent minority is rushing to segregate itself in 'gated communities'—the modern version of medieval walled towns. Gated communities account for 40 per cent of new residential housing in the state of California.

In Britain, the National Health Service (NHS) has dampened inequalities, while the educational and housing systems have powerfully widened them: 90:10 after-tax inequality soared from 3.5 in 1980 to 4.6 in 2000 (but still much less than the US figure). Overseas and homegrown billionaires flock to Britain to live and work, but claim residence in an overseas tax haven, avoiding income tax. London, powerhouse of the British economy, is so unequal that a half-hour Tube ride east from wealthy Kensington and Knightsbridge to poor Bethnal Green spans a sixteen-year gap in male life expectancy.

The high and rising levels of US and UK post-tax income inequality since 1980 are matched by low rates of social mobility, or high rates of transmission of economic status from one generation to the next, compared to other OECD countries (Blanden *et al.* 2005). The irony is rich. The two societies that most advertise the virtues of free markets and open opportunities are themselves moving beyond class towards caste (Wade 2007*b*).

The fast rise of income inequality is not a result of a rising premium on education and skills. Even the typical US male college graduate saw hardly any growth (13 per cent) in real wages over the three decades to 2005. Most of the increase in inequality among college graduates results from the institutions that structure markets in the anglophone countries, which are concentrating a rising share of profits, value-added and rents in the hands of the manipulators of money and the topmost corporate executives, and a falling share in the hands of other employees.

Wealth, of course, is distributed even more unequally than income. It is estimated that 25 per cent of US households in 1999 were in 'net worth asset poverty', with insufficient net worth (including house equity) to survive for three months or more without income by spending down their wealth

(Caner and Wolff 2004). So one household in four in the world's most powerful economy is persistently vulnerable to adversities such as job loss. This matters all the more because, as income inequality has risen, so also has household income volatility. American households now have an almost 20 per cent chance of seeing their income drop by more than half in the following year, more than double the probability in the 1970s.

OECD

The upward redistribution of the anglophone countries is part of a broader, though less extreme, pattern throughout the OECD. The OECD 90:10 ratio of after-tax income increased from 3.4 around 1980 to 3.7 around 2000. The share of labour remuneration in business revenue hovered around 70 per cent for decades after the Second World War, rose to 72 per cent by 1980, then fell steadily to 64 per cent in 2003. The share of profits rose by 8 percentage points of business revenue, an excellent result for shareholders. In the USA, the share of corporate profits taken as personal compensation by the top five executives in the 1,500 largest public companies doubled in the decade from 1995 to 2005, from 5 per cent to 10 per cent, at the expense of wage increases for ordinary workers, funding of pension plans, and reinvestment.

Even Japan's capitalism is being reinstitutionalized to twist income from labour to capital and achieve anglophone levels of income inequality. Among Japan's 5,000+ biggest firms, the recovery of 1986–9 saw dividends to shareholders increase by 6 per cent, directors' salaries and bonuses by 21 per cent, and employee remuneration per capita by 14 per cent. Just over a decade later, the recovery of 2001–4 saw dividends increase by 71 per cent, directors' salaries and bonuses by 59 per cent, and a fall in employee remuneration of 5 per cent.

On the other hand, continental Western Europe and Scandinavia have experienced much less of a rise in after-tax inequality than the anglophone countries, and currently have much lower levels of inequality, even with similar or higher levels of integration into the world economy. They also have rates of 'psychological distress' and mental illness roughly half those of the anglophone countries, and employees work substantially fewer hours per year. The prison population per 100,000 of the national population is around 60 to 70 in Scandinavia, and 85 to 95 in continental Europe, compared to almost 140 in Britain, the highest in the European Union, and 686 in the US, the highest in the world. A UNICEF study of child well-being in twenty-one advanced countries found that the four Scandinavian countries had the four lowest percentages of children (0–17 years) living in households with equivalent income of less than 50 per cent of the median, and were in the top seven positions in terms of child well-being; while Britain and the USA had the highest percentages of children in relative poverty and the lowest positions in child well-being (UNICEF 2007).

KEY POINTS

- The major determinant of income inequality on a world scale is the choice of measures, and the income measure matters most. Studies which use market exchange rates to convert incomes into US dollars find very large income dispersions between countries and sharply rising inequality over (at least) 1980–95. Studies that use PPP-adjusted incomes find smaller dispersions and falling, unchanged, or more slowly rising inequality. The distribution measure is the second most important determinant. Studies using the Gini or other average plus PPP$ are more likely to find less of a change than those that measure relative gaps. The few studies that measure absolute gaps find very fast-rising inequality (though the word 'inequality' is not normally used to refer to absolute gaps).

- Between-country income inequality (population-weighted PPP incomes, distribution measured by the Gini) fell after 1980. This is in line with neo-liberal predictions. But those who celebrate this result often overlook the fact that it is entirely a result of the rapid economic growth in China. Take China out, and even the measure most favourable to the neo-liberal argument shows that between-country income inequality has been rising. Nor is this just the result of Africa's fall. Take Africa out, and the trend of income inequality between countries is still rising. So falling between-country inequality is not a general tendency of the globalizing world system.

- Unweighted between-country income distribution has been widening, and the divergence in performance remains even when Africa is excluded. Since there has been a striking convergence of policy towards the neo-liberal, the fact of divergence between unweighted countries is bad news for the neo-liberal argument.

- Inequality within China and India has increased substantially in recent years.

- Inequality within all English-speaking industrialized economies has increased substantially (Canada may be a partial exception), especially between the 'mega-haves' and the rest. Throughout the OECD, capital income has risen as a share of business revenue, and labour income has fallen, raising the political power of those who own capital.

- Throughout the world, from California to India and beyond, the affluent minority is self-segregating into gated communities and private markets, undercutting democratically expressed preferences for higher-quality public services.

- The predominant pattern of mobility of states in the world income hierarchy is downwards, whichever of several comparators are used (average income of the USA, the OECD, or the lowest country of the OECD). On the other hand, a small number of states are stably at the top. This suggests an analogy between forces of the world economy and forces of gravity and magnetic levitation.

- Absolute income gaps between countries and individuals have been widening fast. The present absolute income gaps in the world economy are so large that they will go on increasing for another half century at least. Many of the negative effects of rising inequality (operating through a sense of deprivation, for example) probably hold when absolute gaps are widening, even if inequality is falling.

Globalization

The above evidence suggests that neo-liberalism—the 'global policy' since the 1980s—is not a sufficient condition for higher growth, lower poverty and falling inequality. It also suggests that *further* neo-liberal-globalization, making more of the world economy behave like a single economy, might accentuate the adverse trends, especially because the world economy lacks redistributive mechanisms akin to those of national welfare systems in the high-income states.

But the case that 'globalization works' could be rescued in two ways. One is to say that globalization since around 1980 has not gone far enough to make much difference; the solution is more globalization. Another is to say that, at the national level, a country can always improve its performance by undertaking more free market reforms. The evidence is not kind to either of these rescues.

Not far enough?

There is no doubt that 'globalization as economic integration' has increased hugely over recent decades. For example, the world trade to world GDP ratio rose from a little under 30 per cent in 1970 to a little under 60 per cent in 2001, according to the World Development Indicators. Similarly, movement of people across borders has accelerated—including borders between the high-income West and the rest. The year 1984 was a milestone, when one day in early summer the number of wide-bodied jets aloft over the Pacific exceeded the number over the Atlantic for the first time ever (Winchester 1991: 23). Outsourcing by business firms has also intensified, as businesses broke up their supply chains and looked to cheap labour sites for components. FedEx enabled companies in the USA to rely on suppliers in Europe (by the late 1970s) and Asia (by the 1980s) almost as intimately as on local suppliers.

In terms of 'globalization as policy', we see the dominance of neo-liberal ideas in the use of the word 'reform' exclusively to denote changes in a free market direction. 'Reform' of a trade regime means reducing protection, not making it work better. 'Reform' of corporate governance means increasing transparency, so that investors can better evaluate the buying and selling of shares, not giving more voice to employees. 'Reform' of public enterprises means 'privatization'. 'Reform' of public services means 'outsourcing of government responsibilities' and making labour contracts 'flexible'. We also see the dominance of neo-liberal ideas in the falls in policy barriers to trade and foreign investment. For example, the world average ratio of tariff revenue to GDP fell from about 27 per cent in 1980 to 10 per cent in 2000. On the other hand, government expenditure as a share of GDP has remained fairly constant, in both developed and developing countries, a disappointment in neo-liberal eyes (Cohen and Centeno 2006).

Of all the globalization changes since 1980, two stand out strongly. One is the entry of China, India, and the former Soviet Union into the 'international' economy since the early 1980s. This resulted, by 2000, in a doubling of workers. Whether transmitted through international trade, international investment, or migration, this is a vast economic shock. The second is the 'financialization of everything'—the rocket-like rise of financial transactions relative to 'real' transactions, both domestically and internationally, and the associated ascendancy of financial interests in national policy-making in the USA, the UK and some other leading capitalist states. With the breakdown of the Bretton Woods system—including the switch to fiat money and removal of capital controls—financial flows across borders have come to dwarf trade and direct investment flows. Not only do they largely determine exchange rates, interest rates and other key prices, but the financial sector has also become the pivot of the bigger Western economies, through both institutional interlocking and normative dominance—such as the dependence of a majority of middle- and upper-class households on the performance of the stock market via their pension funds, and the use of return on capital as the measure of managers' performance (Wade 2001).

It may still be a stretch to say that most of the world is functioning as a single economy. For one thing, this ignores trends towards *macro-regional* integration, such as China–Japan, North-East–South-East Asia, North America, and Western Europe. Macro-regions have become strong and are becoming stronger in terms of (1) correlated fluctuations of major economic variables; (2) trade; and (3) sales of multinational corporations. (Hardly any of the top 500 multinational corporations have 'global' sales, even in the limited sense of at least 20 per cent in each of North America, Europe and East Asia and less than 50 per cent in any one of them). Nevertheless, there is no doubt that economic integration and market liberalization have already gone a long way, which questions the argument that things would improve if only globalization went still further.

Globalization as the key to improved national performance?

Do more globalized economies subsequently experience improved economic performance? That trade liberalization promotes higher welfare probably commands more agreement among economists than any other proposition (at least those educated in the anglophone tradition, as distinct from, say, the French tradition). The proposition appears to be supported by many cross-country studies, which find that more liberal trade and investment policies generate economic dynamism. Let us consider one of the most influential, a high-profile World Bank publication called *Globalization, Growth and Poverty* (World Bank 2002*b*).

The study measured globalizing by *changes* in the ratio of trade to GDP between 1977 and 1997. It ranked a sample of developing countries by the amount of change. It called the top third the globalizing, or more globalized, countries, and the remaining two-thirds, the non-globalizing or less globalized countries; and weighted countries by population. The more globalized countries had faster economic growth, no increase in inequality, and faster reduction of poverty than the less globalized. 'Thus globalization clearly can be a force for poverty reduction', it concluded (World Bank 2002*b*: 51). And it attributed the increase in globalization (measured by trade) largely to trade liberalization, as in, 'the result of this trade liberalization in the developing world has been a large increase in both imports and exports' (World Bank 2002*b*: 56).

Not so fast. First, using 'change in the trade/GDP ratio' as the measure of globalization skews the results (Rodrik 1999, 2001). It is quite possible that 'more globalized' countries are less open than 'less globalized' countries, both in terms of trade/GDP and in terms of the magnitude of tariffs and non-tariff barriers. A country with high trade/GDP and a very free trade policy would still be categorized as 'non-globalized' if its increase in trade/GDP over 1977–97 was not large enough to put it in the top third. On the other hand, some of the so-called globalizing countries initially had very low trade/GDP in 1977 and still had relatively low trade/GDP at the end of the period in 1997 (reflecting more than just the fact that larger economies tend to have lower ratios of trade/GDP). To call relatively closed economies 'globalizers' and economies with much higher ratios of trade/GDP and much freer trade regimes 'non-globalizers' is an audacious use of language.

But it yields the right result. The inclusion of India and China as globalizers—even though India at the end of the period still had relatively low trade/GDP and a trade regime with plenty of protection, and China had lots of market restrictions behind the borders—practically guarantees that 'globalization works'. And excluding countries with high but not fast-rising levels of trade to GDP from the globalizers eliminates many poor countries that have had poor economic performance (Honduras and Kenya, for example).

The second problem is causality. The study finds that faster growth of trade quantities is associated with improved economic performance, and concludes that trade liberalization is the key to faster trade growth. In fact, trade volumes are the outcomes of many factors, including an economy's overall growth, not only of trade policy. And they are not something that the government controls directly. It turns out that there is no systematic relationship between trade policy (indicated by tariffs and non-tariff barriers) and subsequent economic growth—not a conclusion the World Bank study brings out.

The only systematic relationship in the data is that countries lower trade barriers as they become richer. To infer that they became richer because they lowered trade barriers is like inferring that, since rich people tend to live in nice houses, you can become rich by living in a nice house.

With few exceptions, today's rich countries had high tariffs during their rapid growth phase (including the USA) and then lowered trade barriers as their domestic industries became competitive. Japan from the 1950s to the 1970s, and Korea and Taiwan from the 1960s to the 1980s had fast growth of trade together with managed trade regimes. They managed trade so as to intensify the cycle of investment and reinvestment in the domestic economy. This generated rapid growth, which generated fast growth of demand for raw materials and capital goods, and prompted careful trade liberalization (Wade 2004a). More recently, China and India began to open their own markets *after* building up entrepreneurship, industrial capacity, internal integration and fast growth behind high barriers. Their continued fast growth now depends heavily on almost free access to Western markets for their exports, and they have lowered barriers on entry to their own markets. Yet throughout their period of 'openness' they have maintained market restrictions, at or inside the border, that would earn them a bad report card from the World Bank and IMF were they not growing so quickly.

In Latin America, Chile adopted free market policies under Augusto Pinochet in the 1970s and enjoyed substantial economic success. Economists urged other Latin American countries to follow Chile's lead, and many did. Yet they have had poor economic performance. Take this report from Mexico, for example:

> "The three main options for high school graduates—attending college, getting a job in Mexico or crossing the border illegally to work in the United States—have become tougher in the past few years…The result is that the generation being counted on to drive Mexico's future finds itself stuck. A historically high number of Mexicans—more than 20 million people, a fifth of the population, are 15 to 24 years old. These young people have been promised much. They are reaching working age a decade after implementation of a free trade agreement with the United States that was supposed to bring new jobs, higher wages and a better life than their parents had. They are also coming of age as Mexico moves beyond its authoritarian past. But millions are finding more obstacles than opportunities in the new democratic era." (Jordan, *New York Times,* 4 October 2003: A15).

Something is amiss when the good pupils score the low marks and the bad pupils score the high marks.

A large-scale study of the whole body of literature on the relationship between globalization, poverty and inequality concludes, 'any claims regarding growth and poverty, or trade liberalization (even globalization) and poverty, should be interpreted with extreme caution…If we achieve no more than to convince readers to interpret cross-country evidence on inequality, growth and poverty with extreme caution and to eschew generalizations based on such evidence, we would be content' (Mbabzi *et al.* 2003: 113).

On the other hand, while the evidence that globalization drives improvements in growth, poverty and inequality is shaky, the evidence that developing countries have performed badly in growth-propelling manufacturing—notwithstanding the more open opportunities of the globalized world

Table 12.4 Regional Share of World Manufacturing Value-Added (Percentages)

	1980	2000
East Asia	4.0	14.0
Latin America and the Caribbean	6.5	5.0
South Asia	0.8	1.8
Mid East/North Africa	1.7	2.1
Sub-Saharan Africa	0.8	0.7
Total	**13.8**	**23.6**

Note: East Asia includes China and excludes Japan. Latin America and the Caribbean includes Mexico. Middle East/North Africa includes Turkey and excludes Israel. Sub-Saharan Africa includes South Africa. The table refers to manufacturing value-added, not manufacturing output
Source: Lall (2004)

economy—is much clearer. Manufacturing performance can be measured in terms of a country's or region's share in world manufacturing value-added. Table 12.4 shows the percentage share for developing country regions in 1980 and 2000. At first glance, the results look impressive: the share of developing countries went up from 14 per cent to 24 per cent in only twenty years. But all of the gain came from East Asia (including China and excluding Japan). The other regions have, if anything, lost share in world manufacturing value-added. In terms of share of world manufacturing output (as distinct from value-added) Western Europe, North America, and Japan still account for as much as three-quarters, and China accounts for only 9 per cent, up from 4 per cent in 1995.

In short, the neo-liberal argument about the benign effects of globalization on growth, poverty, and income distribution can easily be knocked off its pedestal. But if the evidence is so shaky, why the ringing confidence that neo-liberal globalization is the right direction of *further* travel for the world, as in Wolf's *Why Globalization Works*? Part of the answer comes from 'who gains?' By and large, the beneficiaries of a given political economy arrangement tend to argue that it is good for everyone. As noted earlier, a majority of the increase in world consumption between 1993 and 2001 accrued to those already in the top 10 per cent of world income distribution, four-fifths of whom lived in the West; and within the West, those in the top 1 per cent and top 0.1 per cent have benefited hugely disproportionately.

The bulldozer forces of globalization identified earlier help to explain these unequalizing trends. One is the doubling of the one-world labour force since the 1980s, with the entry of China, India and the former Soviet Union into the Western-dominated international economy. The newcomers are paid much less than their Western counterparts yet have rising levels of skill (roughly $5 a day compared to $200 a day). Their bulk supply tends to cheapen consumer goods in the West while also pushing down wages and raising the return to now scarcer capital. The second is the 'financialization of everything', which makes it easier for the financial sector, centred in the West, to squeeze profits from a wider range of global economic activity and concentrate those profits in the hands of a tiny section of the population. The bonuses (not including salary and wages) paid to about 4,000 employees in the City of London in 2006 equalled about half of the increase in the government's spending on wars, health, education, and low-income tax credits in the previous year.

The business community in the West, with its enormous resources, dominates the public debate about global economic policy. It commissions studies, endows think tanks and university centres, and broadcasts appropriate findings with fanfare. All this helps to generate a positive normative glow around neo-liberalism and globalization, which encourages the idea that 'competent' and 'responsible' economists take neo-liberal positions. Then the 'ideology' mechanism takes over, as explained by former US Treasury Secretary Paul O'Neill: 'Ideology is a lot easier because you don't have to know or search for anything. You already know the answer to everything. It's not penetrable by facts.'

In this atmosphere, anyone who argues for industrial policy, higher taxation, provision of public services through public agencies, labour standards, selective protection, a currency transaction tax, or employee voice in running corporations, is suspected of being 'incompetent' or 'deviant'. The main political parties depend on the business community for finance, not on members, and present what is good for business as what is good for the nation—parties of the centre-left almost as much as parties of the right. The parties compete to win support of the mass media, which is owned for the most part by groups, such as that owned by Rupert Murdoch, aggressively committed to a neo-liberal agenda. No wonder that the British Labour Party, while declaring its commitment to reducing poverty, also advertises its unconcern about inequality. As Prime Minister Tony Blair said in 2001, 'If you end up going after those people who are the most wealthy in society, what you actually end up doing is in fact not even helping those at the bottom end' (Lansley 2006: 24). He unwittingly confirmed that democracy is losing its grip to regulate market competition in line with a common good whose characteristics are defined by political debate.

KEY POINTS

- The argument that globalization—seen at the national level in the form of liberalizing policy shifts and/or rising trade and investment integration into the world economy—has been driving falls in poverty and inequality does not stand up.

- The much-cited World Bank study, *Globalization, Growth and Poverty*, relies on a measure of globalization (changes in the ratio of trade to GDP) that skews the results. Weighting countries by population ensures that the overall results are mainly the results for China and India. The study counts China and India as 'globalizers', even though India continues to have a low trade ratio and substantial trade controls, and China has many market restrictions inside its (relatively free) borders. The study counts economies with slow-growing trade ratios but high levels of trade and liberal trade policy regimes as 'non-globalizers', including many poorly-performing countries in Africa, Latin America, and the Caribbean. It also makes unwarranted assumptions about causality in the relationship between trade policy, trade growth, and economic growth.

- We can say with confidence that as countries become richer they tend to liberalize their trade and their **foreign direct investment** rules.

- The fact that countries vary substantially in after-tax inequality even when holding levels of integration into the world economy suggests that globalization is not itself a bulldozer force eliminating 'policy space' and flattening out national diversity.

- The shakiness of the evidence that neo-liberal globalization is producing catch up growth feeds back only weakly into global policy as practised by organizations such as the World Bank and the IMF. The story is too good not to be true. It legitimizes the hugely disproportionate gains obtained by the top 10 per cent of world income distribution, by global firms based largely in the West, and by the USA which, more than others, has adopted a commitment to continuous expansion of private consumption as the basis for domestic peace. The main public-opinion-shaping media outlets are controlled by groups strongly committed to neo-liberalism.

Does Inequality Matter?

One response to this chapter is that, yes, slow, long-run growth and a rising poverty headcount are world problems, but rising world income inequality is not a problem as long as the poor do not become worse off than before. Indeed, the concentration of income at the top may be a condition for improved living standards at the bottom (Tony Blair's argument, also made more elegantly by the philosopher John Rawls). Inequality provides incentives for effort and risk-taking, and thereby spurs efficiency and productivity, the gains from which will trickle down. Also, today's inequalities tend to be undone by tomorrow's social mobility, within and between nations. So those who worry about inequality are just practising the 'politics of envy'.

On the other hand, most economists do not now accept the once conventional wisdom that they should consider 'efficiency' and 'distribution' separately, and base policy recommendations entirely on efficiency (ignoring distribution)—provided the gainers from an efficiency-enhancing change could *potentially* compensate the losers and still gain. Economists today are more likely to accept that they should not be indifferent to inequality, because today's inequality can drive tomorrow's allocative inefficiency through both market and political chains of causation. But this conceptual concession notwithstanding, most economists are not much bothered about income inequality provided markets are free, because they buy into the belief about inequality as the main source of incentives.

What is the evidence? At the national level, does a rising level of income inequality cause slower or faster subsequent growth? The cross-sectional evidence gives no robust answer; there is too much 'noise', the link depends too much on the specific sources of rising inequality. Even if we found a strong relationship between inequality and subsequent growth, the causality is questionable. The effect on growth might be a result of whatever caused the inequality to be high rather than the inequality itself.

The effects of income inequality on other variables are clearer. There is 'suggestive' to 'good' evidence that higher income inequality within countries goes with: (1) a higher poverty headcount and a lower contribution of economic growth to poverty reduction (lower 'growth elasticity of poverty reduction'); (2) higher unemployment; (3) higher crime; (4) lower average health; (5) weaker property rights; (6) more skewed access to public services and state rule-setting forums, and lower standards of public services; (7) lower social mobility; and (8) slower transitions to democratic regimes, more fragile democracies, and more social unrest (some of this evidence is gathered in World Bank 2005b and UNDP 2006).

Correlation is not causation, of course, and the causation in all these cases is probably two-way. But it is plausible that a strong causality does run from income inequality to the other variables. The link to crime, for example, comes partly through the inability of unskilled men in high inequality societies to play traditional male economic and social roles, including a plausible contribution to family income; and partly through the perception that income differentials have no relationship to effort and social values. But crime and violence are only the tip of a distribution of social relationships skewed towards the aggressive end of the spectrum in high inequality societies, with low average levels of trust and social capital. American states with more equal income distribution, such as New Hampshire, also have more social trust.

The link to political conflict is only too evident in China and India. Many people whose incomes are growing nevertheless feel ever poorer—and more resentful—as they see the gap between themselves and the new money being flaunted all around them. And many people are thrown into new poverty as their land is seized, or as they leave their village for work only to end up alone, unprotected and barely employed in the city. In India, some of the resentment is channelled through electoral politics; so in national and state elections in the mid 2000s most political leaders seen as 'pro-business' lost. In China, incidents of mass protest are increasing, even by official statistics.

There is evidence that higher levels of income and wealth inequality go with weaker property rights and more fragile, less accountable states. However, international development agencies such as the World Bank give high priority to strengthening property rights and making governments more accountable—while they avoid inequality as being too 'political'. Interestingly, the Bank's executive directors from emerging market economies with surging levels of inequality, led by China and Russia, are the ones most opposed to the World Bank analysing inequality, as distinct from poverty. Yet without tackling inequality, efforts to strengthen property rights and enhance democratic accountability in high-inequality societies are like pushing on a piece of string.

Within Europe, Scandinavia has lower after-tax income inequality than other countries. Its 90:10 ratio increased from 2.9 around 1980 to 3.1 around 2000, the latter being two-thirds of the UK figure and just over half the US figure, given earlier. Scandinavia has also shown better economic and social performance than both the rest of Europe and the USA by most of the important yardsticks—economic growth; labour productivity; research and development investment; product and service markets; performance in high technology and telecommunications sectors; rates of employment; physical and social infrastructure; and quality of public services (from transport to education, healthcare and care for the elderly). Scandinavia's better performance suggests that a relatively equal income distribution is compatible with relatively high economic growth, high labour productivity, and entrepreneurial incentives. Yet European governments and the European Commission fix on the United States as the model

of virile capitalism, and look hardly at all to Scandinavia.

Japan is an interesting case to watch. It has had a system of welfare-orientated capitalism, with relatively equal distribution of income and wealth, good public services and especially good education and health services for the poorer half of the population. But recall those figures mentioned earlier, comparing income shares during the recovery of 1986–9 and the one of 2001–4: dividends increased by 6 per cent in the recovery of 1986–9 and 71 per cent in the recovery of 2001–4, while wages increased by 14 per cent in the first recovery and fell by 5 per cent in the second. The sharp tilt in favour of capital income results partly from changes in corporate governance law—much encouraged by the OECD and the USA—to make corporate takeovers easier. Managers who used to worry about protecting the reputation of their firm by paying good wages, and who could concentrate on managing processes and products, are becoming more concerned to manage shareholder anticipation by keeping up the share price in order to protect against takeovers. The quintessential figure of anglophone capitalism, the head-hunter, is beginning to appear, who helps part-time, shareholder-representing directors of major companies to find a corporate saviour with the right charismatic qualities and lures him/her from his/her current employment with a vast salary and a stock-option package. Shareholder interests come increasingly to shape government economic policy, and government legislation explicitly invokes the United States as the shiny model of corporate management. As yet, there has not been much change in practices (external directors have been appointed in many firms, but they rarely have much influence). But the shift in the objectives of managers towards the protection of shareholder interests is palpable. It results not only from changes in corporate law, but also from the coming to power in business, government and universities of a generation of people with MBAs and PhDs in economics and corporate law, soaked in the ideological assumption that neo-liberal economics is like the laws of engineering, or a '"sign of God's irresistible will" as Alexis de Tocqueville described the supposedly inevitable trend to ever-greater equality' (Dore 2004: 21). We may be in the early stages of Japan's transformation from welfare-orientated capitalism to devil-take-the-hindmost capitalism, accompanied by applause from those not in the hindmost.

Even in the United States, where nearly half of the population subscribe to a 'conservative' world view that sees inequality of income and wealth as an essential feature of a moral society, there is a groundswell of resentment. In the words of a recent report, 'the incoming freshmen of the 110th House of Representatives feel under enormous pressure to respond not just to the economic insecurity that middle-class voters feel, but also to voters' resentment at what they see as disproportionately prospering corporate elites' (Summers 2006).

The neo-liberal argument is even less concerned about widening inequality between countries than it is about inequality within countries. Not only does it posit a sharp moral discontinuity of obligation at the national border, it also says that nothing much can be done to change international inequality (short of more liberalization all round), because we do not have an international redistribution mechanism akin to national welfare states. But, on the face of it, the more globalized the world becomes, the more reasons why we should be concerned about within-country inequalities also apply between countries.

Migration is an obvious case in point. The EU-15 have an average FX income fifty times higher than the average of Sub-Saharan Africa, and EU territory can be reached by a small boat from Africa within a few days. The migration incentive is the FX income or wage gap (rather than the PPP gap). Commonly, migrants cut rent of expensive living space by jamming themselves into sub standard accommodation

and remitting the savings back home, where, thanks to the FX–PPP gap, their family can purchase much more than the savings could buy in the migrant's country of residence. The inflow pressures into North America and Europe are intense and set to intensify. Yet immigration is already among the two or three most emotive issues in the politics of high-income societies, with solid majorities declaring that there are already too many 'foreigners' in their midst.

Rising internal inequality in the advanced industrial countries and in the big 'emerging market economies' such as China and India may interact with rising between-country inequality to reinforce the dominance of neo-liberal thinking as global policy, backed up by trade agreements, loan conditionality and the like, intended to drive through market opening and 'harmonization of standards'. Why? Because rising internal inequality tends to reinforce the power of classes opposed to redistributive measures to expand the domestic market. Domestic capitalists are then under more pressure both to find markets abroad and to 'financialize' their assets so as to be able to move in and out of markets quickly. Neo-liberalism provides the 'common interest' justification for public policies aimed at these objectives, and a much safer justification—because it is 'apolitical'—than the ones used to justify eighteenth- and nineteenth-century territorial market openings: namely, nationalism, racism, Christianity, and imperialism. Yet it could properly be called a 'new imperialism'—new because it is without colonies (Harvey 2005). Unfortunately, the clever people who now flock into 'capital management' and dominate opinion about appropriate economic policy include very few like Keynes, who made a fortune manipulating money on behalf of Kings College, Cambridge, while also standing outside such activities and thinking for mankind.

Conclusions

It is a given that average living conditions have improved in most of the world in the past half century or so, and by much more than in the previous half century. In my judgement, the economic development since the Second World War ranks alongside the Renaissance and the Industrial Revolution in the annals of human achievement.

But while average living conditions have improved, the rate of economic growth in most regions has been lower in the past quarter century than in the previous quarter century. Income inequality within countries and—by several plausible measures—between countries has risen. The number of people living in poverty has quite possibly also risen, although the proportion of the world's population in poverty has probably fallen. The gated community is the emblem of the age.

At the same time, free market policies have constituted 'global policy' during the past quarter century, bolstered by a promise that they would produce better results than under the earlier, more 'interventionist', regimes. Yet using two eyes rather than one, it is surprising how little the data supports this promise. To reiterate just one point, much of the evidence adduced for the 'globalization works' story is in fact the story of China. It does not support the idea that a general process of globalization is driving a widely distributed improvement in material living standards sufficiently fast to bring most of the caravan closer together.

There are broadly two criteria of 'truth' in science. One is consistency; and the other, correspondence with evidence. Mathematics is the home of truth as consistency; and observational sciences the home of truth as evidence. Economics contains an uneasy tension. Neoclassical economics emphasizes truth as consistency; and econometrics, evolutionary economics and behavioural economics emphasize truth as correspondence with evidence. Neo-liberal economics, a more ideological and anti-state version

of neoclassical economics, tends to prescribe on the basis of consistent deduction from 'first principles', from simple models of atomistic rational agents and perfectly competitive markets, and to pay selective inattention to data that would upset the deduced prescriptions. It is happy to affirm as a universal truth that 'Government failure is worse than market failure', as though it is just 'common sense'.

Its anti-state bias is consistently deduced—from a framework that conveniently excludes some of the main sources of market failure. The framework assumes that technological learning is exogenous, thereby excluding the real-world market failures in technological learning in developing countries, especially when the learning is discontinuous rather than incremental. It assumes that the willingness of individuals to supply services to the market constitutes a reciprocal demand, precluding a more than temporary gap between aggregate supply and aggregate demand. Keynesian economics displaced this assumption (often known as Says Law), but the neo-liberal counter-reformation of the 1970s and 1980s restored it to the centre of mainstream thought, and with it, the efficacy and morality of free markets. It lies behind the optimistic assumption that trade liberalization changes only the allocation of resources, not the overall utilization of resources; which spirits away possible unemployment, de-industrialization, erosion of skills, and firm-level capacities.

The anti-state bias is further bolstered by the framework's implicit assumption that developing country governments are all of a type—a 'neo-patrimonial' type in Weberian theory, where the structure of state authority is characterized by little organizational or normative separation between the public and private domains. It is as though all developing country governments are like Nigeria's. This too makes it easy to declare that 'Government failure is worse than market failure'.

The political economy of research and statistics

My critique of the neo-liberal globalization argument is based on the empirical conclusion that divergence may be dominating convergence, and that the circle of prosperity may be failing to widen in much of the developing world. The implications are so serious (for international action on apparently distant issues including climate change and nuclear proliferation) that we should mount a co-ordinated worldwide project to get better data on poverty and inequality, just as concerns about global warming gave rise to a co-ordinated worldwide project to access better climatological data.

The World Bank is one of the key actors. It has moved from being a major to a minor source of foreign finance for most developing countries outside Africa. But it remains an important world organization because it wields a disproportionate influence in setting the development agenda, in offering an imprimatur of 'sound finance' that crowds in other resources, and in providing finance at times when other finance is not available. Its research and statistics are crucial to its legitimacy (Kapur 2002). Other regional development banks and aid agencies have largely given up, ceding the ground to the World Bank. Alternative views come only from a few 'urban guerrillas' in pockets of academia and the UN system (for a good example of a heterodox book from a corner of the UN system, see UNDP 2003*b*: the WTO lobbied to prevent its publication). Indeed, so dominant is the Bank as a producer of research and development statistics that if it produced an ordinary commodity it would be liable to anti-trust action.

To see the dangers, think of two models of a research and statistical organization that is part of a larger organization working on politically sensitive subjects. The 'exogenous' model says that the research and statistics are produced by professionals exercising best judgement in the face of difficulties that have no optimal solutions, and who are organizationally insulated from the tactical goals of the organization. The 'endogenous' model says that the research and statistics are produced by staff who act as agents of the senior managers (the principals). The senior managers are guided by Winston Churchill's maxim that the truth may be 'so precious that she should always be attended by a bodyguard of lies'. They expect the researchers and statisticians to help advance the organization's tactical goals, just like other staff. They expect the wish to be mother of the thought. They expect policy-based evidence-making rather than evidence-based policy-making.

The simple, endogenous model does not fit the Bank; but nor does the other. The Bank is committed to an Official View of how countries should seek development; it is exposed to arm twisting by the G7 member states and international non-governmental organizations; it must secure their support and defend itself against criticism. It seeks to advance its market-opening agenda, not mainly by arm-twisting but more by establishing a sense that the agenda is correct, because confirmed by robust empirical evidence. If it seriously qualified its argument that market liberalization is the driver of development it would lose the support of the G7 states, Wall Street, and fractions of developing country elites.

The units of the Bank that produce statistics and research are partly insulated from the resulting pressures, especially by their membership in 'epistemic communities' of professionals both inside and outside the Bank; but not wholly. The bias comes not through management instructions to lie, but rather through more subtle mechanisms such as choice of statistical technique and country sample; one that yields an answer in line with the Official View is likely to be retained without much thought, but one that yields a contrary answer will be subjected to much scrutiny. Or the boss of a unit who wants a result that pleases senior managers or a major state but whose professionals decline to comply may bring in a consultant to write a report that affirms the 'right' answer over the heads of the professionals—and then write negative annual performance evaluations of those professionals. To deny this bias is to deny that the Bank is subject to the Chinese proverb, 'Officials make the figures and the figures make the officials'; or to Goodhart's Law, which states that any statistical regularity will tend to collapse when it is used for control purposes. Charles Goodhart was thinking of monetary policy, but the point also applies to the measurement of variables used to evaluate the performance of multilateral economic organizations. However, little is known about the balance in the Bank between autonomy and compliance, or the ability of researchers and statisticians to challenge the way that senior managers use or modify their results.

Some of the Bank's statistics are also provided by independent sources, which provide a check. Others, including the poverty numbers, are produced only by the Bank, and these are more subject to Goodhart's Law. The Bank should appoint an independent auditor to verify its main development statistics or cede the work to an independent agency, perhaps under UN auspices (but if done by, say, UNCTAD, the opposite bias might be introduced). And it would help if the Bank and other multilateral organizations made clear the margins of error and direction of bias. They should issue health warnings that 'Taking the figures too seriously can seriously damage your decision-making capacity'. The US National Council on Public Polls is a model. It sets principles of disclosure for its members, and findings of the Harris Poll are accompanied by the warning, 'All surveys are subject to several sources of error. These include [a list of types of error]', and a statement about the magnitudes of error associated with each type. The Bank and other such organizations should do the same.

Recently, the Bank has moved a little on the issues highlighted here. For example, having previously de-emphasized the uncertainty around the poverty numbers, the two Bank experts in charge of the poverty numbers declared, 'A cloud of doubt hangs over our knowledge about the extent of the world's progress against poverty' (Chen and Ravallion 2004: 141). And an independent panel established to evaluate the Bank's research over the period 1998–2005—the first-ever such panel—found a lot of evidence consistent with the endogenous model. In the words of its report,

'We see a serious failure in the checks and balances within the system that has led the Bank to repeatedly trumpet these early empirical results without recognizing their fragile and tentative nature . . . once the evidence is chosen selectively without supporting argument, and empirical skepticism selectively suspended, the credibility and utility of the Bank's research is threatened' (Banerjee *et al.* 2006: 53–56).

Policy implications

The arguments and evidence adduced here are a wake-up call to individuals and organizations still convinced that the private sector and market liberalization should be the micro economic core of development strategy. Far from being rooted in evidence, meta-propositions such as 'government failure is always worse than market failure' derive from a distinctively anglophone worldview, which has come to dominate global thinking only because two of the anglophone countries have been the norm-setting hegemonic powers for the past 150 years.

It is reasonably clear from contemporary evidence, and from the nineteenth- and early-twentieth-century history of today's developed countries, that states which eschew the role of nurturing their companies and encouraging sectoral diversification and technological upgrading are unlikely to rise up the world income hierarchy against the analogues of gravity (Chang 2002). An open economy with all its eggs in its comparative advantage basket will lose much of the spillover benefits from firms' profit-maximizing behaviour abroad, while in a more diverse and nationally-integrated economy the spillovers promote the growth of national income. Once we set aside the false dichotomies of open *or* closed economy, globalization as opportunity *or* threat, and government limited to creating a level playing field *or* government intervention to distort resource allocation, we can begin to consider the possibilities of state-sponsored directional thrust without the discussion being hijacked by a preternatural terror of governments 'picking winners', or by a religious conviction that the private sector can do no wrong. The question for policy is not whether 'globalization' is good or bad, *pace* Martin Wolf. It is how to combine the opportunities offered by international markets with co-ordinated strategies for domestic investment and institution building, so as to stimulate domestic entrepreneurs and create a more nationally-integrated economy, and so as to retain some economic sovereignty within the developing country state rather than being externalized to foreign firms and foreign governments, or international organizations.

The direction of travel of the international economic and financial regime is, however, to shrink the space for developing country governments to undertake this role; a tendency likely to be reinforced as inequality continues to soar in the G8 states, even as these same states have long practised disguised industrial policy themselves (the British state has given strong and consistent support to pharmaceuticals and defence, the only sectors with a global presence). The governments and civil society organizations of developing countries should therefore co-ordinated their actions so as to push back against this direction of travel, not only at the national level but also at regional and multilateral levels, including in the World Trade Organization and the World Bank. The regional level is especially important as the space to build alternatives to the hub-and-spokes world economy of the twentieth century, with concerted efforts of governments, firms and trade unions to boost the flow of trade, capital and ideas between the erstwhile spokes—between Greater China, South Asia, South America, and the Middle East, for example.

Elsewhere I have outlined a set of principles that might guide an alternative approach to development strategy with a more active role for the state (Wade 2003*a*, 2003*b*, 2004*a*: ch. 11). But alternative development strategies have to be geared to the authority structure of states, and to leaders' perception of the determinants of their or their group's political survival. Some states are more 'neo-patrimonial' than others, some have a broader class base than others, and both factors affect the degree to which the state is able to concentrate resources on investment (Kohli 2004). Political

leaders base their survival strategies on sponsoring varying combinations of (1) political stability; (2) rapid economic growth and diversification of production; and (3) democracy and the expansion of civil society. The West is keen to promote democracy and the expansion of civil society. But where political parties are weak, a democratic transition may result in business capture of the state, weakened technocracy, popular disgust at politics, and an erosion of a pre-existing growth coalition (as arguably in Indonesia and Malaysia since the Asian crisis of 1997–8). In this area of appropriate state structure we know even less about alternative principles of development strategy. But certainly the contrast between the development trajectory and present-day living conditions in Seoul/South Korea and Manila/Philippines is sobering for those who believe that democracy and civil society—with a much longer history in the Philippines than in South Korea—is the vehicle for development.

For political economists the challenge is to explain state effectiveness and derive policy prescriptions which take account of organizational capacity and leaders' survival strategies; and at the international level, it is to devise global and regional governance arrangements through which to regulate market competition so that it advances a common good whose characteristics are decided through political debate. For scholar-activists the challenge is to formulate 'rules for radicals' on a world scale (Alinsky 1972)—rules on how to foment a mutiny about the bounty, and how to shift US foreign policy away from aggressive interference in other states. For philosophers the challenge is to work up alternatives to liberal political morality, which loses its claim to constitute a universal value scheme when its derived economic policy regime helps to produce—if this is a correct reading of the evidence—an extremely unequal world distribution of individual well-being. Or else we could cheer on neoliberalism and await the maturing of the conditions for a socially owned and planned economy, in the spirit of Marx's dictum, 'what the bourgeosie produces, above all, are its own gravediggers'.

QUESTIONS

1. What arguments do liberal writers use to make the case that globalization increases growth and reduces poverty and inequality?

2. What evidence is there to support the liberal position on the relationship between globalization, growth, poverty, and inequality?

3. What are the advantages and disadvantages of using purchasing power parity measures for comparing incomes across countries?

4. What are the main difficulties in measuring the number of people living in poverty?

5. What are the advantages and disadvantages of the various ways of examining the extent of inequality within and between countries?

6. How much change has there been in the global distribution of income in the last forty years?

7. Why might there be problems with the statistics that the World Bank and other international agencies use on poverty and inequality?

8. How can the neo-liberal argument be tested empirically? And how do its assumptions shape its conclusions about the appropriate role of the state?

9. Should one be concerned about rising levels of inequality in the global economy?

10. What are the implications of the trends in growth, poverty, and inequality for the agendas of the multilateral economic organizations?

FURTHER READING

■ **Brune, N., and Garrett, G. (2005)**, 'The Globalization Rorschach Test: International Economic Integration, Inequality, and the Role of Government', *Annual Review of Political Science*, 8: 399–423.

■ **Chen, S., and Ravallion, M. (2001), 'How Did the World's Poorest Fare in the Early 1990s?', *Review of Income and Wealth*, 47/3: 283–300; and 'How Have the World's Poorest Fared Since the Early 1980s?', *World Bank Research Observer*, 19/2, 2004: 141–169.** Key papers from the two main World Bank experts on poverty trends.

■ **Deaton, A. (2001), 'Counting the World's Poor: Problems and Possible Solutions', *World Bank Research Observer,* 16/2: 125–147.** A non-technical account of some of the issues involved in estimating the number of people living in extreme poverty.

■ **Edward, P. (2006a), 'Examining Inequality: Who Really Benefits from Global Growth?', *World Development,* 34/10: 1667–1695.** A study of the relationship between growth, poverty and unequality.

■ **Edward, P. (2006b), 'The Ethical Poverty Line: A Moral Quantification of Absolute Poverty', *Third World Quarterly*, 27/2: 377–393.** The case for developing an ethically defensible poverty line.

■ **Galbraith, J. K. (2007), 'Global Macroeconomics and Global Inequality', in D. Held and A. Kaya (eds), *Global Inequality: Patterns and Explanations* (Cambridge: Polity Press).** A non-technical discussion of inequality trends, including world wage data.

■ **Kaplinsky, R. (2005), *Globalization, Poverty and Inequality: Between a Rock and a Hard Place* (Cambridge: Polity Press).** Links the globilization of production to trends on poverty and inequality.

■ Korzeniewicz, R., and Moran, T. (2006), 'World Inequality in the Twenty-First Century: Patterns and Tendencies', in G. Ritzer (ed.), *The Blackwell Companion to Globalization* (Oxford: Blackwell). An overview of trends in inequality.

■ Korzeniewicz, R., Stach, A., Patil, V., and Moran, T. (2004), 'Measuring National Income: A Critical Assessment', *Comparative Studies in Society and History*, 46/3: 535–586. The problems involved in using national income and PPP data.

■ Pritchett, L. (1997), 'Divergence, Big Time', *Journal of Economic Perspectives,* 11/3: 3–17. A powerful statement of the argument that inequality has been rising.

■ Reddy, S. G., and Pogge, T. W. (2003), 'How *Not* to Count the Poor', www.socialanalysis.org (accessed 26 March; 2007 www.columbia.edu/~sr793/count.pdf. A detailed examination of the methodological examination of the World Bank's poverty statistics.

■ Rodrik, D. (1999), *The New Global Economy and Developing Countries: Making Openness Work* (Baltimore, Md.: Johns Hopkins University Press for the Overseas Development Council). A powerful argument for development strategy that is not just a liberalization strategy.

■ Wade, R. (2003), 'What Strategies Are Viable for Developing Countries Today? The World Trade Organization and the Shrinking of "Development Space"', *Review of International Political Economy,* 10/4: 621–644. How the WTO contrains the strategies available to developing economies.

■ Wade, R. (2004), *Governing the Market: Economic Theory and the Role of Government in East Asian Industrialization* (Princeton, NJ: Princeton University Press). The descisive role of the state in East Asia's rapid economic growth.

■ Wade, R. (2007), 'Should We Worry About Income Inequality?', in D. Held and A. Kaya (eds), *Global Inequality: Patterns and Explanations* (Cambridge: Polity Press). Potential political repercussions for growing unequalities.

■ Wolf, M. (2000), 'The Big Lie of Global Inequality', *Financial Times,* 8 February. A good summary of the case that global inequality is falling.

■ Wolf, M. (2004), *Why Globalization Works* (New Haven, CO: Yale University Press). The case for globilization from a liberal perspective.

WEB LINKS

- **http://utip.gov.utexas.edu**   University of Texas Inequality Project.

- **www.unido.org**   United Nations Industrial Development Organization.

- **www.columbia.edu/~sr793**   Monitoring Global Poverty.

- **www.worldbank.org/poverty**   World Bank PovertyNet.

- **www.bris.ac.uk/poverty**   Townsend Centre for International Poverty Research.

Visit the Online Resource Centre that accompanies this book for more information:
www.oxfordtextbooks.co.uk/orc/ravenhill2e/

13 Globalization and Development in the South

CAROLINE THOMAS

✔ **Reader's Guide**

After more than half a century of development initiatives since the Second World War, the countries and peoples of the South continue to experience unequal development. Opinion is divided as to the precise contribution of domestic and/or external/structural factors to this situation. This is clear in assessments of the impact of globalization on the South. Despite—or, some would argue, because of—over two decades of intense global economic integration, 2 billion people live in countries experiencing falling incomes and rising poverty. Frustration is widespread at the uneven distribution of the economic benefits of globalization between and within world regions and states. The very poor economic outlook for much of the South is a serious cause for concern, as is the lack of voice for Southern governments and peoples in global development policy. In response, there have been some modifications to global development policy, especially the much publicized Poverty Reduction with Growth strategy. Hope for further significant improvement is vested in the potential of the Monterrey Compact, which specifies the roles and responsibilities of rich and poor governments, and other stakeholders, in improving the situation in the South. Whether this will evolve from rhetoric into policy remains to be seen, and even if it does, there are still questions as to its adequacy or appropriateness.

Introduction

The aim of this chapter is to explore the development impact of globalization on the South. Before we can begin, we must clarify terms. Each of our key terms of reference has been hotly debated.

The meaning of 'development' is heavily contested and the subject of an extensive debate in the literature (for example, Rahnema and Bawtree 1997). Here, we take development to mean more than simply economic growth, understood in early post-Second-World-War decades as an increase in economic output (Rostow 1960). We understand development as structural transformation: the economic growth of national economies, coupled with a material improvement in the lives of their citizens evidenced in poverty reduction and increased equity. In other words, national economic growth must be accompanied by human development—measured by the United Nations Development Programme (UNDP) as an aggregate of income, life expectancy, and literacy—for development to be occurring. The former without the latter does not equal true development (see Box 13.1).

'Globalization' has been interpreted in many ways by scholars, policy analysts, politicians, and global citizens (see Hay, Chapter 10, and McGrew, Chapter 9 in this volume; also Held and McGrew 2000). We use the definition offered by Hans Kohler (2002: 1), former managing director of the International Monetary Fund (IMF): 'the process through which an increasingly free flow of ideas, people, goods, services and capital leads to the integration of economies and societies'. Thus our concern is with the development impact of global economic integration, focusing in particular on the period since the early 1980s when privatization, deregulation, and liberalization have proceeded rapidly.

By 'South' we mean the majority of the world's countries, which do not have the opportunity to play a significant role in global rule-making and policy formulation, and where the overwhelming majority of the world's poorer citizens reside. Many other terms have been used to refer to this grouping, but 'South' has been selected here because it leaves open the issue of membership and is therefore more dynamic than some of the alternatives. It sits more comfortably than some alternatives (for example, Third World) with the political reality of the post-1989 world.

Since the late 1980s, global economic integration has become synonymous with global development policy. In other words, privatization of public enterprises, deregulation, and the liberalization of trade, investment, and finance have together been promoted as a global development policy for the South. But to what extent is global economic integration supporting development? On the basis of available evidence, what do we expect that the future might hold in terms of development outcomes

---

Economic Growth and Human Development

Economic growth is necessary but insufficient for human development. And the quality of growth, not just its quantity, is crucial for human well-being. Growth can be jobless, rather than job creating; ruthless, rather than poverty reducing; voiceless, rather than participatory; rootless, rather than culturally enshrined; and futureless, rather than environmentally friendly. Growth that is jobless, ruthless, voiceless, rootless, and futureless is not conducive to human development.

Source: UNDP 2003*a*: 23.

if we continue on our current path? What, if anything, needs changing to get a better result in development terms? And what are the prospects for the international community reaching agreement on such changes?

In order to address these questions, this chapter is divided into four sections. The first is concerned with the current development challenge, and the response of the international community. The second and third sections explore how we got here. A brief overview of development history from the Second World War to the end of the 1970s is followed by more detailed evaluative study of the period from the early 1980s, since when global economic integration has proceeded rapidly. The fourth section explores what might be done to achieve better development outcomes, and assesses whether the Monterrey Consensus really represents a compact for development. An important theme has occured repeatedly throughout more than fifty years of the North–South development debate, and remains unresolved: the extent to which international and/or domestic structures and policies pose a barrier to development, and what must be done to overcome them.

Getting Our Terms Straight

The literature on North–South relations and development uses a multiplicity of terms—such as Third World, South, or G77—to refer to the poorer countries, or specific subgroups, in the international system. Many of these terms are indicative rather than fixed, reflecting the difficulty of categorizing a very heterogeneous set of countries with diverse histories and changing trajectories. Some relate to ways in which countries define themselves; others, to how they have been classified by commentators and/or international agencies. Some of the most common of these terms are presented in Box 13.2. It would be useful to familiarize yourself with these straight away, as they will crop up frequently.

BOX 13.2

Definitions

Third World A term (*tiers monde*) coined by the French demographer, Alfred Sauvy, used during the Cold War to distinguish the non-industrialized countries, including China, from the industrialized countries of Western Europe, North America, Japan, and Australasia (First World) and the planned economies of the USSR and Eastern Europe (Second World). Despite obvious negative connotations, the term 'Third World' came to refer to a self-defining group of mainly post-colonial states with relatively low per capita incomes. Despite growing diversity in economic achievement among this grouping, a common, unifying experience persists: lack of voice in global affairs and vulnerability to external forces beyond their control—such as commodity price fluctuations, transnational corporate policies, and IMF/World Bank/WTO decisions.

NAM (Non-Aligned Movement) The central defining characteristic of the NAM is a commitment to political independence, and this reflects its inception during the era of anti-colonial struggle and the Cold War. Its origins were in the Asia–Africa Conference held in Bandung, Indonesia, in 1955, which brought together twenty-nine mainly former colonies under the leadership of Prime Minister Nehru of India, President Nasser of Egypt, and President Soekarno of Indonesia.

The aim was to discuss common problems and develop common positions on international affairs that reflected the interests and priorities of developing countries. At the first Conference of Non-Aligned Heads of State, in Belgrade in 1961, twenty-five countries were represented, not on regional grounds, as in Bandung, but rather on commitment to shared principles: support for national liberation, and an independent or non-aligned foreign policy. The latter was considered especially important in the context of the ideological bipolar division of the world between the two superpowers—the United States and the Union of Soviet Socialist Republics. At the time of writing, membership stands at 115. Its remit has expanded beyond the early political interests to embrace policy advocacy on global economic and other issues. This shift has been intensified post-Cold War (www.nam.gov.za/background/history.htm).

G77 The Group of Seventy-Seven was established by seventy-seven developing countries in June 1964 at the end of the first meeting of the United Nations Conference on Trade and Development (UNCTAD) in Geneva. It is the largest grouping of Southern countries in the United Nations system. The membership currently stands at 131 states, but the grouping retains its original name. The G77's aims are threefold: to articulate and promote the collective economic interests of its members; to enhance its joint negotiating capacity on major economic issues in the UN system; and to promote economic and technical co-operation among developing countries (www.g77.org).

LDCs Traditionally used to refer to **less developed countries**, synonymous with the Third World or the South, but used more commonly now to refer to the *least* **developed countries**, as defined by the United Nations. UN criteria for membership are: low per capita income—under $750; human resource weakness, including poor nutrition, heath, education, and adult literacy; and economic vulnerability. Triennial reviews determine membership, which stood at 50 in 2006 (www.un.org/special-rep/ohrlls/ldc/default.htm).

LIC Low-income country.

LLDC Landlocked developing countries, as classified by the UN. Currently includes thirty-one states, sixteen of whom are also classified by the UN as LDCs (www.un.org/special-rep/ohrlls/lldc/list.htm).

MIC Middle-income country.

NIE **Newly industrializing economy**—an economy that seems to be on a sound path towards joining the ranks of rich, industrialized states or, indeed now ranks as an industrial economy. In the early 1960s, commentators applied the label to the Latin-American states of Brazil, Mexico, and Argentina. Later, it was applied most frequently to the East Asian economies of Taiwan, Hong Kong, South Korea, and Singapore. Others, such as Thailand and Malaysia, have had the label applied to them more recently.

SIDS Small Island Developing States—fifty-one identified by the UN, of which twelve are also identified as LDCs (www.un.org/special-rep/ohrlls/sid/default.htm).

The South/the Global South With the ending of the Cold War and the accompanying transition of the former centrally planned economies into the global market, the terminology of First, Second, and Third World seemed to have less relevance. The expectation was that the Second World would join the ranks of the First, and the new line-up would be advanced Northern economies and the rest—the South. However, in practice, the former Second World states have more in common with Third-World countries, being characterized by lack of voice in global affairs and widespread poverty. European Union enlargement may alter this for some.

The new globalizers The term used currently by the World Bank to refer to those countries, such as China, India, Mexico, and Malaysia, which it believes have taken best advantage of the opportunities offered by global economic integration by breaking into global manufacturing markets and making some progress towards poverty reduction.

BRICs A subset of the new globalizers, comprising Brazil, Russia, India, and China, the economies of which, taken together, could by 2025 amount to over half the size of the combined total of those of USA, UK, France, Germany, Japan, and Italy (www2.goldmansachs.com/insight/research/reports/99.pdf).

G20/G20 Plus A bloc of developing countries which emerged at the Cancun trade talks in September 2003, where it was united by clearly articulated economic interests on which it negotiated forcefully with the European Union and the United States. Agriculture lay at the heart of its concerns. The alliance includes twenty-one countries from Africa, Asia and Latin America, including the world's most populous countries and most of its fastest-growing economies—for example India, China, Brazil, Malaysia, Indonesia, South Africa, and Nigeria (www.g-20.mre.gov.br/index.asp).

The Development Challenge in the South

Let us assess where we are. The development experience of the South since the 1950s has not been uniform across space or time. *Differentiation* has been the key defining word. While, broadly speaking, we can identify the 1950s, 1960s, and 1970s as periods of growth for the South, the quality and location of that growth differed greatly, with some regions, countries, and social groups faring better than others at various times. The picture was mixed. What is special about the 1980s and 1990s, however—the period in post-war history when global economic integration proceeded most rapidly—is that these mixed results intensified, with deepening economic differentiation between regions, within regions, and within countries (see Wade, Chapter 12 in this volume). *Polarization* is arguably a more apt term than *differentiation* to describe the impact of globalization on the South since the early 1980s. The message is clear: the potential for global economic integration to support development in the South cannot be assumed, and therefore must come under scrutiny.

The top priority in terms of the global development challenge is those countries where poverty is widespread, deeply entrenched, and even getting worse. Also important, however, are those countries that have made economic progress, such as China, India, Mexico, and Brazil, but where the gaps within the country are widening as certain regions or groups of the populace fail to enjoy the benefits of growth; indeed, the improvement of some groups may even be at the direct expense of others.

A new partnership for development?

How is the development challenge to be tackled? This depends on how the causes of the problem are understood, and how responsibility for action is constructed within the international system. Hitherto, a culture of blame has permeated North–South relations, with a failure to acknowledge shared responsibilities. The North has laid the blame for lack of development on domestic factors in Southern countries, while failing to acknowledge that structural aspects of the global economic order that, for example, have caused changes in the terms of trade (the ratio of export prices to those of imports—see Box 13.3 on page 415), discriminate systematically against Southern countries. Many Southern countries have drawn attention to systemic factors, and Northern policy choices and double standards that have undermined the South, while ignoring their own domestic policy failings, corruption, and so on.

However, we may be witnessing a change. At least at a rhetorical level, we can identify an embryonic development compact based on *collective responsibility*. The development challenge has been articulated in terms of the United Nations' Millennium Development Goals (MDGs) (see Box 13.4 on page 416). Governments of rich and poor states have accepted—at least in theory—their collective responsibility for human development in a world where the benefits of globalization are spread unevenly and where the gap between rhetoric and performance in development policy is stark.

In March 2002, the responsibilities and roles of rich and poor alike were restated in the UN's global level summit in Monterrey, the International Conference on Financing for Development. There, rich and poor countries struck a global deal. The Monterrey Consensus (see Box 13.5 on page 416) proclaimed at this conference acknowledged the existence of two fundamental aspects to the development challenge—the domestic and the external/structural—and this represented a potentially important step forward.

However, a note of caution is in order: the history of North–South relations is littered with unfulfilled

BOX 13.3

Terms of Trade

The price of exports of a given state relative to the price of its imports.

The Prebisch–Singer thesis forecast a consistent, long-run tendency for the prices of primary products to decline in relation to manufactured products, in part because demand for primary products grows more slowly than that for manufactures, as incomes rise, and because of competition among suppliers of primary products (Raffer and Singer 2001: 16).

This forecast has been borne out. The impact on Southern countries that export primary products has been *declining terms of trade*: the price of their primary product exports has grown more slowly than the cost of manufactured imports. In practice, this means that Southern countries have had to run in order to stand still: over time, they have needed to export, for example, larger quantities of tea or coffee in order to generate the foreign exchange necessary for one imported tractor or computer (see Figure 13.1).

Since 2002 there has been an upward trend in commodity prices. Yet, despite this, overall commodity prices in 2005 remained about a third lower than the average for 1975–85. It is important to remember that, month by month, and year by year, there can be huge variations between different commodities, such as metals, minerals and agricultural products, and between the experience of different developing countries as exporters and importers of a variety of commodities (see UNCTAD 2006a: 17–29 for details; also see Box 13.2 above).

Figure 13.1 Non-fuel primary commodity prices, nominal and real, 1960–2005

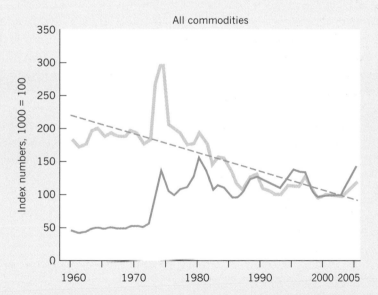

Key: light blue line = real price*; dark blue line = nominal price; dashed line = real price trend
Note: Real price is deflated by the export unit value of manufactured goods of developing countries
Source: UNCTAD 2006a: 20

BOX 13.4

The United Nations' Millennium Development Goals and Targets for 2015

1. *Eradicate extreme poverty and hunger* Halve the proportion of people living on less than a dollar a day, and those who suffer from hunger.

2. *Achieve universal primary education* Ensure that all boys and girls complete primary schooling.

3. *Promote gender equality and empower women* Eliminate gender disparities in primary and secondary education, preferably by 2005, and at all levels by 2015.

4. *Reduce child mortality* Reduce by two-thirds the mortality rate among children under 5.

5. *Improve maternal health* Reduce by three-quarters the ratio of women dying in childbirth.

6. *Combat HIV/AIDS, malaria, and other diseases* Halt and begin to reverse the spread of HIV/AIDS, and the incidence of malaria and other major diseases.

7. *Ensure environmental sustainability* Integrate the principles of sustainable development into country policies and programmes and reverse the loss of environmental resources; reduce by half the proportion of people without access to safe drinking water; by 2020, achieve significant improvement in the lives of at least 100 million slum dwellers.

8. *Develop a global partnership for development* Further develop an open trading and financial system that includes a commitment to good governance, development, and poverty reduction—nationally and internationally; address the least developed countries' special needs, and the special needs of landlocked and small island developing states; deal comprehensively with developing countries' debt problems; develop decent and productive work for youth; in co-operation with pharmaceutical companies, provide access to affordable essential drugs in developing countries; in co-operation with the private sector, make available the benefits of new technologies—especially information and communications technologies.

Source: www.undp.org.

BOX 13.5

The Monterrey Consensus: a Compact for Development

- *Poor states:* Pledged to strengthen the rule of law, reduce corruption, and improve the environment for private-sector growth.

- *Rich states:* Pledged more generous financial assistance, better access to their markets for goods from poor countries, and lasting debt relief.

In addition, the compact included a commitment to enhancing the voice of the South in global governance.

promises. For example, the OECD countries committed as long ago as 1969 to an Official Development Assistance (ODA) target of 0.7 per cent of gross national product (GNP). Yet, nearly four decades later, only a handful of countries have reached this target.

The task is to make the Monterrey compact work. With the UNDP (2003*a*) estimating that, on current performance, Sub-Saharan Africa (SSA) will not even halve extreme poverty until 2147—that is, 140 years away—the responsibility is huge. However, even if both North and South keep to their side of the bargain as expressed in the MDGs and the Monterrey Consensus, the question remains as to whether the collective response is enough to meeting today's challenge. Moreover, with a projected global population of 8 billion by 2025, an even more difficult question is whether it is appropriate to meet tomorrow's challenge.

The question of voice

A key element in making the compact work lies in translating the commitment to enhancing the voice of the South in global governance into practice. As will be shown below, the South has felt aggrieved at its long-standing lack of an effective voice in drawing up the rules and institutions that govern the global economy, and at its lack of opportunity to influence policy evolution within that framework. It is important to note that formal representation at a table does not necessarily translate into influence. Progress on this issue is vital.

KEY POINTS

- The South refers to the states of the world that do not have a significant voice in global rule making and/or where the majority of the world's poor live.

- Too many states and people are being excluded from the economic benefits of globalization.

- The international community of states has signed up to the Millennium Development Goals and Targets for achievement by 2015.

- The Monterrey Consensus represents a potentially significant partnership for development between North and South.

- The issue of enhancing the voice of the South in global governance remains a major challenge.

Development History: 1945 to 1980

Hopes on Independence

When most colonies gained their independence in the 1950s, after the Second World War, nationalist leaders in the South wanted to pursue economic independence and the development imperative was strong. They identified industrialization as the path to growth, wealth, and economic independence. They believed that their countries' poor economic status resulted from the imperial policy of using them as the source of raw materials, and depriving them of the opportunity to produce manufactured goods for local consumption or trade.

Some Southern states, such as India and China, had a rich history of manufacturing. Indeed, in the mid- to late-eighteenth century, the largest manufacturing areas in the world lay in the Yangtze delta in mid-China, and Bengal in India, and it is likely that the average standard of living in Europe at that time was slightly lower than in these regions (Davis 2002: 34). India and China have bitter memories of the military and economic policies of the imperial powers that had been geared towards the destruction of their commercial and manufacturing bases.

Some of the Latin-American states (independent since the nineteenth century), had a more recent experience of industrialization. Although still dependent on primary commodity exports at the end of the Second World War, they had been developing their industrial bases since the 1930s. This had been largely in response to the economic insecurity they experienced during the Depression, when their dependence on the industrialized states for markets for their primary products and as sources of manufactured goods had cost them dearly. The unreliability of export commodity prices in the 1920s and 1930s had hurt them badly, and resulted in a shortage of foreign exchange for imported manufactures. This had made local manufacture for the domestic market essential, rather than relying on imports (Rapley 1996: 12). The Latin-American governments believed that this kind of *import substitution*, which involved both large public and private enterprises, would protect them against the unreliable international market. The newly independent African and Asian countries wanted to follow this example, in the hope of 'catching up' with the industrialized countries of the North and breaking out of their condition of economic dependence.

Were 'breaking out' and 'catching up' realistic goals, and, if so, how might they be achieved? Two schools of thought emerged on this topic, and continue to inform analysis. The first is the structuralist approach, which identified underlying structures in the international economy that worked against the South. Southern countries, because of their colonial history, were tied into structures of production and trade that militated against their advancement. Many, for example, were dependent on the production of one or two primary commodities for sale in the markets of their former colonizer. Hence they were extremely vulnerable to factors outside their control. Structuralists believed that it was possible to reform these patterns to the advantage of the South. The second approach, often termed 'modernization' theory, identified domestic constraints as the obstacle to development, and did not engage with the issue of how international economic structures might have an adverse impact on the South. They too believed development was possible, if the internal context was reformed (see Box 13.6). The writings of several of the key authors associated with the two approaches, plus pertinent critiques, have been drawn together in a useful collection by Seligson and Passe-Smith (1993).

BOX 13.6

Obstacles to Development: Domestic or Structural?

Structuralist theory

- Developed from 1950 on the basis of analyses of North–South trade, and promoted vigorously by the UN's Economic Commission for Latin America in the 1950s.

- Identified the obstacles to Southern development in *structural* differences between production and trade in the North and the South rooted in colonial history.

- Southern economies were dominated by the primary sector—production of raw materials, agricultural products and so on. In Northern economies, the industrial sector was more important.

- The South relied on the export of primary products to pay for manufactured imports from the North, but the price of these manufactured imports rose faster than the price of primary exports.

- Outcome: the South would have to run in order to stand still because of *deteriorating terms of trade*.

- Result: the South could not catch up, and moreover, the gap between South and North would get bigger.

- Conclusion: this could be avoided by reforming the system so that the South would benefit.

- Development required a concentration on the industrial rather than on the primary sector, and a breaking of dependence on the North by increasing intra-South trade.

- Action: the state was to be the catalyst for this change, and should support **import-substitution industrialization** (this could be facilitated by regional co-operation—see Ravenhill, Chapter 6 in this volume).

- Key authors: Frank (1971); Wallerstein (1975); Amin (1976); Baran (1976).

Modernization theory

- Developed in the United States in the 1950s and 1960s in the context of ideological competition between the two superpowers, the USA and the USSR.

- Based on behaviouralism: the belief that scientific study could determine the ingredients of successful development in the North, and these could be applied in the South to deliver similar results.

- Identified a linear path to development, from a traditional, agrarian society to a modern, industrial, mass-consumption one.

- Economic growth would go through set stages, one of which was economic 'take off', indicative of self-sustaining development.

- Identified obstacles to development as domestic: for example, administrative inefficiency, weak legal systems, and insufficient mobilization of domestic resources.

- Structures created by imperialism were irrelevant to future development of the South.

- Action: development required Southern countries to embrace liberal Western values of economics, politics, and society.

- Domestic efforts to mobilize resources would be helped by some private foreign investment.

- Export-led growth was the path to development.

- Key authors: Rostow (1960); Inkeles and Smith (1974).

Development context and experience

From the perspective of the South, the international system of states in 1945 looked very different from that of today. Not only were the African states still colonies, but major Southern countries, such as India and Indonesia, were yet to gain their independence. Post-1945, when colonies achieved independent statehood, they found themselves born into a global economic order in which they were expected to grow through export-led trade, and without any aid or special treatment. Moreover, they had had no effective voice in shaping that order. Southern countries felt that the global economic order inherently discriminated against them. The history of North–South relations thereafter is the story of their struggle to gain a greater voice and a better deal in the global economic order (Thomas 1987; Adams 1993).

As discussed in Chapter 1 in this volume, the essential character and management of the post-war international economy was discussed at **Bretton Woods** in 1944, by invitation of the United States. At the time of Bretton Woods, there was little anticipation that rapid decolonization would occur. Therefore, apart from the Latin-Americans, 'development' seemed to be an issue for individual colonial powers (see Box 13.7).

BOX 13.7

Representation but no Effective Voice: the South's Experience at Bretton Woods

The influence of the underdeveloped countries on the Bretton Woods negotiations, and on the nature of the institutions that emerged was nil or negligible. Of the forty-three countries invited to attend the Bretton Woods Conference, 27 were from the underdeveloped regions of Africa, Asia, and Latin America, with the overwhelming majority (19) being Latin American countries. Indeed there were only three African countries present (Egypt, Ethiopia, and Liberia) and five countries from Asia (India, Iran, Iraq, the Philippines, and China). The bulk of Africa was still under European colonial rule, as was a large part of Asia. Given the complexity of the issues involved, the late stage at which they [the developing countries] were brought into the picture, and the minimal bargaining power that they could in any event exert, it is not surprising that the influence of these countries on the conference and its outcome was minimal (Adams 1993: 22).

Chapter 1 in this volume showed how the Bretton Woods system created two multilateral organizations (the IMF and the World Bank, or International Bank for Reconstruction and Development—IBRD) and one standing conference (the General Agreement on Tariffs and Trade—GATT). While liberal in orientation, this system represented a compromise. The North believed that the economic protectionism of the 1930s had fuelled international instability. Therefore, the recipe for peace and prosperity in future would be economic liberalism. However, Northern leaders were aware of the political imperative in their own states for meeting social issues such as full employment, and thus *they wanted a clear role for governments in the operation of the market* (Ruggie 1982). Thus their desire to meet their own domestic economic objectives would result in breaches of their 'liberal' economic principles; Southern countries, such as textile exporters, were often victims of these breaches when Northern countries limited access to their markets.

In the immediate post-war period, the IMF and the World Bank, unsurprisingly, were preoccupied with the needs of Northern countries. Southern countries soon felt that the Bretton Woods system operated against their interests. The South was dissatisfied with its lack of voice in the IMF and World Bank, and potential violations of sovereignty (Thomas 1987; Woods 2001b). Those institutions operated a system of weighted voting. Moreover, the United States was (and remains) the only state with unilateral veto power in the IMF (Thomas 2000). The problem of lack of representation was made all the more acute because, while theoretically part of the United Nations family, the IMF and World Bank, unlike other arms of the UN, were not (and never have been) accountable to the UN General Assembly, where the principle of 'one state, one vote' operated. Instead, they answer to their major shareholders (see earlier chapters in this volume; also, Raffer and Singer 2001).

Southern countries had many concerns over policies, all stemming from the fact that their special needs were not considered in the establishment of the Bretton Woods structure. Indeed, it was only

after the numerical balance in the United Nations shifted dramatically in the late 1950s with the decolonization of Africa that Southern concerns began to be taken on board. The IBRD, for example, during its early years, concentrated on market-rate finance for reconstruction, rather than concessional (that is, low-interest-rate) finance for development (which was not forthcoming until 1960) (Spero 1977). The IMF was simply not interested in the South in its early years. It was not until 1963 that it responded to calls from the South for special resources, with the creation of the Compensatory Finance Facility (Williams 1994: 60). The Southern experience of the GATT was similar. The General Agreement on Tariffs and Trade promoted trade as the engine of growth, but the South felt that equal treatment rules and reciprocal tariff-cutting arrangements under GATT were unfair, and made things worse rather than better for them. They needed to protect their infant industries, and they needed preferential access to the markets of the North. Moreover, GATT failed to include agriculture. Southern countries needed stable commodity prices, but the GATT was not geared towards this (Raffer and Singer 2001). Indeed, GATT did not even recognize a distinction between developed and developing countries until 1964 (Tussie 1987). Moreover, GATT had relatively few Southern members until the Uruguay Round negotiations in the mid-1980s (Winham 2000).

As regards aid (other than to Northern countries through the Marshall Plan), it was only in the context of the Cold War that this took off. In the mid-1950s, the US government assumed that aid would spur growth and development in the South, and thereby bring these countries into the Western camp. By this time, the United States' priority of rebuilding the European and Japanese economies was well on its way to being achieved.

As more Southern states (particularly those of Africa) gained independence, the early political solidarity of the South expressed through the non-aligned movement (NAM) was transferred to the economic arena. The South was able to start collective organization, both in the General Assembly and in the Economic and Social Council (ECOSOC).

These forums operated on the basis of 'one state, one vote', and therefore provided a more congenial environment than the World Bank and the IMF in which to work collectively to put pressure on the North for a better economic deal. The NAM provided a further impetus for the collective articulation of demands. With the growing competition between the superpowers for allies in the South from the mid-1950s onwards, opportunities opened up not only to receive aid (a mixed blessing, as it was usually accompanied by 'strings'—that is political and economic conditions) but also to bargain for changes.

A noteworthy achievement for the South came in 1964 with the establishment of the United Nations Conference on Trade and Development (UNCTAD), a standing conference outside the West-founded GATT. This was followed by the formation of the G77, through which the South would pursue collective representation in the United Nations (Spero 1977; Adams 1993). The Southern victory had a hollow ring, however. The Western powers did not object to the establishment of UNCTAD, secure in the knowledge that funding and economic policies would be determined through the IMF and the World Bank, where weighted voting operated in their favour. Also, while in 1965 they formally acknowledged the need for sustained and rapid expansion of Southern exports, by adding Part IV to GATT—on 'Trade and Development'—this did not translate substantively into help for the South. Yet UNCTAD's intangible achievements, in terms of its role as a pressure group for the developing world, and as a focus for critiques of mainstream development thinking, were significant in its first decade (see Box 13.8).

The decade of the 1970s was to be the high point of Southern achievement in terms of participating in decisions and producing outcomes on the global economic stage (Williams 1994: 60–62). The

---

BOX 13.8

Development Achievement in the South, 1945–1980

Throughout this period, development in the South was led by the state rather than the market. There were many variations in national policy. Some states (for example, in Latin America, South Asia, and Sub-Saharan Africa (SSA)) pursued import substitution, while others (for example, in East Asia) used selective protection in key industries as preparation for export-led growth. A few (for example, Tanzania, Burma) attempted self-sufficiency. Some (for example, in East Asia) emphasized growth with equity (Watkins 1998: 18). Others (for example, in Latin America) ignored issues of equity and human capital. *The common thread was the important role of the state as the motor of development. This was in accord with the conventional wisdom of development economics of the period.*

The 1950s and 1960s have been described as an *'optimistic'* period of growth for the South (Singer and Roy 1993). However, despite this, the South was still being left further behind by the North. The South's share of world trade fell during the 1950s from a third to a fifth, and expansion of its export earnings decelerated over the decade. Nevertheless, the proportion of the South's people living in absolute poverty fell.

In the 1970s, growth continued in the South, but Singer and Roy identify this as 'illusory', based on the accumulation of debt. Nevertheless, the proportion of people living in absolute poverty continued to fall. When overall averages for per capita growth rates are unpacked, great variation in achievement is apparent, with many states experiencing negative or very low growth rates (for example, SSA), some moderate (Latin America), and some high (East Asia).

But growth alone is an inadequate measure of development. Again, variations are apparent. In the oil states of the Gulf, for example, the high rates of growth experienced after 1973 did not translate into similar achievements in various aspects of human development. Also, the gross inequity that characterized many Latin-American states meant that they needed to grow more than the East Asian states (which they failed to do) to make an impact on poverty reduction.

negotiating environment changed dramatically for the South in the early 1970s (Adams 1993; South Commission 1990). Several factors contributed to this change: the Bretton Woods system of fixed exchange rates was abandoned in 1971; the OPEC countries acting as a cartel quadrupled the price of oil in 1973; commodity prices were strong during the first half of the 1970s. Even though oil-importing Southern countries were in difficulty economically, politically the South remained united, enjoying the new-found empowerment. The North felt insecure; not yet understanding that oil was a special case, it was concerned that the cartel action could be repeated for other commodities, giving even more bargaining power to the South. It was also troubled at this time by inflation and unemployment.

In 1974, the South called for a New International-al Economic Order (NIEO) at the UN General Assembly, and followed this a year later with a Charter on the Rights and Duties of States (Thomas 1985: 122–151). At core, these represented a political demand for sovereignty to be taken seriously. There were a number of economic demands, several geared toward reducing the vulnerability of the South to external factors (for example, index-linking the price of raw materials to the price of manufactured goods) and exercising sovereignty (for example, control over foreign investment and domestic natural resources). At the IMF, the South fought for increased financial flows, and this was realized through a number of mechanisms such as the two-year Oil Facility in 1974, to help countries in difficulties because of the oil price rise, and the Trust Fund in 1976 to support the poorest countries with concessional loans (Williams 1994: 61).

Despite the shock of oil price rises, the Northern states were in no mood to make significant concessions (Hansen 1979; Rothstein 1979; Bhagwati and Ruggie 1984; Zartman 1987). The new lending facilities helped poorer oil-importing countries, but fell far short of offsetting the impact of oil price increases. Larger issues that emanated from the NIEO and the Charter of Economic Rights and Duties of States (CERDS) were sidelined.

This period of heightened diplomatic activity by the South in the United Nations and the IMF coincided with a change of commitment in the World Bank from highly visible infrastructural projects to poverty-focused aid. The presidency of Robert McNamara (1968–81) is best remembered for an emphasis on redistribution with growth, illustrated by the emergence of integrated rural development projects which tackled multiple causes of poverty in parallel—health, education, and rural finance, as well as infrastructure (Mosley and Eeckhout 2000: 133–134). McNamara first highlighted the issue of growth with equity at the joint meetings of the IMF and World Bank in 1973. A year later, the Bank supported the publication of *Redistribution with Growth* (Chenery *et al.* 1974), and in 1978 it published its *First World Development Report,* on the prospects for enhanced growth and poverty alleviation. However, the changed focus of the Bank did not mean that the institution or its president supported the claims of the South for an NIEO. Indeed, by 1979, McNamara was calling at the Manila UNCTAD conference for structural adjustment (see below).

Oil price rises were a double-edged sword for the non-oil-exporting South, and their economic difficulties mounted. In addition to the oil shock, volatile commodity prices in the second half of the 1970s, and declining terms of trade, further weakened their position. Keen to maintain rates of growth comparable to the 1960s, many Southern governments, including the Latin-Americans, borrowed recycled petrodollars at low but floating rates of interest from private banks. SSA states were unable to borrow much from private banks, but borrowed from official creditors. When the United States responded to a second oil price hike in 1979 by raising interest rates, Southern countries found themselves in severe trouble. Interest payments on debts rose, and they needed to borrow more money to deal with deficits and to service their debt (see Pauly, Chapter 8 in this volume). The debt crisis was born, and was to define their development experience over the next two decades.

At the end of the 1970s, the Soviet bloc was still intact, and the G77/non-aligned group, while weak, still functioned—albeit under increasing strain because of growing divisions between oil-exporting and oil-importing developing countries that became apparent at the 1979 UNCTAD Manila Conference. While the calls for an NIEO had receded, the idea and the reality still existed that there was more than one model of development on offer—but not for much longer. Governance in the international system would shift from the relatively open, discursive multilateral UN system of the 1970s, to governance through the narrowly defined IMF and World Bank under the direction of the G7 in the 1980s.

KEY POINTS

- Post-1945, Southern states pursued several paths to development, but all identified the state as the motor of development, and industrialization as the means of catching up with the economic achievement of the North.

- Structuralist theory and modernization theory emerged as the two main approaches to explain the development problem.

- The South felt that the liberal Bretton Woods Economic Order did not address their special needs.

- The South campaigned for changes through the UN system.

- Empowered by the OPEC cartel action, they called for a NIEO in 1974.

- Oil price rises hurt Southern countries, and they tried to maintain earlier growth rates through borrowing.

- The political response of the North to the second phase of oil price rises in the late 1970s sealed the fate of the South. Interest rate rises on floating-rate debt, coupled with falling commodity prices, meant the debt crisis was born.

Development Policy Since 1980: From State-Led to Market-Led

The beginning of the 1980s marked a very significant shift in development policy from state-led to market-led. The overwhelming need of many states in the South for immediate and longer-term external finance was so great that they had no effective bargaining power *vis-à-vis* the First World. This weakness coincided with the ascendancy of a neo-liberal agenda (see below) within the domestic politics of leading industrialized economies. The post-war liberal principle of a state-guided market gave way to neo-liberalism; the scene was set for the expansion of market fundamentalism across the South.

The G7 accorded the World Bank a higher and more exclusive profile in global development policy, and the IMF an entirely new one, as the major Western powers decided to use these institutions to manage Third World debt. They worked on the assumption that needy countries suffered from short-term cash flow problems that could be remedied by policy reforms. Thus loans were made conditional on policy changes: the role of the state was to be reduced and redefined, and the market was to operate unhindered.

By the early 1990s, with the demise of the eastern bloc, the IMF and World Bank were portrayed globally as *the exclusive holders of legitimate knowledge about development*. This meant that the role of external/structural factors in the development challenge was played down. Crucially, these institutions disbursed most of the multilateral aid, and other lenders withheld support unless developing countries first gained approval for a reform package from the international financial institutions (IFIs). The amount and significance of ODA declined substantially in the 1990s, and the majority of the developing countries found it difficult to tap other sources or to resource alternative pathways for development. Middle-income countries, however, such as Malaysia and Thailand, competed to attract growing volumes of private capital (see below), and they enjoyed substantial increases in portfolio capital flows.

Over the period 1986 to 1994, the Uruguay Round GATT trade negotiations were under way, and these too reflected and reinforced the ascendancy of the neo-liberal agenda and the lack of political leverage or bargaining power of the South (UNDP *et al.* 2003).

During the 1990s, the G7 used its summits increasingly to frame development policy politically. Under its direction, since the mid-1990s, the World Bank has pushed forward the harmonization of donor policies and coherence between the policies of the IMF, the World Bank, and the WTO in support of free trade. This has further strengthened the already overwhelming influence of the North on development policy for the South, as bilateral donors line up behind IFIs policies. During the recent Doha Round of trade negotiations, the space for a Southern voice was more evident, but this failed to translate into effective leverage.

Neo-liberal development policy for the South

Neo-liberal development policies are often referred to as the Washington Consensus (WC). These policies are based on the assumption that global economic integration through free trade is the most effective route to promote growth, and that the benefits of growth will trickle down throughout society. Broadly, they involve three stages (Green 1995: 4). The first stage is to control inflation by *stabilization, and to get rid of government spending deficits.* The money supply is reduced by *cutting public spending and raising interest rates.* The second stage is structural adjustment—this involves letting the market operate unhindered by state controls; *privatizing* public enterprises; and *liberalizing* trade, investment, and finance. The third stage is export-led growth—which involves encouraging foreign investors to bring in capital and technology unhindered by government regulation (see Box 13.9).

The WC was applied as a universal blueprint for development throughout the Third World and former Second World. The debt crises in Latin America and Africa in the 1980s gave the IMF and the World Bank an opportunity to institutionalize **structural adjustment programmes** as a debt management strategy in those regions. Post-1989, the treatment was consolidated in the economies in transition, several of which were already borrowing from the IFIs. In the late 1990s, in the context of financial crisis, it was the turn of some East Asian states.

The IMF and World Bank diagnosed the problems of all these regions and their constituent countries in the same way, and made loans conditional on a standard package of policy advice. But their problems were not the same, and uniform solutions were not appropriate. The Latin Americans, for example, had very high inflation, low savings rates, and large **balance-of-payments** problems (Green 1995), whereas the East Asians enjoyed low inflation, high savings, and balanced budgets (Bullard *et al.* 1998). The debts of African states were to public creditors—bilateral and multilateral, while the Latin American states were more indebted to private banks.

From the late 1980s onwards, anxieties grew regarding the model's ability to deliver the promised economic growth, as well as its social and environmental impact (Cornia *et al.* /UNICEF 1987; South Commission 1990; Walton and Seddon 1994).

BOX 13.9

From State-Led to Market-Led Development

- In the context of mounting Southern debt, the IMF and the World Bank were given a prominent new role by the United States in making global development policy and monitoring its implementation.

- Loans to the South were dependent on the adoption of stringent policy conditions.

- They universalized a neo-liberal approach to development: state-led was replaced by market-led development.

- Export-led growth was the route to enable Southern countries to generate the foreign exchange necessary to repay their debts and to promote development through a trickle-down process.

- They identified the causes of poverty and underdevelopment as being *internal* to states, rather than external/structural or a combination of both.

- The state was redefined as an enabler for the private sector; it was to facilitate deregulation, privatization, and liberalization, and regulate activities of the private sector.

- Good governance was the key, including tackling corruption, holding free elections, and developing and enforcing **property rights** and contracts.

- Other possible paths to development were closed off, as IMF/World Bank loans were the necessary green light for finance from other public and private sources.

Moreover, while there had been some reduction in Latin-American debt as a consequence of the Baker and Brady initiatives, for the poorest states in the South, debt continued to mount (see Table 13.1). The conditions attached to loans raised concerns that the model was being externally imposed on needy, vulnerable client states in violation of national sovereignty.

In the early to mid-1990s, the IMF and World Bank responded to these criticisms by attempting to make their prescriptions for growth more palatable on the ground. They offered some support for limited, targeted poverty-reduction actions such as micro-credit, social safety nets, and social funds (Vivian 1995; Subbarao *et al.* 1997); 1996 saw a change in the approach to debt. Up to then, the debt problem had been seen as one of *illiquidity*; in other words, states were perceived as being unable to meet immediate obligations, but there was the expectation that over time they would be able to repay their debts. This assumption underpinned the emphasis on debt collection, debt rescheduling, and aid/structural adjustment. In 1996, however, the international community introduced the Heavily Indebted Poor Countries' (HIPC) initiative, based on the recognition that the least developed

countries (LDCs) were *insolvent*. In other words, there was a recognition that they would never be able to repay their debts. Thus the HIPC was designed to reduce the debt stock of the LDCs and to bring those countries to a position of debt sustainability. It would remove the debt overhang that was seen as a disincentive to private investment, and a barrier to the government expenditures needed to improve physical and human infrastructures.

But while the IMF and World Bank made a few modifications to their prescriptions for the South, the conclusion of the GATT Uruguay Round in 1994 reflected the economic interest and political influence of the United States and the Europeans, for whom trade in services, intellectual property, and investment issues were becoming increasingly important. The special needs of the South in these issues were ignored; for example, in the **trade-related investment measures (TRIMs)** (UNDP *et al.* 2003: 11). Also, for much of the South (especially, but not only, the heavily indebted), trade in agriculture rather than in services was the most pressing issue, yet this was of less interest to the North and was left unresolved.

The basic WC model remained, promoted by a wider group of actors. From the mid-1990s policy co-ordination for development went wider and deeper than before. It involved the IMF, World Bank, and the new World Trade Organization (WTO) in new areas and enmeshed them with new partners, particularly private partners and civil society groups. Most noticeable during this period was the privatization of global governance, in which corporate and private interests hid beneath the apparel of public governance. Examples in the field of development policy are wide-ranging. One is corporate sponsorship of UN conferences, influencing their agendas and outcomes—such as UNCED (the United Nations Conference on Environment and Development), which gave a green light for self-regulation by transnational corporations. Another example is the overt corporate role in shaping policy at the WTO, seen in striking fashion in the formulation of trade-related intellectual property rights (TRIPs) (Drahos 2002) and in the proliferation of bilateral trade agreements.

The results were very disappointing. By the late 1990s, it was no longer politically tenable for the IMF and the World Bank to argue that the WC model had not been applied long enough or fully enough for the expected growth and trickle-down to occur. Evidence was mounting that inequalities had increased between and within states while the model had been applied, and there was no sign of this trend reversing:

1. *Economic growth.* Lower than expected, and often of an insufficient quality (see Box 13.1 on page 411). In SSA, for example, it remained under 2.5 per cent annually during the 1980s and the 1990s (and on a per capita basis was frequently negative) (UNCTAD 2002b). East Asia, which had enjoyed strong rates, suffered reversals in the late 1990s.

2. *Indebtedness.* Remained a serious problem, particularly for the most heavily indebted countries, where the situation actually got worse, with the nominal stock of debt exploding relative to exports. The HIPC did not achieve the desired results; it amounted to 'too little, too late' (see Table 13.1 and Figure 13.2).

   The total debt stock of the net-debtor developing countries almost doubled in the 1990s, from $1.3 trillion to $2.2 trillion, while their debt service payments to export ratio increased from 19.6 per cent in 1991 to 22.3 per cent in 1999.

3. *Trade liberalization.* The share of world trade enjoyed by Southern countries increased, and the composition of Southern exports changed, with the share of manufactured goods growing relative to primary commodities (see Figure 13.3). However, the East Asian newly industrializing economies (NIEs) accounted for much of this growth, having a 75 per cent share of Southern manufactured exports (compared with less than 2 per cent for South Asia and SSA combined) (Oxfam International 2002b: 10) and an increasing role in the high-tech export market. By contrast, the LDCs

---

Table 13.1 External Debt as a Percentage of GDP (Period Average)

Category	1980–4	1985–9	1990–4	1995–2000
HIPC	38	70	120	103
Other IDA countries	21	33	38	33
Other lower-middle-income countries	22	30	27	26

Source: Gautam (for World Bank's OED) 2003: 5

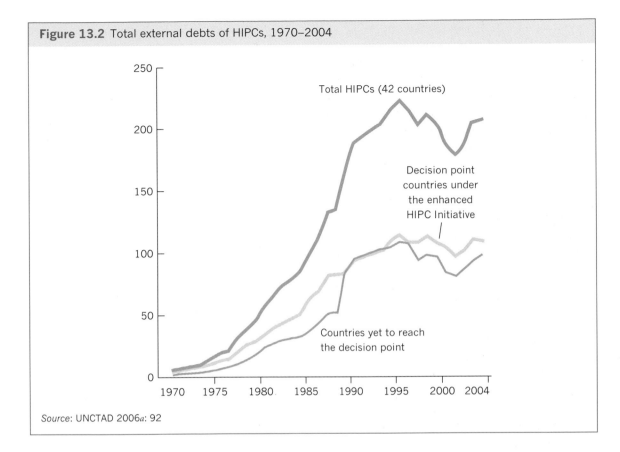

Figure 13.2 Total external debts of HIPCs, 1970–2004

Total HIPCs (42 countries)

Decision point countries under the enhanced HIPC Initiative

Countries yet to reach the decision point

Source: UNCTAD 2006*a*: 92

that relied on the export of primary commodities suffered a continuous, significant decline in market prices (real terms) of their products (see Figures 13.4 and 13.5).

The commodity-exporting countries became far more open to trade, yet they were earning less. Why was this so? UNCTAD (2002*b*) identifies the reasons as their continued concentration on production of primary commodities that have been characterized by stagnant markets and declining prices, and their failure to shift production into technology-intensive products. This experience lends support to the structuralist position outlined earlier. A secular decline in the terms of trade of primary commodity producers occurred, costing SSA, for example, 50

cents for every US dollar received in aid since the late 1970s (Oxfam International 2002*b*: 10; see Box 13.2 on page 412). The Southern countries that were able to develop their exports of manufactures fared much better. This helps to explain increasing polarization within the South between the NIEs and the states of SSA.

The South's share of world trade would be higher were it not for the double standards practised by the North. It has been estimated that if Africa, East Asia, South Asia, and Latin America were each to increase their share of world exports by 1 per cent, then 128 million people could be lifted out of poverty (Oxfam International 2002*b*: 5). In the case of Africa, this 1 per cent increase would

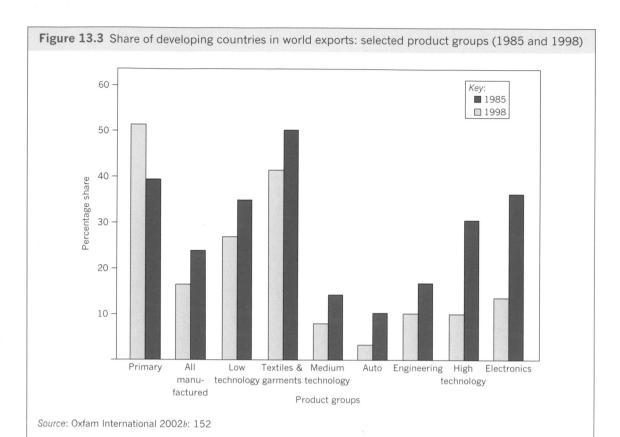

Figure 13.3 Share of developing countries in world exports: selected product groups (1985 and 1998)

Source: Oxfam International 2002*b*: 152

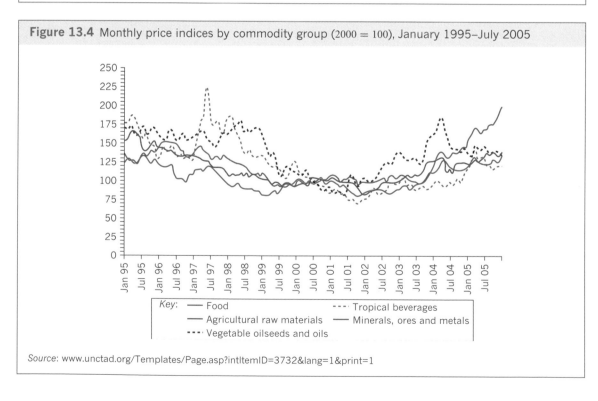

Figure 13.4 Monthly price indices by commodity group (2000 = 100), January 1995–July 2005

Source: www.unctad.org/Templates/Page.asp?intItemID=3732&lang=1&print=1

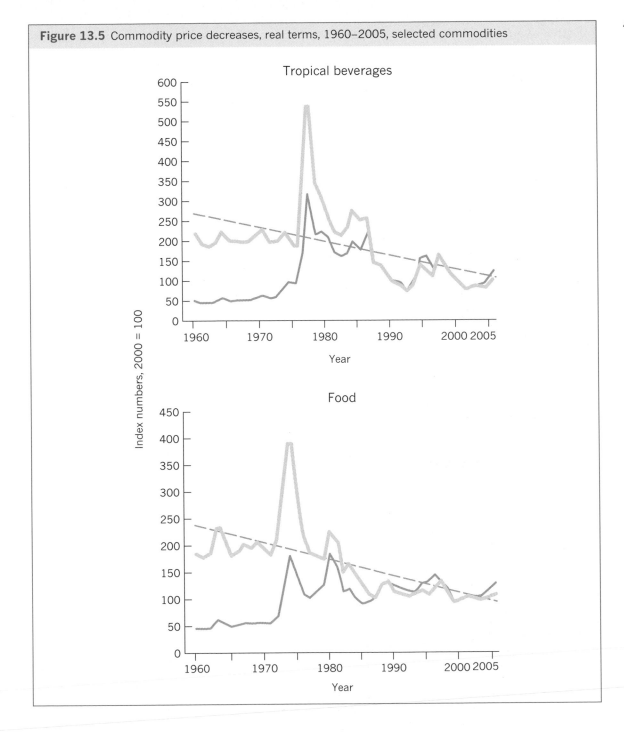

Figure 13.5 Commodity price decreases, real terms, 1960–2005, selected commodities

Figure 13.5 (*continued*)

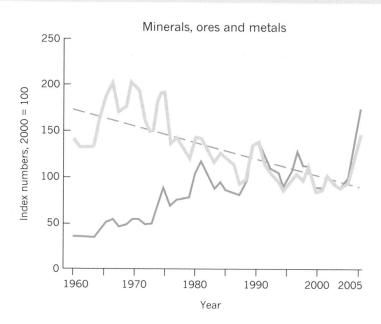

Key: Light blue line = real price*; dark blue line = nominal price; dashed line = real price trend
Note: Real price is deflated by the export unit value of manufactured goods of developing countries
Source: UNCTAD 2006*a*: 20

generate $70 billion—which, as Oxfam noted in 2002 (2002*b*: 8), was five times the amount received through aid and debt relief at that time. Moreover, a 5 per cent increase in the share of world trade for Southern countries would deliver $350 billion—seven times the amount they received in aid.

But the North stands in the way of this expansion of Southern trade. The North demands that the South open its borders to trade, while protecting its own domestic markets from Southern imports—for example, by escalating tariffs on processed goods (as opposed to raw materials). The very products in which Southern countries can most easily develop a manufacturing base and gain a competitive edge—for example, labour-intensive clothing and textiles—meet

Northern protectionist barriers four times higher than those faced by Northern producers (Watkins 2002). Also, the North subsidizes its own domestic production, resulting in global **dumping** and the destruction of Southern production. This is seen starkly in relation to agriculture, where Northern subsidies to domestic farmers have topped $1 billion per day. Livelihoods have been devastated in the South—for example, the cotton growers of West Africa—and local food markets destroyed. The UNDP (2003*a*: 155) notes that the European Union cash subsidy to every dairy cow exceeds total per capita EU aid to SSA.

4. *Social problems.* Global deprivation has spread geographically. The effect of shock therapy on the former Soviet Union was to throw

60 million people below the poverty line in the 1990s. In South-East Asia, severe reversals following the financial crises of the late 1990s (which in some cases, such as Indonesia, compounded political disintegration) threw millions back below the poverty line virtually overnight. In SSA, poverty deepened in the 1980s and 1990s as structural adjustment took its social toll. Public infrastructures such as health, education, and transport eroded as governments were forced to cut public spending, and the World Bank advocated the use of user fees (Save the Children 2001; GUFPC 2003; Thomas and Weber 2004). Privatization, for example of water, failed to expand services to the poorest, as transnational corporations practised 'cherry picking'. Market-based entitlement deprived the poor of access to essential services. In SSA this has happened at the same time as the region and its people have faced their greatest health emergency—the HIV/AIDS pandemic (Poku 2001). Aggressive US trade policy has prevented poor states from taking advantage of the limited opportunities open to them in the WTO's TRIPs to access inexpensive medicines (Thomas 2002).

Trade liberalization can contribute to social problems and polarization. International trade theory assumes that increased openness to trade will result in more equal income distribution within poor countries. But research by Milanovic (2002) found that in countries with a low per capita income level, such as in Sub-Saharan Africa, it is the rich who benefit from trade openness, while in countries where average income has risen, such as Chile or the Czech Republic, openness seems to be related to the rise in the relative income of the poor and middle class relative to the rich.

5. Official Development Assistance. The quantity, quality and distribution of flows were disappointing (see Figure 13.6). Even though Southern states implemented structural adjustment, sufficient new money failed to flow in as expected and, by the mid-1990s, workers' remittances (money sent back to their home countries by nationals working abroad) exceeded ODA (see Figure 13.8). In real per capita terms, ODA to the LDCs fell 46 per cent in the 1990s (UNCTAD 2002b: 215). Over the 1990s, ODA declined from 0.33 per cent of donor country gross national product (GNP), to 0.22 per cent—despite the OECD countries' 1969 commitment mentioned earlier to an ODA target of 0.7 per cent of GNP! The hopes for a 'peace dividend' after the demise of the Eastern bloc came to nothing.

Until 2000 it seemed that debt relief was not additional 'new' money; rather, after the deduction of debt relief, there was in fact a *decline* in aid flows to HIPCs during 1996–2000. From 2001 to 2004, while flows rose, the main beneficiaries were not among the HIPC or poor transitional countries such as the Commonwealth of Independent States (CIS). Rather, there were significant flows to two countries where Western forces were engaged in military conflict: Afghanistan and Iraq (UNCTAD 2006a: 97–98). Middle-income countries with debts did not receive adequate attention.

In terms of quality, the tying of aid to the purchase of goods and services, and technical co-operation, from donor countries eroded its value; for example, in 1997, technical co-operation amounted to 40 per cent of bilateral ODA.

6. Foreign direct investment. Although the South's overall share of global FDI increased during the 1990s—and rose from

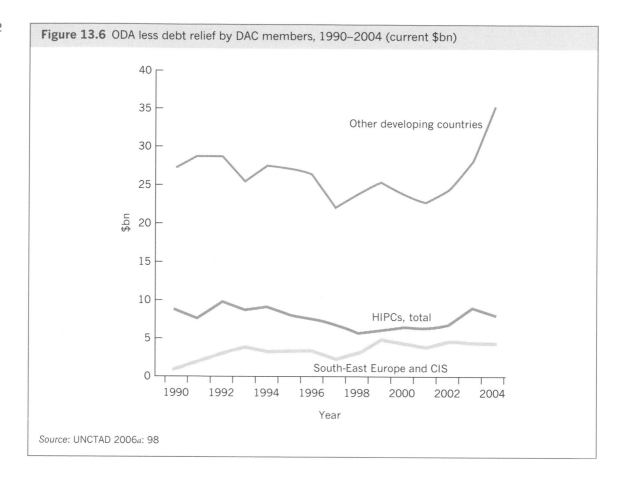

Figure 13.6 ODA less debt relief by DAC members, 1990–2004 (current $bn)

Other developing countries

HIPCs, total

South-East Europe and CIS

Source: UNCTAD 2006*a*: 98

18 per cent in the late 1990s to 28 per cent in 2001 (UNCTAD 2002*c*: 5)—the quantity and quality (its impact) were disappointing for much of the South. The quantity of Southern FDI in 2000 ($240 billion) seems impressive when compared with the amount of ODA ($56 billion) (Oxfam International 2002*b*: 35). But this must be seen against the pattern of distribution: it was highly concentrated in about ten states, with China dominating, and the majority of Southern countries received very little (see Figure 13.7). Indeed, in 2001, five developing countries accounted for 62 per cent of Southern FDI, while forty-nine LDCs attracted just 2 per cent of the Southern FDI, or 0.5 per cent of global FDI. Moreover, FDI still contributes a

relatively small share of gross capital formation in most Southern countries (with some notable exceptions, such as Malaysia and Singapore).

Assessments of the efficacy of this FDI are mixed. While UNCTAD (2002*c*) is generally positive, suggesting that FDI can bring benefits provided that host governments have the correct policy mix in place to encourage spillovers, some other assessments are more cautious. The International Labour Organization (ILO), for example, has voiced significant concerns regarding the conditions for 43 million workers in rapidly expanding Export Processing Zones (EPZs). EPZs, in order to attract FDI, are designed as tax free havens outside standard national social

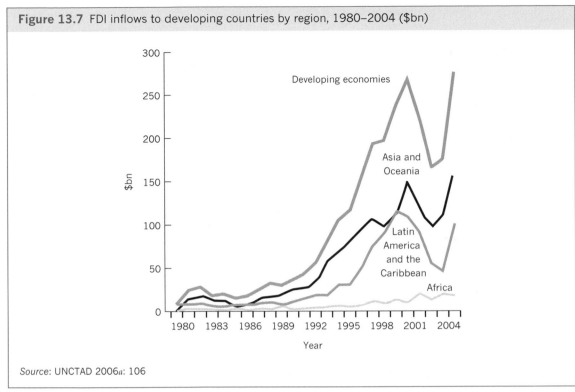

Figure 13.7 FDI inflows to developing countries by region, 1980–2004 ($bn)

Source: UNCTAD 2006*a*: 106

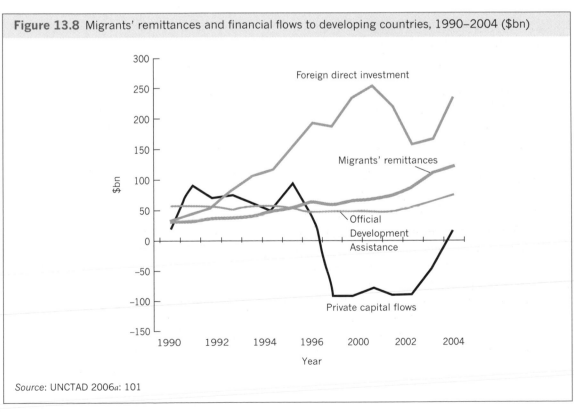

Figure 13.8 Migrants' remittances and financial flows to developing countries, 1990–2004 ($bn)

Source: UNCTAD 2006*a*: 101

or environmental regulation (ILO 2002; Oxfam International 2002*b*: 181).

7. *Private capital flows.* Private flows to the South, which dropped sharply after the debt crisis broke in 1982, increased dramatically in the early 1990s, before tailing off (see Figure 13.8). By 1996, they accounted for 85 per cent of resource flows.

But only about a dozen countries—the middle-income ones—benefited. Moreover, the quality of the flows posed problems for recipients: short-term portfolio investment grew fastest, and its volatile nature had the potential to undermine rather than support development efforts in recipient countries. The East Asian states discovered this to their cost.

KEY POINTS

- A significant shift in development policies from state-led to market-led approaches emerged at the beginning of the 1980s, coinciding with the rise of neo-liberalism.

- The World Bank and the IMF were assigned new roles in managing Third World debt, using conditionality attached to their lending to promote the neo-liberal policy agenda (the 'Washington Consensus') in LDCs.

- Despite an extended experience of structural adjustment, the economic performance of most developing countries has been disappointing.

- Industrialized countries' continuing protection of their markets hampered LDCs' development efforts, as did the relatively small amounts of foreign aid provided.

Post-Washington Consensus

These poor achievements fuelled criticism of the WC, with non-governmental organizations (NGOs) and civil society movements being particularly effective in their attacks. The Jubilee 2000 campaign against Third-World debt became extremely important, impacting on the G7 governments. The effects of financial crises in Mexico, East Asia, and Russia intensified the critique, as it was clearly not only in the poorest states that the WC did not seem to be working. Protests took place at WTO meetings and G7 summits. Criticism of the WC model mounted even within the IMF and the World Bank themselves. Notable individuals such as the World Bank's chief economist and senior vice-president, Joseph Stiglitz, argued that the lessons of the East Asian crisis of the late 1990s

was that inappropriately managed market liberalization was devastating for the poor. Stiglitz believed that globalization had to be made to work for the poor. He called for change, but his message was not well received within the IFIs. He left office in 2000, and published an international bestseller critical of IFI policy in 2002. With such criticisms of the WC mounting, the pace of global economic integration was set to be threatened, unless the benefits of the process were shared more evenly. Concerns about the possible link between poverty and conflict were voiced forcefully by the leaders of the IMF and World Bank (Thomas 2000: 3), and these were to be reinforced by the events of 11 September 2001. The Post-Washington Consensus (PWC) was born.

Whereas the WC aimed for growth, the PWC stresses that growth alone is not enough, it must be made 'pro-poor'; and that poverty reduction is crucial for development. Under the WC, the IMF and World Bank decided on the universal development blueprint; but under the PWC, national governments must own development strategies, and civil society must *participate* in their formulation. Blueprints must not be imposed by external actors. Conditions should relate to *processes* rather than *policies*. A new emphasis on *governance*—in other words, *who decide*—was a distinctive feature of the PWC.

The PWC discourse took off in 1999, with the ideas officially launched in World Bank President James Wolfensohn's Comprehensive Development Framework. The donor/creditor relationship looked set to change, as the language of *partnership* between donors and recipients permeated development discourse. National Poverty Reduction Strategy Papers (PRSPs) were identified by the IMF and the World Bank as the litmus test of a country's suitability for debt relief under the HIPC, and for new funds from multilateral and bilateral lenders. The *Enhanced* HIPC was launched, which moved away from the original HIPC's emphasis on debt sustainability, to a new emphasis on deeper, faster, broader relief linked directly to poverty reduction. Once a country qualified for debt relief under the Enhanced HIPC, *access* to relief would depend on acceptance by the IMF and World Bank Boards of the national PRSP.

The idea of the PRSP has been adopted rapidly by the official aid community, and it is now the centrepiece for policy dialogue in *all* countries seeking concessional funds. In April 2002, Wolfensohn's first recommendation, in setting out a post-Monterrey action plan to the DAC was the use of PRSPs as 'anchors for securing fresh donor support' (Wolfensohn 2002).

The language of the PWC is different from the WC, but in practice has much changed? Previous efforts to change institutional direction—such as the McNamara era of 'Growth with Equity'—do not inspire confidence in the capacity to change the institutional culture in the World Bank (see, for example, Ayres 1983). It is still early days for the PWC. However, critics have raised some legitimate concerns. Two related issues will be discussed here in respect of the PRSP, the central vehicle for the new approach: continuity in the policy focus with the WC, and the issue of ownership/sovereignty.

PRSPs: the issue of ownership

PRSPs were to be country-driven and owned, rather than imposed by outside actors such as the World Bank. But the PRSP infact *enables* the IMF and World Bank to assume even more extensive powers over developing countries than under the WC, as they are able to validate an *entire national development strategy,* including its social and political aspects. This is so even though they are only lending or underwriting a very small part of that strategy (Abugre 2000). Moreover, with the entire spectrum of donors aligning behind a single development strategy, as part of their coherence and harmonization policy, there is little room for flexibility or diversity among borrowers. Thus sovereignty can be further undermined.

PRSPs: the issue of policy

While the PRSPs encourage governments to focus more attention on some poverty issues, such as health and education, an important potential failing is *the continued absence of a real discussion of the link between macroeconomic policy and poverty creation, or inequality, or possible alternatives to the WC orthodoxy.* The primacy of *export-led growth as the route to development is not held up for scrutiny, but rather assumed, as common sense.* Also, some NGOs such as Eurodad (European Network on Debt and Development) argue that Poverty and Social Impact Analysis (PSIA) advocated by the World Bank to map potential effects of reform policies on the poor prior to their adoption does not seem to be working effectively (www.eurodad.org).

Given the emphasis on country ownership, how can we explain the limited nature of the debate? One reason is necessity. The poorest countries, starved of investment resources and crippled with debt burdens, are desperate for immediate debt reduction so as to free up resources for the importing of essential items without which they cannot function. Therefore, they are under intense pressure to develop PRSPs quickly, because without these they cannot receive debt reduction under the Enhanced HIPC, or new loans. They are drawing up these plans, however, in full knowledge that if their plans do not fit with the world view of the World Bank and Fund, they are unlikely to get approval, and this knowledge is bound to affect the shape of the plans. In some cases, the World Bank or IMF have been involved in the drawing up of the national paper. It is well known that in the case of Nicaragua, the draft PRSP was available in English in Washington before it was even available in Managua! A second reason may be the intellectual hegemony of the Bank: 'Through its global and national-level studies, and its extensive network of official, journalist and academic contacts, the Bank has a strong influence on policy debates' (Wilks and Lefrancois 2002: 8). The IFIs even provide a 1,000-page PRSP Sourcebook. Other reasons include the lack of bureaucratic capacity in many HIPCs, and the lack of well-organized domestic NGOs to participate in the process.

Despite the intention that PRSP loan conditions are related to processes, this does not seem to be supported by country experience. This is not entirely surprising. Since the World Bank and Fund understand poverty reduction to occur within the context of a trade-led growth-orientated strategy, the parameters of the national strategy are assumed. An inquiry conducted by a network of leading Southern NGOs of experiences in Latin America, Africa, and Asia suggested that: 'In every case examined the most important element of the PRSPs or interim PRSPs devised are the mandatory policy matrices. These orientations detail the now standardized Bank–Fund assortment of policy "reform" including liberalisation, privatisation, fiscal and administrative reform, assets management' (Jubilee South *et al.* 2002). Many loan conditions are the same as twenty years ago.

The same inquiry revealed that important issues are ignored, such as 'Policy and political measures indispensable in many cases to effective poverty and inequality reduction . . . land and agrarian reform, progressive taxation, support for domestic markets and protection, food sovereignty, the protection of the environment and labour *vis-à-vis* investors, assurances of social rights and entitlements, and other forms of governmental protection *vis-à-vis* the free market' (Jubilee South *et al.* 2002; para 5).

Development: roads to failure and success in the South

The PWC strategy does not seem to be sufficiently different from the WC as to make a crucial difference to outcomes in terms of growth and poverty reduction. In particular, the continued emphasis on the need for domestic policy reform in the South, and the emphasis on growth via trade liberalization,

---

BOX 13.10

Making the Rules: 'Global' in Name Only

'the main problem, from the perspective of poor countries is simply that the rules drawn up, and decisions handed down, at the WTO, the IMF and other international tribunals, are drawn up and handed down almost entirely by the rich countries. They have the negotiators, the expertise, the financial leverage, and in some cases (such as the IMF and World Bank) the weighted vote to win virtually every dispute. Even when rich countries clearly violate an agreement, their poor-country counterparts may lack the resources (meaning, often, simply the lawyers) to lodge a successful protest' (Finnegan 2003: 16).

coupled with the continued neglect of structural issues, is unbalanced. Moreover, the South's perception of lack of voice in global institutions and global rule making remains.

These problems are all too evident in the WTO's Doha Round (WTO 2003c), which began in November 2001, and faltered along until it collapsed in July 2006 (see Winham, Chapter 5 in this volume). The Doha Round was labelled 'the Development Round', and developing countries had high hopes that their concerns regarding trade would finally be addressed. However, both the nature of the agenda setting, and the general conduct of the negotiations, left them sorely disappointed.

At the Doha Conference in November 2001, it was decided through undemocratic means (for example, the exclusive Green Room process—see Box 13.11) that, instead of using its 'Development Round' to redress profound imbalances in its rules and the structure of trade, it would expand its power and remit. Despite the opposition of many developing countries and social movements, the WTO would negotiate agreements on four new areas—the Singapore issues, placed on the agenda at a WTO Ministerial meeting in Singapore in 1996: investment, competition, transparency in government procurement, and trade facilitation (Khor 2001). This undemocratic Green Room process and other unfair practices disadvantageous to the poorer countries have continued throughout the Doha Round (ActionAid 2006).

More than 100 NGOs from North and South joined together to declare the Doha Declaration—touted by supporters as a 'development agenda'—'Everything but development' (Joint Statement by NGOs 2001).

Developing countries and NGOs representing their interests are angry about the lack of attention to fundamental structural issues in WTO negotiations, and lack of respect for their special and different needs which must be addressed if Doha is to be a meaningful development round. Also, they are angry at the way in which the developed countries have pushed further trade liberalization in the South, even as the North has continued to undermine Southern efforts by protection, subsidies, and dumping. When, in May 2002, US president, George W. Bush, introduced a six-year, $51.7 billion farm

---

BOX 13.11

The Green Room Process

GATT negotiations developed a pattern known as the Green Room process. Representatives from a limited number of states sat at a table, exchanged drafts, and negotiated. An 'inner circle' of consensus was developed, and this was then sold to other members, so the circle of consensus expanded (Drahos 2002: 167).

The pattern continued with the WTO, where its supporters argue that the entire membership cannot negotiate on issues as this would take far too long. The process has come under attack from the developing countries and the global NGO community, who argue that democracy should not be sacrificed on the altar of efficiency. They say that while in theory the WTO is based 'on one state, one vote', this type of consensus formation is undemocratic and operates against the spirit of international co-operation.

Participation in Green Room meetings is by invitation only, and there are no published selection criteria for membership. The director-general (or occasionally the chairman) invites a small number of states—perhaps twenty-five—to discuss compromise texts on specific issues, and there is no written record of the discussions. The agenda is set, and the consensus built, among the few, on the behalf of the entire membership. The consensus is then presented to the majority as a take-it-or-leave-it package. The implications are far reaching, as the WTO creates legally binding and enforceable agreements for member governments worldwide.

(Adapted from Khor 1999 and NGO Coalition 2002.)

law, designed to boost crop and dairy subsidies for US farmers, by 67 per cent, this sounded a death knell for many Southern farmers, who would be unable to compete on the world market against these heavily subsidized US exports. The European Union is guilty of the same crime, and its 2003 reform of the Common Agricultural Policy did nothing significant to rectify the problem.

The failure of the WTO to reach agreement in Cancun in September 2003 reflected the South's level of frustration with the North, and consequent unwillingness to go along with new issues while their existing trade problems were sidelined by the North. Importantly, it represented a coming of age of the South within the WTO, as a powerful new bloc of the economically stronger Southern countries—the G20—made its presence felt.

The Doha Round debacle came in July 2006, when the USA refused to make a serious offer on cutting domestic subsidies for US farmers. The WTO's Doha Agenda, despite being billed as a development agenda, has not been perceived as such by the South. The Doha Development Round has failed to open the markets of the rich countries to Southern exports; it has not delivered on access to affordable generic medicine; and it has not dealt with Northern farm subsidies and dumping.

We can conclude that the PWC development strategy and policies advocated for the South by the IMF, World Bank, and WTO are unlikely to deliver the UN-sanctioned outcomes, the MDGs.

In contrast, evidence from the history of development of the East Asian NIEs, plus more recent evidence from India and China, suggests that growth with poverty reduction is achievable by a different route—one that assigns *an important place to the role of the state in development, and within this basic approach, encourages appropriate diversity rather than a policy straitjacket.*

Despite World Bank assessments claiming these countries' achievements as evidence of the market's ability to deliver, many analysts within those countries, and even in UN organizations, argue to the contrary (as do some former high-ranking members of the World Bank who have departed from office) (Bello 1997). As Box 13.12 shows, trade liberalization *followed* rather than *preceded* high growth in India and China.

Opinion remains divided. It is argued forcefully by various Southern governments, and an international network of NGOs from South and North, that progress in the East Asian NIEs, as well as more recently in India and China, has been state—rather than market—led, with a high degree

---

BOX 13.12

Trade Liberalization: Precedes or Follows High Rates of Growth in India and China?

'China and India implemented their main trade reforms about a decade after the onset of higher growth. Moreover, their trade restrictions remain among the highest in the world. The increase in China's growth started in the late 1970s. Trade liberalization did not start in earnest until much later, in the second half of the 1980s and especially in the 1990s—once the trend growth rate had already increased substantially. India's growth rate increased substantially in the early 1980s, while serious trade reform did not start until 1991–93.' (UNDP 2002: 31)

These UNDP findings are extremely important, as they suggest that the unadulterated free-trade mantra that still dominates IMF/World Bank/WTO policy on how to promote global economic integration (and therefore development) may well be misplaced. The study is not suggesting that states should never liberalize trade. Rather, it is suggesting that *the sequencing and intensity of trade liberalization policies may well be crucial for growth, and for human development.* In other words, states need to be mindful in their application of trade liberalization, and not see it as an end in itself that will necessarily bring the desired results.

of government intervention in a form of state-assisted capitalism. State planning was crucial, with governments deciding which 'infant industries' to protect with tariffs, and then encouraging exports when selected industries were strong enough to compete internationally. Governments negotiated favourable local content laws and technology transfer.

In the area of finance, they argue that the evidence suggests that states (and, of course, their people) that went against WC/PWC prescriptions regarding liberalization have weathered the storm of global financial volatility better than those that did not (Bello *et al.* 2000). Malaysia defied IMF prescriptions and imposed **capital controls**, and recovered from the crisis of the late 1990s more quickly than others that did not. The lesson was not lost on countries such as Hong Kong and Taiwan. China and India also have capital controls. Chile is often cited as a successful example of WC policies in Latin America, but this is not strictly true, as it too uses capital controls.

Such views on the central role of governments in development are still not shared by the IMF, or by mainstream economists, and dominant figures in the World Bank hierarchy would also have reservations. However, many are willing to accept that the state in success stories has played a positive role in non-sector-specific intervention—for example, education and technical training—maintaining low rates of inflation, government deficits, and so on. Regarding capital controls (of which there are many different types), they may concede that these are likely to be successful at best only as a temporary, short-term measure in today's globalized financial market, offering countries a breathing space (Hood 2001).

Despite this ongoing debate, one message is clear: the WC/PWC has not delivered growth with equity; in other words, it has not delivered development. However, development is occurring through other routes. Knowledge of these successes must inform future development paths.

KEY POINTS

- Poor performance under structural adjustment programmes led to criticism of the international financial institutions; this was intensified following the financial crises of the late 1990s.

- The international financial institutions and the governments of industrialized economies responded to these criticisms by adopting a new approach that emphasized poverty eradication (the 'Post-Washington Consensus').

- Although the Poverty Reduction Strategy Papers that are at the heart of the post-Washington

Consensus approach were intended to be devised by developing countries, the international financial institutions still dictate their terms.

- Southern countries have not perceived the 'Doha Round' as having development at the heart of its agenda.

- Debate continues over the appropriate role for the state in development, and the lessons to be learned from the success of the East Asian newly industrializing economies.

Development Prerequisites: Signs of Progress?

In this section, the task is to outline some indicative examples of the prerequisites of development in the South, based on experiences since the early 1980s. As recognized in the Monterrey Consensus 2002, discussed in the first section, these include both domestic and external/structural elements. In contrast to that Consensus, however, the evidence from the development successes and failures discussed in the third section suggests *that the appropriateness of market-led policies should be considered mindfully, rather than simply assumed.*

Voice for the South

There must be a greater voice for Southern states and peoples within the global governance of development (see Box 13.10 on page 436). Civil society groups have been campaigning on this issue since the mid- to late 1990s. The impact of their efforts was clear in the Monterrey Consensus, which referred to the need of the IMF and World Bank to 'continue to enhance the participation of all developing countries . . . in their decision-making' (UN 2002: point 63). This has been confined largely to capacity building; for example, supporting the efforts of the two African Executive Directors at the IMF, rather than increasing African representation on the Executive Boards of the IMF and World Bank. This must go much further, ideally to ensure that all member states can represent themselves fairly, and to remove veto power from a single country (Thomas 2004). At the September 2006 meetings of the IMF, it was agreed that China, South Korea, Mexico, and Turkey would increase their shareholdings in the IMF, and thus their voting power. While this is a step in the right direction, it has left the majority of developing countries extremely unhappy. The IMF is committed to further rebalancing of voting by 2008. With regard to the WTO, many Southern countries can afford at best only token representation at Geneva, while Northern delegations are extensive and reflect considerable technical expertise. Again, efforts to enhance the competency of Southern delegations are inadequate, and divert attention from the bigger issue of representation. This profound imbalance must be redressed if these global institutions are to have legitimacy in the eyes of global citizens.

Voice for the South is not simply a matter of *national representation* within the international arena; importantly, it embraces a voice for people at the grass roots within the South. While the PRSPs in theory include civil society in the making of national development plans, in practice this has not developed very far. If the making of PRSPs develops in the spirit that was intended, then the process would represent a potentially very important step towards genuinely expanding grass-roots participation in the formulation, and therefore also ownership, of development policy in the South (Cheru 2001).

Equity: the neglected element of domestic reform

The IFIs and donor states continue to define domestic reform in the South, primarily in terms of reducing corruption, strengthening the rule of law, and fostering an enabling environment for the private sector. These are very important. Yet one of the most important domestic underpinnings for development is *government commitment to growth with equity.*

Differences in income distribution are crucial in explaining interregional differences in poverty reduction (Watkins 1998: 38). In highly unequal societies, such as Brazil, the benefits of growth are distributed highly unequally. This means that unequal countries have to grow much more than more equal countries to bring benefits to the poor. This is supported by recent research by Milanovic regarding the impact of trade liberalization on poverty reduction, cited above.

Where governments have been committed to growth with equity, as in East Asia, progress has been very encouraging—especially when compared with areas where this has not been so, such as Latin America and SSA. East Asian governments have not been large spenders per capita on health and education, but the quality and target of their spending has ensured that *most people have access to basic services.*

More recently, there have been signs that, where debt write-off has taken place, concrete improvements are being experienced by local people within a short time scale. In Zambia, for example, the cancellation by the IMF of its $5 billion debt, was followed quickly by the introduction of universal basic health care. Debt write-off offers the opportunity for committed governments to make a difference to their citizens' lives.

Debt write-off

Civil society groups have campaigned since 1996 under the Jubilee 2000 umbrella for debt write-off for heavily indebted poor countries. For almost a decade, the response of the North was totally inadequate. While the HIPC represented an improvement on what preceded it in terms of dealing with the debt of the poorest, the fact that it was geared towards *sustainable debt* rather than *speedy total debt cancellation* was a major failing. No matter how hard the HIPCs tried, the continuous fall in commodity prices, and the continued deterioration in terms of trade, made sustainable debt repayment a fanciful idea, and outside their control.

An 'historic breakthrough' in the words of British Chancellor Gordon Brown, occurred in 2005 following a global civil society campaign, 'Make Poverty History'. In July, agreement was reached at the G8 summit in Gleneagles on the cancellation of $40 billion of debt owed by the HIPCs to the IMF, the World Bank and African Development Bank.

Countries would be eligible on completion of their HIPC programme. The deal has since been renamed the Multilateral Debt Relief Initiative (MDRI). In the same year, the IMF and World Bank, recognizing implicitly the shortcomings of the approach to debt management of the HIPC, announced a new Debt Sustainability Framework (DSF), which aimed to put debt at the centre of the IFIs' decision-making. Civil society groups have met both initiatives with a mixture of praise and criticism.

Campaigners were pleased with the qualitative change of approach to debt cancellation that came out of Gleneagles, but were disappointed with the quantitative result, which did not cover 100 per cent of countries or 100 per cent of debts. African HIPCs stood to benefit more than those of Latin America, and middle income countries were omitted. Campaigners became critical of delays to implementation. Eurodad (2006: 1) points out that while the IMF delivered $3.3 billion of debt cancellation on 6 January 2006, it took the World Bank and African Development Bank until July 2006 to start delivering on their promised debt cancellation. In the meantime, potential beneficiaries—some of the poorest countries in the world—continued to make debt service repayments. Also, civil society groups continue to emphasize that the overall Gleneagles package needs to be seen in context: low income countries still had $380 billion debt one year after the summit, and middle income countries $1.66 trillion (Eurodad 2006: 2). Campaigners have also been critical of the DSF, which they feel

---

BOX 13.13

UN Secretary General Kofi Annan's Thoughts on the Debt Challenge

The shortcomings of the HIPC and the challenge ahead were noted by the UN Secretary General in his report, *In Larger Freedom*:

'$54 billion ... committed for debt relief to 27 countries ... still falls far short of what is needed. To move forward, we should redefine debt sustainability as the level of debt that allows a country to achieve the Millennium Development Goals and reach 2015 without an increase in debt ratios. For most HIPC countries, this will require exclusively grant-based finance and 100 per cent debt cancellation, while for many heavily indebted non-HIPC and middle-income countries, it will require significantly more debt reduction than has yet been on offer.' (Annan 2005: 18)

should have the objective of reaching the MDGs at its heart.

More—and more effective—aid

Aid flows need both to increase and to become more predictable to have maximum effect. Less developed countries cannot mobilize adequate resources domestically to stimulate self-sustained growth. The World Bank has estimated that reaching the MDGs by 2015 will depend on a number of factors. In addition to the domestic policy reform in the South recommended by the World Bank, *an additional $40–60 billion per year in assistance will be needed until 2015* (World Bank 2002*c*). This figure has been criticized as a gross underestimate by Oxfam International, which suggests that an extra $100 billion is more realistic (Oxfam International 2002*a*).

At the G8 summit in July 2005, promises were made on new aid as well as debt cancellation. This offers some hope that the sharp declines in aid of the 1990s may be reversed, but the situation will need to be monitored closely. The donor community has historically been long on promises and short on delivery regarding ODA. The commitment to increase annual aid by $40 billion by 2010 will need to be honoured in spirit as well as in money, to ensure that new resources reach developing countries to tackle poverty alleviation. A report by a group of respected NGOs (Joint European NGO Report 2006) suggests that, while European member states are fulfilling their collective target set in 2002 of 0.39 per cent of their gross national income in aid by 2006, almost a-third of their ODA in 2005 was spent on debt cancellation for Iraq and Nigeria, foreign students, and refugees in donor states. It is imperative that they are not tied to the purchases of goods or services of Northern donors, and that they are put to the most effective use possible at the point of delivery. UNCTAD (2002*a*: 222) suggests that there should be selective targeting of areas where the money could make a real difference in poverty alleviation, and highlights agriculture as an obvious target.

Donor countries must be encouraged to live up to their commitments, and in this respect NGOs have suggested a legally binding treaty to make donors comply with internationally agreed ODA targets. While this may seem politically unrealistic, history shows us that dramatic changes in attitude often occur unexpectedly.

In addition, new ways of funding additional resources can be explored (CAFOD *et al.* 2003). Several ideas have been put forward. A Tobin Tax—a tax on foreign exchange transactions—could contribute to new development funds (Raffer and Singer 2001; Jetin and de Brunhof 2000). First mooted in the 1970s, it has gained more political momentum in the wake of the global financial crises that have accompanied capital liberalization. The primary aim of the tax would be to reduce the instability that has wreaked havoc with the international financial system and destroyed livelihoods in the South. A secondary benefit of the tax is that it could generate extra resources for development. Another way to raise money for development would be through stronger international co-operation on taxation. For example, it has been suggested that tax havens result in losses to Western governments of $50 billion per annum—money that could be directed to development (Wabl 2002). A third possibility is the idea of development bonds, launched by Chancellor Gordon Brown (CAFOD *et al.* 2003). While sceptics will raise concerns about political acceptability, workability, and so on of such measures, supporters will point to the step-by-step building of a new consensus which they see as gradually eroding the legitimacy of neo-liberalism.

Trade for development

A multilateral trade system serious about development must put the special and different nature of economies at the heart of its agenda. This has been an issue since the 1950s, and it will not go away. The working assumption of the WTO, that trade liberalization equals development, must be unpicked. Trade liberalization can help and it can harm: a blanket approach is not appropriate. Moreover, it is not at all clear that the WTO as currently constituted is the appropriate locus for decisions about development.

Greater efforts must be made to give the South a bigger role in trade decisions and agenda setting. Until this happens, key issues for the well-being of citizens in the South will not be considered appropriately. For example, unless progress is made on commodities—especially basic agricultural commodities—the living conditions of the poor in developing countries will not improve at the rate necessary to meet the Millennium Development Goal on hunger. Urgent action is needed. UNCTAD set up a UN International Task Force on Commodities in 2004; whether this group can challenge and change the WTO agenda remains to be seen. Much rides on this.

Other prerequisites

The list of development prerequisites is long. Aspects not discussed here because of space constraints include, for example, technology transfer; accountability for the North via a commitment to development index (UNDP 2003a: 161); greater South–South co-operation; the regulation of capital in the interests of development; and, increasingly, the productive use of remittances. These can be followed up via the References and Further reading.

KEY POINTS

Experiences since the 1980s suggest the following prerequisites for development:
- An enhanced role for the South in key global institutions;
- Commitment to growth with equity, and to poverty eradication;

- The writing-off of the debts of the HIPC;
- Additional and more effective aid; and
- Reform of the trade **regime** to remove impediments to developing countries' exports.

Conclusion

Since the 1980s, market-led globalization has been substituted for nationally-driven development policies in the South. The result has been unsatisfactory: the deepening impoverishment of entire world regions, states, and the majority of humanity, amid greater but evermore concentrated wealth and opportunity. In these circumstances there is a legitimate worry that the current course of globalization may not be appropriate to meet the development challenge that lies ahead. In continuing to advocate this path for the South, the IMF, World Bank, and the WTO—and the G7 from whom they take their cue—are promoting policies at odds with the achievement of the MDGs accepted by the UN General Assembly.

It will take far more than a tweaking of the prevailing order to promote growth with equity in the South. Reform within developing countries is a necessary but insufficient condition to achieve these goals; it must extend outside the borders of developing countries to encompass global economic and financial structures, and the process of governance itself. Only when both parts of the equation—the domestic and the structural/external—are addressed, will there be a chance for the language of the PWC to be translated into sustainable results for the majority of humankind.

But even that may not be enough. Since 1945, the development challenge has been understood largely in terms of modernization theory or structuralist theory. Both of these approaches allow for gains for the South within the existing global economic order. But to date these gains have not been extensive enough, nor have they reached enough people. Time will tell whether another approach is necessary to promote development for all humanity, one that prioritizes the needs of all human beings rather than capital or a narrow band of humanity. If this is necessary, then it will require a rejection of the current global economic and political order, rather than accommodation of the South within it.

QUESTIONS

1. Why are there so many different terms to refer to the poorer states in the international system?

2. Why did the poorer states find the United Nations a more congenial environment than the International Monetary Fund and the World Bank in the early post-Second-World-War decades?

3. Explain modernization theory and structuralist theory.

4. Why did the developing countries call for a New International Economic Order in 1973, and what did they hope to achieve?

5. What was the 'Washington Consensus'?

6. How far does the World Bank's recent emphasis on national Poverty Reduction Strategy Papers represent a change of policy on development matters?

7. What are the Millennium Development Goals, and to what extent are they owned by North and South?

8. What is the significance of the Monterrey Consensus?

9. Why has trade liberalization not delivered expected results for the least developed countries?

10. How could financial resources for development be increased?

11. What do you think are the most important prerequisites for development in the South, and why?

FURTHER READING

General

 Chossudovsky, M. (1997), *The Globalisation of Poverty: Impacts of IMF and World Bank Reforms* (London: Zed Books Penang: Third World Network). The author draws on examples from the Third World and Eastern Europe to provide a lucid and cogent critique of IFI policies.

 Hoogevelt, A. (1997), *Globalisation and the Postcolonial World: The New Political Economy of Development* (London: Macmillan). A historically and theoretically well-informed comparison of the impacts of globalization and the responses to it in Sub-Saharan Africa, the Middle East, East Asia, and Latin America.

Trade

■ Kiely, R. (2006), *The New Political Economy of Development: Globalization, Imperialism and Hegemony* (Basingstoke: Palgrave Macmillan). An interesting text, which examines development in an historic and political–economic context.

■ Barratt Brown, M. (1993), *Fair Trade* (London: Zed Books).

■ World Bank Institute (2003), *Development Outreach*, July, whole edition on Trade for Development: www1.worldbank.org/devoutreach. Interesting collection of accessible articles from different viewpoints.

Investment

■ Picciotto, S., and Mayne, R. (eds) (1999), *Regulating International Business: Beyond Liberalization* (London: Macmillan).

■ Madeley, J. (1999), *Big Business, Poor Peoples: The Impact of Transnational Corporations on the World's Poor* (London: Zed Books).

Aid

■ Randel, J., German, T. and Ewing, D. (eds) (2000), *The Reality of Aid 2000: An Independent Review of Poverty Reduction and Development Assistance* (London: Earthscan).

Health

■ Kim, J., Millen, J., Irwin, A., and Gershman, J. (eds) (2000), *Dying for Growth: Global Inequality and the Health of the Poor* (Monroe, Me.: Common Courage Press). An excellent reader on effects of WC on health.

■ Farmer, P. (2003), *Pathologies of Power: Health, Human Rights and the War on the Poor* (Berkeley, Calif. and Los Angeles: University of California Press).

Development

■ Greig, A., Hulme, D., and Turner, M. (2007), *Challenging Global Inequality: Development Theory and Practice in the 21st Century* (Basingstoke: Palgrave Macmillan). An accessible overview.

■ Preston, P. (1996), *Development Theory: An Introduction* (Oxford: Basil Blackwell). A good general reader.

■ Sachs, G. (1993), *The Development Dictionary* (London: Zed Books). Thought-provoking definitions which challenge mainstream analyses.

Development and security

■ Duffield, M. (2001), *Global Governance and the New Wars* (London: Zed Books). An original and fascinating book that examines the current framing by donors of the link between security and development.

■ **Rogers, P. (2002),** *Losing Control: Global Security in the Twenty–First Century,* **2nd edn** (London: Pluto). Examines core global security issues, including poverty and inequality.

 WEB LINKS

● Southern NGOs/independent research institutes

www.twnside.org.sg Third World Network (based in Malaysia).

www.focusweb.org Focus on the Global South (based in Thailand).

www.choike.org Choike: a portal on Southern civil societies (based in Uruguay).

www.seatini.org SEATINI: Southern and Eastern African Trade Information and Negotiations Institute (based in Zimbabwe).

● Southern intergovernmental organizations

www.g77.org The Group of 77 at the United Nations.

www.nam.gov.za The Non-Aligned Movement.

www.southcentre.org South Centre.

● Northern NGOs

www.eurodad.org European Network on Debt and Development.

www.brettonwoods.org Bretton Woods Project: scrutinizes and attempts to influence the World Bank and International Monetary Fund (IMF).

● International organizations

www.imf.org International Monetary Fund.

www.worldbank.org International Bank for Regional Development.

www.wto.org/english/tratop_e/dda_e/dda_e.htm Doha Development Agenda.

www.unctad.org UNCTAD.

 Visit the Online Resource Centre that accompanies this book for more information: www.oxfordtextbooks.co.uk/orc/ravenhill2e/

Appendix 13.1

Figure 13.9 Heavily indebted poor countries (HIPC)

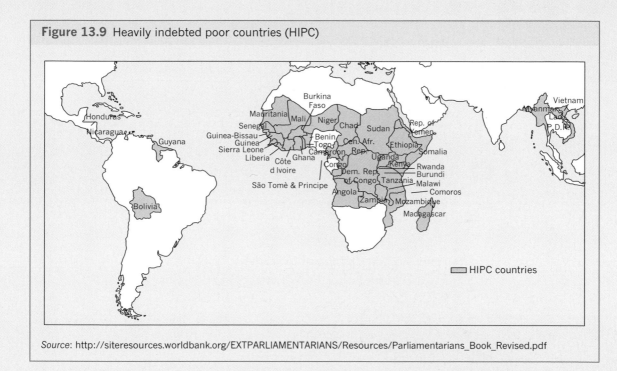

Source: http://siteresources.worldbank.org/EXTPARLIAMENTARIANS/Resources/Parliamentarians_Book_Revised.pdf

14 Globalization and the Environment

PETER DAUVERGNE

Chapter Contents

- Introduction: Globalization and Environmental Change
- History of Global Environmentalism
- Economic Growth, Trade, and Corporations
- A Sustainable Future? Financing and Regimes
- Conclusion

Reader's Guide

Globalization is transforming the health of the planet. There is nothing particularly controversial about this statement. Yet sharp disagreements arise over the nature of this transformation. Is globalization a force of progress and environmental solutions? Or is it a *cause* of our current global environmental crisis? This chapter explores these questions by examining the debates around some of the most contentious issues at the core of economic globalization and the environment: economic growth, production, and consumption; trade; and transnational investment. It begins with a glance at the general arguments about how globalization affects the global environment. Then, to set the stage for an analysis of more specific arguments about the global political economy of the environment, it sketches the history of global environmentalism—in particular the emergence of global environmental institutions (including regimes) with the norm of sustainable development. The last section builds on these arguments to assess the effectiveness of North–South environmental financing and global environmental regimes.

Introduction: Globalization and Environmental Change

Globalization is altering the global environment. Few scholars of global environmental politics would challenge this statement (see Box 14.1). The nature of the change, however, is hotly debated. Some argue it is a source of progress and ingenuity and co-operation, of a future world with much better environmental conditions for all. Others argue it is accelerating the process of the capitalist exploitation of nature and humanity, spinning the globe faster and faster toward an ecological meltdown.

Globalization and a healthy planet

The optimists see globalization as a process that fosters economic growth and raises per capita incomes, both essential to generate the funds and political will for global environmental management. Optimists see other environmental benefits from globalization as well. It is promoting global integration and co-operation as well as common environmental norms and standards, which are enhancing the capacity of a system of sovereign states to manage problems such as ozone depletion and climate change. It is pushing states to liberalize trade and foreign investment, promote specialization, and eliminate subsidies, which in the past have contributed to market failures and suboptimal economic and environmental outcomes. It is enhancing the capacity of developing states for environmental management through the transfer of technologies, knowledge, and development assistance. And it is contributing to a host of domestic reforms to policies—such as better environmental laws, stronger institutions, and more secure property rights.

Optimists such as environmental writers Julian Simon, Gregg Easterbrook, and Bjørn Lomborg see a past full of progress and a future full of hope and socio-ecological triumph. There is every reason

---

BOX 14.1

Globalization

This chapter assumes that globalization is an ongoing and accelerating process that is restructuring and increasing connections among economies, institutions, and civil societies. This dynamic and multidimensional process is integrating trade, production, and finance as well as strengthening global norms and global social forces. A constellation of forces drives globalization, including new and faster technologies (such as computers) as well as the increasing dominance of capitalism and Western ideologies. In the simplest terms, it is leading to a 'world as a single place', where changes in distant lands affect people around the globe more quickly, and with greater frequency and intensity (Scholte 1997: 14). It is, in the words of Thomas Friedman (2002), 'the integration of everything with everything else . . . the integration of markets, finance, and technology in a way that shrinks the world from a size medium to a size small. Globalization enables each of us, wherever we live, to reach around the world farther, faster, deeper, and cheaper than ever before and at the same time allows the world to reach into each of us farther, faster, deeper, and cheaper than ever before.' This does not assume the process of globalization is even or equal within or across countries. The rich in Europe and America are unquestionably benefiting far more than the poor of Africa, Asia, and Latin America. The process is also not inevitable. States and societies can resist and reverse globalization.

to believe that economic growth and technological progress will continue for ever. 'The standard of living,' Simon (1996: 12) argues, 'has risen along with the size of the world's population since the beginning of recorded time. There is no convincing economic reason why these trends toward a better life should not continue indefinitely.' Simon's lifetime of work has stirred a hornet's nest of environmental critics. Writers such as Easterbrook, however, see him as profound and brave. 'There was a time,' Easterbook (1995: xxi) argues, 'when to cry alarm regarding environmental affairs was the daring position. Now it's the safe position: People get upset when you say things may turn out fine.' Writers such as Lomborg add, too, that there is little statistical evidence of a global environmental crisis—that this common misperception is more a result of media hype and non-governmental organization (NGO) fund-raising antics than real problems. 'Mankind's lot,' Lomborg (2001: 4) asserts, 'has actually improved in terms of practically every measurable indicator . . . We are not running out of energy or natural resources . . . Acid rain does not kill the forests, and the air and water around us are becoming less and less polluted.'

Simon, Easterbrook, and Lomborg are at the extreme of the optimistic end of the spectrum of opinion. Most supporters of globalization—those in governments such as the United States and the United Kingdom, and in global institutions such as the World Bank and the World Trade Organization—emphasize the need for a practical view that looks towards future generations. These supporters argue that some degree of ecological change and loss is inevitable, but the consistent trend under globalization is towards a future that looks like Britain, France, and the United States, not one that looks like Ethiopia, Cambodia, and Guyana. History demonstrates the great strides of humanity. Just a hundred years ago cities such as London and New York were filthy and unhealthy. Today, health conditions in virtually every city in the North are vastly improved. One of the greatest feats has been the increase in food production. In the middle of the twentieth century close to half of the people in

the South were starving. By 1970 it was less than a-third; at the time of writing, it is less than a-sixth (WFS 1996: 1; Lomborg 2001: 61).

Just over two hundred years ago, Thomas Malthus (1798) predicted that exponential population growth would, following the laws of basic maths, inevitably surpass arithmetical food production: and mass starvation would thus ensue. Since then, many scholars, now commonly called Malthusians or neo-Malthusians, have continued to tout the same logic. Yet, optimists stress, Malthus was flat-out wrong, primarily because he discounted the ability of human ingenuity to increase agricultural yields. The Green Revolution of the 1960s saw scientists and farmers work together to produce fast-growing, pest-resistant, high-yield crops able to grow just about anywhere (with the help of irrigation, fertilizers, and pesticides). There is, as a result, plenty of food today. And it is far cheaper—global food prices have fallen by two-thirds in real terms since 1957. People starve at present because of inefficient distribution and incompetent governments, not because of insufficient global food supplies. For optimists, perhaps the most revealing statistic of all is global life expectancy: in 1900 it was a mere thirty years; in 1950, forty-six years; at the start up the twenty-first century, it is over sixty-six years (Lomborg 2001: 50–51, 61; World Bank 2002d). Granted, such progress has demanded changes, including some global environmental changes. But, optimists stress, science and human ingenuity have time and again shown the capacity to respond with even more progress.

The view that globalization is a basically positive ecological force dominates global economic and environmental negotiations, and institutional decision-making. The debate here ranges over how best to channel globalization so as to minimize environmental damage and maximize socio-economic progress (which, in the long run, must occur for effective global environmental management). Some argue for few, if any, restraints. Others see a need to guide globalization with national environmental agencies, and strong global norms and institutions. There are, however, many scholars and activists who challenge the core assumptions behind these views—that is, they see globalization as a core cause of the current ecological crisis.

Globalization and ecological collapse

Environmental critics of globalization worry that it is luring humanity towards a global fate not unlike that of Easter Island of 300 years ago, where ecological decay drove a once thriving people to violence and cannibalism in just a few centuries (Rees 2002: 249). Particularly worrying for these critics is that so-called progress and scientific reason has created, in the words of Paul Ehrlich's (1968) infamous book title, 'a population bomb', an explosion from fewer than 300 million people at the time of Christ to over 6.6 billion today (see Figure 14.1). Globalization, critics contend, is compounding the ecological impact of more than 200,000 people being added to the planet every day. It reinforces the neoclassical economic assumption that indefinite economic growth is both possible and desirable. It assumes, too, that it is possible and logical for the South to follow the development path of the North and continue to industrialize and intensify agricultural production. The globe can barely sustain its current

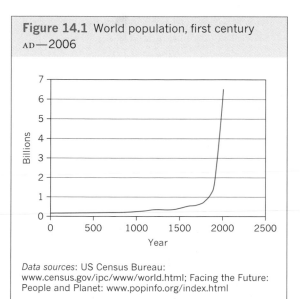

Figure 14.1 World population, first century AD—2006

Data sources: US Census Bureau: www.census.gov/ipc/www/world.html; Facing the Future: People and Planet: www.popinfo.org/index.html

population. How, critics ask, can it sustain another 3 billion in 2050? How can Africa sustain an additional 1 billion people in 2050, more than double its current population? (See Population Reference Bureau 2002: 4.)

The net effect of globalization, moreover, is to enlarge the ecological footprint of *each* person on the planet, by promoting ever more economic growth as well as cultivating an almost religious faith in the value of consumption—in the value of electronic toys, cars, and fast food (Robbins 2002)—all of which requires increasing amounts of natural resources, energy, and infrastructure to produce. The growing integration and disparities among economies are also increasing the extent and number of ecological shadows, which tend to shift the ecological damage of more powerful economies on to weaker economies (see Box 14.2).

Critics contend, too, that globalization is encouraging ever more economic growth and production with no real concern about unequal or unsustainable patterns of consumption. It exacerbates the ecological inequality within and between countries, and marginalizes women, indigenous peoples, and the poor. The global political economy is constructing, for critics such as William Rees and Laura Westra (2003), a world of 'eco-apartheid' and 'eco-violence'. Globalization tears, too, at the fabric of local communities, destroying historic patterns of trust, co-operation, and knowledge so essential to ecological and social balance. In short, it destroys the living environments of much of the world's people.

There can be, in the view of critics, no environmental justice or biological balance in a globalized world where the super-rich like Bill Gates and J. K. Rowling live alongside (metaphorically, that is, in their mansions) the 1.2 billion who live on less than $1 per day, and the 2.7 billion who live on less than $2 per day. Over a billion people do not have access to clean water (UNFPA 2001: 5). Over 800 million people in the South suffer from chronic malnutrition. Unhealthy environments aggravate illnesses—contributing, for example, to the deaths of more than 4.7 million children under the age of

BOX 14.2

Ecological Footprints and Shadows

Ecological footprints

Bill Rees and Mathis Wackernagel created this concept to measure the sustainability of human lifestyles. It translates human consumption of renewable natural resources into hectares of average biologically productive land. A person's footprint is the total area in global hectares (one hectare of average biological productivity) required to sustain his or her lifestyle: food and water, clothing, shelter, transportation, and consumer goods and services. The concept allows an analyst to compare the average ecological impact of people from Africa to Australia to China to the United Kingdom to the United States. The average global ecological footprint in 2003 was 2.2 global hectares per person. There were, however, great differences across the globe. In Africa, it was about 1.1 global hectares (with a low in Somalia of 0.4) and in China it was 1.6. 'In contrast, the average footprint of someone in the United Kingdom was 5.6, and in the United States 9.6.

This measure also allows an analyst to compare the world ecological footprint with the total biological productive capacity of the earth. The total productive capacity of the earth in 1999 was roughly 11.4 billion hectares. Between 1961 and 1999, the world ecological footprint grew by 80 per cent, reaching 13.7 billion hectares in 1999—20 per cent above the earth's biological capacity. The state of the globe, according to this measure, is continuing to worsen—and at the time of writing the world's ecological footprint is 25 per cent above the planet's ability to regenerate. Humanity, the World Wide Find for Nature (WWF) laments, is now 'running an ecological deficit with the Earth'.

Sources: Wackernagel and Rees (1996); WWF (2002): 2–4, 22–28; WWF (2006): 28–34.

Ecological shadows

This concept is designed to capture the extent of the environmental impact of a nation state in jurisdictions beyond its sovereign control. Ecological shadows arise as economies, through both intentional and unintentional patterns of consumption, trade, investment, and financing, transfer the environmental harm of its citizens outside its territory. This concept is particularly useful for analysing the environmental impact of more powerful economies on weaker (dependent) economies. The United States, for example, casts a large ecological shadow over South America. Such shadows can extend down a chain of weaker economies. Japan, for example, casts an ecological shadow over Thailand, which in turn casts a shadow over neighbours such as Cambodia and Laos. Ecological shadows do not arise from straightforward North–South exploitation. Often, elites in weak economies in the South profit personally from these ecological shadows, commonly acting as the agents of the ecological destruction—for example, as miners, fishers, and loggers.

Sources: MacNeill *et al.* (1991); Dauvergne (1997)

---

5 in 2000 (WHO 2002). The future under current patterns of globalization, critics argue, is one of still greater horrors: of pandemics such as AIDS, which UNAIDS (2002) predicts will kill 68 million people between 2000 and 2020. Over 80 per cent of these victims will come from Sub-Saharan Africa, where average life expectancy has already fallen to just 46 years. What is needed, critics like Colin Hines (2000) argue, is not globalization, but localization.

The latest biological trends, critics further note, confirm the beginnings of a global Easter Island. Humans are now the dominant predator in every ecosystem (even in the seemingly limitless Pacific and Atlantic oceans), and unless strict restraints are put in place, humans will exhaust the globe's natural resources, fill its sinks, and overstep the earth's capacity to support life. Half the world's forests and wetlands are already gone. Every day another thirty to 100 species become extinct. One of the more worrying findings in recent years, say critics, is the ten-year survey by Ransom Myers and Boris Worm (2003), which found a 90 per cent decline in the ocean's large predatory fish—such as tuna, swordfish, marlin, cod, and flounder—since the 1950s. The waters of Ernest Hemingway's *The Old Man and the Sea* will soon be empty of the majestic marlin, a startling testimony, critics warn, not to the environmental consequences of the exploits of men such as Hemingway's old man, Santiago, but to the greed of industrial fishing boats plying the oceans to feed global markets.

Supporters and critics of a globalizing world, then, hold starkly different pictures of the current and future state of the global environment. The trends and statistics to support the statement 'globalization is good for the environment' seem convincing. Yet so do the trends and statistics that say 'globalization is bad for the environment'. The truth seems to lie somewhere in the middle: globalization is producing both constructive and destructive ecological processes. The goal is to harness globalization in some way to ensure sustainability. What has the global community done so far to harness globalization and manage global environmental affairs? The next section examines the history of environmentalism with an eye on this question.

KEY POINTS

- Some perceive the net ecological impact of globalization as being positive, as a force for progress and better lives. It fosters economic growth and co-operative institutions—both of these necessary in the long run to manage the global environment.

- Others see the net impact as negative, as a force sinking the globe into a bog of ecological decay. It is accelerating the destructive process of too many people consuming too many natural resources with no concern for equality or justice.

- Both the pro- and anti-globalization camps present persuasive data and arguments. Globalization involves multiple and complex sets of overlapping processes. Inevitably, there will be manifold and at times cross-cutting effects on the global environment.

History of Global Environmentalism

Collective human efforts to control nature began in earnest 8,000 to 15,000 years ago, as nomadic hunters-and-gatherers in various locales began to change to settled agriculture. Great civilizations sprang up, inventing such wonders as the plough (animal drawn), the wheel, writing, and numbers. Often, nature was subsumed in the quest for human progress, and many civilizations cut down regional forests, degraded land, and polluted local waters. Environmental decay even toppled a few great civilizations, such as Mesopotamia (a land between the Tigris and Euphrates rivers, part of contemporary Iraq), where a poorly designed irrigation system gradually poisoned the agricultural land with salt. For most of the history of civilization, however, the scale of human activity has been too small to alter the global environment—that is, to induce climate change, deplete the ozone layer, empty the oceans, or destroy global biodiversity stocks.

This began to change with the dawn of the Industrial Revolution some 300 years ago. Production and energy use (including the burning of coal) began to rise rapidly. The global population of 600 million or so began to multiply. There were a billion people by the early 1800s; and 2 billion by the end of the 1920s. The wealthy began to extract more natural resources, more quickly, from increasingly remote parts of the globe (often through colonial administrations). Such activities strained local and regional environments. The evidence was stark. Smog in cities like London and New York killed thousands in the nineteenth and twentieth centuries. Once seemingly boundless species, like the plains bison of North America, were brought to near extinction. Some, like the passenger pigeon, a bird that once migrated through eastern North America in its millions, became extinct (in 1914).

Governments reacted to these environmental disasters with new national and regional policies. At first these were aimed primarily at either conservation of wildlife or more effective resource management. Canada and the United States, for example, signed the Migratory Birds Treaty in 1918. Colonial powers reacted as well, putting in place policies (like sustained yield management) to try to ensure more efficient and rational resource extraction. After the Second World War, ordinary citizens began to become increasingly worried about the biological impacts of industrialization and agricultural production. Anxiety mounted after Rachel Carson's (1962) best-seller, *Silent Spring*, shocked popular consciousness with images of pesticide-laden food chains and dying ecosystems.

Worries about the health of the 'global environment' also began to emerge around this time. The picture of the earth from space, beautiful and fragile and borderless, became a compelling global ecological image. These concerns fed into the sense of the mutual economic vulnerability of post-war economies (in both the North and the South). Paul Ehrlich's 1968 best-seller, *The Population Bomb*, added a new and perturbing image: the earth left barren by an exploding population. 'In the 1970s,' Ehrlich predicted boldly, 'the world will undergo famines—hundreds of millions of people are going to starve to death' (1968: xi).

Concern over the health of the global environment continued to rise in the late 1960s and early 1970s. Experts met in 1968 at the United Nations Biosphere Conference to discuss global environmental problems. The first Earth Day was held in the United States in April 1970. Twenty million people rallied—one of the largest organized demonstrations in the history of the United States. That same year, the US government founded the Environmental Protection Agency (EPA). Canada created a

Department of the Environment the following year. One outcome of this growing societal and political concern was the United Nations Conference on the Human Environment, held in Stockholm, Sweden, in June 1972.

The Stockholm Conference and the 1970s

The Stockholm Conference, organized by Canada's Maurice Strong, was the first global United Nations conference on the environment for state officials. There were 1,200 delegates from over a hundred countries. Swedish Prime Minister Olaf Palme and Indian Prime Minister Indira Gandhi were the only heads of state to attend. Russia and the communist bloc countries boycotted the conference, to protest against the exclusion of East Germany.

The North was interested initially in addressing industrial pollution, nature conservation, and population growth. The South was more worried about development, and did not want the anxieties of rich conservationists to deny poorer countries the benefits of economic growth and industrialization (an ongoing source of conflict). There were tensions, too, over who would pay, and who was responsible for solving global environmental problems. Many Southern delegates saw global capitalism as a core reason for poverty, and there was general anger that global economic institutions were pushing developing countries to export raw materials on declining terms of trade. The phrase 'the pollution of poverty' was coined at Stockholm, to express the idea that poverty was the greatest global environmental threat. Many delegates from the South called for global economic reforms to help solve the pollution of poverty.

In the end, conference delegates tried to reconcile the desire (need) for economic development in the South with the need to protect the global environment for all. Most governments came to recognize the mutual interdependence and vulnerability of North and South. The official conference documents, however, did not emphasize the Southern calls for global economic reforms. The conference produced a Declaration on the Human Environment (with twenty-six principles), an Action Plan for the Human Environment (with 109 recommendations), and a Resolution on Institutional and Financial Arrangements. These were non-binding on signatory states—and most scholars agree that Stockholm produced few practical commitments to address global environmental change.

The Stockholm Conference did, however, signal a growing concern among national governments over the global environment. It also led to a General Assembly decision to create the United Nations Environment Programme (UNEP), launched officially in 1973, with Maurice Strong as the first executive director. The United Nations Environment Programme was designed as a relatively weak global institution. Its headquarters were in Nairobi, Kenya, rather than New York or Geneva, and it was established as a co-ordinating programme with a small budget rather than as a specialized agency. This was in the interest of all sides: the North did not want to finance a large institution; and the South did not want a global institution with the power to interfere with development goals. And other United Nations agencies did not want to relinquish significant 'turf' (Elliot 1998: 11–13).

After Stockholm, the Organization of Petroleum Exporting Countries' success in raising the price of oil dramatically through limiting output in 1973–4 rocked the global economy. Oil prices quadrupled, inflation soared, and economic growth became sluggish worldwide. Many developing economies, particularly those in Latin America and Africa, began to experience debt crises. This economic turbulence deflated some of the potential for more aggressive global environmental initiatives after Stockholm. The South, in particular, became even more worried about the effects on debt levels and prospects for industrial development. Still, the debate over how to handle global environmental change continued, sparked by groundbreaking books such as the Club of Rome's (1972) *Limits to Growth* and E. F. Schumacher's (1973) *Small*

is Beautiful. The global community also signed noteworthy global environmental treaties just after Stockholm. These include the Convention on the Prevention of Marine Pollution by Dumping of Wastes and other Matter (the London Convention, 1972, which came into force in 1975), and the Convention on International Trade in Endangered Species of Wild Flora and Fauna (CITES, 1973, coming into force in 1975).

Environment slid more into the background of global affairs in the second half of the 1970s and first half of the 1980s, as conservative governments came to power in leading industrialized economies, and Southern economies sank further into debt. There was nevertheless a great deal of environmental activity. Scientists continued to research global environmental change. Non-governmental organizations continued to campaign and pressure governments and firms. Individual states, including some in the South, continued to establish environmental agencies. States also continued to sign and ratify global environmental agreements, such as the 1980 Convention on the Conservation of Antarctic Marine Living Resources (which came into force in 1982). The global community, too, continued to debate and make some headway on how best to manage the need for development (especially in the South) with the need for a healthy global environment. Problems such as the depletion of the ozone layer, and disasters such as the nuclear accident at Three Mile Island in 1979, the Union Carbide chemical leak in Bhopal in 1984, and the Chernobyl nuclear meltdown in 1986, added a sense of urgency. Slowly, environmental issues began to move once more up the global agenda. The debate by the mid-1980s began to focus increasingly on the concept of *sustainable development*. The publication in 1987 of the World Commission on Environment and Development report, *Our Common Future*, synthesized and consolidated the global debates over environment and development, defining sustainable development as 'development that meets the needs of the present without compromising the ability of future generations to meet their own needs' (WCED 1987: 43).

The Brundtland Commission

The World Commission on Environment and Development, commonly known as the Brundtland Commission, was chaired by the former prime minister of Norway, Gro Harlem Brundtland. There were twenty-three members serving in an expert rather than an official state capacity—and thirteen were from the South, including from India, China, and Brazil. Among G7 countries, only France and the United Kingdom did not send representatives. The Commission's report *Our Common Future*, commonly known as the Brundtland Report, is widely seen as a watershed in the evolution of environmental debates within the global community of state representatives. The content of the Brundtland Report is an ingenious compromise. It did not foresee any necessary limits to growth, and industrialization and natural resource production, under correct management, were viewed as being acceptable, indeed inevitable, for some countries. The report called for a transfer of environmental technologies and economic assistance to support sustainable development in the South. It called, too, for more effective controls on population growth, as well as better education and food security in the South. It portrayed poverty as a core cause of unsustainable development. The source of much of the poverty in the South, it argued, is the position of developing economies within the global structure. The best way forward, then, is to stimulate—not slow down—economic growth: not the unchecked growth of the 1960s and 1970s, however, but growth from sustainable development.

States continued to negotiate and sign global environmental treaties leading up to and after the publication of the Brundtland Report. These include the 1985 Vienna Convention for the Protection of the Ozone Layer, the 1987 Montreal Protocol on Substances that Deplete the Ozone Layer, and the 1989 Basel Convention on the Control of Transboundary Movements of Hazardous Waste and their Disposal. By the late 1980s, global environmental issues had again crept back to the top of the global agenda, culminating in a 1989 United Nations General Assembly resolution to hold the first summit of world leaders on the global environment: what became the 1992 United Nations Conference on Environment and Development (UNCED), held in Rio de Janeiro, Brazil.

The Rio (Earth) Summit

The UNCED Conference is popularly known as the Rio or Earth Summit. It was the largest United Nations conference to date, with most countries and 117 heads of state participating. There were thousands of non-governmental representatives at the official conference as well as at a parallel NGO forum. The recommendations in the Brundtland Report and the notion of sustainable development formed the core of the debate at Rio. Most countries endorsed the Brundtland definition of sustainable development. Many developing countries, however, wanted specific assurances of transfers of environmental technologies and economic assistance from the North to support the additional costs of 'green' growth. Many Northern states, on the other hand, were reluctant to assume further financial commitments (Rogers 1993: 238–239).

The Rio Summit put environment and development on the agendas of global leaders. It reinforced, too, the Brundtland Commission's assumption that more growth was compatible with a better global environment. Two official Rio Summit documents of particular note are the Rio Declaration on Environment and Development, and Agenda 21. The Rio Declaration is a set of twenty-seven principles on the rights and responsibilities of states for environment and development. These principles include far more of the South's concerns about the right to development than the Stockholm Declaration on the Human Environment. Agenda 21 was a 300-page action programme to promote sustainable development (UN 1992).

The Rio Summit also produced the Non-legally Binding Authoritative Statement of Principles for a Global Consensus on the Management, Conservation and Sustainable Development of all Types of Forests. The original intent was to sign a legally binding forest treaty, but after irreconcilable differences arose among negotiators over the terms of an agreement, the conference settled for a non-binding statement of principles (Brack *et al.* 2001: 2). Rio also opened two conventions for signature: the United Nations Framework Convention on Climate Change; and the Convention on Biological Diversity. Negotiations began, too, on a treaty on desertification. Finally, the conference established the United Nations Commission on Sustainable Development to monitor and evaluate the progress on meeting the Rio objectives.

The Rio Summit was a historic global conference hailed by many states as a great success. Critics from all sides, however, lamented the inadequate amount of 'promised' funds—especially from the North—to implement Agenda 21. More radical environmentalists, too, attacked the Brundtland definition of sustainable development—in particular its support for more economic growth and industrialization. Among activists, there was, in addition, a general concern that the negotiators had ignored the root cause of global environmental change: the inequalities, unsustainable industrial production and growth, and over-consumption that arise from corporate globalization and free trade. That, in fact, industry captured the agenda at Rio (Chatterjee and Finger 1994), and the outcomes were little more than an incompetent doctor (the state system) slapping a Band-Aid on to a cancerous tumour (capitalism). Other critics also felt the Rio Summit entrenched a top-down set of solutions, without nearly enough focus on the needs of local communities, or the plight of women and indigenous peoples (Shiva 1993; Lohmann 1993).

The decade after Rio saw global environmental issues again slip down the list of state priorities. States turned to the threats of terrorism, chemical and biological warfare, and global financial crises. The global community nevertheless kept signing and ratifying environmental treaties. The Convention on Biological Diversity, for example, was opened for signature in 1992 (and came into force in 1993). The United Nations Convention on the Law of the Sea, though first opened for signature in 1982, eventually came into force in 1994. The United Nations Convention to Combat Desertification in Those Countries Experiencing Serious Drought and/or Desertification, Particularly in Africa was opened for signature in 1994 (and came into force in 1996). The Stockholm Convention on Persistent Organic Pollutants (POPs) was opened for signature in 2001 (and came into force in 2004). The Kyoto Protocol to the United Nations Framework Convention on Climate Change was opened for signature in 1998 (and came into force in 2005) (see Table 14.1).

The global community also continued to discuss and review the progress of Agenda 21 and the implementation of sustainable development, including a 1997 special session of the United Nations General Assembly, known as the Earth Summit + 5. The global community also prepared for the World Summit on Sustainable Development, eventually held in Johannesburg, South Africa, in 2002.

Johannesburg and beyond

The World Summit on Sustainable Development is popularly called Rio + 10, or the Johannesburg Summit. The purpose was to evaluate the progress of sustainable development since the Rio Summit in 1992. It was also designed to establish specific targets to improve implementation of the Rio goals as well as to develop a strategy to implement the United Nations' Millennium Development Goals (Mehta 2003: 122). The Johannesburg Summit—with over 180 nations, over 10,000 delegates, at least 8,000 civil society representatives, and 4,000 members of the press, as well as countless ordinary citizens—was even larger than the Rio Summit. Revealingly, however, there were only about 100 heads of state, fewer than at Rio.

The official documents of Johannesburg were similar to Rio and Stockholm in their broad calls for global sustainability. The two most important were the Johannesburg Declaration on Sustainable Development, a list of challenges and general commitments; and the Johannesburg Plan of Implementation, to meet these. These are

Table 14.1 Examples of International Environmental Agreements

Name of the agreement	Opened for signature	Entered into force	Website address
International Convention for the Regulation of Whaling	1946	1948	www.iwcoffice.org
Convention on Wetlands of International Importance Especially as Waterfowl Habitat (Ramsar)	1971	1975	www.ramsar.org
Convention on the Prevention of Marine Pollution by Dumping Wastes and Other Matter (London Convention)	1972	1975	www.imo.org
Convention on the International Trade in Endangered Species of Wild Flora and Fauna (CITES)	1973	1975	www.cites.org
Convention on the Conservation of Antarctic Marine Living Resources	1980	1982, as part of the Antarctic Treaty System	www.ccamlr.org
Montreal Protocol on Substances that Deplete the Ozone Layer	1987	1989	www.ozone.unep.org
Basel Convention on the Control of Transboundary Movements of Hazardous Wastes and their Disposal	1989	1992	www.basel.int
Convention on Biological Diversity	1992	1993	www.cbd.unt default.shtml
United Nations Convention on the Law of the Sea (LOS)	1982	1994	www.un.org/Depts/los
United Nations Convention to Combat Desertification in Those Countries Experiencing Serious Drought and/or Desertification, Particularly in Africa	1994	1996	www.unccd.int
Stockholm Convention on Persistent Organic Pollutants (POPs)	2001	2004	www.chem.unep.ch/pops
Kyoto Protocol to the United Nations Framework Convention on Climate Change	1998	2005	www.unfccc.int

non-binding, but nevertheless represent significant political compromises. One of the most contentious issues (as was the case too at Rio) was financing. But Johannesburg also added two equally tough topics: the impact of globalization on sustainable development as well as specific timetables/targets to meet goals (Mehta 2003: 122). The Johannesburg Declaration on Sustainable Development (2002) reflects the debates over globalization. Point 12 declares: 'The deep fault line that divides human society between the rich and the poor and the ever-increasing gap between the developed and developing worlds pose a major threat to global prosperity, security and stability.' Point 14 states: 'Globalization has added a new dimension to [global environmental problems]. The rapid integration of markets, the increasing mobility of capital and significant upsurge in investment flows around the world have opened new challenges and opportunities for the pursuit of sustainable development. But the benefits and costs of globalization are unevenly distributed, with developing countries facing special difficulties in meeting this challenge.'

Was the Johannesburg Summit a success? The answer, naturally, depends on your definition of success. No doubt, like Stockholm and Rio, it helped to focus the attention of world leaders on global environmental change. The preparation and outcomes also cemented sustainable development as the core organizing concept for global and national environmental institutions. Some see the outcomes as being constructive and more realistic than the outcomes of Rio. Others, though, see the conference as a symbol of the global failure to tackle sincerely global environmental problems. They see the targets and timetables as weak, and the Johannesburg Declaration as little more than a restatement of the past, doing little to promote global sustainability (Burg 2003: 116–118). These critics also see the official statements on globalization as being little more than bland and evasive whitewash. The Johannesburg Summit added yet another layer to global environmentalism, but as with Stockholm and Rio, it seems highly unlikely that it will stem the tide of ecological decay. Paul Wapner (2003: 7), in his assessment of the Johannesburg Summit outcomes, sums this up nicely: 'The strains on the earth's sources, sinks and sites

have intensified dramatically since Rio and show no sign of decreasing in the near future.' In short, critics worry that environmentalism, piloted by the principle of sustainable development, is too weak to manage global environmental change. It does not, in particular, have the depth or content to restrain the ecological impacts of the globalization of production, consumption, trade, and corporations—the focus of the next section of this chapter.

KEY POINTS

- Environmental change began to accelerate some 300 years ago, after the Industrial Revolution intensified production and colonizers reached into distant lands.

- By the late 1960s, governments had begun to recognize the need to co-operate to address global environmental problems. The result was the 1972 United Nations Conference on the Human Environment.

- A global compromise gradually emerged in the 1970s and 1980s around the concept of sustainable development, as defined by the Brundtland Commission in 1987.

- The Rio Summit in 1992 set an ambitious agenda for global sustainable development. Progress, however, was slow and uneven over the following decade. Ten years later, the Johannesburg Summit endeavoured to facilitate the implementation of the Rio goals.

- The net result has left thick layers of global environmentalism (treaties, norms, and institutions) with the Brundtland Commission's concept of sustainable development at the core. Supporters see this as evidence of the global community's capacity to handle global environmental change, while critics see it as camouflage for 'business as usual'.

Economic Growth, Trade, and Corporations

What is the ecological impact of economic growth, trade, and corporations under globalization? Some see the net impact as being positive for the health of the planet. It pulls destitute people—who are prone to degrade surrounding environments to survive—out of poverty. And it raises national per capita incomes, which generate the funds, technologies, and political will to implement sustainable development. In the short run, such growth produces more food and better medical care, which in turn lengthens life expectancy and allows the global population to rise. Undeniably, this creates global ecological pressures. But, advocates of economic growth contend that this is a temporary problem. The global population will stabilize at 9 to 10 billion, probably around 2060, in part because globalization is raising the standards of living and education levels of women in the South, a development associated historically with smaller family size.

Others see economic growth and corporate globalization as core causes of the global environmental crisis. These forces are distributing environmental effects unequally, where the rich get richer and the poor remain confined in ever-worsening environments. It is also driving up per capita consumption in the South (without improving well-being) and over-consumption in the North. Already, the number of human beings is well beyond the earth's carrying capacity. The global population may well stabilize in around fifty years' time, but that is still another 3 to 4 billion people to feed, clothe, and shelter. How many earths, these critics wonder, are we planning to live on?

Which side is correct? To begin to address this question, the next section outlines the environmental arguments for more economic growth, more free trade, and more foreign investment.

Trading for growth and a better environment

A world free of poverty, say economists at institutions such as the World Bank, is critical for the long-term health of the planet. The struggle of the poor to survive is a core cause of problems such as deforestation, desertification, and unsanitary water. The poor forage for wood to cook with and to heat homes. They exhaust nearby natural resources, such as fresh water, seafood, and wildlife. They cultivate unsuitable land to grow food and earn income. And they despoil local waterways with rubbish and sewage. Stating these facts, advocates of economic growth argue, is not an attempt to assign blame. Rather, the point is far simpler: poor people have little choice if they wish to survive.

The poor and uneducated, too, tend to have more children than the rich, which creates a spiral of poverty and ecological collapse as ever more people forage for food, water, and shelter on increasingly fragile lands. This spiral occurs for many reasons besides weak economic growth. Other factors include insecure property rights, the failure of family planning, inadequate government services and regulations, trade distortions, and insufficient investment and development assistance. The downward spiral accelerates during times of slow growth—that is, during an economic recession or depression—since firms are less willing to invest in cleaner technologies, and states are less willing and less able to enforce environmental laws. A quick glance at environmental management in Asia during the 1997–9 financial crisis confirms this (Dauvergne 1999).

Admittedly, advocates note, economic growth can worsen environmental conditions in the short run. Air and water quality, for example, can deteriorate in the early stages of industrial production. Yet, in the long run, once a society harnesses sufficient per capita wealth, environmental standards will invariably rise. Advocates of economic growth commonly illustrate this with the Environmental Kuznets Curve (see Figure 14.2). This curve demonstrates that pollution (such as smog and lead) will rise along with economic growth during the early stages of industrial development. This occurs because governments focus on increasing industrial growth and national income rather than on pollution controls. Yet this is a temporary phenomenon. Once per capita income reaches high levels (in the past, often between $5,000 and $8,000), pollution begins to fall (Grossman and Krueger 1995). This occurs partly because citizens demand better living environments, and partly because firms and governments now have the financial and institutional capacity to respond effectively. It arises partly, too, because strong economies naturally tend to move away from heavy industry, and towards service and information industries. The Environmental Kuznets Curve usually draws on data for industrial pollution rather than depletion of natural resources. A recent study, however, found a correlation between lower deforestation and higher national income in Asia, Latin America, and Africa (Bhattarai and Hammig 2001).

Japan's environmental history fits the Environmental Kuznets Curve well. After the Second World War, industrial production and economic growth in Japan soared, and by the 1960s Japan was suffering from acute pollution, 'not unlike many of the heavily polluted areas of India, China, and Southeast Asia today' (Schreurs 2002: 36). Citizen protests over the health consequences of pollution escalated in the 1960s and 1970s. In response, the Japanese government brought in strict environmental regulations, and Japanese business developed new environmental technologies (McKean 1981; Broadbent 1998). The result was a dramatic improvement in the domestic environment.

Environmental advocates of economic growth do not generally propose that states with low per capita incomes should blindly pursue economic growth. For most, the Environmental Kuznets Curve suggests two critical lessons: first, that, in the long run, economic growth will improve environmental institutions and governance; and second, that, following the logic of the Environmental Kuznets Curve, it is feasible to use measures such as ecological markets, technological advances, sound policies, and global institutions to help countries with low per capita incomes to 'tunnel' through the middle of the curve, attaining high per capita incomes with less environmental damage.

The globalization of free trade—following the principles of absolute and comparative advantage—will also help these weak economies to tunnel through the Environmental Kuznets Curve. Free trade fosters efficient worldwide production as well as the transfer of environmental technologies and higher environmental standards from the North to the South (Neumayer 2001; WTO 1999b). This means that humanity is able to produce more goods with fewer resources, which stimulates global economic growth and raises national per capita incomes. The extra income from efficient production is necessary, too, for sustainable development. More income means that more can be spent to preserve the environment as well as to enforce environmental regulations. World Trade Organization director-general, Mike Moore, succinctly explains the logic: 'Every WTO Member Government supports open trade because it leads to higher living standards for working families which

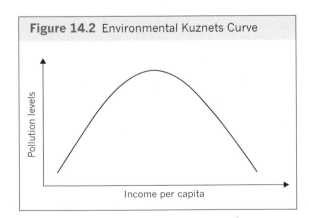

Figure 14.2 Environmental Kuznets Curve

Pollution levels

Income per capita

in turn leads to a cleaner environment' (WTO 1999b).

Trade liberalization, too, produces significant environmental rewards. Trade barriers distort price signals for natural resources. Prices therefore do not reflect real scarcities or pollution costs, which in turn creates waste and overconsumption. Liberalization also fosters cleaner production processes, as firms that produce goods behind trade barriers face less competition and have fewer incentives to upgrade facilities or use resources efficiently. States with more liberal trade policies are also, advocates argue, more likely to meet global environmental standards. 'Liberalized trade', the World Bank (1992: 67) explains, 'fosters greater efficiency and higher productivity and may actually reduce pollution by encouraging the growth of less-polluting industries and the adoption and diffusion of cleaner technologies.' Trade liberalization can further pressure producers with low environmental standards to raise these standards to gain access to markets with higher standards. This 'trading up' of environmental standards, David Vogel (1995) argues, occurred, for example, when California's strict auto emission standards pushed up standards across the United States as well as in Japan and Germany. Germany's willingness to support tougher European Union standards in part reflected its experience in the US market.

Restricting trade for environmental reasons, advocates of open trade argue, is on occasion necessary—such as to protect endangered species or to control the dumping of hazardous waste and dangerous chemicals. Yet far more often, restricting trade on environmental grounds is illogical and counter-productive. Sound policies and incentives within an open trading structure lead to much better long-term environmental management. Green markets—where prices throughout a trade chain internalize environmental and social costs, and where consumers voluntarily pay higher prices for these products—are another effective means of promoting sustainable development.

The globalization of corporations, argue supporters, will further promote sustainable development.

Transnational corporations (TNCs) transfer critical technologies, expertise, and funds into the South. Without this investment, economies stagnate, slip backwards, and sustain environmental degradation—a quick glance at North Korea or Sub-Saharan Africa confirms this. Transnational corporations that invest in the South also tend to employ higher environmental standards than local laws require—what Ronie Garcia-Johnson (2000) calls exporting environmentalism. This occurs for a host of reasons: partly because of more sophisticated technologies and management techniques; partly because of pressure from states, NGOs, shareholders, and consumers; partly because of internal codes of conduct and risk-management strategies; and partly because the resulting efficiencies can provide a competitive advantage.

There is also a trend among all firms since the 1980s to 'green' operations voluntarily (Schmidheiny 1992). For example, Responsible Care—an environmental and safety code for the chemical industry—was established in 1985. The Global Environmental Management Initiative (GEMI) was created by the International Chamber of Commerce in 1990 to implement the Chamber's business charter for sustainable development (Sklair 2001: 204). There was a flood of voluntary industry codes after the 1992 Rio Summit. The ISO 14001 certifiable standards for environmental management have been adopted widely by business since the mid-1990s (see Box 14.3). Industry founded the World Business Council of Sustainable Development in 1995 to address 'the challenges and opportunities of sustainable development based on three fundamental and inseparable pillars: the generation of economic wealth, environmental improvement and social responsibility' (Holme and Watts 2000: 5). The Johannesburg Summit saw the business community stress the need for voluntary corporate leadership to promote sustainable development. Corporations are now embracing the principle of corporate social responsibility. Chairman and chief executive officer of AT&T, C. Michael Armstrong, explains the logic of the greening of the company. 'AT&T understands the need for a global alliance

BOX 14.3

ISO 14000 and ISO 14001

The International Organization for Standardization (ISO), headquartered in Geneva, advances voluntary international standards for particular products, and for environmental management. The ISO develops these standards relying on consensus and voluntary participation among ISO member countries. ISO 14000 is a series of voluntary environmental standards, including for environmental auditing, performance, labelling, and most importantly, the ISO 14001 Environmental Management System (EMS) Standard. The ISO 14001 standard allows for certification from an external authority. It requires a community or organization to implement practices and procedures that together comprise a system of environmental management. It also requires a policy to prevent pollution and continually improve environmental performance.

Source: www.iso14000.com

of business, society and the environment. In the 21st century, the world won't tolerate businesses that don't take that partnership seriously, but it will eventually reward companies that do' (quoted in Holme and Watts 2000: 1).

Most states and global institutions accept the need for more economic growth, more open trade and more foreign investment. There are critics, however, many of whom see the relentless pursuit of growth, trade, and investment under globalization as a primary cause of the global environmental crisis.

Trading away the earth for unequal consumption

Critics contend that the Environmental Kuznets Curve is misleading. They see the link between growth and lower long-term pollution as being simplistic. It is possible, critics argue, for economies to get stuck along the curve, never reaching a point where pollution declines (Arrow *et al.* 1998; Tisdell 2001: 187). The Curve does not account for the integrity of the ecosystem as a whole, and it ignores irreplaceable losses (such as biodiversity and species loss). It discounts, too, the potential for cumulative ecological change to erupt into a sudden and uncontainable crisis. It does not address the possibility that, as the amount of one toxic substance declines, the amount of another may rise. The Curve, moreover, only works for a limited range of pollutants and resources. It fails, for example, for CO_2 emissions (the leading cause of global warming), which have been rising steadily alongside growth. Finally, a decline of a particular pollutant in one country may occur because industrial production shifts offshore. Japan's domestic environment was able to improve, for example, partly because dirty industries shifted into South-East and North-East Asia (Hall 2002).

Environmental critics of economic growth argue further that production patterns and unequal consumption—rather than poverty—are the driving forces of global environmental decay. The earth is already beyond its carrying capacity. The push for constant economic growth under globalization, critics contend, means that industrialization, intensive agriculture, and unsustainable natural resource extraction will continue to rise. Globalization also 'distances' production from consumption, so end users do not 'see' the ecological effects of individual purchases or disposal (Princen 1997; Clapp 2002). Products like computers often become obsolete in a few years, partly because of the design. This, along with advertising, is contributing to ever higher levels of consumption in both the North and the South. Total consumption, for example, doubled in real terms from 1973 to 1998. There has been a fourfold rise in the consumption of fossil fuels since 1950. These rises, moreover, have not solved the gross inequalities between consumption in the South and the

North. Africa's per capita consumption has been declining since the 1980s. Meanwhile, the North, with about 15 per cent of the global population, accounts for about three-quarters of global consumption expenditure (UNDP 1998: 46, 50). The United States alone, with a mere 5 per cent of the global population, consumes 30 per cent of the world's resources (Myers 1997: 34). Much of this consumption, critics argue, is wasteful and excessive—creating a world where obesity is the latest crisis of the North and malnutrition the everlasting crisis of the South.

Global free trade, critics contend, merely adds to the earth's unsustainable ecological burden (Daly 1993, 1996, 2002). The prices of traded goods generally do not reflect the full environmental and social costs of production—the value, for example, of an old-growth tree as a source of biodiversity—leaving consumer prices far too low and consumption far too high for global sustainability (Arden-Clarke 1992). Environmental critics further argue that trade and trade agreements put downward pressure on environmental standards. This occurs because governments, in a bid to become more competitive in global markets, sometimes lower, or fail to strengthen, environmental management. Some see this as creating a race to the bottom; while others see it as leaving countries 'stuck at the bottom' (Esty 1994; Porter 1999). For many, the only solution to the ecological drawbacks of trade is to impose strict controls over trade.

Production under free trade may well become more 'efficient', critics add, but the steady increase in the production of goods overrides any environmental gains—creating, for example, a world full of billions of fuel-efficient cars rather than millions of fuel-inefficient cars. Global free trade, moreover, is in fact far from 'free'. Nor is it equal or fair, as highly mobile capital exploits the so-called comparative advantages of weak economies. The ideology of free trade in reality translates into patterns of exchange that exploit the labour and environments of the South and protect the interests of the North (such as farmers). The South ends up exporting unsustainable quantities of natural resources and absorbing ecological damage so that the North can prosper. Production-for-export from the South tends to rely on either unsustainable quantities of natural resources, or on dirty and unsafe factories (and, of course, cheap labour). Logging and mining sites, and textile and electronic factories in Latin America, Africa, and the Asia-Pacific highlight the ecological damage of such production (Marchak 1995; Karliner 1997; Gedicks 2001). Global trade, critics conclude, in effect allows the North to live beyond its carrying capacity, doing so by using up the carrying capacity of the South.

Critics see corporate globalization as a fundamental cause of the escalating global ecological crisis. Transnational corporations are viewed as engines of environmental exploitation, plundering the globe's limited resources for quick profits. In particular, critics see *pollution havens* and *double standards* as real or potential threats to sustainability. A pollution haven refers to governments using low environmental standards to induce firms to invest, thus creating a haven for polluters. It does not, as David Wheeler (2002: 1) points out, 'necessarily refer to a region that is seriously polluted'. What really matters is 'the willingness of the host government to "play the environment card" to promote growth'. A double standard refers to cases where a firm applies one set of standards at home and another set overseas (generally lower standards in countries with weaker laws). Double standards are common and, most economists would agree, a normal outcome of the process of development. The case of the American TNC, Union Carbide, in Bhopal, India, the site of the worst industrial accident in history, is perhaps the best-known case of double standards (the US headquarters was responsible for the plant's design) (MacKenzie 2002). But there are countless others, too (Ofreneo 1993; Karliner 1997; Frey 1998). The American firms General Electric, Ford, General Motors, and Westinghouse all, for example, operate plants in Northern Mexico, thus avoiding California's much tougher regulations on toxic emissions. Critics blame these TNCs for polluting local rivers, soil, and water supplies near these plants (Bryant and Bailey 1997: 109).

There is, then, little controversy as to whether double standards exist. The existence of pollution havens, however, is hotly debated. Critics of TNCs commonly assert that corporate globalization is producing pollution havens around the globe. The process of globalization spreads these, because corporations are increasingly willing to relocate for the smallest differences in costs. Governments, meanwhile, are more likely to use lax regulations to entice investors. Most economists, however, argue that the reason for double standards is *not* a result of host governments intentionally and explicitly playing the environment card. There are, they claim, in fact few, if any, permanent pollution havens anywhere in the world (Wheeler 2002). There are many reasons for this. For some industries, it is impractical or too risky to relocate for market or infrastructural reasons. The main reason, however, is that, for most industrial sectors, other costs, such as those for labour and technology, are far higher than environmental costs (Ferrantino 1997: 52). It therefore does not make

financial sense for a firm to relocate on environmental grounds alone.

A second and much larger strand of the environmental literature, which is critical of corporations, focuses less on the differential environmental practices of firms across countries and more on practices 'on the ground'. These critics have filled libraries documenting the destructive and illegal practices of loggers, miners, oil companies, chemical companies, and so on (Clapp 2001; Dauvergne 2001; Gedicks 2001). This research not only documents the activities of well-known transnational corporations, but also local and regional firms, such as Malaysian and Indonesian loggers in South-east Asia and the South Pacific. Besides academics, research institutes such as the World Resources Institute and countless numbers of NGOs also research and publish such findings. This research leads popular writers such as Joshua Karliner (1997) to call the world a 'Corporate Planet', and David Korten (1995) to conclude that 'Corporations Rule the World'.

KEY POINTS

Advocates argue that the wealth from the globalization of trade and TNCs creates:

- Poverty alleviation, better education, population controls, and a stronger capacity of states and global institutions to implement sustainable development.

- Technological innovation and less harmful forms of production (for example, a shift from industry and agriculture to service and knowledge).

- Corporate investment that 'exports environmentalism' by transferring funds, new technologies, and higher standards to the South.

- Opportunities to use creative policies and incentives to tunnel through the Environmental Kuznets Curve.

Critics see unequal and destructive economic growth, trade, and investment that:

- Burden the South with unequal environmental costs and low environmental standards.

- Allow corporations to plunder the globe's fragile ecosystems.

- Generate consumer prices that ignore environmental and social costs of production.

- Drive overconsumption in the North and unbalanced consumption in the South, putting total global consumption well beyond the earth's carrying capacity.

PETER DAUVERGNE

A Sustainable Future? Financing and Regimes

There is, then, a great divide between environmentalists who support and those who oppose globalization. Most agree, however, that it will no doubt require new consumption patterns, innovative markets, technological advances, corporate ethics, and co-operation to ensure a sustainable global economy. There are indeed reforms going on in all these areas. Yet the global community has put much of its energy into funding sustainable development, and into forming and strengthening global environmental agreements. Is sustainable development an effective core principle? Is funding sufficient? Can international agreements and sustainable development ensure globalization is a positive environmental force? Many in the global community—states and state negotiators in particular—believe in sustainable development and environmental agreements. Others, however, see them as, at best, harmless, and at worst, themselves causes of global environmental harm as the effort to reach a compromise lowers expectations, creates long delays, and ultimately contributes to ineffective policies. The next section addresses these issues, with particular attention to global environmental financing and the political economy of three international regimes: ozone depletion, climate change, and forestry.

Financing sustainable development: the GEF

Few deny that the South requires assistance to implement sustainable development. How else can the South find the funds and personnel to address issues such as climate change or global biodiversity? Yet critics lament the failures of existing environmental assistance. Some see total development assistance as being far too low—far below the repeated global promise of total overseas development assistance of 0.7 per cent of gross national income. The OECD average is just 0.22 per cent, while the United States is the lowest of the major donors, supplying a mere 0.11 per cent in 2001. Assistance for sustainable development is even lower. At the Rio Summit, for example, the North was only willing to commit to $125 billion of the $625 billion estimated as being needed to implement Agenda 21 (UNEP 2002: 17).

Other critics see development assistance as a cause of global ecological stress. These critics see the conditions attached to this 'aid' as a tool of donors and corporate allies to exploit labour and natural resources in the South. Multilateral donors such as the World Bank and bilateral donors such as Japan (the world's largest bilateral aid donor during the 1990s), for example, use loans to require governments to eliminate trade barriers and support foreign investors. Heavy foreign debts, these critics contend, further aggravate ecological pressures as states export natural resources to earn the foreign exchange to service and repay the debt (Rich 1994).

The Global Environment Facility (GEF) is one of the few financial sources to fund specific global environmental initiatives in the South. The GEF was first set up as a pilot facility in 1991, just before the Rio Summit, becoming a permanent body formally in 1994. The GEF has three implementing agencies—the World Bank; the United Nations Development Programme (UNDP); and the UNEP—although the World Bank is the most influential. The Global Environment Facility is housed formally in the World Bank, though it is functionally independent. The UNDP handles technical assistance and the UNEP co-ordinates between the GEF and global environmental agreements. There are fourteen donor states, eighteen recipient states, and ten NGOs on the GEF Council. GEF finances global environmental policies and programmes in developing countries, including ozone depletion, biodiversity, climate change, and persistent organic pollutants (Streck 2001). The GEF currently supports more than 1,800 projects in over 140 countries. The total amount of GEF grants by 2006 was over $6 billion. The GEF has also managed to leverage $20 billion in co-financing from other sources.

The GEF disburses grants and technical funds to cover the additional costs for developing countries of a project targeting a global environmental objective (such as to mitigate climate change or protect biodiversity). Some see GEF as a critical step forward to help the South absorb the financial costs of global sustainability. Others, like Bruce Rich of the NGO Environmental Defense, have lashed out at GEF, especially during the pilot phase: 'The formulation of the Global Environment Facility', he argues (1994: 176–177), 'was a model of the Bank's preferred way of doing business: Top-down, secretive, with a basic contempt for public participation, access to information, involvement of democratically elected legislatures, and informed discussion of alternatives'. These critics see GEF as little more than a financial Band-Aid that stresses top-down technological fixes rather than long-term solutions (Young 2003). These critics worry, too, that the World Bank is tying GEF grants to other World Bank loans financing projects that damage the environment. Korinna Horta of Environmental Defense states: 'The World Bank mocks the principles and policies of the GEF by hypocritically funding and mitigating environmental destruction. The GEF "greenwashes" business as usual for the Bank' (Halifax Initiative 2002; also see Horta *et al.* 2002).

Without doubt, funding for global sustainability is far from adequate. The global community has in some ways made more progress in developing and strengthening environmental regimes.

Explaining outcomes: the political economy of environmental regimes

The global community has put great faith in international environmental agreements to guide globalization, promote co-operation, rein in free riders, and avoid the natural drift of a system of sovereign states toward a tragedy of the commons (see Box 14.4). There has been a steady increase since the 1970s in the number of international and regional environmental negotiations, and today there are several hundred agreements (see Table 14.1 on page 458, for examples).

An international environmental regime encompasses more than just international legal agreements. Steven Krasner's (1983: 2) definition of an international regime is the classic one: 'sets of implicit or explicit principles, norms, rules and decision-making procedures around which actors' expectations converge in a given area of international relations' (see Aggarwal and Dupont, Chapter 3 in this volume). Yet most international environmental regimes revolve around an international agreement. Such regimes tend to evolve in four phases. They begin with the recognition of a problem, including the scientific debates about the

---

BOX 14.4

Tragedy of the Commons

Garrett Hardin (1968), in a now famous article in *Science*, drew a vivid analogy of access and historical collapse of the English commons with access and future collapse of modern-day commons (like the high seas, or the atmosphere, or an unregulated forest). Look, he says, at a grazing pasture 'open to all'. It is in the rational self-interest of a farmer to breed and graze as many animals as possible. The addition of one more animal will enhance the wealth of the owner far more than it will degrade the pasture for the owner's herd. Without controls, however, the logic of personal gain will inevitably overfill and destroy the pasture. The process is the same for all commons with rising populations and unrestricted access. 'Ruin is the destination toward which all men rush,' he argues, 'each pursuing his own best interest in a society that believes in the freedom of the commons. Freedom in a commons brings ruin to all.' The only solution, he concludes, is 'mutual coercion, mutually agreed upon by the majority of the people affected'.

causes and severity, and the emergence of an agenda. The science here is often speculative, especially if, as with climate change, it involves looking hundreds of years into the future. Working through the science can create decades of delay during this phase as various 'experts' make claims and counter-claims. Dramatic events, such as an oil spill or chemical leak, or a 'hole' in the ozone layer, can catalyse action toward the next stage—the negotiation of the rules and decision-making procedures. Here, coalitions of states or a powerful state such as the United States can play a critical role either in the emergence or the veto of an agreement. States may also shift gears during this phase—for example, signing an agreement then withdrawing later (by refusing to ratify, say). As with the emergence of an agenda, scientists or experts with collective policy preferences can play a key role in defining the content of an agreement (Haas 1992). So can networks of activists who work across traditional sovereign borders (Keck and Sikkink 1998). Once an agreement comes into force, parties to the agreement need to implement policies that meet their obligations. This phase can further strengthen or weaken a regime, as many states, even those striving legitimately to meet obligations, may be unable (or unwilling) to do so for technical or political reasons. Finally, regimes continue to evolve even after implementation begins, strengthening and weakening as norms shift (or sometimes as negotiators amend the formal rules).

There is a growing literature on evaluating the effectiveness of international environmental regimes (Victor *et al.* 1998; Young 1999, 2002; Vogler 2000, 2003). Many global environmental regimes are weak, with little influence over the behaviour of states and firms or, if there is influence, with little impact on global ecological conditions. An array of factors can undermine regime effectiveness. Ongoing research (and resulting debates) within the scientific community can make it hard to create and maintain a scientific consensus on the causes, consequences and solutions for particular ecological problems. Corporations can exploit the resulting uncertainty common to the scientific

method to further delay negotiations or weaken regimes (as well as to fund scientific research to try to prolong uncertainty). The domestic political influence of corporations can also weaken the formal rules and procedures for international agreements, undermine international financial commitments to support compliance, and stall national implementation, even in countries with reasonable local environmental records. The priority of all states on maintaining economic growth—and the insistence of many governments in developing countries on ensuring the opportunity to one day reach the levels of economic prosperity the North currently enjoys—can also mean that international negotiators compromise and avoid strict measures entailing economic costs. These factors all shape the scope and nature of international agreements, as well as the strength of the national policies and implementing agencies designed to meet international obligations.

National agencies are generally responsible for monitoring and enforcing international environmental laws. To encourage compliance, however, parties generally submit implementation data to secretariats as well as attend regular meetings to review implementation. Some agreements also link financing to compliance (especially important in the South). The secretariats, however, often lack the staff and funds to verify data (as well as push laggards to submit). The combined total in 1999 of professional staff of the Framework Convention on Climate Change, the Convention on Biological Diversity, the Montreal Protocol, CITES, and the Convention to Combat Desertification was a mere 100 people. The combined total budget was just $43.5 million (Porter *et al.* 2000: 150). Both figures are tiny in comparison with the international financial institutions (see Winham, Chapter 5 in this volume). Non-governmental organizations also play a key role here, publicizing violations and conducting independent studies of national implementation. The NGO Environmental Defense, for example, has been 'critical' in ensuring US regulations in fact implement the Montreal Protocol (Porter *et al.* 2000: 149).

Implementation can pose great technical and political problems for governments in the South. Often, these governments do not have the finances, personnel, or technologies to monitor and enforce environmental legislation. Systemic corruption may further hinder enforcement. The cost of compliance, too, is frequently greater in the South than in the North, as the South has less infrastructure and experience in meeting environmental obligations, although, as mentioned earlier, funds such as the ones from the GEF can help to offset the higher costs of compliance in the South. Countries in the North, however, also struggle with implementing international environmental agreements. The process of confirming scientific explanations may create long bureaucratic delays in implementation. Lobby groups and bureaucracies may work to weaken national legislation designed to meet international obligations. In democratic federations, such as Canada, the federal government may sign and ratify an agreement, but then face stiff opposition from some of the provinces, as happened after the federal government ratified the Kyoto Protocol in 2002.

For all these reasons, then, it is a formidable challenge for state negotiators and implementers to develop and uphold an effective international environmental regime. Perhaps the most common example of a 'successful' regime is the one to reduce the production and consumption of chlorofluorocarbons (CFCs), the main cause of the depletion of the ozone layer.

Ozone depletion regime

Production and consumption of CFCs, first invented in 1928, rose quickly from the 1950s to the 1970s. The main use was in aerosols, refrigerators, air conditioners, insulation, and solvents. In 1974, Mario Molina and F. Sherwood Rowland (1974) (who went on to win the 1995 Nobel Prize in Chemistry) published an article hypothesizing that CFCs were drifting into the atmosphere, breaking apart, releasing chlorine, then reacting to deplete the ozone layer. Ozone is a molecule of three oxygen atoms able to absorb harmful ultraviolet light. The ozone layer refers to the region of high concentrations of ozone in the stratosphere. (The stratosphere is 10–50 kilometres above the earth's surface. Below this is the troposphere, where weather occurs.) The ozone layer protects us from the harmful effects of ultraviolet radiation from the sun, which can contribute to skin cancer and cataracts, decrease our immunity to diseases, and make plants less productive.

In the decade after Molina and Rowland's seminal article, global negotiators worked slowly towards a collective consensus on the causes and consequences of ozone depletion. This effort gained momentum in 1985 after British scientists found a 'hole' (in fact, a severe thinning) in the ozone layer over Antarctica. This hole, which persisted for three months, was the size of North America. That same year, the global community signed the Vienna Convention for the Protection of the Ozone Layer, a framework convention with no legally binding targets. The 1987 Montreal Protocol on Substances that Deplete the Ozone Layer was adopted two years later, setting mandatory targets to reduce the production of ozone-depleting CFCs and halons (halons are another significant ozone-depleting substance found, for example, in fire extinguishers).

Significantly, in 1990 the South agreed to phase out consumption of CFCs and halons by 2010. The Parties to the Montreal Protocol created the Multilateral Fund for the Implementation of the Montreal Protocol to assist developing countries with implementation. This is unusual, as most international agreements do not contain a funding mechanism, and instead rely on traditional development assistance and, more recently, the GEF. So far, this Fund has approved more than $2 billion to phase out the consumption of ozone-depleting substances in the South. Partly as a result, many developing countries were already 'on track' by the mid-1990s to phase out CFCs and halons ahead of schedule (Greene 1997: 329), and the South was able to reduce CFC consumption by about 60 per cent from the mid-1990s to 2004 (UNEP 2005).

Conferences of the Parties in London in 1990, Copenhagen in 1992, Montreal in 1997, and Beijing in 1999 amended and strengthened the Montreal Protocol. These conferences also added other ozone-depleting substances and accelerated the phase-out schedules. Over this time, the Vienna Convention and the Montreal Protocol became truly global agreements, and today both have over 180 Parties. The result has been a dramatic fall in global CFC production (see Figure 14.3).

The damage to the ozone layer, it is important to emphasize, is still a serious problem. Today, the thickness of ozone over Antarctica, for example, is generally 40–55 per cent of its pre-1980 level (UNEP 2000: 5). The stratospheric concentration of CFCs also continues to increase, because the long life of CFCs means that 'old' emissions are still rising into the stratosphere. Nevertheless, the World Meteorological Organization (2006) now predicts that the ozone layer will repair itself and return to pre-1980 levels by 2065, thus preventing millions of cases of melanoma cancer and eye cataracts (UNEP 2003:

4). This is indeed an exceptional turnaround. 'The ozone layer regime is remarkable,' Marvin Soroos (1997: 169) argues, 'not only for the series of agreements limiting and phasing out the production and use of ozone-depleting substances but also for the broad acceptance of them and the apparent high rate of compliance with the controls.' Most other scholars would agree. Edward Parson (2003: vii) calls it a 'striking success', noting: 'With near-universal participation of nations and energetic support from industry, the ozone regime has reduced worldwide use of ozone-depleting chemicals by 95 per cent, and use is still falling.'

Yet in many ways this was an exceptional case, one that may well tell us little about our ability to handle future global environmental crises such as climate change. The consequences of less ozone were easy for the general public to understand, with skin cancer a particular worry in the North. Even more important, the causes and solutions were relatively straightforward. In the mid-1980s, twenty-one firms in sixteen countries were

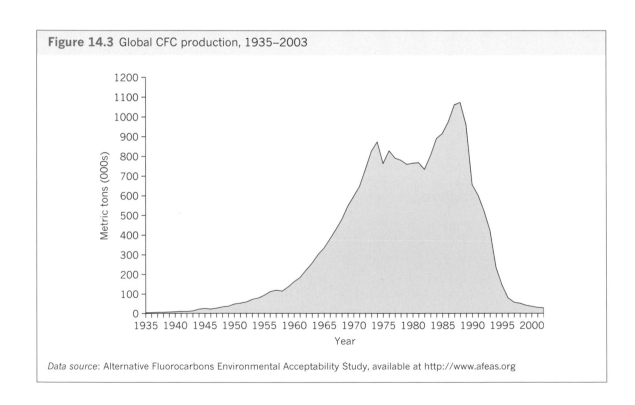

Figure 14.3 Global CFC production, 1935–2003

Data source: Alternative Fluorocarbons Environmental Acceptability Study, available at http://www.afeas.org

responsible for CFC production, with the North accounting for about 88 per cent of this. Especially notable, by 1986, the chemical company DuPont, the largest producer of CFCs (accounting for a-quarter of global production), had decided to seek substitutes for CFCs (Grundmann 2001; Parson 2003). Two years later, DuPont announced that it would phase out production of CFCs. The shift to CFC substitutes did not harm its profits; indeed, in many ways it gave DuPont a competitive edge as other producers soon followed suit.

Climate change regime

Most other global environmental problems involve far greater complexities and uncertainties, and will require far greater sacrifices to solve. Climate change is perhaps the most complex of all (see Dressler and Parson 2006). Human activities are altering the relative volumes of greenhouse gases—such as carbon dioxide, methane, and nitrogen oxides—in the earth's atmosphere. Figure 14.4, for example,

shows the rapid increase in global emissions of carbon dioxide during the twentieth century. The planet is warming as the 'new' atmosphere traps more heat, a process akin to rolling up a car window on a hot day. The Intergovernmental Panel on Climate Change (IPCC 2001) calculates that the mean global surface temperature has already risen by 0.3–0.6 degrees Celsius since the end of the nineteenth century. This may seem minor, but it was the largest rise of any century in the last millennium. And the problem appears to be getting worse. The 1990s was the warmest decade, and 2005 was the warmest year, since records began. The twenty-first century could be even hotter. Various studies predict a rise of between 1.4 and 5.8 degrees Celsius by 2100—the fastest rate of change since the last Ice Age. The IPCC (2001) estimates that seas could rise by as much as 88 centimetres by the end of the twenty-first century, displacing millions in low-lying coastal areas in countries such as Bangladesh and submerging low-lying countries such as the Marshall Islands and the Maldives.

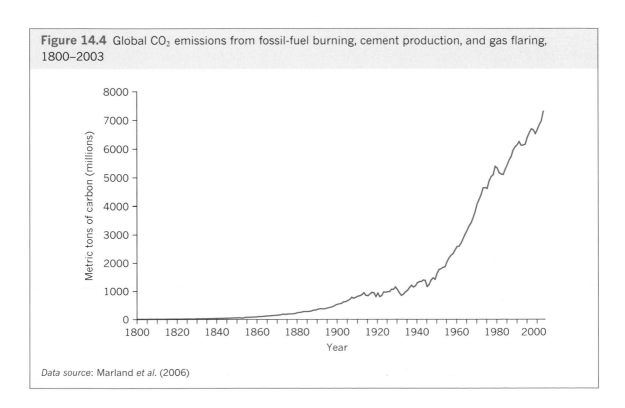

Figure 14.4 Global CO_2 emissions from fossil-fuel burning, cement production, and gas flaring, 1800–2003

Data source: Marland *et al.* (2006)

Climate change alarms environmental critics of economic globalization in particular, as the primary greenhouse gases arise from core economic activities, such as automobiles, power plants, oil refineries, factories, agriculture, and deforestation. At the same time, many of the consequences, such as melting polar ice, rising seas, severe storms, new diseases, and drought, are beyond the lifetimes of politicians and business leaders. No doubt, to lower greenhouse gas emissions will require significant changes to global economic production and consumption patterns. It will require, too, governmental, corporate, and personal sacrifices. Replacing CFCs, these critics note, is simply not a comparable sacrifice (Paterson 1996; Newell 2000).

The South sees the North as being largely responsible for climate change, because developed countries accounted for three-quarters of cumulative emissions of carbon dioxide between 1950 and 1992. The North, on the other hand, often notes the need for global efforts, as carbon dioxide emissions from the South are likely to equal those from the North by 2035. Nevertheless, specific views on climate change do not split cleanly along North–South lines. The European Union, Japan, and Canada, for example, have supported global efforts to combat climate change, while the United States and Australia have remained sceptical, at times even questioning the science of global warming. Meanwhile, the states in OPEC oppose efforts to reduce the global dependence on oil while, predictably, the thirty countries in the Alliance of Small Island States support every possible effort to halt the rise of sea levels.

The 1997 Kyoto Protocol to the 1992 Climate Change Convention is the core agreement in the climate change regime. It requires developed countries (including Russia) to reduce emissions of six greenhouse gases, on average, by 5 per cent below 1990 levels between 2008 and 2012 (calculated as an average over these years). If this is achieved, emissions levels in 2010 would be about 20 per cent lower than they would have been without the Protocol. But not all governments have the same 'target'. The European Union agreed to reduce emissions by 8 per cent below 1990 levels; the United States by 7 per cent; and Japan and Canada by 6 per cent. The Russian Federation agreed to stabilize emissions at 1990 levels. Australia managed to negotiate an increase of 8 per cent above 1990 levels. Developing countries are exempt from legally binding commitments in the Kyoto Protocol, although some, like India and China, set voluntary reduction targets.

The rules of the Kyoto Protocol require it to come into force ninety days after at least fifty-five Parties, accounting for at least 55 per cent of the 1990 carbon dioxide emissions of the developed country signatories, ratify it. This seemed unlikely to occur after the United States, which accounts for 36.1 per cent of 1990 carbon dioxide emissions of developed countries, withdrew support in 2001, and instead vowed to reduce greenhouse gases 'by 18 per cent over the next decade through voluntary, incentive-based, and existing mandatory measures' (Switzer 2004: 293). The Kyoto Protocol did, in the end, come into force in 2005 even without the United States, after Russia, which accounts for 17.4 per cent of 1990 levels, tipped the total over the 55 per cent mark. Many see this as a sign of the determination of the global community (minus the United States and Australia) to tackle climate change. Still, most analysts agree that, even with full compliance, the Kyoto Protocol will not lower greenhouse gas emissions to levels that will 'solve' climate change. More radical groups, such as Greenpeace, argue for a global emission reduction closer to 80 per cent.

Forests regime

Most environmental regimes, as with ozone and climate change, contain a core international agreement. But some, like the international forests regime, are emerging without a core global treaty. The international forests regime includes the norms and principles arising from numerous global meetings since the Rio Summit to discuss the benefits and drawbacks of negotiating a global treaty for forest management. It consists, too, of the forest-related clauses of international conventions such as the ones on biodiversity, desertification, climate change, and wetlands. It also includes the sustainable forest principles of institutions such as the International Tropical Timber Organization (ITTO), and the standards of organizations such as the Forest Stewardship Council (FSC) (see Box 14.5). At the core of the regime is the concept of sustainable forest management. Humphreys (1999: 251) writes, 'The forests regime has coalesced around the core concept of sustainable forest management (SFM) and the norm that forests should be conserved and used in a sustainable manner.' Other global principles include the value of conservation, ecosystem integrity, protected areas, indigenous knowledge and values, and the participation of civil society (Humphreys 1999, 2003, 2006; also, see Cashore *et al.* 2004).

Yet global norms and principles are only a small part of the basket of rules—both formal and informal—that shape forest management. National and local leaders often ignore the concept of sustainable forest management as well as the non-binding principles of institutions such as the ITTO and FSC. The international forests regime is particularly weak and ineffective in Asia, Africa, and South America, most notably where timber profits prop up corrupt politicians, bureaucrats, and military officers. This explains in part why tropical deforestation has persisted largely unimpeded over the last few decades despite a global outcry and repeated government promises to do better (Dauvergne 2001).

International regimes, then, can solve global environmental problems. The history of the depletion of the ozone layer confirms this. Yet the regimes for climate change and deforestation, for different reasons, are still largely ineffective. Supporters of regimes argue this reflects in part the complexity of the causes and consequences of these problems, as well as the need for economic sacrifices to solve them. For them, this suggests a need to work even

---

BOX 14.5

ITTO and FSC

International Tropical Timber Organization (ITTO)

The 1983 International Tropical Timber Agreement (in force from 1985) created the International Tropical Timber Organization (ITTO), with its headquarters in Yokohama, Japan. A successor agreement was negotiated in 1994 (in force since 1997). The ITTO's mandate is to facilitate consultation and co-operation among member countries that produce and consume tropical timber. There are fifty-nine members (as of 2004), representing 90 per cent of world trade in tropical timber. The organization is committed to assisting members with meeting the so-called Year 2000 Objective, which calls for members, by the year 2000, to trade only tropical timber products that originate from sustainably managed forests. (This is still being pursued despite the passing of the target year.) The Bali Partnership Fund is designed to assist producers with implementing sustainable forest management. *Source*: ITTO website, at www.itto.or.jp/live/index.jsp

Forest Stewardship Council (FSC)

The non-profit Forest Stewardship Council was founded in 1993 to promote more effective forest management. Its members include environmental organizations, forest industries, indigenous and community groups, and forest certification bodies. The FSC accredits and monitors organizations that certify that forest products come from 'a well-managed forest'—that is, a forest that meets the FSC's Principles and Criteria of Forest Stewardship. The FSC visits certified forests to ensure compliance. It further supports the development of regional, national, and local standards that implement these principles and criteria. The FSC logo on a wood product is ultimately designed to provide a 'credible guarantee' to the consumer 'that the product comes from a well-managed forest.' *Source*: FSC website, at www.fsc.org/en

harder to strengthen these regimes. For critics of regimes, however, the failure to slow climate change and deforestation suggests the innate limitations of regimes as a mechanism to constrain and guide economic globalization. The energy expended on seemingly endless international negotiations on climate change and deforestation, some critics argue, would be better spent elsewhere, perhaps in labs developing new technologies, or in communities developing new ethics. A few of these critics even see the focus on the development of agreements, such as an international forests convention, as a strategic move by powerful actors to delay real action and ensure that 'business as usual' continues for as long as possible (Dauvergne 2005).

KEY POINTS

- All sides agree that the South needs financial and technical support to pursue global sustainability.

- Some see current efforts—for example the GEF—as a critical lifeline for weak economies. Others see such financing as being too small to matter, and still others see global development assistance as a cause of the global environmental crisis, with states exporting natural resources to service and repay foreign debt.

- Environmental regimes are the primary global mechanism for co-ordinating environmental management across states. It is exceedingly difficult, however, to create and maintain an effective environmental regime.

- Most agree that the ozone regime has been effective, largely because the causes, consequences, and solutions of ozone depletion are straightforward.

- The climate and deforestation regimes are much weaker than the ozone regime. Advocates of regimes see this as temporary, a result of the sheer complexity and difficulty of the science, politics, and economics of climate change and deforestation. Critics, on the other hand, see weak regimes for problems such as climate change and deforestation as inevitable within the current global political economy; for some, these are not a part of the solution but rather a part of the reasons for failure.

- Most advocates and critics of regimes agree, however, that solutions to climate change and deforestation will require far more than financing and regimes. Solving them will require a level of innovation, co-operation, and sacrifice never seen before in the history of global environmental politics.

Conclusion

What, then, is the nature of global environmental change in an era of globalization? Is globalization a force for environmental progress or crisis? Are global environmental regimes and the norm of sustainable development effectively channelling globalization to ensure a sustainable future? The record is mixed. For some problems, such as ozone depletion, global co-operation has indeed been effective. But for problems such as tropical deforestation, the global community appears to be making no headway at all. Perhaps the greatest environmental problem of all is climate change. Here, it also appears that global efforts are failing. Can sustainable development and regimes alone 'solve' deforestation and climate change? The answer seems clear: no. These may indeed help. But such great problems will require new national policies, new corporate ethics, more North–South financial transfers, innovative markets, technological advances, and new forms of co-operation. It will be a bumpy path forward: one that will, because of the nature of the global political economy and global environmental change—no doubt, most unjustly—impose the greatest hardships on the world's poorest and least powerful peoples. That much seems certain.

The chapter did not strive to convince the reader to believe in a particular set of arguments. Already far too many globalization and anti-globalization 'environmental ideologues' preach or chant at, rather than talk to, each other. The goal was instead to deepen the understanding of the range of reasonable and logical arguments about the environmental impacts of the ongoing changes to the global political economy. The hope is that, one day, those who choose to act on their beliefs—from joining the World Bank's environment team to protesting at an anti-globalization rally—will do so with the humility of knowing the complexities and uncertainties of the relationship between globalization and the environment.

 ## QUESTIONS

1. What, in the broadest terms, is the relationship between globalization and global environmental change?

2. What is the globalization of environmentalism? Is the overall trend positive or negative?

3. Is the Environmental Kuznets Curve a useful policy tool?

4. Which is more common: 'pollution havens' or 'exporting environmentalism'?

5. What are the effects of inequality and consumption on global environmental conditions?

6. What are the effects of trade and corporations on global environmental conditions?

7. What are the effects of financing and regimes on global environmental conditions?

8. Is there a global environmental crisis? If yes, why? If no, why?

9. Can we solve global environmental problems within the current political and economic structures? If yes, how? If no, why?

FURTHER READING

■ Brown, J. W., Chasek, P. S., and Downie, D. L. (2006), *Global Environmental Politics*, 4th edn (Boulder, CO: Westview Press). Introduces the academic study of global environmental politics with a focus on international agreements.

■ Clapp, J., and Dauvergne, P. (2005), *Paths to a Green World: The Political Economy of the Global Environment* (Cambridge, MA: MIT Press). Maps out an original typology to classify the dominant world views regarding the impact of the global political economy on the global environment.

■ Conca, K., and Dabelko, G. D. (eds) (2004), *Green Planet Blues: Environmental Politics from Stockholm to Johannesburg*, 3rd edn (Boulder, CO: Westview Press). Surveys and extracts core concepts and arguments from seminal articles in global environmental politics.

■ **Dauvergne, P. (ed.) (2005),** *Handbook of Global Environmental Politics* **(Cheltenham: Edward Elgar).** Collection of original and cutting-edge articles by many of the world's premier scholars of global environmental politics.

■ **Dryzek, J. S. (2005),** *The Politics of the Earth: Environmental Discourses*, **2nd edn (Oxford: Oxford University Press).** Analysis of the history of environmental discourses. Collection of accompanying readings is available in: J. S. Dryzek and D. Schlosberg (eds) (2005), *Debating the Earth: The Environmental Politics Reader*, 2nd edn (Oxford: Oxford University Press).

■ *Global Environmental Politics* **(www.mitpressjournals.org/loi/glep?cookieSet=1).** Scholarly journal that contains the latest innovative and original research on environment and the global political economy (first issue February 2001).

■ **Haas, P. M. (ed.) (2003),** *Environment in the New Global Economy* **(Cheltenham: Edward Elgar).** A collection of sixty seminal articles on environment, globalization, and the global political economy (previously published, dating from 1944 to 2001).

■ **Lipschutz, R. D. (2004),** *Global Environmental Politics: Power, Perspectives, and Practice* **(Washington, DC: CQ Press).** A text on the politics of the global environment, that among other issues, examines green thought, capitalism, power, and international environmental policies.

■ **Paterson, M. (2000),** *Understanding Global Environmental Politics: Domination, Accumulation, Resistance* **(London: Macmillan/St. Martin's Press).** Draws on the literature in international relations to provide a critical account of the environmental impacts of the global political economy.

■ **Pojman, L. P. (ed.) (2004),** *Environmental Ethics: Readings in Theory and Application*, **4th edn (Belmont, CA: Wadsworth Publishing).** Balanced collection of many of the most influential articles in environmental philosophy and politics, including deep ecology, generational obligations, population, hunger, economics, and sustainability.

■ **Princen, T., Maniates, M. F., and Conca, K. (eds) (2002),** *Confronting Consumption* **(Cambridge, MA: MIT Press).** Breaks new ground in the understanding of consumption as a core problem for the global political economy.

■ **Young, O. R. (2002),** *The Institutional Dimensions of Environmental Change: Fit, Interplay, and Scale* **(Cambridge, MA: MIT Press).** Leading scholar of environmental regimes analyses the role of institutions in causing and constraining environmental change.

WEB LINKS

● **www.unep.org** United Nations Environment Programme and **www.undp.org** United Nations Development Programme. Provide entries into environment and development data and projects of the United Nations.

● **www.gefweb.org** Global Environment Facility. Outlines projects and programmes to finance protection of the global environment in developing countries.

● **www.wri.org** World Resources Institute. Source of scientific environmental research and non-governmental policy proposals. Includes agriculture, biodiversity, forests, climate change, marine ecosystems, water, and health.

● **www.iisd.org**   International Institute for Sustainable Development. Monitors the proceedings of global environmental negotiations and conferences.

● **www.worldwatch.org**   WorldWatch Institute. Source of data on the global environmental 'crisis'. Challenges some of the data (and interpretations) of the United Nations, World Bank, and governments.

 Visit the Online Resource Centre that accompanies this book for more information: www.oxfordtextbooks.co.uk/orc/ravenhill2e/

Glossary

Absolute advantage Where a country produces one or more goods or services at lower cost than other countries.

Adjustable peg A form of international monetary system in which governments are permitted to change their currencies' exchange rates, normally fixed in value against other currencies.

Anarchy The absence of a centralized authority in the international system capable of enforcing agreements.

Autarchy When a country attempts to maximize its self-sufficiency by minimizing contacts with the global economy.

Balance of payments An account of a country's transactions with foreign countries and international institutions in a specific period. Transactions are divided into current account, which consists of the balance of trade in goods and services plus profits and interest on overseas assets less those paid to foreign owners of domestic assets, plus net transfers such as worker remittances. The capital account consists of inflows and outflows of money for investment, and for grants and loans (and their repayment). The balance of payments is an accounting identity: the entries in the account should sum to zero with, for example, any imbalances on the current account being offset by net movements of capital.

Balance of trade *see* Balance of payments

Bounded rationality Rational decision-making in a context of incomplete knowledge.

Bretton Woods New Hampshire village where the Mount Washington Hotel is located—the site of the 1944 United Nations Monetary and Financial Conference: the birthplace of the International Monetary Fund and the World Bank. 'Bretton Woods' is often used as shorthand for post-war international financial regimes.

Capital account *see* Balance of payments

Capital controls Restrictions placed by governments on private actors' moving funds into or out of the territories they control.

Coase Theorem The argument that economic efficiency will be optimized as long as property rights are fully allocated, and completely free trade in these rights is possible.

Collaboration games A type of game where the Pareto-optimal solution the players desire may not be an equilibrium outcome; for example, the pursuit of strategies that are rational for individual players produces a sub-optimal outcome, as in the Prisoner's Dilemma.

Common market A customs union that also allows free movement of factors (capital, labour) within its boundaries.

Common pool resources Goods that cannot be withheld from those that do not pay for them, and whose consumption comes at the expense of other potential consumers.

Comparative advantage Where a country is relatively more efficient at producing at least one product than others, even though it may lack absolute advantage in producing that good or service. Production according to comparative advantage enables specialization in relatively more efficient production, thereby increasing welfare.

Competitive advantage The competitive strength of an economy that derives from the capacity of its firms in various sectors. Whether government intervention can enhance an economy's competitive advantage remains a matter of considerable controversy.

Conditionality The stipulation by lenders of conditions that borrowers must meet if they are to continue to receive instalments of their loans.

Co-ordination games A type of game that typically has multiple Nash Equilibria, some of which are more preferred by one or more players.

Current account *see* Balance of payments

Customs unions Agreements between two or more countries to trade freely between themselves, and to adopt a common tariff on imports from countries outside the customs union.

Dollarization The adoption by foreign countries of the US dollar as their national currency.

Dumping A situation where a country's exports are sold in foreign markets at a price less than that at which they are sold at home.

Ecological footprint A measure (translated into hectares of average biologically productive land) of the resources required to sustain a person's lifestyle.

Ecological shadow A concept that attempts to capture the environmental impact of a country in jurisdictions beyond its sovereign control.

Economic union A common market that has also adopted common monetary and fiscal policies.

Economies of scale Realized when longer production runs enable firms to produce at a lower average unit cost.

Embedded liberalism A concept put forward by John Gerard Ruggie, following Karl Polanyi, to capture the compromise in post-war economic regimes between liberalization and the pursuit of domestic social and political objectives.

Enabling clause Formally, the 1979 Decision on Differential and More Favourable Treatment, Reciprocity and Fuller Participation of Developing Countries, it legitimizes Special and differential treatment in the trade regime for less developed countries.

Environmental Kuznets Curve A graphical representation of the relationship between level of per capita income and pollution showing that levels of pollution initially increase with economic growth but then decline once per capita income reaches high levels.

Epistemology What knowledge is and how it is acquired.

Export-oriented industrialization Strategy for economic development based on domestic production targeted primarily at international markets.

Exporting environmentalism The use by TNCs in less developed economies of more environmentally-friendly technologies than are required by local laws.

Externalities Consequences for societal welfare (costs and benefits) that are not captured in the market price of a good; for example, pollution is a negative externality if the producers do not pay the financial costs it imposes on society. Innovation can be a positive externality if pricing does not capture the full benefits that flow from innovators to the broader society. Externalities are a type of market failure.

Factor price equalization The process whereby trade generates a tendency for the prices of factors (capital or labour) to be equalized (a process predicted by the Stolper-Samuelson Theorem).

Feldstein–Horioka Puzzle In a world of unfettered capital mobility, savings will flow to those countries offering the highest interest rates, while investment will be financed from the lowest-cost source. Feldstein and Horioka, however, found in a 1980 study that national savings and domestic investment were highly correlated in sixteen OECD countries, suggesting the presence of segmented capital markets and low capital mobility.

Financial intermediaries Institutions that provide links between those with surplus savings and those who desire to use these funds for investment purposes.

Fiscal policies Government budgetary policies on taxation and expenditure.

Foreign direct investment (FDI) The establishment by domestic firms of a foreign subsidiary, or their acquisition of a controlling interest in an existing foreign company.

Free riders Actors who fail to contribute appropriately to the cost of the goods or services from which they benefit.

Free trade area Agreements between two or more countries to remove tariff and non-tariff barriers on trade between themselves.

General Agreement on Tariffs and Trade (GATT) A 1947 agreement that became the principal component of the international trade regime following the failure of the international community to establish the International Trade Organization. Its provisions were incorporated in the World Trade Organization when it was established in 1995.

Generalized System of Preferences (GSP) Non-reciprocal programmes of tariff preferences on selected goods for less developed countries introduced by industrialized countries after GATT in 1971 permitted a waiver of the MFN requirement to facilitate special and differential treatment for LDCs.

Gini coefficient A measure of income inequality devised by the Italian statistician, Corrado Gini. The Gini coefficient is a number between zero and one where zero represents perfect equality (everyone has the same income) and one represents perfect inequality (one person has all the income, all others have zero). The Gini coefficient is calculated using the Lorenz curve, a graph showing the relationship between the percentage of households and the share of the country's income they receive.

Global Environmental Facility (GEF) A fund established in 1991, jointly managed by the World Bank, the United Nations Development Programme, and the United Nations Environment Programme, which finances environmental projects in less developed economies.

Global value chain The sequence of activities involved in the production of a good or service through which technology is combined with material and labour inputs.

Gold exchange standard An international monetary system in which it is possible for central banks to convert their foreign exchange holdings into gold (one or more countries must guarantee that they will permit others to convert their currencies into gold, as the USA did in the period from 1945 to 1971).

Gold standard A monetary system in which the money supply is linked directly to the country's holdings of gold; citizens are usually entitled to exchange banknotes for gold. An international gold standard is an international monetary system in which the value of all currencies is set in terms of a unit of gold, and settlement of trade imbalances occurs through the transfer of gold reserves.

Graduation The process by which less developed economies are removed from the list of countries given special trade benefits by industrialized countries once they reach a certain level of development.

Gross Domestic Product (GDP) The total value of goods and services produced by an economy in a specific time period.

Gross National Product (GNP) Gross domestic product plus the income earned by domestic residents from investment abroad less the income earned by foreigners in the domestic market.

Heckscher–Ohlin Principle Countries will export those commodities that are intensive in the factor (land, labour, capital) in which they are best endowed.

Hegemonic stability Argument that liberal (open) international economic regimes are associated with the presence of a dominant state.

Heavily Indebted Poor Countries (HIPC) A grouping of the world's poorest countries, identified as those eligible for concessional assistance from the World Bank group's International Development Association and from the IMF's Poverty Reduction and Growth Facility that face an unsustainable debt situation after the full application of traditional debt relief mechanisms. A debt initiative for HIPC was proposed by the World Bank and the IMF in 1996.

Import-substitution industrialization (ISI) Strategy pursued by less developed economies to promote industrialization by domestic production of goods previously imported (usually undertaken behind high levels of tariff protection).

Inclusive club goods Goods that can be withheld from those who do not pay for them, and whose consumption does not reduce their availability to other potential consumers.

Infant industry promotion Idea that recently-established industries require protection until they are able to produce efficiently and withstand import competition from more advanced economies.

Interdependence A network of relationships among actors that is costly for any of the actors to break.

Intermediation The process whereby financial institutions link savers and investors of funds.

International Bank for Reconstruction and Development The original component of the World Bank group, created at the Bretton Woods conference in 1944. Subsequently, two other institutions, the International Finance Corporation (1956) and the International Development Association (1960) were added to the group. Most writers today simply refer to the group of institutions as the 'World Bank'.

Private goods Goods and services that can be withheld from those who do not pay for them, and that cannot be used by others without additional production taking place.

Property rights The legal right of owners of resources to be paid for their usage; for example, fees paid to patent or copyright owners.

Public goods Goods that cannot be withheld from consumers who do not pay for them, and whose consumption does not reduce their availability to other consumers.

Purchasing power parity (PPP) A method of computing an appropriate exchange rate between currencies (rather than that determined by the market or fixed by governments), which rests on determining domestic purchasing power by calculating the price of a basket of goods in the two countries in local currencies. To compute the PPP exchange rate between the two currencies, one takes the ratio of the prices for the baskets of goods in local currencies. PPP exchange rates are often used as a means of presenting a more accurate comparison of standards of living across countries than those given by actual exchange rates.

Race to the bottom The idea that, in a globalized economy, some governments will attempt to increase their attractiveness to investors by offering minimal requirements on, for example, environmental and labour standards and taxation.

Reciprocity The principle in international trade that countries benefiting from trade liberalization by others should offer equivalent (but not necessarily identical) concessions in return.

Regime A set of international governing arrangements (including rules, norms, and procedures) that are intended to regularize the behaviour of state and non-state actors, and control its effects.

Rules of origin Regulations negotiated as part of free trade agreements that specify the conditions that goods must meet if they are to be considered as originating in a partner country (for example, that a specific share of the good's value must be added locally). Intended to prevent non-partner countries from trans-shipping goods to take advantage of the lower tariffs offered within a free trade agreement.

Safeguards Provisions enabling countries with problems in specific sectors or their economy more generally to seek temporary exemptions from some of their obligations in the trade regime.

Seigniorage The profit that results from the difference between the cost of producing and distributing money and the face value of that money. Originally, the difference between the face value of a coin and the cost of the metal that went into that coin.

Singapore issues The 1996 WTO ministerial meeting in Singapore began exploratory work on co-operation on policy harmonization in four areas: investment, competition, transparency in government procurement, and trade facilitation. These subsequently became known as the 'Singapore issues'.

Single undertaking The principle within the GATT/WTO that members must accept all parts of the agreement rather than signing on selectively to individual components.

Special and differential treatment Exemptions for less developed countries from some of the obligations imposed on other members of the trade regime.

Special Drawing Rights (SDR) An international reserve asset created by the International Monetary Fund in 1969. Over 30 billion SDRs have been created; these were distributed by the IMF to member countries in proportion to the size of their IMF quota. The SDR is valued in terms of a basket of sixteen major currencies.

Specific Factors Model Movement of factors of production to different uses following trade liberalization may be difficult: the effects of trade, therefore, contrary to the Stolper–Samuelson Theorem, may not benefit/harm different factors across various sectors but rather hurt/benefit *all* factors *within* the same industrial sector.

Sterilization Efforts by monetary authorities to counter the impact of international monetary flows on domestic economic activity by issuing/selling financial instruments to reduce or increase the domestic money supply.

Stolper–Samuelson Theorem Trade benefits the owners of factors of production that are relatively abundant in an economy while lowering the returns to owners of relatively scarce factors; for example, trade for labour-rich countries such as China should benefit (their relatively-abundant) labour.

Strategic trade policies Efforts by governments to promote domestic companies in international industries characterized by oligopoly through policies (for example, investment subsidies) intended to permit them to move strategically (for example, enable them to become early developers of a product).

Structural adjustment programmes These are often designed in association with the international financial institutions, and pursued by countries experiencing debt problems. They usually include privatization of assets, reductions in government expenditure to reduce budgetary deficits, trade liberalization, encouragement of foreign investment, and currency devaluation.

Sunk costs Costs that are difficult for investors to recover; for example, investment in physical infrastructure, plant and machinery.

Supranational institutions International institutions to which states have ceded some of their sovereignty; for example, the European Union.

Swiss formula A method of reducing tariffs based on a mathematical equation, which results in higher tariffs being reduced more than lower ones. It was used in the Tokyo Round of GATT negotiations.

Terms of trade The price of a country's exports relative to the price of its imports.

Trade creation Where a preferential trade agreement leads to the replacement of domestic production by lower-cost imports from a party to the trade agreement.

Trade diversion Where a preferential trade agreement leads to the displacement of goods previously imported from a non-preferred trading partner by imports from a party to the preferred agreement (because these preferential imports now enter the local market at a reduced tariff).

Tragedy of the commons Garrett Hardin, in a paper published in *Science* in 1968, first put forward the idea that individuals rationally pursuing their self-interest where they have access to a freely available good (a 'commons') will inevitably act in a way that is collectively irrational; for example, through over-grazing a pasture.

Transaction costs The costs other than the monetary price that are involved in trading goods and services; for example, costs of search and information, bargaining and decision-making, and policing and enforcement. High transaction costs are often viewed as a significant example of externalities.

Transnational corporations (also Multinational enterprises) Companies that engage in Foreign direct investment; that is, which own, control, and manage assets in more than one country.

Triffin Dilemma Yale University economist Robert Triffin pointed out in a 1960 book that the Bretton Woods monetary system rested on the confidence of other countries in the gold exchange standard—that is, that they could convert their dollar holdings into gold—yet the capacity of the USA to guarantee this conversion was being undermined by dollar outflows that were the principal source of new liquidity in the system. If outflows stopped, the system would have insufficient liquidity; if they continued, confidence in the system would be undermined.

TRIMs (Trade-related investment measures) The title of a Uruguay Round WTO agreement that prohibits governments from applying measures that discriminate against foreign companies or foreign products; for example, requirements that foreign investors must source a certain value of their inputs locally ('local content' requirements) or export a certain value of their output ('trade balancing' requirements).

TRIPs (Trade-related aspects of intellectual property rights) A Uruguay Round WTO agreement that establishes minimum levels of protection that governments must give to the intellectual property of fellow WTO members.

Two-level game Term coined by Robert Putnam to refer to negotiations in which governments must negotiate simultaneously at two levels: with domestic constituencies, and with one or more foreign partners.

Voluntary export restraint An agreement between an exporting and an importing country under which the exporting country agrees to limit the total (value or volume of) exports of particular products. Outlawed by the GATT Uruguay Round Agreements.

Washington Consensus (WC) Phrase coined by John Williamson to refer to the prevailing views held in the late 1980s and early 1990s by the international financial institutions and governments of most industrialized countries regarding the desirable policy agenda for less developed economies; for example, liberalization of their trade regimes, privatization of state-owned enterprises, and reduction of state intervention in the economy.

Other Useful Sources

Print

Bannock, G., R. E. Baxter and E. Davis (2003), *The Penguin Dictionary of Economics*, 7th edn (London: Penguin).

Black, J. (2003), *A Dictionary of Economics*, 2nd edn (Oxford: Oxford University Press).

Pearce, D. W. (1992), *The MIT Dictionary of Modern Economics*, 4th edn (Cambridge, Mass.: MIT Press).

Online

- Deardorff's Glossary of International Economics
  http://www-personal.umich.edu/~alandear/glossary

- Economics—Wikipedia, the free encyclopedia
  http://en.wikipedia.org/wiki/Economics

- *The Economist*'s Economics A–Z
  http://economist.com/research/Economics

References

Abbott, A. J., and De Vita, G. (2003), 'Another Piece in the Feldstein–Horioka Puzzle', *Scottish Journal of Political Economy,* 50/1: 68–89.

Abbott, K. W., and Snidal, D. (2000), 'Hard and Soft Law in International Governance', *International Organization,* 54/3: 421–456.

Abdelal, R. (2007), *Capital Rules: The Construction of Global Finance* (Cambridge, Mass.: Harvard University Press).

Abernathy, F. H., Dunlop, J. T., Hammond, J. H., and Weil, D. (1999), *A Stitch in Time: Lean Retailing and the Transformation of Manufacturing* (Oxford: Oxford University Press).

Abugre, C. (2000), 'Who Governs Low Income Countries? An Interview with Charles Abugre on the PRS Initiative', *News and Notices for IMF and World Bank Watchers,* 2/3, Autumn.

ActionAid (2006), 'The Doha Deception Round: How the US and EU Cheated Developing Countries at the WTO Hong Kong Ministerial', June, www.actionaid. org.uk/doc_lib/doha_deception_round.pdf

Adams, N. (1993), *Worlds Apart: The North–South Divide and the International System* (London: Zed Books).

Aggarwal, V. K. (1985), *Liberal Protectionism: The International Politics of Organized Textile Trade* (Berkeley, Calif. and Los Angeles: University of California Press).

—— (1994), 'Comparing Regional Cooperation Efforts in Asia-Pacific and North America', in A. Mack and J. Ravenhill (eds), *Pacific Cooperation: Building Economic and Security Regimes in the Asia-Pacific Region* (Sydney: Allen & Unwin).

—— (1996), *Debt Games: Strategic Interaction in International Debt Rescheduling* (Cambridge: Cambridge University Press).

—— (ed.) (1998), *Institutional Designs for a Complex World: Bargaining, Linkages and Nesting* (Ithaca, NY: Cornell University Press).

—— (2001), 'Economics: International Trade', in P. J. Simmons and C. de Jonge Oudraat (eds), *Managing Global Issues: Lessons Learned* (Washington, DC: Carnegie Endowment for International Peace).

—— and Dupont, C. (1999), 'Goods, Games and Institutions', *International Political Science Review,* 20/4: 393–409.

—— —— (2002), '"Goods, Games, and Institutions": A Reply', *International Political Science Review,* 23/4: 402–410.

Alinsky, S. (1972), *Rules for Radicals: A Practical Primer for Realistic Radicals* (New York: Vintage Books).

Allen, J., and Thompson, G. F. (1997), 'Think Global, and Then Think Again: Economic Globalization in Context', *Area,* 29/3: 213–227.

Allen, M. (2003), 'Some Lessons from the Argentine Crisis: A Fund Staff View', in J. J. Teunissen and A. Akkerman (eds), *The Crisis That Was Not Prevented: Lessons for Argentina, the IMF, and Globalisation* (The Hague: FONDAD).

Alt, J., and Gilligan, M. (1994), 'The Political Economy of Trading States', *Journal of Political Philosophy,* 2/2: 165–192.

Amin, S. (1976), *Unequal Development* (New York: Monthly Review Press).

—— (1997), *Capitalism in the Age of Globalization* (London: Zed Books).

Amsden, A. (1989), *Asia's Next Giant: South tored and Late Industrialisation* (New York: Oxford University Press).

Anderson, J. E., and van Wincoop, E. (2001), 'Gravity with Gravitas: A Solution to the Border Puzzle', NBER Working Paper 8079 (Cambridge, Mass.: National Bureau of Economic Research).

Andrews, D., and Willett, T. (1997), 'Financial Interdependence and the State', *International Organization,* 51/3: 479–511.

Annan, K. (2005), *In Larger Freedom: Towards Security, Development and Human Rights For All,* Report of the Secretary General (New York: United Nations).

Archibugi, D. (ed.) (2003), *Debating Cosmopolitics* (London: Verso).

Arden-Clarke, C. (1992), 'South–North Terms of Trade: Environmental Protection and Sustainable Development', *International Environmental Affairs,* 4/2: 122–139.

Arndt, S. W., and Kierzkowski, S. (2001), *Fragmentation: New Production Patterns in the World Economy* (Oxford: Oxford University Press).

Arrow, K., Bolin, B., Costanza, R., Dasgupta, P., Folk, C., Holling, C. S., Jansson, B., Levin, S., Mäler, K., Perrings, C., and Pimentel, D. (1998), 'Economic Growth, Carrying Capacity and the Environment', *Science,* 268 (28 April 1995), in J. Dryzek and D. Schlosberg (eds), *Debating the Earth: The Environmental Politics Reader* (Oxford: Oxford University Press).

Arup, C. (2000), *The New World Trade Organization Agreements: Globalizing Law through Services and Intellectual Property* (Cambridge: Cambridge University Press).

Aslanbeigui, N., and Summerfield, G. (2000), 'The Asian Crisis, Gender and the International Financial Architecture', *Feminist Economics,* 6/3: 81–103.

Axelrod, R., and Keohane, R. O. (1986), 'Achieving Cooperation under Anarchy: Strategies and Institutions', *World Politics,* 38/1: 226–254.

488

Ayres, R. L. (1983), *Banking on the Poor: The World Bank and World Poverty* (Cambridge, Mass.: MIT Press).

Bachrach, P., and Baratz, M. S. (1970), *Power and Poverty: Theory and Practice* (New York: Oxford University Press).

Backhouse, R. (2002), *The Penguin History of Economics* (London: Penguin).

Bair, J. (2005), 'Global Capitalism and Commodity Chains: Looking Back and Going Forward', *Competition & Change*, 9/2: 153–180.

Bairoch, P. (1996), 'Globalization Myths and Realities: One Century of External Trade and Foreign Investment', in R. Boyer and D. Drache (eds), *States against Market: The Limits of Globalization* (London: Routledge).

Baker, A. (2006), *The Group of Seven: Finance Ministries, Central Banks and Global Financial Governance* (London/New York: Routledge).

Baldwin, C. Y., and Clark, K. B. (1997), 'Managing in an Age of Modularity', *Harvard Business Review*, 75/5: 84–93.

—— —— (2000), *Design Rules, Vol. 1: The Power of Modularity* (Boston, Mass.: MIT Press).

Baldwin, R. E. (1997), 'The Causes of Regionalism', *World Economy*, 20/7: 865–888.

—— (2006), 'Multilateralising Regionalism: Spaghetti Bowls as Building Blocs on the Path to Global Free Trade', *World Economy*, 29/11: 1451–1518.

Banerjee, A., and Zanghieri, P. (2003), 'A New Look at the Feldstein–Horioka Puzzle Using an Integrated Panel', CEPII Working Paper 2003–22 (Paris: Centre d'Etudes Prospectives et d'Informations Internationales).

—— Deaton, A., Lustig, N., Rogoff, K., with Hsu, E. (2006), 'An Evaluation of World Bank Research, 1998–2005', September.

Baran, P. A. (1976), *The Political Economy of Growth* (Harmondsworth: Penguin).

Barber, W. (1991), *A History of Economic Thought*, reprinted edn (London: Penguin).

Barr, N. (1998), *The Economics of the Welfare State*, 3rd edn (Oxford: Oxford University Press).

Bauer, R. A., Pool, I., and Dexter, L. A. (1972), *American Business and Public Policy*, 2nd edn (Chicago: Aldine Atherton).

Baxter, M., and Crucini, M. J. (1993), 'Explaining Saving–Investment Correlations', *American Economic Review*, 83/3: 416–436.

Bayoumi, T. (1990), 'Savings–Investment Correlations', *IMF Staff Papers*, 37: 360–387.

—— (1997), *Financial Integration and Real Activity* (Manchester: Manchester University Press).

—— and Rose, A. D. (1993), 'Domestic Savings and Intra-national Capital Flows', *European Economic Review*, 37/6: 1197–1202.

Beason, R., and Weinstein, D. E. (1993), 'Growth, Economies of Scale, and Targeting in Japan, 1955–90', Harvard

Institute for Economic Research Discussion Paper No. 1644 (Cambridge, Mass.: Harvard University).

Beck, U. (1992), *The Risk Society* (London: Sage).

Beeson, M. (2000), 'Mahathir and the Markets: Globalisation and the Pursuit of Economic Autonomy in Malaysia', *Pacific Affairs*, 73/3: 35–51.

Bekaert, G., Hodrick, R. J., and Zhang, X. (2005), 'International Stock Return Comovements', NBER Working Paper 11906 (Cambridge, Mass.: National Bureau of Economic Research).

Bello, W. (1997), 'Fast Track Capitalism, Geo-economic Competition, and the Sustainable Development Debate in East Asia', in C. Thomas and P. Wilkin (eds), *Globalization and the South* (London: Macmillan).

—— Bullard, N., and Malhotra, K. (eds) (2000), *Global Finance: New Thinking on Regulating Speculative Capital Markets* (London: Zed Books).

Benton, T., and Craib, I. (2001), *Philosophy of Social Science* (London: Routledge).

Berger, S. (2006), *How We Compete: What Companies Around the World Are Doing to Make it in Today's Global Economy* (New York: Currency Doubleday).

—— and Dore, R. (eds) (1996), *National Diversity and Global Capitalism* (Ithaca, NY: Cornell University Press).

Bergsten, C. F. (1997), 'The Dollar and the Euro', *Foreign Affairs*, 76/4: 83–95.

—— (1999), 'America and Europe: Clash of the Titans', *Foreign Affairs*, 78/2: 20–34.

Bernard, M., and Ravenhill, J. (1995), 'Beyond Product Cycles and Flying Geese: Regionalization, Hierarchy, and the Industrialization of East Asia', *World Politics*, 47/2: 171–209.

Bernhard, W., and Leblang, D. (1999), 'Democratic Institutions and Exchange Rate Commitments', *International Organization*, 53/1: 71–97.

Bhagwati, J. (1988), *Protectionism* (Cambridge, Mass.: MIT Press).

—— (1991), *The World Trading System at Risk* (New York: Harvester Wheatsheaf).

—— (1995), 'US Trade Policy: The Infatuation with Free Trade Areas', in J. N. Bhagwati and A. O. Krueger (eds), *The Dangerous Drift to Preferential Trade Agreements* (Washington, DC: AEI Press).

—— and Ruggie, J. G. (eds) (1984), *Power, Passions, and Purpose: Prospects for North–South Negotiations* (Cambridge, Mass.: MIT Press).

—— Brecher, R., Dinopoulos, E., and Srinivasan, T. N. (1987), 'Quid Pro Quo Foreign Investment and Welfare: A Political-Economy-Theoretic Model', *Journal of Development Economics*, 27/1–2: 127–138.

Bhattarai, M., and Hammig, M. (2001), 'Institutions and the Environmental Kuznets Curve for Deforestation: A Crosscountry Analysis for Latin America, Africa and Asia', *World Development*, 29/6: 995–1010.

BIS (Bank for International Settlements) (2003), *International Banking and Financial Market Developments* (Geneva: BIS).

—— (2005), *Triennial Central Bank Survey: Foreign Exchange and Derivatives Market Activity in 2004* (Basel: BIS).

—— (2006), *OTC Derivatives Market Activity in the First Half of 2006* (Basel: BIS). *BIS Quarterly Review* (2001) (Geneva: Bank for International Settlements).

—— (2005) (Geneva: Bank for International Settlements).

Blackhurst, R. (1998), 'The Capacity of the WTO to Fulfill its Mandate', in A. O. Krueger (ed.), *The WTO as an International Organization* (Chicago: University of Chicago Press).

Blanden, J., Gregg, P., and Machin, S. (2005), 'Intergenerational Mobility in Europe and North America', Centre for Economic Performance (London: London School of Economics).

Blaug, M. (1996), *Economic Theory in Retrospect*, 5th edn (Cambridge: Cambridge University Press).

Blonigen, B., and Feenstra, R. (1996), 'Protectionist Threats and Foreign Direct Investment', NBER Working Paper 5475 (Cambridge, Mass.: National Bureau of Economic Research).

Blustein, P. (2001), *The Chastening: Inside the Crisis that Rocked the Global System and Humbled the IMF* (New York: Public Affairs).

—— (2005), *And the Money Kept Rolling In (And Out): Wall Street, the IMF, and the Bankrupting of Argentina* (New York: Public Affairs).

Blyth, M. (2003), 'Same As It Never Was: Temporality and Typology in the Varieties of Capitalism', *Comparative European Politics*, 1/2: 215–226.

Bomberg, E. E., and Stubb, A. C. G. (2003), *The European Union: How Does It Work?* (Oxford: Oxford University Press).

Bordo, M. (2005), 'Historical Perspectives on Global Imbalances', NBER Working Paper 11383 (Cambridge, Mass.: National Bureau of Economic Research).

—— and Eichengreen, B. (2002), 'Crises Now and Then: What Lessons from the Last Era of Financial Globalization', NBER Working Paper W8716 (Cambridge, Mass.: National Bureau of Economic Research).

—— and Helbling, T. (2003), 'Have National Business Cycles Become More Synchronized?', NBER Working Paper 10130 (Cambridge, Mass.: National Bureau of Economic Research).

—— Eichengreen, B., and Irwin, D. A. (1999), 'Is Globalization Today Really Different than Globalization a Hundred Years Ago?', NBER Working Paper 7195 (Cambridge, Mass.: National Bureau of Economic Research).

—— —— and Kim, J. (1998), 'Was There Really an Earlier Period of International Financial Integration Comparable to Today?', NBER Working Paper 6738 (Cambridge, Mass.: National Bureau of Economic Research).

Borjas, G. J. (1999), 'The Economic Analysis of Immigration', in O. Ashenfelter and D. Card (eds), *Handbook of Labor Economics* (Amsterdam: North-Holland).

—— Freeman, R., and Katz, L. (1996), 'Searching for the Effect of Immigration on the Labor Market', *American Economic Review*, 86/2: 247–251.

Borrus, M., and Zysman, J., (1997), 'Globalization with Borders: The Rise of Wintelism as the Future of Global Competition', *Industry and Innovation*, 4/2: 141–166.

Boughton, J. (2001), *Silent Revolution: The International Monetary Fund, 1979–1989* (Washington, DC: International Monetary Fund).

Bovard, J. (1991), *The Fair Trade Fraud* (New York: St. Martin's Press).

Boyer, R., and Drache, D. (eds) (1996), *States against Markets* (London: Routledge).

Brack, D., Calder, F., and Dolun, M. (2001), 'From Rio to Johannesburg: The Earth Summit and Rio+10', Royal Institute of International Affairs Briefing Paper New Series No. 19 (London: RIIA)

Brawley, M. (2005), *Power, Money, and Trade: Decisions that Shape Global Economic Relations* (Plymouth: Broadview Press).

Brenner, N. (1999), 'Beyond State-Centrism? Space, Territoriality and Geographic Scale in Globalization Studies', *Theory and Society*, 28/1: 39–78.

—— (2004), *New State Spaces: Urban Governance and the Rescaling of Statehood* (Oxford: Oxford University Press).

Brewer, T. L., and Young, S. (1998), *The Multilateral Investment System and Multinational Enterprises* (Oxford: Oxford University Press).

Broadbent, J. (1998), *Environmental Politics in Japan: Networks of Power and Protest* (Cambridge: Cambridge University Press).

Broz, J. L., and Frieden, J. A. (2001), 'The Political Economy of International Monetary Relations', *Annual Review of Political Science*, 4/1: 317–343.

Brune, N., and Garrett, G. (2005), 'The Globalization Rorschach Test: International Economic Integration, Inequality, and the Role of Government', *Annual Review of Political Science*, 8: 399–423.

Bryant, R. C. (2003), *Turbulent Waters: Cross-Border Finance and International Governance* (Washington, DC: Brookings Institution).

Bryant, R. L., and Bailey, S. (1997), *Third World Political Ecology* (London: Routledge).

Bullard, N., Bello, W., and Malhotra, K. (1998), 'Taming the Tigers: The IMF and the Asian Crisis', *Third World Quarterly*, 19/3: 505–555.

Burch, K., and Denemark, R. A. (1997), *Constituting International Political Economy* (Boulder, Colo.: Lynne Rienner).

Burg, J. (2003), 'The World Summit on Sustainable Development: Empty Talk or Call to Action?', *Journal of Environment and Development*, 12/1: 111–120.

490

REFERENCES

Burki, S. J., Perry, G. E., and Dillinger, W. R. (1999), *Beyond the Center: Decentralizing the State* (Washington, DC: World Bank).

Burtless, G., Lawrence, R. Z., Litan, R. E., and Shapiro, R. J. (1998), *Globaphobia: Confronting Fears about Free Trade* (Washington, DC: Brookings Institution).

Busch, A. (2000), 'Unpacking the Globalization Debate: Approaches, Evidence and Data', in C. Hay and D. Marsh (eds), *Demystifying Globalization* (Basingstoke: Palgrave).

Buzan, B., Held, D., and McGrew, A. (1998), 'Realism Versus Cosmopolitanism: A Debate', *Review of International Studies*, 24/3: 387–398.

CAFOD, Christian Aid, Eurodad and Jubilee Research (2003), *Debt and the Millennium Development Goals: A New Deal for Low-Income Countries: Financing Development through Debt Cancellation and Aid*, www.oxfam.org.uk/what_we_do/issues/debt_aid/debt_mdgs.htm

Cai, F., and Warnock, F. E. (2006), 'International Diversification at Home and Abroad', NBER Working Paper 12220 (Cambridge, Mass.: National Bureau of Economic Research).

Calleo, D. (1976), 'The Historiography of the Interwar Period: Reconsiderations', in B. Rowland (ed.), *Balance of Power or Hegemony: The Interwar Monetary System* (New York: New York University Press).

—— (1987), *Beyond American Hegemony* (New York: Basic Books).

Callinicos, A. (2003), *An Anti-Capitalist Manifesto* (Cambridge: Polity Press).

Calvo, G. A., and Talvi, E. (2005), 'Sudden Stop, Financial Factors and Economic Collapse in Latin America: Learning from Argentina and Chile', NBER Working Paper 11153 (Cambridge, Mass.: National Bureau of Economic Research).

Cameron, D. R. (1978), 'The Expansion of the Public Economy: A Comparative Analysis', *American Political Science Review*, 72/4: 1243–1261.

Caner, A., and Wolff, E. (2004), 'Asset Poverty in the United States, 1984–1999', *Challenge: The Magazine of Economic Affairs*, 47/1: 5–52.

Carlos, A. M., and Nicholas, S. (1988), 'Giants of an Earlier Capitalism: The Chartered Trading Companies as Modern Multinationals', *Business History Review*, 62/Autumn: 398–419.

Carr, E. H. (1939/1946), *The Twenty Years' Crisis 1919–1939: An Introduction to the Study of International Relations*, 2nd edn (London: Macmillan).

Carrere, C., and Schiff, M. (2004), 'On the Geography of Trade: Distance is Alive and Well', World Bank Policy Research Working Paper 3206 (Washington, DC: World Bank).

Carson, R. (1962), *Silent Spring* (Boston, Mass.: Houghton Mifflin).

Carver, T., and Thomas, P. (1995), *Rational Choice Marxism* (London: Macmillan).

Cashin, P., McDermott, C. J., and Scott, A. (1999), 'Booms and Slumps in World Commodity Prices', IMF Working Paper 99/155 (Washington, DC: IMF).

Cashore, B., Auld, G., and Newsom, D. (2004), *Governing Through Markets: Forest Certification and the Emergence of Non-state Authority* (New Haven, Conn.: Yale University Press).

Castells, M. (1996), *The Rise of the Network Society* (Oxford: Basil Blackwell).

—— (1997), *The Power of Identity* (Oxford: Basil Blackwell).

—— (1998), *End of the Millennium* (Oxford: Basil Blackwell).

—— (2000), *The Rise of the Network Society* (Oxford: Basil Blackwell).

Castles, S., and Miller, M. (2002), *The Age of Global Migration* (Basingstoke: Palgrave).

Caves, R. E. (1982), *Multinational Enterprise and Economic Analysis* (Cambridge: Cambridge University Press).

Centre for Economic Policy Reform (2002), 'Making Sense of Globalization', CEPR Policy Paper 8 (Paris: CEPR).

Cerny, P. G. (1994), 'The Dynamics of Financial Globalization: Technology, Market Structure, and Policy Response', *Policy Sciences*, 27/4: 319–342.

—— (1995), 'Globalization and the Changing Logic of Collective Action', *International Organization*, 49/4: 595–625.

—— (1997), 'Paradoxes of the Competition State: The Dynamics of Political Globalization', *Government and Opposition*, 32/2: 251–274.

Chandler, A. D. (1977), *The Visible Hand: The Managerial Revolution in American Business* (Cambridge, Mass./London: Harvard University Press).

Chang, H.-J., (2002), *Kicking Away the Ladder: Development Strategy in Historical Perspective* (London: Anthem).

Chase, K. A. (2003), 'Economic Interests and Regional Trading Arrangements: The Case of AFTA', *International Organization*, 57/1: 137–174.

—— (2005), *Trading Blocs: States, Firms, and Regions in the World Economy* (Ann Arbor, Mich.: University of Michigan Press).

Chatterjee, P., and Finger, M. (1994), *The Earth Brokers: Power, Politics and World Development* (London: Routledge).

Chen, S., and Ravallion, M. (2004), 'How Have the World's Poorest Fared Since the Early 1980s?', *World Bank Research Observer*, 19/2: 141–169.

Chenery, H., M. S. A Sluwalici, C. L. G. Bell, J. H. Duloy, and R. Jolly (1974), *Redistribution with Growth: Policies to Improve Income Distribution in Developing Countries in the Context of Economic Growth*, Joint study [commissioned] by the World Bank's Development Research Center and the Institute of Development Studies, University of Sussex (London: Oxford University Press).

Cheru, F. (2001), 'Foot Dragging on Foreign Debt', www.southcentre.org/info/southbulletin/bulletin10/bulletin10web-03.htm

China News Digest (2006), 'Survey of China's Second-Tier Cities', 15 June.

Chiswick, B. R., and Hatton, T. J. (2003), 'International Migration and Integration of Labor Markets', in M. D. Bordo, A. M. Taylor, and J. G. Williamson (eds), *Globalization in Historical Perspective* (Chicago: Chicago University Press).

Chortareas, G. E., and Pelagidis, T. (2004), 'Trade Flows: A Facet of Regionalism or Globalisation?', *Cambridge Journal of Economics*, 28/2: 253–271.

Citrin, J., Green, D., Muste, C., and Wong, C. (1997), 'Public Opinion toward Immigration Reform: The Role of Economic Motivations', *Journal of Politics*, 59/3: 858–881.

Clapp, J. (2001), *Toxic Exports: The Transfer of Hazardous Wastes from Rich to Poor Countries* (Ithaca, NY: Cornell University Press).

—— (2002), 'What the Pollution Havens Debate Overlooks', *Global Environmental Politics*, 2/2: 11–19.

Clark, W. R., and Hallerberg, M. (2000), 'Strategic Interaction between Monetary and Fiscal Actors under Full Capital Mobility', *American Political Science Review*, 94/2: 323–346.

—— and Reichert, U. N. (1998), 'International and Domestic Constraints on Political Business Cycles in OECD Economies', *International Organization*, 52/1: 87–120.

Cline, W. R. (ed.) (1983), *Trade Policy in the 1980s* (Washington, DC: Institute for International Economics).

Club of Rome (authors D. H. Meadows, D. L. Meadows, W. W. Behrens, and J. Randers) (1972), *The Limits to Growth* (New York: Universe Books).

Coakley, J., Fuertes, A.-M., and Spagnolo, F. (2004), 'Is the Feldstein–Horioka Puzzle History?', *The Manchester School*, 72/5: 569–590.

—— Kulasi, F., and Smith, R. (1998), 'The Feldstein–Horioka Puzzle and Capital Mobility: A Review', *International Journal of Finance and Economics*, 3/2: 169–188.

Coase, R. H. (1937), 'The Nature of the Firm', *Economica*, 4/16: 386–405.

—— (1960), 'The Problem of Social Cost', *Journal of Law and Economics*, 3: 1–44.

Coe, D. T., Subramanian, A., Tamirisa, N. T., and Bhavnani, R. (2002), 'The Missing Globalization Puzzle', IMF Working Paper No. 02/171 (Washington, DC: IMF).

Cohen, B. (1998), *The Geography of Money* (Ithaca, NY: Cornell University Press).

—— (2002), 'US Policy on Dollarization: A Political Analysis', *Geopolitics*, 7/1: 63–84.

—— (2003), 'Can the Euro Ever Challenge the Dollar?', *Journal of Common Market Studies*, 41/4: 575–595.

Cohen, J., and Centeno, M. (2006), 'Neoliberalism and Patterns of Economic Performance, 1980–2000', *Annals of the American Academy of Political and Social Sciences*, 606/1: 32–67.

Colander, D. (2001), *The Lost Art of Economics: Essays on Economics and the Economics Profession* (Cheltenham: Edward Elgar).

Condliffe, J. B. (1950), *The Commerce of Nations* (New York: W. W. Norton).

Conybeare, J. A. C. (1980), 'International Organization and the Theory of Property Rights', *International Organization*, 34/3: 307–334.

—— (1984), 'Public Goods, Prisoners' Dilemmas and the International Political Economy', *International Studies Quarterly*, 28/1: 5–22.

Cooke, W. N., and Noble, D. S. (1998), 'Industrial Relations Systems and US Foreign Direct Investment Abroad', *British Journal of Industrial Relations*, 36/4: 581–609.

Cooper, R. N. (1968), *The Economics of Interdependence* (New York: McGraw-Hill).

—— (1972), 'Economic Interdependence and Foreign Policy in the Seventies', *World Politics*, 24/2: 159–181.

—— (1975), 'Prolegomena to the Choice of an International Monetary System', *International Organization*, 29/1: 63–97.

Cornes, R., and Sandler, T. (1996), *The Theory of Externalities, Public Goods, and Club Goods*, 2nd edn (New York: Cambridge University Press).

Cornia, A., Jolly, R., and Stewart, F./UNICEF (eds) (1987), *Adjustment with a Human Face* (Oxford: Oxford University Press).

Cox, R. W. (1981), 'Social Forces, States and World Orders: Beyond International Relations Theory', *Millennium*, 10/2: 126–155.

—— (1987), *Production, Power, and World Order: Social Forces in the Making of History* (New York: Columbia University Press).

—— (2000), 'Explaining Business Support for Regional Trade Agreements', in J. A. Frieden and D. A. Lake (eds), *International Political Economy: Perspectives on Global Wealth and Power*, 4th edn (New York: St. Martin's Press), 366–376.

—— with Sinclair, T. (1996), *Approaches to World Order* (Cambridge: Cambridge University Press).

Crafts, N., and Venables, A. J. (2003), 'Globalization in History: A Geographical Perspective', in M. D. Bordo, A. M. Taylor, and J. G. Williamson (eds), *Globalization in Historical Perspective* (Chicago: Chicago University Press).

Crawford, J.-A., and Florentino, R. V. (2005), 'The Changing Landscape of Regional Trade Agreements', WTO Discussion Paper 8 (Geneva: World Trade Organization).

Croome, J. (1995), *Reshaping the World Trading System: A History of the Uruguay Round* (Geneva: World Trade Organization).

Crouch, C., and Streeck, W. (1997), 'Introduction: The Future of Capitalist Diversity', in C. Crouch and W. Streeck (eds), *Political Economy of Modern Capitalism* (London: Sage).

492

Crystal, J. (1994), 'The Politics of Capital Flight: Exit and Exchange Rates in Latin America', *Review of International Studies*, 20/2: 131–147.

—— (2003), *Unwanted Company: Foreign Investment in American Industries* (Ithaca, NY: Cornell University Press).

Cumings, B. (1984), 'The Origins and Development of the Northeast Asian Political Economy: Industrial Sectors, Product Cycles, and Political Consequences', *International Organization*, 38/1: 1–40.

Cutler, A. C. (2003), *Private Power and Global Authority* (Cambridge: Cambridge University Press).

—— Haufler, V., and Porter, T. (eds) (1999), *Private Authority and International Affairs* (Albany, NY: State University of New York Press).

Dahl, R. A. (1963), *Modern Political Analysis* (Englewood Cliffs, NJ: Prentice-Hall).

Daly, H. (1993), 'The Perils of Free Trade', *Scientific American* (November): 50–57.

—— (1996), *Beyond Growth: The Economics of Sustainable Development* (Boston, Mass.: Beacon Press).

—— (2002), 'Uneconomic Growth and Globalization in a Full World', *Natur und Kultur*, www.puaf.umd.edu/faculty/daly/unecon.pdf

Dam, K. W. (1970), *The GATT: Law and International Economic Organization* (Chicago: University of Chicago Press).

Dash, K., Cronin, P., and Goddard, R. (2003), 'Introduction', in R. Goddard, P. Cronin, and K. Dash (eds), *International Political Economy: State–Market Relations in a Changing Global Order*, 2nd edn (Basingstoke: Palgrave).

Dauvergne, P. (1997), *Shadows in the Forest: Japan and the Politics of Timber in Southeast Asia* (Cambridge, Mass.: MIT Press).

—— (1999), 'Asia's Environment after the 1997 Financial Meltdown: The Need of a Regional Response', *Asian Perspective: A Journal of Regional and International Affairs*, 23/3: 53–77.

—— (2001), *Loggers and Degradation in the Asia-Pacific: Corporations and Environmental Management* (Cambridge: Cambridge University Press).

—— (2005), 'The Environmental Challenge to Loggers in the Asia-Pacific: Corporate Practices in Informal Regimes of Governance', in D. L. Levy and P. J. Newell (eds), *The Business of Global Environmental Governance* (Cambridge, Mass.: MIT Press).

Davey, W. J. (2000), 'The WTO Dispute Settlement System', *Journal of International Economic Law*, 3: 15–18.

Davis, M. (2002), 'The Origins of the Third World: Markets, States and Climate', Corner House Briefing 27 (Dorset: Corner House), www.thecornerhouse.org.uk/pdf/briefing/27origins.pdf

Deagon, B. (2006), 'Electronics—Contract Manufacturing', *Investor's Business Daily*, 17 April.

Deaton, A. (2002), 'Is World Poverty Falling?', *Finance and Development*, 39/2: 4–7.

De Goede, M. (2000), 'Mastering Lady Credit: Discourses of Financial Crisis in Historical Perspective', *International Feminist Journal of Politics*, 2/1: 58–81.

De Gregorio, J. (2001), 'Something for Everyone: Chilean Exchange Rate Policy Since 1960', in J. Frieden, P. Ghezzi, and E. Stein (eds), *The Currency Game: Exchange Rate Politics in Latin America* (New York: Inter-American Development Bank).

Deibert, R. (1997), *Parchment, Printing and Hypermedia* (Ithaca, NY: Cornell University Press).

Denemark, R., and O'Brien, R. (1997), 'Contesting the Canon: International Political Economy at UK and US Universities', *Review of International Political Economy*, 4/1: 214–238.

Desai, P. (2003), *Financial Crisis, Contagion, and Containment* (Princeton, NJ: Princeton University Press).

Destler, I. M. (1995), *American Trade Politics*, 3rd edn (Washington, DC: Institute for International Economics).

—— and Balint, P. (1999), *The New Politics of American Trade: Trade, Labor, and the Environment* (Washington, DC: Institute for International Economics).

—— and Henning, R. C. (1989), *Dollar Politics: Exchange Rate Policymaking in the US* (Washington, DC: Institute for International Economics).

Dicken, P. (2003), *Global Shift: Reshaping the Global Economic Map in the 21st Century*, 4th edn (London: Sage).

Diebold, W. (1952), *The End of the GATT* (Princeton, NJ: Princeton University Press).

Dikhanov, Y., and Ward, M. (2003), 'Evolution of the Global Distribution of Income in 1970–99', Proceedings of the Global Poverty Workshop, Initiative for Policy Dialogue, Columbia University dos Santos, T. (1970), 'The Structure of dependence', American Economic Review, 60/2: 231–236.

Dormael, A. van (1978), *Bretton Woods: Birth of a Monetary System* (London: Macmillan).

dos Santos, T. (1970), 'The Structure of Dependence', *American Economic Review*, 60/2: 231–236.

Downs, G. W., and Rocke, D. M. (1995), *Optimal Imperfection? Domestic Uncertainty and Institutions in International Relations* (Princeton, NJ: Princeton University Press).

Dowrick, S., and DeLong, J. B. (2003), 'Globalization and Convergence', in M. D. Bordo, A. M. Taylor, and J. G. Williamson (eds), *Globalization in Historical Perspective* (Chicago: Chicago University Press).

—— and Akmal, M. (2005), 'Contradictory Trends in Global Income Inequality: A Tale of Two Biases', *Review of Income and Wealth*, 51/2: 201–229.

Drahos, P. (2002), 'Negotiating Intellectual Property Rights: Between Coercion and Dialogue', in P. Drahos and R. Mayne (eds), *Global Intellectual Property Rights* (Basingstoke: Palgrave Macmillan).

Dressler, A. E., and Parson, E. A. (2006), *The Science and Politics of Global Climate Change* (Cambridge: Cambridge University Press).

Dryzek, J. (2006), *Deliberative Global Politics: Discourse and Democracy in a Divided World* (Cambridge: Polity Press).

Duchacek, I. D. (1990), 'Perforated Sovereignties: Towards a Typology of New Actors in International Relations', in H. J. Michelman and P. Soldatos (eds), *Federalism and International Relations* (Oxford: Oxford University Press).

Dunne, T. (2001), 'Liberalism', in J. Baylis and S. Smith (eds), *The Globalization of World Politics*, 2nd edn (Oxford: Oxford University Press).

Dunning, J. H. (1981), *International Production and the Multinational Enterprise* (London: Allen & Unwin).

—— (1988), 'The Eclectic Paradigm of International Production: An Update and Some Possible Extensions', *Journal of International Business Studies*, 19/1: 1–32.

—— (1993), *Multinational Enterprises and the Global Economy* (Wokingham: Addison-Wesley).

—— (2000), 'The New Geography of Foreign Direct Investment', in N. Woods (ed.), *The Political Economy of Globalization* (Basingstoke: Palgrave).

Dupont, C. (1998), 'European Integration and APEC: The Search for Institutional Blueprints', in V. K. Aggarwal and C. Morrison (eds), *Asia-Pacific Crossroads: Regime Creation and the Future of APEC* (New York: St. Martin's Press).

—— and Hefeker, C. (2001), 'Integration Linkages: Between Trade-offs and Spillovers', Paper presented at the Fourth Pan-European IR conference, Canterbury, United Kingdom, 8–10 September.

Durbin, A., and Welch, C. (2002), 'The Environmental Movement and Global Finance', in J. A. Scholte (ed.), *Civil Society and Global Finance* (London: Routledge).

Easterbrook, G. (1995), *A Moment on the Earth: The Coming Age of Environmental Optimism* (New York: Penguin).

ECLA (2001), *Panorama Social De America Latina 2000–01* (Santiago: ECLA (CEPAL)).

—— (2002), *Globalization and Development* (Santiago: ECLA (CEPAL)).

Edward, P. (2006a), 'Examining Inequality: Who Really Benefits from Global Growth?', *World Development*, 34/10: 1667–1695.

—— (2006b), 'The Ethical Poverty Line: A Moral Quantification of Absolute Poverty', *Third World Quarterly*, 27/2: 377–393.

Edwards, S. (2005), 'Capital Controls, Sudden Stops and Current Account Reversals', NBER Working Paper 11170 (Cambridge, Mass.: National Bureau of Economic Research).

Ehrlich, P. (1968), *The Population Bomb* (New York: Sierra Club–Ballantine).

Eichengreen, B. J. (ed.) (1985), *The Gold Standard in Theory and History* (New York: Methuen).

—— (1992), *Golden Fetters: The Gold Standard and the Great Depression: 1919–1939* (New York: Oxford University Press).

—— (1996), *Globalizing Capital: A History of the International Monetary System* (Princeton, NJ: Princeton University Press).

—— (2000) 'The International Monetary Fund in the Wake of the Asian Crisis', in G. W. Noble and J. Ravenhill (eds), *The Asian Financial Crisis and the Architecture of Global Finance* (Cambridge: Cambridge University Press).

—— (2002), *Financial Crises and What to Do about Them* (Oxford: Oxford University Press).

—— (2003), *Capital Flows and Crises* (Cambridge, Mass.: MIT Press).

Elliott, L. (1998), *The Global Politics of the Environment* (New York: New York University Press).

Encarnation, D. J. (ed.) (1999), *Japanese Multinationals in Asia: Regional Operations in Comparative Perspective* (New York/Oxford: Oxford University Press).

Energy Information Administration, Department of Energy, US Government (2001), 'Indonesia: Environmental Issues', Energy Information Administration October, www.eia.doe.gov/emeu/cabs/indoe.html

Enright, S., Scott, E. E., and Chang, K. (2005), *Regional Powerhouse: The Greater Pearl River Delta and the Rise of China* (Singapore: John Wiley).

Epstein, G. (1996), 'International Capital Mobility and the Scope for National Economic Management', in R. Boyer and D. Drache (eds), *States against Markets: The Limits of Globalization* (London: Routledge).

Ernst, D. (2006), 'Searching for a New Role in East Asian Regionalization: Japanese Production Networks in the Electronics Industry', in P. J. Katzenstein and T. Shiraishi (eds), *Beyond Japan: The Dynamics of East Asian Regionalism* (Ithaca, NY/London: Cornell University Press).

—— and Ravenhill, J. (2000), 'Convergence and Diversity: How Globalization Reshapes Asian Production Networks', in M. Borrus, D. Ernst, and S. Haggard (eds), *International Production Networks in Asia: Rivalry or Riches?* (London: Routledge).

Espenshade, T. J., and Calhoun, C. A. (1993), 'An Analysis of Public Opinion toward Undocumented Immigration', *Population Research and Policy Review*, 12: 189–224.

Esping-Andersen, G. (1996a), 'After the Golden Age? Welfare State Dilemmas in a Global Economy?', in G. Esping-Andersen (ed.), *Welfare States in Transition: National Adaptations in Global Economies* (London: Sage).

—— (1996b), 'Positive-sum Solutions in a World of Trade-Offs', in G. Esping-Andersen (ed.), *Welfare States in Transition: National Adaptations in Global Economies* (London: Sage).

Esty, D. (1994), *Greening the GATT: Trade, Environment and the Future* (Washington, DC: Institute for International Economics).

494

Eurodad (2006), 'G8 Debt Deal One Year On: What Happened and What Next?', June, www.eurodad.org/uploadedFiles/Whats_New/Reports/G8_debt_deal_one_year_on_final_version.pdf

European Commission (1990), 'One Market, One Money', *European Economy*, 44.

Evans, J. W. (1971), *The Kennedy Round in American Trade Policy: The Twilight of the GATT* (Cambridge, Mass.: Harvard University Press).

Evans, P. B. (1979), *Dependent Development: The Alliance of Multinational, State, and Local Capital in Brazil* (Princeton, NJ: Princeton University Press).

——Jacobson, H. K., and Putnam, R. D. (eds) (1993), *Double-Edged Diplomacy: International Bargaining and Domestic Politics* (Berkeley, Calif., and Los Angeles: University of California Press).

Feldstein, M. (1983), 'Domestic Savings and International Capital Movements in the Long Run and the Short Run', *European Economic Review*, 21: 139–151.

——and Bacchetta, P. (1991), 'National Saving and International Investment', in D. B. Bernheim and J. B. Shoven (eds), *National Saving and Economic Performance* (Chicago: Chicago University Press).

——and Horioka, C. (1980), 'Domestic Savings and International Capital Flows', *Economic Journal*, 90/358: 314–329.

Fernandez, R., and Portes, J. (1998), 'Returns to Regionalism: An Analysis of Nontraditional Gains from Regional Trade Agreements', *World Bank Economic Review*, 12/2: 197–220.

Ferrantino, M. (1997), 'International Trade, Environmental Quality and Public Policy', *World Economy*, 20/1: 43–72.

Fewsmith, J. (2001) *China Since Tiananmen* (Cambridge: Cambridge University Press).

Finnegan, W. (2003), 'The Economics of Empire: Notes on the Washington Consensus', *Harpers Magazine* (May), www.mindfully.org/WTO/2003/Economics-Of-EmpireMay03.htm

Firebaugh, G. (2003), *The New Geography of Global Income Inequality* (Cambridge, Mass.: Harvard University Press).

Fischer, S. (2000), *On the Need for an International Lender of Last Resort* (Princeton, NJ: International Economics Section, Department of Economics, Princeton University).

Flandreau, M., and Zumer, F. (2004), *The Making of Global Finance, 1880–1913* (Paris: OECD Development Centre).

Foroutan, F. (1998), 'Does Membership in a Regional Preferential Trade Arrangement Make a Country More or Less Protectionist?', *World Economy*, 21/3: 305–336.

Frank, A. G. (1971), *Capitalism and Underdevelopment in Latin America: Historical Studies of Chile and Brazil* (Harmondsworth: Penguin).

Frankel, J. (2005), 'Contractionary Currency Crashes in the Developing Countries', CID Working Paper 117 (Cambridge, Mass.: Center for International Development at Harvard University).

Frankel, J. A. (1991), 'Quantifying International Capital Mobility in the 1980s', in D. Bernheim and J. Shoven (eds), *National Saving and Economic Performance* (Chicago: Chicago University Press).

——(1997), *Regional Trading Blocs in the World Economic System* (Washington, DC: Institute for International Economics).

——(ed.) (1998), *The Regionalisation of the World Economy* (Cambridge, Mass.: National Bureau of Economic Research).

Freeman, R. B. (2006), 'People Flows in Globalization', NBER Working Paper 12315 (Cambridge, Mass.: National Bureau of Economic Research).

Frey, B. S. (1984), 'The Public Choice View of International Political Economy', *International Organization*, 38/1: 199–223.

Frey, R. S. (1998), 'The Export of Hazardous Industries to the Peripheral Zones of the World System', *Journal of Developing Societies*, 14/1: 66–81.

Frieden, J. A. (1991), 'Invested Interests: The Politics of National Economic Policies in a World of Global Finance', *International Organization*, 45/4: 425–451.

——(1994), 'Exchange Rate Politics', *Review of International Political Economy*, 1/1: 81–98.

——(1997), 'Monetary Populism in Nineteenth-Century America: An Open Economy Interpretation', *Journal of Economic History*, 57/2: 367–395.

——Ghezzi, P., and Stein, E. (eds) (2001), *The Currency Game: Exchange Rate Politics in Latin America* (New York: Inter-American Development Bank).

——and Lake, D. (1995), 'Introduction: International Politics and International Economics', in J. Frieden and D. Lake (eds), *International Political Economy: Perspectives on Global Power and Wealth*, 3rd edn (London: Routledge).

Friedman, M. (1953), 'The Case for Flexible Exchange Rates', in M. Freidman, *Essays in Positive Economics* (Chicago: University of Chicago Press).

Friedman, T. (2000), *The Lexus and the Olive Tree* (New York: Anchor Books).

——(2002), 'Techno Logic', in 'States of Discord: A Debate between Thomas Friedman and Robert Kaplan', *Foreign Policy*, 129/March—April: 64–65.

Fujii, E., and Chinn, M. (2001), '*Fin de Siècle* Real Interest Parity', *Journal of International Financial Markets, Institutions and Money*, 11/3–4: 289–308.

Funabashi, Y. (1988), *Managing the Dollar: From the Plaza to the Louvre* (Washington, DC: Institute for International Economics).

Galbraith, J. R. (2002), 'A Perfect Crime: Inequality in an Age of Globalization', *Daedalus*, 131/1: 11–25.

Gamble, A., and Payne, A. (eds) (1996), *Regionalism and World Order* (New York: St. Martin's Press).

Garcia-Johnson, R. (2000), *Exporting Environmentalism: US Multinational Chemical Corporations in Brazil and Mexico* (Cambridge, Mass.: MIT Press).

Gardner, R. N. (1969), *Sterling–Dollar Diplomacy: The Origins and the Prospects of Our International Economic Order*, 2nd edn (New York: McGraw-Hill).

—— (1980), *Sterling–Dollar Diplomacy in Current Perspective: The Origins and the Prospects of Our International Economic Order* (New York: Columbia University Press).

Garrett, G. (1995), 'Capital Mobility, Trade, and the Domestic Politics of Economic Policy', *International Organization*, 49/4: 657–687.

—— (1998a), 'Global Markets and National Politics: Collision Course or Virtuous Circle?', *International Organization*, 52/4: 787–824.

—— (1998b), *Partisan Politics in the Global Economy* (Cambridge: Cambridge University Press).

—— (2000a), 'The Causes of Globalization', *Comparative Political Studies*, 33/6: 945–991.

—— (2000b), 'Shrinking States? Globalization and National Autonomy', in N. Woods (ed.), *The Political Economy of Globalization* (Basingstoke: Palgrave).

—— and Lange, P. (1996) 'Internationalization, Institutions and Political Change', in R. O. Keohane and H. V. Milner (eds), *Internationalization and Domestic Politics* (Cambridge: Cambridge University Press).

—— and Weingast, B. R. (1993), 'Ideas, Interests, and Institutions: Constructing the European Community's Internal Market', in J. Goldstein and R. O. Keohane (eds), *Ideas and Foreign Policy: Beliefs, Institutions and Political Change* (Ithaca, NY: Cornell University Press).

Gautam, M. (2003), *Debt Relief for the Poorest: An OED Review of the HIPC Initiative* (Washington, DC: Operations Evaluation Department, World Bank).

Gedicks, A. (2001), *Resource Rebels: Native Challenges to Mining and Oil Corporations* (Boston, Mass.: South End Press).

Gee, S., and Kuo, W. J. (1997), 'Export Success and Technological Capability: Textiles and Electronics in Taiwan Province of China', in D. Ernst, T. Ganistasos, and L. Mytelka (eds), *Technological Capabilities and Export Success* (London: Routledge).

Gereffi, G., and Korzeniewicz, M. (eds) (1994), *Commodity Chains and Global Capitalism* (Westport, Conn.: Praeger).

—— and Pan, M. L. (1994), 'The Globalization of Taiwan's Garment Industry', in E. Bonacich, L. Cheng, N. Chinchilla, N. Hamilton, and P. Ong (eds), *Global Production: The Apparel Industry in the Pacific Rim* (Philadelphia, Pa.: Temple University Press).

—— Humphrey, J., and Sturgeon, T. (2005), 'The Governance of Global Value Chains', *Review of International Political Economy*, 12/1: 78–104.

Germain, R. (1997), *The International Organization of Credit* (Cambridge: Cambridge University Press).

Geyer, M., and Bright, C. (1995), 'World History in a Global Age', *American Historical Review*, 100/4: 1034–1060.

Ghosh, A. R. (1995), 'International Capital Mobility amongst the Major Industrialised Countries: Too Little or Too Much?', *Economic Journal*, 105/1: 173–180.

Giannone, D. and Lenza, M. (2004), 'The Feldstein–Horioka Fact', CEPR Discussion Paper 4610 (Paris: Centre for Economic Policy Research).

Giavazzi, F., and Pagano, M. (1988), 'The Advantage of Tying One's Hands: EMS Discipline and Central Bank Credibility', *European Economic Review*, 32/5: 1055–1075.

Giddens, A. (1984), *The Constitution of Society* (Cambridge: Polity Press).

—— (1990), *The Consequences of Modernity* (Cambridge: Polity Press).

Gill, S. (1990), *American Hegemony and the Trilateral Commission* (Cambridge: Cambridge University Press).

—— (1995), 'Globalization, Market Civilization, and Disciplinary Neoliberalism', *Millennium*, 24/3: 399–424.

—— (1998), 'European Governance and New Constitutionalism: Economic and Monetary Union and Alternatives to Disciplinary Neoliberalism in Europe', *New Political Economy*, 3/1: 5–26.

—— (2003), *Power and Resistance in the New World Order* (Basingstoke: Palgrave).

—— and Law, D. (1988), *The Global Political Economy: Perspectives, Problems and Policies* (London: Harvester-Wheatsheaf).

—— —— (1989), 'Global Hegemony and the Structural Power of Capital', *International Studies Quarterly*, 33/4: 475–499.

Gilligan, M. (1997), *Empowering Exporters; Reciprocity and Collective Action in Twentieth Century American Trade Policy* (Ann Arbor, Mich.: University of Michigan Press).

Gilpin, R. (1975), *US Power and the Multinational Corporation* (New York: Basic Books).

—— (1981), *War and Change in World Politics* (Cambridge: Cambridge University Press).

—— (1987), *The Political Economy of International Relations* (Princeton, NJ: Princeton University Press).

—— (2001), *Global Political Economy: Understanding the International Economic Order* (Princeton, NJ: Princeton University Press).

—— (2002), *The Challenge of Global Capitalism: The World Economy in the 21st Century* (Princeton, NJ: Princeton University Press).

Goddard, R., Cronin, P., and Dash, K. (eds) (2003), *International Political Economy: State–Market Relations in a Changing Global Order*, 2nd edn (Basingstoke: Palgrave Macmillan).

Goldberg, L. G., Lothian, J. R., and Kunev, J. (2003), 'Has International Financial Integration Increased?', *Open Economies Review*, 14/3: 299–317.

496

REFERENCES

Goldin, C. (1994), 'The Political Economy of Immigration Restriction in the United States, 1890 to 1921', in C. Goldin and G. Libecap (eds), *The Regulated Economy: A Historical Approach to Political Economy* (Chicago: University of Chicago Press).

Goldstein, J. (1993), *Ideas, Interests, and American Trade Policy* (Ithaca, NY: Cornell University Press).

—— and Keohane, R. O. (eds) (1993), *Ideas and Foreign Policy: Beliefs, Institutions and Political Change* (Ithaca, NY: Cornell University Press).

Goodhart, C., and Illing, G. (eds) (2002), *Financial Crises, Contagion, and the Lender of Last Resort* (Oxford: Oxford University Press).

Goodin, R. E. (2003), 'Choose Your Capitalism?', *Comparative European Politics*, 1/2: 203–214.

Goodman, J., and Pauly, L. (1993), 'The Obsolescence of Capital Controls? Economic Management in an Age of Global Markets', *World Politics*, 46/1: 50–82.

Gordon, D. (1988), 'The Global Economy: New Edifice or Crumbling Foundations?', *New Left Review*, 168: 24–64.

Gorodnichenko, Y., and Tesar, L. (2005), 'A Re-examination of the Border Effect', NBER Working Paper 11706 (Cambridge, Mass.: National Bureau of Economic Research).

Gowa, J. (1983), *Closing the Gold Window* (Ithaca, NY: Cornell University Press).

—— (1994), *Allies, Adversaries, and International Trade* (Princeton, NJ: Princeton University Press).

Graham, E., and Krugman, P. R. (1995), *Foreign Direct Investment in the United States* (Washington, DC: Institute for International Economics).

Gray, J. (1998), *False Dawn: The Delusions of Global Capitalism* (London: Granta).

Green, D. (1995), *Silent Revolution: The Rise of Market Economics in Latin America* (London: Frank Cassell, with the Latin American Bureau).

Greene, O. (1997), 'Environmental Issues', in J. Baylis and S. Smith (eds), *The Globalization of World Politics: An Introduction to International Relations* (Oxford: Oxford University Press).

Greider, W. (1997), *One World, Ready or Not: The Manic Logic of Global Capitalism* (New York: Simon & Schuster).

Grieco, J. M., and Ikenberry, G. J. (2002), *State Power and World Markets* (New York: W. W. Norton).

—— —— (2003), *State Power and World Markets: The International Political Economy*, 1st edn (New York: W. W. Norton.).

Grimes, W. (2003), 'Internationalization of the Yen and the New Politics of Monetary Insulation', in J. Kirshner (ed.), *Monetary Orders: Ambiguous Economics, Ubiquitous Politics* (Ithaca, NY: Cornell University Press).

Grossman, G. M., and Helpman, E. (1994), 'Protection for Sale', *American Economic Review*, 84/4: 833–850.

—— —— (1995). 'The Politics of Free-Trade Agreements', *American Economic Review* 85: 667–690.

—— and Krueger, A. (1995), 'Economic Growth and the Environment', *Quarterly Journal of Economics*, 110/May: 353–377.

Grundmann, R. (2001), *Transnational Environmental Policy: Reconstructing Ozone* (London: Routledge).

GUFPC (Grow up Free from Poverty Coalition) (2003), *80 Million Lives: Meeting the Millennium Development Goals in Child and Maternal Survival* (London: GUFPC); September, www.savethechildren.org.uk/scuk_cache/scuk/cache/cmsattach/1019_80MillionLives.pdf

Haas, E. B. (1958), *The Uniting of Europe: Political, Social and Economic Forces, 1950–1957* (Stanford, Calif.: Stanford University Press).

—— (1975), *The Obsolescence of Regional Integration Theory* (Berkeley, Calif.: Institute of International Studies, University of California).

—— (1980), 'Why Collaborate? Issue-Linkage and International Regimes', *World Politics*, 32/3: 357–405.

Haas, P. M. (1992), 'Introduction: Epistemic Communities and International Policy Coordination', *International Organization*, 46/1: 1–35.

Haggard, S. (1990), *Pathways from the Periphery: The Politics of Growth in the Newly Industrializing Economies* (Ithaca, NY: Cornell University Press).

—— (1997), 'Regionalism in Asia and the Americas', in E. D. Mansfield and H. V. Milner (eds), *The Political Economy of Regionalism* (New York: Columbia University Press), 20–49.

—— (2000), *The Political Economy of the Asian Financial Crisis* (Washington, DC: Institute for International Economics).

—— and MacIntyre, A. (2000), 'The Political Economy of the Asian Financial Crisis: Korea and Thailand Compared', in G. Noble and J. Ravenhill (eds), *The Asian Financial Crises and the Global Financial Architecture* (Cambridge: Cambridge University Press).

Halifax Initiative (2002), 'Green Band-Aid Won't Save the Environment', Press Release, 29 August, www.halifaxinitiative.org/index.php/PR_HI_Other/ART3e9f13c05f3d1

Hall, D. (2002), 'Environmental Change, Protest and Havens of Environmental Degradation: Evidence from Asia', *Global Environmental Politics*, 2/2: 20–28.

Hall, P. A. (ed.) (1989), *The Political Power of Economic Ideas* (Princeton, NJ: Princeton University Press).

—— and Soskice, D. (eds) (2001), *Varieties of Capitalism: The Institutional Foundations of Comparative Advantage* (Oxford: Oxford University Press).

Hansen, R. D. (1979), *Beyond the North–South Stalemate* (New York: McGraw-Hill [for] the 1980s Project Council on Foreign Relations).

Hardin, G. (1968), 'The Tragedy of the Commons', *Science*, 162/3859: 1243–1248.

Hardt, M., and Negri, A. (2000), *Empire* (Cambridge, Mass.: Harvard University Press).

Harmes, A. (1998), 'Institutional Investors and the Repro-duction of Neoliberalism', *Review of International Political Economy*, 5/1: 92–121.

Harrison, A. E., and McMillan, M. S. (2006), Outsourcing Jobs? Multinationals and US Employment', NBER Working Paper 12372 (Cambridge, Mass.: National Bureau of Economic Research).

Harvey, D. (1989), *The Condition of Postmodernity* (Oxford: Basil Blackwell).

—— (2005), *The New Imperialism* (Oxford: Oxford University Press).

Hay, C. (2000), 'Contemporary Capitalism, Globalization, Regionalization and the Persistence of National Variation', *Review of International Studies*, 26/4: 509–531.

—— (2002a), 'Globalization as a Problem of Political Analysis: Restoring Agents to a "Process Without a Subject" and Politics to a Logic of Economic Compulsion', *Cambridge Review of International Affairs*, 15/3: 379–392.

—— (2002b), *Political Analysis* (Basingstoke: Palgrave).

—— (2003), 'What's Globalisation Got To Do With It?', Inaugural Lecture, University of Birmingham, www.polsis. bham.ac.uk/department/staff/publications/ hay_inaugural.htm

—— (2004), 'Common Trajectories, Variable Paces, Divergent Outcomes? Models of European Capitalism Under Conditions of Complex Economic Interdependence', *Review of International Political Economy*, 11/2: 231–262.

—— and Rosamond, B. (2002), 'Globalisation, European Integration and the Discursive Construction of Economic Imperatives', *Journal of European Public Policy*, 9/2: 147–167.

—— and Watson, M. (1998), 'Rendering the Contingent Necessary: New Labour's Neo-Liberal Conversion and the Discourse of Globalisation', *Center for European Studies Working Paper* (Boston, Mass.: Center for European Studies, Harvard University).

Heilbroner, R. (2000), *The Worldly Philosophers: The Lives, Times and Ideas of the Great Economic Thinkers*, rev. 7th edn (London: Penguin).

—— —— (eds) (2000), *The Global Transformations Reader* (Cambridge: Polity Press).

Held, D., and McGrew, A. (2002), *Globalization/Anti-Globalization* (Cambridge: Polity Press).

—— —— Goldblatt, D., and Perraton, J. (1999), *Global Transformations: Politics, Economics and Culture* (Cambridge: Polity Press).

Helleiner, E. (1994), *States and the Reemergence of Global Finance* (Ithaca, NY: Cornell University Press).

—— (1997), 'Braudelian Reflections on Economic Globalization: The Historian as Pioneer', in S. Gill and J. Mittleman (eds), *Innovation and Transformation in International Studies* (Cambridge: Cambridge University Press).

—— (2003), *The Making of National Money: Territorial Currencies in Historical Perspective* (Ithaca, NY: Cornell University Press).

—— (2005), 'Conclusion: The Meaning and Contemporary Significance of Economic Nationalism', in E. Helleiner and A. Pickel (eds), *Economic Nationalism in a Globalizing World* (Ithaca, NY: Cornell University Press).

Helleiner, G. K. (1996), 'Why Small Countries Worry: Neglected Issues in Current Analyses of the Benefits and Costs for Small Countries of Integrating with Large Ones', *The World Economy*, 19/6: 759–763.

Henning, C. R. (1987), *Macroeconomic Diplomacy in the 1980s* (London: Croom Helm).

—— (1998), 'Systemic Conflict and Regional Monetary Integration: The Case of Europe', *International Organization*, 52/3: 537–573.

—— (2002), *East Asian Financial Cooperation,* Policy Analyses in International Economics 68 (Washington, DC: Institute for International Economics).

Herrigel, G. (1996), *Industrial Constructions: The Source of German Industrial Power* (Cambridge: Cambridge University Press).

Hilferding, R. (1910/1981), *Finace Capital: A Study of the latest Phase of Capitalist Development*, transl. by M. Watrick and G. Gordon (London: Routledge & Kegan Paul).

Hines, C. (2000), *Localization: A Global Manifesto* (London: Earthscan).

Hirschman, A. O. (1945), *National Power and the Structure of Foreign Trade* (Berkeley, Calif. and Los Angeles: University of California Press).

Hirst, P., and Thompson, G. (1996), *Globalization in Question,* 1st edn (Cambridge: Polity Press).

—— —— (1999), *Globalization in Question*, 2nd edn (Cambridge: Polity Press).

—— —— (2003), 'Globalization: A Necessary Myth?', in D. Held and A. McGrew (eds), *The Global Transformations Reader,* 2nd edn (Cambridge: Polity Press).

Hiscox, M. J. (1999), 'The Magic Bullet? The RTAA, Institutional Reform, and Trade Liberalization', *International Organization*, 53/4: 669–698.

—— (2002), *International Trade and Political Conflict* (Princeton, NJ: Princeton University Press).

Hobson, J. A. (1902/1948), *Imperialism* (London: Allen & Unwin).

Hoekman, B., and Kostecki, M. (1995), *The Political Economy of the World Trading System* (Oxford: Oxford University Press).

Hoffmann, M. (1998), 'Long Run Capital Flows and the Feldstein–Horoika Puzzle: A New Measure of International Capital Mobility and Some Historical Evidence from Great Britain and the United States', EUI Working Paper 1998/30 (Florence: European University Institute).

Hoffmann, S. (1966), 'Obstinate or Obsolete? The Fate of the Nation-State in Europe', *Daedalus*, 95/3: 862–915.

498

Holme, R., and Watts, P. (2000), *Corporate Social Responsibility: Making Good Business Sense* (Conches-Geneva: World Business Council for Sustainable Development).

Holsti, O. R. (1996), *Public Opinion and American Foreign Policy* (Ann Arbor, Mich.: University of Michigan Press).

Hood, R. (2001), *Malaysian Capital Controls*, Policy Research Working Paper No. 2536 (Washington, DC: World Bank), January.

Hoogvelt, A. (1997), *Globalisation and the Postcolonial World: The New Political Economy of Development* (London: Macmillan).

——(2001), *Globalization and the Post-Colonial World* (Basingstoke: Palgrave).

Horta, K., Round, R., and Young, Z. (2002), *The Global Environmental Facility: The First Ten Years—Growing Pains or Inherent Flaws?* (Washington, DC and Ottawa: Environmental Defense and Halifax Initiative).

Hoyningen-Huene, P. (1993), *Reconstructing Scientific Revolutions: Thomas S. Kuhn's Philosophy of Science*, trans. A. Levine (Chicago: University of Chicago Press).

Huang, Y., and Khanna, T. (2003), 'Can India Overtake China?', *Foreign Policy*, 137/July–August: 74–81.

Huber, E., Ragin, C., Stephens, J. D., Brady, D., and Beckfield, D. (2004), *Comparative Welfare States Data Set* (Northwestern University and University of North Carolina), www.lisproject.org/publications/welfaredata/welfareaccess.htm

Hudec, R. E. (1975), *The GATT Legal System and World Trade Diplomacy* (New York: Praeger).

Hufbauer, G. C., and Wong, Y. (2004), 'China Bashing 2004', *International Economics Policy Briefs*, Number PB04-5/September: 1–53.

Hummels, D. (2001), 'The Nature and Growth of Vertical Specialization in World Trade', *Journal of International Economics*, 54/1: 75–96.

Humphrey, J., and Memedovic, O. (2003), *The Global Automotive Value Chain* (Vienna: United Nations Industrial Development Organization).

——and Schmitz, H. (2000), 'Governance and Upgrading: Linking Industrial Cluster and Global Value Chain Research', IDS Working Paper 120 (Brighton: Institute of Development Studies, University of Sussex).

————(2001), 'Governance in Global Value Chains', *IDS Bulletin*, 32/3: 19–29.

Humphreys, D. (1999), 'The Evolving Forests Regime', *Global Environmental Change*, 9/3: 251–254.

——(2003), 'Life Protective or Carcinogenic Challenge? Global Forests Governance under Advanced Capitalism', *Global Environmental Politics*, 3/2: 40–55.

——(2006), *Logjam: Deforestation and the Crisis of Global Governance* (London: Earthscan).

Hymer, S. (1976), *The International Operations of National Firms* (Cambridge, Mass.: MIT Press).

Ikeda, S. (2004), 'Zonal Structure and the Trajectories of Canada, Mexico, Australia, and Norway under Neo-liberal Globalization', in M. G. Cohen and S. Clarkson (eds), *Governing Under Stress: Middle Powers and the Challenge of Globalization* (London: Zed Books).

Ikenberry, G. J. (2001), *After Victory* (Princeton, NJ: Princeton University Press).

——and Kupchan, C. A. (1990), 'Socialization and Hegemonic Power', *International Organization*, 44/3: 283–315.

ILO (International Labour Organization) (2002), *Export Processing Zones: Addressing the Social and Labour Issues* (Geneva: Bureau for Multinational Enterprises, ILO).

IMF (International Monetary Fund) (2002), *World Economic Outlook: Trade and Finance* (Washington, DC: International Monetary Fund).

——(2003*a*), Independent Evaluation Office, 'The Role of the IMF in Argentina, 1991–2002', *Issue Paper* (Washington, DC: International Monetary Fund).

——(2003*b*), *World Economic Outlook: Trade and Finance* (Washington, DC: International Monetary Fund).

——(various years), *Financial Statistics Yearbook* (Washington, DC: IMF).

IOM (International Organization for Migration) (2005), *World Migration 2005: Costs and Benefits of International Migration* (Geneva: International Organization for Migration).

Inkeles, A., and Smith, D. (1974), *Becoming Modern: Individual Change in Six Developing Countries* (Cambridge, Mass.: Harvard University Press).

IPCC (Intergovernmental Panel on Climate Change) (2001), *Climate Change 2001: The Scientific Basis* (Cambridge: Cambridge University Press for IPCC).

Irwin, D. A. (2002), 'Long-Run Trends in World Income and Trade', *World Trade Review*, 1/1: 89–100.

——(2003), 'Explaining America's Surge in Manufacturing Exports, 1880–1913', *Review of Economics and Statistics*, 85/2: 364–376.

——and Kroszner, R. S. (1997), 'Interests, Institutions and Ideology in the Republican Conversion to Trade Liberalization, 1934–45', NBER Working Paper 6112 (Cambridge, Mass.: National Bureau of Economic Research).

Isard, P. (2005), *Globalization and the International Financial System* (Cambridge: Cambridge University Press).

Iversen, T., Pontusson, J., and Soskice, D. (eds) (2000), *Unions, Employers and Central Banks: Macroeconomic Coordination and Institutional Change in Social Market Economies* (Cambridge: Cambridge University Press).

Jackson, J. H. (1969), *World Trade and the Law of the GATT* (Indianapolis, Ind.: Bobbs-Merrill).

——(1998), *The World Trade Organization: Constitution and Jurisprudence* (London: Pinter).

Jackson, R. H. (1993), 'The Weight of Ideas in Decolonization: Normative Change in International Relations', in J. Goldstein and R. O. Keohane (eds), *Ideas and Foreign Policy: Beliefs, Institutions and Political Change* (Ithaca, NY: Cornell University Press).

James, H. (1995), 'The Historical Development of the Principle of Surveillance', *IMF Staff Papers*, No. 42, December: 762–791.

—— (1996), *International Monetary Cooperation Since Bretton Woods* (Washington, DC: International Monetary Fund).

—— (2001), *The End of Globalization: Lessons from the Great Depression* (Cambridge, Mass.: Harvard University Press).

Jenkins, R. (1987), *Transnational Corporations and Uneven Development* (London: Methuen).

Jessop, B. (1998), 'The Rise of Governance and the Risks of Failure: The Case of Economic Development', *International Social Science Journal*, 50/155: 29–45.

—— (2002), *The Future of the Capitalist State* (Cambridge: Polity Press).

Jetin, B., and de Brunhof, S. (2000), 'The Tobin Tax and the Regulation of Capital Movements', in W. Bello, N. Bullard, and K. Malhotra (eds), *Global Finance* (London: Zed Books).

Jevons, W. S. (1871/1970), *The Theory of Political Economy* (Harmondsworth: Pelican).

Johannesburg Declaration on Sustainable Development (2002), Official Document of the 2002 World Summit on Sustainable Development, 4 September.

Johnson, C. (1982), *MITI and the Japanese Miracle* (Stanford, Calif.: Stanford University Press).

Joint European NGO Report (2006), 'EU Aid: Genuine Leadership or Misleading Figures?', April, www.eurodad.org/uploadedFiles/Whats_New/Reports/Eurodad%202006EUAidReport.pdf

Joint Statement by NGOs (2001), 'International Civil Society Rejects WTO Doha Outcome and WTO's Manipulative Process', *Third World Resurgence*, 135–136: 15–17.

Jones, R. (1971), 'A Three-Factor Model in Theory, Trade, and History', in B. Jagdish, R. Jones, R. A. Mundell, and J. Vanek (eds), *Trade, Balance of Payments, and Growth* (Amsterdam: North-Holland).

Jones, V. C. (2006), 'WTO: Antidumping Issues in the Doha Development Agenda', CRS Report for Congress (Washington, DC: Congressional Research Service, Library of Congress).

Josselin, D. (2001), 'Trade Unions for EMU: Sectorial Preferences and Political Opportunities', *West European Politics*, 24/1: 55–74.

JSBRI (Japan Small Business Research Institute) (2003), *White Paper on Small and Medium Enterprises* (Tokyo: Japan Small Business Research Institute).

Jubilee South, Focus on the Global South–Bangkok, AWEPON (Kampala) and Centro de Estudos Internacionales (Managua) (2002), 'The World Bank and the PRSP: Flawed Thinking and Failing Experiences', January www.focusweb.org/publications/2001/THE-WORLD-BANK-AND-THE-PRSP.html

Kahler, M. (1992), 'Multilateralism with Small and Large Numbers', *International Organization*, 46/3: 681–708.

Kaltenthaler, K. (1998), *Germany and the Politics of Europe's Money* (Durham, NC: Duke University Press).

Kaplan, E., and Rodrik, D. (2002), 'Did the Malaysian Capital Control Work?', in S. Edwards and J. A. Frankel (eds) (2002), *Preventing Currency Crises in Emerging Markets* (Chicago: University of Chicago Press).

Kaplinsky, R. (2000), 'Governance and Unequalisation: What Can Be Learned from Value Chain Analysis?', *Journal of Development Studies*, 37/2: 117–146.

—— (2005), *Globalization, Poverty and Inequality: Between a Rock and a Hard Place* (Cambridge: Polity Press).

Kapstein, E. B. (1994), *Governing the Global Economy: International Finance and the State* (Cambridge, Mass.: Harvard University Press).

—— (2000), 'Winners and Losers in the Global Economy', *International Organization*, 54/2: 359–384.

Kapur, D. (2002), 'The Changing Anatomy of Governance of the World Bank', in J. Pincus and J. A. Winters (eds), *Reinventing the World Bank* (Ithaca, NY: Cornell University Press).

—— and McHale, J. (2003), 'Migration's New Payoff', Foreign Policy, 139/November–December: 49–57.

Karliner, J. (1997), *The Corporate Planet, Ecology and Politics in the Age of Globalization* (San Francisco: Sierra Club).

Kasman, B., and Pigott, C. (1988), 'Interest Rate Divergences amongst the Major Industrial Nations', *Federal Reserve Bank of New York Quarterly Review*, 13/3: 28–44.

Katada, S. (2002), 'Japan and Asian Monetary Regionalization: Cultivating a New Regional Leadership after the Asian Financial Crisis', *Geopolitics*, 7/1: 85–112.

Katzenstein, P. J. (ed) (1978), *Between Power and Plenty: Foreign Economic Policies of Advanced Industrial States* (Madison, Wisc.: University of Wisconsin Press).

—— (1985), *Small States in World Markets: Industrial Policy in Europe* (Ithaca, NY: Cornell University Press).

Kearney, A. T., and *Foreign Policy* Globalization Index (2003), 'Measuring Globalization: Who's Up, Who's Down?', *Foreign Policy*, 134/January–February: 60–72.

—————— (2005), 'Measuring Globalization', *Foreign Policy*, 148/May–June: 53–60.

—————— (2006), 'The Globalization Index', *Foreign Policy*, 157/November–December: 74–81.

Keck, M. E., and Sikkink, K. (1998), *Activists beyond Borders: Advocacy Networks in International Politics* (Ithaca, NY: Cornell University Press).

Keegan, J. (1998), *The First World War* (London: Random House).

Keohane, R. O. (1984), *After Hegemony: Cooperation and Discord in the World Political Economy* (Princeton, NJ: Princeton University Press).

—— (1997), 'Problematic Lucidity: Stephen Krasner's "State Power and the Structure of International Trade"', *World Politics*, 50/1: 150–170.

—— and Nye, J. S. (eds) (1972), *Transnational Relations and World Politics* (Cambridge, Mass.: Harvard University Press).

—— —— (1977), *Power and Interdependence* (Boston, Mass.: Little, Brown).

—— —— (2003), 'Globalization: What's New? What's Not? (And So What?)', in D. Held and A. McGrew (eds), *The Global Transformations Reader* (Cambridge: Polity Press).

Keynes, J. M. (1925), *The Economic Consequences of Mr. Churchill* (London: L. and V. Woolf).

—— (1933), 'National Self-Sufficiency', *Yale Review,* 22: 755–769.

—— (1936), *General Theory of Employment, Interest and Money* (New York: Harcourt, Brace).

—— (1980), *The Collected Writings of J. M. Keynes Volume 25, Activities, 1940–44: Shaping the Post-War World, the Clearing Union*, ed. Donald Moggridge (Cambridge: Cambridge University Press).

Keynes, J. N. (1891/1970), *The Scope and Method of Political Economy*, reprinted 4th edn (New York: Augustus M. Kelley).

Khor, M. (1999), 'Letter Sent by 11 Countries to WTO Chair Criticising Green Room Process', 15 November, www.globalpolicy.org/socecon/bwi-wto/wto/1999/letter.htm

—— (2001), 'Manipulation by Tactics and Conquest by Drafts: How the WTO Produced its Anti-development Agenda at Doha', *Third World Resurgence*, 135–136: 11–14.

Kindleberger, C. P. (1951), 'Group Behavior and International Trade', *Journal of Political Economy*, 59/1: 30–46.

—— (1969), *American Business Abroad: Six Lectures on Direct Investment* (New Haven, Conn.: Yale University Press).

—— (1973), *The World in Depression, 1929–1939* (Berkeley, Calif. and Los Angeles: University of California Press).

—— (1975), 'The Rise of Free Trade in Western Europe', *Journal of Economic History*, 35/1: 20–55.

—— (1978), *Manias, Panics, and Crashes: A History of Financial Crises* (New York: Basic Books).

Kirshner, J. (1995), *Currency and Coercion: The Political Economy of International Monetary Power* (Princeton, NJ: Princeton University Press).

—— (ed) (2003), *Monetary Orders: Ambiguous Economics, Ubiquitous Politics* (Ithaca, NY: Cornell University Press).

Kiser, E., and Laing, A. M. (2001), 'Have We Overestimated the Effects of Neoliberalism and Globalization? Some Speculations on the Anomalous Stability of Taxes on Business', in

J. L. Campbell and O. K. Pedersen (eds), *The Rise of Neoliberalism and Institutional Analysis* (Princeton, NJ: Princeton University Press).

Kitschelt, H., Lange, P., Marks, G., and Stephens, J. D. (1999), *Continuity and Change in Contemporary Capitalism* (Cambridge: Cambridge University Press).

Klein, N. (2002), *No Logo* (New York: Picador).

Kleinknecht, A., and ter Wengel, J. (1998), 'The Myth of Economic Globalization', *Cambridge Journal of Economics,* 22/5: 637–647.

Knight, J. (1992), *Institutions and Social Conflict* (Cambridge: Cambridge University Press).

Kohler, H. (2002), 'Working for a Better Globalization', 28 January, www.imf.org/external/np/speeches/2002/012802.htm

Kohli, A. (2004), *State-Directed Development: Political Power and Industrialization in the Global Periphery* (Cambridge: Cambridge University Press).

Koremenos, B., Lipson, C., and Snidal, D. (2001), 'The Rational Design of International Institutions', *International Organization* 55/4: 761–799.

Korten, D. C. (1995), *When Corporations Rule the World* (West Hartford, Conn. & San Francisco: Berrett-Koehler and Kumarian Press).

Korzeniewicz, R., and Moran, T. (2006), 'World Inequality in the Twenty-First Century: Patterns and Tendencies', in G. Ritzer (ed), *The Blackwell Companion to Globalization* (Oxford: Blackwell).

—— Stach, A., Patil, V., and Moran, T. (2004), 'Measuring National Income: A Critical Assessment', *Comparative Studies in Society and History*, 46/3: 535–586.

Krasner, S. D. (1976), 'State Power and the Structure of International Trade', *World Politics*, 28/3: 317–347.

(Zem) (1978), *Defending the National Interest: Raw Material Investments and us foreign Policy* (Princeton, NJ: Princeton University Press).

—— (ed) (1983), *International Regimes* (Ithaca, NY: Cornell University Press).

—— (1985), *Structural Conflict: The Third World against Global Liberalism* (Berkeley, Calif. and Los Angeles: University of California Press).

—— (1991), 'Global Communications and National Power: Life on the Pareto Frontier', *World Politics*, 43/3: 336–366.

—— (1994), 'International Political Economy: Abiding Discord', *Review of International Political Economy*, 1/1: 13–19.

—— (1999), *Sovereignty: Organized Hypocrisy* (Princeton, NJ: Princeton University Press).

Krueger, A. O. (1995), *Trade Policies and Developing Nations* (Washington, DC: Brookings Institution).

—— (1999), 'Are Preferential Trading Arrangements Trade-Liberalizing or Protectionist?', *Journal of Economic Perspectives*, 13/4: 105–124.

—— (2002), 'A New Approach to Sovereign Debt Restructuring', Pamphlet Series (Washington, DC: International Monetary Fund).

Krugman, P. R. (1990), 'Import Protection as Export Promotion: International Competition in the Presence of Oligopoly and Economies of Scale', in P. R. Krugman (ed.), *Rethinking International Trade* (Cambridge, Mass.: MIT Press), 185–198.

—— (1994), 'Does Third World Growth Hurt First World Prosperity?', *Harvard Business Review*, July, 113–121.

—— and Obstfeld, M. (2000), *International Economics: Theory and Policy*, 5th edn (New York: Addison-Wesley).

Kuhn, T. (1970), *The Structure of Scientific Revolutions*, 2nd edn (Chicago: University of Chicago Press).

Kurzer, P. (1993), *Business and Banking: Political Change and Economic Integration in Western Europe* (Ithaca, NY: Cornell University Press).

Lall, S. (2004), 'Reinventing Industrial Strategy: The Role of Government Policy in Building Industrial Competitiveness', G-24 Discussion Paper Series No. 28 (New York and Geneva: United Nations).

Lamfalussy, A. (2000), *Financial Crises in Emerging Markets* (New Haven, Conn.: Yale University Press).

Landreth, H., and Colander, D. (1994), *History of Economic Thought*, 3rd edn (Boston, Mass.: Houghton Mifflin Company).

Lasswell, H. D. (1936), *Politics: Who Gets What, When, How* (New York: Whittlesey House, McGraw-Hill).

Lane, P. R., and Milesi-Ferretti, G. M. (2003), 'International Financial Integration', *IMF Staff Papers* 50/Special Issue: 82–100.

Lansley, S. (2006), *Rich Britain: The Rise and Rise of the New Super-Wealthy* (London: Politico).

Lawrence, R. Z. (1996a), *Regionalism, Multilateralism, and Deeper Integration* (Washington, DC: Brookings Institution).

—— (1996b), *Single World, Divided Nations? International Trade and OECD Labor Markets* (Washington, DC: Brookings Institution).

Leamer, E., and Levinsohn, J. (1995), 'International Trade Theory: The Evidence', in G. Grossman and K. Rogoff (eds), *Handbook of International Economics*, vol. III (Amsterdam: North-Holland).

Lee, D. (2008), 'The "Orthodoxy": Neorealism and Neoliberalism', in D. Lee, J. Steans, C. Hay, D. Hudson, A. Morton and M. Watson, *International Political Economy* (Oxford: Oxford University Press, forthcoming).

Lenin, V. I. (1902/1903), *What is to be Done?* Transl. by S.V. Vtechin (Oxford: Oxford University Press).

—— (1917/1996), *Imperialism, the Highest Stage of Capitalism: A Popular Outline* (London: Pluto Press).

Levinson, M. (2006), *How the Shipping Container Made the World Smaller and the World Economy Bigger* (Princeton, NJ: Princeton University Press).

Lewis, A. (1981), 'The Rate of Growth of World Trade, 1830–1973', in S. Grassman and E. Lundberg (eds), *The World Economic Order: Past and Prospects* (London: Macmillan).

Leys, C. (2001), *Market-Driven Politics: Neoliberal Democracy and the Public Interest* (London: Verso).

Lindberg, L. N. (1963), *The Political Dynamics of European Economic Integration* (Stanford, Calif.: Stanford University Press).

Lindert, P. H., and Williamson, J. G. (2001), 'Does Globalization Make the World More Unequal?', NBER Working Paper W8228 (Cambridge, Mass.: National Bureau of Economic Research).

—— —— (2003), 'Does Globalization Make the World More Unequal?', in M. D. Bordo, A. M. Taylor, and J. G. Williamson (eds), *Globalization in Historical Perspective* (Chicago: Chicago University Press).

Lipschutz, R. D. (1992), 'Reconstructing World Politics: The Emergence of Global Civil Society', *Millennium*, 21/3: 389–420.

Lissakers, K. (1991), *Banks, Borrowers and the Fstabushment* (new york: Basic Books).

List, F. (1841/1977), *The National System of Political Economy*, reprinted edn (New York: Augustus M. Kelley).

Locke, R., and Kochan, T. (1985), 'The Transformation of Industrial Relations? A Cross-National Review of the Evidence', in R. Locke, T. Kochan, and M. Piore (eds), *Employment Relations in a Changing World* (Cambridge, Mass.: MIT Press).

Locke, R. M. (1995), *Remaking the Italian Economy* (Ithaca, NY: Cornell University Press).

—— (2003), 'The Promise and Perils of Globalization: The Case of Nike', in T. A. Kochan and R. Schmalensee (eds), *Management: Inventing and Delivering Its Future* (Boston, Mass.: MIT Press).

Lohmann, L. (1993), 'Resisting Green Globalism', in W. Sachs (ed.), *Global Ecology: A New Arena of Political Conflict* (London: Zed Books).

Lohmann, S. (1997), 'Linkage Politics', *Journal of Conflict Resolution*, 41/1: 38–67.

Lomborg, B. (2001), *The Skeptical Environmentalist* (Cambridge: Cambridge University Press).

Longin, F. and Solnik, B. (1995), 'Is the Correlation in International Equity Returns Constant: 1960–1990?', *Journal of International Money and Finance*, 14/1: 3–26.

Loriaux, M. (1991), *France after Hegemony* (Ithaca, NY: Cornell University Press).

Lowenstein, R. (2001), *When Genius Failed: The Rise and Fall of Long-Term Capital Management* (London: Fourth Estate).

Lukes, S. (1974), *Power: A Radical View* (London: Macmillan).

Lynn, B. (2005), *End of the Line: The Rise and Coming Fall of the Global Corporation* (New York: Doubleday).

McCall Smith, J. (2000), 'The Politics of Dispute Settlement Design: Explaining Legalism in Regional Trade Pacts', *International Organization*, 54/1: 137–180.

McCord, N., (1958), *The Anti-Corn Law League 1838–1846* (London: George Allen & Unwin).

McCullagh, C. B. (1998), *The Truth of History* (London: Routledge).

McDowell, L. (1997), *Capital Culture: Gender at Work in the City* (Oxford: Basil Blackwell).

McGillivray, F. (1997), 'Party Discipline as a Determinant of the Endogenous Formation of Tariffs', *American Journal of Political Science*, 41/2: 584–607.

McGinnis, M. D. (1986), 'Issue Linkage and the Evolution of International Cooperation', *Journal of Conflict Resolution*, 30/1: 141–170.

McGrew, A. (2002), 'Liberal Internationalism: Between Realism and Cosmpolitanism', in D. Held and A. McGrew (eds), *Governing Globalization: Power, Authority, and Global Governance* (Cambridge: Polity Press).

McKean, M. A. (1981), *Environmental Protest and Citizen Politics in Japan* (Berkeley, Calif. and Los Angeles: University of California Press).

McKendrick, D. G., Doner, R. F., and Haggard, S. (2000), *From Silicon Valley to Singapore: Location and Competitive Advantage in the Hard Disk Drive Industry* (Stanford, Calif.: Stanford University Press).

MacKenzie, D. (2002), 'Fresh Evidence on Bhopal Disaster', *New Scientist*, 4 December.

McKenzie, R., and Lee, D. (1991), *Quicksilver Capital: How the Rapid Movement of Wealth Has Changed the World* (New York: Free Press).

McLaren, L. (2001), 'Immigration and the New Politics of Inclusion and Exclusion in the European Union: The Effect of Elites and the EU on Individual-level Opinions Regarding European and Non-European Immigrants', *European Journal of Political Research*, 39/1: 81–108.

McNamara, K. (1998), *The Currency of Ideas: Monetary Politics in the European Union* (Ithaca, NY: Cornell University Press).

MacNeill, J., Winsemius, P., and Yakushiji, T. (1991), *Beyond Interdependence: The Meshing of the World's Economy and the Earth's Ecology* (New York: Oxford University Press).

Maddison, A. (1987), 'Growth and Slowdown in Advanced Capitalist Economies: Techniques of Quantitative Assessment', *Journal of Economic Literature*, 25/2: 649–698.

—— (1989), *The World Economy in the 20th Century* (Paris: Development Centre of the Organisation for Economic Co-operation and Development).

—— (2001), *The World Economy: A Millennial Perspective* (Paris: Development Centre of the Organisation for Economic Co-operation and Development).

Maeil Kyongjae [Maeil Business Newspaper] (2005), 'Global Sourcing: Samsung Electronics', 22 February.

Magee, S. P. (1980), 'Three Simple Tests of the Stopler–Samuelson Theorem', in P. Oppenheimer (ed.), *Issues in International Economics* (London: Oriel Press).

—— Brock, W. A., and Young, L. (1989), *Black Hole Tariffs and Endogenous Policy Theory* (Cambridge: Cambridge University Press).

Maggi, G. (1999), 'The Role of Multilateral Institutions in International Trade Cooperation', *American Economic Review*, 89/1: 190–214.

Malthus, T. R., (1798), *Essay on the Principle of Population,* 1st edn, www.econlib.org/library/Malthus/malPop.html

Mandeville, B. (1714/1755), *Fable of the Bees; Or, Private Vices, Public Benefits*, 9th edn (Edinburgh: W. Gray and W. Peter).

Manheim, J. M. (1991), *All of the People All of the Time: Strategic Communication and American Politics* (Armonk, NY: M. E. Sharpe).

Mann, M. (2003), *Incoherent Empire* (London: Verso).

Marchak, M. P. (1995), *Logging the Globe* (Montreal: McGill-Queen's University Press).

Margolis, H. (1993), *Paradigms and Barriers: How Habits of Mind Govern Scientific Beliefs* (Chicago: University of Chicago Press).

Marland, G., Boden, T. A., and Andres, R. J. (2006), 'Global, Regional, and National Fossil Fuel CO_2 Emissions', in *Trends: A Compendium of Data on Global Change* (Oak Ridge, Tenn.: Carbon Dioxide Information Analysis Center, Oak Ridge National Laboratory, US Department of Energy), http://cdiac.ornl.gov/trends/emis/meth_reg.htm

Marshall, A. (1920), *Principles of Economics*, 8th edn (London: Macmillan).

Martin, L. L. (1992), 'Interests, Power, and Multilateralism', *International Organization*, 46/4: 765–792.

—— (2000), *Democratic Commitments: Legislatures and International Cooperation* (Princeton, NJ: Princeton University Press).

—— (2002) 'International Political Economy: From Paradigmatic Debates to Productive Disagreements', in M. Brecher and F. P. Harvey (eds), *Conflict, Security, Foreign Policy, and International Political Economy: Past Paths and Future Directions in International Studies* (Ann Arbor, Mich.: University of Michigan Press).

Marugami, T., Mimura, T., Saito, K., Suzuki, M., and Kotaka, T. (2005), 'Survey Report on Overseas Business Operations by Japanese Manufacturing Companies', *JBICI Review*, No. 13 (Tokyo: Japan Bank for International Cooperation, September).

Marugami, T. Toyoda, T., Kasuga, T., and Suzuki, M. (2003), 'Survey Report on Overseas Business Operations by Japanese Manufacturing Companies', *JBICI Review*, No. 7 (Tokyo: Japan Bank for International Cooperation, August).

Marx, K. (1890/1930), *Capital: A Critique of Political Economy*, trans. from 4th German edn by E. and C. Paul (London: Dent).

—— (1973), *Grundrisse: Foundations of the Critique of Political Economy (Rough Draft)*, trans. from German edn by M. Nicolaus (Harmondsworth: Penguin).

—— and Engels, F. (1848/1948), *The Communist Manifesto* (London: Lawrence & Wishart).

Maskus, K. E. (2000), *Intellectual Property Rights in the Global Economy* (Washington, DC: Institute for International Economics).

Mazur, J. (2000), 'Labor's New Internationalism', *Foreign Affairs*, 79/1: 79–93.

Mbabazi, J., Morissey, O., and Milner, C. (2003), 'The Fragility of Empirical Links Between Inequality, Trade Liberalization, Growth and Poverty', in R. van der Hoeven and A. Shorrocks (eds), *Perspectives on Growth and Poverty* (Tokyo: United Nations Press).

Mearsheimer, J. J. (1990), 'Back to the Future: Instability in Europe after the Cold War', *International Security*, 15/1: 5–56.

Mehta, S. (2003), 'The Johannesburg Summit from the Depths', *Journal of Environment and Development*, 12/1: 121–128.

Mellor, D. H. (1995), *The Facts of Causation* (London: Routledge).

Meltzer, A. (2001), 'The World Bank One Year after the Commission's Report to Congress', *Hearings before the Joint Economic Committee, US Congress*, 8 March.

Menger, C. (1871/1950), *Principles of Economics*, trans. and ed. by J. Dingwall and B. Hoselitz (Glencoe, Ill.: Free Press).

METI (Ministry of Economy, Trade and Industry, Japan) (2000), 'The Economic Foundations of Japanese Trade Policy—Promoting a Multi-Layered Trade Policy', Ministry of Economy, Trade and Industry, www.meti.go.jp/english/report/data/g00Wconte.pdf

—— (2004), 'The Report of the Joint Study Group on the Possible Trilateral Investment Arrangements among China, Japan, and Korea' (Tokyo: METI), 29 November.

—— (2006), 'White Paper on International Economy and Trade 2006' (Tokyo: METI), June.

Milanovic, B. (2002), 'Can We Discern the Effect of Globalization on Income Distribution? Evidence from Household Budget Surveys', Policy Research Working Paper 2876 (Washington, DC: World Bank).

—— (2003), 'The Two Faces of Globalization: Against Globalization As We Know It', *World Development*, 31/4: 667–683.

—— (2005), *World Apart: Measuring International and Global Inequality* (Princeton, NJ: Princeton University Press).

Mill, J. S. (1970), *Principles of Political Economy, with Some of Their Applications to Social Philosophy* (Harmondsworth: Penguin).

Milner, H. V. (1997*a*), *Interests, Institutions, and Information: Domestic Politics and International Relations* (Princeton, NJ: Princeton University Press).

—— (1997*b*), 'Industries, Governments, and the Creation of Regional Trading Blocs', in E. D. Mansfield and H. V. Milner (eds), *The Political Economy of Regionalism* (New York: Columbia University Press), 77–106.

Milward, A. S. (1984), *The Reconstruction of Western Europe 1945–51* (London: Routledge).

—— (1992), *The European Rescue of the Nation-State* (London: Routledge).

Mitchell, B. R. (1992), *International Historical Statistics: Europe 1750–1988*, 3rd edn (London: Macmillan).

—— (1993), *International Historical Statistics: The Americas 1750–1988*, 2nd edn (London: Macmillan).

Molina, M. J., and Rowland, F. S. (1974), 'Stratospheric Sink for Chlorofluoromethanes: Chlorine Atom Catalyzed Destruction of Ozone', *Nature*, 249: 810–814.

Moran, T. H. (1998), *Foreign Direct Investment and Development* (Washington, DC: Institute for International Economics).

Moravcsik, A. (1998), *The Choice for Europe: Social Purpose and State Power from Messina to Maastricht* (Ithaca, NY: Cornell University Press).

Morgenthau, H. (1948/1960), *Politics Among Nations: The Struggle for Power and Peace*, 3rd edn (New York: Knopf).

Morse, E. L. (1976), *Modernization and the Transformation of International Relations* (New York: Free Press).

Mosley, L. (2003), *Global Capital and National Governments* (Cambridge: Cambridge University Press).

Mosley, P., and Eeckhout, M. J. (2000), 'From Project Aid to Programme Assistance', in F. Tarp (ed.), *Foreign Aid and Development: Lessons Learnt and Directions for the Future* (London: Routledge).

Motta, M., and Norman, G. (1996), 'Does Economic Integration Cause Foreign Direct Investment?', *International Economic Review*, 37/4: 757–783.

Multilateral Trade Negotiations: Evaluations and Further Recommendations Arising Therefrom (1979), UNCTAD V (UN Doc. TD/227).

Mun, T. (1664/1928), *England's Treasure by Forraign Trade*, reset and reprinted edn (Oxford: Basil Blackwell).

Munck, R. (2002), *Globalisation and Labour* (London: Zed Books).

Mundell, R. (1961), 'A Theory of Optimum Currency Areas', *American Economic Review*, 51/3: 657–665.

—— (1963), 'Capital Mobility and Stabilization Policy under Fixed and Flexible Exchange Rates', *Canadian Journal of Economics and Political Science*, 29/4: 475–485.

Murphy, C., and Nelson, D. (2001), 'International Political Economy: A Tale of Two Heterodoxies', *British Journal of Politics and International Relations*, 3/3: 393–412.

—— and Tooze, R. (1991), 'Introduction', in C. Murphy and R. Tooze (eds), *The New International Political Economy* (Boulder, Colo.: Lynne Rienner).

Mussa, M. (1974), 'Tariffs and the Distribution of Income: The Importance of Factor Specificity, Substitutability, and Intensity in the Short and Long Run', *Journal of Political Economy,* 82/6: 1191–1203.

—— (2002), *Argentina and the Fund: From Triumph to Tragedy* (Washington, DC: Institute for International Economics).

Myers, N. (1997), 'Consumption in Relation to Population, Environment and Development', *The Environmentalist,* 17: 33–44.

Myers, R., and Worm, B. (2003), 'Rapid Worldwide Depletion of Predatory Fish Communities', *Nature,* 423/6937: 280–283.

Nadvi, K., and Schmitz, H. (1998), 'Industrial Clusters in Less Developed Countries: Review of Experiences and Research Agenda', in P. Cadène and M. Holström (eds), *Decentralized Production in India: Industrial Districts, Flexible Specialization, and Employment* (Thousand Oaks, Calif.: Sage).

Naím, M. (2002), 'Post-Terror Surprises', *Foreign Policy,* 132: 96, 95.

Neumayer, E. (2001), *Greening Trade and Investment: Environmental Protection without Protectionism* (London: Earthscan).

Newell, P. (2000), *Climate for Change: Non-State Actors and the Global Politics of the Greenhouse* (Cambridge: Cambridge University Press).

Ng, F., and Yeats, A. (1999), 'Production Sharing in East Asia: Who Does What for Whom, and Why?', World Bank Policy Research Working Paper No. 2197 (Washington, DC: World Bank).

NGO Coalition (2002), 'NGOs Call on Trade Ministers to Reject Exclusive Mini-Ministerials and Green Room Meetings in the Run-Up to, and at, the 5th WTO Ministerial', www.ciel.org/Tae/WTO_5 Min_112002.html

Notermans, T. (2000), *Money, Markets, and the State: Social Democratic Economic Policies Since 1918* (Cambridge: Cambridge University Press).

—— (2001), *Social Democracy and Monetary Union* (New York: Berghahn).

Nye, J. S., Jr. (1990), 'Soft Power', *Foreign Policy,* 80: 153–171.

Oatley, T. (1997), *Monetary Politics: Exchange Rate Cooperation in the European Union* (Ann Arbor, Mich.: University of Michigan Press).

—— (2006), *International Political Economy: Interests and Institutions in the Global Economy,* 2nd edn (London: Pearson Longman).

O'Brien, Richard (1992), *The End of Geography: Global Financial Integration* (London: Pinter).

O'Brien, Robert and Williams, M. (2004), *Global Political Economy: Evolution and Dynamics* (Basingstoke: Palgrave Macmillan).

Obstfeld, M. (1993), 'International Capital Mobility in the 1990s', NBER Working Paper 4534 (Cambridge, Mass.: National Bureau of Economic Research).

—— and Rogoff, K. (1996), *Foundations of International Macroeconomics* (Cambridge, Mass.: MIT Press).

—— and Taylor, A. M. (1998), 'The Great Depression as a Watershed: International Capital Mobility in the Long Run', in M. D. Bordo, C. Goldin, and E. N. White (eds), The *Defining Moment: The Great Depression and the American Economy in the Twentieth Century* (Chicago: Chicago University Press).

—— —— (2003), 'Globalization and Capital Markets', in M. D. Bordo, A. M. Taylor, and J. G. Williamson (eds), *Globalization in Historical Perspective* (Chicago: University of Chicago Press).

—— —— (2004), *Global Capital Markets: Integration, Crisis, and Growth* (Cambridge: Cambridge University Press).

Odell, J. S. (1982), *US International Monetary Policy: Markets, Power, and Ideas as Sources of Change* (Princeton, NJ: Princeton University Press).

—— (2002), 'Making and Breaking Impasses in International Regimes: The WTO, Seattle and Doha', Paper prepared for the Conference on Gaining Leverage in International Negotiations, Yonsei University, Seoul.

OECD (Organisation for Economic Co-operation and Development) (2002), Regional Trade Agreements and the Multilateral Trading System: Consolidated Report, 20 November, www.olis.oecd.org/olis/2002doc.nsf/ 43bb6130e5e86e5fc12569fa005d004c/ db1bbc3ddbadceeec1256c770042bc1b/$FILE/ JT00135547.PDF

Offer, A. (1989), *The First World War: An Agrarian Interpretation* (Oxford: Clarendon Press).

Officer, L. H. (2001), 'Gold Standard', EH.Net Encyclopedia 1 October, http://eh.net/encyclopedia/article/officer.gold. standard

Ofreneo, R. (1993), 'Japan and the Environmental Degradation of the Philippines', in M. Howard (ed.), *Asia's Environmental Crisis* (Boulder, Colo.: Westview Press).

Ohmae, K. (1990), *The Borderless World* (London: Collins).

—— (1995), *The End of the Nation State: The Rise of Regional Economies* (New York: Free Press).

Oi, J. C. (1992), 'Fiscal Reform and the Economic Foundations of Local State Corporatism in China', *World Politics,* 45/1: 99–126.

Okimoto, D. I. (1988), 'Political Inclusivity: The Domestic Structure of Trade', in T. Inoguchi and D. I. Okimoto (eds), *The Political Economy of Japan,* II: *The Changing International Context* (Stanford, Calif.: Stanford University Press).

Olson, M. (1965), *The Logic of Collective Action: Public Goods and the Theory of Groups* (Cambridge, Mass.: Harvard University Press).

Onuf, N. (1997), 'Hegemony's Hegemony in IPE', in K. Burch and R. Denemark (eds), *Constituting International Political Economy* (Boulder, Colo.: Lynne Rienner).

O'Rourke, K. H., and Williamson, J. G. (1999), *Globalization and History: The Evolution of a Nineteenth-Century Atlantic Economy* (Cambridge, Mass.: MIT Press).

Osherenko, G., and Young, O. R. (1993), 'The Formation of International Regimes: Hypotheses and Cases', in O. R. Young and G. Osherenko (eds), *Polar Politics: Creating International Environmental Regimes* (Ithaca, NY: Cornell University Press), 1–21.

Osler, C. L. (1991), 'Explaining the Absence of International Factor-Price Convergence', *Journal of Money and Finance*, 10/1: 89–107.

Ostrom, E. (2000), 'Reformulating the Commons', *Swiss Political Science Review*, 6/1: 29–52.

Oxfam International (2002*a*), 'Last Chance in Monterrey: Meeting the Challenge of Poverty Reduction', Oxfam Briefing Paper No. 17 (Oxford: Oxfam), March.

—— (2002*b*), *Rigged Rules and Double Standards: Trade, Globalisation, and the Fight against Poverty*, www.maketradefair.com/assets/english/report_english.pdf

Oye, K. A. (1985), 'Explaining Cooperation under Anarchy: Hypotheses and Strategies', *World Politics*, 38/1: 1–24.

—— (1992), *Economic Discrimination and Political Exchange: World Political Economy in the 1930s and 1980s* (Princeton, NJ: Princeton University Press).

Paarlberg, R. L. (1997), 'Agricultural Policy Reform and the Uruguay Round: Synergistic Linkage in a Two-Level Game', *International Organization*, 51/3: 413–444.

Palan, R. (2003), *The Offshore World: Sovereign Markets, Virtual Places and Nomad Millionaires* (Ithaca, NY: Cornell University Press).

Palmeter, D. N., and Mavroidis, P. C. (1999), *Dispute Settlement in the World Trade Organization: Practice and Procedure* (The Hague: Kluwer).

Palmisano, S. J. (2006), 'The Globally Integrated Enterprise', *Foreign Affairs*, 85/3: 127–136.

Parker, B. (1998), *Globalization and Business Practice: Managing across Boundaries* (London: Sage).

Parson, E. A. (2003), *Protecting the Ozone Layer: Science and Strategy* (Oxford: Oxford University Press).

Pastor, R. (1980), *Congress and the Politics of US Foreign Economic Policy, 1929–1976* (Berkeley, Calif. and Los Angeles: University of California Press).

Paterson, M. (1996), *Global Warming and Global Politics* (London: Routledge).

—— (2001), 'Risky Business: Insurance Companies in Global Warming Politics', *Global Environmental Politics*, 1/4: 18–42.

Pauly, L. W. (1992), 'The Politics of European Monetary Union: National Strategies, International Implications', *International Journal*, 47/1: 93–111.

—— (1997), *Who Elected the Bankers? Surveillance and Control in the World Economy* (Ithaca, NY: Cornell University Press).

Pearson, F., and Rochester, M. (1998), *International Relations: The Global Condition in the Twenty-First Century*, 4th edn (New York: McGraw-Hill).

Perraton, J., Goldblatt, D., Held, D., and McGrew, A. (1997), 'The Globalization of Economic Activity', *New Political Economy*, 2/2: 257–278.

Perroni, C., and Whalley, J. (1994), 'The New Regionalism: Trade Liberalization or Insurance?', NBER Working Paper 4626 (Cambridge, Mass.: National Bureau of Economic Research).

Petras, J., and Veltmeyer, H. (2001), *Globalization Unmasked: Imperialism in the 21st Century* (London: Zed Books).

Petrella, R. (1996), 'Globalization and Internationalization: The Dynamics of the Emerging World Order', in R. Boyer and D. Drache (eds), *States against Market: The Limits of Globalization* (London: Routledge).

Pharr, S. J., and Putnam, R. D. (eds) (2000) *Disaffected Democracies: What's Troubling the Trilateral Countries?* (Princeton, NJ: Princeton University Press).

Pierson, P. (1994), *Dismantling the Welfare State? Reagan, Thatcher and the Politics of Retrenchment* (Cambridge: Cambridge University Press).

—— (1996), 'The New Politics of the Welfare State', *World Politics*, 48/2: 143–179.

Pilling, D., and Mitchell, T. (2007), 'Japan in Yields to China's Lure', *Financial Times*, 5 April: 7.

Pinto, P. M. (2003), 'Tying Hands vs. Exchanging Hostages: Domestic Coalitions, Political Constraints, and FDI', Paper presented at the Annual Meeting of the American Political Science Association, Philadelphia, Pa.

Piore, M., and Sabel, C. (1984), *The Second Industrial Divide: Possibilities for Prosperity* (New York: Basic Books).

Poku, N. (2001), 'The Crisis of AIDS in Africa and the Politics of Response', in N. Poku (ed.), *Security and Development in Southern Africa* (Westport, Conn.: Praeger).

Polanyi, K. (1944), *The Great Transformation* (New York: Rinehart).

Population Reference Bureau (2002), '2002 World Population Data Sheet of the Population Reference Bureau: Demographic Data and Estimates for the Countries and Regions of the World', www.prb.org/pdf/WorldPopulationDS02_Eng.pdf

Porter, m.e. (1990) *The Competitive Advantage of nations* (new york: Free Press).

Porter, G. (1999), 'Trade Competition and Pollution Standards: "Race to the Bottom" or "Stuck at the Bottom"?', *Journal of Environment and Development*, 8/2: 133–151.

—— Brown, J. W., and Chasek, P. (2000), *Global Environmental Politics*, 3rd edn (Boulder, Colo.: Westview Press).

Prebisch, R. (1963), *Towards a Dynamic Development Policy for Latin America* (New York: United Nations).

—— (1970), *Change and Development: Latin America's Great Task* (Washington, DC: Inter-American Development Bank).

Preeg, E. H. (1970), *Traders and Diplomats: An Analysis of the Kennedy Round under the General Agreement on Tariffs and Trade* (Washington, DC: Brookings).

—— (1995), *Traders in a Brave New World: The Uruguay Round and the Future of the International Trading System* (Chicago: University of Chicago Press).

Princen, T. (1997), 'The Shading and Distancing of Commerce: When Internalization is not Enough', *Ecological Economics*, 20/3: 235–253.

Putnam, R. D. (1988), 'Diplomacy and Domestic Politics: The Logic of Two-Level Games', *International Organization*, 42/3: 427–460.

—— and Bayne, N. (1987), *Hanging Together: Cooperation and Conflict in the Seven-Power Summits* (Cambridge, Mass.: Harvard University Press).

Raffer, K., and Singer, H. (2001), *The Economic North–South Divide: Six Decades of Unequal Development* (Cheltenham: Edward Elgar).

Rahnema, M., and Bawtree, V. (eds) (1997), *The Post Development Reader* (London: Zed Books).

Raphael, D. D., and Macfie, A. L. (1982), 'Introduction', in A. Smith (1759/1982), *The Theory of Moral Sentiments*, Glasgow Edition of the Works and Correspondence of Adam Smith, ed. D. D. Raphael and A. L. Macfie (Indianapolis, Ind.: Liberty Fund).

Rapley, J. (1996), *Understanding Development* (Boulder, Colo.: Lynne Rienner).

Ravenhill, J. (1995), 'Competing Logics of Regionalism in the Asia-Pacific', *Journal of European Integration*, 18/2–3: 179–199.

—— (2001), *APEC and the Construction of Asia-Pacific Regionalism* (Cambridge: Cambridge University Press).

—— (2003), 'The New Bilateralism in the Asia-Pacific', *Third World Quarterly*, 24/2: 299–317.

—— (2004), 'Back to the Nest? Europe's Relations with the African, Caribbean and Pacific Group of Countries', in V. K. Aggarwal and E. A. Fogarty (eds), *EU Trade Statistics: Between Regionalism and Globalization* (Basingstoke: Palgrave Macmillan), 118–147.

—— (2005), 'The Study of Global Political Economy', in J. Ravenhill (ed.), *Global Political Economy* (Oxford: Oxford University Press).

—— (2006a), 'Is China an Economic Threat to Southeast Asia?', *Asian Survey*, 46/5: 653–674.

—— (2006b), 'The Political Economy of the New Asia-Pacific Bilateralism: Benign, Banal or Simply Bad?', in V. K. Aggarwal and S. Urata (eds), *Bilateral Trade Agreements in the Asia-Pacific: Origins, Evolution, and Implications* (London: Routledge), 27–49.

Reddy, S. G., and Pogge, T. W. (2002), 'How *Not* to Count the Poor!—a Reply to Ravallion', 15 August, www.columbia.edu/~sr793/poggereddyreply.pdf

—————— (2003), 'How *Not* to Count the Poor', 26 March, www.columbia.edu/~sr793/count.pdf

Rees, W. E. (2002), 'Globalization and Sustainability: Conflict or Convergence?', *Bulletin of Science, Technology & Society*, 22/4: 249–268.

—— and Westra, L. (2003), 'When Consumption Does Violence: Can There Be Sustainability and Environmental Justice in a Resource-limited World?', in J. Agyeman, R. Bullard, and B. Evans (eds), *Just Sustainabilities: Development in an Unequal World* (London: Earthscan).

Reich, R. (1992), *The Work of Nations* (New York: Vintage Books).

Rhodes, M. (1996), 'Globalization and West European Welfare States: A Critical Review of Recent Debates', *Journal of European Social Policy*, 6/4: 305–327.

—— (1997), 'The Welfare State: Internal Challenges, External Constraints', in M. Rhodes, P. Heywood, and V. Wright (eds), *Developments in West European Politics* (London: Macmillan).

Ricardo, D. (1817/2002), *On the Principles of Political Economy and Taxation*, reprinted version of 3rd edn (London: Empiricus Books).

Rich, B. (1994), *Mortgaging the Earth: The World Bank, Environmental Impoverishment, and the Crisis of Development* (London: Earthscan).

Rieger, E., and Leibfried, S. (2003), *Limits to Globalization: Welfare States and the World Economy* (Cambridge: Polity Press).

Robbins, R. H. (2002), *Global Problems and the Culture of Capitalism*, 2nd edn (Boston, Mass.: Allyn & Bacon).

Robertson, R. (2003), *The Three Waves of Globalization: A History of Developing Global Consciousness* (London: Zed Books).

Robinson, J. (1964), *Economic Philosophy*, 2nd edn (Harmondsworth: Pelican).

Rodrik, D. (1989), 'Promises, Promises: Credible Policy Reform via Signalling', *Economic Journal*, 99/397: 756–772.

—— (1995), 'Political Economy of Trade Policy', in G. Grossman and K. Rogoff (eds), *Handbook of International Economics*, vol. III (Amsterdam: Elsevier).

—— (1996), 'Why Do More Open Economies Have Bigger Governments?', NBER Working Paper 5537 (Cambridge, Mass.: National Bureau of Economic Research).

—— (1997), *Has Globalization Gone Too Far?* (Washington, DC: Institute for International Economics).

—— (1999), The *The new Economy and Developing Countries: makingopennes work* (Baltimore: Johns hopkins University Press for Overseas Development Council).

—— (2006), 'The Social Cost of Foreign Exchange Reserves', NBER Working Paper 11952 (Cambridge, Mass.: National Bureau of Economic Research).

Rødseth, A. (2000), *Open Economy Macroeconomics* (Cambridge: Cambridge University Press).

Roemer, J. E. (1988), *Free to Lose: An Introduction to Marxist Economic Philosophy* (London: Radius).

Rogers, A. (1993), *The Earth Summit: A Planetary Reckoning* (Los Angeles: Global View Press).

Rogowski, R., (1987), 'Trade and the Variety of Democratic Institutions', *International Organization*, 41/2: 203–223.

—— (1989), *Commerce and Coalitions* (Princeton, NJ: Princeton University Press).

Rosamond, B. (2001), 'Discourses of Globalization and European Identities', in T. Christiansen, K. Jorgensen, and A. Wiener (eds), *The Social Construction of Europe* (London: Sage).

Rosecrance, R. (1986), *The Rise of the Trading State: Commerce and Conquest in the Modern World* (New York: Basic Books).

—— (1999), *The Rise of the Virtual State* (New York: Basic Books).

Rosen, D. (2003), 'Low-tech bed, high-tech dreams', *China Economic Quarterly*, 4: 20–27.

Rosenberg, A. (1995), *Philosophy of Social Science* (Boulder, Colo.: Westview Press).

Rosenberg, J. (2000), *The Follies of Globalization Theory* (London: Verso).

—— (2005), 'Globalization Theory: A Post Mortem', *International Politics*, 42/1: 2–74.

Rostow, W. (1960), *The Stages of Economic Growth* (New York: Cambridge University Press).

Rothstein, R. L. (1979), *Global Bargaining: UNCTAD and the Quest for a New International Economic Order* (Princeton, NJ: Princeton University Press).

Roubini, N., and Setser, B. (2004), *Bailouts or Bail-ins? Responding to Financial Crises in Emerging Markets* (Washington, DC: Institute for International Economics).

Rowthorn, R., and Wells, J. (1987), *De-industrialization and Foreign Trade* (Cambridge: Cambridge University Press).

Ruggie, J. G. (1982), 'International Regimes, Transactions, and Change: Embedded Liberalism in the Postwar Economic Order', *International Organization*, 36/2: 379–415.

—— (1992), 'Multilateralism: The Anatomy of an Institution', *International Organization*, 46/3: 561–598.

—— (1998), *Constructing the World Polity* (London: Routledge).

Rugman, A. (2000), *The End of Globalization* (London: Random HouseNew York: Amacom–McGraw Hill).

Ruigrok, W., and Tulder, R. V. (1995), *The Logic of International Restructuring* (London: Routledge).

Sako, M. (2003), 'Modularity and Outsourcing: The Nature of Co-evolution of Product Architecture and Organization Architecture in the Global Automotive Industry', in A. Prencipe, A. Davies, and M. Hobday (eds), *The Business of Systems Integration* (Oxford: Oxford University Press).

—— (2006), 'Outsourcing and Offshoring: Implications for Productivity of Business Services', *Oxford Review of Economic Policy*, 22/4: 499–512.

Samuelson, P. (1987), *The Collected Scientific Papers: Volume 5* (Cambridge, Mass.: MIT Press).

Sandholtz, W. (1993), 'Choosing Union: Monetary Politics and Maastricht', *International Organization*, 47/1: 1–39.

—— and Stone Sweet, A. (eds) (1998), *European Integration and Supranational Governance* (Oxford: Oxford University Press).

—— and Zysman, J. (1989), '1992: Recasting the European Bargain', *World Politics*, 42/1: 95–128.

Sandler, T. (1992), *Collective Action: Theory and Applications* (Ann Arbor, Mich.: University of Michigan Press).

Santiso, J. (2006), *Latin America's Political Economy of the Possible* (Cambridge, Mass.: MIT Press).

Sassen, S. (2006), *Territory, Authority, Rights: From Medieval to Global Assemblages* (Princeton, NJ: Princeton University Press).

Saul, J. R. (2005), *The Collapse of Globalism* (London: Atlantic Books).

Save the Children (2001), *The Bitterest Pill of All: The Collapse of Africa's Health Systems* (London: Save the Children), 21 May.

Sayer, A. (2000), *Realism and Social Science* (London: Sage).

Schelling, T. C. (1960), *The Strategy of Conflict* (Cambridge, Mass.: Harvard University Press).

Schiff, M. W., and Winters, L. A. (2003), *Regional Integration and Development* (New York: Oxford University Press for the World Bank).

Schiller, R. J. (2001), *Irrational Exuberance* (Princeton, NJ: Princeton University Press).

Schirato, T., and Webb, J. (2003), *Understanding Globalization* (London: Sage).

Schirm, S. A. (2002), *Globalization and the New Regionalism* (Cambridge: Polity Press).

Schmidheiny, S. (with World Business Council for Sustainable Development) (1992), *Changing Course: A Global Business Perspective on Development and the Environment* (Cambridge, Mass.: MIT Press).

—— and Zorraquin, F. (1996), *Financing Change: The Financial Community, Eco-efficiency, and Sustainable Development* (Cambridge, Mass.: MIT Press).

Schmidt, V. (2002), *The Futures of European Capitalism* (Oxford: Oxford University Press).

Schmitter, P., and Lehbruch, G. (eds) (1979), *Trends Towards Corporatist Intermediation* (Beverly Hills, Calif.: Sage).

Schnietz, K. (1994), 'To Delegate or Not to Delegate: Congressional Institutional Choice in the Regulation of Foreign Trade, 1916–1934', Ph.D. dissertation (Berkeley, Califo., University of California).

Scholte, J. A. (1997), 'The Globalization of World Politics', in J. Baylis and S. Smith (eds), *The Globalization of World Politics: An Introduction to International Relations* (Oxford: Oxford University Press).

508

—— (2000), *Globalization: A Critical Introduction* (Basingstoke: Palgrave).

—— (2005), *Globalization: A Critical Introduction*, revd and updated 2nd edn (Basingstoke: Palgrave Macmillan).

Schreurs, M. A. (2002), *Environmental Politics in Japan, Germany, and the United States* (Cambridge: Cambridge University Press).

Schubert, A. (1992), *The Credit-Anstalt Crisis of 1931* (Cambridge: Cambridge University Press).

Schumacher, E. F. (1973), *Small is Beautiful: Economics as if People Mattered* (New York: Harper & Row).

Schumpeter, J. (1954/1994), *History of Economic Analysis* (New York: Oxford University Press).

Schwartz, H. (2001), 'Round up the Usual Suspects: Globalization, Domestic Politics, and Welfare State Change', in P. Pierson (ed.), *The New Politics of the Welfare State* (Oxford: Oxford University Press).

Scollay, R., and Gilbert, J. (2001), *New Regional Trading Arrangements in the Asia Pacific?* (Washington, DC: Institute for International Economics).

Seligson, M., and Passe-Smith, J. (eds) (1993), *Development and Underdevelopment: The Political Economy of Global Inequality* (Boulder, Colo.: Lynne Rienner).

Sen, A. (1999), *Development as freedom* (Oxford: Oxford University Press).

Shah, A., and Thompson, T. (2002), 'Implementing Decentralized Local Governance: A Treacherous Road with Potholes, Detours, and Road Closures', Paper presented at 'Can Decentralization Help Rebuild Indonesia?', Andrew Young School of Policy Studies, Georgia State University, Atlanta, Georgia, 1–3 May.

Shiva, V. (1993), 'The Greening of the Global Reach', in W. Sachs (ed.), *Global Ecology: A New Arena of Political Conflict* (London: Zed Books).

Shonfield, A. (ed.) (1976), *International Economic Relations of the Western World 1959–1971, I: Politics and Trade* (London: Oxford University Press).

Silver, B. J. (2003), *Forces of Labor: Workers' Movements and Globalization Since 1870* (Cambridge: Cambridge University Press).

Simmons, B. A. (1994), *Who Adjusts? Domestic Sources of Foreign Economic Policy During the Interwar Years* (Princeton, NJ: Princeton University Press).

—— (1999), 'The Internationalisation of Capital', in H. Kitschelt, P. Lange, G. Marks, and J. D. Stephens (eds), *Continuity and Change in Contemporary Capitalism* (Cambridge: Cambridge University Press).

Simon, J. L. (1996), *The Ultimate Resource 2* (Princeton, NJ: Princeton University Press).

Sinclair, T. (1994), 'Between State and Market', *Policy Sciences*, 27/4: 447–466.

Singer, H., and Roy, S. (1993), *Economic Progress and Prospects in the Third World* (Aldershot: Edward Elgar).

Singh, A., and Zammit, A. (2000), 'International Capital Flows: Identifying the Gender Dimension', *World Development*, 28/7: 1249–1268.

Skidelsky, R. (2003), 'Keynes's Road to Bretton Woods: An Essay in Interpretation', in M. Flandreau, C.-L. Holtfrerich, and H. James (eds), *International Financial History in the Twentieth Century* (Cambridge: Cambridge University Press).

Sklair, L. (2001), *The Transnational Capitalist Class* (Oxford: Blackwell).

—— (2002), *Globalization: Capitalism and its Alternatives* (Oxford: Oxford University Press).

Smith, A. (1776/1976), *An Inquiry into the Nature and Causes of the Wealth of Nations* (Oxford: Oxford University Press), www.econlib.org/library/Smith/smWN.html

—— (1759/1982), *The Theory of Moral Sentiments*, Glasgow Edition of the Works and Correspondence of Adam Smith, ed. D. D. Raphael and A. L. Macfie (Indianapolis, Ind.: Liberty Fund).

—— (1776/1981), *An Inquiry into the Nature and Causes of the Wealth of Nations*, Glasgow Edition of the Works and Correspondence of Adam Smith, ed. R. H. Campbell and A. Skinner (Indianapolis, Ind.: Liberty Fund).

Snidal, D. (1985*a*), 'Coordination versus Prisoners' Dilemma: Implications for International Cooperation and Regimes', *American Political Science Review*, 79/4: 923–942.

—— (1985*b*), 'The Limits of Hegemonic Stability Theory', *International Organization*, 39/4: 579–614.

Snyder, R. (2001), 'Scaling Down: The Subnational Comparative Method', *Studies in Comparative International Development*, 36/1: 93–110.

Soederberg, S. (2002), 'A Historical Materialist Account of the Chilean Capital Controls: Prototype for Whom?', *Review of International Political Economy*, 9/3: 490–512.

Solis, M. (2003), 'On the Myth of *Keiretsu* Network: Japanese Electronics in North America', *Business and Politics*, 5/3: 303–333.

Soroos, M. S. (1997), *The Endangered Atmosphere* (Columbia, SC: University of South Carolina Press).

Soros, G. (1997*a*), 'The Capitalist Threat', *Atlantic Monthly*, February.

—— (1997*b*), Letter to the Editor, *Atlantic Monthly*, May.

—— (1998), *The Crisis of Global Capitalism* (New York: Public Affairs).

South Commission (1990), *The Challenge to the South* (Oxford: Oxford University Press).

Spero, J. (1977), *The Politics of International Economic Relations* (London: George Allen & Unwin).

—— (1980), *The Failure of the Franklin National Bank* (New York: Columbia University Press).

Spiro, D. (1999), *The Hidden Hand of American Hegemony: Petrodollar Recycling and International Markets* (Ithaca, NY: Cornell University Press).

Sraffa, P. with the collaboration of Dobb, M. (1951/1981), 'Introduction', in P. Sraffa and M. Dobb (eds), *The Works and Correspondence of David Ricardo, Volume 1: On the Principles of Political Economy and Taxation*, reprinted edn (Cambridge: Cambridge University Press).

Stasavage, D. (2003), 'When Do States Abandon Monetary Discretion? Lessons from the Evolution of the CFA Franc Zone', in J. Kirshner (ed.), *Monetary Orders: Ambiguous Economics, Ubiquitous Politics* (Ithaca, NY: Cornell University Press).

Steans, J., and Pettiford, L. (2001), *International Relations: Perspectives and Themes* (Harlow: Pearson Education).

Stein, A. A. (1982), 'Coordination and Collaboration: Regimes in an Anarchic World', *International Organization*, 36/2: 294–324.

Steinmo, S. (2003), 'The Evolution of Policy Ideas: Tax Policy in the Twentieth Century', *British Journal of Politics and International Relations*, 5/2: 206–236.

Stiglitz, J. E. (2002), *Globalization and its Discontents* (New York: W. W. Norton)

—— (2006), *Making Globalization Work* (New York: W. W. Norton).

Stolper, W., and Samuelson, P. A. (1941), 'Protection and Real Wages', *Review of Economic Studies*, 9: 58–73.

Strange, S. (1986), *Casino Capitalism* (Oxford: Basil Blackwell).

—— (1988), *States and Markets* (London: Pinter).

—— (1998a), 'International Political Economy: Beyond Economics and International Relations', *Economies et Sociétés*, 34/4: 3–24.

—— (1998b), *Mad Money: When Markets Outgrow Government* (Ann Arbor, Mich.: University of Michigan Press).

Streck, C. (2001), 'The Global Environment Facility—a Role Model for International Governance?', *Global Environmental Politics*, 1/2: 71–94.

Sturgeon, T. (2002), 'Modular Production Networks: A New American Model of Industrial Organization', *Industrial and Corporate Change*, 11/3: 451–496.

Subbarao, K., A. bonnerjee, J. Braitnwaite et al. (1997), *Safety Net Programs and Poverty Reduction: Lessons from Cross-Country Experience* (Washington, DC: World Bank).

Summers, L. (2006), 'Only Fairness Will Assuage the Anxious Middle', *Financial Times*, 10 December.

Suskind, A. (2004), *The Prince of Loyalty: George W Bush, the White House, and the Education of Paul O'neill* (new york: Simon & Schuster).

Svedberg, P. (2003), 'World Income Distribution: Which Way?', Institute for International Economics Seminar Paper 724 (Stockholm: Stockholm University).

Swank, D. (2002), *Global Capital, Political Institutions and Policy Change in Developed Welfare States* (Cambridge: Cambridge University Press).

Swenson, P. (2000), *Capitalists against Markets* (Oxford: Oxford University Press).

Switzer, J. V. (2004), *Environmental Politics: Domestic and Global Dimensions*, 4th edn (Belmont, Calif.: Thomson/Wadsworth).

Tasca, H. J. (1938), *The Reciprocal Trade Policy of the United States* (New York: Russell & Russell).

Taylor, A. M. (1996), 'Domestic Saving and International Capital Flows Reconsidered', NBER Working Paper 4892 (Cambridge, Mass.: National Bureau of Economic Research).

—— (2002), 'Globalization, Trade and Development: Some Lessons from History', NBER Working Paper 9326 (Cambridge, Mass.: National Bureau of Economic Research).

Taylor, M. (1987), *The Possibility of Cooperation* (Cambridge: Cambridge University Press).

Teeple, G. (1995), *Globalization and the Decline of Social Reform* (Toronto: Garamond Press).

Teivainen, T. (2002), *Enter Economism, Exit Politics* (London: Zed Books).

Tesar, L. L. (1991), 'Saving, Investment and International Capital Flows', *Journal of International Economics*, 31/1: 55–78.

Thun, E. (2000), 'Growing Up and Moving Out: Globalization in the Taiwanese Textile/Apparel and Automotive Sectors', MIT IPC Working Paper 00–007 (Cambridge, Mass.: Industrial Performance Center, Massachusetts Institute of Technology), June.

—— (2006), *Changing Lanes in China: Foreign Direct Investment, Local Governments, and Auto Sector Development* (New York: Cambridge University Press).

Thomas, C. (1985), *New States, Sovereignty and Intervention* (London: Gower).

—— (1987), *In Search of Security: The Third World in International Relations* (Brighton: Wheatsheaf/Boulder, Colo.: Lynne Rienner).

—— (2000), *Global Governance, Development and Human Security* (London: Pluto Press).

—— (2002), 'Trade Policy and the Politics of Access to Drugs', *Third World Quarterly*, 23/2: 251–264.

—— (2004), 'The International Financial Institutions' Relations with Sub-Saharan Africa: Insights from the Issue of Representation and Voice', in P. Williams and I. Taylor (eds), *Into Africa: External Involvement in the African Continent after the Cold War* (London: Routledge).

—— and Weber, M. (2004), 'The Politics of Global Health Governance: Whatever Happened to "Health for All by the Year 2000"?', *Global Governance*, 10/2: 187–205.

Thompson, G. (2006), 'The Supra-national Regionalization of the International Financial System: How Far and With What Prospects?', Paper prepared for the GARNET Conference, Amsterdam, 28–30 September.

510

Tichenor, D. J. (2002), *Dividing Lines: The Politics of Immigration Control in America* (Princeton, NJ: Princeton University Press).

Tirole, J. (2002), *Financial Crises, Liquidity, and the International Monetary System* (Princeton, NJ: Princeton University Press).

Tisdell, C. (2001), 'Globalization and Sustainability: Environmental Kuznets Curve and the WTO', *Ecological Economics*, 39/2: 185–196.

Traxler, F., and Woitech, B. (2000), 'Transnational Investment and National Labour Market Regimes: A Case of "Regime Shopping"?', *European Journal of Industrial Relations*, 6/2: 141–159.

Triffin, R. (1960), *Gold and the Dollar Crisis* (New Haven, Conn.: Yale University Press).

Truman, E. (2006), 'A Strategy for International Monetary Fund Reform', *Policy Analyses in International Economics 77* (Washington, DC: Institute for International Economics).

Tullock, G. (1983), *The Economics of Income Distribution* (Boston, Mass.: Kluwer-Nijhoff).

Turner, P. (1981), 'Capital Flows in the 1980s: A Survey of Major Trends', *BIS Economic Papers*, No. 30 (Geneva: Bank for International Settlements).

Tussie, D. (1987), *The Less Developed Countries and the World Trading System: A Challenge to the GATT* (London: Frances Pinter).

Tyers, R., and Anderson, R. K. (1992), *Disarray in World Food Markets* (Cambridge: Cambridge University Press).

Ugur, M. (ed.), (2001), *Open Economy Macroeconomics: A Reader* (London: Routledge).

UN (United Nations) (1992), *Agenda 21: The United Nations Programme of Action from Rio* (New York: United Nations).

—— (2002), 'Report of the International Conference on Financing for Development (or the Monterrey Report)', 18–22 March, A/Conf.198/11, www.unctad.org/en/docs/aconf198d11_en.pdf

—— (2006), *World Economic and Social Survey 2006: Diverging Growth and Development* (New York: United Nations).

UNAIDS (2002), 'The Impact of HIV/AIDS', *Fact Sheet 2002* (UNAIDS).

—— (1999), *World Investment Report 1999: Foreign Direct Investment and the Challenge of Development* (New York and Geneva: United Nations).

—— (2000), *World Investment Report 2000: Cross-border Mergers and Acquisitions and Development* (New York/Geneva: United Nations).

UN Commission on Transnational Corporations (1978), *Transnational Corporations in World Development: A Re-examination* (New York: UN Publications).

UNCTAD (United Nations Conference on Trade and Development) (1999), *World Investment Report 1999: foreign Direct Investment and the Challenge of Development* (Geneva: UNCTAD).

—— (2000), *World Investment Report 2000: Cross-Border mergers and Acquisitions and Development* (Geneva: UNCTAD).

—— (2001), *World Investment Report: Promoting Linkages* (Geneva: UNCTAD).

—— (2002a), *The Least Developed Countries Report* (Geneva: UNCTAD).

—— (2002b), *Trade and Development Report 2002: Developing Countries in World Trade* (Geneva: UNCTAD).

—— (2002c), *World Investment Report 2002: Transnational Corporations and Export Competitiveness* (Geneva: UNCTAD).

—— (2003), *World Investment Report 2003: FDI Policies for Development: National and International Perspectives* (Geneva: UNCTAD).

—— (2004a), *Development and Globalization: Facts and Figures* (Geneva: UNCTAD).

—— (2004b), 'The New Geography of International Economic Relations', TD/B/51/6 Trade and Development Board, 51st Session, Geneva, 4–15 October, GE.04–52426.

—— (2005), *Trade and Development Report 2005: New Features of Global Interdependence* (Geneva: UNCTAD).

—— (2006a), *Trade and Development Report 2006: Global Partnership and National Policies for Development* (Geneva: UNCTAD).

—— (2006b), *World Investment Report 2006: FDI from Developing and Transition Economies: Implications for Development* (Geneva: UNCTAD).

UNDP (United Nations Development Programme) (1998), 'Consumption in a Global Village—Unequal and Unbalanced', in *Human Development Report 1998* (Oxford: Oxford University Press).

—— (2002), *Human Development Report 2002: Deepening Democracy in a Fragmented World* (New York/Oxford: Oxford University Press for UNDP).

—— (2003a), *Human Development Report 2003: Millennium Development Goals: A Compact among Nations to End Human Poverty* (New York/Oxford: Oxford University Press for UNDP).

—— (2003b), *Making Global Trade Work for People* (London: Earthscan).

—— (2006), *Human Development Report 2005: International Cooperation at a Crossroads: Aid, Trade and Security in an Unequal World* (New York: UNDP).

—— Heinrich Boll Foundation, Rockefeller Brothers Fund, Rockefeller Foundation, and Wallace Global Fund (2003), *Making Global Trade Work for People* (London: Earthscan).

UNEP (United Nations Environment Programme) (2000), *Action on Ozone* (Geneva: UNEP), www.unep.ch/ozone/pdf/ozone-action-en.pdf

—— (2002), *Global Environment Outlook 3* (London: Earthscan).

—— (2003), 'Backgrounder: Basic Facts and Data on the Science and Politics of Ozone Protection', www.unep.org/ozone/pdf/Press-Backgrounder.pdf

——(2005), 'Basic Facts and Data on the Science and Politics of Ozone Protection', November Media Release (Nairobi: UNEP).

UNFPA (United Nations Fund for Population Activities) (2001), *The State of the World Population 2001. Footprints and Milestones: Population and Environmental Change* (New York: UNFPA).

UNICEF (United Nations Children's Fund) (2007), 'Child Poverty in Perspective: An Overview of Child Well-being in Rich Countries', Report Card 7 (Florence, Italy: UNICEF Innocenti Research Centre).

van der Pijl, K. (1998), *Transnational Classes and International Relations* (London: Routledge).

Van Dormael, A. (1978), *Bretton Woods: The Birth of a Monetary System* (London: Macmillan).

van Staveren, I. (2002), 'Global Finance and Gender', in J. A. Scholte (ed.), *Civil Society and Global Finance* (London: Routledge).

Vaubel, R. (1986), 'A Public Choice Approach to International Organization', *Public Choice*, 51/1: 39–57.

——(1991), 'The Political Economy of the International Monetary Fund', in R. Vaubel and T. D. Willett (eds), *The Political Economy of International Organizations: A Public Choice Approach* (Boulder, Colo.: Westview Press).

Veloso, F. (2000), 'The Automotive Supply Chain Organization: Global Trends and Perspectives', MIT Working Paper (Cambridge, Mass.: MIT).

Verdier, D. (1994), *Democracy and International Trade: Britain, France, and the United States, 1860–1990* (Princeton, NJ: Princeton University Press).

Vernon, R. (1971), *Sovereignty at Bay* (New York: Basic Books).

——(1995), 'The World Trade Organization: A New Stage in International Trade and Development', *Harvard International Law Journal*, 36: 329–340.

Victor, D., Raustiala, K., and Skolnikoff, E. (1998), *The Implementation and Effectiveness of International Environmental Commitments: Theory and Practice* (Cambridge, Mass.: MIT Press).

Viner, J. (1948), 'Power Versus Plenty', *World Politics*, 1/1: 1–29.

——(1950), *The Customs Union Issue* (New York: Carnegie Endowment for International Peace).

Viotti, P., and Kauppi, M. (1993), *International Relations Theory: Realism, Pluralism, Globalism* (London: Macmillan).

Vivian, J. (ed.) (1995), *Adjustment and Social Sector Restructuring* (Geneva: UNRISD).

Vogel, D. (1995), *Trading Up: Consumer and Environmental Regulation in a Global Economy* (Cambridge, Mass.: Harvard University Press).

Vogler, J. (2000), *The Global Commons: Environmental and Technological Governance*, 2nd edn (Chichester: John Wiley).

——(2003), 'Taking Institutions Seriously: How Regime Analysis can be Relevant to Multilevel Environmental Governance', *Global Environmental Politics*, 3/2: 25–39.

Wabl, M. G. (2002), 'A "Monterrey Consensus" Might Replace the Washington Consensus', *UN Chronicle*, 39/1.

Wackernagel, M., and Rees, W. (1996), *Our Ecological Footprint: Reducing Human Impact on the Earth* (Gabriola Island, British Columbia: New Society Publishers).

Wade, K. (1990), *Governing the market: Economic Theory and the Role of Government in East Asian Industralization* (Princeton: Princeton University Press).

Wade, R. (2001), 'The US Role in the Long Asian Crisis of 1990–2000', in A. Lukauskas and F. Rivera-Batiz (eds), *The Political Economy of the East Asian Crisis and its Aftermath: Tigers in Distress* (Northampton, Mass.: Edward Elgar).

——(2003a), 'What Strategies Are Viable for Developing Countries Today? The WTO and the Shrinkage of Development Space', *Review of International Political Economy*, 10/4: 621–644.

——(2003b), 'The Invisible Hand of the American Empire', *Ethics and International Affairs*, 17/2: 77–88.

——(2004a), *Governing the Market: Economic Theory and the Role of Government in East Asian Industrialization* (Princeton, NJ: Princeton University Press).

——(2004b), 'Is Globalization Reducing Poverty and Inequality?', *International Journal of Health Services*, 34/3: 381–414.

——(2007a), 'The Washington Consensus', in *International Encyclopedia of the Social Sciences* (New York: Macmillan).

——(2007b), 'Economic Liberalism and the "Outward Alliance" of State, Finance and Big Companies: A Perspective from the United Kingdom', in P. Bowles, H. Veltmeyer, S. Cornelissen, N. Invernizzi, and K.-L. Tang (eds), *National Perspectives on Globalization: A Critical Reader* (Basingstoke: Palgrave Macmillan).

——and Veneroso, F. (1998), 'The Asian Crisis: The High Debt Model Versus the Wall Street–Treasury–IMF Complex', *New Left Review*, 228: 3–23.

Walker, R. B. J. (1993), *Inside/Outside: International Relations as Political Theory* (Cambridge: Cambridge University Press).

Wallace, H. (2000), 'The Policy Process: A Moving Pendulum', in H. Wallace and W. Wallace (eds), *Policy-Making in the European Union*, 4th edn (Oxford: Oxford University Press).

——and Wallace, W. (eds) (2000), *Policy-making in the European Union*, 4th edn (Oxford: Oxford University Press).

Wallerstein, I. (ed.) (1975), *World Inequality: Origins and Perspectives on the World System* (Montreal: Black Rose Books).

——(1979), *The Capitalist World-System: Essays by Immanuel Wallerstein* (Cambridge: Cambridge University Press).

——(1983), *Historical Capitalism* (London: Verso).

512

Walras, L. (1874/1984), *Elements of Pure Economics: Or the Theory of Social Wealth*, trans. W. Jaffé (Philadelphia, Pa.: Orion Editions).

Walton, J., and Seddon, D. (1994), *Free Markets and Food Riots: The Politics of Global Adjustment* (Oxford: Basil Blackwell).

Waltz, K. N. (1979), *Theory of International Politics* (Reading, Mass.: Addison Wesley).

Wapner, P. (2003), 'World Summit on Sustainable Development: Toward a Post-Jo'burg Environmentalism', *Global Environmental Politics*, 3/1: 1–10.

Warnock, F. E., and Warnock, V. C. (2006), 'International Capital Flows and US Interest Rates', NBER Working Paper 12560 (Cambridge, Mass.: National Bureau of Economic Research).

Warr, P. G. (1998), 'Thailand', in R. H. McLeod and R. Garnaut (eds), *East Asia in Crisis: From Being a Miracle to Needing One?* (London: Routledge).

Watkins, K. (1998), *Economic Growth with Equity: Lessons from East Asia* (Oxford: Oxfam).

—— (2002), 'Is the WTO Legit?', *Foreign Policy*, 132/September–October: 78–9.

Watson, M. (2001), 'International Capital Mobility in an Era of Globalization: Adding a Political Dimension to the "Feldstein–Horioka Puzzle"', *Politics*, 21/2: 81–92.

—— (2003), 'Ricardian Political Economy and the Varieties of Capitalism Approach: Specialisation, Trade and Comparative Institutional Advantage', *Comparative European Politics*, 1/2: 227–240.

—— (2005), *Foundations of International Political Economy* (Basingstoke: Palgrave Macmillan).

Watts, J. (2005), 'The Tiger's Teeth', *Guardian*, 25 May.

WCED (World Commission on Environment and Development) (1987), *Our Common Future* (Oxford: Oxford University Press).

Webb, M. (1995), *The Political Economy of Policy Coordination: International Adjustment Since 1945* (Ithaca, NY: Cornell University Press).

Weber, M. (1913/1958), 'The Social Psychology of the World Religions', in H. H. Gerth and C. Wright Mills (eds), *Max Weber: Essays in Sociology* (New York: Oxford University Press).

Weingast, B., Shepsle K., and Johnsen, C. (1981), 'The Political Economy of Benefits and Costs', *Journal of Political Economy*, 89/4: 642–664.

Weiss, L. (1998), *The Myth of the Powerless State: Governing the Economy in a Global Era* (Cambridge: Polity Press).

Wendt, A. (1992), 'Anarchy Is What States Make of It', *International Organization*, 42/2: 391–422.

—— (1995), 'Constructing International Politics', *International Security*, 20/1: 71–81.

—— (1998), 'On Constitution and Causation in International Relations', *Review of International Studies*, 24/5: 101–117.

West, E. G. (1976), *Adam Smith: The Man and His Works* (Indianapolis, Ind.: Liberty Fund).

WFS (World Food Summit) (1996), Technical Background Documents, Rome, 13–17 November, www.fao.org/docrep/003/w2612e/w2612e00.htm

Whalley, J. (1999), 'Why Do Countries Seek Regional Trade Agreements?', in J. Frankel (ed.), *The Regionalization of the World Economy* (Cambridge, Mass.: National Bureau of Economic Research).

Wheeler, D. (2002), 'Beyond Pollution Havens', *Global Environmental Politics*, 2/2: 1–10.

Whiting, S. H. (2001), *Power and Wealth in Rural China* (Cambridge: Cambridge University Press).

WHO (World Health Organization) (2002), *Healthy Environments for Children: An Alliance to Shape the Future of Life* (Geneva: WHO).

Wilensky, H. L. (2002), *Rich Democracies: Political Economy, Public Policy and Performance* (Berkeley, Calif. and Los Angeles: University of California Press).

Wilks, A., and Lefrancois, F. (for Bretton Woods Project and World Vision) (2002), 'Blinding with Science or Encouraging Debate? How World Bank Analysis Determines PRSP Policies', www.brettonwoodsproject.org/article.shtml? cmd[126]=i-126-e8e879f3bf130d8b04c2069806658c71

Wilkins, M. (2003), 'Conduits for Long Term Foreign Investment in the Gold Standard Era', in M. Flandreau, C.-L. Holtfrerich, and H. James (eds), *International Financial History in the Twentieth Century: System and Anarchy* (Cambridge: Cambridge University Press).

Williams, M. (1994), *International Economic Organizations and the Third World* (Hemel Hempstead: Harvester Wheatsheaf).

Williamson, O. E. (1975), *Markets and Hierarchies, Analysis and Anti-Trust Implications: A Study in the Economics of Internal Organization* (New York: Free Press).

—— (1981) 'The Modern Corporation: Origins, Evolution, Attributes', *Journal of Economic Literature*, 19/4: 1537–1568.

Winchester, S. (1991), *Pacific Rising* (New York: Prentice-Hall)

Winham, G. R. (1986), *International Trade and the Tokyo Round Negotiation* (Princeton, NJ: Princeton University Press).

—— (1998a), 'Explanations of Developing Country Behaviour in the GATT Uruguay Round Negotiation', *World Competition*, 21/3: 109–134.

—— (1998b), 'The World Trade Organization: Institution-Building in the Multilateral Trade System', *World Economy*, 21/3: 349–368.

—— (2000), 'The Uruguay Round and the World Economy', in R. Stubbs and G. Underhill (eds), *Political Economy and the Changing Global Order*, 2nd edn (Oxford: Oxford University Press).

Wintrobe, R. (1998), *The Political Economy of Dictatorship* (Cambridge: Cambridge University Press).

Wolf, D., and Zangl, B. (1996), 'The European Economic and Monetary Union: "Two-level Games" and the Formation of International Institutions', *European Journal of International Relations*, 2/3: 355–393.

Wolf, M. (2004*a*), *Why Globalization Works* (New Haven, Conn.: Yale University Press).

—— (2004*b*), 'States are Cure and Disease', Special Report: World Economy, *Financial Times*, 1 October.

Wolfensohn, J. (2002), 'World Bank President Outlines Post-Monterrey Action Plan to Development Committee', News Release No. 2002/280/S, 15 April.

Womack, J. P., Jones, D. T., and Roos, D. (1990), *The Machine That Changed the World* (New York: Harper Perennial).

Wood, A. (1994), *North–South Trade, Employment and Inequality* (Oxford: Oxford University Press).

Wood, E. M. (2003), *Empire of Capital* (London: Verso).

Woods, N. (2001*a*), 'International Political Economy in an Age of Globalization', in J. Baylis and S. Smith (eds), *The Globalization of World Politics: An Introduction to International Relations*, 2nd edn (Oxford: Oxford University Press).

—— (2001*b*), 'Making the IMF and World Bank More Accountable', *International Affairs*, 77/1: 83–100.

—— (2003), 'Order, Justice, the IMF and the World Bank', in R. Foot, J. L. Gaddis, and A. Hurrell (eds), *Order and Justice in International Relations* (Oxford: Oxford University Press).

—— (2006), *The Globalizers: The IMF, the World Bank and Their Borrowers* (Ithaca, NY: Cornell University Press).

World Bank (1992), *World Development Report 1992* (New York: Oxford University Press).

—— (1993), *The East Asian Miracle: Economic Growth and Public Policy* (Oxford: Oxford University Press).

—— (1999*a*), *Global Development Finance* [electronic resource] (Washington, DC: International Bank for Reconstruction and Development/The World Bank), computer disks; 3 1/2 in.

—— (1999*b*), *Global Economic Prospects and the Developing Countries 1998/99: Beyond Financial Crisis* (Washington, DC: World Bank).

—— (1999*c*), *World Development Report 1999/2000: Entering the 21st Century* (Washington, DC: World Bank).

—— (2000), *Trade Blocs* (New York: Oxford University Press).

—— (2002*a*), *Global Development Finance: Financing the Poorest Countries* [electronic resource] (Washington, DC: World Bank), 1 CD-ROM; 4 3/4 in. 11 insert.

—— (2002*b*), *Globalization, Growth, and Poverty: Building an Inclusive World Economy* (New York: Oxford University Press).

—— (2002*c*), 'World Bank Estimates Cost of Reaching the Millennium Development Goals at $40–60 Billion Annually in Additional Aid', Press Release No. 2002/212/S, 21 February.

—— (2002*d*), *World Development Indicators 2002* (Washington, DC: World Bank).

—— (2005*a*), *World Development Indicators 2005* (Washington, DC: World Bank).

—— (2005*b*), *World Development Report 2006: Equity and Development* (New York: World Bank and Oxford University Press).

—— (2006), *Global Economic Prospects 2007: Managing the Next Wave of Globalization* (Washington, DC: World Bank).

World Meteorological Organization (2006), 'New Report Projects Later Recovery of Ozone Layer', Press Release WMO No. 757, 18 August (Geneva/Nairobi: World Meteorological Organization).

WTO (World Trade Organization) (1999*a*), 'World Trade Growth Slower in 1998 after Unusually Strong Growth in 1997', Press Release, PRESS/128, 16 April, www.wto.org/english/news_e/pres99_e/pr128_e.pdf

—— (1999*b*), *WTO, Trade and Environment*, Special Studies 4 (Geneva: WTO), Press Release, www.wto.org/english/tratop_e/envir_e/stud99_e.htm

—— (2000*a*), 'Developing Countries Merchandise Exports in 1999 Expanded by 8.5%—About Twice as Fast as the Global Average', Press Release, Press/175, 6 April, www.wto.org/english/news_e/pres00_e/pr175_e.htm

—— (2000*b*), 'Mapping of Regional Trade Agreements: Note by the Secretariat', Committee on Regional Trade Agreements, WT/REG/W/41 (Geneva: World Trade Organization) 11 October, www.wto.org/english/tratop_e/region_e/wtregw41_e.doc (Chart 2: 5).

—— (2000*c*), 'Overview of the State of Play of WTO Disputes' (Geneva: WTO Informal Paper).

—— (2001*a*), *World Trade Report* (Geneva: WTO).

—— (2001*b*), 'WTO Successfully Concludes Negotiations on China's Entry', *WTO Press Release* (PRESS/243), 17 September.

—— (2002), *World Trade Report* (Geneva: WTO).

—— (2003*a*) *Annual Report* (Geneva: WTO).

—— (2003*b*), 'Decision Removes Final Patent Obstacle to Cheap Drug Imports', WTO Press Release, PRESS/350/Rev. 1, 4 September 2003.

—— (2003*c*), *World Trade Report* (Geneva: WTO), www.wto.org/english/res_e/booksp_e/anrep_e/world_trade_report_2003_e.pdf

—— (2005), *World Trade Report 2005: Exploring the Links between Trade, Standards and the WTO* (Geneva: WTO).

—— (2006*a*), *International Trade Statistics 2006* (Geneva: WTO).

—— (2006*b*), *Report (2006) of the Committee on Regional Trade Agreements to the General Council*, WT/REG/17, http://docsonline.wto.org/

—— (2006*c*), *World Trade Report 2006: Subsidies, Trade and the WTO* (Geneva: WTO).

514

WTO (2007), 'Notification of RTAs in Force to GATT/WTO', www.wto.org/english/tratop_e/region_e/summary_e.xls

WWF (World Wide Fund for Nature) (2002), *Living Planet Report 2002* (Gland, Switzerland: WWF—World Wide Fund for Nature), www.panda.org/downloads/general/LPR_2002.pdf

—— (2006), *Living Planet Report 2006* (Gland, Switzerland: WWF—World Wide Fund for Nature).

Yabuchi, M. (2000), 'Changing Determinants for Manufacturing Investment: The Availability of Parts', *JETRO China Newsletter*, 6/149: 1–2.

Yandle, B. (1984), 'Intertwined Interests, Rent Seeking and Regulation', *Social Science Quarterly*, 65/4: 1002–1012.

Young, B. (2002), 'On Collision Course: The European Central Bank, Monetary Policy and the Nordic Welfare Model', *International Feminist Journal of Politics*, 4/3: 295–314.

Young, O. R. (ed.) (1999), *The Effectiveness of International Environmental Regimes: Causal Connections and Behavioral Mechanisms* (Cambridge, Mass.: MIT Press).

—— (2002), *The Institutional Dimensions of Environmental Change: Fit, Interplay, and Scale* (Cambridge, Mass.: MIT Press).

Young, Z. (2003), *A New Green Order: The World Bank and the Politics of the Global Environment Facility* (London: Pluto Press).

Zaller, J. (1992), *The Nature and Origins of Mass Opinion* (New York: Cambridge University Press).

Zartman, I. W. (ed.) (1987), *Positive Sum: Improving North–South Negotiations* (New Brunswick, NJ: Transaction Books).

Zevin, R. (1992), 'Are World Financial Markets More Open? If so, Why and With What Effects?', in T. Banuri and J. B. Schor (eds), *Financial Openness and National Autonomy: Opportunities and Constraints* (Oxford: Oxford University Press).

Zimmerman, H. (2002), *Money and Security: Troops, Monetary Policy and West Germany's Relations with the United States and Britain 1950–71* (Cambridge: Cambridge University Press).

Zolo, D. (1997), *Cosmopolis: Prospects for World Government* (Cambridge: Polity Press).

Zürn, M. (1992), *Interessen und Institutionen in der internationalen Politik. Grundlegung und Anwendung des situationsstrukturellen Ansatzes* (Opladen, Germany: Leske & Budrich).

Zysman, J. (1984), *Governments, Markets and Growth: Financial Systems and the Politics of Industrial Change* (Ithaca, NY: Cornell University Press).

Index

Italic numbers denote references to Boxes